Corporate Finance

Principles of investment, financing and valuation

Robert Hutchinson

Stanley Thornes (Publishers) Ltd

00062575290010

First published 1995 by
Stanley Thornes (Publishers) Ltd
Ellenborough House
Wellington Street
CHELTENHAM GL50 1YW

96 97 98 99 00 / 10 9 8 7 6 5 4 3 2

ISBN 0 7487 1818 4

A catalogue record for this book is available from the British Library

Typeset by Paston Press Ltd, Loddon, Norfolk

Printed in Great Britain by T.J. Press (Padstow) Ltd, Padstow, Cornwall

Contents

Preface

In recent years there has been an increasing emphasis placed on the study of corporate finance in degree programmes specialising in Banking and/or Finance and/or Accounting, and in the more generally based areas of Economics, Business and Management. In writing a corporate finance book for these markets I was aware of two factors. First, that a relatively long book would be unsuitable in the context of the module based system of teaching which is being adopted throughout the United Kingdom university sector. Second, that in writing a relatively compact text, there can be a temptation to avoid formal presentation of technical material which, even at an introductory level, is essential for guiding students through the difficult issues and controversies of corporate finance. Consequently, my over-riding aims have been to:

- produce a relatively short book, in keeping with the module based system
- avoid over-emphasis on the technical nature of the subject while not losing sight of the formal relationships, and economic model based approach, which provide unique insights into corporate financial management.

As the content summary has already indicated, this book provides a comprehensive introductory treatment of corporate finance. It covers the essential principles and applications of investment, financing and valuation and incorporates some of the most recent research in this area.

Special features

Throughout the book, attention is drawn to the importance of:

- the Required Rate of Return, a concept which is often treated in isolation, leading to difficulties in understanding its role in valuation and its relationship to the cost of capital; and
- Agency Theory, in explaining debt and equity financing decisions, investments in tangible and intangible assets, small firm financing and leveraged buyouts.

In addition to covering the standard topics of the subject (accounting numbers, compounding and discounting, equity and debt valuation, investment appraisal, capital structure, dividends, working capital, and international investment and financing) the book devotes full chapters to:

- small firm investment and financing;
- futures and options;
- mergers and reorganisation;
- the efficient market hypothesis; and
- joint investment and financing decisions.

Academic level

The book is principally aimed at undergraduates, from any discipline in Social Sciences or Business and Management, and postgraduates on an MBA programme, taking a module in corporate finance/financial management.

Technicalities

Corporate finance cannot be properly understood without developing a number of simple, but technical, relationships. When confronted with these, students are sometimes panicked. I am confident, however, that all students are capable, with a reasonable amount of perseverance, of grasping the concepts that these relationships succinctly convey. Indeed, on past experience, it appears that once students have mastered these technicalities they appreciate their contribution to an understanding of corporate finance and become more aware of the elegance of the corporate finance models which are built around these technicalities. In Appendix B, a brief review of some of the technical relationships, used throughout this book, is presented. It is primarily for those students who are totally unfamiliar with, for example, the equation of a straight line and the concept of a summation.

Finally, a set of questions and exercises is included at the end of each chapter. Answers to these questions appear at the end of the book, in Appendix C.

Acknowledgements

Thanks to Kate McCaffery and Ken Dyson who each prepared the initial drafts of two chapters. Very helpful comments on the book as a whole were provided by Robert Jackson, who read at least two full drafts, Kate McCaffery, and an anonymous referee. Michael Thompson's advice on Accounting was much appreciated. The views expressed in this book and any errors are, of course, entirely my responsibility.

The book could not have been completed without Avril McNamee who typed and retyped various drafts and who showed her usual inexhaustible patience in handling equations and tables.

Finally, most authors acknowledge the support of their families. I did not fully realise the essential role this support played until I embarked on this book. So to Linda, Claire, Mark and Rebecca: your forbearance has been invaluable.

Permission for the use of Copyright Material is gratefully acknowledged in respect of:

> Kluwer Academic Publishers
> The Bank of England
> The Financial Times
> The London Business School

In memory of my parents:
Robert and Nora

1 Preliminary issues

Introduction

This chapter begins by outlining the nature of corporate finance and the links between investment, financing and valuation. As a preparatory background, it then presents a brief review of accounting information which is directly relevant to corporate finance. This information is applied in the context of the DuPont system, to demonstrate how accounting numbers can be used to obtain a summary view of some of the key aspects of a company's performance.

While accounting numbers are important, it is the market value of a company, which differs from its accounting value, which is central to the analysis of a company's investment and financing behaviour. Consequently, since the market values of publicly quoted companies are determined in the stock market, this preliminary chapter continues with an outline of the role that the stock exchange, and other financial markets, play in valuation. The chapter draws to a close with a discussion of the risk–return relationship.

Corporate finance

Industrial economics, and the sections of microeconomic courses which deal with the theory of the firm, are primarily concerned with the levels of competition which companies face in product and/or service markets. They are also concerned with the production and cost function relationships involved in creating a company's output. The emphasis is on firm conduct, in terms of marketing and pricing policies; on a firm's ability to minimise its cost of production, at each level of output; and on the possibilities it has of exploiting production economies of scale and scope. While paying some attention to a company's investment and financing decisions, micro-economics and industrial economics normally assume that these decisions have already been taken. In other words, the choice of goods and/or services which a company wishes to sell, and the production technology it uses, have already been determined.

It is in the discipline of corporate finance that detailed investigation and analysis of a company's investment and financing decisions are undertaken. Briefly, corporate finance views a company as being composed of a set of investment projects. (The easiest way to conceive of projects is in terms of the output of distinct products, or groups of products, that a company produces now, or may wish to produce in the future.) On this basis, the emphasis of corporate finance is on establishing the criteria that a company should use in choosing its most appropriate investment projects, and on determining the most appropriate ways in which the chosen investment projects should be financed.

Investment, financing and valuation

Making a decision on whether or not to invest in a potential project involves estimating its expected future series of net cash flows and then determining how this series would affect the current total market value of the company. Net cash flows consist of cash inflows, or revenues, from selling the potential project's output, less cash outflows, or costs, from producing that output.

The investment decision, once made, determines the asset base of a company. This consists, for example, of capital equipment, inventories of raw materials and accounts receivable (trade credit made available to the company's customers). The asset base is necessary to the generation of the expected future net cash flows of the company's projects.

The financing decision determines the ways in which a company raises funds to procure its assets. These funds can consist, for example, of a mixture of borrowing (debt capital), share issues (equity capital) and accounts payable (trade credit taken by a company from its suppliers). Each of these sources of capital has a cost, for example, the interest rate on debt and the return on equity that shareholders, as the owners of a publicly quoted company, expect and require.

The way in which the available sources, or components, of financing are combined determines what is referred to as a company's capital structure. While the investment decision affects a company's market value, there is a great deal of controversy, as explained in Chapter 8, surrounding the effect that capital structure, and hence the financing decision, has on valuation.

Overall objective
To develop criteria to enable a company to make the most appropriate, or optimal, investment and financing decisions, an overall, or core, objective is required. Formulating this objective in terms of the ownership rights to a company, the assumption is normally made that shareholders have the singleminded aim of maximising their wealth. This aim is achieved through the maximisation of a company's current total market value, that is through maximising the current total market value of its assets, or investment projects.

In the case of publicly quoted companies, which are the central focus of corporate finance, achievement of wealth maximisation requires an additional assumption: that the management of a company always acts in the interest of the company's shareholders. This assumption is necessary because of the divorce of ownership from control. It is needed to avoid the possibility that management, who are in day-to-day control of a company, and who, at most, only own an insignificant fraction of its shares, will have different objectives from the majority of shareholders.

Agency theory

The problem of differing objectives is not simply confined to a potential conflict of interest between management and shareholders but extends to a potential conflict of interest between shareholders and debtholders. (The primary debtholders of a company are banks, who provide overdraft facilities and short and intermediate-term loans, and bondholders who supply long-term debt capital through the ownership of corporate bonds.) While focusing on the maximisation of the current total market value of a company, discussion of these conflicts, in terms of what is known as Agency Theory, forms a significant strand of this book.

Agency Theory has become one of the important developments in corporate finance in recent years. It focuses on the relationships between principals, as the owners of an asset, and the agents who operate the asset on the principals' behalf.

Agency costs of equity

At one level Agency Theory examines the relationship between shareholders, as principals, and management as their agents. Because markets for information are imperfect, shareholders experience difficulties in gaining access to the inside knowledge which managers possess on the current and future prospects of the company they control. With this information asymmetry operating against shareholders, managers have the potential to act in their own interests, to the disadvantage of shareholder objectives. This potential creates what is referred to as moral hazard and implies, to the extent that shareholder objectives will not be met, that there are potential costs to owning equity, arising from the agency problem.

Recognising these potential agency costs of equity, shareholders may require some form of compensation in terms of a surcharge or premium on their return on equity. Alternatively, shareholders may seek some mechanism which ensures that managers make greater public disclosure of information. As it will be explained at various points in the book, this can influence the type of financial capital that management raises and may have an influence on the way in which shareholders want to receive their equity income.

There are two basic forms in which equity income is received: capital gains (losses), resulting from share price appreciation (depreciation), and dividends. In a perfect environment, where information is freely available to both managers and shareholders, and there is no agency problem, shareholders are indifferent between capital gains and dividends. In the presence of agency costs, however, the amount of dividends which a company pays, in any given period, may not be a matter of indifference to shareholders. Consequently, management's dividend payout decision may affect the market value of their company. Like the capital structure valuation debate, there is considerable controversy surrounding the dividend valuation relationship, which will be discussed in Chapter 9.

Agency costs of debt

Assuming that management acts in the interests of shareholders, the other level on which the principal–agent problem operates is in relation to debtholders. Here, with debtholders modelled as principals, agency costs associated with debt capital arise because management, especially in situations where a company experiences financial distress, may make investment decisions which potentially favour shareholders at the expense of debtholders.

It will be discussed in Chapter 3 how, with information asymmetry and the potential for moral hazard operating against debtholders, the agency problem can be used to explain some of the terms and conditions on which debt is issued. The agency problem explains why companies pledge part of their existing assets as security, or collateral, to a lender and/or why lenders may place a surcharge, or premium element, on the loan interest rates that they levy. Collateral and/or interest rate premiums partly compensate debtholders for the agency costs they would otherwise anticipate from making loans.

Market values

Leaving the agency problem aside, and assuming that managers maximise the current total market value of the company that they operate, corporate finance demonstrates how investment and financing policy should be formulated to achieve this goal. In this context, investment activity is ultimately judged in terms of the contribution it makes to the current, or present, value of the company. In technical terms, potential investment projects are judged on the net present value (NPV) which they are expected to create. NPV is discussed in Chapters 6 and 7.

Similarly, to the extent that different combinations of the components of finance (or capital) can have a market value impact, management should determine the optimal combination which maximises total market value. Confining the components of capital to long-term debt and equity, the optimal capital structure, if one exists, is defined in terms of the optimal ratio of debt to equity, that is, what is known as the optimal level of financial leverage.

Given the core importance of market value, the issue of how it is measured becomes crucial. The total assets of a company are created as a result of the investment projects a company undertakes. These investment projects must be financed. Assume that a company only uses financial capital traded in the stock market and that investment and financing decisions are independent. Then, given these assumptions, the total market value of a company's assets is measured by the combined market value of its financial capital.

Restricting financing to actively (or regularly) traded long-term corporate bonds and equity, the total market value of a company (V) is simply defined as the current market value of its corporate bonds (B) plus the current market value of its equity, or share capital (S), that is:

$$V = B + S \qquad (1.1)$$

It is important to note that the current market value of a company's equity, its share price times the number of shares it has outstanding (that is the number of shares it has issued), only measures the total market value of a company's assets when the company has no debt capital outstanding.

The asset base

The assets of a company consist of capital investment in plant and equipment, land and buildings. These are known as long-term physical, or fixed, assets. They are tangible in nature and are referred to as long term because their useful economic lives extend over a considerable period of time. A company also invests in financial assets, in the form of short-term cash balances and short-term (and sometimes long-term) marketable securities. The latter enables a company to avoid holding cash balances which would otherwise be surplus to current requirements. Marketable securities are financial assets which are actively traded in the financial markets.

As part of its short-term investment policy, a company often holds inventories of raw materials, spare parts, semi-finished and finished goods, and creates accounts receivable. These, together with cash and marketable securities, constitute a company's short-term, or current, assets and form an essential part of a company's working capital policy.

Working capital refers to current assets and current liabilities (defined below), both of which are needed to execute the day-to-day operations of a company. Inventories of spare parts may be needed, for example, to provide back-up for a company's after-sales service which may be an essential element in generating sales. Readily available spare parts would, therefore, enhance the company's reputation and increase its ability to sell its products. Similarly, trade credit offered to customers, that is accounts receivable, is a current asset which can represent a necessary element in fostering sales growth. Working capital will be explored in detail in Chapter 12.

The total market value of a company also takes into account any intangible assets that a company employs. These can represent an important element in a company's total asset base. Intangible assets include investments in human capital, education and training, and investments to develop a company's marketing and research and development capabilities. Intangible assets can enhance the reputation of a company and, to that extent, are sometimes referred to as reputational assets. The importance of the distinction between tangible and intangible assets will be discussed in Chapter 10, when the assumption that investment and financing decisions are taken independently is relaxed, and joint decisions in these areas are considered.

Sources of financing

It has been assumed, for simplicity, that a company's capital structure is composed only of long-term debt and equity. As will be explained at later stages in the book, there are other important sources of capital which a company can use. On a long-term basis these include convertible bonds, bonds issued with warrants, lease financing (all of which will be analysed in Chapter 11) and preferred shares (discussed briefly in Chapter 3).

Part of a company's profits, that is its earnings after meeting interest charges on debt and corporate taxes levied by the government, can also be used as a source of financing. Since profits belong to shareholders, these retained earnings are, in effect, a form of equity financing. The role of retained earnings in financing investments will be discussed in Chapter 3, under the investment opportunities approach to share valuation.

Where short-term financing is concerned, the main sources include bank loans (which are also the dominant form of medium-term financing), overdraft facilities and trade credit taken from a company's suppliers (accounts payable). These short-term sources of finance are referred to as short-term, or current, liabilities. They form an integral part of a company's working capital and are most often used to finance current assets. If, for example, a company increases its inventories of raw materials, it can finance the increase through a short-term bank loan or on the basis of trade credit made available by its suppliers, that is, accounts payable.

The maturity structure of assets and liabilities

There is nothing to stop a company financing its current assets on a long-term basis, or indeed, using short-term sources of finance to fund its long-term fixed assets. When a company uses current liabilities to finance current assets and long-term sources of finance to fund long-term assets, it is said to match the maturity structure of its assets and liabilities. This results in a company hedging risk since any change in the value of its liabilities is matched directly by a change in the value of its assets.

It is often difficult for a company to match the maturity structure of its assets and liabilities; hence it can face the risk that the value of its assets will fall below the value of its liabilities, creating negative net worth. This could occur as a result of macroeconomic changes in the economies in which the company operates. Macro-economic changes come about through, for example, government policy changes which affect interest rates, changes in exchange rates and in the level of consumer confidence, among other factors. Negative net worth could also occur as a result of microeconomic changes in the specific markets in which the company operates, for example, a change in the level of competition which affects its expected future profit performance.

The maturity structure of assets and liabilities, and some of the alternative strategies that a company can use to hedge its risk exposure, will be discussed at various points in Chapter 11 (on working capital), Chapter 15 (on international investment and financing) and Chapter 16 (on futures and options).

Note, as a general point, that there are no definitive time periods specified in respect of the medium and long term. As a rough rule, medium-term corporate assets and liabilities are defined as having life lengths and terms to maturity of, respectively, between one and ten years, the long term referring to over ten years.[1] In the case of working capital, current assets and current liabilities are normally defined as having, respectively, life lengths and terms to maturity of up to one year.

Accounting values and accounting numbers

The prices of the stock exchange assets, on which the current total market value of a company is based, are determined in a supply and demand framework. The main participants in the stock exchange are individuals, financial institutions and other financial market traders making buying and selling decisions. These decisions are based on expectations about future macroeconomic activity and about the future performance of each publicly quoted company. Expectations are formed on the currently available information that stock exchange investors have at their disposal.

At the individual company level, expectations about future performance are based on the future growth prospects of the industrial sectors in which a company operates, on the level of competition it faces and on its financial strengths. All of these factors are closely interrelated.

One of the most important sources of information is a company's accounts or financial statements. These are produced on an annual basis and record key aspects of a company's financial performance over the most recent financial year.[2] Accounts of publicly traded companies are prepared under legal requirements and in accordance with specific standards laid down by professional accounting bodies. In the UK, for example, the Accounting Standards Board, whose criteria extend to the Republic of Ireland, defines the way in which profits, fixed assets, equity share capital and other elements in a financial statement are to be measured.

In an important sense, therefore, the 'accounting numbers' which appear in financial statements have specifically defined meanings. They are meant to convey what auditors refer to as 'a true and fair view of the state of affairs of a company', in accordance with the Accounting and Auditing Standards currently in place. Consequently, accounting information is intended to present sound measures of the recent financial state of a company and, on this basis, can be used to deduce an implicit, although slightly complex, view of a company's current market value.

From a corporate finance point of view, however, there are two crucial aspects to accounting numbers which, while not detracting from their importance, place highly significant qualifications on their use in determining the current total market value of a company. These qualifications relate to the historic cost base of many accounting numbers and to controversy surrounding what is referred to as the Efficient Market Hypothesis (EMH).

Historic cost
First and foremost, many of the accounting numbers in a financial statement are based on historic cost information and special accounting formula used to depreciate capital assets. As will be explained in Chapter 2 (which sets out the principles of valuation) and Chapter 6 (which sets out the principles of investment appraisal), market values are current measures of worth, not historic measures.

Current market values are based on the level and timing of the future net cash flows, not the past net cash flows, which a company is expected to generate. That is, market values are determined by considering current and future cash inflows and current and future cash outflows, on the dates on which they actually occur.

Consider the case, for example, of the purchase today of a piece of capital equipment costing £100,000. In determining the current market value of the investment project it is associated with, its full cost is taken account of now. In accounting number terms, however, the £100,000 cost will not be entered in the company's financial statement for the current financial year. It will be entered, quite properly under accounting standards, on an annual depreciation basis, in accordance with the accounting depreciation method being used. If, for example, depreciation is on a straight-line basis, over a five-year period, only £100,000/5 = £20,000 will be entered annually in the company's accounts, over the next five financial years.

In addition, economic depreciation, which is essential for market valuation, may differ from accounting depreciation, especially if a country's tax regime has special depreciation rules for tax purposes. In this capital expenditure example, accounting depreciation renders the value of the equipment as zero, at the end of five years, ignoring residual or resale value. If, however, the equipment has a useful economic life of 20 years, it would need, in economic terms, to be depreciated accordingly. Economic depreciation allows the opportunity cost of the equipment, at any point in time, to be taken into account when making new investment decisions in the future which potentially involve use of this equipment.

The Efficient Market Hypothesis

The second qualifying factor, in respect of accounting numbers, relates to the controversy surrounding the usefulness of the information which these convey. This qualifying factor also involves the issue of whether or not the quality of accounting numbers matters, that is, whether or not accounting standards are necessary. One school of thought, which supports the Efficient Market Hypothesis, argues that the current market value of a publicly quoted company will have largely taken account of the information contained in the company's accounts, before the date on which these accounts are published. Supporters of the EMH also imply that the quality of the accounting reporting standards imposed on companies is irrelevant to valuation. The controversy surrounding the EMH will be examined in Chapter 5.

Notwithstanding the above two points, the understanding of corporate finance is enhanced through awareness of the information which company accounts contain. In addition, knowledge of how company accounts can be used, to provide accounting based summary views of a company's performance, is of direct relevance to investors considering buying and selling corporate bonds and equity. An example of such a summary approach is shown in the context of the DuPont system. Before this, two of the core financial statements in company accounts are outlined. These are: consolidated profit and loss accounts and balance sheets.

Consolidated profit and loss accounts

The profit and loss accounts of a company, or the consolidated profit and loss accounts of a group of companies, present a financial statement of revenues, expenses and profits generated over a financial year. A simplified example is given in Table 1.1, in respect of Hypothetical plc for the year ended 31 December 1994.

The first item in Table 1.1 records Hypothetical's turnover, or sales revenue, and the second item, the cost of producing the goods[3] and/or services it sold in 1994. Deducting the cost of sales from turnover determines Hypothetical's gross profit.

Operating profit

Taking distribution costs and administrative expenses from gross profit, after adding other operating income, determines the company's operating profit. Administrative expenses may include depreciation, the hire of plant and machinery, directors' remuneration and auditors' fees, etc. Other operating income includes, for example, royalties and licensing income which the company has received during the year. Any profits on the sale of fixed assets, or any losses on the sale and termination of operations, are then taken into account to determine the company's profit on ordinary activities, before interest.

Earnings before interest and taxes

In corporate finance texts, profit on ordinary activities, before interest, is referred to as operating income (sometimes net operating income) or, more often, earnings before interest and taxes: EBIT.

Table 1.1: Hypothetical plc: consolidated profit and loss account[1]

For the year end 31 December 1994	£m
Turnover	2000.00
Cost of sales	(1375.00)
Gross Profit	625.00
Distribution costs	(300.00)
Administrative expenses	(110.00)
Other operating income	20.00
Operating Profit	235.00
Profit on sale of fixed assets	5.00
Losses on sale and termination of operations	(10.00)
Profit on ordinary activities before interest	230.00
Share of profits of associated companies	2.00
Interest receivable and similar income	18.00
Amounts written off investments	(4.00)
Interest payable and similar charges	(95.00)
Profit on ordinary activities before taxation	151.00
Tax on profit on ordinary activities	(51.00)
Profit on ordinary activities after tax	100.00
Equity minority interests	(3.00)
Non-equity minority interests	(1.00)
Profit for the financial year	96.00
Preference dividends on non-equity shares	(1.00)
Profit attributable to ordinary shareholders	95.00
Ordinary dividends on equity income	(52.25)
Transferred to reserves	42.75
Earnings per ordinary share[2]	30.16p
Dividends per ordinary share	16.59p

[1] Cost figures to be subtracted are bracketed.
[2] Assumes Hypothetical plc has 315m shares outstanding.

Earnings after interest but before taxes

The next profit figure, which is of key importance from a corporate finance point of view, is profit on ordinary activities before taxation. This is typically referred to as earnings after interest charges but before tax payments: EAI. Given that debt capital is one of the two primary components of a company's capital structure the focus of attention, in determining EAI, is on the interest charges which a company has to meet. In the case of corporate bonds the interest charges are normally fixed. Table 1.1 indicates, however, that in calculating EAI, the consolidated profit and loss account takes other items into consideration. Any interest income a company receives (from its financial investments), and the profits of its associated companies, are added to profit on ordinary activities, before taxation. Any amounts written off on investments are subtracted.

Earnings after interest and taxes

Profit on ordinary activities, after taxation, is determined by deducting the company's tax liabilities. Netting out other payments, for example equity minority interests, produces profits attributable to ordinary shareholders. It is these profits which represent the earnings available to ordinary, or common, shareholders. These are referred to as earnings after tax or, more often, earnings after interest and taxes: EAIT.

EAIT represents the amount of operating income which is owned by a company's common shareholders. Management has discretion over how these earnings are used, and normally retains a proportion of EAIT for investment purposes. In the accounts these retained earnings are entered as funds transferred to reserves.

Retention and payout ratios

The proportion of funds retained determines what is referred to as the retention ratio: b. The remainder of EAIT which is not retained is paid out as dividends to ordinary shareholders. This total dividend payout defines the payout ratio which is equal to one minus the retention ratio, that is:

$$\text{payout ratio} = 1 - \text{retention ratio} = 1 - b \qquad (1.2)$$

Hypothetical plc has EAIT of £95.00m for the financial year ending 31 December 1994. As Table 1.1 indicates, with a total dividend payout of £52.25m and retained earnings of £95.00m − £52.25m = £42.75m, the retention ratio is:

$$b = £42.75m/£95.00m = 0.45$$

In other words, Hypothetical plc retained 45% of its EAIT for investment purposes during 1994. The payout ratio is:

$$£52.25/£95.00m = 0.55 \text{ or } 1 - b = 1 - 0.45$$

In other words, 55% of EAIT was paid out in dividends during 1994.

Earnings per share and dividends per share

A company's EAIT, and its total dividend payout (D), are often expressed on a per share basis. Given the total number of shares which a company has outstanding (n), earnings per share (EPS) are defined as:

$$\text{EPS} = \text{EAIT}/n \qquad (1.3)$$

Dividends per share (d) are defined as:

$$d = D/n \qquad (1.4)$$

For Hypothetical plc, which has n = 315m shares outstanding,

$$\text{EPS} = £95.00m/315m = 30.16p$$

and

$$d = £52.25/315m = 16.59p$$

Note that dividends per share are equal to EPS multiplied by the dividend payout ratio, that is:

$$d = (1 - b)\text{EPS} \qquad (1.5)$$

In Hypothetical's case:

$$d = (1 - .45)(30.16p) = 0.55(30.16p) = 16.59p$$

Table 1.2: Hypothetical plc: balance sheets[1]

At 31 December 1994	£m
Fixed Assets	
Tangible assets	700.00
Investments	60.00
	760.00
Current Assets	
Stocks	450.00
Debtors (accounts receivable)	435.00
Investments	10.00
Cash at bank and in hand	200.00
	1095.00
Creditors – amounts falling due within one year (Current Liabilities)	
Bank overdrafts	(30.00)
Other creditors (accounts payable)	(710.00)
	(740.00)
Net current assets/(liabilities): Net working capital	355.00
Total assets less current liabilities: Capital Employed	1115.00
Creditors – amounts falling due after more than one year[2]	(450.00)
Provisions for liabilities and charges	(50.00)
Net assets	615.00
Capital and Reserves	
Called up share capital	157.50
Share premium account	195.50
Other reserves	220.00
Shareholders' Funds	573.00
Equity minority interests	32.00
Non-equity minority interests	10.00
Total Capital and Reserves	615.00

[1] Figures to be subtracted are bracketed
[2] Medium to long-term liabilities

Balance sheets

The profit and loss account of a company presents a statement of its revenues, expenses and profits over a financial year. The balance sheets present a statement of a company's assets, liabilities and shareholders' funds at a given point in time, usually the financial year end. A simplified version of the balance sheets of Hypothetical plc is given in Table 1.2, at 31 December 1994.

As Table 1.2 indicates, the balance sheets divide a company's assets into two components: long-term (fixed) assets and short-term (current) assets. The company's liabilities are also divided into two components: current, and medium to long-term liabilities. As explained, current assets and current liabilities form the core of a company's working capital policy. Shareholders' funds, which are essentially long term in nature, are divided into equity share capital and reserves.

Most of the fixed assets in the balance sheets are book value concepts, in that they are based on historic values. In the case of plant and equipment, for example, value is recorded in terms of the purchase prices paid for these assets when they were acquired, less accumulated depreciation, that is, less the accounting depreciation to date. (Allowance is sometimes made for revaluation of assets although, if this occurs, it is stated in the company's accounts.) Thus the value of fixed assets is measured on their historic cost, not their current resale value or their current replacement value. Similarly, long-term liabilities, such as bonds, are valued at par and not at their current market price. Shareholders' funds are also measured on a book value basis. Short-term, or current, assets and liabilities are valued, almost by definition, at their current prices.

Assets and liabilities
Looking specifically at the balance sheets of Hypothetical plc, the first items record the value of fixed tangible (or physical) assets plus investments (financial assets). Next, the value of current assets is recorded. These assets include stocks (physical inventories of raw materials, etc.), debtors (accounts receivable), investments (short-term marketable securities), and cash in the bank and in hand. The section entitled 'Creditors – amounts falling due within one year' refers to current liabilities.

Net working capital
The next item, current assets/(liabilities), is often referred to as working capital or, possibly more appropriately, net working capital. That is:

Net Current Assets = Current Assets − Current Liabilities

In Hypothetical's case,

Net Current Assets = £1095.00m − £740.00m = £355.00m

Total assets are defined as:

Total Assets = Fixed Assets + Current Assets

= £760.00m + £1095.00m = £1855.00m

in Hypothetical's case.

Total assets less current liabilities
Total assets less current liabilities, sometimes referred to as capital employed, appear next. For Hypothetical plc,

Total Assets − Current Liabilities

= £1855.00m − £740.00m = £1115.00m

This figure can be obtained, alternatively, as:

Fixed Assets + Net Current Assets

= £760.00m + £355.00m = £1115.00m

Long/medium-term liabilities
Long and medium-term liabilities come under the section 'Creditors – amounts falling due after one year'. Long-term liabilities may include corporate bonds and other long-term debt, while medium-term liabilities may include bank loans.

Net assets
Netting all liabilities out of capital employed, as well as provisions for liabilities and charges (for example, any deferred taxation), defines the net assets of Hypothetical plc:

Net Assets

= Capital Employed − Medium and Long-term Liabilities − Provisions

= £1115.00m − £450.00m − £50.00m = £615m

Shareholders' funds
The section in the balance sheets dealing with capital and reserves looks at a company from the shareholders' point of view. Since shareholders are the owners of a company, shareholders' funds (plus minority[4] interests) must balance with net assets. That is, the total capital plus reserves of Hypothetical plc are equal to its net asset value of £615.00m.

Shareholders' funds, which represent shareholders' net worth, are composed of called-up capital, a share premium account and other reserves. Called-up capital is measured in book value terms as the number of shares outstanding (or called up) times the nominal, or par value, on the share's certificate. In Hypothetical's case the nominal value of each share is 50p. With 315m shares outstanding, Hypothetical has a called-up book value of 315m(50p) = £157.5m. The share premium account, which is part of the reserves, measures the difference between the price at which shares were issued and their par value. Other reserves refer to the cumulated, past and current, sums of money which have been retained for investment purposes and, additionally, to any asset revaluations.

Confusion of terms
Note above that capital employed was referred to as total assets less current liabilities and, in Hypothetical's case, was £1115.00m. There can be confusion over the use of this term. Sometimes it is used to refer to net assets but more often to total capital and reserves (basically shareholders' funds) plus long-term debt. These three alternative uses of the term, capital employed, are entirely different.

Cumulative capital requirement
Note also the concept of a company's cumulative capital requirement: the amount of capital required to fund a company's total assets at a given point in time. The cumulative capital requirement is equal to shareholders' funds (including any minority interests) plus the value of all liabilities (current, medium to long-term, and provisions). In Hypothetical's case, the cumulative capital requirement is:

£615.00m + £740.00m + £450.00m + £50.00m = £1855.00m

In other words, Hypothetical's cumulative capital requirement is equal to its total assets (fixed plus current) of:

£760.00m + £1095.00m = £1855.00m

The cumulative capital requirement concept will be considered in the chapter on working capital (Chapter 12).

Goodwill
Note finally that there is no measure of intangible assets in the balance sheets.

Intangible assets are roughly equivalent to goodwill. If Hypothetical's assets were all valued in current market prices, the difference between the current value of its assets and the accounting value would represent the value of intangible assets. Some companies do report measures of goodwill in their accounts, others do not.

The DuPont system

In corporate finance one of the central aims is to measure company performance. From an accounting perspective, performance can be assessed by examining various ratios, and rate of return concepts, based on accounting numbers. At this stage in the book the focus of attention is on overall performance measurement and on gaining a general understanding of the way in which the principal sources of long-term capital, debt and equity, might be related. An interesting approach to this is contained in the DuPont system, a method developed by the DuPont company in the earlier part of this century to analyse its financial performance. Some aspects of the DuPont system, which is now in widespread use, are presented next.

The return on the book value of equity

Given that the overall objective in corporate finance is to maximise shareholder wealth, the obvious focus of attention is on the returns to equity ownership. In accounting numbers this is measured as the return on equity, ROE, which is defined as EAIT (the total earnings available to common shareholders) divided by the book value of equity, EQ, that is:

$$\text{ROE} = \text{EAIT}/\text{EQ} \qquad (1.6)$$

The book value of equity measures shareholders' net worth and is defined as shareholders' funds or the net asset value of a company.

The ROE, which is an accounting investment ratio, indicates how effective management is from the shareholders' point of view. In Hypothetical's case, EAIT = £95m (see Table 1.1). Shareholders' funds, and thus EQ, are £157.50m (see Table 1.2). Therefore,

$$\text{ROE} = £95\text{m}/£157.50\text{m} = 0.6032 \text{ or } 60.32\%$$

The two fundamental factors directly affecting the ROE are: the return on total assets, ROA, and the financial leverage ratio, L. The ROA, which is another investment ratio, is defined as the ratio of EAIT to total assets, A, that is:

$$\text{ROA} = \text{EAIT}/\text{A} \qquad (1.7)$$

In Hypothetical's case, with total assets equal to £1855m,

$$\text{ROA} = £95\text{m}/£1855\text{m} = 0.0512 \text{ or } 5.12\%$$

ROA measures the productivity of the overall funds a company is using, that is, how efficiently a company's total assets are being employed. The higher the ROA, the greater the efficient and productive utilisation of a company's total asset base.

Financial leverage

The financial leverage ratio, which is one of a set of debt management ratios, measures a company's reliance on debt capital. It can be defined in a number of ways, which will be explained in Chapter 8. For current purposes L is defined on a total debt basis as the ratio of the book value of total assets to the book value of equity, that is, as:

$$L = A/EQ \qquad (1.8)$$

In Hypothetical's case,

$$L = £1855m/£157.50m = 11.78$$

The higher the ratio of the book value of assets to the book value of equity, the greater the amount of debt used in financing a company's assets.

ROA and financial leverage

Inspecting the above three equations (1.6 to 1.8), the return on equity can be expressed as a product of the return on assets and financial leverage:

$$ROE = ROA \times L \qquad (1.9)$$

that is,

$$\frac{EAIT}{EQ} = \frac{EAIT}{A} \times \frac{A}{EQ} \qquad (1.9a)$$

In Hypothetical's case:

$$ROE = 0.0512 \times 11.78 \simeq 0.603 \text{ or } 60.3\%$$

On the basis of Equation 1.9a, an assessment can be made of the relative importance of the ROA and L in determining the ROE. A numerical example on this follows shortly. If the ROA is relatively more important than leverage, it could be argued that a company is in a relatively 'strong' position, since its ROE is largely being generated by the productive and efficient employment of its assets. There is a 'good' prospect of the company maintaining its ROE into the future.

If, alternatively, financial leverage appears relatively more important, some might argue that the ROE is largely being determined by the company's financial, or capital structure, policy. In this situation the ability of the company to maintain a 'sound' ROE into the future is much more problematical. (There is considerable debate over this issue, which, as already explained, will be discussed in Chapter 8.)

Deciding whether L or ROA is more important can be difficult. In the case of financial leverage, the effects on the return on equity depend on relatively complex relationships between EBIT and EAIT. The central issue focuses, however, on the probability of a company not being able to meet its fixed interest charge obligations in the future.

The return on equity and financial leverage

Consider the financial leverage argument in more detail. Equity capital entitles shareholders to dividend payments; however, whether or not these are made is at the discretion of a company's management. Debt capital generally offers fixed interest payments which management are obligated to meet. Debt capital is, therefore, less risky than equity capital from an investor's point of view. Consequently, from management's point of view, debt is a cheaper source of financing than equity. Under specific circumstances this means that increases in financial leverage can increase a company's profitability and, therefore, its ROE.

The problem with financial leverage

There is a potential problem with using increased leverage, however, since increased fixed interest charges have to be met out of EBIT (earnings before interest and taxes). If circumstances in the future result in these interest charges taking up nearly all of a company's EBIT, the company may experience financial distress. In the extreme, if EBIT fall below interest charges the company defaults on part of its fixed interest obligations and may, ultimately, be forced into bankruptcy. The probability that this will happen in the future increases with the amount of financial leverage a company currently employs and may, therefore, adversely affect the company's ROE.

To get a better flavour of this argument on debt, Equation 1.9a can be expanded, to produce the following relationship:

$$\frac{EAIT}{EQ} = (1 - t_c)[i + L(EP - i)] \qquad (1.9b)$$

Here, the return on equity is a function of the corporate tax rate (t_c), the average interest rate on a company's debt (i), its financial leverage ratio (L), and the earnings power of its assets (EP). EP is defined as earnings before interest and taxes (EBIT) divided by total assets (A).

Before explaining and interpreting ROE, in the context of Equation 1.9b, it is helpful to show how this equation is derived. To do this EAIT and the ROA have to be determined in more detail.

Determining EAIT

Consider how EAIT are determined. First, the total fixed interest charges on debt, I, are calculated. Second, since interest charges are tax deductible, they are taken out of EBIT before a company's tax liabilities are calculated. Thus earnings after interest charges but before tax, EAI, are:

$$EAI = EBIT - I \qquad (1.10)$$

Third, a company's total tax charges, T, are determined by the corporate tax rate, t_c, and are:

$$T = t_c(EBIT - I) \qquad (1.10a)$$

Fourth, EAIT are calculated by deducting the total tax charge from EAI, that is:

$$EAIT = EBIT - I - t_c(EBIT - I) \qquad (1.10b)$$

Equation 1.10b can be regrouped into the neater expression:

$$EAIT = (1 - t_c)(EBIT - I) \qquad (1.10c)$$

To illustrate the above, consider the following example. A company has EBIT =

£10.00m. It calculates its total interest charges as I = £1.00m; therefore, from Equation 1.10:

$$EAI = £10.00m - £1.00m = £9.00m$$

It faces a corporate tax rate of $t_c = 35\%$ so its total tax charges, from Equation 1.10a, are:

$$T = (.35)(£9.00m) = £3.15m$$

Thus EAIT are:

$$EAIT = EAI - T = £9.00m - £3.15m = £5.85m$$

This is equivalent to Equation 1.10b,

$$EAIT = £10.00m - £1.00m - (.35)(£10.00m - £1.00m) = £5.85m$$

and similarly to Equation 1.10c,

$$EAIT = (1 - .35)(£10.00m - £1.00m) = (.65)(£9.00m) = £5.85m$$

Determining the ROA

To achieve the desired objective of relating the ROE to financial leverage, a few more steps are required. Consider the total fixed interest charge, I, which is determined by applying the debt interest rate to the value of debt. Assuming that there is only debt and equity in a company's capital structure, the book value of debt is equal to total assets, A, less the book value of equity, EQ. Thus, given the average interest rate on debt, i, the total interest charges in book value terms are:

$$I = i(A - EQ) \tag{1.11}$$

In the above example, with I = £1.00m, and assuming A = £44.667m and EQ = £28.00m, the implied rate of interest is i = 6%, since

$$A - EQ = £44.667m - £28.00m = £16.667m$$

$$I = 0.06(£16.667) = £1.00m$$

Returning to the abstract, substituting Equation 1.11 into Equation 1.10c gives an expression for EAIT:

$$EAIT = (1 - t_c)[EBIT - i(A - EQ)] \tag{1.12}$$

If Equation 1.12 is divided by total assets, the following expression for the ROA is determined:

$$ROA = \frac{EAIT}{A} = \frac{(1 - t_c)[EBIT - i(A - EQ)]}{A} \tag{1.13}$$

In other words:

$$ROA = (1 - t_c)\left[\frac{EBIT}{A} - i\left(1 - \frac{EQ}{A}\right)\right] \tag{1.13a}$$

Looking at Equation 1.13a, the term EBIT/A defines the before interest and taxes rate of return on a company's assets. It is known as a company's earnings power, EP, that is, it measures the ability of the company's asset base to generate its operating income. From Equation 1.8, EQ/A is the reciprocal, or inverse of the leverage ratio, that is, EQ/A = 1/L.

Explaining ROE

Putting the EP and L terms into Equation 1.13a, and multiplying by L, gives the return on equity:

$$ROE = ROA \times L = (1 - t_c)\left[EP - i\left(1 - \frac{1}{L}\right)\right] \times L \qquad (1.14)$$

Finally, a slight rearrangement of Equation 1.14 produces:

$$ROE = (1 - t_c)[i + L(EP - i)] \qquad (1.14a)$$

Equation 1.14a demonstrates that the return on the book value of equity, measuring the return to shareholders, is a function of:

● the corporate tax rate, t_c;
● the average interest rate, i, on the book value of debt;
● the leverage ratio, L; and
● the earnings power of a company's assets, EP.

Breakeven point

The interesting aspect of this equation is the level of the financial leverage ratio in respect of the 'breakeven' point between the earnings power and the average interest rate on debt. Above the breakeven point, when the earnings power exceeds the average rate of interest, EP > i, an increase in financial leverage increases the ROE. If, alternatively, EP < i, an increase in financial leverage reduces the ROE.

To illustrate the above, a summary example is given. A fuller example is presented shortly. Assume t_c = 30%, i = 5%, EP = 10% and L = 2. Then,

$$ROE = (1 - .30)[.05 + 2(.10 - .05)] = .105 \text{ or } 10.5\%$$

The earnings power of this company's assets exceeds the average interest rate on its debt, that is, EP − i = 10% − 5% = 5 percentage points. Thus an increase in leverage, that is, an increase in the ratio of the book value of assets to the book valued equity, increases the company's return on equity. If, for example, L rises from 2.00 to 2.50, all other things being equal, the ROE rises from 10.5% to 12.25%, that is

$$ROE = (1 - .30)[.05 + 2.5(.10 - .05)] = 0.1225 \text{ or } 12.25\%$$

Now consider the case where EP = 6% and i = 9%. The company is below the breakeven point, with EP − i = 6% − 9% = −3 percentage points. If L = 2,

$$ROE = (1 - .30)[.09 + 2(.06 - .09)] = 0.021 \text{ or } 2.1\%$$

If L rises to 2.50, all other things being equal, ROE falls from 2.1% to 1.05%, since:

$$ROE = (1 - .30)[.09 + 2.5(.06 - .09)] = 0.0105 \text{ or } 1.05\%$$

Interpreting the return on equity

Now consider one way in which Equation 1.14a could be used to analyse ROE, that is, to analyse the recent performance and short-term future prospects of a company from its shareholders' point of view. The Always Optimistic Company prospered a few years ago during an upturn in the business cycle. Its earnings power increased sharply during a period when the government pursued a low interest rate policy. The EP of Always Optimistic plc exceeded the average rate of interest on its debt. The company at the same time decided to boost its ROE in order to impress its shareholders. To do this, it significantly increased the amount of debt in its capital structure; in other words, it increased financial leverage. Since EP > i, this had the desired effect of boosting the company's ROE.

Unfortunately, somewhat like the 1989/90 recession in the UK, the business cycle, and company-specific market conditions, have now just turned against Always Optimistic plc. Recent government policy has resulted in a sharp rise in interest rates and the earnings power of Always Optimistic's assets has fallen, as a result of the recession in sales. Always Optimistic's earnings power[5] is now below the average rate of interest on its debt, that is, EP < i. For Always Optimistic the rise in i, and fall in EP below i, are compounded by the company's high financial leverage ratio.

If Always Optimistic plc finds itself in short-term financial problems, because of its relatively high leverage ratio, it may find it awkward to ease its difficulties by raising further debt. This would arise because bankers and other suppliers of debt capital are usually unwilling to increase lending in a recessionary period to a company which already has a relatively high ratio of debt to equity. Even if Always Optimistic plc could further increase its financial leverage, because EP − i < 0, this would lead to an additional reduction in the return to its shareholders, since ROE would fall.

Financial policy implications

The optimal policy, if the above description is valid, is to reduce the level of financial leverage when EP < i, thus raising the ROE. This illustrates two general points in respect of debt financing. A company should:
- avoid excessive debt financing, as a prudent policy in the face of future unanticipated adverse changes in business conditions; and
- attempt to build flexibility into its debt financing policy, that is, build in an ability to adjust its financial leverage ratio relatively rapidly, in response to changing business conditions.

These issues, of whether or not there is such a concept as 'excessive debt' financing and of whether or not debt financing flexibility is required and, if it is, how it can be achieved, are major issues in the rest of this book.

An example

To give a numerical illustration to some of the above points, consider the data, in Table 1.3, taken from the financial statements of Always Optimistic plc. These relate to one of the previous financial years during which Always Optimistic was 'prospering'. In the second half of the table, the various accounting ratio measures are calculated. Also the ROE is expressed, using Equation 1.14a, in terms of the

Table 1.3: Illustrating aspects of the DuPont system

Always Optimistic plc: Extracts of Profit and Loss Accounts and Balance Sheets

Earnings Before Interest and Taxes:	**EBIT** = £30.00m
Interest Charges on Debt:	**I** = £10.00m
Corporate Tax Rate:	t_c = 35%

Earnings After Interest and Taxes

$$EAIT = (1 - t_c)(EBIT - I) = (1 - .35)(£30m - £10m) = £13.00m$$

Total Assets:	**A** = £225.00m
Book Value of Equity[1]	**EQ** = £100.00m
Book Value of Debt	**A − EQ** = £125.00m

Implied average rate of interest on debt:

$$i = I/(A - EQ) = £10m/£125m = 0.08 \text{ or } 8\%$$

Return on Assets: **ROA** =   EAIT/A =   £13m/£225m =0.0577 or 5.77%

Return on Equity: **ROE** = EAIT/EQ =   £13m/£100m =0.13 or 13%

Financial Leverage: **L** =   A/EQ = £225m/£100m =2.25

Earnings' Power: **EP** =   EBIT/A =   £30m/£225m =0.133 or 13.3%

ROE = ROA × L = 0.0577 × 2.25 = 0.1298 or 13%

From Equation 1.14a

ROE = (1 − t_c)[i + L(EP − i)]
= (1 − .35)[0.08 + 2.25(0.133–0.08)]
= (.65)[0.08 + 2.25(0.053)]
= (.65)[0.08 + 0.119] = 0.1294 or 13%

[1] Book Value of Equity = Shareholders' Funds = Net Assets

corporate tax rate, the average rate of interest on debt, earnings power and financial leverage.

From Table 1.3, given t_c = 35%, i = 8%, L = 2.25 and EP = 13.3%, Always Optimistic's ROE is approximately 13%, that is:

ROE = (1.35)[0.08 + 2.25(0.133 − 0.08)] = 0.1294 or 13%

Always Optimistic's earnings power exceeds its average interest rate on debt, by EP − i = 5.3 percentage points. Thus, all other things being equal, any increase in financial leverage increases the ROE. If, for example, L rises from 2.25 to 2.6, Always Optimistic's ROE rises to 14.2%, that is:

ROE = (1 − .35)[0.08 + 2.60(0.133 − 0.08)] = 0.142 or 14.2%.

Note that in changing its capital structure, it is assumed that the company does not alter its total assets. In other words the company increases debt but reduces equity, that is, it sells debt using the funds raised to repurchase equity. An additional assumption is implicit here: that the company's financing decision does not affect its asset investments.[6]

The above referred to an earlier 'prosperous' period in Always Optimistic's operations. Assume, however, that in the recession which has just now begun,

Always Optimistic's EBIT fall sharply, causing its EP to fall to 7%. With L = 2.25, and all other things being equal, Always Optimistic's ROE is 3.74%, that is:

ROE = (1 − .35)[0.08 + 2.25(0.07 − 0.08)] = 0.0374 or 3.74%

In this situation EP − i = −1.0 percentage points. The company is below its breakeven point so that a rise in L, from 2.25 to 2.60, lowers its ROE from 3.74% to 3.51%, that is:

ROE = (1 − .35)[0.08 + 2.60(0.07 − 0.08)] = 0.351 or 3.51%

Financial analysts

Analysts, using the above approach, can examine how close any company is to its breakeven point. They can make assessments of likely future changes in a company's circumstances which might lead to a deterioration in EP and/or a rise in i and assess if, and how far, EP is likely to fall below the average interest rate on the company's debt. This would permit an assessment of the future sensitivity of ROE. Indeed, analysts translate this type of analysis, as it will be argued in Chapter 3, into their assessment of a company's current total market value.

Analysis of the above type of equation represents, however, only a part of the overall assessment of a company. Note also that an industry analysis is important, with rates of return for a company, based on accounting numbers, being compared to the rates of return for the industry sector in which the company is based.

Debt management ratios

The debt management issue is a core consideration in corporate finance. Other ratios are used to assess a company's exposure to potential difficulties, arising from its debt financing policy. One of these ratios is the times interest earned ratio, which is defined as earnings before interest and taxes divided by annual interest charges:

$$\text{Times Interest Earned} = \frac{\text{EBIT}}{\text{I}}$$

This ratio measures the number of times in a year that operating income can cover interest charges. A relatively high ratio indicates that the probability of a company being unable to cover its interest payments, in the foreseeable future, is relatively low.

Debt is not the only instrument which exposes a company to fixed interest charges. Instead of purchasing all of its assets, a company may lease some of them, in which case it faces obligations on fixed rental, or lease, payments as well as debt interest. Leasing, as it will be explained in Chapter 11, is a form of debt financing. A more comprehensive ratio than the times interest earned ratio, is the fixed charge coverage ratio which includes lease payments:

$$\text{Fixed Charge Coverage} = \frac{\text{EBIT} + \text{Lease Payments}}{\text{Interest} + \text{Lease Payments}}$$

Its interpretation is similar to the times interest earned ratio.

The return on equity and the return on assets

Recall from Equation 1.9 above that the ROE is determined by financial leverage and the rate of return on assets. Assume that you have analysed these two rates in respect of a particular company. You have come to the conclusion that the financial leverage policy that the company is pursuing is 'about right' and that the ROE is strongly influenced by the ROA. An insight into the effect that the ROA has, can be determined by considering its decomposition into two components: the net profit margin and the asset turnover ratio.

Net profit margin
The net profit margin, PM, which is one of a set of profitability ratios, measures the profit productivity of sales and is defined as the ratio of EAIT to turnover:

$$PM = EAIT/Turnover \qquad (1.15)$$

A low net profit margin can indicate that a company is not generating enough sales relative to its expenses, and/or that its expenses are out of control.

Asset turnover ratio
The asset turnover ratio, which is one of a set of asset management or activity ratios, measures how effective a company is in using its total asset base to generate sales. It is a measure of the intensity of utilisation, or productivity, of assets. The asset turnover ratio, ATR, is defined as the ratio of turnover to total assets:

$$ATR = Turnover/A \qquad (1.16)$$

Interpreting ROA
Given the definition of the return on assets, it is clear from Equations 1.15 and 1.16 that the ROA can be defined as the product of the net profit margin and the asset turnover ratio, that is as:

$$ROA = PM \times ATR \qquad (1.17)$$

or

$$\frac{EAIT}{A} = \frac{EAIT}{Turnover} \times \frac{Turnover}{A} \qquad (1.17a)$$

If the ROA is largely determined by the asset turnover ratio, this might imply that a company is subject to a relatively high level of sales volatility. In turn, its ROA and consequently its ROE might be relatively sensitive to the business cycle. Alternatively, a relatively high net profit margin might indicate that the company is in a relatively 'strong' position.

A great deal of caution must, however, be exercised in interpreting these ratios. As explained above, they must be analysed in the context of the industry in which a company is based and compared to the average ratios for that industry. In the food retailing sector, for example, the net profit margin tends to be relatively low, the ROA being strongly influenced by high asset turnover. In other words, by the nature of the food retailing sector there is high sales volume relative to the sector's asset base. In addition, a high level of competition makes companies in the sector highly price competitive, with the consequent effect of producing a relatively low net profit margin. Alternatively, at the quality end of the retail jewellery sector, companies can be expected to experience relatively low sales volume but relatively high net profit margins.

Market based rates of return

Rate of return measures based on accounting numbers are useful aids to analysing company performance. These measures and the broader range of accounting ratios will be presented and discussed at later stages in this book, particularly in Chapter 12, on working capital, and in the final chapter (Chapter 17). It is, however, market based rates of return which figure prominently in corporate finance.

There are two fundamental market based rate of return measures in respect of debt and equity. In the case of debt capital, the market rate of return measure is the expected yield. This yield relates the annual fixed interest payment on a bond to the bond's current market price and its term to maturity. Where equity capital is concerned, the expected rate of return on a share takes account of the expected capital gain (or loss): the difference between the market price at which a share is purchased and the market price at which it is expected to be sold. The expected rate of return on equity also includes the dividend per share expected to be paid during the period the share is to be held. Each of these market rate of return measures are formally introduced and analysed in Chapter 3, which sets out the principles of market valuation in respect of bonds and equities.

Financial institutions and markets

The financial services industry in any advanced economy covers a wide range of financial activities; however, these activities centre on a small number of basic but interrelated services: lending and borrowing, buying and selling physical and financial assets, and altering or transforming risk. Financial institutions, or financial intermediaries, intermediate between these activities.

Financial institutions

UK financial intermediaries may be grouped loosely into the following overlapping categories:
- the banking sector, which includes retail banks, merchant or investment banks (which provide long-term loans to businesses and general business services) and the discount houses (which operate as intermediaries between retail banks and the Bank of England);
- non-bank financial intermediaries, such as building societies (some of which have become banks), insurance companies, and finance houses (which, among other activities, provide factoring and leasing services to businesses); and
- specialist fund managers[7] who manage, for example, pension funds, unit trusts and investment trusts.

Financial markets

All of these financial intermediaries, together with the general public, use financial markets to buy and sell financial assets, that is, financial instruments or securities.

As explained, it is this buying and selling activity, in both primary and secondary markets, that is essential to the determination of market values. It is through the primary markets, for example, that companies make additional issues of shares.

Secondary markets involve the trading of outstanding financial assets, that is, the buying and selling of assets subsequent to their initial issue. While there is a clear distinction between primary and secondary markets, the success of primary markets in the core financial assets in an economy (equities, gilt-edged stocks and corporate bonds) is fundamentally dependent on the existence of secondary markets in these assets. In other words, it is the existence of secondary markets in shares, for example, that enables companies to make new equity issues. While the prospects of a company's new share issue being taken up partly depend on the new issue's price, in relation to investor expectations, the subsequent marketability[8] of the new issue is a prerequisite. New issues markets are important, and will be discussed briefly below; however, it is secondary markets which dominate in the determination of a company's current total market value.

Marketability

The marketability of a company's bonds and equities depends on a number of specific factors, the creditworthiness of the company being prominent among these. Generally, however, marketability is enhanced when financial assets are actively traded regularly on a daily basis, as opposed to thinly traded on an irregular basis.

The efficiency of a financial market also promotes marketability. As will be explained in Chapters 3 and 5, market efficiency refers to the extent to which, for example, the price of a company's shares fully reflects all the relevant information on the company's future prospects. To the extent that it does, the market price represents a 'fair' measure of the intrinsic, or 'true', value of the company's equity.

Both marketability and efficiency are closely related to the levels of transactions costs involved in using secondary markets. Transactions costs refer to brokerage fees, that is, the costs of actually trading in a financial asset. These costs reduce any profits, and accentuate any losses, which investors anticipate from making buying and selling decisions. Consequently, the higher the transactions costs, the less frequently will investors be willing to trade, thus potentially reducing marketability and increasing information inefficiencies.

The main UK markets

The main financial markets in the UK, which are more international in nature than they are domestic, cover a broad range of assets. Equities and bonds are traded on the London Stock Exchange, futures and options on LIFFE (the London International Financial Futures Exchange) and foreign currencies on the London foreign exchange markets. There is an Unlisted Securities Market (USM) with lenient listing requirements, relative to the main Stock Exchange. The USM was introduced to encourage small to medium-sized, privately owned companies to go public. Lloyds represents an important international insurance market. London has also the largest Euromarket where eurocurrencies, eurobonds and euronotes are traded.

Another set of markets is the Sterling Money Markets where Treasury Bills (short-term securities issued by the Bank of England), Certificates of Deposit (issued by major banks) and Commercial Bills and Commercial Paper (issued by companies) are traded. These markets are referred to as the discount markets, the discount houses having a role in making a market in these financial instruments. Discount houses have the ability to borrow from the Bank of England as the lender of last resort.

The latter facility distinguishes the discount markets from the wholesale, or parallel, money markets where there is no lender of last resort. The parallel money markets include the very important inter-bank market, where banks borrow and lend among themselves, and UK local authority loan markets.

In developing investment and financing principles for publicly quoted companies, this text only deals with financial assets directly involving the markets for bonds, equities, foreign currencies and futures and options. The rudiments of trading in foreign currencies and futures and options will be discussed in Chapters 15 and 16 respectively. At this stage, it is helpful to present a brief outline of the share dealing system whose principles also apply, approximately, to bond trading and the trading of financial assets in general.

Market making

Under the old Stock Exchange system of trading dealing took place at stalls, or pitches, on the floor of the Exchange under a Single Capacity system, with minimum commission or transaction charges. The Single Capacity system involved two distinct classes of market participant:
- stockbrokers who dealt directly with clients wishing to buy and sell shares;
- stockjobbers who only dealt directly with stockbrokers.

Stockjobbers had the right to own shares themselves, and traded directly with stockbrokers by quoting two prices:
- the bid price at which the stockjobber was willing to buy shares;
- the offer price at which the stockjobber was willing to sell shares.

The bid–offer spread, the offer price less the bid price, represented the jobber's turn or profit. The stockbroker received his/her income from the commissions charged to clients. If, for example, a jobber bid £1.20 and offered £1.22 for a share, he/she was willing to buy the share for £1.20 and sell it for £1.22. The bid–offer spread or jobbers turn in this example is 2p per share.

Big Bang

By the early 1980s the London stock market was experiencing significant limitations on its development, largely from the increasing competition it faced from other international stock markets (mainly in the United States, Japan and continental Europe). London's main problems appeared to arise from:
- the Single Capacity system;
- minimum commissions; and
- developing new markets, in particular the telephone or over-the-counter market, and the exchange traded market where trade in UK shares did not have to be based in London.

The Stock Exchange resolved these problems by radically changing its trading methods through the introduction of Big Bang in October 1986.

Under this new system, Single Capacity has been replaced by Dual Capacity and minimum commissions have been abolished. Most of the buying and selling of shares is no longer carried out on the floor of the Exchange but by telephone, with dealing aided by computer screens. In the Dual Capacity system there are now broker/dealers and market makers (the equivalent of stockjobbers). The broker/dealer can be a market maker and own shares in his/her own right. Shares are still traded on a bid–offer basis and are classified according to their frequency of trading as:

- Alpha stocks, which are most actively traded and roughly equivalent to the concept of a 'blue chip' stock;
- Beta stocks, which have a steady daily turnover; and
- Gamma stocks, which are thinly or inactively traded.

The new issue market

Companies, when raising equity capital through a new share issue, have to decide the price at which the new issue is to be sold and the number of shares in the new issue. This determines the amount of funds expected to be raised. When raising debt capital, through an issue of bonds, the rate of interest which is to be offered has to be determined, together with the number of bonds to be issued. Corporate bonds normally have a face, or par, value of £100 at which each bond is issued. An outline of the factors influencing the interest rate to be offered, when a new bond issue is floated, is contained in Chapter 3.

Issue costs

In the case of new equity issues (and indeed corporate bonds) a company will use the advisory services of a merchant or investment bank in determining the terms and conditions of the issue, and will normally have the issue underwritten. Underwriters contract, for a fee, to buy any part of the new issue which is not taken up by the market. Issue costs make this method of financing relatively expensive. In effect, only the net funds raised through a new issue, that is the gross funds raised less the issue costs, are available for investment.

The issue costs normally include expenses associated with advertising, meeting Stock Exchange regulatory requirements and publishing a prospectus (which presents information on the company and the terms and conditions of the issue), as well as advisory and underwriting fees. Total issue, or flotation, costs will normally represent at least 3% of the funds raised, making it uneconomical to raise relatively small amounts of capital through the financial markets.

Ways of issuing equity

There are a number of ways in which a company can raise additional equity,[9] by:
- an offer for sale, where the share price is specified;
- an offer by tender, where investors are invited to bid for shares at, or above, a minimum price;
- a placement, where shares are sold to, that is placed with, private or institutional investors; and
- a rights issue,[10] where existing shareholders are offered additional shares at a significant discount to the current market price on outstanding shares.

A placement lowers issue costs since underwriting fees and advertising and allotment expenses are avoided. Allotment expenses arise where there is an excess demand for the issue and some method of apportioning shares to the applicants has to be determined. A placement, like a rights issue, will be offered below current market price so that the gains from lower issue costs are likely to be offset, other things being equal, by the discount induced reduction in the amount of funds raised.

Securitisation and disintermediation

In this section on financial institutions and markets, attention has focused on the intermediating role of financial institutions and on the tradability of marketable securities. There are financial assets which are not normally tradable, for example, mortgage and hire-purchase agreements. Recently there has been a securitisation trend, where some untradable assets are transformed into tradable securities. In the United States, for example, mortgages and hire-purchase agreements have been put into tradable bonds. If the issuer of such a bond defaults on the loan, the holder of the bond takes over receipt of the payments from the mortgage and/or hire-purchase agreements, which represent the bond's security.

A further development is disintermediation. Banks, for example, as borrowing and lending intermediaries earn significant off-balance sheet fee income from arranging loans for companies. With the possibilities that securitisation has opened up, companies have realised that they do not always need to use intermediaries to arrange loans. Consequently, companies are increasingly making direct agreements with other companies and investors to borrow and lend funds, using securitisation.

The risk–return relationship

The risk–rate-of-return relationship underlies all financing and investment activities. This basic principle, which will be fully demonstrated in Chapter 4, states that the higher the return that an asset is expected to generate, the greater will be the risk surrounding the asset's expected return.

The normal probability distribution
In corporate finance this risk–return relationship is modelled at its most basic level, by assuming that the return on an asset is normally distributed. In other words if you hold a share, for example over the coming year, the actual return that you will realise on the share, at the end of the year, cannot be known with certainty: This realised return will depend on how the company prospers, whether or not it experiences strike activity in its plants, discovers a revolutionary cost-reducing method of production, faces increased competition from competitors, experiences a rise or fall in interest rates and a change in exchange rates, among a host of other factors.

Taking all these factors into account you could probably make an estimate of what, on the average, you would expect this return to be. In probability terms, where the rate of return on the ith share is r_i, this average would be defined as the expected rate of return, $E(r_i)$. Assuming that the realised return will be normally distributed, this

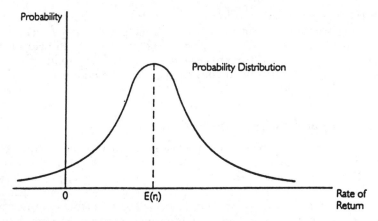

Figure 1.1   The normal probability distribution

expected return is the mean (or mathematical expectation) of the distribution. An example of a normal probability distribution is shown in Figure 1.1.

A measure of risk

The realised return on a share is unlikely to be equal to its expected return. It may be close to the expected return (either above or below it) or significantly above or below the expected return. In statistical terms the standard deviation of a normal distribution, σ, measures the range of the likely outcomes around the mean. Thus the standard deviation is the underlying measure of risk used in corporate finance. Note that, by assuming a normal distribution, the characteristics of the return on an asset are fully described since a normal distribution is fully specified by only two parameters: its mean and standard deviation.[11]

Figure 1.2 shows the returns on two assets, A and B. Since $E(r_A) < E(r_B)$, asset A has a lower expected rate of return than asset B. The spread of asset B's distribution is, however, higher than the spread of asset A's, since $\sigma_A < \sigma_B$. In other words, asset B, with the higher expected rate of return, has a greater spread to its distribution relative to asset A's distribution. In absolute terms, asset B has greater risk because its distribution has a higher standard deviation than asset A's distribution. This example characterises the general principle of what is referred to as the positive risk–return relationship.

The degree of risk

In relative terms the degree of risk an asset possesses can be defined by its coefficient of variation, that is, the ratio of the expected rate of return on the asset to its standard deviation. The coefficient of variation measures the expected rate of return per unit of risk. In the above example, if

$$\frac{E(r_A)}{\sigma_A} = \frac{E(r_B)}{\sigma_B}$$

both assets would have the same degree of risk. If, alternatively,

$$\frac{E(r_A)}{\sigma_A} > \frac{E(r_B)}{\sigma_B}$$

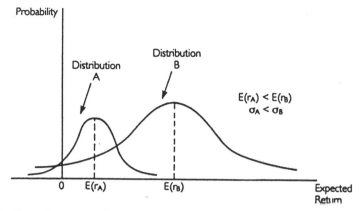

Figure 1.2   *Illustrating expected return and risk*

asset A would have a higher degree of risk than asset B (despite asset A having a lower rate of return and standard deviation than asset B).

Summary

This chapter has presented a preliminary view of corporate finance, explaining the central role that market value maximisation has in deriving the principles on which investment and financing decisions are based. Accounting numbers in financial statements contain important information on company performance and can be used in interesting ways, for example, in the DuPont system. It would, however, be inappropriate to derive investment and financing principles from accounting values.

This chapter has also identified the medium through which the current total market value of a publicly traded company is determined: financial markets. In addition it has introduced the concept of the risk–return relationship which underlies all investment and financing decisions.

The investment and financing concepts introduced in this preliminary chapter are fully developed, explained and subjected to critical appraisal throughout the book. The key principle of discounting, which is used to translate the expected future net cash flows into a current, or present, monetary value, is introduced in the next chapter. This chapter explores the general principles of both compounding and discounting and discusses the main ways in which loan interest charges can be determined.

Questions

1 Outline the main ways in which the assets of a company can be categorised.

2 Explain the differences between gross profits and operating income and between

operating income and earnings after interest and taxes. Who owns earnings after interest and taxes?

3 What is meant by the payout and retention ratios?

4 Consider the following information from the XYZ company's latest profit and loss account:

	£m
Turnover	250.00
Cost of sales	100.00
Distribution/administrative expenses	50.00
Interest payable	15.00
Tax on profit on ordinary activities	37.00
Ordinary dividends on equity income	19.20

XYZ has n = 100m shares outstanding

Determine
a) earnings before interest and taxes (EBIT)
b) the payout ratio $(1 - b)$
c) the retention ratio (b)
d) earnings per share (EPS)
e) dividends per share (d).

5 Consider the following information from the ABC company's latest profit and loss account and balance sheets:

	£m
Turnover	200.00
Earnings before interest and taxes	70.00
Interest payable	30.00
Tax on profit on ordinary activities	20.00
Fixed assets	600.00
Current assets	400.00
Current liabilities	300.00
Medium to long-term liabilities	620.00
Shareholders' funds	80.00

a) Show that net assets = shareholders' funds.
b) What is the value of ABC's net working capital?
c) Calculate the return on equity and the return on assets.
d) Calculate the ratio of the book value of assets to the book value of equity. What does this measure?

6 Given the information in question 5
a) Show that the return on equity is equal to the return on assets times financial leverage.
b) Calculate the net profit margin and the asset turnover ratio. Show that the product of these ratios equals the return on assets.
c) Calculate the earnings power of ABC's assets, its implied corporate tax rate and its implied average interest rate on debt. Show that the return on equity can also be determined from the equation:

$$ROE = (1 - t_c)[i + L(EP - i)]$$

7 Why is it important for an asset to possess marketability?

Exercises

1 What do you understand by the agency problem?

2 Over the past year, Relatively Cautious plc has produced an earnings power (EP) of 12%. It faced an average interest rate on debt (i) of 7% and a corporate tax rate (t_c) of 40%. Its capital structure policy resulted in a financial leverage ratio (L) of 5.0. The company is relatively satisfied with this performance, although it believes that its return on equity (ROE) is on the low side and wishes to raise it by 15% next year.

Management have looked at next year's prospects and have a finely balanced opinion on how the economy is likely to change. The focus is on two scenarios.

Scenario A: The average interest rate on debt will fall by one percentage point and the company's sales will increase, raising the EP of Relatively Cautious to 14%. The corporate tax rate is expected to stay at 40%.

Scenario B: The average interest rate on debt will rise to 9% and the EP will remain at 12%. In this scenario, the government is expected to raise the corporate tax rate to 45%.

a) Calculate the current ROE and the ROE expected next year, under each scenario, assuming that Relatively Cautious plc does not change its financial leverage.

b) Assume that Relatively Cautious plc can, at this stage, take a flexible approach to its capital structure policy. How would financial leverage have to change under each scenario, if a 15% increase in the ROE is to be achieved?

c) In the case of Scenario B, would it be prudent to attempt to raise the ROE by 15%?

Endnotes

1. In the case of British government gilt-edged securities, a short-term gilt has a term to maturity of up to five years; a medium-term gilt, a term of between five and fifteen years; and a long-term gilt, a term in excess of fifteen years. In the case of bank loans a medium-term loan is usually defined as having a maturity of between one and ten years. UK banks normally avoid making long-term company loans which have a maturity in excess of ten years.

2. Annual company accounts relate to a financial year which may or may not coincide with the end of a calendar year. Different companies, even within the same industry sector, may use different financial year end dates, for example 30 June or 31 December. This makes a comparative analysis of companies, on the basis of their financial statements, quite difficult. Other difficulties arise since there are ambiguities surrounding the way in

which certain types of activities have to be recorded in a company's accounts, for example the use of operating leases. Complexities, in addition to these off-balance sheet activities (that is, activities which do not have to be recorded), arise where there is a certain amount of flexibility available to companies in the way they record some of the activities that they are required to report.

3. Goods sold in the financial year 1994 may have been manufactured in the previous financial year but held in stock, that is, as part of the company's inventories of finished goods.

4. A consolidated balance sheet refers to a group of companies. In the present example, Hypothetical plc is the holding company's name. Minority interests refer to subsidiary companies shareholders' funds which are not held as an integral part of the holding company. It is the direct shareholders of the holding company who are of primary interest.

5. Note that $EP = EBIT/A$, so that if $EP < i$, this does not imply that EBIT are insufficient to cover total debt interest charges I.

6. In this case with A remaining at £225m but L rising to 2.60, EQ falls to £86.54m. Since $L = A/EQ$, $EQ = £225m/2.6$. The book value of debt rises to $A - EQ = £225m - £86.54m = £138.46m$. With i remaining at 8%, $I = 0.08(£138.46m) = £11.077$. With $EBIT = £30m$, $EAIT = (1 - .35)(£30m - £11.077m) = £12.3m$. As a result of the increased debt, ROA falls to £12.3m/£225m = 5.47% but with increased financial leverage the ROE rises to $ROA \times L = 0.0547 \times 2.60 = 0.1422$ or 14.2% approximately. Note that the ROE obtained directly as EAIT/EQ is equivalent since £12.3m/£86.54m = 0.142 or 14.2%.

7. Fund management activities can be carried out by independent fund managers as well as fund managers employed within insurance companies and other financial intermediaries.

8. A bank loan, for example, is a primary market operation, but normally bank loans once they are issued cannot be traded. Similarly, National Savings Certificates and Certificates of Tax Deposits are not marketable financial assets.

9. A flotation of shares can refer to a 'first time' issue when a privately owned company is going public and seeking a Stock Exchange listing.

10. A stock split is another term involved with equity. Here a company simply increases the number of shares outstanding by, for example, replacing one of each of the existing shares by two shares. No new capital is raised in the process. A consolidation is the opposite of a stock split.

11. If the distribution is not normal the standard deviation only partially measures risk. In the non-normal case additional measures of risk, such as the skewness of the distribution, have to be taken into account.

References

Cobham, D. (Ed.), *Markets, Dealers and the Economics of the London Financial Markets*, London, Longman, 1992

Coggan, P., *The Money Machine: How the City Works*, London, Penguin Books, 1989

Fuller, R. and J. Farrell, *Modern Investments and Security Analysis*, New York, McGraw-Hill, 1987

Maxwell, C.E., *Financial Markets and Institutions: The Global View*, New York, West Publishing Company, 1994

Parker, R.H., *Understanding Company Financial Statements*, London, Penguin Books, 1988

Pizzey, A., *Accounting and Finance: A Firm Foundation*, London, Cassell, 1993

Steinherr, A., *The New European Financial Market Place*, London, Longman, 1992

Wood, F., *Business Accounting 1 and 2*, London, Pitman, 1993

2 The time value of money

Introduction

Investment and financing decisions are concerned with activities which produce future cash inflows and future cash outflows. The amounts of these cash flows and their timing have a major impact on the current market prices of the traded assets which produce them. Similarly, the present and future amounts of borrowing and lending that individuals, companies and governments are willing to undertake are influenced by the level and time pattern of the cash flows associated with these decisions.

The cash flow timing effect arises because money has a time value which is most easily understood in terms of an interest rate at which money can be borrowed and lent. At minimum, an interest rate reflects a pure time preference rate, arising from society's general preference for current, over future, consumption. This implies that if current investment can only be increased by postponing current consumption, each £1 of consumption forgone today must be compensated by £1 plus interest tomorrow. An interest rate, however, normally exceeds the pure time preference rate by premiums which compensate for anticipated inflation, which will erode the purchasing power of £1 through time, and by the risk which surrounds future outcomes in general.

Consequently, the above implies that an amount of money invested today will have a future value dependent on the rate at which interest is compounded over the investment period. By analogy, £1 received in the future will have a value today of less than £1, since the future £1 must be discounted to the present by taking account of the opportunity to earn interest over time. These concepts of compounding and future values, and discounting and present values, form the core of this chapter.

While compounding and discounting concepts are essential to the development of techniques for analysing investment and financing decisions in the corporate sector, they are equally applicable to the personal sector. This sector, in the United Kingdom, is being confronted by an increasing array of personal financial products: Peps, Tessas, endowment mortgages, fixed rate mortgages, building society deposit accounts, assurance policies, income annuities, alternative pension schemes, unit trusts, investment trusts, the privatisation programme, and of course personal financial advisors. A basic knowledge of how to apply the time value of money principles can aid the personal sector's decision processes and help avoid the purchase of financial products which are not particularly relevant to an individual's needs.

In developing these concepts it is initially assumed that future cash flows are known with certainty and occur on an annual, year end, basis. The certainty assumption is important in that it permits the use of a single interest, or discount, rate. It will be seen as the book develops that once risk is introduced, discount rates change to reflect differences in risks among financial assets. For ease of computation, compounding and discounting tables, A.1 to A.4, are contained in Appendix A, at the end of the book.

Compounding and future values

The basic relationship between future value and compound interest is:

$$FV_t = PV(1 + r)^t \tag{2.1}$$

PV is the principal or initial amount of money to be invested now, that is, in the present.
t is the number of investment periods, defined in years.
r is the per period compound rate of interest. It is earned on the principal amount invested and on the interest payments credited at the end of each year.
FV_t is the future value of the initial investment at the end of t years, given the rate of interest r.

To understand the general application of the above equation, assume initially that PV = £100, r = 10% and t = 1. Then,

$$FV_1 = £100(1 + .10)^1 = £100 + £100(.10) = £110$$

In other words, £100 is invested for one year, with the interest of £10, 10% of £100 or £100(.10), credited at the end of the year. The future value of the investment, one year from now, is equal to £110 which is the initial amount invested plus the interest payment.

If the principal is invested for two years, interest will be earned at the end of the second year, on both the principal of £100 and the £10 interest credited at the end of year one.[1] This is equivalent to stating that £110 at the end of year one, FV_1, is invested for a subsequent year, raising the value of the investment to £110(1 + .10) = £121 at the end of year two, that is,

$$FV_2 = FV_1(1 + .10)$$

By substituting for FV_1 = £100(1 + .10), the future value of the two year investment can be expressed as:

$$FV_2 = £100(1 + .10)(1 + .10) = £100(1 + .10)^2$$

the value which would have been obtained directly from Equation 2.1. Extending the investment for a further year produces a value, at the end of year three, of £121(1.10) = £133.10, that is,

$$FV_3 = FV_2(1.10)$$

Again a similar substitution, this time for FV_2 = £100(1 + .10)^2, demonstrates the equivalence with Equation 2.1:

$$FV_3 = £100(1 + .10)^2(1 + .10) = £100(1 + .10)^3$$

Equation 2.1 can be used to determine the future value of any present amount of money invested for t periods at r. If, for example, £500 is invested for t = 15 years at r = 7%, its future value is:

$$FV_{15} = £500(1 + .07)^{15} = £1379.52$$

Future value interest factors
The complicated part of Equation 2.1 is the term $(1 + r)^t$ which is the future value interest factor: $FVIF_{t,r}$. This measures the future value of £1 invested over t periods at r. To simplify, Equation 2.1 can be re-expressed as:

$$FV_t = PV(FVIF_{t,r}) \tag{2.1a}$$

Table A.1 presents the FVIFs, for specified rates of interest over a number of time periods. In the last example, $FVIF_{15,7} = 2.759$, and is determined by reading down the rows of Table A.1 to period 15, and across the interest rate columns to 7%. Consider another example: if PV = £5000, t = 3 and r = 8%, $FVIF_{3,8} = 1.26$ and the future value at the end of year three is:

$$FV_3 = £5000(1.26) = £6300$$

Discounting and present values

The future value formula can be reversed to define another fundamental concept in valuation, the present value. If, for example, an individual is to receive £5000 three years from now and r = 7%, the question can be asked: what cash amount would the individual have to invest now to produce £5000 in three years time? In this case, since FV_3 = £5000, Equation 2.1 can be solved for PV, that is, for the initial or present value. Given

$$£5000 = PV(1 + .07)^3$$

the answer to the question is:

$$PV = \frac{£5000}{(1 + .07)^3} = £4080$$

In other words, instead of applying the compounding principle to find the future value of a present amount of money, a discounting principle can be applied to determine today's value of a future cash flow. The interest rate used in obtaining present values is referred to as the discount rate.

This last example illustrates the opportunity cost concept of the time value of money. £5000, three years from now is not worth £5000 today. Given the opportunity to lend money at r = 7%, £5000 can be produced in three years by lending £4080 now.

Alternatively, if you know that you will receive £5000 three years from now, this future sum can be transformed into a current loan. The £5000 could be used, for example, to repay the principal amount borrowed and the cumulated interest charges, all in one single amount at the end of three years. This is illustrated in Table

Table 2.1: Borrowing with cumulated interest charges

	Total Value of Loan (£s)	Interest (£s)
End Year zero[1]		
Principal value of loan	4080.00	
End Year 1		
Interest £4080(0.07)		285.60
Loan outstanding £4080 + £285.60	4365.60	
End Year 2		
Interest £4365.60(0.07)		305.60
Loan outstanding £4365.60 + £305.60	4671.20	
End Year 3		
Interest £4671.20(0.07)		327.00
Loan outstanding £4671.20 + £327.00	4998.20[2]	
Cumulative Interest Charges		
End Year 3		918.20

[1] When referring to the current or present point in time, a zero subscript is often used.
[2] Rounding error.

2.1 on the assumption that the rate of interest at which money can be borrowed equals the rate of interest at which money can be lent: in the present example at r = 7%. Only £4080 can be borrowed (now) since, with r = 7%, total interest due at the end of three years is £920.

Thus, given common borrowing and lending rates, the present value of £5000 three years from now is £4080.

Present value interest factors
Generalising, if a cash flow X_t is to be received t periods in the future and r is the discount rate, measured as a per period compound rate of interest, the present value of X_t is:

$$PV = \frac{X_t}{(1 + r)^t} = X_t(1 + r)^{-t} \qquad (2.2)$$

The term $1/(1 + r)^t$ or $(1 + r)^{-t}$ is the present value interest factor, $PVIF_{t,r}$, and measures the present value of £1 to be received t periods from now, given r. It is the reciprocal, or inverse, of the future value interest factor given in Equation 2.1a. To simplify, Equation 2.2 can be expressed as:

$$PV = X_t(PVIF_{t,r}) \qquad (2.2a)$$

Table A.2 presents the PVIFs for specified rates of interest, over a number of time periods. In the last example, given t = 3 and r = 7%, the present value interest factor, $PVIF_{3,7} = 0.816$, is substituted into Equation 2.2a, together with $X_3 = $ £5000, to produce the present value: £5000(0.816) = £4080.

To further illustrate these present value interest factors a number of examples are given in Table 2.2 using r = 8%. Taking the fourth example in this table, where

Table 2.2: Cash flows and discount factors

Year t	X_t = Future Cash Flow[1] (£'s)	Discount Factor $1/(1+r)^t = PVIF_{t,r}$	Present Value $PV = X_t(PVIF_{t,r})$ (£'s)
0	$X_0 = 500$	$1/(1.08)^0 = PVIF_{0,8} = 1.000$	500
1	$X_1 = 1000$	$1/(1.08)^1 = PVIF_{1,8} = 0.926$	926
2	$X_2 = 1000$	$1/(1.08)^2 = PVIF_{2,8} = 0.857$	857
3	$X_3 = 2000$	$1/(1.08)^3 = PVIF_{3,8} = 0.794$	1588
4	$X_4 = 3000$	$1/(1.08)^4 = PVIF_{4,8} = 0.735$	2205

$\sum_{t=0}^{4} = 0 X_t/(1+r)^t$ = Present value of the cash flow series = £6076

[1] The first example refers to £500 which is to be received at the end of year zero, representing the present. Since this is available now, its PV=£500. Formally, the PVIF for year zero is $1/(1+r)^0$. Any number raised to the power of zero is automatically one, thus $1/(1+r)^0 = 1$.

£2000 is to be received at the end of three years, $PVIF_{3,8} = 0.794$, and the present value is: £2000(0.794) = £1588.

The present value of a future series

Each cash flow in Table 2.2 has been valued in isolation. If, however, these cash flows are viewed as a future series, for example annual gifts from a parent to a student, the present value of the whole series can be determined by adding the present values of the individual cash flows. Formally, the present value of a cash flow series X_t, t = 0, 1, 2, ..., n is:

$$PV = \frac{X_0}{(1 + r)^0} + \frac{X_1}{(1 + r)^1} + \frac{X_2}{(1 + r)^2} + \cdots + \frac{X_n}{(1 + r)^n} \qquad (2.3)$$

This can be expressed in a more compact form using the summation concept, as:

$$PV = \sum_{t=0}^{n} \frac{X_t}{(1 + r)^t} \qquad (2.3a)$$

or in terms of the PVIFs, as:

$$PV = \sum_{t=0}^{n} X_t(PVIF_{t,r}) \qquad (2.3b)$$

Consider, as another example, the guaranteed cash flow series in Table 2.3. This series occurs over a six-year period, starting at the end of year one. Using Equation 2.3a, since there is no payment in year zero and n = 6, the summation runs from t = 1 to t = 6 and the present value of the series is:

$$\sum_{t=1}^{6} \frac{X_t}{(1 + r)^t} = \frac{X_1}{(1 + r)} + \frac{X_2}{(1 + r)^2} + \cdots + \frac{X_6}{(1 + r)^6}$$

With an assumed discount rate of 8%, the present value of the series in Table 2.3 is £4058.90. If the discount rate is raised to 10%, the present value is reduced to

Table 2.3: Illustrating present values and present value interest factors

Year t	Cash flows X_t (£'s)	Present Value Interest Factors $PVIF_{t,8}$	$PVIF_{t,10}$	$X_t(PVIF_{t,8})$ (£'s)	$X_t(PVIF_{t,10})$ (£'s)
1	400	0.926	0.909	370.40	363.60
2	500	0.857	0.826	428.50	413.00
3	1000	0.794	0.751	794.00	751.00
4	2000	0.735	0.683	1470.00	1366.00
5	1000	0.681	0.621	681.00	621.00
6	500	0.630	0.564	315.00	282.00

$$\text{Present value of series } \sum_{t=1}^{6} X_t (PVIF_{t,8}) = £4058.90$$

$$\sum_{t=1}^{6} X_t (PVIF_{t,10}) = £3796.60$$

Table 2.4: Present values with varying interest rates

Year t	Cash flow (£'s)	Present Value (£'s)	Present Value (£'s)
1	400	$400 (PVIF_{1,6})$	= 377.20
2	500	$500 (PVIF_{2,6})$	= 445.00
3	1000	$1000 (PVIF_{1,8})(PVIF_{2,6})$	= 824.14
4	2000	$2000 (PVIF_{2,8})(PVIF_{2,6})$	= 1525.46
5	1000	$1000 (PVIF_{1,10})(PVIF_{2,8})(PVIF_{2,6})$	= 693.32
6	500	$500 (PVIF_{2,10})(PVIF_{2,8})(PVIF_{2,6})$	= 315.00
Present value of series			£4180.20

£3796.60. This illustrates that there is, for a given series of positive future cash flows, an inverse relationship between the present value of the series and its discount rate:[2] the higher (the lower) the discount rate, the lower (the higher) the present value.

Varying interest rates

The compounding and discounting principles can be used to determine future and present values when interest rates vary through time.

In the case of compounding, consider an initial amount of £1000 invested over a nine-year period and assume that the annual compound rates of interest are: 4% in the first four years, 6% in the next three years and 8% in the final two years. Using Equation 2.1a and the FVIFs in Table A.1, the future value of this investment[3] is:

$$£1000(FVIF_{4,4})(FVIF_{3,6})(FVIF_{2,8}) = £1000(1.17)(1.191)(1.166) = £1624.79$$

The value of the investment at the end of the first four years is £1000(1.17) = £1170. This sum then earns 6% annual compound interest for three years producing a value, at the end of seven years, of £1170(1.191) = £1393.47. With r = 8% in years eight and nine the future value, at the end of year nine, is £1393.47(1.166) = £1624.79. If new deposits can be made at some future point over the nine-year period, their contribution to future value can easily be determined.[4]

To see how variations in interest rates can be accommodated in the present value formulation, consider the cash flow series in Table 2.4 and assume that the average annual discount rates are as follows: 6% for years one and two, 8% for years three and four and 10% for years five and six. The PVIFs in Table A.2 are used to calculate the present value of each cash flow. The PVs of the cash flows in years one and two are straightforward. To determine the PV of the year three cash flow, the 8% discount rate over year three has to be taken into account by multiplying £1000 by $PVIF_{1,8} = 0.926$, yielding £926. The latter number is then multiplied by $PVIF_{2,6} = 0.890$, yielding £824.14. Intuitively, it is as if an individual moved in a time machine from the present to the end of year two and then viewed the year three cash flow: it is discounted for one year at 8% and valued at the end of year two, as £926. The time machine then moves back over two years, taking £926 with it, but discounting this amount by the appropriate 6% rate for years one and two. Where the cash flow at the end of year four is concerned, it has first to be discounted at 8% for two years and then at 6% for two years. The PVs of the cash flows at the end of years five and six are obtained by a similar process, taking account of the 10% discount rate over years five and six.

Present value of a fixed annuity

Having developed the general formula for obtaining the present value of a future series of cash flows, attention is turned to the special case of a fixed annuity which is defined as a series of fixed annual cash flows over a given time span. Assume that an annual cash flow of £I is to be received for t = n years, beginning at the end of year one. In terms of the present value formula in Equation 2.3, $X_1 = X_2 = \ldots = X_n = I$. There is no payment in year zero, hence $X_0 = 0$.

The present value of this annuity is, therefore:

$$PVA = \frac{I}{(1 + r)} + \frac{I}{(1 + r)^2} + \cdots + \frac{I}{(1 + r)^{n-1}} + \frac{I}{(1 + r)^n} \tag{2.4}$$

Since I is common to all terms on the right-hand side of the equation,

$$PVA = I \left[\frac{1}{(1 + r)} + \frac{1}{(1 + r)^2} + \cdots + \frac{1}{(1 + r)^{n-1}} + \frac{1}{(1 + r)^n} \right] \tag{2.4a}$$

This latter equation can be manipulated[5] to produce a more compact expression:

$$PVA = I \left[\frac{1 - (1 + r)^{-t}}{r} \right] \tag{2.4b}$$

The present value interest factor of an annuity

In Equation 2.4b the term inside the bracket [ ] is the present value interest factor of an annuity, $PVIFA_{t,r}$, and measures the present value of £1 to be received annually for t (equal to n) periods, given r. Table A.3 presents these factors, for specified interest rates over a range of time periods. Writing Equation 2.4b in terms of PVIFAs:

$$PVA = I(PVIFA_{t,r}) \tag{2.4c}$$

Assume, for example, that an annuity of £500 is to be paid for t = 12 years given r = 12%; then

$$PVA = £500(PVIFA_{12,12}) = £500(6.194) = £3097$$

In other words, if £500 is received annually for the next 12 years and the discount rate is 12%, the present value of this future series is £3097. Alternatively, if I = £2000, t = 6 and r = 5%, $PVIFA_{6,5} = 5.076$, and the present value is £10,152.

Basic decision rules

The annuity formula can be used to illustrate, at a simplified level, how some decision rules can be formulated to help choose between investment alternatives.

Assume that a relative has just retired from employment and is considering using part of a retirement gratuity to purchase a ten-year annuity. A financial advisor has offered a choice of one from two:
- Annuity A, price £10,000, producing annual income of £1652
- Annuity B, price £15,000, producing annual income of £2235

The relative wants advice on which annuity to purchase. Assuming no risk of default, someone unfamiliar with the concept of the time value of money might suggest Annuity B; it costs more than Annuity A but, of course, it offers higher annual income payments. To reach an informed decision, a common base is needed on which to compare the two annuities.

An average annual rate of return, which assesses the income generated by an investment, relative to its initial cost, enables such a comparison to be made. Using the annuity formula, the average annual rate of return is the discount rate which equates the present value of each annuity's future payments to its initial price. In the case of Annuity A, the question is being asked: what discount rate, r_A, if applied to the future annual payments of £1672 would produce a PV of £10,000? From Equation 2.4c,

$$£10,000 = £1652(PVIFA_{10,r_A})$$

therefore,

$$PVIFA_{10,r} = £10,000/£1652 = 6.053$$

Turning to Table A.3, since t = 10 is known, read across this row to find the PVIFA closest to 6.053. It is 6.145 which, as the PVIFA for 10 years at r = 10%, indicates that the rate of return on Annuity A is $r_A \simeq 10\%$. Following a similar process for Annuity B,

$$£15,000 = £2235(PVIFA_{10,r_B})$$

therefore,

$$PVIFA_{10,r} = 6.711 \text{ and } r_B \simeq 8\%$$

On comparison, although the annual income of Annuity A is lower than that of Annuity B, when the incomes from the two annuities are related to their respective prices Annuity A provides a higher rate of return and is to be preferred.

Internal rate of return

The discount rate which renders the discounted sum of a future cash flow series equal to its initial price or cost, is known as the Internal Rate of Return and denoted as IRR. Use of this form of the discount rate is valid in the above example. Annuity A is chosen because it has a higher IRR than annuity B. The direct application of the IRR as a decision rule for choosing among investment alternatives is limited, however, to a set of special circumstances. These circumstances are discussed fully in Chapter 6.

Net present value

The annuity formula can be used in a slightly different way to illustrate an alternative decision rule based on the direct use of present values.

Assume a financial institution wishes to sell a fifteen-year annuity, producing annual payments of £1000, and that there is no default risk. To decide the price at which the annuity is to be sold, the institution must estimate its opportunity cost of capital: the return that could be earned on these funds in their best alternative use. Assume this is 10%; the annuity will be priced at $£1000(PVIFA_{15,10}) = £7606$. A potential investor who is considering purchasing this annuity must make a personal assessment of its present value based on his/her own discount rate. If this discount rate is 12%, the investor's valuation is $£1000(6.811) = £6811$ and the investor would not purchase the annuity since the institution's price for the annuity exceeds the investor's own assessment of its present value or present worth.

Looking at the annuity from this angle, the concept of Net Present Value, NPV, is introduced. The NPV of an investment is defined as the difference between the present value of its future cash inflows and the present value of its future cash outflows. Viewing the potential purchase of the annuity from the investor's point of view, NPV is the difference between his/her present valuation of the future cash inflows from owning the annuity (£6811) and the present cost of purchase (£7606). The NPV is negative,

$$NPV = £6811 - £7606 = -£795$$

and the investor rejects the annuity.

If the investor used a different discount rate, say 8%, his/her present value assessment of the annuity income would be £8560 and the NPV would be positive:

$$NPV = £8560 - £7606 = £954$$

In this case the investor would probably consider the annuity to be a bargain and purchase it. If the investor and the financial institution concurred on a discount rate of 10%, the investor would probably consider the annuity to be fairly priced and assess it as having a zero NPV. In this case the investor's present valuation of the future cash inflows from owning the annuity would now be £7606, which equals the present cost of purchase. As it will be argued in Chapters 6 and 7, the NPV concept underlies most accept/reject decision rules in corporate finance.

Required and expected rates of return

This last annuity example can also be used to illustrate the concepts of required and expected rates of return which are fully discussed in Chapter 3. An investor who is interested in purchasing this annuity views it as having an expected rate of return of 10%, the discount rate used by the financial institution to determine its price. The investor's own discount rate is what is known as his/her required rate of return. If this required rate of return is 12%, it exceeds the expected rate of return. In other words, the annuity is expected to produce a rate of return below the rate the investor requires and the annuity is not purchased; vice versa if the required rate is 8% and the expected rate is 10%. If the annuity is an asset traded in a financial market, and the required rate exceeds the expected rate, the market price will fall to bring the two rates into equality; vice versa if the required rate is less than the expected rate. When the required and expected rates are equal, NPV = 0, and the asset is fairly priced.

The future value of a fixed annuity

Individuals, and some companies, often have regular savings plans where a fixed amount of money is added to a savings account on a regular periodic basis. The future value of such an investment can be determined by a simple manipulation of the present value annuity formula in Equation 2.4b:

$$PVA = I \left[\frac{1 - (1 + r)^{-t}}{r} \right]$$

Assume that this present amount of money, PVA, is invested for t periods at r. Using the compounding formula in Equation 2.1, its future value at the end of t years, is $PVA(1 + r)^t$, or

$$FVA = I \left[\frac{1 - (1 + r)^{-t}}{r} \right] (1 + r)^t$$

With a slight rearrangement the future value of the annuity is:

$$FVA = I \left[\frac{(1 + r)^t - 1}{r} \right] \qquad (2.5)$$

In effect the fixed cash flows which are discounted in the present value annuity formula are now being viewed as regular periodic deposits, each of which is compounded from the time period when the deposit is made to the end of the term of the investment.[6] To simplify, Equation 2.5 can be written as:

$$FVA = I(FVIFA_{t,r}) \qquad (2.5a)$$

$FVIFA_{t,r}$ is the future value interest factor of a £1 annuity invested for t periods at r and is given in Table A.4. If, for example, £1000 is invested annually for seven years at r = 10%, $FVIFA_{7,10} = 9.487$, and the future value is £1000(9.487) = £9487.

This formula can be used to determine the fixed amount of money, earning interest, that needs to be deposited on a regular basis to meet some future commitment or savings target. If, for example, a company estimates that it will need to replace a piece of capital equipment three years from now, at a future net cost of £100,000, it might decide to meet this future commitment by setting aside a fixed annual amount of £I. Assuming that this can earn annual interest at 8%, the annual amount of set-aside is determined from Equation 2.5a as £30,807 per year, for the next three years. That is,

$$£100,000 = I(FVIFA_{3,8}) = I(3.246)$$

therefore,

$$I = £100,000/3.246 = £30,807$$

Loan amortisation

The annuity concept can also be used to illustrate a loan amortisation schedule. Here a principal amount of money is borrowed and repaid in fixed regular instalments over a given time interval. Each repayment includes an element of interest and a contribution towards the repayment of the principal or capital amount borrowed. Interest payments are determined on a declining balance basis which means that the interest rate is levied on the principal value of the loan outstanding, after deducting the appropriate principal repayments at the end of the previous period. At the end of the term of the loan all capital and interest charges have been met. Given the term of the loan and the interest rate, the level of the fixed repayments can be determined.

Assume that a loan of £4080 is to be taken out over a three-year period, at $r = 7\%$, with repayments made in equal annual instalments at the end of each year. The loan can be viewed, from the lender's point of view, as the purchase of a three-period annuity of £I which has a PV of £4080. Using Equation 2.4c, each instalment of £I can be determined as:

$$£4080 = I(PVIFA_{3,7})$$

therefore,

$$I = \frac{£4080}{PVIFA_{3,7}} = \frac{£4080}{2.624} = £1554.90$$

The loan amortisation schedule is shown in Table 2.5. In year one, for example, the 7% interest rate produces an interest charge of $(0.07)(£4080) = £285.60$. With the year one repayment of £1554.90, the implied repayment of the capital amount borrowed is $£1554.90 - £285.60 = £1269.30$. Thus, at the end of year one only $£4080.00 - £1269.30 = £2810.70$ of the principal amount borrowed remains outstanding. The interest charge for year two is determined by applying the 7% rate to this outstanding value, that is, $(0.07)(£2810.70) = £196.75$.

The above approach is also employed by building societies and banks to determine monthly mortgage repayments. Here, however, one small variation applies: the interest payment in each month is not deducted from the principal value of the mortgage until the end of the financial year.

Table 2.5: Loan amortisation

Year End	Repayment Instalment[1] (£'s)	Loan Interest (£'s)	Principal Repayment (£'s)	Loan Outstanding (£'s)
1	1554.90	285.60	1269.30	2810.70
2	1554.90	196.70	1358.20	1452.50
3	1554.90	101.70	1453.20	≈0.00

[1] Initial loan £4080

Opportunity cost

From the example in Table 2.5, the discount rate used to determine present value can be viewed as an opportunity cost since it automatically takes account of the alternative possibilities open to the lender. As the lending institution receives the future repayment instalments on the loan of £4080, it can relend these at r = 7%. Using Equation 2.5a, the formula for the future value of an annuity, the lender would have £1554.90(FVIFA$_{3,7}$) = £1554.90(3.215) ≈ £5000 at the end of three years. Since, however, the present value of the future £5000 is £5000(PVIF$_{3,7}$) = £4080, the reinvestment of the instalments is equivalent to the amount that the institution is currently going to lend. There is, therefore, no need to take explicit account of the reinvestment possibilities.

This is demonstrated, yet again, by going back to Table 2.1 which involved an example of borrowing £4080 and using a gift of £5000, at the end of three years, to repay the principal and meet the cumulative compound interest charges. An equivalent alternative to the example in Table 2.1 has now been established, where an individual could have borrowed successive yearly amounts matching the instalments in Table 2.5. Therefore, a discount rate always represents the opportunity cost of capital, that is, the opportunity cost of funds borrowed or lent. Thus, applying the appropriate discount rate in a present value calculation automatically takes account of all the alternative borrowing and lending possibilities.

The present value of a perpetuity

A perpetuity is an annuity which has a perpetual, that is unlimited, future series of annual fixed cash flows. In technical terms, since the future series never ends, t tends to infinity (t –> ∞). Given the present value of the annuity, specified in Equation 2.4b, and assuming r > 0, as t –> ∞, $1/(1 + r)^t$ –>0 and the present value becomes:

$$PVP = \frac{I}{r}$$

(2.6)

In other words the present value of a perpetuity is simply the annual fixed payment divided by the discount rate. If, for example, an annual cash flow of £10,000 is to be received in perpetuity and r = 10%, its present value is £100,000. If r = 5%, then PVP = £200,000.

There are assets which in practice make regular fixed payments in perpetuity, for example, British Government Consols. In addition, in developing theory in corporate finance the perpetuity is sometimes used as a simplifying assumption.

Within-year compounding and discounting

In most of the problems examined in this chapter the time period, t, has been defined as a year. In many instances an annual interest rate is applied at regular intervals within a year. Some examples are: government bonds which pay interest on a semi-annual basis and deposit accounts which offer interest on a semi-annual compounding basis.

The compounding and discounting formulas can easily be adapted to accommodate a within-year problem. No adaptation is required in the case of the interest factor Tables A.1 to A.4, since the first column of each refers to periods. If, for example, interest on a principal amount is to be compounded on a six-monthly basis, over three years, then the number of compounding periods is six. Generalising, if interest is compounded m times within a year, over t years, then the total number of compounding periods is mt.

Interest rates, and discount rates, are normally quoted on an annual basis; therefore, if there are m compounding periods within a year, the per period rate of interest is r/m. Assuming, for example, that a 6% annual rate of interest is compounded semi-annually, the per period rate of interest is 3%. If £100 is invested under these conditions for t = 2 years, since there are four compounding periods (mt = 4) the future value, at the end of two years, is: $£100(1.03)^4 = £112.6$.

Generalising, if interest is compounded m times within a year over t years, Equation 2.1 is adapted to give a future value:

$$FV_{mt} = PV\left[1 + \frac{r}{m}\right]^{mt} \tag{2.7}$$

In terms of future value interest factors:

$$FV_{mt} = PV(FVIF_{mt, r/m}) \tag{2.7a}$$

As an example, assume PV = £100, r = 12%, t = 5 and m = 4; then $FVIF_{20,3} = 1.806$ and the future value over twenty periods, or a five-year term, is $FV_{20} = £180.6$. If interest is compounded at the end of each year only, that is if m = 1, then the future value falls to £179.60.

When a future cash flow is to be discounted and the annual interest rate is compounded m times within a year, Equation 2.2 is adapted to give the present value as:

$$PV = \frac{X_t}{\left(1 + \frac{r}{m}\right)^{mt}} \tag{2.8}$$

In terms of PVIFs:

$$PV = X_t(PVIF_{mt, r/m}) \tag{2.8a}$$

As an example, assume t = 4, r = 9%, m = 3 and X_t = £500; then PV = £500($PVIF_{12,3}$) = £350.50. Alternatively, if the discount rate is applied annually, that is if m = 1, PV = £354.

The value of m can be large, for example if interest is compounded daily; or very large, if interest is compounded every second. In the limit, letting m tend to become infinitely large, compounding and discounting become continuous. These concepts are explored further in the Appendix to this chapter.

Effective rates of interest

In the analysis so far, it has been assumed that a rate of interest is:

(i) defined over a given period,
(ii) applied on an end of period compound basis, and
(iii) in the case of a multi-period loan, applied using the declining balance approach.

To bring this chapter to a close, the implications of these assumptions are now examined.

Any comparison of interest rates is only valid if the rates are calculated on a common basis. To standardise the approach to this, an effective rate of interest is defined on the basis of the effective interest charge at the end of a given period, divided by the effective amount borrowed at the beginning of that period. If nominally quoted interest rates satisfy the above assumptions they are effective rates of interest.

In the case of the period over which a rate is quoted, the length of the period – a day, a month, or a year – is irrelevant, provided that each nominal rate is quoted in relation to the specified period. If, for example, a six-month, end of period, compound rate is quoted at 6%, then this nominal rate is the effective six-month rate. Here, a loan of £1000 will have an interest charge of £60 at the end of six months, so that the effective rate of interest is:

$$\frac{\text{Interest Charge}}{\text{Principal}} = \frac{£60}{£100} = 6\%$$

This interest rate could, however, have been applied on a discount basis, in which case the interest charge would be deducted from the principal value of the loan at the beginning of the period. In this case a borrower would receive the principal value less interest: £1000 − £60 = £940. At the end of the period, the borrower repays the principal of £1000 which includes a payment covering the interest charge. Thus the effective six-month rate of interest is:

$$\frac{\text{Interest}}{\text{Principal} - \text{Interest}} = \frac{£60}{£1000 - £60} = 6.38\%$$

This is not equal to the nominally quoted six-month rate of 6%.

Effective annual rate

Normally interest rates are quoted on an annual basis but, as shown previously, often compounded at regular intervals within a year. The effective annual compound rate of interest, r_{ef}, cannot, therefore, be equal to the nominally quoted rate r_{nom}. The reason should be clear: the end year value of £1 invested now, will increase as m increases.

The definition of r_{ef} is explained as follows. First, consider the compounding formula in Equation 2.7 and assume £1 is invested for one year, with m within year compounding periods. With $t = 1$, and a per period compound rate of interest of r_{nom}/m, the future value is:

$$\left(1 + \frac{r_{nom}}{m}\right)^m = FVIF_{m, r_{nom}/m}$$

Second, consider a hypothetical one-year investment where £1 is deposited to produce this future value but with interest compounded, in one lump sum, at the end of the year. Third, ask the question: what rate of interest, r_{ef}, would produce this future value for the hypothetical alternative? Since the future value of the hypothetical alternative must be $(1 + r_{ef})$, then

$$1 + r_{ef} = FVIF_{m, r_{nom}/m}$$

that is,

$$r_{ef} = FVIF_{m, r_{nom}/m} - 1 \tag{2.9}$$

Thus the effective annual rate of interest is the relevant future value interest factor, less one.

If a deposit account offers a nominal annual rate of interest of 10%, with $m = 5$, then:

$$r_{ef} = FVIF_{5,2} - 1 = 1.104 - 1 = 0.104 \text{ or } 10.4\%$$

If another account offers $r_{nom} = 12\%$, with $m = 6$:

$$r_{ef} = FVIF_{6,2} - 1 = 1.126 - 1 \text{ or } 12.6\%$$

If the same nominal rate is offered with m increased to 12:

$$r_{ef} = FVIF_{12,1} - 1 = 1.127 - 1 \text{ or } 12.7\%$$

Annual percentage rate (APR)

In the case of most term loans offered by banks and finance houses, where repayments are made in fixed regular instalments, interest charges are determined neither at the end of each instalment period nor using the declining balance approach.[7] These factors violate assumptions (i) and (iii) above.

Instead, the nominally quoted rate of interest is applied annually, over the whole term of the loan, to the principal amount borrowed. The amount of each fixed regular instalment is then determined by adding the total interest charges to the principal amount borrowed, and dividing by the total number of instalment periods over the term.

In effect, interest is being determined on what is referred to as an add-on basis, as opposed to a compounding basis. In these cases effective comparisons can be made between alternative loans by using the concept of the Annual Percentage Rate or APR.

An example

To exemplify, assume £2000 is borrowed at a nominal annual rate of 13.44%. The term of the loan is two years. Thus, the annual rate of interest is applied to the principal value of the loan to determine the annual interest charge: $(0.1344)(£2000) = £268.80$. This interest charge is made in each of the two years of the loan and equals, in total, £537.60. Repayments are made in 12 regular instalments per year, so that there are 24 instalments in all. The fixed repayment instalment is determined by adding the total interest charge to the principal value of the loan and dividing by the number of instalments. That is, $(£2000 + £537.60) \div 24$. The profile of this loan is summarised as follows:

Principal amount borrowed or actually received	£2000.00
Total interest charge £2000(0.1344)(2)	£537.60
Face value of loan £2000 + £537.60	£2537.60
Instalment repayment (£2537.60)/24	£105.73

Determining the APR

To determine the APR, the financial institution making the loan is viewed as having purchased a 24-period annuity, at a price equal to the principal value of the loan. Since each instalment represents the per period annuity payment to the financial institution, Equation 2.4c can be solved for the instalment period annuity rate of interest, r_{pa}, that is:

$$£2000 = £105.73(PVIFA_{24,rpa})$$

therefore,

$$PVIFA_{24,rpa} = £2000/105.73 = 18.92$$

Given $t = 24$, r_{pa} can be found from Table A.3, it is 2%.

The APR is then defined as r_{pa} times the number of instalment repayment periods (m) per year:

$$APR = m(r_{pa}) \qquad (2.10)$$

Given that there are 12 instalment periods per year in this example, the APR is $12(2\%) = 24\%$.

Note that the instalment period annuity rate, a one-month rate of $r_{pa} = 2\%$, exceeds the nominal one-month instalment period rate of 1.12%. This latter rate is the nominal annual rate of 13.44% divided by m, that is $13.44\% \div 12 = 1.12\%$. Consequently, the APR must exceed the nominal annual rate.

Another example

As a final example, assume you own a small business and wish to borrow £100,000 over four years. You have approached two banks and both are willing to advance

Table 2.6: Determining APRs

	Bank A $r_{nom} = 18.50\%$, m = 6 t = 4	Bank B $r_{nom} = 19.58\%$, m = 2 t = 4
	(£'ths)	(£'ths)
PV: Principal amount borrowed	100.00	100.00
TIC: Total interest charge $t(r_{nom})(PV)$	74.00	78.32
FAC: Face value borrowed PV + TIC	174.00	178.32
IR: Instalment repayment FAC/mt	7.25	22.29
$PVIFA_{mt,r_{pa}} = PV/IR$	13.793	4.487
r_{pa}: per period rate of interest	5.00%	15.00%
APR = m(r_{pa})	30.00%	30.00%

[1] t is the term of the loan in years, m the number of instalment periods within a year, r_{nom} the nominal annual rate of interest.

the loan. Bank A quotes a nominal annual rate of interest of 18.5%, with repayments in six regular instalments per year. Bank B quotes a nominal rate of 19.58%, with two regular instalments per year. The choice of loan depends on the respective APRs. These are calculated in Table 2.6. Since the APRs are equal, you would conclude, on the basis of this statutory measure, that there is no difference between the two loans offered.[8]

All financial institutions offering term loans will quote their interest rates on both a nominal annual and an APR basis. Before approaching such an institution to attempt to arrange a loan, you must find out if there are other fees and charges and whether or not these are included in the quoted APR. You might be charged an interview fee for meeting a bank manager to discuss the possibility of being given a loan and, if the loan is granted, a further arrangement fee. If these fees are included in the APR, well and good. If not, you must find out what the APR is, including non-interest fees and charges, before a formal approach is made.

Real and nominal rates of interest

Reference is often made to the real rate of interest. Providing that there is no default risk associated with an investment, the nominal annual rate of interest includes the real rate of interest (r^*) and an adjustment for expected inflation. To explain this, take the base rate of interest,[9] or the minimum lending rate determined by a central bank, as a crude measure of the general level of interest rates in an economy. Then, measuring the rate of inflation (r_{RPI}) in terms of a retail price index, the base rate (r_b) can be expressed as:

$$(1 + r_b) = (1 + r^*)(1 + r_{RPI}) \qquad (2.11)$$

In other words, in the absence of inflation money has a real time value. In the presence of inflation, however, the compounding (and discounting) process must recognise that the postponement of the purchase of a bundle of goods today involves added, inflation induced, expenditure tomorrow. If, for example, the nominal base rate is 15% and the expected rate of inflation is 5%, the real rate of interest is determined from Equation 2.11 as:

$$1 + r^* = \frac{(1 + r_b)}{(1 + r_{RPI})}$$

$$= \frac{1.15}{1.05} = 1.095$$

(2.11a)

That is, the real rate is $r^* = 1.095 - 1.00$ or 9.5%. Removing the brackets in Equation 2.11:

$$1 + r_b = 1 + r^* + r_{RPI} + (r^*)(r_{RPI})$$

Since $(r^*)(r_{RPI})$ is relatively small, in the example it is $(.15)(.05) = 0.0075$, the nominal rate is often expressed as $r_b \simeq r^* + r_{RPI}$ and the real rate as the nominal rate less the expected inflation rate:

$$r^* \simeq r_b - r_{RPI}$$

(2.11b)

In the example, with the approximate real rate at 10%, the approximation is not that close.

Summary

This chapter has concentrated on the basic techniques of compounding and discounting. It has demonstrated how a future series of cash flows can be expressed as a single amount of money through either compounding to obtain a future value, or discounting to obtain a present value. If asked to identify one of the key concepts which underlies most of the rest of this book, it would be the present value. Many of the decisions made in corporate finance are based on the current prices, or present values, of assets whose entire function is to produce future cash flows.

It is worth formally defining the concept of present value once again. From Equations 2.3 and 2.3a, if r is the per period discount rate and X_t represents a series of cash flows at the end of the time periods $t = 0, 1, 2 \ldots, n$, then the present value of the series, at time zero, is:

$$PV = X_0 + \frac{X_1}{1 + r} + \frac{X_2}{(1 + r)^2} + \cdots + \frac{X_n}{(1 + r)^n}$$

or

$$PV = \sum_{t=0}^{n} \frac{X_t}{(1 + r)^t}$$

Since some of the issues in valuation are highly complex, academics involved in corporate finance have developed simplified models to attempt to focus on the key factors which determine the market value of particular assets. This process of model building is aided by making simplifying assumptions. Given its simplicity, perpetuity valuation has been used in developing some of the basic share valuation models. These are explored in the next chapter. Perpetuity valuation has also been used to help focus attention on one of the major, and continuing, controversies in corporate finance: the capital structure, valuation debate.

To restate the perpetuity valuation principle, if r is the per period discount rate and £1 represents a fixed cash flow to be received from the end of period one in perpetuity, then the present value of the perpetuity, at time zero, is (as Equation 2.6 demonstrated):

$$PVP = \frac{1}{r}$$

Questions

1 Assume you wish to invest £1000. What will this sum of money have grown to if it is deposited for:
   a) t = 5 years at an annual compound rate of interest of r = 15%
   b) t = 10 at r = 8%
   c) t = 30 at r = 6%?

2 Find the present value of the following series of cash flows, assuming a discount rate of 5%.

Year	0	1	2	3	4
Cash Flow(£s)	500	3000	6000	1000	500

How would the present value of this series change if the discount rate
   a) rises to 7%
   b) falls to 3%?

3 Find the present value of an annual fixed sum of £4000, to be received for ten years, beginning at the end of year one. Assume the discount rate is 6%. What is the present value of this annual sum if it is to be received for 15 years at a discount rate of 8%? What is its present value if it is to be received in perpetuity and r = 8%?

4 You are offered a choice between two ten-year annuities. Annuity A costs £7360 and offers an annual sum of £1000. Annuity B costs £9266 and offers an annual sum of £1200.
   a) Find the rate of return on each annuity and indicate which one is 'better value'.
   b) In the case of Annuity A, assume that your opportunity cost of funds is 8%. Explain whether or not you would make an outright decision to reject this annuity.

5 You are going to borrow £10,000 to be repaid in four annual fixed instalments. The quoted annual rate of interest is 10% and interest is to be charged on a declining balance basis. Show the loan amortisation schedule, indicating the annual interest charge and capital repayments.

6 You are going to invest £500 for three years at a quoted annual rate of interest r. What sum of money will you have at the end of three years if:

a) r at 8% is credited at the end of each year
b) r at 8% is credited semi-annually
c) r at 8% is credited eight times within a year?
Find the effective annual rate of interest in each case.

7 Assume an instalment loan manager quotes a six-month rate of interest of 14.7% on a £4000 loan which has monthly repayments over a two-year period. Find the APR.

8 The nominal annual rate of interest is 9% and the expected annual rate of inflation is 4.81%. Find
a) the approximate real rate of interest
b) the exact real rate of interest.

Exercises

1 Assume an instalment loan manager quotes an annual rate of interest of 38.05% on a £1000 loan over a two-year period. Fixed repayments are to be made at the end of each two-month period. Find the APR.

2 You are 65 years of age. A pension fund manager offers to sell you an annuity for £20,000. This annuity will pay £4000 a year for the next ten years. What is the approximate annual rate of return (to the nearest whole number) on this investment? All other things being equal, would you undertake, reject or be indifferent to this investment if the opportunity cost to you was
a) 10%
b) 15% or
c) 20%?
What is the NPV in each case?

3 Assume an annual market rate of interest of 10%. You have five years to retirement and your salary for the next five years (paid year end) is as follows: £10,000, £15,000, £15,000, £20,000 and £25,000. You will receive, on retirement, a gratuity of £20,000 and a pension of £4000 per year for a subsequent ten years.

You are now offered early retirement with a lump sum of £50,000 and a pension of £5000 per year for the next 15 years. From a purely financial perspective, what would you do: take early retirement or continue working?

Endnotes

1. If an investor receives interest annually on a simple interest basis, the interest rate would only be applied to the principal amount invested. Thus, applying simple interest in this example, the total interest calculated at the end of year two is £10. The interest credited, and not withdrawn, at the end of year one is ignored.

2. An inverse relationship may not exist over a range of discount rates if a cash flow series

changes sign more than once. This is known as the multiple roots problem and will be discussed in Chapter 6.

3. Such an investment opportunity could arise if a financial institution wanted to attract and maintain more long-term deposits. Future stepped-up interest rates could be offered over a specified time interval, provided no withdrawals were made over that interval. Alternatively, if the certainty assumption is relaxed, the example could reflect an investor's assessment of future interest rate movements.

4. Assume that an additional deposit of £1000 is made at the end of year six. The future value, at the end of year nine, will be increased by $£1000(FVIF_{1,6})(FVIF_{2,8}) = £1235.96$, taking the total future value of the investment to £2860.75.

5. Consider Equation 2.4a

$$PVA = I\left[\frac{1}{(1+r)} + \cdots + \frac{1}{(1+r)^{n-1}} + \frac{1}{(1+r)^n}\right] \tag{i}$$

Multiplied on both sides by $(1 + r)$.

$$PVA(1+r) = I\left[1 + \frac{1}{(1+r)} + \cdots + \frac{1}{(1+r)^{n-2}} + \frac{1}{(1+r)^{n-1}}\right] \tag{ii}$$

By subtracting Equation (i) from Equation (ii), the common terms which appear inside the brackets [ ] in both equations cancel, so that

$$PVA(1+r) - PVA = I\left[1 - \frac{1}{(1+r)^n}\right]$$

$$PVA(1 + r - 1) = I\left[1 - \frac{1}{(1+r)^n}\right]$$

Therefore, $PVA(1 + r - 1) = I[1 - (1+r)^{-n}] = I\left[\dfrac{1 - (1+r)^{-n}}{r}\right]$

6. Each individual deposit has a future value at the end of period t so that the future value of the annuity is the sum of these individual future values. Note that the final deposit does not earn interest, since it occurs right at the end of the term of the investment.

7. Recall that this is not the way in which a bank or building society determines mortgage repayments. These are determined using the declining balance approach explained in Table 2.5, where the interest rate is applied at the end of the current period on the principal outstanding at the beginning of this period, that is, at the end of the previous period.

8. The APR is a statutory measure introduced under consumer credit legislation to produce a standardised method of quoting interest rates on various loans. Technically the APR is not an effective annual rate of interest since it is not based on an effective interest charge at the end of a year. It is based on the effective rate for the instalment period, multiplied by the number of annual instalments. Given the effective annuity (instalment) period rates in the example, effective annual rates can be calculated using Equation 2.9. For Bank A, $FVIF_{6,5} - 1 = 1.340 - 1$ or 34.00%, and for Bank B, $FVIF_{2,15} - 1 = 1.322 - 1$ or 32.20%.

9. The closest approximation to a default free, or risk free, nominal rate of interest is the rate of return that can be earned on short-term government debt: the Treasury Bill rate.

Appendix 2.1   Continuous compounding and discounting

In Chapter 2 compounding and discounting is carried out on a discrete basis, that is, at the end of a specified time interval. Given that interest is compounded m times within a year, the future value formula, Equation 2.7, is:

$$FV_{mt} = PV\left(1 + \frac{r}{m}\right)^{mt}$$

Letting P_0 denote the initial investment, instead of PV, and defining the future value at the end of t years, V_t, this equation becomes:

$$V_t = P_0\left(1 + \frac{r}{m}\right)^{mt}$$

Multiplying mt by r/r,

$$V_t = P_0\left[\left(1 + \frac{r}{m}\right)^{m/r}\right]^{rt} \text{ or}$$

$$V_t = P_0\left[\left(1 + \frac{1}{m/r}\right)^{m/r}\right]^{rt}$$

For continuous compounding, m→∞, in which case:

$$\lim_{m\to\infty}\left(1 + \frac{1}{m/r}\right)^{m/r} = e$$

Thus, in terms of an exponential, the future value can be expressed as:

$$V_t = P_0 e^{rt}$$

If £100 is invested now, for five years, at a continuously compounded rate, r = 8%, the investment will have grown to:

$$V_5 = £100e^{(0.081)(5)} = £100e^{0.4} = £100(1.4918) = £149.18$$

For continuous discounting:

$$P_0 = V_t e^{-rt}$$

If £1000 is to be received six years from now, given r = 5%, its present value is

$$P_0 = £1000e^{-(0.05)(6)} = £1000e^{-0.03} = £1000(7.74) = £741$$

Note that in the continuous case e^{rt} and e^{-rt} are, respectively, the future value and present value interest factors.

Reference

Fisher, I. *The Theory of Interest*, New York, Augustus M. Kelly, 1965 (reprint of original edition, 1930)

3 Debt and equity valuation

Introduction

The confidence that can be placed in an asset's current market price as a fair measure of its true or intrinsic value, is an essential component of investment and financing decisions in a complex world. To gain an understanding of how asset prices are determined and to assess the information they convey, this chapter presents basic models of bond and share price determination. Since an asset's price is a function of its future net cash flows, formal valuation techniques are applied, based on the discounting principle developed in Chapter 2. The role of the investment analyst industry in assessing information and interpreting the core factors which determine bond and equity market prices is also outlined.

In applying the formal techniques it is assumed that fixed interest and dividend payments occur on an end of period basis, each period representing a year. It is also assumed that there are no transactions charges in buying and selling assets and no tax effects to be taken into account. Finally, the asset price determined by a valuation model represents the mid-price between the market's bid–offer spread.

Characteristics of long-term debt and equity

Equity, or common shares, convey ownership and voting rights in a company and entitlement to future dividend payments. Per period dividend payments are made at the discretion of the management of a company and vary through time. Once issued, equity is normally not retired so that dividend entitlements exist in perpetuity or, at minimum, over the future life of a company.

Bonds are the primary method of raising long-term debt capital. Unlike equity, which has a perpetuity feature and does not have to make a dividend payment in any given year, bonds make committed regular fixed interest payments over a specified number of years or term to maturity. At the end of the bond's term, when it is retired (or redeemed), the last fixed interest payment is made and the par or face value of the bond is repaid. This par value is the nominal amount of capital raised when the bond is first issued. At any point over its term, a bond's market price might or might not be equal to its par value.

There are two broad classes of long-term debt: government bonds and corporate bonds. In the former case, these are referred to as gilt-edged securities since it is highly improbable that a government in an advanced capitalist democracy will default on its interest payments. Corporate bonds do, however, possess default risk since companies can experience cash flow difficulties which can jeopardise their ability to meet fixed interest commitments.

For gilts which have known fixed interest payments, market prices are determined by the general level of interest rates in the economy. This level depends on a number of interrelated factors: the real rate of interest, anticipated inflation, the risk of unanticipated inflation and the government's economic policy stance. The latter will determine how a government increases or decreases base rates of interest in response to changes in unemployment levels, balance of payments and associated exchange rate problems and its own estimate of expected inflation.

The absence of default risk on gilts results in these assets earning a lower rate of return than corporate bonds. In turn, corporate bonds earn a lower rate of return than equities. With the payment of dividends being subject to the discretion of management, equity has a more risky future cash flow series, relative to the committed fixed interest payments on corporate debt.

Bond valuation

The market value of a bond can be explained, using the present value principle presented in Equation 2.3a, as:

$$BV_0 = \sum_{t=1}^{n} \frac{I}{(1 + r_d)^t} + \frac{M}{(1 + r_d)^n} \qquad (3.1)$$

BV_0 is the market price of the bond at $t = 0$.
M is its par or face value.
n is the number of periods outstanding, or term to maturity, before the bond is retired or redeemed and the par value repaid.
I is the fixed interest or coupon payment in period t, $t = 1, 2, \ldots, n$. It is assumed that the fixed interest payment due at $t = 0$ has just been received.[1]
r_d is the yield to maturity or yield to redemption. It is the internal rate of return on the bond, that is, the discount rate which equates the discounted sum of future interest payments and the par value to the bond's current price.
r_c is the implicit coupon interest rate, I/M. It is the fixed interest payment divided by the par value.

With a bond making fixed interest payments, the first term on the right-hand side of Equation 3.1 is the present value of an annuity and the second term is the present value of a future cash flow. Equation 3.1 can therefore be expressed as:

$$BV_0 = I(PVIFA_{n,rd}) + M(PVIF_{n,rd}) \qquad (3.1a)$$

The fixed interest payments, the par value and the current market price of the bond are known. Assuming there is active trading in the bond markets, then with investors willing to trade at BV_0, the yield to maturity or IRR represents the rate of return that the market requires for trade to take place at this price.

Gilts[2]

To understand how the factors on the right-hand side of Equation 3.1 determine a bond's price, it is useful to begin by considering how the interest payments are set in relation to the par value when a bond is first issued. To abstract from default risk, only gilt-edged securities are considered at this stage.

Assume that the government wishes to raise £100m via a new gilt issue. The issue is to have a 25-year term and is to be sold at its par value, normally £100 in the United Kingdom's case. This incidentally determines the number of bonds in the issue: £100m/£100 = 1m. To ensure that the gilt issue is sold at par, the officials setting its terms must equate the coupon interest rate to the appropriate discount rate.

The discount rate is found by observing the yield to maturity on an existing traded bond which has, as nearly as possible, identical terms and conditions to the new bond which is about to be issued. This required rate of return is the cost of capital of the new issue since it is the minimum rate of return that the new issue must offer if it is to be taken up in the market. This is the rate at which the new issue's future cash flows will be discounted; therefore, to ensure that it sells initially at its par value of £100, r_c must equal r_d.

Assume $r_d = 8\%$ then, with $r_c = I/M$, this 25-year bond has a fixed interest payment of $I = r_c(M) = £8$. Substituting into Equation 3.1a yields:

$$BV_0 = £8(PVIFA_{25,8}) + £100(PVIF_{25,8})$$
$$= £8(10.675) + £100(.146) = £100$$

It is important to note that, irrespective of the term to maturity, the market price of a new or an outstanding issue will always equal its par value, if the coupon rate equals the yield to maturity. Assuming, in this example, that the bond has been outstanding for five years and that the required rate of return has remained constant, then with 20 years to maturity:

$$BV_0 = £8(PVIFA_{20,8}) + £100(PVIF_{20,8})$$
$$BV_0 = £8(9.818) + £100(.215) = £100$$

The problem of mispricing a new issue

Returning to the new issue case, if the officials setting the terms and conditions miscalculate the discount rate, the bond will be mispriced at its par value. Similarly, if between the time that the terms and conditions are set and the new issue is actually floated a change in market conditions changes the required rate of return, the bond will be mispriced at its par value. If, for example, the market's required rate is 10% and $r_c = 8\%$, the market will price the bond below its par value and the issue will not be taken up, since:

$$BV_0 = £8(PVIFA_{25,10}) + £100(PVIF_{25,10})$$
$$= £8(9.007) + £100(.092) = £81.26$$

If, alternatively, the required rate is only 6%, with $r_c = 8\%$, the market will price the bond above its par value. Investors who committed themselves to purchasing it at par in the primary market have the prospect of making a positive abnormal return through resale in the secondary market, since:

$$BV_0 = £8(12.783) + £100(.233) = £125.56$$

The difficulty of attempting to ensure that the pre-set coupon rate will equal the market's current discount rate on the date the gilt is actually issued, explains why the Bank of England does not make new gilt issues at par. One of the approaches used by the Bank is an offer by tender where the coupon rate is set above the market's required discount rate. This means that the issue will sell below par; however, by taking a view on the market conditions expected at the time of issue, a minimum price is set, or struck. Tender offers above the minimum price are given priority. If the full issue cannot be sold at or above its minimum price, the remaining bonds become part of the tap stock and are sold at a later date as market conditions warrant.

Once a bond is issued it can trade at varying prices over its term since the inverse relationship between bond prices and yields to maturity holds in general.

Yield to maturity

The yield to maturity on a bond should be distinguished from the interest yield and, in turn, the coupon interest rate. Whereas the coupon rate is the fixed interest payment on a bond divided by its par value, the interest yield is the fixed interest payment divided by a bond's current market price. The interest yield is not appropriate for making comparisons between bonds with finite redemption dates, since it concentrates on interest income alone and ignores the potential capital gain or loss element in owning a bond.

Consider, for example, a bond priced at £74.85 with $M = £100$, $n = 7$ and $r_c = 4\%$. The interest yield is $£4/£74.83 = 5.35\%$ but as the bond is priced below par it will, other things being equal, experience a pure time capital gain. With the bond repaying a par value of £100 seven years from now, its market price will automatically move towards its par value as time elapses and the redemption date gets nearer. The yield to maturity reflects both the interest income and capital gains.

The yield to maturity is found by solving for r_d in the following equation:[3]

$$£74.85 = £4(\text{PVIFA}_{7,rd}) + £100(\text{PVIF}_{7,rd})$$

The yield to maturity is 9% and exceeds the interest yield, thus reflecting the potential capital gain. Note that, given $r_d = 9\%$, the bond's price one year from now, when it has six years to maturity, will have risen to:

$$£77.54 = £4(\text{PVIFA}_{6,9}) + £100(\text{PVIF}_{6,9})$$

If the above bond, with seven years to maturity, sold at £112.99, a premium above par, the interest yield would be 3.54%. The yield to maturity would be only 2%, reflecting a potential capital loss.[4] The latter yield is found by solving the equation:

$$£112.99 = £4(\text{PVIFA}_{7,rd}) + £100(\text{PVIF}_{7,rd})$$

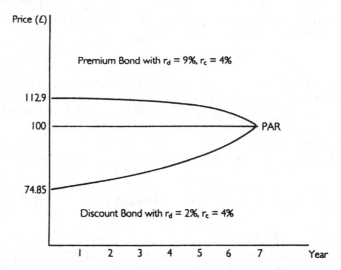

Figure 3.1   Bond prices and pure time effects

This pure time price effect is demonstrated for these two examples in Figure 3.1.

While the redemption yield reflects both interest income and potential capital gains or losses, it has its own weaknesses. By being measured at a given point in time it does not reflect the possibility that there will be changes in interest rates, and hence yields to maturity, over the outstanding term of a bond. It is in effect a promised yield, assuming nothing changes in the future, rather than the actual or realised yield over a given holding period.

Interest rate risk and term to maturity

While a bond's price varies inversely as its yield to maturity varies, the percentage change in its price, in response to a given unexpected percentage change in yields, increases with the term to maturity. This reflects what is known as interest rate risk, or price risk.

Consider two outstanding bonds with the following profiles:

Bond A: $n = 10$, $r_c = 5\%$, $M = £100$, $r_d = 5\%$
Bond B: $n = 2$, $r_c = 5\%$, $M = £100$, $r_d = 5\%$

With $r_d = 5\%$ both bonds are priced at par. Next, assume that the yield on each bond rises unexpectedly to 8% as the result, for example, of a tightening of the government's monetary policy. In this case the bonds' prices fall to:

Bond A: $£5(PVIFA_{10,8}) + £100(PVIF_{10,8}) = £79.85$
Bond B: $£5(PVIFA_{2,8}) + £100(PVIF_{2,8}) = £94.62$

There has been a three percentage point rise in yields. Bond A, with a ten-year term to maturity, experiences a price fall of 20.15% but Bond B, with a two-year term, only experiences a fall of 5.38%. Similarly, the greater the term to maturity, the greater the rise in price resulting from a given fall in yields. This price risk, resulting

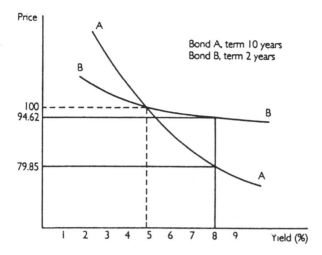

Figure 3.2   *Interest rate risk and term to maturity*

from interest rate risk, is demonstrated diagrammatically in Figure 3.2 where each bond's price, or present value schedule, is drawn by varying yields to maturity.[5]

The term structure of interest rates

In general, yields on gilts are represented by the term structure of interest rates. At a given point in time this shows the relationship between bond yields and their term to maturity, holding all other factors constant. An example of yield curves, estimated by the Bank of England (Bank of England, *Quarterly Bulletin*, February 1994), is shown in Figure 3.3. For most periods of time yield curves are upward sloping, reflecting a required higher rate of return on long-dated bonds, relative to shorts. This results from the former's higher price risk in response to interest rate risk. The term structure of interest rates is discussed in more detail at the end of Chapter 11.

Interest rate opinions

Interest rate risk and induced price risk effects are important considerations for corporate treasurers and fund managers. When current cash inflows significantly exceed current cash outflows, a company will invest part of the surplus in marketable securities to avoid excessive cash balances earning zero interest. The intention is to realise these investments at some future estimated date when the company expects cash outflows to significantly exceed cash inflows. While the levels of prospective interest income partly determine the type of marketable securities that a company chooses, an overriding concern may be the amount of funds realised when it becomes necessary to sell these marketable securities. An insurance company, for example, invests part of its policy premiums in marketable

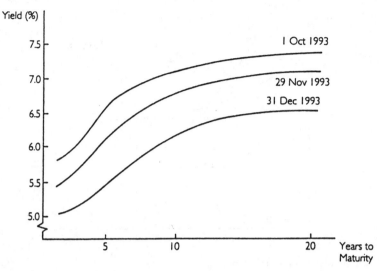

Figure 3.3   UK gilts and term structure

securities, using the interest income to meet part of its estimate of normal policy payouts. It may, however, have to sell marketable securities at future points in time to meet, for example, unexpectedly large claims resulting from exceptional storm or flood damage. Thus, price risk will be an important consideration.

Given a concern about price risk, investment analysts and fund managers will want to assess the future macroeconomic performance of the economy – its unemployment, inflationary and balance of payments prospects – to determine how interest rates are likely to behave. If investment analysts and fund managers take the opinion that base rates are likely to fall in the future, the gilt yield curve will move downwards, reflecting the anticipated fall in yields over its whole term structure. This is demonstrated in Figure 3.4. Given the yield curve YY_t, the fall in base rates implies that existing bonds, with fixed coupon payments, become more attractive; but the resulting increase in demand raises their market prices and lowers their yields to maturity, thus lowering the yield curve to YY_{t+1}.

While remaining upward sloping the yield curve might tilt in some way, the fall in yields being more marked in the case of long-dated bonds relative to short-dated bonds. This could arise because investors, believing that future interest rates will fall, place a greater emphasis on their current demand for longs. These will experience the biggest future price rises if it turns out that interest rates do fall. With an increased demand for all existing bonds, but particularly for longs, there will be a more marked increase in the prices of longs and, consequently, a more marked fall in their yields. Alternatively, if the opinion is that rises in base rates are likely, the decision might be to concentrate on shorts since these will experience the lowest price falls.

The change in the yield curve will depend on a whole range of factors: the existing supply of bonds in terms of different maturities and levels of coupon interest rates; the possibility that bond analysts and investors will take different opinions on future base rate changes; and the different investment needs of fund managers. The

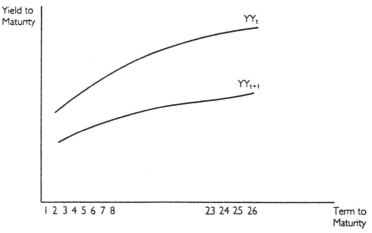

Figure 3.4   Changes in the term structure of interest rates

above illustrates, however, in a simplified way how analysts' assessments of an economy's fundamentals will be brought to bear on the gilt markets, altering prices and yields to maturity.

Bond market efficiency

The above has illustrated some active bond management strategies where investors believe that they can form opinions about future interest rate behaviour. There is, however, a very subtle problem with this. In a market where investment decisions are being made on new information about future prospects, prices and yields will start to reflect the new information through the forces of demand and supply. If the market experiences highly active trading then, in a very short period of time, market prices will have fully adjusted to new information. In this respect bond prices can be interpreted as representing the market's consensus view of future outcomes, based on the information available.

The efficient market hypothesis argues that in an advanced capitalist economy, the period of time necessary for financial markets to reflect new information is so short as to be instantaneous. The implication of this is that current yields and bond prices already fully reflect what can be deduced about the future performance of the economy. The trading described above, however, is necessary to ensure that this happens. In the example above, if the expected fall in interest rates induces an immediate increase in demand for bonds, thus raising current bond prices and lowering current yields, the market will have already reflected the anticipated future fall in interest rates.[6]

It is when markets are informationally efficient, and the likelihood of future changes are properly discounted into current prices, that assets can be described as being fairly priced. Belief in market efficiency leads to passive management strategies where investors accept that current prices are fair prices and that there is no advantage in attempting to effectively guess the future. There is also the additional implication that if markets already reflect the currently available information on, for example, future interest rate changes, there is no point in attempting to forecast the optimal time to make a new bond issue. In an efficient market the current price that can be obtained for a new bond issue and the yield the issuer is required to offer, as a current cost or price of capital, are fair prices.

Corporate bonds[7]

Bonds issued by companies to raise long-term debt capital have the same characteristics as gilts, their prices and yields to maturity being subject to general interest rate movements in the economy. The yield to maturity on a corporate bond represents the cost of long-term debt capital for the company which made the issue. The distinguishing feature of corporate bonds is the existence of default risk, which is a function of the probability that a company will experience financial distress or, in the limit, go into bankruptcy. On average the market requires a premium on corporate bond yields, relative to gilts, to compensate for the risk of default. The higher the default risk, other things being equal, the higher the required yield.

Default risk and agency costs

The concept of agency costs was introduced in Chapter 1. Recall that the agency costs of debt arise because debtholders have limited information on how debt capital is being used within a company. Assuming that management always acts in the best interests of shareholders, debtholder agency problems can be particularly acute in periods of financial distress. Here, in a make or break situation, a company's management can choose effectively to gamble and take on higher risk projects than warranted. Given a positive risk–return trade-off, if these high risk projects are successful they will produce high pay-offs which can considerably ease the company's financial distress and benefit shareholders. For the suppliers of debt capital, however, these pay-offs will not produce added benefits above the previously committed fixed interest receipts. If, alternatively, the high risk projects fail, it is the suppliers of debt capital who bear the brunt of failure through the company defaulting on its fixed interest payments.

This problem of information asymmetry could be resolved by monitoring a company's investment policy. Since monitoring involves relatively high costs, one of the market's solutions is to compensate for the agency problem of debt by requiring a further premium on corporate bond yields, thus increasing the cost of debt capital.

Default risk and agency problems can also be controlled by building restrictions into a bond's terms and conditions, or indenture provisions. These restrictions can take the form of limits on the amount of additional debt capital to be raised in the future. Existing assets, such as property, can also be pledged as collateral for the bond.[8] While this lowers the risk surrounding the fixed income stream to bondholders, and hence the yield or cost of debt capital to the company, it reduces a company's flexibility in respect of funding future attractive investment opportunities which might arise.

One way in which a company can potentially enhance this flexibility is through the inclusion of a call feature in a bond. This gives the company the right to buy back a bond, before its redemption date, at some pre-specified price. This call price feature can, however, operate to the disadvantage of bondholders. If, for example, general interest rates fall and bond market prices rise above the bond's call price, an exercise of the call by the company will result in bondholders receiving a price below market value. If a call feature is included then, other things being equal, bondholders will require higher yields on callable bonds, relative to non-callable bonds, to compensate for the risk of the call being exercised by the company.

Assessing default risk

Taking the indenture provisions and the general level of interest rates into account corporate bond analysts determine the level of default risk, which can change through time, by assessing company fundamentals. This includes an analysis of a company's financial ratios, its product market prospects, the propensity for strike activity in its plants, its research and development capabilities, its cost competitiveness within the industry sectors in which it operates, and all other factors which are likely to influence the company's ability to meet its fixed interest commitments in the future. The multinational nature of a company will also be taken into account, with assessments made of the political risks in the countries in which it operates and exchange rate risk. As is explained in Chapter 15, the latter influences the levels of export revenues, import costs and the profit variability of foreign subsidiaries.

Analysis of financial ratios focuses on the level of debt to total assets, as a measure of the overall commitment to debt capital and hence interest charges. Other ratios will also be taken into account, such as the times interest earned ratio (earnings before interest and taxes divided by interest charges) which measures the number of times a year's interest payments can be covered by a company's current annual earnings. A detailed discussion of financial ratios is contained in Chapters 12 and 17.

The risk structure of interest rates

A comprehensive assessment of all of the above factors is carried out by a number of investment analyst companies and summarised, for all corporate bonds, in regularly updated publications of default risk ratings. Two of the major rating agencies are Moody's Investment Services and Standard and Poor's Corporation. In the former case, the rankings begin with Aaa, as high or best quality bonds with minimal default risk. The next category begins with Baa, medium grade bonds with speculative investment characteristics. Here there is a low, but not insignificant, probability that companies will experience some difficulty in meeting future fixed interest commitments. The high default risk category begins with a Caa rating. Using these ratings, the upward sloping risk structure of interest rates can be measured where, other things being equal, the higher the default risk rating, the higher the required rate of return on a corporate bond.

Assessing new information as it becomes available, and responding through buying and selling activities on the markets, cause the prices and yields on corporate bonds to change. In terms of the market efficiency argument, changes in required rates of return will be instantaneous, implying that corporate bond prices are efficient prices representing all that can be known, now, about the probability of default risk at some future date.

Semi-annual interest

For ease of exposition, it has been assumed that bond interest payments are made on an end of year basis. In practice most bonds pay interest semi-annually. In this case, the fixed interest payment, determined by the quoted annual coupon rate, is divided by two and the basic bond valuation model, in Equation 3.1, is adapted to read:

$$BV_0 = \frac{I}{2} \sum_{t=1}^{2n} \frac{1}{\left(1 + \frac{r_d}{2}\right)^t} + \frac{M}{\left(1 + \frac{r_d}{2}\right)^{2n}} \qquad (3.2)$$

or

$$BV_0 = \frac{I}{2} (PVIFA_{2(n),\, rd/2}) + M(PVIF_{2(n),\, rd/2}) \qquad (3.2a)$$

Solving for the IRR produces a six-month yield to maturity.

Consider a bond with semi-annual payments, where $n = 12$, $r_c = 8\%$ and $M = £100$. The bond's current price is £116.94. With an annual coupon rate of 8% on a par value of £100, the fixed annual interest payment of £8 is made in two six-month interest payments of £4. There are 24 payment periods to redemption. The six-month yield to maturity is determined from the following equation:

$$£116.94 = £4(PVIFA_{24,\, rd/2}) + £100(PVIF_{24,\, rd/2})$$

The six-month yield is $r_d/2 = 3\%$ and the annual yield to maturity, on an APR basis,[9] is 6%.

Equity valuation[10]

Having examined the basic principles underlying corporate debt valuation, attention is now turned to the basic approaches to share valuation. Two of these are presented: one based on future dividend receipts and the other on the investment opportunities open to a company. Both approaches rely on internal financing models where future financing is based entirely on retained earnings. While this rules out the use of corporate debt and excludes new equity issues, allowance for external funding will not affect the following results providing it is assumed that investment and financing decisions are independent. The implications of this independence assumption are examined in Chapters 8 and 10.

Before developing the basic share valuation models the relationship between dividends and retained earnings, originally introduced in Chapter 1, is briefly reviewed.

Shareholders own the residual earnings of a company[11] but give discretion to management over how these earnings are split between dividends, on the one hand, and retained earnings for investment purposes, on the other. The amount of earnings per share (EPS) which a company retains determines its retention ratio:

$$b = \frac{\text{Retained EPS}}{\text{EPS}}$$

Since dividends per share (d) are equal to EPS less retentions per share, the dividend payout ratio is determined as:

$$1 - b = \frac{d}{\text{EPS}}$$

To illustrate, assume that a company with 10 million shares on issue has current earnings of £2.5m, of which £1.2m are retentions. With EPS = £0.25 and retentions per share of £0.12, b = 0.48. The payout ratio is $1 - b = 0.52$. Since 52% of EPS is paid out as dividends, d = £0.13, and the total dividend payout is £1.3m.

The dividend valuation model

In the dividend valuation model the future cash flow series determining a company's share price is comprised entirely of future expected dividend payments. This is based on the assumption that a company is never liquidated or involved in a merger, so that the owners of its common shares have an entitlement to an infinite series of dividend payments. Using the present value principle presented in Equation 2.3a, the dividend valuation model is formally expressed as:

$$P_0 = \sum_{t=1}^{\infty} \frac{d_t}{(1 + r_e)^t} \tag{3.3}$$

$$= \frac{d_1}{1 + r_e} + \frac{d_2}{(1 + r_e)^2} + \ldots + \frac{d_n}{(1 + r_e)^n} + \ldots +$$

P_0 is the market price of the share at $t = 0$.
d_t is the expected dividend per share in period t, $t = 1, 2, \ldots, n, \ldots, \infty$; assuming that the current, or $t = 0$, dividend has just been paid.
r_e is the IRR on the share or the discount rate which equates the discounted sum of future dividends per share to P_0.

The Gordon Growth Model

Since dividends can be expected to vary through time, the calculation of a share's price involves an estimate of the expected dividend per share in each future period. To simplify, the Gordon Growth Model assumes that dividends per share grow at a constant annual compound rate, g, with each future expected dividend payment expressed as a function of the time zero payment, d_0. Since d_0 has already been paid it does not, in its own right, enter the valuation equation.

Through the principle of compounding, the expected dividend per share in period one can be expressed as:

$$d_1 = d_0(1 + g)$$

For period two:

$$d_2 = d_1(1 + g) = d_0(1 + g)^2$$

Analogously:

$$d_3 = d_0(1 + g)^3, \ d_4 = d_0(1 + g)^4 \ ...$$

Therefore, Equation 3.3 can be rewritten as:

$$P_0 = \sum_{t=1}^{\infty} \frac{d_0(1 + g)^t}{(1 + r_e)^t} \qquad (3.3a)$$

Assuming that the growth rate is less than the discount rate and using a simple transformation process,[12] Equation 3.3a becomes:

$$P_0 = \frac{d_1}{r_e - g} \qquad (3.3b)$$

From Equation 3.3b, the current share price is equal to the dividend per share expected in period one (d_1), divided by the discount rate (r_e) less the annual expected growth rate (g). The assumption that $g < r_e$ ensures that the share price cannot be negative or, if g tended to r_e, cannot be infinitely large. Since the share is being valued in terms of its future dividend stream, the annual rate at which this stream grows determines the annual rate of growth in the share's price, that is, the share's price appreciation (capital gain) or depreciation (capital loss).

Consider a company with $r_e = 12\%$ which is expected to announce a dividend per share of 10p next year. The future annual growth rate in dividends, and hence capital gains, is expected to be 4%. By Equation 3.3b, the company's share price is:

$$P_0 = \frac{0.10}{0.12 - 0.04} = £1.25$$

If, for another company, $r_e = 8\%$, $g = -1\%$ and $d_1 = 2.7\text{p}$,

$$P_0 = \frac{0.027}{0.08 + 0.01} = £0.30$$

The required rate of return on equity
If a share is actively traded at the observed price of P_0, and the market provides a consensus view of the expected growth rate and next period's expected dividend per share, then r_e is the share's required rate of return. This represents the equity capitalisation rate[13] or cost of equity capital to the company. By rearranging

Equation 3.3b, the required rate of return is shown to be determined by the dividend yield (the expected dividend per share divided by the current share price) plus the annual rate of capital gains, or losses:

$$r_e = \frac{d_1}{P_0} + g \tag{3.3c}$$

(For the rest of this chapter, the required rate of return on a company's equity is assumed to be given.)

This form of the Gordon Growth Model indicates that the dividend yield, like the interest yield on a bond, is an income measure which ignores capital gains. Only in the case of a zero growth company, when $g = 0$, can the expected dividend yield be used to measure the required rate of return.

Consider two companies, A and B, with expected dividends per share of respectively 10p and 16p, and share prices of respectively £1.67 and £2.00. Company A's expected dividend yield is 6% and company B's 8%. If, however, Company A's expected growth rate is 4% and company B's only 2%, both will have identical required rates of return and would be perfect substitutes. From Equation 3.3c, the required rate of return on company A's shares is:

$$r_e = \frac{.10}{1.67} + 0.04 = 0.06 + 0.04 = 0.10 \text{ or } 10\%.$$

For company B:

$$r_e = \frac{.16}{2.00} + 0.02 = 0.08 + 0.02 = 0.10 \text{ or } 10\%.$$

Single-period valuation

The above results hold, irrespective of the year in which shareholders intend selling their shares to realise their capital gains or losses. This can be demonstrated by considering a holding period of one year. In this case, the present value of a share is the discounted sum of the dividend per share and the future share price, both expected at the end of year one:

$$P_0 = \frac{d_1}{1 + r_e} + \frac{P_1}{1 + r_e}$$

Given the capital gains rate g, P_1 can be expressed as $P_1 = P_0(1 + g)$. Using this expression and reorganising the above equation gives:

$$P_0(1 + r_e) = d_1 + P_0(1 + g)$$

Solving for P_0,

$$P_0(1 + r_e - 1 - g) = d_1$$

in which case

$$P_0 = \frac{d_1}{r_e - g}$$

This is identical to the result achieved in Equation 3.3b. The equivalence with the infinite dividend series model is due to single period valuation (or indeed n period valuation) implicitly including all of the future dividends associated with a share. This arises because the price at which the share is expected to be sold, at the end of period one (P_1), will be based on the discounted sum of the future expected dividend receipts, beginning from the end of year two: d_2, d_3, d_4, ...

Investment opportunities and valuation

While dividends per share cannot be expected to increase or decrease at a constant annual rate indefinitely, the Gordon Growth Model nevertheless captures in a succinct way the relatively stable trend that dividends exhibit in practice. It does not, however, identify any of the factors which are likely to determine the growth rate. One way of making the growth rate explicit is by using the investment opportunities approach to share valuation. Here, a share's price is determined by the earnings which the company's management is capable of generating from the company's existing investments, which determine its existing asset base, and the earnings from additional new future investments.

Formally, the current price of a share is defined as the present value of EPS from existing assets (PV_1), plus the net present value of future growth opportunities. This NPV is the present value of EPS from future investments (PV_2) less the present cost of these future investments (PV_3).

The discount rate used in the investment opportunities approach is the equity capitalisation rate, r_e. Since an internal financing model is being used, retained earnings are the sole source of capital for funding future investments. These earnings are, however, owned by shareholders, who have foregone the opportunity to receive them directly in the form of dividends. Thus, the cost of retained earnings to a company must equal its required rate of return on equity, r_e.

The results of two variants of the investment opportunities approach are presented: the Miller–Modigliani (MM) Model, which is the more frequently used in corporate finance, and the Solomon Model. The latter is included for two reasons. First, an understanding of how a growth rate is being determined can only be achieved by gaining insight into the workings of the model which produces it. The formal proof of the Solomon Model is relatively straightforward and is presented in full. Second, in some ways this model can be used to give more direct meaning to financial growth.

Solomon's Model

The investment outlays and returns in this model are shown in detail in Table 3.1. It is assumed that a company's existing assets generate, in perpetuity, a constant

Table 3.1: Investment opportunities approach to equity valuation (The Solomon Model)

					PRESENT VALUE
Year	1	2	3	4 … ∞	
EPS Existing Assets	E	E	E	E …	$PV_1 = E/r_e$
Investment Outlay per Year	bE	bE	bE	bE …	$PV_3 = bE/r_e$

Returns Series on each Investment Outlay

Year				
1				
2	kbE			
3	kbE	kbE		
4	kbE	kbE	kbE	
5	kbE	kbE	kbE	kbE
6	kbE	kbE	kbE	kbE
.	.	.	.	.
.				
∞				

					Total PV of Returns Series
Year	1	2	3	4 … ∞	
PV of Returns Series at date of investment outlay	kbE/r_e	kbE/r_e	kbE/r_e	kbE/r_e …	$PV_2 = kbE/r_e^2$

PV of Share	$P_0 = PV_1 + PV_2 - PV_3$
	$= E/r_e + kbE/r_e^2 - bE/r_e$
	$= E/r_e + bE/r_e [\pi^* - 1]$, where $\pi^* = k/r_e$

annual amount of EPS: £E. Thus, using the perpetuity valuation principle, the present value of EPS from the company's existing assets is:

$$PV_1 = \frac{E}{r_e}$$

Next, each future investment is assumed to earn, in perpetuity, a constant annual rate of return k which exceeds the company's required rate of return. To exploit these investment opportunities the company retains, in perpetuity, a constant annual proportion, b, of EPS from existing assets. Therefore, with the company investing an amount of £bE each year, the present cost of future investment outlays is:

$$PV_3 = \frac{bE}{r_e}$$

Each year's investment produces a perpetual future series of annual returns: kbE. The present value of each of these series, at the year in which the associated investment is made, is kbE/r_e. Since, however, the latter is itself one element in a perpetual series of investments, the present value of EPS from all future investments is:

$$PV_2 = \frac{kbE}{r_e^2}$$

With the present value of the share defined as $PV_1 + PV_2 - PV_3$:

$$P_0 = \frac{E}{r_e} + \frac{kbE}{r_e^2} - \frac{bE}{r_e}$$

$$= \frac{E}{r_e} + \frac{bE}{r_e}\left[\frac{k}{r_e} - 1\right]$$

$$= \frac{E}{r_e} + \frac{bE}{r_e}[\pi^* - 1] \qquad (3.4)$$

From Equation 3.4, the share price is equal to the present value of EPS from existing assets (E/r_e) plus the present cost of future investment outlays per share (bE/r_e), times an index of their profitability ($\pi^* - 1$).

With $\pi^* = k/r_e$, the profitability of future investments is defined in terms of the extent to which the rate of return on new investment exceeds the equity capitalisation rate. To illustrate the model, assume E = £0.37, b = 0.4, k = 15% and r_e = 12%, then

$$P_0 = \frac{0.37}{0.12} + \frac{(0.4)(0.37)}{0.12}\left[\frac{0.15}{0.12} - 1\right] = £3.39$$

In other words, the current share price is determined by the present value of EPS from existing assets,

$$\frac{0.37}{0.12} = £3.08$$

plus the cost of financing investment outlays per share,

$$\frac{(0.04)(0.37)}{0.12} = £1.233,$$

times the index of profitability

$$\left[\frac{0.15}{0.12} - 1\right] = 0.25$$

Thus,

$$P_0 = £3.08 + £1.233[0.25]$$
$$= £3.08 + £0.308 = £3.39$$

Note that the NPV of future investments is 30.8p per share.

Implications of Solomon's Model

The Solomon Model clearly identifies the nature of the growth process in valuation. Zero growth occurs when b = 0. In this case, with no future investments being made and no earnings being retained, all EPS are paid out as dividends and the share price is simply the present value of EPS from existing assets:

$$P_0 = \frac{E}{r_e} \qquad (3.4a)$$

Using the previous example, the share is valued at £3.08, that is:

$$P_0 = \frac{0.37}{0.12} = £3.08.$$

More interestingly, even if earnings are retained ($b \neq 0$) and new investments are made, the company will fail to grow if $\pi^* = 1$. In this case, with $k = r_e$, investments can only earn a return equal to the company's cost of capital.[14] This implies that while a company may be investing and creating growth in terms of employment numbers, sales revenue and/or the number of plants it operates, etc., this will not induce financial growth unless k exceeds r_e.

In the above example, if $k = r_e$, the share's price will remain unchanged at £3.08. That is, with $k = r_e = 12\%$,

$$P_0 = \frac{0.37}{0.12} + \frac{(0.4)(0.37)}{0.12}\left[\frac{.12}{.12} - 1\right]$$

$$= \frac{0.37}{0.12} + \frac{(0.4)(0.37)}{0.12}[0.0] = £3.08$$

In other words, even with 40% of EPS from existing assets being retained ($b = 0.4$) the new investments are incapable of raising future EPS above the level generated by existing assets.

In conclusion, no growth arises if $k = r_e$, or $b = 0$, or both. Growth requires $b \neq 0$ and $k > r_e$.

The Miller–Modigliani Model

By investing a constant proportion of EPS from existing assets, the Solomon Model ignores the possibility of retaining a proportion of the additional EPS generated by new investments. The MM Model takes account of these additional earnings by assuming that a constant proportion of each future year's total EPS is retained.[15] In this case, the present value of the share is:

$$P_0 = \frac{(1 - b)E}{r_e - bk} \tag{3.5}$$

The advantage of the MM Model is that the growth rate is simply defined. It is the retention ratio times the rate of return on new investment: $g = bk$. The share price in the MM Model could, however, be expected to be higher because greater future amounts of EPS are being invested.[16]

The MM Model has the same implications as the Solomon Model. Zero growth occurs with either $r_e = k$, or $b = 0$, or both. In, for example, the case where $r_e = k$, Equation 3.5 reduces to:

$$P_0 = \frac{(1 - b)E}{r_e - br_e} = \frac{E}{r_e}$$

In other words, zero growth under the MM Model produces a share price equal to the present value of EPS from existing assets.

Price–earnings ratios

Another way of assessing a share's value is in terms of its price–earnings ratio, PE, defined as the current share price divided by current EPS. While it might seem that this ratio, or multiple, measures the price which the market is willing to pay for each £1 of current EPS, it also reflects the future growth prospects of a company. This is demonstrated by dividing Equation 3.4 by EPS, yielding:

$$\frac{P}{E} = \frac{1}{r_e} + \frac{b}{r_e} [\pi^* - 1] \qquad\qquad (3.6)$$

In the no growth situation the PE ratio, or base PE, is simply the reciprocal of the equity capitalisation rate, representing the present value of £1 of EPS from existing assets. That is, if $b = 0$ or $k = r_e$,

$$\frac{P}{E} = \frac{1}{r_e}$$

Consider a company with $r_e = 8\%$. Its base PE rate is $1/.08 = 12.5$. If this company has attractive future investments, $k = 15\%$, and retains 60% of EPS from existing assets ($b = 0.6$), its PE is raised to 19.06. That is:

$$\frac{P}{E} = \frac{1}{0.08} + \frac{0.6}{0.08} \left[\frac{.15}{.08} - 1 \right] = 19.06$$

This reflects the future growth potential of retaining and investing earnings at attractive rates of return.

Generally PE ratios are reasonably robust measures of future growth potential. Growth prospects, because they represent a potential which has not yet been realised, are intangible assets. As time passes and growth potential is realised, these intangible assets are transformed into tangible assets and EPS begin to increase, other things being equal, lowering the PE ratio. In the limit, when most of the potential growth prospects have been realised, a company's PE ratio will approach its base PE.

Towards the end of the 1980s some doubts were expressed about the usefulness of PE ratios, when a major divergence developed between the average PE ratio for Japanese companies (about 50) and the average for American companies (about 16). Investigation of these differentials has, however, tended to support the view that high PE ratios do reflect enhanced future growth prospects.

Dividends and investment opportunities

The dividend and investment opportunities approaches to valuation give equivalent results. This is easily demonstrated in the MM Model. Dividends per share in year one are paid out of EPS from existing assets. Since the dividend payout ratio equals one minus the retention ratio, $d_1 = (1 - b)E$ can be substituted into Equation 3.5, producing the Gordon Growth Model equation:[17]

$$P_0 = \frac{d_1}{r_e - bk} = \frac{d_1}{r_e - g}$$

In other words, the share price in the MM Model is identical to the share price determined by discounting the dividend stream produced by the MM investment strategy. Also, the required rate of return (defined in Equation 3.3c as the dividend yield plus the growth rate) can now be expressed as:

$$r_e = \frac{d_1}{P_0} + bk \tag{3.7}$$

Expected and required rates of return

Taking the required rate of return on a share as given, and assuming that the market can form a consensus view of a company's expected dividend yield and growth rate, any change in market expectations will produce a change in a share's observed market price. In this context, an equilibrating mechanism is at work, determined by the relationship between expected and required rates of return. If the expected rate of return on a share exceeds its required rate, demand for the share will increase and produced a rise in price. This causes the expected rate of return to fall, with the price rise terminating when the expected rate equals the required rate.

Using the MM Model as an illustration, assume that for a given share in equilibrium: $d_1 = £0.09$, $b = 0.5$, $P_0 = £2.25$, $k = 12\%$ and $r_e = 10\%$. The required rate of return equals the expected rate of return determined from Equation 3.7:

$$\frac{0.09}{2.25} + (.5)(.12) = 0.10$$

That is, the required rate of return of 10% is determined by the expected dividend yield, 4%, plus the expected growth rate, $g = bk$, of 6%.

Next, assume that the market makes an upward revision of k to 14%. All other things being equal, the expected rate of return on the share rises to 11% since, with $k = 14\%$,

$$\frac{0.09}{2.25} + (.5)(.14) = 0.11$$

With the expected rate exceeding the required rate of 10%, the share price rises. The new equilibrium price, at which the expected and required rates are equal, is £3.00 since

$$\frac{0.09}{3.0} + (.5)(.14) = 0.10$$

Equity market efficiency

By taking views on the relationships between expected and required rates of return, based on continuously updated analysis of company fundamentals, equity analysts have a major role to play in the above process. Their views are translated into buy and sell recommendations:

Buy: on anticipation of price rises, when expected rates exceed required rates.

Sell: on anticipation of price falls, when expected rates are below required rates.

There is a perceived need among equity analysts to act quickly to exploit an expected price advantage before the price actually changes to its new equilibrium level. The speed of reaction to new information which alters expectations will determine how quickly a price changes from its old to its new equilibrium level. In the context of equity market efficiency, this change will be instantaneous. In these circumstances current equity prices, by being equilibrium prices based on consensus market expectations, will be fair prices and represent the best available estimate of intrinsic value.

If equity markets are efficient, then buy and sell decisions based on perceived price advantages will not enable investors to earn more than their required rates of return. The price advantages will not exist since current prices are fair prices. Paradoxically, for equity markets to be efficient, equity analysts are essential to ensuring that new information, which alters expectations, is properly discounted in market values.

Investors who believe that equity markets are efficient adopt passive buy and hold strategies. Investors who reject market efficiency adopt active strategies in the expectation of earning returns above their required rates. An outline of the two approaches on which active strategies are based – fundamental analysis and technical analysis – brings this chapter to a close.

Fundamental analysts

Fundamental analysts can formulate their views on intrinsic value, directly, by using historic company data to estimate the parameters in the equity valuation models. Using the Gordon Growth form of the dividend discounting model, Equation 3.3b, and assuming that the required rate of return is given, two parameter estimates are needed: dividends per share expected next period and the annual dividend growth rate. When company dividends exhibit relatively stable trends, the growth rate can be estimated on the basis of the actual change in dividends per share over the last five or six years. Similarly, the next period's expected dividend per share can be based on this estimated trend.

Alternatively, given the explicit definition of the growth rate, as $g = bk$, an analyst can obtain an estimate of the retention ratio based on the retention policy followed by a company in recent years. In the case of the expected rate of return on new investment, some analysts believe that it will equal the existing accounting rate of return on the book value of equity, ROE. Recall from Chapter 1 that this is defined as EAIT divided by the book value of equity. Here the growth rate, $g = b(ROE)$, is known as the long-run sustainable growth rate.

The general problem with using historic data is that past trends in dividends and EPS cannot necessarily be projected into the future without modification. By making detailed assessments of company fundamentals, similar to those described in corporate bond analysis, equity analysts can make a more critical appraisal of the parameter values relevant to the future. The DuPont system described in Chapter 1 can, for example, be used to assess the sensitivity of the components of ROE – the profit margin, asset turnover ratio and, if debt is included, financial leverage – to future prospects in the domestic and international economy.

At a general level equity analysts attempt to assess changing trends within a given economy in order to identify growth prospects for different industry sectors. In the United Kingdom examples of changing trends are: the fall in birth rates, the increasing proportion of elderly in the population and the changing balance of the workforce towards part-time female employment. These and other likely future changes will alter the pattern of future consumption and thus demand across various industries. At an international level identification of foreign markets with major growth potential and the companies which are likely to benefit by exporting to these markets or by providing direct foreign investment is also important.

Because of the complex factors affecting share prices, some analysts prefer to avoid direct application of discounting models and instead focus on PE ratios. Using their knowledge and expertise they produce estimates of PE ratios which they believe are justified by company fundamentals. Buy and sell recommendations are then based on a comparison of the justified price–earnings ratio, JPE, with the market PE ratio. If a JPE exceeds a market PE, a buy recommendation may be made; vice versa when a JPE is less than a market PE. In effect, an indirect estimate of an intrinsic share price can be obtained by multiplying expected EPS by the JPE. JPEs still require analysts to make their own estimates of prices and expected EPS but by using the JPE neither is made explicit.

Technical analysts

There are two approaches to technical analysis, one using mechanical trading rules and the other using charts. Technical analysts ignore company fundamentals, believing that current and past prices by themselves convey all the information that is necessary to predict how prices will behave in the future.

Mechanical trading rules are based on the belief that market prices tend to vary around an established equilibrium price, thus producing secondary price movements. When, however, a new piece of information comes onto the market which changes expectations and implies a new equilibrium, the belief is that the market will take time to adjust to the new level, but will do so with a systematic trend. This defines a primary price movement. (Note that the efficient market hypothesis, discussed in Chapter 5, argues that price would jump instantaneously to its new equilibrium level and that there is no systematic price movement.)

Mechanical trading rules are established with the aim of distinguishing between primary and secondary movements. The most common approach is a filter strategy where price changes within a given range, or filter, are deemed to be secondary. A price rise above the upper limit of the filter is viewed as indicating a primary upward movement, eliciting a buy recommendation. A price fall below the lower limit indicates the start of a primary price fall, eliciting a sell recommendation. Figure 3.5

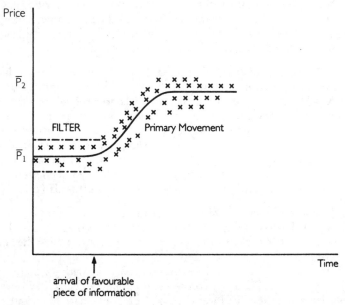

Figure 3.5   Primary and secondary price movements

demonstrates the above argument for a new piece of favourable information, one which implies a rise in the equilibrium price level from $\overline{P}_1$ to $\overline{P}_2$.

The major weakness of the filter strategy is that if technical analysts set too fine a filter, say 2%, there is a danger of intervening in the market when only secondary price movements are taking place. Alternatively, if a wide filter is set, say 15%, there is a danger of intervening after a primary price movement has taken place.

Chartists base their analysis on charts of past price movements. They believe that they can determine historical patterns in these charts which had formed before a major price rise or fall and that if, at a current point in time, a particular pattern begins to emerge history will repeat itself. A favourite approach by chartists involves using a point and figure chart. Here, chartists enter an 'x' each time price rises by a pre-specified amount, say 2p, and an 'o' each time price falls by the prescribed amount. Each time price changes direction the chart moves on to a new column. An example of a point and figure chart is shown in Figure 3.6. The idea is to identify areas of congestion where price is oscillating within a clear range and then determine when it is about to break out from an area of congestion.

Summary

Explaining gilt prices and determining yields to maturity is relatively straight-forward since the fixed coupon interest payments, par value and term to maturity on most gilts are known. Where corporate bonds are concerned, the additional factor to be considered is default risk. An estimate of this factor requires knowledge of the current and prospective financial strength of the company whose bond is being analysed.

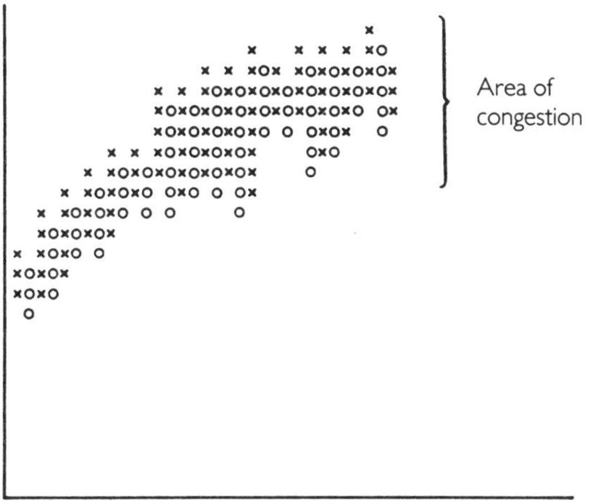

Figure 3.6   Point and figure chart

Equity valuation is by far the most difficult since all of the factors determining the future cash flows in the valuation equations, and the required rate of return, have to be estimated. An analyst obtains a set of these estimates with a view to determining the intrinsic price of a share which may differ from the market price. If a difference does arise, it may be due to the market's failure to reflect intrinsic value but could also be due to errors made by the analyst who is assessing company fundamentals. Technical analysts ignore fundamentals and concentrate their buy and sell recommendations on filter strategies or expected price patterns determined from charts.

There have been two recurring concepts in this chapter: the required rate of return and market efficiency. Required rates of return on bonds and shares, as measures of the cost of long-term debt and equity capital, are the minimum rates of return which must be offered on these assets if they are to be acceptable to investors. Market efficiency which is dependent on the speed at which new relevant information is reflected in market prices, has a major impact on the confidence that can be placed in financial markets, in terms of their ability to measure the intrinsic value of assets. It is only in efficient markets that observed prices are fair prices, produced by properly discounting all currently available, and relevant, information on future outcomes.

These concepts of the required rate of return and market efficiency need further exploration. The required rate of return, which in this chapter was assumed given to avoid overcomplicating the analysis, is primarily determined by risk. It is examined in Chapter 4 in the context of Modern Portfolio Theory and the Capital Asset Pricing Model. The extent to which equity markets are efficient markets is addressed in Chapter 5. Formal treatment of the risk–rate-of-return trade-off is a prerequisite to gaining insight into the market efficiency debate.

Questions

1 A new 20-year bond is to be issued at a par value of £100. The discount rate appropriate for this new issue is $r_d = 5\%$.

a) Assuming that fixed interest is to be paid at the end of each year, at what level must the coupon interest rate be set to ensure that the bond sells at its par value?

b) Assume that the above issue has been successful and that ten years have elapsed. What is the bond's current price if (i) $r_d = 5\%$, (ii) $r_d = 10\%$ and (iii) $r_d = 3\%$.

2 Consider the following two bonds:
Bond A: n = 15, $r_c = 10\%$ M = £100
Bond B: n = 5, $r_c = 10\%$ M = £100

a) What will be the price of each bond if r_d, in each case, is 10%?

b) Assuming that the common yield to maturity on each bond unexpectedly falls from 10% to 6%, determine the price at which each bond will now sell.

c) Compare the percentage price change on each bond and explain what concept these changes illustrate.

3 What is the main distinguishing factor between gilts and corporate bonds?

4 Briefly describe the work of bond rating agencies.

5 Using the Gordon Growth Model, calculate the share price of a company under the following scenarios:
Scenario A: $r_e = 5\%$, g = 3% and $d_1 = 15p$
Scenario B: $r_e = 8\%$, g = 4% and $d_1 = 18p$.

6 Use Solomon's Model to determine the price of a share where E = 50p, $r_e = 10\%$, b = 0.35 and k = 13%. In this example, what is the present value of EPS from existing assets? Under what circumstances would the present value of EPS from existing assets represent the price of the share in question?

7 What is the main difference between Solomon's and Miller and Modigliani's share price models? Use the data in question 6 to calculate the share price under the MM Model. Why is the share price higher under the MM Model?

8 Explain the concepts of the required and expected rates of return on a share. Illustrate your answer using the MM share valuation model.

9 Describe briefly the approach that fundamental analysts take in assessing equity values.

Exercises

1 Describe briefly the approach that technical analysts take towards the assessment of equity values.

2 Consider the following information on an all equity financed company.
EPS from existing assets: 25p
Retention ratio b = 0.45
Equity capitalisation rate $r_e = 14\%$
Rate of return on the book value of equity: ROE = 16%

a) Calculate the share price of the company using (i) Solomon's and (ii) Miller–Modigliani's investment opportunity models.

b) Calculate the long-run sustainable growth rate.

c) Use the long-run sustainable growth rate to calculate the share price using the Gordon Growth Model.

d) Explain why identical share prices are achieved using Gordon's dividend based approach and MM's investment opportunities approach.

e) Assume, all other things being equal, that the required rate of return on this share falls to 12%. Find, using Gordon's Model, the new equilibrium price. Explain briefly why price changes as a result of a fall in the required rate of return.

Endnotes

1. When a bond is first issued, its initial interest payment is due at the end of the first time period.

2. Gilt-edged securities are often referred to as shorts, when their term to maturity is under five years; mediums, when their term is between five and 15 years; and longs, when their term exceeds 15 years. For an existing issue the term to maturity automatically declines as time passes, for example, a long with 20 years to maturity will become a medium five years from now. The majority of gilts are dated, that is, have a term to maturity and make fixed interest payments. Two other types of government bonds exist in the United Kingdom: undated, such as consols; and index linked, where the per period interest payment is tied to the retail price index in order to take account of inflation. There are also Treasury Bills which are issued with a three-month or six-month maturity.

3. An approximate method of obtaining the yield to maturity, or IRR, is presented in Chapter 6 which formally examines the main capital appraisal techniques, of which IRR is one. For the moment a quick check of the interest factor tables will demonstrate that a discount rate of 9% produces a PV of £74.85.

4. The interest yield and redemption yield on UK gilt-edged securities are published regularly in the *Financial Times*. Look at a recent copy of the FT and identify gilts selling above and below par, then compare their interest and redemption yields.

5. Note also, by inspecting the curvature of the bond price schedules in Figure 3.2, that the effect of a given change in yields on price also depends on the yield level at which the change takes place. This is a standard elasticity concept. There are other factors, such as the level of the coupon interest rate, which will influence the effect that a given change in yields has on a bond's price.

6. Interest rates might not fall in the future; the point of the efficient market argument is that given the currently available information this is the market's current anticipation. This anticipation may change, leading to further changes in yield curves, as new information becomes available in the future.

7. The corporate bonds being analysed here are straight debt issues. Two prominent hybrid debt issues are convertible bonds and bonds with warrants. While initially issued as pure debt instruments these bonds have special features which, in the case of warrants, enable the warrant holder to buy equity at a specified price. Convertibles and warrants are examined in Chapter 11.

8. In the United Kingdom corporate bonds which are backed by a company's existing

assets are referred to as debentures. Corporate bonds which do not have this feature are referred to as subordinated debentures.

9. The effective annual yield to maturity, determined from Equation 2.9, is:

$$1 + r_{ef} = FVIF_{2,3} - 1 = 1.601 \text{ or } r_{ef} = 6.01\%$$

10. This section develops valuation models based on existing or outstanding issues of common shares. Many companies also have outstanding issues of preferred shares which normally entitle holders to a fixed dividend payment. Management have discretion over the timing of the fixed dividend payments, but when these are deferred the cumulative dividends over the deferment period must be paid before, or in preference to, dividend payments on common shares. Because of the fixed nature of dividend payments, preferred shares are viewed as a hybrid form of debt financing.

11. If a company is using debt financing and operating in a corporate tax environment, earnings per share available to common shareholders are defined after interest and tax payments have been made.

12. Writing Equation 3.3a for n periods only:

$$P_0 = d_0 \left[\frac{(1 + g)}{(1 + r_e)} + \frac{(1 + g)^2}{(1 + r_e)^2} + \cdots + \frac{(1 + g)^n}{(1 + r_e)^n} \right] \qquad (i)$$

Multiply equation (i) by $\left(\dfrac{1 + r_e}{1 + g} \right)$, giving

$$P_0 \left[\frac{1 + r_e}{1 + g} \right] = d_0 \left[1 + \frac{(1 + g)}{(1 + r_e)} + \cdots + \frac{(1 + g)^{n-1}}{(1 + r_e)^{n-1}} \right] \qquad (ii)$$

Next, subtract equation (i) from equation (ii). Since most of the terms in the brackets [ ] on the right-hand side of both equations are common, they disappear in the subtraction, giving

$$P_0 \left[\frac{1 + r_e}{1 + g} - 1 \right] = d_0 \left[1 - \frac{(1 + g)^n}{(1 + r_e)^n} \right] \qquad (iii)$$

Assuming $r_e > g$, then given an infinite series where $n \to \infty$,

$$\frac{(1 + g)^n}{(1 + r_e)^n} \to 0$$

therefore equation (iii) becomes:

$$P_0 \left[\frac{1 + r_e - 1 - g}{1 + g} \right] = d_0, \text{ or}$$

$$P_0 \left[\frac{r_e - g}{1 + g} \right] = d_0, \text{ that is}$$

$$P_0 = \frac{d_0 (1 + g)}{r_e - g} = \frac{d_1}{r_e - g}$$

since $d_1 = d_0(1 + g)$.

13. The discount rate in equity valuation is often referred to as the equity capitalisation rate. With the current price representing the capital value of a share, in the form of a stock concept, and future dividends representing a flow concept, the discount rate applied to the future dividend stream is capitalising a future series of cash flows.

14. In the no growth case, defined where $\pi^* = 1$, all EPS do not have to be paid out as dividends. Any retentions earn r_e, the rate of return that existing investors require for holding the company's shares.

15. Given EPS from existing assets of £E, the first year's investment of bE produces additional EPS of kbE. With total EPS in the second year equal to kbE + E, the next investment outlay per share is b(kbE + E), instead of just bE in the Solomon Model. This process in the MM Model is carried out in perpetuity. Applying perpetuity principles produces the result in Equation 3.5.

16. Care has to be exercised in making comparisons using different valuation models since the growth rate and the required rate of return are interrelated. A change in a company's investment policy can cause the market to change its required rate of return, if, for example, this was accompanied by a change in the risks surrounding a company's operations. Taking r_e as given at 12%, with E = £0.37, b = 0.4 and k = 15%, the share price rises from £3.39 in the Solomon Model to £3.70 in the MM Model:

$$\frac{(1 - .4)(.37)}{0.12 - (.4)(.15)} = 3.70$$

17. In a similar fashion, the share price determined in the Solomon Model is identical to the share price that would be determined by discounting this model's dividend payout stream. Given Equation 3.4, where

$$P_0 = \frac{E}{r_e} + \frac{bE}{r_e}[\pi^* - 1]$$

since

$$E = \frac{d_1}{1 - b}$$

the substitution of dividends per share for EPS produces

$$P_0 = \frac{d_1}{r_e} + \frac{bE\pi^*}{r_e}$$

Formulating the latter equation in terms of the required rate of return:

$$r_e = \frac{d_1}{P_0} + \frac{bE\pi^*}{P_0}$$

References

Bank of England, Quarterly Bulletin, 1994

Constand, R.L., L.P. Freitas and M.J. Sullivan, 'Factors Affecting Price Earnings Ratios and Market Values of Japanese Firms', Financial Management, 1991

Fuller, R.J. and J.L. Farrell, *Modern Investments and Security Analysis*, New York, McGraw-Hill, 1987

Gordon, M.J., *The Investment, Financing and Valuation of a Corporation*, Homewood, Ill., Irwin, 1962

Johnson, L.D., 'Growth Prospects and Share Prices: A Systematic View', Journal of Portfolio Management, 1987

Leibowitz, M.L. and S. Kogelman, 'Inside the PE Ratio: The Franchise Factor', Financial Analysts Journal, 1990

Mao, J.C.T., *Quantitative Analysis of Financial Decisions*, New York, Macmillan, 1969

Miller, M.H. and F. Modigliani, 'Dividend Policy, Growth and the Valuation of Shares', Journal of Business, 1961

Muller, F.L. and B.D. Fielitz, 'Standard and Poors Quality Rankings Revisited', Journal of Portfolio Management, 1987

Rutterford, J., *Introduction to Stock Exchange Investments*, London, Macmillan, 1993

Solomon, E., *The Theory of Financial Management*, New York, Columbia University Press, 1963

Valdez, S., *An Introduction to Western Financial Markets*, London, Macmillan, 1993

4 Modern portfolio theory and the capital asset pricing model

Introduction

In the previous chapter three distinct forms of long-term financing were identified: gilts, corporate bonds and equity. In a world of perfect certainty, where all future outcomes are known, there would be no effective distinction between these assets because market forces would equalise their rates of return. If, for example, it was known with certainty that equity provided a higher rate of return than corporate bonds, rational wealth-maximising investors would demand equity. This would cause the price of equity to rise to the point where its return equalled that on all other assets. It is the presence of risk which creates a distinction between financial assets and induces investors to require higher rates of return, in compensation for being exposed to higher levels of risk.

Most decisions in finance are taken in the context of this positive risk, rate-of-return trade-off. Indeed, a major part of investment activity focuses on risk reduction via diversification. This explains why investors hold portfolios of different types of assets and identifies one of the main functions of the fund management industry: risk management. Since portfolio diversification is a widespread activity it has a major impact on how a company's shares are valued and, consequently, on a company's cost of equity capital.

This chapter outlines Modern Portfolio Theory, of which the Capital Asset Pricing Model is a part. It demonstrates how this theory can be used in practice: to explain share price behaviour, to help choose investments, and to measure the cost of capital.

Measuring risk and return

Recall, from the end of Chapter 1, that risk measurement in corporate finance is based on the assumption that asset returns can be characterised by a normal probability distribution (see for example Figure 1.1). Before developing the Portfolio Selection Model a brief review of this underlying approach is presented.

Consider a one-year investment in a share. The share's potential rate of return will depend, among other factors, on the level of inflation, changes in government policy, changes in exchange rates and the possibility of a recession developing or a recovery beginning. In these circumstances the rate of return can be characterised by a probability distribution, assumed normal. The mean of the probability distribution indicates the expected rate of return on the share, E(r). The actual rate of return will depend, however, on how the above factors have interrelated over the year and may not necessarily equal the expected rate.

Loosely speaking, the actual rate of return might be just above, moderately above or well above the expected return; or it might be just below, moderately below, or well below it. The range of potential outcomes around the mean represents the risk of the share and, given normality, is measured by the distribution's standard deviation, σ, that is the square root of its variance. The greater σ is, the greater the risk is that the actual return will be significantly above or significantly below the expected return.

Only two parameters are needed to fully specify a normal distribution: the mean and standard deviation. Thus, assuming that the returns on all assets are normally distributed, an investor only needs to use E(r) and σ to make investment choices.

These choices will depend on investors' general attitudes to risk and on the actual levels of risk they are willing to be exposed to. While wishing to maximise the expected utility or satisfaction they gain from undertaking risky investments, their general attitude is one of risk aversion. This implies that the gain in pleasure, or expected utility, from adding £1 to their wealth is less than the displeasure experienced from losing £1. Technically, investors exhibit diminishing marginal utility of wealth and therefore need to be compensated by higher expected returns for any willingness to increase their risk exposure.[1]

The essence of diversification

The ability of a risk averse investor to maximise expected utility is constrained by the investment opportunities which are available. To illustrate these opportunities and explain the rationale behind portfolio diversification, consider the following example. An individual has £1000 to invest in two available shares, or assets, whose expected return and risk characteristics are:

A_1: $E(r_1) = 10\%$ and $\sigma_1 = 15\%$

A_2: $E(r_2) = 15\%$ and $\sigma_2 = 25\%$

These are illustrated in Figure 4.1. The investor has three alternatives: invest only in A_1, or only in A_2, or combine both in a portfolio. The expected return on this two-asset portfolio, $E(r_p)$, is a simple weighted average of the expected returns on A_1 and A_2, with the weights, W_i, defined as the proportions of wealth invested in each ($W_1 + W_2 = 1$):

$$E(r_p) = W_1 E(r_1) + W_2 E(r_2) \qquad (4.1)$$

Taking A_1 as a base line for comparison,[2] if all funds were invested in this asset the expected return would be 10%. Consider the case where the individual invests £400 in A_1 and £600 in A_2. With $W_1 = 0.4$ and $W_2 = 0.6$, the expected return on the portfolio is:

$$E(r_p) = (.4)(.10) + (.6)(.15) = 0.13 \text{ or } 13\%$$

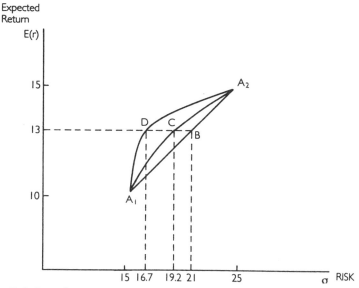

Figure 4.1   Risk diversification on a two-asset portfolio

Has the investor, relative to the base line, achieved any benefits from investing in both shares? The answer depends on what has happened to risk. If the risk of the portfolio, σ_p, is a simple weighted average of the risks of the two shares,

$$\sigma_p = W_1\sigma_1 + W_2\sigma_2 = (.4)(.15) + (.6)(.25) = 0.21 \text{ or } 21\%$$

then the answer is no. Compared to a single investment in A_1, the expected return on the portfolio has risen from 10% to 13% but risk has risen, in the same proportion, from 15% to 21%, thus offsetting any benefits from the increase in expected return. This is demonstrated generally in Figure 4.1 for any combination of investments in the two assets: the line A_1BA_2 showing the risk–return combination from varying the investment proportions W_i.

The risk of the portfolio, however, will only be equal to a simple weighted average of the risks of the individual assets under the special condition where the returns on the two assets are perfectly positively correlated. If the asset returns are less than perfectly positively correlated, the investor will benefit from diversification.

Benefits of diversification

The above can be explained using standard statistical analysis, where the variance of two random variables is the sum of their individual variances plus twice their co-variance (COV). Formally[3] the risk of the two-asset portfolio is:

$$\sigma_p = \sqrt{W_1^2\sigma_1^2 + W_2^2\sigma_2^2 + 2W_1W_2COV(1,2)} \qquad (4.2)$$

By substituting for the correlation coefficient (COR), which is equal to the co-variance of the two assets divided by the product of their standard deviations,

$$COR(1,2) = \frac{COV(1,2)}{\sigma_1\sigma_2}$$

the above equation becomes:

$$\sigma_p = \sqrt{W_1^2\sigma_1^2 + W_2^2\sigma_2^2 + 2W_1W_2COR(1,2)\sigma_1\sigma_2} \qquad (4.2a)$$

Leaving the value of the correlation coefficient unspecified for the moment, the risk of the portfolio in the present example is:

$$\sigma_p = \sqrt{(.4)^2(.15)^2 + (.6)^2(.25)^2 + 2(.4)(.6)COR(1,2)(.15)(.25)}$$
$$= \sqrt{0.0261 + 0.018COR(1,2)}$$

The correlation coefficient, which lies between -1 and $+1$, measures the degree of association between the two assets' returns. If $COR(1,2) = 1.0$, the assets are perfectly positively correlated. In this situation, with a 1% rise (fall) in A_1's rate of return being accompanied by a 1% rise (fall) in A_2's,

$$\sigma_p = \sqrt{0.0261 + 0.018} = \sqrt{0.441} = 0.21 \text{ or } 21\%$$

This is identical to the simple weighted average of the individual assets' risks.

If the assets are less than perfectly positively correlated, $COR(1,2) < 1$, the risk of the portfolio will be less than this simple weighted average. If, for example, $COR(1,2) = 0.6$,

$$\sigma_p = \sqrt{0.0261 + (0.018)(.6)} = \sqrt{0.0369} = 0.192 \text{ or } 19\%$$

Consider the base line case where all funds were invested in asset A_1. There is now, relative to this base line case, a less than proportionate rise in risk. Risk rises from 15% to 19.2%, instead of from 15% to 21%, when asset returns were perfectly positively correlated. The rise in the expected rate of return is as before: from 10% to 13%. (The expected rate of return on a portfolio always remains a simple weighted average of the expected returns on the individual assets.) This less than proportionate effect is demonstrated on the curve A_1CA_2, in Figure 4.1, which indicates the risk–return combination from varying the proportions of wealth invested in each asset, given $COR(1,2) = 0.6$.

The curve A_1DA_2, in Figure 4.1, shows the case for $COR(1,2) = 0.1$ where, with $W_1 = 0.4$ and $W_2 = 0.6$, $\sigma_p = 16.7\%$. That is:

$$\sigma_p = \sqrt{0.0261 + (0.018)(0.1)} = \sqrt{0.0279} = 0.167 \text{ or } 16.70\%$$

Markowitz's opportunity set

The above highlights the benefits of portfolio investment in assets which are less than perfectly positively correlated. Since the risk of the portfolio is less than a simple weighted average of individual asset risks, part of each asset's risk is removed in the diversification process.

Generalising, if there are n assets available, all of the possible ways in which they can be combined defines the risky set of investment opportunities open to an individual. This opportunity set of available risky portfolios is shown in Figure 4.2. By Markowitz's mean-variance maxim, risk averse investors will always choose portfolios on the frontier, ABC, of the opportunity set. Consider portfolio P_1: an investor can obtain a higher expected rate of return for the same level of risk by investing in P_2. Alternatively, a lower level of risk can be achieved for the same expected return by investing in portfolio P_3.

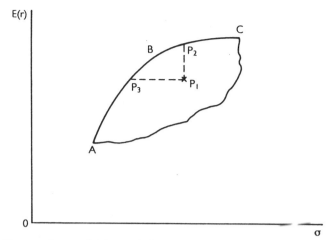

Figure 4.2   Opportunity set of risky portfolios

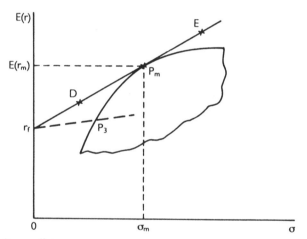

Figure 4.3   The linear efficient set

Preference for a risk-free asset

If an opportunity exists to borrow and lend money at a common risk-free rate of interest, r_f, whose $\sigma = 0$, an investor will always prefer to combine this risk-free asset with a portfolio of risky assets chosen from the frontier ABC. This is shown in Figure 4.3. In this situation, the investor's optimal portfolio of risky assets is determined by drawing a straight line from r_f tangential to the frontier ABC. The point of tangency determines the optimal risky portfolio, P_m.

In terms of risk–return combinations, the line r_fDE, in Figure 4.3, represents the linear efficient set of investments available to the individual. If, for example, the investor locates at point D, part of the investor's available funds will be used to purchase a proportion of portfolio P_m, the remainder being lent on the market at r_f. A point to the left of P_m, such as D, indicates that the investor is seeking stability of income and exhibiting a preference for lending. The higher the proportion of wealth invested in risk-free lending, the lower the exposure to risk. Alternatively, the greater the proportion of the risky portfolio P_m which is purchased, the greater the exposure to risk and, because of risk aversion, the higher the expected return required to compensate for this exposure.[4]

If an investor had located at a point to the right of P_m, in Figure 4.3, such as E, all of his/her personal available investment funds and an additional amount borrowed from the market at r_f would have been used to purchase a proportion of P_m. A preference for borrowing would have been exhibited, with the investor indicating a willingness to be exposed to relatively high levels of risk, in anticipation of relatively high expected returns.[5]

That the line r_fDE represents the efficient combination of investments available to the individual can be easily demonstrated. Consider risky portfolio P_3, in Figure 4.3. If this portfolio is combined with the risk-free asset, the line from r_f through P_3 shows the combinations of the risk-free asset and P_3 available to the investor. These combinations are inefficient, however, since by Markowitz's mean-variance maxim the highest possible expected return, for a given level of risk, can be achieved by shifting to portfolio P_m and combining it with investments at r_f.

The Capital Asset Pricing Model

In deriving the equilibrium position for the individual investor the following assumptions were made:

(i)   Rates of return on all assets are normally distributed.
(ii) Investors are risk averse expected utility maximisers.
(iii) Rates of return on all pairs of assets are less than perfectly positively correlated.
(iv) Borrowing and lending opportunities are available at a common risk-free rate of interest.

This equilibrium analysis can be extended to the capital markets as a whole under what is known as the Capital Asset Pricing Model (CAPM). The CAPM includes the following additional assumptions:

(v)   Capital markets are perfect with information freely available to all.
(vi) Decisions are made in a one-period time horizon.
(vii) Investors have homogeneous expectations.

Assumption (v) implies that there are no transaction costs in buying and selling shares and no taxes. All investors have access to the same information which is costlessly available. Assets are infinitely divisible so that a fraction of an individual asset can be bought and sold. This assumption also implies a common borrowing and lending rate. Assumptions (vi) and (vii) imply that all investors make decisions on a common single-period basis. They take identical views of expected inflation and of the probability distributions of returns on all assets available in the capital markets.

The market equilibrium portfolio

Under the above sets of assumptions each individual investor faces the same linear efficient set of investment opportunities depicted in Figure 4.3. Each investor is able to borrow and lend at r_f and each identifies P_m as their optimal portfolio of risky assets. When P_m is chosen by all investors, it becomes the market equilibrium portfolio of risky assets (the market portfolio). $E(r_m)$ and σ_m are, respectively, the expected return and risk on the market portfolio. In equilibrium this portfolio includes all of the assets in the capital or stock markets, each asset being held according to its market value weight. An asset's market value weight is the market value of the asset divided by the total value of the market portfolio. Also in equilibrium aggregate borrowing equals aggregate lending, at r_f.

The capital market line

This common linear efficient set of investment opportunities is known as the Capital Market Line, CML. It demonstrates that there is a linear, upward sloping, risk–return trade-off for the whole capital market, in equilibrium. The benefit of this approach is that the CML has reduced the complexity of analysing risky investments by:

- producing a linear form of the risk–return trade-off for the whole capital market, and
- demonstrating that each and every investor has only to consider two factors in choosing their overall portfolios: the risk-free asset, or rate of interest, and the market portfolio of risky assets.

As it is linear, the CML has an intercept term, r_f, and a slope coefficient. The latter is defined as the expected return on the market portfolio less the risk-free rate of interest, both divided by the risk of the market portfolio. The equation of the CML is:

$$E(r_p) = r_f + \left[\frac{E(r_m) - r_f}{\sigma_m} \right] \sigma_p \qquad (4.3)$$

With σ_p representing a chosen portfolio's risk exposure, the expected and, in equilibrium, required rate of return on the chosen portfolio is equal to the risk-free rate of interest plus the market risk premium times the risk exposure σ_p.

The market risk premium, $E(r_m) - r_f$, shows the degree of risk aversion in the capital market. Since r_f is the rate of return that can be earned in the absence of risk, the higher that $E(r_m)$ is in relation to r_f, the greater is the degree of risk aversion in the market, or, in other words, the greater is the average return that investors require from stock market investments. In Equation 4.3 the market risk premium is standardised by expressing it per unit of market risk.

All investors are located on the CML, either to the right or the left of P_m, according to their willingness to be exposed to risk. Investors determine their own σ_p's by constructing personal portfolios which combine either borrowing or lending with investment in the market portfolio.

A practical interpretation of the CAPM

A practical view of the CAPM can be taken by conceptualising the capital market as a giant unit trust, with each investor purchasing the number of units which, when combined with borrowing and lending, exposes the individual to their desired level of risk. In stock market terms, the market portfolio can be represented by a stock exchange index, such as the FT All-Share Index. The return on the index represents the average return on the market portfolio and the movement of the index represents market risk. In a similar vein, the risk-free rate of interest can be approximated by the rate of return on short-term government debt such as a Treasury Bill. Since Treasury Bills have no default risk and have a very short term to maturity, they exhibit the lowest return variations in practice.

Personal and corporate leverage

Note, for future reference, that an investor who chooses a point to the right of P_m is using personal leverage, that is, borrowing in relation to their own personal funds. By engaging in personal leverage, expected return is increased above the market average of $E(r_m)$ but is accompanied by an increase in risk above the market risk of σ_m. Analogously, companies which engage in corporate leverage do so to enhance expected returns to shareholders, but in the process expose shareholders to higher risk. This is an important issue when considering the corporate leverage, or capital structure, debate in Chapter 8.

Diversifiable and undiversifiable risk

When pairs of assets are less than perfectly positively correlated, the rationale for diversifying investments across a range of risky assets was shown to result from the possibilities of risk reduction. In the market portfolio all possible risk reduction has been achieved. This implies that the variation in the rate of return on the market portfolio is subject only to the general macroeconomic conditions in the economy: changes in an economy's inflation rate, its balance of payments, government policy, the threat of wars, political instability and oil crises, among other factors. In this context market risk, σ_m, defines the level of systematic or undiversifiable risk in the economy. (A moment's thought on how stock exchange indices, as proxies for the market portfolio, behave in respect of the above factors should clarify this point.)

Rates of return on each individual company's shares will vary, not just in response to systematic factors, but in response to factors peculiar to each company's own operations. The latter defines unique, or company-specific, risk. This is a function of the quality of management, labour and technology within a company; its labour relations; the specific market(s) in which it operates and the strength of its close competitors, among other factors. Since the market portfolio is subject only to systematic risk it must be these specific risks which are removed, or avoided, in the diversification process. Consequently, in determining the rate of return required to hold a share in the market portfolio, only that part of the share's risk which contributes to market risk will be relevant.

The security market line

The relevant market risk of a share can be judged by assessing how the share's rate of return varies with the return on the market portfolio. In formal statistical terms, this

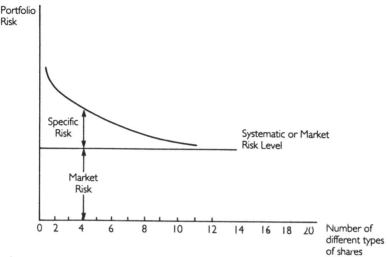

Figure 4.4

is measured by the ith share's beta coefficient, β_i, defined as the co-variance between the returns on the share and the market portfolio, $COV(r_i, r_m)$, per unit of market risk, σ_m:

$$\beta_i = \frac{COV(r_i, r_m)}{\sigma_m} \tag{4.4}$$

A share's required rate of return, which in equilibrium will equal its expected rate of return $E(r_i)$, is related to its β via the Security Market Line, SML. Since each individual share is being valued in overall capital market equilibrium, the SML reflects the positive and linear risk–return trade-off implied by the CML. For each share, the requirement is that its rate of return must rise to adequately compensate for any increase in risk which is due to systematic or market factors. The equation of the SML is:

$$E(r_i) = r_f + [E(r_m) - r_f]\beta_i \tag{4.5}$$

By partitioning a share's risk into two elements – market, or undiversifiable, risk; and specific, or diversifiable, risk – an economic rationale has now been provided for diversification. Assuming that shares are held in the market portfolio, or in practice a well-diversified portfolio, investors have totally avoided, or completely diversified, the risk factors specific to each company's operations. Since the required rate of return, determined by the SML, is the discount rate used in share valuation models, the market value of a share is, by implication, independent of its specific risk. These are not simply theoretical points devoid of empirical meaning. Research has shown that in practice the level of market risk is approached when a portfolio is made up of as little as between 10 and 15 different types of common shares.

This risk diversification effect is demonstrated in Figure 4.4, where the risk of a portfolio is shown as falling as the number of different types of shares in the portfolio is increased. The risk of the portfolio approaches the systematic risk level, below which it can never fall.

Interpreting βs

The β coefficient can be used to define three classes of assets or shares: average, aggressive and defensive. To help explain these concepts and the SML, assume $r_f = 4\%$ and $E(r_m) = 12\%$. From Equation 4.5,

$$E(r_i) = 4 + [12 - 4]\beta_i$$

A share is defined as average if $\beta_i = 1$. In this case, the rate of return varies exactly with the market's average rate, a 1% rise (fall) in the market average being accompanied by a 1% rise (fall) in the share's rate of return. For an average share, the expected rate of return is 12% since

$$E(r_i) = 4 + [12 - 4](1.0) = 12\%$$

In other words, assuming that the stock market is in equilibrium, the rate of return which an investor requires to hold an average share in a well-diversified portfolio, is equal to the average rate expected on the market.

If a share's $\beta > 1$, the share is aggressive and its rate of return varies more than in proportion to the market's average rate. If, for example $\beta_i = 1.5$, the share will perform well in an upward trending market, with a 1% rise in the market average being accompanied by a 1.5% rise in the share's rate of return. In a downward trending market, however, the share's rate of return will fall by 1.5% when the market average falls by 1%. If an aggressive share is to be included in a well-diversified portfolio, the market will require it to earn an above-average rate of return since it possesses more than average market risk. With $\beta_i = 1.5$, $E(r_i)$ exceeds $E(r_m)$ by four percentage points since,

$$E(r_i) = 4 + [12 - 4](1.5) = 16\%$$

If a share's $\beta < 1$, it is a defensive share with a rate of return which varies less than in proportion to the market average. While a defensive share underperforms in a market rise, it performs relatively better than the average share when the market falls. Thus, depending on the extent to which a share is defensive, that is, on the extent to which β_i falls below one, the required rate of return will be correspondingly less than the required rate of return on the market portfolio. If, for example $\beta_i = 0.4$,

$$E(r_i) = 4 + [12 - 4](0.4) = 7.2\%$$

The SML can also be used to explain the risk structure of interest rates. In this case the debt segment of the SML is being viewed. Bond risk can be measured either in terms of the bond ratings described in Chapter 3 or in terms of debt βs, with the latter measured, using Equation 4.4, as the co-variance between the rates of return on the ith bond and the market portfolio, per unit of market risk.

Portfolio βs

A portfolio beta, β_p, is a simple weighted average of the n individual assets comprising a portfolio:

$$\beta = \sum_{i=1}^{n} w_i \beta_i \qquad (4.6)$$

The weights, W_i, are the value proportions in which the assets are held. Analogous to the above, a portfolio is defined as defensive if $\beta_p < 1$, or average if $\beta_p = 1$, or aggressive if $\beta_p > 1$. Assuming that a portfolio is well diversified and that the CAPM provides a good description of stock market behaviour, β_p can be used to interpret portfolio performance.

Consider a situation where a stock market is experiencing a bullish period, with relatively strong rises in the main indices in the market. Analysts demonstrate that particular unit trusts, investment trusts and some other funds managed by insurance companies and pension trustees have been significantly outperforming the market over this period. How can such 'exceptional' performance be explained? According to the CAPM, it arises solely because these portfolios are dominated by aggressive shares, producing β_ps greater than one. Consequently, because they possess more than average market risk, these portfolios could have been expected to outperform the average in an upward trending market. If their composition is not altered, however, they can be expected to perform worse than the market average when the market eventually falls.

Similarly, if particular portfolios are shown to underperform in a rising market this should not be judged, according to the CAPM, as indicating bad performance per se. If investors have chosen to be exposed to significantly lower levels of risk in these cases, then fund managers have invested correctly in predominantly defensive shares, producing defensive portfolios. The return appropriate to this risk exposure could only be expected to be below the market's average.

Equity valuation

In Chapter 3, when presenting equity valuation models, share prices were examined in terms of expected dividend yields and growth rates. The required rate of return, or discount rate, was held constant. Using the CAPM, the discount rate has now been specified by solely market-determined and, therefore, objective factors. This market-determined discount rate is a function of the market's risk-free rate of interest, the market's risk premium and the level of market risk in the share. Given the MM share valuation model (Equation 3.3b) the price of the ith share can now be specified as:

$$P_{0i} = \frac{d_{1i}}{r_f + (E(r_m) - r_f)\beta_i - g}$$

To examine how the share price will change as a result of a change in the required

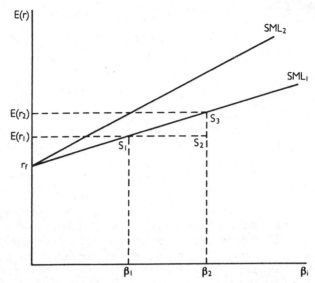

Figure 4.5   The security market line

rate of return, all other things being equal, consider SML$_1$ in Figure 4.5. In equilibrium, with expected and required rates of return equal, all shares will plot along this SML. Shares with identical risks will have identical expected, and required, rates of return.

A change in β_i

Assume there is a temporary disequilibrium, as the result of a rise in a share's risk from β_1 to β_2. The share which originally plotted at S$_1$, has an expected return of E(r$_1$). Now, however, the market requires it to earn E(r$_2$), consistent with β_2. With the expected rate below the required rate, the share is overvalued and will plot below SML$_1$, at S$_2$. For equilibrium to be re-established, the share's price must fall to the point where the share plots, once again, on SML$_1$ but this time at S$_3$.

As a general rule, shares which plot below the SML are overvalued and can be expected to experience price falls. Conversely, shares which plot above the SML are undervalued and can be expected to experience price rises.

A change in r$_f$

The rates of return on all shares will change if r$_f$ changes. The risk-free rate of interest includes the real rate of interest and a premium for expected inflation. A rise in the expected rate of inflation will raise the SML in parallel fashion, increasing the rates of return that the market requires at each level of risk. This produces a general fall in share prices until all shares plot on the new SML.

A change in the market risk premium

Where changes in the market risk premium are concerned, again all share prices will change but differentially. The market risk premium measures the average degree of risk aversion in the capital markets. This can change over the business cycle with, for example, the average investor becoming more risk averse in recessionary periods and, consequently, requiring a higher return from stock market investments relative to the risk-free rate. This changes the slope of the SML, which tilts upwards from, for example, SML_1 to SML_2 in Figure 4.5. The resultant impact on share prices varies with the level of β since the market risk premium is weighted by β_i:

$$[E(r_m) - r_f]\beta_i$$

Consequently, aggressive shares can be expected to experience greater price rises (falls), relative to defensive shares, in response to a given fall (rise) in market risk aversion.

The cost of capital

With the required rate of return representing the minimum rate of return that investors require on an asset, the SML can be used to calculate the cost of capital. In the all equity case, this is determined by using the equity β. In general the key benefit of using the CAPM is that it provides an objective method of calculating the cost of capital using a market-determined risk premium.

It can be argued that this approach is preferable to the ad hoc procedures which predated the CAPM: the 'bond yield plus risk premium' or the 'dividend yield plus growth rate'. In the former case, for example, a risk premium is added to the rate of interest on company or government debt. Shares are classified into low, medium and high risk categories, with subjective risk premia in the ranges (say): 1%–2%, 2%–3% and 3%–5% respectively. Alternatively, the cost of equity capital can be computed by taking a share's current dividend yield and adding a somewhat subjective estimate of its future dividend growth rate.

Asset βs
In the case of a levered company, where assets have been financed by both debt and equity, the CAPM uses an asset β in calculating the cost of capital. Here a company's required rate of return is determined as:

$$r_{assets} = r_f + [E(r_m) - r_f]\beta_{assets} \qquad (4.7)$$

The asset β is a weighted average of the βs associated with the market value of debt and equity in the levered company, the weights being defined as the respective proportions of each source of finance in the company's capital structure. The asset β is measured as:

$$\beta_{assets} = \beta_{debt}\left[\frac{Debt}{Debt + Equity}\right] + \beta_{equity}\left[\frac{Equity}{Debt + Equity}\right] \qquad (4.8)$$

For companies using high quality debt, a simplifying assumption is sometimes made that $\beta_{debt} = 0$; in which case:

$$\beta_{assets} = \beta_{equity}\left[\frac{Equity}{Debt + Equity}\right] \qquad (4.8a)$$

Under certain circumstances, further modification is necessary if the CAPM is used to estimate the cost of capital. These modifications and the general use of the CAPM

Table 4.1: Constructing portfolios

Company	Estimated β_i	Average	Portfolio Type Aggressive	Defensive
		Investment Weights (W_i)		
Alliance Trust Co.	1.01	0.30	0.15	0.10
British Gas	0.96	0.15	0.10	0.10
Ladbroke Group	1.55	0.12	0.30	0.05
Pilkington	1.28	0.03	0.30	0.05
Sainsbury (J)	0.78	0.20	0.05	0.40
Wellcome	0.85	0.20	0.10	0.30
			Portfolio Beta[1]	
For each portfolio		Average	Aggressive	Defensive
		1.0	1.22	0.91

[1] $\beta_p = \sum_{i=1}^{6} W_i \beta_i$, with for each portfolio $\sum_{i=1}^{6} W_i = 1.0$

Source: London Business School 'Risk Measurement Service' January–March, 1994

in measuring the cost of capital are discussed in Chapters 6 and 7 when capital investment appraisal is considered.

Using a β book

Practical use of β has been advanced with the development of β books by many of the major investment analyst companies in the United States. These books provide detailed estimates of βs for all listed companies on the New York stock market. One example is the quarterly publication *Security Risk Evaluation* by Merrill Lynch, Pierce, Fenner and Smith Incorporated.

For the London stock market, the London Business School (LBS) produces a quarterly publication entitled the *Risk Measurement Service*, which provides β estimates for all British and Irish companies with a Stock Exchange listing. The β is based on monthly returns,[6] over the most recent five-year period, relative to monthly returns on the FT All-Share Index.

The return in month t on the All-Share Index, FT_t, and its monthly standard deviation, σ_{FT}, are used as approximations for the return on the market portfolio and portfolio risk respectively. The estimates of each company's β, β_i, are produced from Equation 4.4 as:

$$\beta_i = \frac{COV(r_{it}, FT_t)}{\sigma_{FT}} \qquad (4.9)$$

To illustrate a number of theoretical points raised in this chapter, Table 4.1 reports β estimates relating to the five-year period preceding January 1993 for a small selection of British companies.

Equity βs

To summarise the earlier discussion, British Gas and Alliance Trust have βs reasonably close to one, indicating that they are average shares whose rates of return

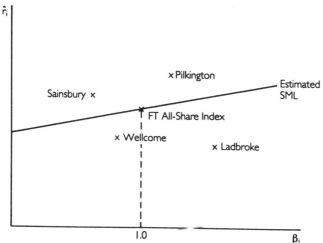

Figure 4.6   Using the SML

vary approximately in proportion to the FT All-Share Index. The Ladbroke Group and Pilkington are aggressive shares, more risky than the average share in the market, and consequently require rates of return higher than the market average. Sainsbury and Wellcome are defensive shares with required rates of return lower than the market average.

Assuming that these shares are held in well-diversified portfolios, the CAPM argues that, in an upward or downward trending stock market, the rates of return on Ladbroke and Pilkington can be expected to rise or fall faster than the market average, vice versa for Wellcome. British Gas and Alliance Trust are so essentially linked to the British economy (Alliance Trust appears to be an index tracking investment trust) that their performances could be expected to move in line with the economy in general. Ladbroke operates in the hotel and catering sector which tends to flourish in boom periods but be relatively depressed in slump conditions, hence its $\beta_i > 1$. A similar conclusion might be drawn about Pilkington, which operates in the building materials sector. In the case of Wellcome, by being health care based and thus an essential as opposed to luxury item of consumption, performance varies less than in proportion to the broadly based FT All-Share Index, hence $\beta_i < 1$. A similar conclusion might be drawn about Sainsbury, which operates in food retailing.

Intrinsic value

Assume that, at a given point in time, market prices do not necessarily reflect the intrinsic value of a company. In this case some investment analysts argue that the CAPM can be used to identify overvalued and undervalued shares, according to whether or not their rates of return plot, respectively, below or above the SML. This is illustrated in Figure 4.6, using the LBS concept of quarterly abnormal returns.[7] Four of the shares – Ladbroke, Pilkington, Sainsbury and Wellcome – are plotted, together with the FT All-Share Index. Since this index is approximating the market portfolio, it automatically has a $\beta = 1$ and automatically plots on the estimated SML.

The extent to which it can be confidently stated that, for example, Sainsbury and Pilkington are underpriced and Ladbroke and Wellcome are overpriced, depends on the accuracy of the estimated SML but more importantly on whether or not investment analysts can develop trading rules to earn abnormal returns. This in turn focuses on the issues associated with market efficiency, discussed in the next chapter (Chapter 5).

Portfolio choice

Investors, whether individuals or managers of corporate treasury departments, unit trusts, investment trusts or pension funds, can build their own portfolios with the aid of a β book. This is illustrated in Table 4.1 with the shares in the above example. Given the definition of a portfolio β in Equation 4.6, sets of investment weights are chosen to achieve an average, an aggressive and a defensive portfolio.

Note that, with only a small number of shares, these portfolios are imperfectly diversified, that is, they contain elements of specific risk. Since the LBS publishes information on the total and specific risk of each share in terms of percentage standard deviations, this information can be used to assess the extent to which a particular portfolio has been diversified. This assessment is based on the formulae, given below, for calculating the total risk, market risk and specific risk of a portfolio.

The total risk of a portfolio is defined as:

$$\sigma_p = \sqrt{(\text{Market Risk of Portfolio})^2 + (\text{Specific Risk of Portfolio})^2} \qquad (4.10)$$

The market risk is,

$$\sqrt{\beta_p^2 \sigma_{FT}^2} \qquad (4.10a)$$

and portfolio specific risk, which is a function of each share's specific risk, δ_i, is:

$$\sqrt{\sum_{i=1}^{n} (W_i \delta_i)^2} \qquad (4.10b)$$

Using the aggressive portfolio (in Table 4.1) as an example, where $\beta_p = 1.22$, the above formulae are applied in Table 4.2. This table records the total and specific risk for each of the above shares and the FT All-Share Index. Since the latter is being used to approximate the market portfolio it has, by definition, no specific risk.

From the calculations in Table 4.2, note that all of the specific risk has not been removed from this portfolio because, as explained, there is an insufficient number of different shares for the full benefits of diversification to be achieved. The specific risk of this portfolio is, however, less than the total risk of an individual share,

Table 4.2: Calculating portfolio risk[1]

Company	Total Risk (%)	Specific Risk (δ_i) (%)	$(W_i\delta_i)^2$
Alliance Trust Co.	18	7	$[(.15)\ (7)]^2$
British Gas	23	16	$[(.10)(16)]^2$
Ladbroke Group	33	21	$[(.30)(21)]^2$
Pilkington	37	30	$[(.30)(30)]^2$
Sainsbury (J)	23	19	$[(.05)(19)]^2$
Wellcome	37	34	$[(.10)(34)]^2$
FT All-Share Index	17	–	

Portfolio:

$$\text{Market Risk} = \sqrt{\beta_p^2\sigma_I^2} = \sqrt{(1.22)^2(17)^2} = 20.74\%$$

$$\text{Specific Risk} = \sqrt{\sum_{i=1}^{6}(W_i\delta_i)^2} = \sqrt{136.82} = 11.70\%$$

$$\text{Total Risk} = \sigma_p\ \sqrt{(\text{Market Risk})^2 + (\text{Specific Risk})^2} = 23.81\%$$

[1] This example uses the aggressive portfolio in Table 4.1 with its associated investment weights.
Source: as in Table 4.1

demonstrating the effect that even a modest number of shares has on risk reduction via diversification.[8]

Appraising the CAPM

The CAPM can be judged on three criteria: the validity of its assumptions, empirical testing and the confidence that can be placed in estimated βs. The appraisal begins by examining the assumptions.

Appraising the assumptions
Since rates of return on shares are in practice less than perfectly positively correlated, there is unquestioned support for this assumption which is crucial to risk diversification. Where risk aversion is concerned, it might appear that the maximisation of expected utility is not straightforward since individuals exhibit both risk aversion, reflected in their purchase of assurance policies, and risk preference, reflected by gambling on football games and horse races. Gambling, however, is generally perceived as a pleasure orientated activity, independent of serious wealth orientated, and therefore risk averse, investment decisions. The assumption that asset returns are normally distributed is reasonable, provided that the time interval over which returns are calculated is relatively short: a day, a week or a month. If returns are not normally distributed then additional information, such as a measure of the skewness of a distribution, would be needed to help make effective investment choices.

Moving to the assumptions which produce capital market equilibrium, if investors have heterogeneous expectations, each taking a different view of an asset's returns' distribution, investors will not face a common SML. It will therefore not be possible to identify an objective, market-determined, risk premium. Differences in time horizons between investors would also make it difficult to identify a common SML.

With respect to the assumption of perfect capital markets, the presence of transaction costs implies that investors will not always fine tune their portfolios, because the benefits of responding to small price changes will be offset by transaction charges. The absence of this assumption would partly explain why assets and portfolios lie above or below the SML. Similarly, inability to subdivide individual shares will inhibit portfolio adjustment, as will imperfect information and the presence of taxes.

If the perfect capital market assumption is broken because borrowing and lending rates differ, the SML will lose the linearity property which is important to the model's ease of application. For major financial institutions and blue chip companies, however, the rates at which funds can be borrowed or lent only differ marginally.

In practice a true risk-free asset does not exist since the return on Treasury Bills is subject to inflation risk. This has led to the development of a zero-beta version of the CAPM, where the equivalent of a risk-free rate is defined in terms of an asset whose rate of return varies (it has a non-zero standard deviation) but not in response to the market portfolio, that is, its $\beta = 0$.

Empirical tests
Irrespective of its assumptions, the CAPM can be tested empirically to determine whether or not it provides a good description of stock market behaviour. There has been a large number of such tests.[9] In general, they support the positive and linear relationship predicted by the model but suggest that it overestimates the risk-free rate of interest and underestimates the market risk premium. This implies that returns on aggressive investments will be underestimated and returns on defensive investments overestimated. (The zero-beta version of the CAPM was introduced in an attempt to correct for this problem.) Empirical tests also indicate some ambiguity over the role which specific risk factors play in determining rates of return but tests largely confirm the CAPM's prediction that they are irrelevant.

The tests themselves have been queried. Under Roll's Critique they appear to be tautological, since they are not tests of whether the CAPM predicts market behaviour but tests of whether the chosen stock market index is a good proxy for the theoretical market portfolio. According to Roll (1977), if an index is a good proxy the tests will automatically support the CAPM. More recently, empirical tests by Fama and French (1992) conclude that the positive risk–return relationship characterised by the CAPM is only weakly supported, when examined over the period 1941–1990. Over the period 1963–1990 the relationship appears to have disappeared with β having no discernible effect on average returns.

Applying the CAPM
Finally, in applying the CAPM to estimate the cost of capital or analyse portfolios, estimates of r_f, $E(r_m)$ and β have to be based on historic data. This raises the problem of the appropriateness of using historic data to formulate investment decisions which are concerned with future events. Historic βs have been shown to vary considerably over different estimation periods, the problem being most acute for

thinly, as opposed to actively, traded shares. While ways have been developed to cope with thin trading, the problem still persists in respect of shares in general. In the case of portfolio βs there is considerably less estimation period volatility, with the conclusion being drawn that historic portfolio βs can be projected into the future with a reasonable degree of confidence.

Arbitrage Pricing Theory

The CAPM views the rate of return on an asset as a function of a single factor, the market portfolio. The impact of this factor is determined by the asset's β times a risk premium, both measured in relation to the market portfolio: $[E(r_m) - r_f]\beta_i$.

Arbitrage Pricing Theory, APT, argues that returns on asset i are subject to a series of factors. A share's returns are measured in relation to the returns on each factor j, giving rise to a β_{ij} on each factor, and a factor j risk premium. In equilibrium, the return on asset i is a linear function of these factors, with each factor's impact measured as: $[E(r_j) - r_f]\beta_{ij}$. Given k factors, the required rate of return on asset i is:

$$E(r_i) = r_f + [E(r_1) - r_f]\beta_{i1} + [E(r_2) - r_f]\beta_{i2} + \ldots + [E(r_m) - r_f]\beta_{ik} \qquad (4.11)$$

The CAPM, as a single factor model, is a special case of APT.

APT is based on a smaller set of assumptions than the CAPM. In particular, it does not assume a single period time horizon or view investment decisions on a mean-variance efficiency basis. The reduction in the number of assumptions has a cost, however, in that APT does not theoretically identify any of the factors which are relevant, including the market portfolio. All factors have to be determined empirically so that a certain amount of objectivity is lost. The main factors identified to date are: the market portfolio, which tends to dominate; unexpected changes in inflation, industrial production and a company's size, PE ratio and dividend yield.

Summary

Recognising the limitations of its assumptions and its empirical weaknesses, the CAPM provides an objective method of assessing risk and calculating risk adjusted rates of return. APT has attempted to replace the CAPM but, so far, has failed to do so. No doubt other models will surface. Even if successful, they will not detract from the formal recognition that the CAPM gave to rational investor intuition: if you seek high returns, be prepared for the possibility of losses because the higher the returns which are sought, the greater the exposure to risk.

As an important part of Modern Portfolio Theory, developed on the pioneering work of Markowitz (1952) and Tobin (1958), the CAPM re-emphasises that risk management is central to investment diversification. It argues that the role given by investors and financial journalists to the behaviour of stock market indices has a sound theoretical rationale. These indices reflect systematic risk factors which reasonably diversified portfolios of common shares are subject to, specific risk factors having been removed in the process of diversification. Indeed, developments in this general field have enhanced the practical uses to which such indices can be put, for example, in the passive fund management strategy of constructing a portfolio to match, or track behaviour in, a particular market index.

The CAPM also implies that, in an efficient market, unit trusts, investment trusts and other well-diversified portfolios which outperform the market average (or indeed underperform it) do so, not as a result of superior (inferior) fund management techniques, but purely as a consequence of the risk complexion of the portfolio. Whether or not stock markets are efficient is the subject of the next chapter.

Questions

1 Consider the following two assets whose expected return and risk characteristics are:

A_1: $E(r_1) = 8\%$ and $\sigma_1 = 10\%$

A_2: $E(r_2) = 12\%$ and $\sigma_2 = 16\%$

Assume that a two-asset portfolio is created by investing 30% of wealth in asset A_1 and 70% of wealth in asset A_2.
a) Calculate the expected return on the portfolio.
b) Obtain a simple weighted average of the risks of the two assets, using the portfolio wealth weights.
c) Calculate the risk of the portfolio assuming a correlation coefficient between the two assets of 1.0. Are there any benefits to diversification in this case?
d) Calculate the risk of the portfolio assuming a correlation coefficient between the two assets of 0.6. Are there any benefits to diversification in this case?

2 In moving from the equilibrium condition for the individual investor to equilibrium for the capital markets as a whole, what additional assumptions have to be made to produce the CAPM?

3 Assume that the return on the market equilibrium portfolio is 16% and that the risk-free rate of interest is 6%.
a) Calculate the expected rate of return on three shares which have the following β coefficients: $\beta_A = 1.0$, $\beta_B = 2.5$ and $\beta_C = 0.2$.
b) Explain the relationship of each share's expected rate of return to the market's average rate.

4 How can the SML be used to explain the share price equilibriating process in the context of expected and required rates of return?

5 What implications does the absence of the perfect capital market assumption have for the CAPM?

6 Consider the following information taken from the LBS Risk Measurement Service (January–March 1995):

Company	β	Total Risk	Specific Risk	Investment Weight
Euromoney Publication	0.49	26	25	0.05
Highland Distillers Co.	0.70	24	21	0.10
Hogg Robinson	1.09	33	28	0.20
Gartmore	1.26	28	19	0.35
Automated Security	1.20	42	38	0.30
FT All-Share Index	1.0	16.0	–	–

A portfolio is constructed using the indicated investment weights.

a) Calculate the portfolio's β coefficient. How might this portfolio's returns be expected to behave in (i) an upward trending market, (ii) a downward trending market?

b) Calculate the market risk, specific risk and total risk of this portfolio.

c) Why is the specific risk of this portfolio less than the total risk of any of the individual shares in the portfolio?

d) Why has the specific risk of this portfolio not been totally removed?

Exercises

1 Repeat question 6 given the following investment weights:

Euromoney (0.25), Highland (0.30), Hogg (0.20), Gartmore (0.15) and Automated (0.1).

2 Explain the concepts of market and specific risk.

3 On balance, to what extent do empirical tests support the predictions of the CAPM?

Endnotes

1. Contrast this with an individual who, by gambling, exhibits risk preference. Here the expected utility from gaining £1 outweighs the displeasure, or reduction in expected utility, from losing £1.

2. The analysis is equally valid if A_2 is taken as a base line.

3. By the laws of variance, if X is a random variable and a is a constant, $Var(ax) = a^2 Var(x)$. If X and Y are two random variables,

$$Var(X + Y) = Var(X) + Var(Y) + 2COV(X, Y)$$

In the example, the returns on the two assets are random variables and the proportions of investment in each, the W_is, are treated as constants.

4. There are two investments, the risk-free asset and the risky portfolio P_m. Applying Equations 4.1 and 4.2a and assuming asset A_1 is the risk-free asset, since σ_1 is by definition zero the risk of this combination is:

$$\sigma_p = \sqrt{W_2^2\sigma_m^2} = W_2\sigma_m$$

The expected return on the combination is:

$$E(r_p) + W_1 r_f + W_2 E(r_m)$$

Assume $\sigma_m = 20\%$, $r_f = 4\%$ and $(Er_m) = 12\%$. If 40% of wealth is lent, $W_1 = 0.4$ and since $W_1 + W_2 = 1$, $W_2 = 0.6$. Thus,

$$\sigma_p = (.6)(20) = 12\%$$

and

$$E(r_p) = (.4)(4) + (.6)(12) = 8.8\%$$

Now increase the proportion of wealth invested in P_m to $W_2 = 0.8$. With greater exposure to risk, that is

$$\sigma_p = (.8)(20) = 16\%$$

the expected return on the portfolio has risen to

$$E(r_p) = (.2)(4) + (.8)(12) = 10.4\%$$

5. The investor's actual location on the line $r_f DE$ depends on his/her utility function. This can be expressed in terms of indifference curve analysis with the indifference curves specified in terms of expected return and risk.

6. The rate of return is defined in terms of the price change at the beginning and end of a month. Any dividends are taken into account by assuming that the payments, when received, are used to purchase more of the shares. Similarly, rights issues are included by taking account of the discount offered in relation to the current price. Stock splits or scrip issues, where the number of outstanding shares are increased by some multiple, are also included. This opportunity cost or reinvestment rate approach to determining a rate of return is also used in the compilation of stock market indices.

7. The LBS reports quarterly and annual abnormal returns. The abnormal return is the actual return over the specified period less the return, given the shares β_i, implied from the estimated SML. The Risk Measurement Service is available from the London Business School, Sussex Place, Regents Park, London NW1 4SA. Tel: 0171 262 5050.

8. It is important when considering performance from the position of abnormal returns, that the actual return on the portfolio is not compared with the average return on the market. The actual return on a portfolio should be compared with the return implied by the SML, given the particular portfolio's β. For further discussion of the use of β coefficients see either Rutterford (1993) or Blake (1990).

9. A comprehensive review of this work is contained in Levy and Sarnat (1984) and Copeland and Weston (1988).

References

Black, F., 'Capital Market Equilibrium with Restricted Borrowing', Journal of Business, 1972

Blake, D., *Financial Market Analysis*, London, McGraw-Hill, 1990

Brealey, R., *An Introduction to Risk and Return*, Oxford, Basil Blackwell, 1983

Copeland, T. and J. Weston, *Financial Theory and Corporate Policy*, Addison-Wesley, 1988

Dhrymes, P. 'The Empirical Relevance of Arbitrage Pricing Models', Journal of Portfolio Management, 1984

Dimson, E., 'Risk Measurement when Shares are subject to Infrequent Trading', Journal of Financial Economics, 1979

Fama, E.F., and J. MacBeth, 'Risk, Return and Equilibrium: Empirical Tests', Journal of Political Economy, 1973

Fama, E.F., and K.R. French, 'The Cross-Section of Expected Returns', Journal of Finance, 1992

Journal of Portfolio Management, 'Risk and Return: A Critique of Theory and an Analysis of Practice', Tenth Anniversary Issue, Journal of Portfolio Management, 1984

Latane, H. and W. Young, 'Tests of Portfolio Building Rules', Journal of Finance, 1969

Levy, H. and M. Sarnat, *Portfolio and Investment Selection*, Englewood Cliffs, N.J., Prentice Hall, 1984

Markowitz, H., 'Portfolio Selection', Journal of Finance, 1952

Reilly, F. and D. Wright, 'A Comparison of Published Betas', Journal of Portfolio Management, 1988

Roll, R., 'A Critique of the Assets Pricing Theory's Tests: Part I: On Past and Potential Testability of the Theory', Journal of Financial Economics, 1977

Ross, S.A., 'The Arbitrage Pricing Theory of Capital Asset Pricing', Journal of Economic Theory, 1976

Rutterford, J., *An Introduction to Stock Market Investments*, London, Macmillan, 1993

Sharpe, W.F. 'Capital Asset Prices: A Theory of Market Equilibrium Under Conditions of Risk', Journal of Finance, 1964

Tobin, J., 'Liquidity Preference as Behaviour Towards Risk', Review of Economic Studies, 1958

5 The efficient market hypothesis

Introduction

In Chapter 3 the concept of an efficient market was introduced. Recall that it explains the conditions under which an asset's price represents fair value: when it fully reflects all existing information on the asset's future net cash flows. In addition the Efficient Market Hypothesis (EMH) implies that market prices adjust instantaneously, to reflect any new information when it becomes available. If markets are not efficient, there is a worthwhile return to be made from identifying the extent to which assets are mispriced. In these circumstances investors and companies have a potential to beat the market.

The CAPM, presented in Chapter 4, provides a reference point for judging whether or not the market can be beaten. For a given level of risk, beating the market involves investors demonstrating a consistent ability to earn abnormal returns in excess of the required rate determined from the SML. For companies it involves a consistent ability to issue shares or bonds when market prices are above their intrinsic values. This implies that, in raising new funds, the cost of capital will be consistently below the cost required by the market, at the appropriate level of risk.

Consistent abnormal performance is only possible in an inefficient market. In an efficient market abnormal returns will be random with, over a period of sufficient length, positive and negative abnormal returns netting out to zero. In an efficient market any persistent performance above the SML must arise from the inclusion of specific risk in an imperfectly diversified portfolio. If, for any reason, a well-diversified portfolio began to demonstrate consistent abnormal returns, that in itself would constitute information to which the market would rapidly respond.

Since the presence or absence of market efficiency has profound implications for investment and financing strategies, this chapter examines the debate on the EMH in more depth. It begins by assessing the practical extent of market efficiency. Given, however, the very extensive literature on this topic, only a general view of the empirical evidence can be presented.[1] The chapter also explores the main implications of the EMH as they relate to accounting regulation, the roles of the investment analyst and fund management industries, the level of market trading and corporate financial management.

Testing the EMH

Tests of the EMH are concerned with determining the extent to which an asset's price reflects existing relevant information and the speed with which an asset's price reacts to relevant new information when it becomes available. The tests are primarily based on the possibilities of using information based trading rules to beat the market. To facilitate testing, three forms of market efficiency have been postulated: the weak, the semi-strong and the strong-form. Each of these are examined in turn.

Weak-form efficiency

Under the weak-form of market efficiency, a share's current price reflects all information contained in its past price history. Consequently, trading rules based solely on past price histories cannot be used to beat the market.[2] This arises because a share's current price fully and instantaneously responds to relevant new information, which, by definition, comes onto the market randomly. If future information was in any way predictable it would not constitute new information.

A common way of testing for the randomness of share price changes, induced by the random arrival of new information, is through examination of correlation coefficients. Since price changes are being analysed through time, these are often referred to as serial correlation, or autocorrelation, coefficients. If there is a discernible trend in a share's price, its serial correlation coefficient will be significantly different from zero.

The evidence from a number of studies pertaining to all the major stock markets is that there is no worthwhile correlation to speak of and, consequently, that there are no discernible trends in the past price histories of individual shares. This implies that the historical price patterns on which chartists base their trading rules are illusory and that this group of technical analysts cannot beat the market.

Where technical analysts who use mechanical trading rules are concerned, a similar conclusion has been deduced from empirical studies. Here, for example, tests are based on filter strategies formulated to buy and sell shares over a set time period, usually five years. The return from the filters, ranging from under 1% to 20% of price movements, is compared to returns from buy and hold strategies, where an initial set of share purchases is held throughout the test period. Interestingly the buy and hold strategies tend to outperform filter strategies. In a classic study by Fama and Blume (1966), the average rate of return on a range of filter strategies was 2.7%, before transaction costs were taken into account, as against a buy and hold strategy which yielded 9.9%. Very fine filters of around 1% did tend to outperform buy and hold positions, but any advantage disappeared when transactions costs were netted out.

In general, therefore, stock markets are weak-form efficient, with next to no prospects of developing trading rules, based on price information, to beat the market.[3]

Semi-strong form efficiency

Under the semi-strong form of market efficiency, share prices fully and instantaneously reflect all relevant publicly available information. Consequently, publicly available information cannot be used to develop trading rules to beat the market. Here, besides focusing on the reaction time to announcements of new information, the EMH argues that the market is capable of ignoring information which is only superficially relevant to valuation. This form of the EMH has important implications for fundamental analysts, since it implies that current market prices will already include all possible, and relevant, publicly available information on company fundamentals.

Information announcements

Basing trading rules on announcements of information does not, on balance, produce abnormal returns. In cases involving earnings or dividend announcements most of the information has already been assimilated by the market before announcements are made. Similarly, most of the information in company accounts appears to have been incorporated in market prices before the date on which the accounts are published. In the case of earnings announcements the research has been highly sophisticated, the information content being separated into anticipated and unanticipated announcement components. Ball and Brown (1968), for example, found that around 15% of the information is unanticipated and that there is a lagged price adjustment to unanticipated announcements after the announcement date. It is in this situation that there is some prospect of earning abnormal returns.

Attempts to develop trading rules based on the announcement of rights issues fail to beat the market; however, the new issue market appears to be inefficient for at least one month after a new issue takes place. In other words new issues are consistently underpriced, implying that the cost of new equity capital is consistently above the cost required by the market.[4]

Block trades and stock splits

Two other tests, relating to block trades and stock splits (or scrip issues), are worthy of mention.

A block trade occurs when a large number of shares in one company is offered for sale in one lot. A possible implication is that the seller of the block is acting on adverse information. Evidence by Kraus and Stoll (1972) indicates that there is an immediate price response when a block trade comes onto the market, thus supporting the EMH. There are, however, two elements to the price fall, one indicating a permanent information effect and the other indicating a temporary liquidity effect. The latter results from the size of the trade; it is as if a discount inducement is necessary to attract a buyer. This liquidity effect can disappear within 15 minutes of the block trade taking place and is apparently too small to formulate a trading rule: buy when a block trade comes onto the market to take advantage of the temporary liquidity effect.

A stock split, or scrip issue, simply involves splitting existing shares in some multiple and does not affect company fundamentals. Consequently prices should not react when a stock split is announced. Evidence by Fama et al. (1969) indicates that for a considerable period before a company announces a stock split, its price trends upwards and may continue to do so after the split. The price trend has been shown to be the result of favourable information which the market has already been anticipating in the pre-split price rise, with the stock split coinciding with other announcements concerning, for example, dividend changes. By itself, therefore, the stock split is irrelevant to valuation, although it may be used by a company as a signal, confirming an underlying change in fundamentals.

Irrelevant information

Further evidence that the market ignores irrelevant information is provided in a study by Kaplan and Roll (1972). They examined United States companies who boosted reported profits by switching from accelerated depreciation, which the companies still had to use for tax purposes, to straight line depreciation. The switch did not alter actual earnings after taxes and shareholders were not misled, since share prices did not respond to the superficial change in the method of accounting reporting. In other words, in an efficient market it is not accounting numbers per se which are determining share prices but the information they convey about the expected future cash generating ability of a company. In addition the EMH argues that the use of any accounting techniques which improve reported earnings without affecting the underlying magnitude and/or timing of a company's taxes, or other elements of its cash flows, has no effect on share prices.

'Accounting for Growth'

The view that the market reflects all relevant information in company accounts has recently been challenged by Smith (1992), who examined the accounting techniques used by the top 200 British companies listed on the London stock market. His argument is that a number of companies used 'accounting/financial engineering' techniques to create illusory growth in the 1980s which, it is implied, was reflected in strong upward movements in their share prices. Using case studies in relation to Polly Peck, British and Commonwealth, Coloroll and the Maxwell group of companies, Smith argues that the underlying financial weaknesses that these techniques were apparently masking were exposed as the recession developed at the end of the 1980s. The consequences for the share prices of these four companies were disastrous.

It is difficult to determine whether Smith's study, which provides major insights into accounting practices, constitutes evidence against the EMH. There are a number of points which need further clarification through formal statistical analysis before any definitive conclusion can be reached.

First, while the share prices in the subsequently failed companies did rise in the mid-1980s, there is no way of telling, without statistical analysis, what proportions (if any) of these rises were attributable to illusory growth conveyed by accounting information.

Second, the suggestion is that in some of the cases it was the recession which produced the serious problems. This raises the issue of whether the market could have been expected, on the basis of the macroeconomic information available in the mid-1980s, to predict that a severe recession would occur.[5]

Third, the share prices of companies such as Dixons and Next, which were identified as using a significant number of 'financial engineering' techniques, did not perform badly over the recessionary period examined.

Fourth, as specific information became publicly available indicating difficulties in a number of companies, their share prices did experience downward trends, as Smith readily admits; they accelerated, the more unfavourable the information.

This fourth and final point raises one of the most interesting issues in relation to Smith's work: whether, if the study does constitute evidence against market efficiency, it is evidence against the semi-strong form or the strong-form. In other words, if there was a lack of market perception it may have been due not to semi-strong form inefficiencies, reflected in a failure to interpret properly the information which was publicly available in company accounts, but to strong-form inefficiencies arising from tightly held, and therefore private, information. Once, for example, it becomes known that a company is under investigation for potential malpractice, private information starts to become publicly available and share prices respond accordingly.[6]

Strong-form efficiency

Under the strong-form of market efficiency, share prices reflect all relevant information even if it is not publicly available. In this case, with the focus on privately held or inside knowledge, the EMH argues that monopoly access to information cannot be used to earn abnormal returns. Strong-form efficiency is important in a wider context, in that it argues that management cannot benefit their own companies by exploiting inside knowledge on their companies' prospects at the expense of the market. In other words, management cannot involve themselves in private actions which materially affect intrinsic value without market prices responding appropriately. The recent examples in relation to the Guinness and Maxwell corporations certainly tend to refute this view of strong-form efficiency.

The task of testing strong-form efficiency is naturally very difficult given the secret nature of private information. In addition, there are legal consequences for insider dealers and corporate executives if they disclose that they have used private information in their own share dealings or to knowingly misrepresent their company's value. Tests based on specialist market makers who legally deal on their own account and tests based on insider dealing indicate that consistent abnormal returns can be earned. In the case of specialist market makers who execute trades for their clients, these specialists represent the first point of entry of private information into the public domain. They have, therefore, the opportunity to exploit the information they glean from observing their clients' buying and selling behaviour, in the context of the clients' background, before the rest of the market.

Other tests of strong-form efficiency have been based on the performance of managed funds and the behaviour of returns surrounding merger announcements. In the latter case abnormal returns are apparently available in the months preceding the announcement of mergers. There is no evidence of abnormal returns after announcements. This might, or might not, suggest that insider dealing is taking place on the basis of privileged information. In the case of managed funds one hypothesis is that fund managers may have access to private information. Abnormal fund returns could, however, result from superior analysis of publicly available information, in which case semi-strong form efficiency is being tested. In either situation the EMH would argue that any tendency for unit trusts or investment trusts to demonstrate consistent abnormal returns would be interpreted by the market as indirect information on superior expertise or access to privileged knowledge, to which the market would rapidly respond. Tests of the performance of managed funds indicate that their returns, after transactions costs, do not outperform buy and hold strategies. Managed fund performance is largely explained, in a CAPM context, by fund βs. This empirical evidence therefore supports the EMH.

Market anomalies

On the basis of most of the empirical work referred to above, a sort of consensus view developed towards the end of the 1970s that markets were at least efficient in their semi-strong form. In recent years, however, studies have produced contrary evidence which is often referred to as market anomalies. The term is used because an underlying view of efficiency persists, with attempts being made to rationalise results which break with convention.

Market anomalies are associated with what is referred to as the January effect, the monthly effect and the daily and day of the week effects. Summarising the anomalies identified across a number of studies, it appears that investors are capable of earning the highest positive abnormal returns in the first five days of January, the worst month for negative abnormal returns being October. There is a monthly effect, with higher returns being possible from trading in the first half of any month relative to its second half. There is a daily effect with, on average, returns appearing to be highest in the last 15 minutes of trading in any given day. There is also a day of the week effect, with returns being highest on a Friday (except the 13th) and lowest on a Monday.

In an efficient market the above effects could not be expected to persist since, once identified, the market would act on the information and the abnormal returns would disappear. In the limit, investors might tend to concentrate their activities on the first Friday in January and want to trade only in the last 15 minutes. Trade would virtually cease in the second half of the month of October. That this has not happened implies that markets are either not efficient in their weak and semi-strong forms, or are efficient but the above results are anomalous.

Explanations for some of the anomalies relate to the possibility that firms tend to announce unfavourable information at the beginning of the week. There may be a weekend (Friday–Monday) effect arising from traders 'clearing their desks' on a Friday (causing price buoyancy) and experiencing 'Monday morning blues' (causing price depressions). Liquidity constraints have been put forward as an explanation for the monthly effect. The major explanations for the anomalies, in particular the January effect, have concentrated on the tax selling hypothesis, the ability to develop trading rules based on PE ratios and/or firm size, and the empirical problems associated with testing the anomalies via the CAPM.

Research by Keim (1983), which confirmed previous evidence that abnormal returns could be made by trading in portfolios comprised of small-sized firms, indicates that almost 50% of these abnormalities occur in the first five days of January trading. In an attempt to explain this, attention has focused on the observation that firms with small capitalisations are subject to greater β risks than large-sized firms; however, adjustments for risk have not produced an adequate explanation. This, in turn, brought the reliability of β estimates into question, especially since small firms tend to be thinly or inactively traded. As indicated in the previous chapter, least confidence can be placed in β estimates associated with thinly traded shares. Subsequent application of estimating techniques which corrected for thin trade biases has still not completely resolved the small firm effect.

One of the difficulties faced with interpreting the evidence on firm size and abnormal returns is that abnormal returns have been shown to be available through trading in portfolios comprised of firms with low PE ratios. Low PE ratios are associated with small firms and it is not completely clear whether the abnormalities are the result of a PE effect or a small firm effect. If the PE effect dominates, attempts to rationalise abnormalities using risk and estimation bias arguments directly related to size effects would be spurious.

An alternative explanation for the January effect involves a tax selling hypothesis. According to this, shares are sold at the end of a year to create capital losses for tax purposes and then repurchased early in January, the buying pressure causing excessive price rises. This hypothesis has tended to be dismissed since small firms which did not exhibit price declines at the end of a year still exhibited strong price rises in early January. In addition the January effect is a worldwide phenomenon occurring in stock markets where capital gains tax considerations are not important.

Instead of accepting the EMH and attempting to explain away market anomalies, recent work by Jackobs and Levy (1988), for example, suggests that an alternative to the EMH may be necessary. In particular, it can be argued that the EMH is fundamentally flawed since it relies on the underlying premise that investors act rationally. Instead, investors may act irrationally, trading on relevant but complex information, using rule of thumb decision processes, and trading when no useful information is available, creating what is referred to as 'noise' in the markets. In these cases market behaviour is analysed on a cognitive psychology based model. Thus, abnormal returns are not anomalous but the direct result of irrational behaviour which also creates excessive market volatility. Even if there is a sub-set of professional market traders who act rationally, to exploit identified abnormal returns, market prices are prevented from approximating intrinsic values because of continuous psychological behaviour by other market participants.

Short-termism

In the United Kingdom a more general challenge has been presented to the EMH by the recent debate on short-termism. The argument, supported by both politicians and industrialists, is that shareholders focus on short-term company performance, causing management to concentrate on short-term factors which will support current share prices at the expense of neglecting investment in long-term projects. Short-termism also promotes a greater degree of share price volatility than there should be, and thus encourages beating the market strategies.

In technical terms the short-termism hypothesis states that there is a capital market prejudice against companies making long-term investments, which is reflected by the average investor exhibiting an abnormally high required rate of return. This, it is argued, reinforces general inefficiencies in capital markets and, by imposing abnormally high costs of capital on companies, produces sub-optimal levels of long-term investment.

While the short-termism debate, until recently, has been based on anecdotal evidence, Miles (1993) has tested the hypothesis using a sample of nearly 500 United Kingdom quoted companies. Applying CAPM methodology, the results do not lead to a weakening of a short-termism view. The discount rates implied by the London stock market indicate, for example, that cash flows expected in five years' time are, on average, discounted as if they are expected in nine years' time. From management's point of view the stock market appears to require projects with five years to maturity to be 40% more profitable than is optimal, if their acceptance by a company is not to lead to a fall in its market value.

Short-termism and market efficiency could be rationalised if, following one of the arguments in the previous chapter, the average degree of risk aversion, reflected in the market risk premium, changes through time. This could also explain the above normal volatility in share prices. Such an explanation is not satisfactory, however, since risk premia would have to be highly variable and increasing. Miles concedes that there may be an explanation for his results but argues that it has not yet been put forward by EMH proponents.

Critics of short-termism argue that share prices do respond to the announcement of new projects which are expected to exploit future profit opportunities, and that such growth potential is reflected in PE ratios which are significantly above their base levels. In response, Miles comments that:

> Perhaps in an efficient market share prices of UK stocks would rise even more than they do on investment announcements and P/E multiples be far higher.

EMH implications

The presence or absence of market efficiency raises a number of issues in respect of corporate investment and financing decisions and the accounting framework in which they are taken. There are also implications for the fund management industry and the level of capital market regulation. These are examined below, beginning with the implications for accounting reporting.

The need for accounting standards

The Accounting Standards Board in the United Kingdom recently introduced changes in reporting requirements in relation to cash flow statements, extra-ordinary items, and goodwill; and it is considering potential change to performance measurement and the valuation of assets. This type of regulation tends to be resented by company managements because of the direct and indirect costs it imposes.[7] The direct costs arise in relation to gathering, collating and publishing information in compliance with reporting requirements. There are indirect costs associated with having to disclose private information which might, on publication, convey operational insights to a company's main competitors and/or be used against a company in litigation. Other objections arise with respect to possible subjectivity, where there is a requirement to report values for tangible and intangible assets which are not traded in active secondary markets.

In an inefficient market where the manipulation of accounting numbers can give a distorted view of future net cash flows, the above costs tend to be outweighed by the benefits of improved reporting standards. In an increasingly complex financial world, improved reporting standards help to enhance the quality of published data and maintain the high level of credibility, by and large already associated with accounting numbers. If, on the other hand, markets are at least semi-strong form efficient, assessment of the intrinsic values of publicly traded companies will be independent of the standards of reporting information which is already publicly available in some form or another. Consequently the resources devoted to improving standards and monitoring their implementation, and the costs imposed on companies required to adopt them, may appear unnecessary in an efficient market.

The latter view, based on the conventional wisdom that markets are at least semi-strong form efficient, necessitated a revision of the underlying rationale for accounting regulation and produced one which is largely management orientated. The crux of the modern argument is that accounting information is important in helping companies establish managerial accountability and effective internal monitoring procedures. In the case, for example, of a company head office acting as a mini capital market, internal assessments must be made of the company's semi-autonomous divisions. An accounting standards framework employed by the head office can enhance monitoring and reduce potential managerial conflict over internal resource allocation. This conflict might arise if the reporting criteria are not seen to be determined by a professional body outside the company. In these senses, standards can indirectly improve efficiency and hence market value.

Accounting numbers are often important items in financial contracts so that confidence in accounting numbers, which is in part associated with the objectivity argument, is essential. In the case of financing, for example, various restrictive covenants relating to bank or open market forms of debt are expressed in terms of accounting numbers, such as coverage ratios. The development of management incentive schemes also produces terms and conditions of employment where part of management compensation is tied to reported accounting figures, such as earnings per share.

Externally, accounting numbers can have a very important effect in cases where arguments are being put for increased subsidies and/or reductions in profit and employment taxes. If the aim is to improve future investment and competitive strategies in particular industries, the credibility of the arguments, as viewed by governments and public sector agencies, will partly depend on the use of reliable reporting conventions. In the European Union, for example, these interactions between interest groups – in economic, social and political terms – are becoming an integral part of corporatism and are helping to define developments in the Single Market. Thus for firms and industries which wish to maximise the benefits of EU membership, there is a strong rationale for supporting and adapting recent and potential future changes in accounting reporting standards despite the costs of implementation.

Market efficiency, by arguing that markets can see behind accounting numbers in whatever form they are presented, does not, therefore, imply that accounting regulation is irrelevant. On the contrary, the EMH has helped redefine some of the objectives of regulation and focused much more on the role of accounting within a company.

Other corporate finance implications

Apart from the implications relating to the internal use of accounting reporting, it has already been argued that market efficiency has implications for the timing of new debt and equity issues. In the latter case there is no reason to believe that, on average, better or worse prices will be available in the future, relative to the present. If there are strong-form inefficiencies, however, management may be able to retain information which, when it eventually becomes publicly available, will have a detrimental (or favourable) effect on price.

In general the EMH implies that careful consideration must be given to all corporate finance decisions so that superficial reasoning can be isolated and disregarded. If, for example, a company is diversifying into new product markets it would be erroneous for a management, in an efficient market, to base decisions on the prospect of enhancing share values through a reduction in their company's risk exposure. Assuming investors hold well-diversified portfolios, all possible risk reduction in respect of an individual company will have been achieved. Investors will only be willing to pay a premium for the company's shares if product market diversification is based on the potential to exploit profitable investment opportunities.

The EMH also has implications for the price companies are willing to pay for mergers and acquisitions, for the general efficiency with which managers run companies and for the prospects of managers pursuing their own objectives at the expense of shareholder wealth maximisation. To the extent that capital markets are efficient, management will be constrained into an optimal deployment of a company's resources and into pursuing shareholder objectives. Persistent failure in these areas would induce a takeover by another management team keen to exploit profit advantages. In this situation, however, the usual EMH paradox arises, in that once shareholders are confronted by a takeover they will only be willing to sell shares at a price which reflects the potential acquirer's ability to run the company efficiently. Consequently, from the acquiring company's point of view, the value additivity principle operates, where the market value of the acquiring company will simply rise by the price paid for the acquisition.

Another area where the EMH raises questions is in respect of the apparently expensive ways in which companies announce information, for example, through stock splits which involve significant administrative costs. This touches on the relatively new area of information signalling which is associated with agency costs. Information signalling is addressed in later chapters (particularly Chapters 8 and 9), as are the reasons for mergers, acquisitions and management buyouts (Chapter 13).

Zero NPV transactions

Many of the investment and financing implications of market efficiency can be summed up in the view that, if capital markets are efficient, financial investments are zero NPV transactions. This arises because, in equilibrium, all financial assets will lie on the SML. Expected and required rates of return will be equal and asset prices will, on average, reflect intrinsic values.

Consider the case of share price valuation in Equation 3.1:

$$P_0 = \sum_{t=1}^{\infty} \frac{d_t}{(1 + r_e)^t}$$

From a potential buyer's point of view, P_0 represents the cost of purchasing the share. This, in equilibrium, is equal to the market's, and the buyer's, assessment of the present value of the expected future dividend entitlements from ownership. The NPV of transacting in the share is, therefore, equal to this present value assessment less the initial cost of purchase, that is,

$$NPV = \sum_{t=1}^{\infty} \frac{d_t}{(1 + r_e)^t} - P_0 = 0$$

The company whose shares are being traded views buying and selling transactions between investors in a similar light since, in an efficient market, the equilibrium required and expected rates of return represent the company's cost of equity capital. Thus all participants in an efficient market view market transactions as having zero NPVs.

The above does not imply an absence of profitable product market investment opportunities with positive NPVs. Under the EMH it is the capital markets' abilities to fully reflect, in a company's share price, that company's potential to undertake such positive NPV projects which cause investments in shares to be zero NPV transactions.

Capital market investment activities

The EMH implies that, since abnormal returns cannot be made, individual investors and professional fund managers should adopt passive investment strategies, choosing investments to suit their desired exposure to risk. Portfolios still have to be adjusted, of course, to maintain particular risk exposures as economic conditions change, or to alter risk exposures in the light of these changing conditions. To the extent that markets are efficient, active investment strategies to gain abnormal returns are irrelevant but costly. The costs arise from higher than necessary levels of resources devoted to portfolio management functions and higher than necessary transactions costs from over-frequent trading, which reduce the net returns to investors.

Active trading is essential, however, to ensure that capital markets are efficient, hence the paradox; although whether the paradox is more apparent than real depends on investor motivation in formulating buy and sell decisions. Investors who believe that markets are efficient will not be motivated to buy and sell on the anticipation of making abnormal returns. On the contrary, they may interpret and act upon new information on the motivation that, if they do not, they will make abnormal losses and, in effect, be beaten by an efficient market. The real question, if the EMH holds, is whether the level of trading activity exceeds that which is necessary to ensure that efficiency is maintained. While this question is practically impossible to answer, it is just conceivable that high share price volatility does not constitute evidence in support of short-termism but evidence of overtrading, or portfolio churning, in an efficient market.

Where stock market regulation is concerned, if markets are at least efficient in their semi-strong form, there is no necessity for government intervention to regulate day-to-day market activities. Indeed the conventional view that, on balance, markets are semi-strong form efficient can partly explain the United Kingdom's emphasis, during the 1980s, on deregulation. This culminated in Big Bang, and persists in the general attitude of government: that when some form of control is necessary, self-regulation is often sufficient.

If there are serious doubts about strong-form efficiency, then there is a rationale for legislation against insider dealing. With the EMH being essentially an information based hypothesis, however, there is a strong case for such legislation to be supported by policies which aim to create an environment which enforces the disclosure of information. By promoting, at minimum, easier access to privately held, valuation relevant knowledge, there is a better chance of preventing insider dealing and increasing the degree of strong-form efficiency.

Summary

To date, the bulk of empirical evidence supports the view that markets are efficient in their weak-form and, therefore, that price trading rules cannot be used to consistently beat the market. While, on balance, statistically based research suggests that fundamental analysts cannot beat the market either, there is some evidence of semi-strong form inefficiencies. Whether, in the long run, Smith's work contributes to a greater degree of scepticism in respect of this form of the EMH is another question. This will largely depend on whether the relationship between share price changes and the 'accounting/financial engineering' techniques identified by Smith is the subject of formal statistical testing and, if it is, on the results of such tests.

Strong-form efficiency receives the least statistically based empirical support, relative to the two other forms of efficiency. Where anomalies and short-termism are concerned, fervent supporters of the EMH believe that, with further theoretical advances and improvements in testing techniques, these will be shown to be spurious.

To the extent that markets are efficient the volume of market trading may be above its optimal level, as might the existing levels of resources devoted to fund management functions and various forms of regulation. To the extent that markets are efficient, investors can be confident that market prices are, on average, the best available value for money measures. Similarly, corporate finance executives can relax and be confident in the knowledge that, if they wish to raise additional debt or equity, there is no better time than the present; on average, there is no possibility of forecasting a better, or worse, price in the future.

Finally, while investment in an efficient capital market represents a zero NPV transaction, this does not necessarily imply that capital projects which companies undertake have zero NPVs. It implies that each company's potential to undertake project investments with positive NPVs is fully reflected in each company's share price. Project or capital investment appraisal is the subject of the next two chapters.

Questions

1 What do you understand by the concept of 'beating the market'? What does the EMH imply about the possibility of 'beating the market'?

2 Why can Smith's study of 'Accounting for Growth' not be taken as evidence against the EMH?

3 What do you understand by the 'small firm effect'?

4 What is the EMH 'paradox'?

5 What implications does the EMH have for a company's costs of capital?

Exercises

1 What do you understand by the concept of short-termism?

2 What implications does the EMH have for accounting reporting standards?

3 What are the main market anomalies?

Endnotes

1. Reasonably comprehensive reviews of the empirical literature are contained in Fisher and Jordan (1991); and Radcliffe (1990).

2. The emphasis in weak-form efficiency is on price changes. An examination of price levels through time might suggest that the prices of individual shares, or indeed stock exchange indices, demonstrate particular patterns or trends. According to the EMH, however, these are superficial because when the underlying changes in price levels are examined a random pattern will be exposed. In very general terms, instead of looking at successive price levels – P_1, P_2, P_3 ..., P_{t-1}, P_t – when price changes are examined – $(P_2 - P_1)$, $(P_3 - P_2)$, ..., $(P_t - P_{t-1})$ – these are determined by a random error component. There are a number of ways in which the random error term can behave, one of which is known as a Random Walk. Weak-form efficiency is often loosely referred to as the Random Walk Hypothesis, although in strictly statistical terms this is misleading.

3. On the basis of these arguments, changes in stock market indices are also random variables.

4. An important issue in the EMH debate is that of consistency. The EMH does not argue that abnormal returns cannot be earned but rather that they cannot be earned consistently. During the UK government's privatisation programme in the early to mid-1980s, for example, companies were underpriced at the time of their privatisations. Any investor operating on the rule, apply for shares in each privatisation and sell within one month of flotation, would have been able to make abnormal returns up to October 1987. At this point the stock market crash occurred and one of the biggest privatisations, of BP, was caught in the middle.

5. This point is supported in a more general sense, when the two major stock market crashes of this century are considered. There have been a number of after the event studies trying to explain the October 1987 crash and the classic 1929 crash. While a debating point can be made of whether or not any of the explanations are satisfactory, there is no evidence of before the event ability to predict when either crash was about to occur, or either's extent.

6. As Smith himself argues in the Polly Peck case:

   Even now it is difficult to judge whether Polly Peck failed because of malpractice or from fundamental flaws in currency mismatching, working capital controls, or even just the absolute level of debt.

7. The apparent proliferation of accounting reporting requirements is not confined to the United Kingdom. Many of the major non-accounting businesses in the United States argue that it has become a 'growth' industry in its own right which has placed, and is likely to continue to place, significant reporting compliance costs on the corporate sector. In a European Union context, as the Single Market evolves, it is probable that in the medium to long term a comprehensive set of reporting requirements will be developed which, again, impose costs on publicly traded companies.

References

Aczel, M., 'After the Crash: The Opportunities According to Benjamin Graham', Investment Analyst, 1988

Ball, J., 'Short-Termism – Myth or Reality?' National Westminster Bank Quarterly Review, 1991

Ball, R. and P. Brown, 'An Empirical Evaluation of Accounting Income Numbers', Journal of Accounting Research, 1968

Damant, D.C., 'The Efficient Market Model and the Stock Market', Investment Analyst, 1986

Davison, E. and P. Marsh, 'The Smaller Companies Puzzle', Investment Analyst, 1986

Fama, E., et al., 'The Adjustment of Stock Prices to New Information', International Economic Review, 1969

Fama, E. and M. Blume, 'Filter Rules and Stock Market Trading', Journal of Business, 1966

Fisher, D.E. and R.J. Jordan, Security Analysis and Portfolio Management, Englewood Cliffs, Prentice-Hall, 1991

Hutchinson, R. and K. McCaffery, 'Accounting for Growth, Market Anomalies and Short-termism', Studies in Accounting and Finance, 1994

Jackobs, B. and K. Levy, 'On the Value of "Value"', Financial Analysts Journal, 1988

Joy, M.M. and C.P. Jones, 'Should We Believe Tests of Market Efficiency?', Journal of Portfolio Management, 1986

Kaplan, R. and R. Roll, 'Investor Evaluation of Accounting Information: Some Empirical Evidence', Journal of Business, 1972

Keim, D.B., 'Size Related Anomalies and Stock Return Seasonality: Further Empirical Evidence', Journal of Financial Economics, 1983

Kraus, A. and H. Stoll, 'Price Impacts of Block Trading on the New York Stock Exchange', Journal of Finance, 1972

Miles, D., 'Testing for Short-Termism in the UK Stock Market', The Economic Journal, 1993

Radcliffe, R.C., Investment: Concepts, Analysis and Strategy, Glenview, Illinois, Scott, Foresman, 1990

Smith, T., Accounting for Growth: Stripping the Camouflage from Company Accounts, London, Century Business, 1992

Watts, R., 'Does it Pay to Manipulate EPS?', in J.M. Stern and D.H. Chew, The Revolution in Corporate Finance, Oxford, Blackwell, 1992

6 Principles of capital investment appraisal

Introduction

When equity valuation was considered in Chapter 3, the capital market's assessment of the growth potential that a company was capable of exploiting was shown to be a fundamental component of a company's share price. This growth potential was expressed in terms of the net present value of available future investments which earned attractive rates of return in excess of a company's cost of capital. While a company's share price will be influenced by short-term factors associated, for example, with a company's working capital policy, its future growth is primarily determined by the strategy it adopts towards investment in capital projects.

Given that a company's capital investment, or capital budgeting decisions, have a crucial bearing on its expected future growth rate, this chapter examines the principal factors which a company takes into account in making these decisions. The chapter begins by outlining the nature of capital projects. This is followed by an analysis of the strengths and weaknesses of the techniques that can be used to choose, from the range of available projects, those which should be selected and those which should be rejected. The four principal investment appraisal techniques are: the Net Present Value (NPV), the Internal Rate of Return (IRR), the Pay-Back, and the Accounting Rate of Return.

It is the intention, at this stage in the chapter, to identify which technique is the most appropriate. Consequently, to simplify the analysis, the future net cash flows and initial capital costs of projects are taken as given. In addition it is assumed that these are known with certainty, and that capital markets are perfect. With these latter two assumptions, there is a single market determined opportunity cost of capital to which all projects are subject, and at which any amount of project finance can be raised.

After indicating that NPV is the most appropriate investment appraisal technique, the chapter proceeds by discussing the factors which should be taken into account in formulating project cash inflows and cash outflows. The emphasis is placed on identifying the relevant costs associated with operating a project and on showing how depreciation and taxes should be treated when obtaining net cash flows. The assumption of certainty is relaxed at this point but a formal analysis of risk, in the context of the cost of capital, is delayed to the next chapter. Some of the implications of relaxing the perfect capital market assumption, by introducing limitations to the supply of capital, are also examined in the next chapter.

The nature of capital projects

Capital projects are largely concerned with investment in plant and equipment. In essence they involve medium to long-term production commitments in order to exploit anticipated sales opportunities in the existing markets in which a company operates and in any new markets it identifies. Even in a no growth situation, where a company is striving to maintain its existing level of operations, capital investment is still necessary to replace existing plant and equipment as it wears out or depreciates.

Capital investment is not, however, exclusively limited to tangible assets such as plant and equipment. In highly competitive markets it may also involve investment expenditures on intangible assets such as research and development (R and D) into new and/or improved products and cost-saving production processes. It may involve investments in reputational assets, in the form of brand names and associated advertising campaigns, and appropriate investment in the education and training of a company's workforce.

Cash inflows and cash outflows

In considering individual projects the key factor, apart from the project's cost of capital, is the current and future cash inflows (or revenues) and the current and future cash outflows (or costs) that the project is likely to generate. These determine the project's series of net cash flows (NCFs) which must be estimated on a net of tax basis. In general, given that capital projects have a gestation period of more than a year, the early or initial NCFs are primarily composed of the capital, or purchase, costs associated with plant and machinery and their installation costs. Therefore the initial NCF, or net investment outlay, which is usually designated as occurring at time zero, is normally negative.

Only when the plant has been completed will the project begin to generate operating revenues. These are largely determined by the expected future levels of sales of the product (or service) associated with the intended project. In each future time period the expected operating costs of running the plant and selling the product are deducted from the expected operating revenues, to give the expected net operating cash flows. There may be further capital expenditure over the life of the project; however, it is the overall NCF in any future period, including additional capital expenditure in that period, which is relevant. After the initial investment period, NCFs are normally assumed to be positive over the remaining life of a project.

There may be terminal NCFs at the end of a project's operating life involving, for example, terminal revenues from the sale of plant and equipment or terminal costs associated with restoring a factory site to its original condition.

Incremental net cash flows

NCFs are often referred to as incremental or marginal NCFs. This emphasises the point that only the costs and revenues which the project itself generates are relevant in assessing the project's viability. Any costs which would be incurred independently of whether a project was accepted or rejected, would not be incremental and would not form part of a project's assessment.

Identifying projects

A significant amount of resources is involved in undertaking project appraisal:

estimating the future sales levels of new or improved products through market research, surveying sites for factories and offices and producing engineering specifications for production processes, among other factors. Therefore, in looking at the range of potential new investments, company management have to employ ad hoc procedures based on experience and intuition, to identify a relatively small set of projects to which formal appraisal techniques can then be applied.

Categorising projects

The projects to which formal appraisal techniques are applied are placed into three categories: independent projects, mutually exclusive projects and linked projects.

If a set of independent projects is being appraised, the acceptance or rejection of any one of the set has no influence on the acceptance or rejection of any other. Independent projects are unrelated to each other. Consider, for example, a company operating in both the leisure and food processing industries. It is considering expanding its business by building a new hotel and by establishing an additional cheese processing plant. Assuming any amount of finance is available to the company at the market determined opportunity cost of capital, acceptance (or rejection) of one of these projects has no implications for the decision to accept (or reject) the other.

A set of mutually exclusive projects involves what is sometimes referred to as an option appraisal. Here each project defines an alternative way of undertaking a particular investment intention. On selecting the 'best option' all the other projects in the appraisal are automatically rejected. In the case, for example, of a Japanese car manufacturer who is considering building an assembly plant in the European Union, an option appraisal might involve considering alternative regional locations within the EU.

If two or more projects are interlinked they are mutually dependent, so that acceptance or rejection of one of the projects automatically necessitates, respectively, acceptance or rejection of those which are linked to it. Consider, for example, a retailing company which wishes to use its customer base to expand into financial services. It believes, however, that acquisition of a competitor's chain of stores is necessary to achieve the size of customer base consistent with the development of banking products. In this case both the potential acquisition, or merger, project and the financial services project are interrelated. If, eventually, the company decides that the price to be paid for the competitor's chain of stores is 'too high', rejection of the acquisition will lead automatically to the rejection of the development of a financial services' arm to the company's operations. Note that, where possible, potential projects which are interlinked should be considered in their totality as one overall project, ensuring that the joint or shared effects are identified and taken into account in such a way that double counting is avoided.

NPV and IRR

Turning to the main appraisal techniques, the analysis begins by considering the NPV and IRR approaches, both of which are based on the discounting principles developed in Chapter 2 on the Time Value of Money.

Obtaining the NPV of a project involves estimating its future net cash flows; discounting these at the appropriate opportunity cost of capital to obtain their present value; and subtracting the initial capital cost, or net investment outlay, at the beginning of the project. Formally,[1]

$$NPV = \sum_{t=1}^{n} \frac{NCF_t}{(1 + r)^t} - I_0 \qquad (6.1)$$

where,

NCF$_t$ is the net cash flow received at the end of each year or period t, t = 1, 2, ..., n.
r is the project's opportunity cost of capital.
I$_0$ is the net investment outlay in time zero.

Expressing Equation 6.1 in terms of present value interest factors:

$$NPV = \sum_{t=1}^{n} (NCF_t)(PVIF_{t,r}) - I_0 \qquad (6.1a)$$

The IRR on a project is based on the NPV concept and is found by solving for the discount rate which makes the NPV on a project equal to zero. In a more formal sense the IRR is the discount rate which, if applied to the future NCF series, equates the present value of that series to the initial or net investment outlay. From Equation 6.1,

$$NPV = \sum_{t=1}^{n} \frac{NCF_t}{(1 + IRR)^t} - I_0 = 0 \qquad (6.2)$$

or

$$\sum_{t=1}^{n} \frac{NCF_t}{(1 + IRR)^t} = I_0 \qquad (6.2a)$$

A conventional NPV schedule

To obtain a clearer understanding of these two methods it is useful to consider the NPV schedule, defined in relation to a standard or conventional project. A conventional project is one which always generates positive future NCFs, subject to the usual initial negative net investment outlay.

Consider project B, detailed in Table 6.1, which has an initial net investment outlay of £700 and which produces a series of NCFs over a subsequent five-year period. Given r, the NPV for this project is:

$$NPV = \frac{200}{1 + r} + \frac{150}{(1 + r)^2} + \frac{200}{(1 + r)^3} + \frac{200}{(1 + r)^4} + \frac{600}{(1 + r)^5} - 700$$

Table 6.1: Net investment outlays and NCFs for three independent projects

Year	A £s	Projects B £s	C £s	
		Net Investment Outlay		PVIFs @ r = 8%
0	−2000	−700	−700	1.00
		Net Cash Flows		
1	200	200	300	0.926
2	500	150	100	0.857
3	400	200	200	0.794
4	600	200	300	0.735
5	500	600	800	0.681
NPV @ 8%	−£287.30	£327.91	£587.25	
IRR	2.94%	21.29%	30.09%	

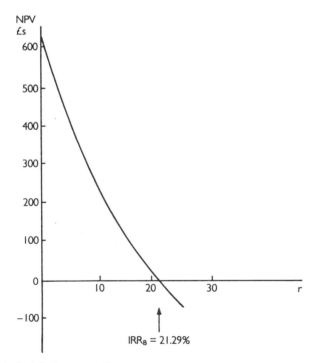

NPV
£s

Figure 6.1   NPV schedule for project B

Its NPV schedule is sketched in Figure 6.1. The NPV is measured on the vertical axis and the discount rate on the horizontal axis.

As an illustration of the relationship between NPV and r, the following four discount rates are applied to project B: 0.00%, 10%, 20% and 25%. If the discount rate is zero the NPV is simply the sum of the future NCFs minus the initial net investment outlay, that is, NPV = £650. At r = 10% the NPV = £265.20; at r = 20% the NPV = £24.15; and at r = 25% the NPV = −£63.07. Thus for this project, and its standard type, the NPV is inversely related to the discount rate: the higher the discount rate the lower the NPV.

From the NPV schedule in Figure 6.1, the IRR is clearly illustrated. Since the IRR is determined as the discount rate which makes the NPV of a project zero, the IRR always occurs where the NPV schedule of a conventional project crosses the horizontal axis. In the case of project B, this point is achieved at a discount rate of 21.29%. Appendix 6.1 demonstrates how an approximate estimate of the IRR can be obtained.

Selecting independent investments

Under the NPV investment selection rule, all independent projects are acceptable provided that, for each project i,

$$NPV_i \geq 0 \qquad (6.3)$$

That is, all independent projects which at the chosen discount rate have positive, or at minimum zero, NPVs should be accepted. A project with a negative NPV is automatically rejected. In the specific example of project B above, providing the opportunity cost of capital, or discount rate, is not in excess of approximately 21%, a positive NPV would occur and the project would be accepted.

The reasoning behind the NPV is straightforward. It measures the extent to which the present value of a project's cash inflows exceeds the present value of its cash outflows and, therefore, the extent to which shareholder wealth will be increased if the project is accepted. A company is indifferent to a project with a zero NPV since the funds that a zero NPV project generates are just capable of covering the project's net investment outlay and meeting the company's required rate of return. Zero NPV projects do not, however, make a net contribution to wealth. Projects with negative NPVs would reduce value, if accepted.

In general, under the IRR investment selection rule, all independent projects are acceptable providing that, for each project i,

$$IRR_i \geq r \qquad (6.4)$$

That is, only independent projects whose IRRs exceed, or at minimum are equal to, the cost of capital would be acceptable. In the specific example of project B, if the cost of capital is greater than 21.29%, the project would be automatically rejected. If the cost of capital is equal to, or below, this cost of capital the project would be acceptable. Since the IRR is determined from the NPV schedule, its accept/reject decision rule has implications for wealth creation similar to NPV. Generally, when the IRR exceeds the cost of capital, NPV > 0; when it falls below it, NPV < 0. There are, however, some problems with applying the IRR rule which are discussed in the next section.

To illustrate the above two investment appraisal rules, consider all three independent projects in Table 6.1 and assume an opportunity cost of capital of 8%. The PVIFs at r = 8% are given in the final column of the table. The NPVs of projects B

Table 6.2: Mutually exclusive projects and incremental cash flows

| | Mutually Exclusive Projects | | Incremental Project |
| | D | E | Z |
Year	£s	£s	£s
		Net Investment Outlay	
0	−800	−800	0.00
		Net Cash Flows	
1	100	400	−300.00
2	200	300	−100.00
3	200	100	100.00
4	400	400	0.00
5	1000	500	500.00
NPV			
@ 8%	£597.42	£541.26	£56.16
IRR	25.08%	30.35%	12.69%

and C are positive and both would be accepted; however, with a negative NPV, project A would be rejected. Similarly, projects B and C would be accepted using the IRR decision rule[2] since each one's IRR exceeds the cost of capital of 8%. Project A would be rejected, however, since its IRR is less than 8%.

One of the advantages of using NPV is that it conforms to what is referred to as the value additivity principle, since the overall NPV of a set of independent projects is simply the sum of the individual project NPVs. In the present example the overall NPV of accepting projects B and C is: £327.91 + £587.25 = £915.16.

The technical superiority of NPV

For technical reasons the NPV investment selection rule is superior to the IRR rule, especially in a situation where a choice has to be made between a set of mutually exclusive projects.

In the mutually exclusive case, when using NPV, the project with the highest positive NPV is chosen. Under the IRR method the project with the highest IRR is chosen, providing the project's IRR is at least equal to the opportunity cost of capital. If, for example, the projects in Table 6.1 were mutually exclusive, instead of independent, project C would be selected by both methods. In the case of mutually exclusive projects, however, a straight application of the IRR method can produce an incorrect project choice.

This is exemplified in Table 6.2, where the net investment outlays and future NCFs are recorded for two mutually exclusive projects: D and E. The discount rate is 8% which, assuming certainty and perfect capital markets, is the market determined opportunity cost of borrowing and lending.

If the two projects in Table 6.2 had been independent there would be no ambiguity, since both projects would have been acceptable using either NPV or IRR. Both projects have positive NPVs and each project's IRR exceeds the opportunity cost of capital. Since the two projects are mutually exclusive, however, there is an obvious problem. Under the NPV rule, project D with its higher NPV would be chosen in preference to project E. Using the IRR rule, project E with its higher IRR would be chosen in preference to project D. The correct choice is made on the basis of NPV.

The conflict between the two decision rules arises because, in diagrammatic terms, the NPV schedules of the two projects cross over. This is demonstrated in Figure 6.2 where the NPV schedules for these two projects are sketched. The cross-over point occurs at a discount rate of 12.69%. If the opportunity cost of capital had been above 12.69%, the NPV method would have yielded the same project choice as the IRR method. The opportunity cost of capital of 8% is below this, giving rise to alternative choices under each selection method. The problem is that, while NPV changes as the opportunity cost of capital changes, the IRR is constant and independent of the cost of capital.

The importance of the discount rate

The conflict is resolved in favour of the NPV method because of the assumptions which underlie the market determined discount rate. Recall that the cost of capital, as an opportunity cost concept, indicates the rate of return that can be earned on resources in their best alternative use. In the example in Table 6.2, the discount rate used to determine each project's NPV is the rate of return at which a company can both borrow and lend funds. Consider, for example, project D which has an initial net investment outlay of £800. If a company has this amount of funds available in cash to invest in the project, the opportunity cost implication is that the company has willingly forgone the opportunity to invest these funds in the market at the market rate of interest of 8%. Extending the argument, if a company has only £400 of its own funds available, it could raise the additional funding from the market at $r = 8\%$. Alternatively, if it has more than £800, the best alternative use for the excess funds is to lend them at 8%.

A straight application of the IRR method implicitly assumes that the opportunity cost of funds is the IRR itself. If, for example, insufficient funds are available to undertake project D, use of the IRR method would incorrectly imply that additional finance would be raised, not at a cost of 8%, but at a cost of 25.08%.

Incremental projects

The IRR method can be adapted to produce a project choice consistent with the NPV method, by considering the incremental cash flows between the two projects. To explain this, assume project choice is based on the direct application of the IRR; consequently, project E would be chosen. The question to be asked is: what has been given up by rejecting project D? This is answered by considering the difference between the NCF profiles of the two projects. These incremental NCFs, which are simply determined by subtracting (on a per period basis) all the NCFs associated with project E from those associated with project D, are shown in the final column of Table 6.2.

Hypothetically these incremental NCFs can be thought of as representing another project, Z. By choosing project E, in preference to project D, it is this hypothetical or incremental project which has been given up or, in general opportunity cost terms, forgone. When the NPV on this incremental project Z is calculated, using $r =$

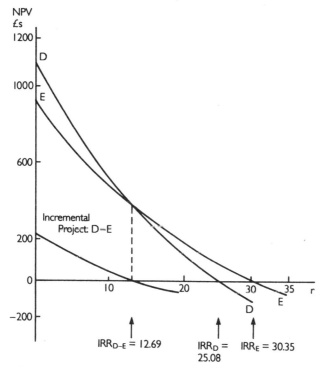

Figure 6.2   NPV schedules for mutually exclusive projects

8%, it is found to be positive and equal to £56.16. Project Z's IRR is 12.69% which is greater than the opportunity cost of capital; yet, by choosing project E, project Z has been implicitly rejected.

The NPV schedule for the incremental project Z is shown in Figure 6.2. Note that $NPV_Z = NPV_D - NPV_E$ and, consequently, that the IRR on project Z occurs where the NPV schedules for D and E intersect.

Now consider what the rejected project D is made up of. It is composed of project E (which would be chosen under the direct application of the IRR method) and the incremental project Z, both of which have positive NPVs and both of which have IRRs in excess of the opportunity cost of capital. It should be obvious that project D is preferable, since it includes both project E and the incremental project Z. The sum of the NPVs of these latter two projects (£541.26 + £56.16 = £597.42) is equal to the NPV of project D. Of course if choice had been based solely on the NPV method, project D would automatically have been accepted and project E rejected. Since the corrected form of the IRR (with incremental cash flows) chooses project D, the preference for using NPV is reinforced.[3]

In general, if for some reason financial managers wish to use the IRR in order to choose from a set of mutually exclusive projects, they must always combine their analysis with an examination of incremental cash flows between projects. This becomes complex when more than two projects are being considered since the incremental cash flows between all possible pairs of projects must be considered.

Table 6.3: Illustrating the multiple roots problem

Year	Project NCFs £m	PVIF @ 6%
0	−4.00	1.0
1	10.00	0.943
2	−6.20	0.890
NPV @ 6%	−£0.09	
IRR	13.80% or 36.20%	

Why embark on tedious computations when the straight application of the NPV method would give the correct choice in the first place?

Non-conventional projects

Up to this point conventional projects have been considered where all future NCFs are positive. Projects can have non-standard NCF patterns where in some future year there is a major cash cost, or outflow, which produces a negative NCF in that year. When this occurs the multiple roots problem is encountered where there is more than one IRR associated with a particular project. In other words, such a project's NPV schedule is not of the standard type indicated in Figures 6.1 or 6.2 because it crosses the horizontal axis more than once. In general the number of roots, or IRR solutions, is equal to the number of times that cash flows change sign.[4]

As an illustration of the multiple roots problem, consider the highly simplified example in Table 6.3. To vary a theme, assume that the market determined opportunity cost of funds is 6%. The net investment outlay for this project is, as normally expected, negative in year zero. There is a positive NCF in year one, but year two's NCF is negative. There are two sign changes, therefore two IRRs. The problem is illustrated in Figure 6.3 where the project's NPV schedule is sketched. The schedule is quadratic in form[5] and crosses the horizontal axis at two points, giving two IRRs: 13.8% and 36.2%.

In this project's case the IRR appraisal rule appears to give a contradictory decision, relative to the NPV appraisal rule. With both IRRs greater than the opportunity cost of capital of 6%, it might appear that the project should be accepted. At the 6% discount rate, however, the NPV of the project is negative, indicating that the correct decision is to reject it since its acceptance would result in a reduction in shareholder wealth. Thus another potential technical problem in directly applying the IRR rule has been identified. One possible way of producing an IRR under the multiple roots problem, which yields a correct decision consistent with the NPV rule, is presented in Appendix 6.2.

Non-discounting appraisal methods

There are two other prominently used methods of investment appraisal: the Pay-Back (PB) and the Accounting Rate of Return (ARR). These methods, which do not take the time value of money into account, are examined next.

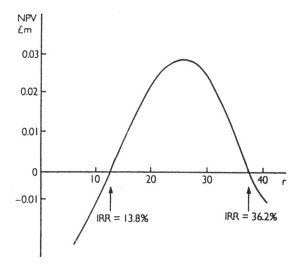

Figure 6.3   Non-standard NPV schedule

Pay-back

The PB method of appraisal is based on the number of periods taken for the future NCFs on a project to pay back the initial net investment outlay. Normally, in formulating PB decision rules a maximum pay-back period, PB^{max}, is specified.

All independent projects under consideration are acceptable providing that, for each project i,

$$PB_i \leq PB^{max} \tag{6.5}$$

Independent projects with PB_is in excess of PB^{max} would be considered to take too long to pay back the initial investment and would be rejected.

For a set of mutually exclusive projects the best option is chosen on the basis of the shortest PB_i, providing $PB_i \leq PB^{max}$.

To illustrate, consider the four projects specified in Table 6.4. If these are independent, and PB^{max} has been set at four years, project F will be rejected, and the other projects accepted. Under the NPV decision rule, however, with a discount rate of 10%, project I would be rejected but project F accepted. If, alternatively, the four projects are assumed to be mutually exclusive, project H, with the smallest PB of three years, would be the preferred option. Under the NPV decision rule, however, project F would be preferred.

The PB method is defective on a number of counts. First, by not considering the time value of money, it gives equal weight to all future NCFs over each project's PB period. Consider the case in respect of projects G and I which have equal PBs of four years. The PB selection method is incapable of recognising that, in early years, the large NCFs on project G, relative to project I, are more valuable than the latter's. Second, once the PB period on a project has been determined, subsequent NCFs which occur beyond this period are ignored in their entirety. This is particularly important in project I's case where the NCFs in the last two years are

Table 6.4: Illustrating pay-back

Year	Project F £s	G £s	H £s	I £s	Discounted NCFs Project G @ 10%
			Net Investment Outlay		
0	−1000	−1500	−2000	−1500	−1500
1	200	1000	500	100	909
2	400	400	400	400	330
3	100	50	1100	500	38
4	200	50	300	700	34
5	100	150	500	−50	93
6	2000	200	100	−100	113
Standard Pay-Back	5 yrs	4 yrs	3 yrs	4 yrs	Discounted Pay-Back Project G } 5.85 yrs
NPV @ 10%	£915.17	£17.42	£183.38	−£477.53	

negative. Third, there is no objective criteria for determining PB^{max}. Fourth, there is ambiguity in respect of defining the initial period of net investment outlays. If, for example, net investment outlays on one project occurred only in year zero, but on another project over the first three years of its life, there is no guidance on the point in time at which counting the number of PB periods should begin.

Some attempt has been made to partially accommodate the time value of money in the PB appraisal method, with the suggestion that Discounted PB should be used. Here the PB on a project is based on its discounted future NCFs; however, this simply reduces the amount of future NCFs which are ignored, subsequent to the discounted PB period. As an example the NCFs for project G are discounted at 10% and presented in the final column of Table 6.3. The discounted PB for project G is 5.85 years compared to its standard PB of four years.

Accounting rate of return[6]

The ARR is based on a definition of the average annual accounting profits from a project divided by a definition of the annual average investment outlays over a project's life. The ARR is then compared to some hurdle rate arbitrarily set by the company. The ARR, as a non-discounting method, is subject to the same types of criticism as the PB, although the ARR does give consideration to all the accounting profits over the life of a project.

There is a serious additional problem with the ARR, arising from the possibility that the use of accounting numbers may give a misleading view of the NCFs generated by a project. This partly arises because depreciation of the initial capital costs over the future life of a project are treated as explicit cash costs. Further, the accounting definition of profit and the accounting treatment of investment outlays will depend on the accounting conventions operated within individual companies and on the accounting standards which happen to be in force at the time when particular project appraisals are being made. These issues are more fully discussed below, when the factors which should be taken into account in formulating a project's NCF profile are specified. Before considering these factors, however, it is useful to reflect on the general superiority of NPV as an investment appraisal method.

The general superiority of NPV

The NPV approach to investment appraisal has been shown, in a technical sense, to be superior to the IRR approach and now, in a general sense, to be superior to the other commonly used approaches of PB and the ARR. The merit of the principle of NPV is that it measures the net wealth-creating potential of capital projects, and investments in general, by considering all of a project's NCFs and discounting these at the project's opportunity cost of capital. Maximising the NPV of project investment maximises shareholders' wealth. Even in the presence of risk and imperfect capital markets, the most appropriate investment choices are made using investment appraisal techniques which are founded on the NPV principle. Some of these are discussed in the next chapter.

Despite the theoretical superiority of NPV, surveys which have investigated the appraisal techniques used in practice indicate that all four methods appeal to corporate executives. Looking across a wide range of these surveys, there is even the suggestion that, on balance, the PB approach is most favoured. The PB is followed, in order of preference, by the ARR, the IRR and finally the NPV. The preference ordering does, however, appear to vary with the size of company, with very large companies undertaking highly sophisticated investment appraisals based on NPV; although even here the other techniques might have a supplementary usage.

One argument in favour of using the IRR is that as a percentage rate of return it is conceptually more familiar than NPV which, as an absolute measure, is somewhat abstract. The rate of return concept combined with managements' familiarity with accounting numbers can explain use of the ARR.

In the case of PB it may be used as a convenient screening device to make an initial selection of projects which would then become subject to detailed formal appraisal using NPV. In addition, since capital projects are medium to long term, full appraisals involve forecasting all future NCFs. Forecasting, even in the short term, can be problematical. (Just consider the difficulties in using macroeconomic models to forecast short-term behaviour in the UK economy.)

Consequently, in those situations where management believe that a very low level of confidence can be placed in forecasting revenues and costs which occur in eight, nine or ten years' time, there may be a rationale for using PB (or better still, discounted PB). If a project can pay back the net investment outlay over the early years of its operation, when NCFs can be measured with a reasonable level of confidence, the project is acceptable. By monitoring the project once it is operational and gaining more information as time passes, on the likely future NCFs beyond the initial PB period, abandonment or continuation decisions can be made at a later date.

Fervent supporters of NPV might well view this as heresy. The argument would be that NPV should always be used, if necessary in combination with simulation and sensitivity analysis. Here, probabilities are assigned to future outcomes and changes in a project's NPV analysed as assumptions about the future are varied. Such an argument is correct, providing decision makers are operating in an environment of risk where, as Knight (1921) argues, probabilities can be measured objectively or subjectively. Using Knight's distinction between risk and uncertainty, this is not possible in the latter situation since, by definition, uncertainty exists where numerical probabilities (either objective or subjective) cannot be assigned to future outcomes.

Cash flows for capital budgeting purposes

Leaving the latter issues and assuming that sufficient information is available to estimate NPVs, attention is turned to the main constituents of a cash flow profile. Before examining these in detail some general principles governing what should, and should not, be included in such a profile are discussed.

Timing
From the perspective of the time value of money, all relevant cash flows must be taken into account at the time they occur. Normally, all the cash flows over a given year are viewed as occurring on an end of year basis.[7]

Incremental cash flows
Since decision makers are concerned with determining a project's net addition to value, only incremental cash flows are considered. Inflows and outflows which would arise independently of a project's acceptance or rejection must not be included. This, for example, rules out apportioning any element of the fixed costs of a company's head office operations to a potential project, if these costs would occur independently of the project's accept/reject decision.

Sunk costs
Before a project's evaluation any costs which have already been incurred must be excluded. If, for example, an idea for a project has been generated by past R and D activity, the expenditure which would have been involved is not relevant to the future development of the project. Similarly, past advertising expenditure which has helped to develop an overall brand name, under which a potential new product or service will be sold, is a sunk cost.

Future R and D expenditures that are necessary to improve a potential product's design, in the light of anticipated competition, must be included; as should relevant future advertising expenditures.

Interlinkages
Any interlinkages that exist between a potential new project and a company's existing projects must be taken into account. If, for example, a soap and detergents manufacturer is considering a new brand of washing powder, the net impact on the company's existing product range must be assessed. In this case the obvious effect is the loss of sales on existing brands, resulting from the introduction of the new washing powder. This loss of sales would represent a cost which must be included in the potential project's cash flow profile.

Double counting

Revenues and costs should only be counted once. This is crucial when considering how a potential project is to be financed, whether by debt, equity or a combination of both. The costs of capital, for example debt interest charges, must not be included in the cash flow profile. These are automatically included in the discount rate which, when applied to the cash flow profile, determines the project's NPV. The discount rate measures the opportunity cost of financing the project.

Opportunity costs

If a company has existing resources which it intends using in a potential project and these resources have an alternative use, then their opportunity cost must be included. Assume, for example, that a company owns an existing building which is to be used if a potential project is accepted. The opportunity cost of this resource must be included either by incorporating the price at which the building could be sold into the project's initial net investment outlay, or by adding an annual rental value to the stream of future operating costs.[8]

Optimism/pessimism

Decision makers should, where possible, make objective assessments of the costs and benefits (revenues) of potential projects. Management may have 'pet projects' or preconceived views on particular issues, which cause them to be over-optimistic (or over-pessimistic) about future outcomes. This may encourage them to 'slant' their assessments of expected future revenues and costs in a subjective manner. Serious biases in NPV assessments can therefore arise and may go undetected, especially in situations where there is a high level of risk and/or limited information in respect of future outcomes.

Cash flow profiles

There are four major elements making up a cash flow profile: the initial net investment outlay; the future net operating cash flows (operating revenues minus operating costs); the net terminal cash flows arising at the end of a project's life (when it has ceased operating); and the relevant tax charges. The latter are partly determined by the extent to which taxes on net operating cash flows can be offset by capital expenditure. This in turn depends on the permitted method of depreciating capital expenditure for tax purposes.

Initial net investment outlay

The initial net investment outlay consists of the initial capital expenditure on plant and equipment (often referred to as expenditure which can be capitalised or depreciated); installation costs; and any initial increase in net working capital, that is, increases in current assets less increases in current liabilities. In the case of working capital, increases in current assets may be necessary: in the form of inventories of raw materials, to support the production process; in the form of accounts receivable, to facilitate sales expansion; and in the form of cash, to support the project in general. In terms of current liabilities there may be initial increases in accounts payable.

Future increases in net investment outlays on plant and equipment or net working capital represent future cash outflows which must be included as part of the future series of cash flows. Future increases in net working capital cannot, however, be offset against tax. Future capital expenditure can, but only to the extent of allowable depreciation.

Net operating cash flows

Once the initial investment has been completed and the project begins operations, the future net operating cash flows can be expected to come on stream.

The operating revenues of a project are primarily determined by sales volume times sales price. In an environment of risk it will be necessary to forecast the level of sales in each year, taking into account the strength of competition that a new or improved product can be expected to face and the speed with which a company's main competitors can produce a close substitute. The level and timing of expected changes in competition will partly determine how a company formulates its future pricing strategy. If a new product can be patented, an estimate of the expected future royalties arising from licensing agreements with other companies should be added to the project's operating revenues.

The sales volume forecast will play a primary role in estimating future operating costs, together with forecasts of the future trends in input prices, or cost inflation. (The role of inflation is discussed in the next chapter.)

Taxation and depreciation

Since a project's accept/reject decision is based on its net addition to value, net after-tax operating cash flows, $NOCF_t$, have to be determined.

Capital expenditure is depreciated for tax purposes, reducing the amount of taxable net operating cash flows. The tax effects depend on the depreciation method that the tax authorities permit a company to use.[9] To illustrate, assume straight-line depreciation where the net initial expenditure on capital equipment is averaged over a project's life,[10] yielding an average annual depreciation charge which can be set against the annual tax liability. Defining CE_0 as the net initial capital expenditure, and n as a project's life length in years, the annual depreciation charge[11] D_t, t = 1, 2, ... n, is:

$$D_t = \frac{CE_0}{n} \qquad\qquad (6.6)$$

An example

To illustrate how a project's cash flow profile should be determined, Table 6.5 presents the projections of operating revenue, R_t, and operating cost, C_t, for a project with a five-year life. The net investment outlay is assumed to consist of capitalisable expenses, $CE_0 = £40,000$, and an initial increase in net working capital of £5000 which is fully recoverable at the end of the project's life. The capital equipment has no salvage value. Under straight-line depreciation, the annual depreciation charge is $D_t = £8000$. Thus taxable profit per year is:

Table 6.5: Calculating net after-tax cash flows[1]

Row/Year	1 £'000	2 £'000	3 £'000	4 £'000	5 £'000
(1) Revenue: R_t	30.00	45.00	50.00	60.00	80.00
(2) Cost: C_t	15.00	25.00	35.00	40.00	70.00
(3) Net Operating Cash Flow: $R_t - C_t$	15.00	20.00	15.00	20.00	10.00
(4) Depreciation: D_t	8.00	8.00	8.00	8.00	8.00
(5) Net Taxable Cash Flow: $R_t - C_t - D_t$	7.00	12.00	7.00	12.00	2.00
(6) Tax: $t_c \times$ Row (5)	2.80	4.80	2.80	4.80	0.80
(7) $NOCF_t$: Row (3) − Row (6)	12.20	15.20	12.20	15.20	9.20
(8) Incremental Net Working Capital	–	–	–	–	5.00
(9) **NCF_t:** Row (7) + Row (8)	12.20	15.20	12.20	15.20	14.20
(10) **$PVNCF_t$** @ 12%	10.89	12.11	8.69	9.67	8.05
(11) Accounting Profit $NOCF_t - D_t$	4.20	7.20	4.20	7.20	1.20

$$NPV = \sum_{t=1}^{5} N\hat{C}F_t(PVIF_{t,12}) - I_0 = £4410; \; IRR = 15.8\%; \; Pay\text{-}Back = 3.36$$

$ARR = (£4800)/(£22,500) = 0.213$ or 21.3%, where average annual accounting profit is £24,000/5 = £4800 and the average investment over the life of the project (including the initial increase in net working capital) is £45,000/2 = £22,500. If accounting profits are defined after depreciation but before taxes, row (6) is added to row (9), and average annual accounting profits rise to £8200, increasing the ARR, given this alternative definition, to 36.44%

---

[1] The initial capital investment is CE_0 = £40,000 with an initial incremental increase in net working capital of £5000. This gives an initial net investment outlay of I_0 = £45,000

Using straight-line depreciation $D_t = \dfrac{CE_0}{n} = \dfrac{£40,000}{5} = £8000$

$$R_t - C_t - D_t \tag{6.7}$$

This is shown in row (5) of Table 6.5. Given a corporate profits tax rate, t_c, of 40%, the tax payable in each year (row (6)) is:

$$t_c(R_t - C_t - D_t) \tag{6.8}$$

The net after-tax operating cash flow is determined by deducting the tax payable in each year from the net operating cash flow, that is:

$$NOCF_t = R_t - C_t - t_c(R_t - C_t - D_t) \tag{6.9}$$

The NOCF profile for this project is given in row (7) of Table 6.5. Finally, the net after-tax cash flows, adjusting for the terminal net working capital, are given in row (9).

As will be explained, at the beginning of the next chapter, the discount rate applied to a project must be calculated on an after-tax and risk adjusted basis. Assuming that the appropriate after-tax risk adjusted discount rate for the project in Table 6.5 is 12%, the project's NPV is £4410 and its IRR is 15.8%. The project's NPV is calculated as:

$$NPV = \sum_{t=1}^{5} NCF_t(PVIF_{t,12}) - I_0$$

It is the sum of the present values of the net cash flows in row (10), that is £49,410, less the net investment outlay of £45,000.

Depreciation tax shield

Equation 6.9 can be rearranged (slightly) to give an alternative, and interesting, definition to the net after-tax operating cash flow:

$$NOCF_t = (R_t - C_t)(1 - t_c) + t_c D_t \qquad (6.9a)$$

The first term on the right-hand side of this equation is the net operating cash flow $(R_t - C_t)$ times one minus the corporate tax rate. It measures the after-tax operating cash flow before allowance for depreciation.

The allowance for depreciation is measured by the second term, $t_c D_t$, and is known as the depreciation tax shield:

$$Depreciation\ Tax\ Shield = t_c D_t \qquad (6.10)$$

It is the amount of allowable depreciation in a given year times the corporate tax rate. It measures the amount of tax which can be offset due to depreciation.[12] In the current example, since the annual depreciation charge is £8000 and the corporate tax rate is 40%, the annual depreciation tax shield is £3200. That is:

$$Depreciation\ Tax\ Shield = (.4)(£8000) = £3200$$

In other words £3200 of tax payments can be avoided annually in this example, if straight-line depreciation is the tax authorities' permitted method.

Accounting profit v. economic profit

It should be evident from Equation 6.9a that, while depreciation is used to determine the $NOCF_t$, it only enters the calculations in the indirect sense that it determines the depreciation tax shield. Depreciation charges are not deducted from the net operating cash flows in their own right, since they are a non-cash cost. The definition of NOCF in Equation 6.9a is an economics based measure of profit.

The accounting definition of profit, on the other hand, deducts depreciation in full from the net operating cash flows.[13] (There are various definitions of accounting profits.) In the above example the accounting profits are defined net of tax and shown in row (11) of Table 6.5.

Therefore, use of accounting profits in an NPV assessment involves double counting since the initial capital expenditure, on which depreciation is based, is already included in the net investment outlay of the NPV. The net investment outlay is automatically, and correctly, deducted at the time the initial cash outflow on capital equipment occurs.

Independently the accounting definition of profit represents one of the reasons why use of the ARR is inappropriate as a method of investment selection. It is a depreciation based measure of profit which does not take account of cash flows when they occur. In the simple example in Table 6.5 the ARR is based on the average annual accounting profit divided by the average net investment outlay. (The average net investment outlay is taken as half of both the initial capital expenditure and the initial increase in net working capital.) The ARR is 21.3% compared to the time value of money based IRR of 15.8%. (There are other problems with the accounting definition of profits; for example, it treats sales as an inflow, even if the cash payment has not been received.)

Net terminal cash flow

Finally, an assessment must be made of the net terminal cash flows, with appropriate tax consequences, which are likely to arise when a project is completed. These flows will be associated with the residual or scrap value of the capital plant and equipment, which is usually based on the expected sale price at the end of a project's life. Net terminal cash flows will also include any costs of decommissioning a plant, such as stripping out its equipment and taking necessary environmental remedies, and the cumulated increases in net working capital over the life of a project. Only a portion of cumulated net working capital can be expected to be recovered and converted into cash, since there are likely to be some accounts receivable which will never be paid and some inventory which may not be capable of being sold. The recoverable net working capital represents a cash inflow but, as explained, there are no resulting tax consequences.

Depreciable asset base and residual value

By basing straight-line depreciation on the initial capital expenditure of a project, there is an implicit assumption that a project's scrap value is zero. This arises because, at the end of a project's life, the book value of its capital equipment is equal to the equipment's initial cost which represents the project's depreciable asset base. In the above example (Table 6.5), with a depreciable asset base of £40,000, the annual depreciation is £8000. Cumulating this depreciation over the five-year life of the project produces a book value of the equipment equal to £40,000. This is the initial capital cost of the project; hence the equipment has no residual value.

From the aspect of the tax benefits of depreciation, the overall contribution which the annual depreciation tax shield makes to a project's NPV is measured by this tax shield's present value over the life of the project. In the above example, the annual depreciation tax shield is:

$$t_c D_t = (0.4)(£8000) = £3200$$

The present value of this shield given the discount rate of 12% is:

$$PV \text{ Depreciation Tax Shield} = £3200 \text{ (PVIFA}_{5,12}) = £3200(3.605) = £11,536$$

If equipment has a residual value at the end of a project's life, this can be included in the depreciable asset base. In the last example assume that the initial capital equipment has an end of life value of £10,000. The depreciable asset base is, therefore, reduced to a book value of £30,000, that is £40,000 − £10,000. In consequence there are reductions in: the annual depreciation charge, the annual depreciation tax shield, and the present value of this tax shield.

From Equation 6.6, the annual depreciation charge becomes:

$$\frac{£30,000}{5} = £6000$$

From Equation 6.10, the annual depreciation tax shield becomes:

$(0.4)(£6000) = £2400$

The present value of this tax shield becomes, therefore:

$£2400(3.605) = £8652$

In the original example, the present value of the depreciation tax shield was £11,536. Thus with the inclusion of a scrap value of £10,000, the fall in the present value of this shield (£11,536 − £8652), leads to a reduction of £2884 in the project's NPV.[14]

Non-monetary values

Normally in corporate project appraisals, money values can be assigned to all relevant benefits and costs: in terms of either the market prices of inputs and outputs or imputed money values. This is not always possible since there are situations, especially in public sector investment appraisals, where benefits cannot be measured in money terms. In public sector education and health care, for example, the benefits of building a new school or hospital are extremely difficult to value. In these situations a set of objectives can be formulated and ranked, or weighted, in some order of priority. In health care one of the objectives might be a reduction in hospital waiting lists. The benefits of a project can then be judged, somewhat subjectively, on the extent to which it meets the relevant set of objectives.

There is an increasing awareness that some of these problems exist in the private sector. Samuels et al. (1990), for example, identify difficulties which began to emerge at the beginning of the 1980s with formal appraisals of advanced manufacturing technologies, particularly related to computer integrated and flexible manufacturing systems. In parts of the corporate sectors of the United States and the United Kingdom, straight appraisal of these new technologies had a propensity to produce negative NPVs, indicating project reject decisions. It appeared, however, that there were significant intangible benefits which could only be qualitatively assessed and which, when included, offset the negative money measure of NPV.

When such circumstances arise, capital investment appraisal may need to be placed in an overall Strategic Management context where, as in the public sector, a company's overall objectives are specified. By dividing a company's operations into strategic areas, or Strategic Business Units, these objectives can be formulated in terms of overall strategies for each unit. A unit's potential investment projects can then be judged on their money NPVs and any identifiable intangibles assessed in a wider strategy framework.

Project review and post-audit

Once a project is accepted and is operational, it is useful to subject it to periodic review. This is especially important if, at the time of its initial appraisal, there was a significant level of risk surrounding its expected future outcomes. During a particular review, if it becomes apparent that a deterioration in revenues, or a substantial increase in costs, is likely over the remaining life of a project, the review may become a formal abandonment/continuation appraisal. In these circumstances the project should not be judged on the basis that substantial investment outlays have already been made. At the time of the review, such outlays are past investments which, to the extent that they are unrecoverable in the form of scrap value, are sunk costs and irrelevant.

Finally, when a project has terminated, a post-audit of its performance relative to what was expected at the beginning of its life may provide useful insights into the strengths and weaknesses of a company's general investment appraisal policy.

Summary

The principles of capital investment appraisal centre on the NPV method. It selects projects on the basis that they are the most likely to meet the objective of shareholder wealth maximisation. The confidence that can be placed in the practical application of this method depends on decision makers' abilities to estimate each potential project's cost of capital (examined in the next chapter), and to identify and measure all the relevant factors which should be included in each project's incremental cash flow profile.

The difficulties involved in doing this should not be underestimated, especially in a complex and competitive corporate environment. Because of high levels of risk and, in a not insubstantial number of cases, uncertainty, a significant amount of scepticism can be expressed about the ability to forecast cash inflows and outflows beyond a three or four-year period. Consequently, methods of appraisal which businessmen have tried and tested and have confidence in, such as pay-back or even the ARR, may be as appropriate as a more sophisticated method.

Even if NPV is not the most widely used method in practice, it is still very relevant to the analysis of corporate financial decision making. Businessmen who do not use the method may make investment decisions which implicitly maximise NPV, although they are not aware that they are doing so. In other words, as an economic model which explains investment behaviour NPV has much to commend it. In previous chapters it was shown to be relevant in explaining the determination of share prices and to be implicit in the analysis of market efficiency. The analysis of short-termism, for example, was best understood in the context of NPV, the implications of this hypothesis being that excessively high discount rates reduce NPVs and cause companies to make sub-optimal long-term investment decisions. NPV as an explanatory model can also be used to guide policy makers in respect of the effect that capital grants, tax breaks and other incentives might have on the level of investment.

The next chapter looks at some other aspects of capital investment appraisal, beginning with estimation of a project's cost of capital. Don't be surprised – it's variations on a theme, it's NPV again!

Questions

1 What are the basic NPV and IRR accept/reject decision rules in respect of independent investments?

2 Consider the following two mutually exclusive one year projects

NCFs

Year	Project A	Project B
0	−£1000	−£800
1	£1250	£1024

The opportunity cost of capital is 10%.
a) Calculate the IRR on each project and indicate which one you would accept using the IRR decision rule.
b) Calculate the NPV on each project and indicate which one you would accept using the NPV decision rule.
c) Explain, using the incremental cash flows between these two projects, how project choice using IRR can be made consistent with project choice using NPV.
d) Roughly sketch the NPV schedules for projects A and B and the incremental project. At what discount rate do the NPV schedules for projects A and B cross over?

3 Consider the NCFs on the following project:
Year 0: −£13.9   Year 1: £40   Year 2: −£27.83
The opportunity cost of capital is 10%. Use this project to illustrate the multiple roots problem.

4 Consider the NCFs from the following three independent projects:

NCFs

Year	Project A £s	Project B £s	Project C £s
0	−1000	−2000	−3000
1	300	500	2000
2	300	1000	1000
3	200	500	500
4	20	−3000	1000
5	7000	−5000	2000

The discount rate is 7% and $PB^{max} = 3$ years.
a) Select projects using the NPV and calculate the total NPV of the projects selected.
b) Select projects using the PB and calculate the total NPV of the projects selected.
c) Explain why project choice is different under these two methods of investment selection.

5 Outline the general principles governing what should and should not be included when determining a project's cash flow profile.

Exercises

1 Explain from a theoretical point of view why NPV, relative to IRR, PB and ARR, is the preferred method of investment selection.

2 Why, in practice, might companies prefer to use the pay-back method of investment appraisal?

3 A company uses straight-line depreciation. It purchases a piece of capital equipment for £100,000 which has a ten-year life. The opportunity cost of capital is 10% and the company's corporate tax rate is 30%.
   a) Assuming that the equipment has no residual value, calculate the annual depreciation tax shield and the present value of this shield.
   b) Repeat these calculations assuming that the equipment has a residual value of £20,000.

Endnotes

1. Since the net investment outlay in period zero is simply a part of a project's net cash flow series, with $I_0 = NCF_0$, the NPV can be defined as:

$$NPV = \sum_{t=0}^{n} \frac{NCF_t}{(1 + r)^t}$$

The period zero NCF is conventionally identified separately, however, because as explained, it is primarily composed of capital costs which normally occur at the beginning of a project. In this way the future NCF series is sometimes referred to as being generated by the initial capital investment.

2. When using the IRR for investment selection, the opportunity cost of capital is often referred to as the hurdle rate. That is, the rate of return which a project must 'get over' or 'jump' to be acceptable.

3. In the example in Table 6.2, the two projects have the same initial net investment outlays and last for equal lengths of time. There is an increased tendency for the direct application of the IRR to give misleading results, relative to NPV, when the scale or size of the initial net investment outlays and the life lengths of mutually exclusive projects differ. IRR as a percentage rate of return has a tendency to be incorrectly biased in favour of the projects in an option appraisal which are of relatively smaller size and/or have the shorter life lengths.

4. This is known as Descartes rule of signs. For a conventional project the initial negative net investment outlay is followed by a future series of net cash flows, all of which are positive. With only one sign change (between year zero and year one) there is, therefore, only one IRR solution.

5. The IRRs for this project are obtained, as normal, by setting the project's NPV equal to zero. Given the data in Table 6.3, IRR is found by solving the following equation:

$$-4 + \frac{10}{1 + IRR} - \frac{6.2}{(1 + IRR)^2} = 0 \qquad (i)$$

To obtain a solution, multiply equation (i) by $(1 + IRR)^2$, giving

$$-4(1 + IRR)^2 + 10(1 + IRR) - 6.2 = 0 \qquad (ii)$$

Equation (ii) is now in the standard quadratic form

$$aX^2 + bX + C$$

where $X = 1 + IRR$. The solution of this quadratic equation is given by the familiar formula:

$$X = \frac{-b \pm \sqrt{b^2 - 4ac}}{2a}, \text{ providing } b^2 < 4ac$$

Substituting the values of Equation (ii) into this formula gives:

$$1 + IRR = \frac{-10 \pm \sqrt{(10)^2 - 4(-4)(-6.2)}}{2(-4)}$$

$$= \frac{-10 \pm \sqrt{0.8}}{-8} = \frac{-10 \pm 0.894}{-8}$$

Therefore,

$$1 + IRR = \frac{-9.106}{-8} = 1.138, \text{ that is, } IRR = 13.8\%$$

or

$$1 + IRR = \frac{-10.894}{-8} = 1.362, \text{ that is, } IRR = 36.2\%$$

6. The accounting rate of return is alternatively referred to as the average return on investment or the average return on capital employed.

7. In cases where large cash flows occur irregularly over a year, some account should be taken of their timing within the year.

8. Another example relates to farming, where the NPV of crop production should include the opportunity cost of the land used. In most cases the most appropriate measure is the rental value of the land.

9. Companies are given a relative amount of freedom under professional accounting standards to adopt particular depreciation methods in preparing annual reports to shareholders. The depreciation method which must be used in assessing tax liability might differ from that used for reporting purposes.

10. Under straight-line depreciation future capital expenditure is capitalised for tax purposes from the date of expenditure to the end of the project's life.

11. There are a number of different depreciation methods. An alternative is to use a reducing balance approach where depreciation in year one is based on a percentage of the net capital expenditure. This percentage is then applied in year two to the undepreciated amount, and so on. For example, if $CE_0 = £2000$ and a 40% depreciation rate is used, $D_1 = (0.4)(2000) = £800$, $D_2 = (0.4)(2000 - 800) = £480$, etc.

12. Currently in the United Kingdom, capital expenditure on industrial buildings is depreciable at 4% per annum on a straight-line basis. Where plant and machinery are concerned, writing-down allowances of 25% per annum are available on a reducing balance basis.

13. From an accounting perspective there are two categories of expenditures: items which are expensed immediately they occur, such as operating costs; and items which are capitalised or depreciated. The latter, like capital expenditure, are not deducted when they occur but in increments over the whole or part of a project's life.

14. Alternatively, if depreciation is based solely on the initial capital expenditure, a tax liability on the sale of the asset in year five would be incurred. With a £10,000 residual value, the tax liability is (.40)(£10,000) = £4000. In this case the original NPV on the project, £4410, would only be reduced by £2268, that is £4000(PVIF$_{5,12}$) = £4000(0.567) = £2268.

Table A6.1.1: Estimating the IRR on project B[1]

Year	Future NCFs £s	PVIF @ 25%	PV NCFs @ 25% £s	PVIF @ 18%	PV NCFs @ 18% £s
1	200	0.800	160.00	0.847	169.40
2	150	0.640	96.00	0.718	107.70
3	200	0.512	102.40	0.609	121.80
4	200	0.410	82.00	0.516	103.20
5	600	0.328	196.80	0.437	262.20
Average NCF = 270			PV$_2$ = 637.20		PV$_1$ = 764.30

[1] Initial net investment outlay, I$_0$ = −£700

Appendix 6.1   Estimating an IRR

As an illustration of how an approximate estimate of an IRR can be obtained, consider project B in Table 6.1. Part of its NPV schedule is reproduced in Figure A6.1.1 below. To estimate the IRR, the idea is to find two discount rates (r_1 and r_2) which will produce two points on the NPV schedule, one on each side of the horizontal axis. Using the equation of a straight line drawn through these two points, the approximate IRR is determined where this line crosses the horizontal axis. The formula for the IRR approximation, defining $r_1 < r_2$ is:

$$IRR \simeq r_1 + \left[\frac{PV_1 - I_0}{PV_1 - PV_2} \right] [r_2 - r_1]$$

The notation in this equation is explained in presenting the steps for calculating an IRR.

Step I
To get the first discount rate the future NCFs on a project are averaged over the project's life. The average future NCF is then set equal, via the formula for the present value of an annuity, to the project's initial net investment outlay. Given t, PVIFA$_{t,r}$ is used to determine r.

For project B, whose future NCFs are given in Table A6.1.1, the average future NCF is £270. Since

£270(PVIFA$_{5,r}$) = £700

PVIFA$_{5,r}$ = 2.59, yielding a discount rate of approximately 25%.

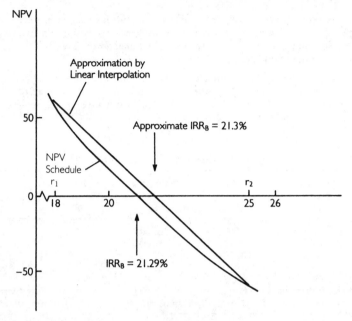

Figure A6.1.1   Section of NPV schedule, project BPI

Step II

This discount rate is applied to the actual future NCF series of the project to determine its present value (see Table A6.1.1). This is compared to the project's net investment outlay to determine whether the project's NPV is positive (in which case a point on its NPV schedule is identified which is above the horizontal axis) or negative (identifying a point below the horizontal axis).

In the case of project B, the 25% discount rate is to the right of the actual IRR (see Figure A6.1.1), hence r_2 has been identified. This is verified since the present value of the NCFs at r_2 is $PV_2 = £637.20$ which, given $I_0 = £700$, produces a negative NPV. In other words, a point on project B's NPV schedule which is below the horizontal axis has been found.

Step III

If a point below (above) the horizontal axis has been identified, the second discount rate must be chosen sufficiently lower than (higher than) the first, to produce a positive (negative) NPV and hence a point above (below) the horizontal axis.

In the case of project B, r_1 must be chosen to be sufficiently less than r_2. There is a certain amount of trial and error in this. In the present example, r_1 is chosen as 18%. Applying r_1 to project B's future NCFs produces a present value of $PV_1 = £764.30$. Given I_0, NPV is positive and the necessary discount rates to obtain the IRR approximation have been found.

Step IV

Using the values for r_1, r_2, PV_1, and I_0, the approximate IRR is computed. In the case of project B:

$$IRR \approx 0.18 + \left[\frac{764.30 - 700}{764.30 - 637.20}\right][0.25 - 0.18]$$

$$= 0.18 + 0.035 = 0.215 \text{ or } 21.5\%$$

The actual IRR, obtained from a financial calculator, is 21.29%.

Step V

If a more accurate estimate of the IRR is required using this approximation approach, steps II to IV can be repeated by narrowing the differential between the two discount rates. In the limit, the straight line becomes just tangential to the project's NPV schedule, at the point at which the schedule crosses the horizontal axis, and the precise IRR is found.

Appendix 6.2   One solution to the multiple roots problem

Given the multiple roots example in Table 6.3, an IRR consistent with the NPV appraisal rule's rejection of this project can be obtained, by redefining the IRR in an opportunity cost context. Here the question is asked: if the initial funds for this project are to be borrowed, for example from a bank, what is the maximum rate of interest, k, that can be paid on this loan? In effect k is the hypothetical maximum possible rate of interest that management could afford to meet out of the funds generated by this project, taking into account the actual opportunities of borrowing and lending at the market rate of interest. The answer to the question is presented in Table A6.2.1.

The initial loan required, as indicated in row (a) of Table A6.2.1, is £4m. The cumulative debt, based on k, at the end of year one is given in row (b). At the end of this year there is a net cash receipt of £10m. This is added to the cumulative debt, giving the outstanding balance in row (e). The outstanding balance could be

Table A6.2.1: IRR and the multiple roots case

Row No.	Description of Loan Financing	£m
(a)	Loan required at time 0	-4
(b)	Maximum interest payable at time 1	$-(k)4$
(c)	Cumulative debt at time 1	$-(1 + k)4$
(d)	Net cash inflow time 1	10
(e)	Outstanding balance at time 1	$-(1 + k)4 + 10$
	Outstanding balance financed at the opportunity cost of capital (6%) over year 2	
(f)	Interest payable/receivable at year 2	$.06[-(1 + k)4 + 10]$
(g)	Cumulative debt at time 2 = e+f	$(1.06)[-(1 + k)4 + 10]$
(h)	Net cash inflow time 2	-6.2
(i)	Outstanding balance at time 2	$(1.06)[-(1 + k)4 + 10] - 6.2$

Row i is set at zero to solve for k
$-(1 + k)4 + 10 = 5.849$
$-(1 + k) = -1.038$ k = 3.8% which is less than the opportunity cost of capital

positive, in which case it would represent a cash surplus. Taking account of financial market opportunities, this could be lent on the market at the company's opportunity cost of capital of 6%. Alternatively, if the outstanding balance is negative, it represents net debt which can be funded at 6%. In row (f) the interest payable (in the case of net debt) or receivable (in the case of a net surplus) is added to row (e) to obtain, in row (g), the cumulative debt at the end of year two. Finally, the NCF in year two (a negative sum of money in this example) is added to obtain the outstanding balance at the end of the project's life.

The value of k is determined by setting the equation in row (i) of Table A6.2.1 equal to zero. $\dot{k} = 3.8\%$, which is less than the opportunity cost of capital of 6%. The project would be rejected, as originally indicated by its NPV of $-£0.9m$.

k is the IRR adjusted by taking account of the market determined opportunity cost of capital; but this opportunity cost is automatically, and fully, reflected in the direct application of NPV.

References

Channon, D.P., *Bank Strategic Management and Marketing*, John Wiley and Sons, 1986

Coulthurst, N.J., 'The Application of the Incremental Principle of Capital Investment Project Evaluation', Accounting and Business Research, 1986

De Canio, S.J., 'Agency and Control Problems in US Corporations: The Case of Energy Efficient Investment Projects', Journal of the Economics of Business, 1994

Dudley, C.L., 'A Note on Reinvestment Assumption in Choosing between Net Present Value and Internal Rate of Return', Journal of Finance, 1972

Gitman, L.J. and V.A. Mercurio, 'Cost of Capital Techniques used by Major US Firms: Survey and Analysis of Fortune's 1000', Financial Management, 1982

Hamada, R.S., 'The Effect of the Firm's Capital Structure on the Systematic Risk of Common Stocks', Journal of Finance, 1972

Knight, F., *Risk, Uncertainty and Profit* (first published: Hart, Schnaffner and Marx, 1921), New York, Harper and Row, 1965

Levy, H. and M. Sarnat, *Capital Investment and Financial Decisions*, New York, Prentice Hall, 1990

Pike, R.H. 'A Review of Recent Trends in Formal Capital Budgeting Procedures', Accounting and Business Research, 1983

Samuels, J.M., F.M. Wilkes and R.E. Brayshaw, *Management of Company Finance*, London, Chapman and Hall, 1990

Sangster, A., 'Capital Investment Appraisal Techniques: A Survey of Current Usage', Journal of Business Finance and Accounting, 1993

Wilkes, F.M., 'On Multiple Rates of Return', Journal of Business Finance and Accounting, 1980

7 NPV: variations on a theme

Introduction

Chapter 6 presented some of the basic principles of capital investment appraisal: demonstrating how cash flows for capital budgeting purposes should be specified and explaining why appraisal rules should be based on project NPVs. In the present chapter some further aspects of investment appraisal are introduced, beginning with the estimation of a project's cost of capital. The other topics discussed are: NPV and inflation, capital rationing and the duration problem.

Before development of the CAPM, project discount rates were estimated on the basis of what is known as the Weighted Average Cost of Capital. Here the components of the capital structure are identified, for example debt and equity, and their individual costs estimated. An overall, or average, cost of capital is then calculated by weighting each component cost by the proportions of each source of capital being used. While outlining this method, the present chapter emphasises the modern CAPM based approach which produces a weighted average cost of capital but on a risk adjusted basis.

Next, NPV is shown to be both a real and a nominal measure of net investment worth. In other words, discounting nominal cash flows by a nominal cost of capital is equivalent to discounting real cash flows by a real cost of capital.

To aid identification of the most appropriate method of investment selection, it was assumed in Chapter 6 that capital markets were perfect. This implied that any amount of finance could be raised at a given opportunity cost of capital and, consequently, that all independent projects with NPVs ≥ 0 could be undertaken. If, however, capital is rationed in some way, with limits placed on the amount of investment expenditure that can be undertaken in a given period, the basic NPV selection rules have to be modified.

To demonstrate how NPV could be used in option appraisals, it was also assumed in Chapter 6 that mutually exclusive projects had equal durations or lives. When such projects have unequal lives the duration problem is encountered. Again this can be handled by modifying the standard NPV decision criteria.

The weighted average cost of capital

In its original form prior to the development of the CAPM, the weighted average cost of capital that was widely used, and still is to some extent, took explicit account of the costs of equity and the after-tax cost of debt. As explained in Chapter 4 the cost of equity, r_e, was calculated, and still can be, on the basis of either the bond yield plus risk premium or the dividend yield plus growth rate.

In the case of debt financing, having determined the type of bond it wishes to issue, a company can base its cost of debt on the yield to maturity, r_d, on an existing traded bond with similar maturity and risk. This was discussed in Chapter 3.

In the presence of corporate taxes, while the yield to maturity represents a bondholder's minimum required rate of return for holding a new bond, this yield is not the effective cost of debt capital from a company's perspective. Companies are allowed to set interest charges on debt against their tax liabilities; therefore, it is the after-tax cost of debt capital which is relevant. This is measured, assuming a corporate tax rate t_c, as: $r_d(1 - t_c)$.

Calculating the weighted average

Given the costs of debt and equity, the weighted average cost of capital, r_a, was usually calculated on the basis of a company's target capital structure. The target was based on a view that a company would have a particular mix of debt and equity, which under certain assumptions (discussed in the next chapter) would maximise its market value. While this mix might not be attainable in the short run, it represented the target debt:equity ratio which management would aim for. Defining B as the target market value of debt and S as the target market value of equity, the weighted average cost of capital is:

$$r_a = r_d(1 - t_c)\left[\frac{B}{S + B}\right] + r_e\left[\frac{S}{S + B}\right] \qquad (7.1)$$

To take a simple example, assume that a company with a corporate tax rate of 35% has a 1:1 target debt:equity ratio. It has estimated its component costs of capital as: $r_e = 9\%$ and $r_d = 4\%$. On an after-tax basis the company has only to earn 2.6% on debt financing, $0.04(1 - 0.35) = 0.026$. The average cost of capital is:

$$r_a = 4(1 - .35)[.5] + 9[.5] = 5.8\%$$

Using this specific form of the weighted average cost of capital, it is assumed that additional finance will be raised in line with the target capital structure and that new projects will not alter a company's existing risk levels. As will be shown below, the development of the CAPM enabled the restrictive risk assumption to be relaxed. Before explaining this approach, some further comments on the component costs of capital are appropriate.

Other sources of capital

There are two forms of equity in a company's capital structure: share issues and retained earnings. As explained in Chapter 3, retained earnings are owned by shareholders and simply represent funds not paid out as dividends. The cost of retained earnings is, therefore, equal to the equity capitalisation rate. This cost is not adjusted for corporate taxes, unlike debt capital, since dividends are paid out on an after-tax basis.

Retained earnings normally represent a cheaper source of funds than new equity issues, since the latter are often sold at a discount below a company's current share price to encourage the market to take them up. This effectively raises the rate of

Table 7.1: Weighted average cost of capital

Component	Target Capital Structure (%)	Component Cost (%)	After-Tax[1] Component Cost (%)	Weighted After-Tax Cost
Long-Term Debt	30	4.00	2.40	0.72
Preferred Shares	10	8.00	8.00	0.80
Equity	60	12.00	12.00	7.20

Weighted Average Cost = 8.72%

[1] Corporate Tax Rate = 40% After-tax cost of debt = 4(1−0.4) = 2.4%

return that has to be offered on the new issue. In addition new issues are subject to flotation costs associated with advertising, the printing of prospectuses and under-writing fees. These can represent around 3% of the funds raised externally and, once again, effectively raise the cost of new equity issues above the cost of retained earnings.

Another source of funds is preferred share financing which, as explained in Chapter 3, is a form of hybrid debt. Since it is equity based, however, there are no tax effects to be taken into account. Preferred shares are a perpetuity with a fixed annual dividend. Given the total annual dividend payment, D, and the amount of funds to be raised, I_p, the component cost of this source of capital, r_p, is: D/I_p. If, for example, £4m is to be raised in terms of preferred share financing, with a total annual dividend payment of £0.24m, $r_p = 0.24/4 = 0.06$ or 6%.

As another example, calculation of the weighted average cost of capital is shown in Table 7.1 for a company using three sources of finance: long-term debt, preferred shares and equity.

Why a weighted average?

The weighted average is a composite cost of capital taking account of all the components in the capital structure, even if, at a given point in time, particular components are not being used to finance a new project. As will be seen in the next chapter, a composite cost of capital is used because of its role in determining a company's overall market value. It is an individual project's contribution to this value which is being assessed in project appraisal.

In the meantime a simple (slightly inexact) example will illustrate the point. Assume that a company's costs of debt and equity capital are, respectively, 8% and 12%. It has a target capital structure or debt:equity ratio of 1:1. The company has a potential project with an IRR of 9% which it has decided to finance with debt capital only. Assuming that there are no problems with interpreting the IRR, it might appear that the project should be accepted since its IRR exceeds the opportunity cost of debt.

Assume the project is accepted but that, for some reason, this will result in no further debt capital being raised. Assume that a new project arises with an IRR of 11%. With only equity capital being available at a cost of 12%, this more attractive project has to be rejected. If the weighted average cost of capital had been used, based on the target capital structure, the hurdle rate, from Equation 7.2, would have been:

$$8[.5] + 12[.5] = 10\%$$

The first project would have been rejected and the second, which makes a greater contribution to the market value of the company, would have been accepted.

Project costs of capital

The analysis of risk and return in Chapter 4 implies that the discount rate to be applied in calculating a project's NPV must take account of a project's risk. In the context of risk diversification, it is a project's systematic risk that is relevant. Consequently, a company can base its estimate of a project's cost of capital on the CAPM. In the simplest case a project's required rate of return can be estimated using Equation 4.7, where,

$$r_{project} = r_{assets} = r_f + [E(r_m) - r_f]\,\beta_{assets} \tag{7.2}$$

Recall that the asset β (from Equation 4.8) is a weighted average of the βs associated with the market values of debt and equity:

$$\beta_{assets} = \beta_{debt}\left[\frac{B}{S + B}\right] + \beta_{equity}\left[\frac{S}{S + B}\right] \tag{7.3}$$

To illustrate the use of Equations 7.2 and 7.3, consider a company whose existing capital structure consists of 40% debt and 60% equity, and whose $\beta_{debt} = 0.24$ and $\beta_{equity} = 1.46$. The company's asset β is:

$$\beta_{assets} = 0.24[0.4] + 1.46[0.6] = 0.972$$

Further, with an estimate of the risk-free rate of interest of $r_f = 3.2\%$, based on short-term government debt, and an estimate of the return on the market of $E(r_m) = 12\%$, based on a stock exchange index, the cost of capital for any potential project the company considers is:

$$r_{project} = 3.2 + [12 - 3.2](0.972) = 11.75\%$$

Tax and risk effects

Equations 7.2 and 7.3 represent the underlying principles on which a risk adjusted cost of capital can be measured; however, they are based on three highly restrictive assumptions that:
- there are no tax effects to be taken into consideration;
- a potential new project will not alter the systematic risk associated with a company's existing assets; and
- the project is to be financed using additional debt and equity capital raised in proportion to the amounts of debt and equity currently in use.[1]

In general, these three assumptions will not hold.

First there are tax effects to be taken into account since companies are allowed to set interest charges on debt against their tax liabilities. Under certain cases, discussed in the next chapter, the benefit of tax deduction can be viewed (in a fashion similar to a depreciation tax shield) as a debt interest tax shield. The debt interest tax shield is measured by the corporate tax rate, t_c, times the market value of debt, that is as:

$$\text{Debt Interest Tax Shield} = t_c B \qquad (7.4)$$

If, for example, the market value of debt used to finance a project, in a given year, is £4m and a company's corporate tax rate is 40%, the debt interest tax shield is $(.4)(£4m) = £1.6m$. Thus the effective amount of debt being used by the company is only £2.4m or $B(1 - t_c)$, that is £4m$(1 - .4)$.

Second, the risk of a project may differ from a company's existing risk, especially if a project is associated with areas of activity which are new to the company.

Third, the proportions in which additional debt and equity are raised may differ from a company's existing capital structure.

The capital structure, tax and risk issues bring to the fore, once again, the view that it is a project's incremental effect on value which is important. Thus it is the incremental, or marginal, cost of capital which is of interest. That is, the minimum required rates of return that have to be offered on raising additional equity and/or debt, and the (marginal) tax rate that acceptance of a project causes a company to be exposed to.

Taking account of tax and risk effects

To take account of the risk relating to a particular project, β_{project}, and the effect of the debt interest tax shield, Equation 7.3 must be modified. Given the corporate tax rate, the project cost of capital becomes:

$$r_{\text{project}} = r_f + [E(r_m) - r_f]\, \beta_{\text{project}} \left[\frac{S + B(1 - t_c)}{S + B}\right] \qquad (7.5)$$

Consider the last example, where $r_f = 3.2\%$ and $E(r_m) = 12\%$. Assume, however, that the company's initial capital expenditure on the project is £10m and that the company's capital structure remains constant. It finances the project by raising £4m of debt and £6m of equity (issue costs are assumed zero). The company is subject to a marginal tax rate of 40% and has calculated its project risk as $\beta_{\text{project}} = 1.64$. The tax adjustment effect in Equation 7.5 is measured as:[2]

$$\left[\frac{S + B(1 - t_c)}{S + B}\right] = \left[\frac{6 + 4(1 - .4)}{10}\right] = 0.84$$

Thus the project cost of capital,[3] from Equation 7.5, is:

$$r_{\text{project}} = 3.2 + [12 - 3.2][1.64][.84] = 15.32\%$$

Project βs

How did this company arrive at its project β estimate of 1.64?

If a company is contemplating undertaking a project whose characteristics differ from its existing operations, the use of the company's own β in its cost of capital calculations will be inappropriate. In this situation a company may be able to identify the industry sector in which the project would be located. If it can identify an individual company in this sector whose operations are closely similar to its own potential project, then it can use this company's equity β in calculating project risk. Alternatively, if an individual company cannot be identified, an industry β, based on an average of the βs of the companies within the specific industrial sector, may be used.

Assume that the company in the above example, Sellright plc, operates in the retail food sector. It is considering investing in a private health club project and has identified a company in the leisure industry, Jimnasium plc, which is exclusively involved in this area. Jimnasium's $\beta_{debt} = 0.20$ and its $\beta_{equity} = 2.24$. Jimnasium is subject to a marginal tax rate of 30% and has a capital structure consisting of a 3:5 debt:equity ratio.

Sellright plc estimates the risk of its project, based on Jimnasium's asset risk, using a modified version of Equation 7.3. The modification is necessary to take account of the debt interest tax shield. The adjusted equation is:

$$\beta_{project} = \beta_{assets} = \beta_{debt}\left[\frac{B(1 - t_c)}{S + B(1 - t_c)}\right] + \beta_{equity}\left[\frac{S}{S + B(1 - t_c)}\right] \qquad (7.6)$$

Substituting the appropriate values for Jimnasium plc produces a project β for Sellright's potential health club investment of:

$$\beta_{project} = (0.2)\left[\frac{3(1 - .30)}{5 + 3(1 - .30)}\right] + (2.24)\left[\frac{5}{5 + 3(1 - .30)}\right] = 1.64$$

It was this β estimate which was substituted into Equation 7.5 (as was demonstrated above) along with both the debt:equity proportions in which Sellright intended financing the project and Sellright's marginal tax rate. This produced the project cost of capital of 15.32%.

Unlevering and relevering βs
In estimating a project cost of capital, a number of factors are being taken into account. Prominent among these is the effect that capital structure, or financial leverage, has on risk. Embedded in the approach just described is a process of unlevering and then relevering β coefficients. This is necessary because equity βs include both the systematic risk of a company and the financial risk to which shareholders are exposed when companies engage in debt financing.

In the above example Sellright had to remove the effect of Jimnasium's financial risk (unlever Jimnasium's β) before Sellright could include the effect of its own leverage level, and hence its own financial risk (relever Jimnasium's β). The underlying rationale for leverage adjustments can only be understood in the wider context of the capital structure, valuation debate. This will be explored in the next chapter, Chapter 8.

Marginal weights

Finally, while the project cost of capital approach is markedly different from the traditional Weighted Average Cost of Capital it is, nevertheless, based on a weighted average principle.

Table 7.2: Real and nominal net cash flows

Year	Nominal NCFs £s	PV Nominal[1] NCF @ 10% £s	Real NCFs £s	PV Real[1] NCF @ 10% £s
0	−1000.00	−1000.00	−1000.00	−1000.00
1	400.00	363.60	$(400)/(1.0578) = 378.14$	363.77
2	600.00	495.60	$(600)/(1.0578)^2 = 536.24$	496.02
3	300.00	225.30	$(300)/(1.0578)^3 = 253.46$	225.33
4	700.00	478.10	$(700)/(1.0578)^4 = 559.10$	478.04

NPV 562.60   NPV 563.16

[1] Subject to rounding errors   NPV(Nom) ≈ NPV(Real) ≈ £563.00

As explained, the average cost of capital is a marginal concept; therefore, use of fixed weights based on a company's target capital structure implies that an accurate measure of the cost of capital will only be obtained if finance for a project is raised in line with the targets. It is unlikely that a company will fund each new project in this way so that a certain amount of inaccuracy will exist in practice. Providing, however, that companies can adjust actual to target levels relatively quickly, this will not be a factor to be overly concerned about. If adjustment is slow, then marginal weights based on changes in capital structure, brought about by new financing, should be used.

Capital budgeting and inflation

As explained in the previous chapter, estimating the cash flow profile of a project involves forecasting trends in output and input prices. In the latter case this may involve estimates of expected cost inflation across a range of inputs, especially if a project has a relatively complex production function. Whatever the complexities, the end result is a future series of NCFs expressed in nominal cash terms.

The discount rate which is applied to this nominal series is based on a rate of return concept, calculated using the market prices of debt and equity. Since market prices include an allowance for inflation, the discount rate is a nominal cost of capital measure. Consequently project NPVs, which have been analysed in the previous chapter, are nominal NPVs.

Consider the example in Table 7.2. Given the nominal NCFs for this four-year project and a nominal cost of capital of 10%, the project's nominal NPV is £563.

Real NCFs
A company may decide that it wishes to convert the nominal NCFs on a project into real NCFs. While allowance may have been made for project-specific inflation, through estimates of cost inflation relating to individual parts of the project, conversion of the resulting nominal NCFs to real NCFs should be based on a macroeconomic measure of inflation. If, for example, a company's operations are largely located within the United Kingdom, an appropriate measure of inflation would be the Retail Price Index (RPI).

A macroeconomic measure of inflation is used to calculate real NCFs since it is the general purchasing power of the NCFs that is being assessed. As was explained at the end of Chapter 2, real measures take into account the fact that the purchase of a bundle of goods today involves added, inflation induced, expenditure tomorrow.

Given the rate of inflation, as measured by the anticipated change in the RPI, the real NCF in period t is found by discounting the nominal NCF by this rate, that is

$$NCF_t(\text{Real}) = \frac{NCF_t(\text{Nom.})}{(1 + r_{RPI})^t} \qquad\qquad (7.7)$$

The real NCFs for the present example are shown in Table 7.2.

The real cost of capital
To obtain the NPV using real NCFs, the real cost of capital must be used as the discount rate. Given the relationship between real and nominal interest rates specified in Chapter 2 (Equation 2.11a), the real cost of capital, r^*, is determined as:

$$1 + r^* = \frac{(1 + r_{nom})}{(1 + r_{RPI})}$$

Given $r_{nom} = 10\%$, and assuming that $r_{RPI} = 5.78\%$,

$$r^* = \frac{(1.10)}{(1.0578)} - 1.0 = 1.0398 - 1.0 \simeq 0.04 \text{ or } 4\%$$

Applying $r^* = 4\%$ to the real NCFs (see the final column of Table 7.2) produces a real NPV of £563 which is equal to the nominal NPV.

NPV as a real and a nominal measure[4]
In general, providing inflation is treated consistently in NPV calculations, with

• nominal NCFs discounted by the nominal cost of capital, and
• real NCFs discounted by the real cost of capital,

the NPV under each approach will be both a real and a nominal measure.

In practice, companies in the private sector focus on nominal measures of NPV since most of the estimates of the cost of capital are market based and therefore nominal. In addition, if a real measure of NCF is used, the nominal values in the series have to be computed anyway, before they are discounted by a general measure of inflation.

Internal capital rationing

There are two main categories of capital rationing, one involving some form of capital constraint imposed externally on a company by the capital markets. The other, which is discussed first, involves internal capital rationing, when a company's management imposes its own limits on capital investment even though the company is capable of raising any amount of funds externally.

Internal capital rationing can arise for a number of reasons; for example, the head office of a multidivisional company may act as a mini capital market in relation to its semi-autonomous divisions. A capital expenditure constraint is imposed as some form of control mechanism, with head office easing or tightening the constraints on each division according to divisional profit performance. Alternatively, a company may feel that, at a given point in time, its existing management team does not have the capacity to deal with all the available investment opportunities. Consequently, it may introduce a self-imposed short-term limit on capital expenditure until the management problems are addressed.

Where an internal limit has been imposed on capital budgets, the most commonly advocated methods of project selection are the benefit–cost ratio (BCR) and the profitability, or present value, index (PVI). Both give the same result and are adaptations of the NPV principle. They seek to identify the combination of projects which will yield the maximum feasible NPV, given the limited capital budget.

Either method can only be used under relatively strict assumptions. These are that:
- the projects under consideration are independent;
- they are infinitely divisible;
- the capital budget constraint, as already stated, is imposed internally; and
- the budget constraint is a single period constraint lasting for the current period only; in all future periods of time a company can obtain whatever level of funding it desires, at the predetermined cost of capital.

The benefit–cost ratio

The BCR is defined as the NPV of a project divided by its initial net investment outlay:

$$BCR = \frac{NPV}{I_0} \qquad (7.8)$$

It measures the NPV of a project per unit of scarce resources, that is, per unit of the resources which are being limited or rationed in the initial investment period.

When examining a set of independent projects, any project i can be considered for selection if:

$$BCR_i \geq 0 \qquad (7.8a)$$

If a project's BCR < 0, the automatic implication is that its NPV < 0. Given this condition, project choice is determined by ranking projects from the highest to the lowest BCR.

Consider the eight independent projects specified in Table 7.3. The present values of their future NCFs have already been calculated and are recorded in column (2). Column (3) records the initial cost of each project and column (4) each project's NPV. If there is no budget constraint, projects would be chosen using the standard NPV criteria. Under the standard NPV approach projects D and F would be rejected since they have negative NPVs; however, the other six projects would be accepted, giving a total NPV of £87m at a total initial net investment outlay of £75m.

Assume that for the current financial year only, capital investment expenditure is limited to £38m; then all of the projects in Table 7.3 with positive NPVs cannot be undertaken. A possible but incorrect solution, given this constraint, is to rank

Table 7.3: Illustrating the benefit–cost ratio and the present value index

(1) Projects	(2) Present Value of Future NCFs £m	(3) Initial Capital Cost £m	(4) NPV Col(2)–Col(3) £m	(5) Ranking by NPV	(6) BCR Col(4)/Col(3)	(7) Ranking by BCR	(8) PVI Col(2)/Col(3)	(9) Ranking by PVI
A	18	5	13	5	2.60	2	3.60	2
B	30	20	10	6	0.50	6	1.50	6
C	34	20	14	4	0.70	5	1.70	5
D	2	8	−6	8	−0.75	8	0.25	8
E	27	10	17	2	1.70	3	2.70	3
F	10	15	−5	7	−0.33	7	0.67	7
G	33	15	18	1	1.20	4	2.20	4
H	20	5	15	3	3.00	1	4.00	1

projects by their NPVs. The NPV ranking, one for the highest, is recorded in column (5) of Table 7.3. On the assumption that projects are infinitely divisible, the following choice, in order of preference, would be made: G, E, H and two-fifths of C. This would just satisfy the budget constraint,

$$£15m + £10m + £5m + \frac{2}{5} \times £20m = £38m,$$

and would produce a total NPV of £55.6m:

$$£18m + £17m + £15m + \frac{2}{5} \times £14m = £55.6m$$

The aim of investment selection is to maximise NPV, given the constraints in force. Ranking by BCR meets this aim; ranking by NPV (or for that matter IRR) does not.

BCR ranking

The BCR project rankings, one for the highest, are shown in column (7) of Table 7.3. They yield a project choice, in order of preference, of: H, A, E, G and three-twentieths of project C. (Note that project A is now included, it wasn't under the NPV ranking, and that a smaller proportion of project C is now undertaken.) Under the BCR the budget constraint of £38m is exactly exhausted:

$$£5m + £5m + £10m + £15m + \frac{3}{20} \times £20m = £38m$$

Using the BCR ranking, the total NPV achieved is composed of: £15m from project H + £13m from project A + £17m from project E + £18m from project G + £2.1m from project C. This gives a total NPV of £65.1m compared to only £55.6m under the NPV ranking.

The present value index

As an alternative, the PVI could have been used. It is defined as the present value of the future NCFs (PVFNCF) divided by the initial net investment outlay:

$$PVI = \frac{PVFNCF}{I_0} \qquad (7.9)$$

The basic decision rule in relation to the PVI is that any project i can be considered for selection, providing:

$$PVI_i \geq 1 \qquad (7.10)$$

If a project's PVI < 1, the automatic implication is the PVFNCF $< I_0$ and the project has a negative NPV.

The PVI is linked directly to the BCR,[5] since

$$BCR = PVI - 1 \qquad (7.11)$$

Thus the PVI gives exactly the same ranking as the BCR and leads to exactly the same result. This is demonstrated in the final two columns of Table 7.3, where the

Table 7.4: Feasible sets of projects[1]

Set 1		Set 2	
Includes Mutually Exclusive Project E	NPV £m	Includes Mutually Exclusive Project G	NPV £m
H	15.00	H	15.00
A	13.00	A	13.00
E	17.00	G	18.00
90% of C	12.60	65% of C	9.10
Total NPV	57.60		55.10

[1] Based on Table 7.2, assuming projects E and G are mutually exclusive

Table 7.5: Choosing amongst independent but non-divisible projects

Projects	Present Value Future NCFs £m	Initial Capital Cost £m	NPV £m	Ranking by NPV £m	BCR	Ranking by BCR
I	12.00	4.00	8.00	4	2.00	3
J	24.00	12.00	12.00	2	1.00	4
K	21.50	11.50	10.00	3	0.88	5
L	7.00	2.00	5.00	6	2.50	2
M	34.00	20.00	14.00	1	0.70	6
N	8.00	2.00	6.00	5	3.00	1

PVI of each project and the PVI ranking, one for the highest, are recorded respectively.

Mutually exclusive projects

The BCR, and by implication the PVI, can only be directly applied when making choices among independent projects. If mutually exclusive projects are present then the alternative feasible sets of projects, each including one of the mutually exclusive projects, must be examined. Assume, in Table 7.3, that projects E and G are mutually exclusive. With the budget constraint of £38m, the two alternative feasible sets of projects are shown in Table 7.4. The set with the highest NPV would be chosen.

Project divisibility

When choosing among independent projects, the BCR can only be used if projects are perfectly divisible. If this assumption does not hold, each project can only be accepted or rejected in its totality. Consequently, project choice must be made by considering all the alternative sets of possible projects which are feasible within the budget constraint and selecting the set with the highest total NPV. To illustrate this, six projects are presented in Table 7.5, on the assumption that they are independent but not divisible. If there is no budget constraint, all of the projects can be undertaken at a cost of £51.5m, yielding a total NPV of £55m.

Table 7.6: Project choice and divisibility and non-divisibility[1]

Level of Budget Constraint £m	Method of Project Selection	Project Choice	Total Capital Cost of Projects £m	Total NPV
		Perfect Divisibility		
No Constraint	NPV	All projects I to N	51.50	55.00
£18m	Ranking by NPV	90% of M	18.00	12.60
£18m	Ranking by BCR	N, L, I @ 80% of J	18.00	29.00
		Non-divisibility		
£18m	Ranking by BCR	N, L, I	8.00	19.00
£18m	Ranking by NPV	Must reject project M		
£18m	Choosing amongst alternative sets to max. NPV	J, I, N	18.00	26.00

[1] Based on projects in Table 7.5

Assume that a budget constraint of £18m is in operation. If projects are ranked by the BCR, only N, L and I can be undertaken at a cost of £8m, yielding a total NPV of £19m but leaving a budget surplus of £10m.

The correct choice is determined by considering all the alternative sets of possible projects which are feasible within the budget constraint. One of these would be to invest only in project J, at a cost of £12m, with an NPV of £12m. Another possibility would be to invest £18m, in projects J, I and L, yielding a total NPV of £25m. The optimal choice, just exhausting the budget constraint, is J, I and N, yielding a total NPV of £26m. No other feasible combination would yield a higher total NPV.

The choices under divisibility and non-divisibility are summarised in Table 7.6. In the first half of this table perfect divisibility is assumed. As indicated, with no capital constraint, project choice would be such that a total NPV of £55m would be achieved. With a capital constraint of £18m, the optimal feasible choice, using the BCR, produces a total NPV of £29m. (Note that if a straight NPV ranking is used, a sub-optimal choice is achieved, with a total NPV of only £12.6m.)

In the second half of the table it is assumed that no project can be subdivided. With a capital constraint of £18m, the optimal project choice yields a total NPV of £26m, against £19m achieved under the BCR. Note, of course, that in moving from perfect divisibility to its complete absence, the optimal feasible total NPV falls from £29m to £26m. Note also that in the absence of divisibility, the best individual project, in terms of the highest NPV (project M), has to be rejected. This arises because its individual cost exceeds the capital constraint, thus illustrating that ranking by NPV is again unacceptable.

The single-period expenditure constraint

The BCR is used to select independent, divisible projects on the assumption that the limit on expenditure is imposed for the current year only and that, in all subsequent years, any amount of funds can be raised at the predetermined cost of capital. If budget constraints extend beyond year zero, the BCR cannot be adapted and defined, for example, as the NPV of a project divided by the present value of the project's costs over the periods of capital rationing. The ranking which would result in this situation would be meaningless.

Consider a simple example where there is an expenditure constraint of £4.5m now and £7.5m in year one. A project is under consideration which has a capital cost of £4m now and £8m in year one. Assuming a cost of capital of 6%, the present value of the investment outlays (£4m + £8m(.943) = £11.54m) are less than the present value of the capital constraint (£4.5m + £7.5(.943) = £11.57m). All looks well. Assume that by using the BCR on this project, defined as its NPV divided by £11.54m (the present value of the net investment outlay), the project achieved, among other projects under consideration, first in the rank. Could the project be undertaken? The answer is no. There is no difficulty in the current year, since year zero costs (£4m) are less than the year zero budget constraint (£4.5m). When year one is considered, however, the budget limit of £7.5m will be violated by the year one cost of £8m. This is not directly obvious from the BCR as defined.

Under single-period capital rationing, if a project with a positive NPV is rejected now, there is an automatic implication that it can be accepted in the future. Once the single-period assumption is broken and budget constraints extend into future time periods, this implication no longer holds. In these circumstances the impact of future constraints must be considered now.

The standard way of handling multi-period capital constraints is through the use of linear-programming techniques, in the case of independent, divisible projects; or integer programming, in the case of non-divisible, independent projects. These techniques are beyond the scope of an introductory text.

External capital rationing

Under internal capital rationing any amount of funds can be raised externally at the appropriate cost of capital. Management may have a self-imposed limit on capital expenditure, but in market terms this limit is arbitrary, artificial and redundant. Consequently, it is the market determined opportunity cost of capital which is used internally as the discount rate determining project NPVs when internal capital rationing is employed.

In a situation of external capital rationing, where the capital markets impose some type of limit on the funds available at a given cost of capital, or impose an absolute limit on the overall funds available, the appropriate project discount rate may not be readily observable. In certain circumstances it may have to be imputed, sometimes in a complex way.

In opportunity cost terms, when capital is rationed externally, the cost of capital is the marginal rate of return on the last £ of project investment undertaken. The problem is that this rate might not be revealed until the optimal investment programme is actually determined.

There is controversy over the extent of external capital rationing. One argument, for example, is that it would arise if a company had issued bonds with restrictive covenants under which no further debt capital could be raised while the existing debt issue was outstanding. In one sense it can be argued that this is a form of

Table 7.7: Mutually exclusive projects with unequal lives

	Project NCFs (£s)			Present Value of NCFs (£s)	
Year	A	B	PVIFs @ 6%	A	B
0	−1200.00	−1700.00	1.000	−1200.00	−1700.00
1	600.00	400.00	0.943	565.80	377.20
2	800.00	400.00	0.890	712.00	356.00
3	1000.00	500.00	0.840	840.00	420.00
4		500.00	0.792		396.00
5		900.00	0.747		672.30
6		900.00	0.705		634.50

internal capital rationing, since a company itself will have chosen to issue this type of debt to reduce its cost of debt financing. Another, more compelling argument, is that agency problems and informational assymmetries, linked to the probability of financial distress, may have an influence on capital rationing. Recall from Chapter 3 that agency costs cause suppliers of debt and equity capital to raise their required rates of return and, in extreme circumstances, to impose restrictions on the absolute amount of funds made available.

In essence, those who reject the existence of external capital rationing believe that in a highly developed economy capital markets will be efficient, at least to the extent that a project exhibiting a positive NPV will be capable of being funded. It will be funded, of course, at the opportunity cost of capital, reflecting project risk. The higher the project risk, the higher the project's cost of capital. This argument might well be true for large publicly quoted companies; however, the recent debate on small business financing in the United Kingdom argues that entrepreneurs in the small business sector believe that they face external capital rationing. The small firm financing issue is discussed in Chapter 14.

Projects with different lives

In many cases investment selection has to be made among mutually exclusive projects which have different lives or durations. When confronted with the duration problem there is some controversy in respect of the circumstances under which standard or 'raw' NPVs can be applied in making project choices. There is general agreement, however, that modification is necessary when projects compete for the use of a common physical resource, for example, a plot of land; or when a project would normally have to be repeated,[6] at the end of its life. In these circumstances use of a standard NPV could lead to incorrect accept/reject decisions.

There are three alternative ways of tackling the duration problem: the Common Lifespan approach, the Annual Equivalent Value approach and the Constant Scale Replication approach. Each method yields identical accept/reject decisions and all three are based on a common set of assumptions about the nature of project replacement chains.

Common lifespans

Consider the two mutually exclusive projects specified in Table 7.7. Project A has a life of three years and project B a life of six years. The standard NPV on each

Table 7.8: Common lifespan for project A

Year	Project A NCFs (£s)	Project A NCFs replicated to give common lifespan with B	Project A Replicated Total NCFs NCFs (£s)	Present Value Total NCFs (£s)
0	−1200		−1200	−1200.00
1	600		600	565.80
2	800		800	712.00
3	1000	−1200	−200	−168.00
4		600	600	475.20
5		800	800	597.60
6		1000	1000	705.00

NPV of project A under common lifespan approach = £1687.60

project, calculated using a cost of capital of 6%, indicates that project B, with an NPV(Std.) = £1156, is preferable to project A which has an NPV(Std.) = £917.8.

By calculating each project's standard NPV, the difference in their durations has been ignored. One way of dealing with this is to judge each project on the basis of a minimum common lifespan (CLS). In the example, the minimum CLS is six years, implying that project B should be compared with project A, on the assumption that project A is repeated or replicated once, beginning at the end of year three. The new cash flow profile for project A, and its replication, is given in Table 7.8. The NPV (CLS) of project B is as before (£1156), since it does not need to be replicated. Under the CLS approach, however, the NPV (CLS) for project A is £1687.6, indicating that project A should be accepted and not project B.

Under the CLS approach, project A's replication begins at the end of period three on the assumptions that:
- its technological characteristics have not changed;
- its initial costs, at the end of year three, are identical to those in year zero; and
- its subsequent cash flows over years four to six are identical to those over years one to three.

Leaving these assumptions aside for the moment, the difficulty with this approach is that calculations become tedious when there are a number of projects which have different lifespans. If, for example, there are three projects – C, D and E – with respective lifespans of three, five and six years, the minimum common duration would be 30 years. This would hypothetically require, after initial completion of each project, replacement chains involving nine sequential replications for project C, five for project D and four for project E. The lengthy calculation of present values over a 30-year period can be avoided by using either the Annual Equivalent Value approach or the Constant Scale Replication approach.

Annual Equivalent Value

Under the Annual Equivalent Value approach (AEV), the standard NPV of each project is calculated and, the question is asked: what constant annual sum of money (the AEV), paid over the life of the project, would have given rise to this project's NPV?

In other words, the constant annual NCF is found which is equivalent to the NPV on the project. For mutually exclusive projects, the project with the highest AEV is accepted.

In effect, the AEV approach applies the annuity principle, where:

$$NPV(Std.) = AEV[PVIFA_{t,r}] \qquad (7.12)$$

Therefore,

$$AEV = \frac{NPV(Std.)}{PVIFA_{t,r}} \qquad (7.12a)$$

Consider, once again, the two projects in Table 7.7. Project A has a three-year life and, at r = 6%, an NPV(Std.) = £917.80. With PVIFA$_{3,6}$ = 2.673,

$$AEV_A = \frac{£917.80}{2.673} = £343.40$$

Project A's NPV is equivalent to an annual net cash flow of £343.40, over a three-year period. Project B has a six-year life and an NPV(Std.) = £1156.00. With PVIFA$_{6,6}$ = 4.917,

$$AEV_B = \frac{£1156.00}{4.917} = £235.10$$

The AEV method leads to the acceptance of project A, since it has the higher AEV.

Constant Scale Replication

The Constant Scale Replication (CSR) approach is similar to the Common Lifespan approach; however, instead of taking a minimum common lifespan, CSR assumes that projects are replicated to infinity, and calculates NPV under these conditions.

The NPV under CSR is obtained from the following formula:[7]

$$NPV(CSR) = \frac{NPV(Std.)}{1 - PVIF_{t,r}} \qquad (7.13)$$

That is, assuming that the replacement chain of a project goes to infinity, NPV(CSR) is equal to the standard NPV of a project divided by one minus the present value interest factor for t periods (the initial life of the project) at r.

Consider the two mutually exclusive projects in Table 7.7. In project A's case, with t = 3 and r = 6%, PVIF$_{3,6}$ = 0.840 and

$$NPV(CSR)_A = \frac{£917.80}{1 - .840} = £5736.25$$

For project B, with t = 6, PVIF$_{6,6}$ = 0.705 and

$$NPV(CSR)_B = \frac{£1156.00}{1 - .705} = £3918.60$$

As in the case of the other two modifications, CSR indicates that project A, with the higher NPV(CSR), and not project B, should be accepted.[8]

Table 7.9: Summary of alternative approaches to the duration problem

	Project A (£'s)	Project B (£'s)
Standard Net Present Value @ 6%	917.80	1156.00
Net Present Value using **Common Lifespan approach** (Common Lifespan = 6 years)	1687.60	1156.00
Annual Equivalent Value[1]	343.40	235.10
Net Present Value using **Constant Scale Replication**[2]	5736.25	3918.60
Annual Equivalent Value[3]	.06 × 5736.25	.06 × 3918.6
= Discount rate × NPV achieved under Constant Scale Replication	= 344.2	= 235.1

[1] $AEV = \dfrac{NPV(Std.)}{PVIFA_{t,r}}$

[2] $NPV(CSR) = NPV(Std.)\left[\dfrac{1}{1 - PVIF_{t,r}}\right]$

[3] $AEV = r[NPV(CSR)]$, alternatively

$NPV(CSR) = \dfrac{1}{r}[AEV]$

Implications

These three methods of investment appraisal are closely interrelated. The relationship between the minimum Common Lifespan and Constant Scale Replication approaches is obvious. The former determines a minimum common lifespan and calculates each project's NPV on this basis. The latter takes the common lifespan to infinity.

Constant Scale Replication is directly linked to Annual Equivalent Values, with the AEV of a project being equal to the discount rate times its NPV(CSR):

$$AEV = r[NPV(CSR)] \qquad (7.14)$$

In project A's case, AEV_A = £343.40 and $NPV(CSR)_A$ = £5736.25. Given r = 6%,

$$AEV_A = 0.06(£5736.25) = £344.20$$

(There is a small rounding error coming from use of the interest factor tables.) In the case of project B, AEV_B = £235.10 and $NPV(CSR)_B$ = £3918.60, thus

$$AEV_B = 0.06(£3918.60) = £235.10$$

The three approaches are summarised in Table 7.9.

Any of these approaches can be used. On balance, companies tend to favour Annual Equivalent Values when they view differences in project duration as being important. As it has been shown, however, use of the AEV implies Constant Scale Replication, the generalisation of the Common Lifespan approach. The latter is based on the restrictive assumptions that the initial costs, subsequent cash flows and technological characteristics of the initial project remain the same over each replication. Thus using AEV implies that these hold over an infinite series of replications.

These assumptions may not hold when making comparisons between projects. Particular projects may be more adaptable to anticipated technological change, some may have rates of cost inflation which will vary over the business cycle and some may be more easily expanded or contracted in the future in response to unanticipated demand changes. If these types of project are identified, such factors must be accommodated as best they can in the appraisal process and in arriving at a particular measure of investment worth.

Summary

This chapter has examined some of the more advanced issues in capital budgeting. It demonstrated that NPV is both a real and a nominal measure and showed how investment selection criteria could be adapted: to appraise projects which have different durations and to cope with capital rationing.

The chapter began by considering how a project's cost of capital should be estimated, with the main emphasis on applying the concepts of the CAPM. The after-tax, risk adjusted, weighted average cost of capital was shown to depend on an assessment of project risk, debt interest tax shields and capital structure.

The underlying relationships between the cost of capital, capital structure and company valuation are the subject of the next chapter.

Questions

1 Given that a company has a cost of debt capital of 4%, a cost of equity capital of 12%, and a corporate tax rate of 40% and that it has a target debt:equity ratio of 7:11, calculate its weighted average cost of capital on the assumption that the risk which it is exposed to is constant.

2 Food Processors plc, whose principal activity is in the food industry, has a capital structure consisting of 30% debt capital and 70% equity capital. It has $\beta_{\text{debt}} = 0.2$ and $\beta_{\text{equity}} = 1.7$. Its marginal tax rate is 25%.

This company is considering expanding into the leisure industry by building a hotel complex. Given the potential location of the hotel and the holiday and conference facilities it hopes to offer, Food Processors plc has identified an existing hotel complex which is equivalent to Food Processor's potential project. The existing hotel, Holiday and Conference plc is quoted on the stock market. It has an equity β of 2.2 and a debt β of 0.3 and finances its operations with 60% debt capital and 40% equity capital. Holiday and Conference plc has a marginal tax rate of 35%.

The risk-free rate of interest is 5% and the expected return on the market 15%.

Calculate the project cost of capital which Food Processors plc should use in determining whether or not to diversify into the leisure industry. Assume Food Processors plc intends financing the new project in line with its existing capital structure.

3 Consider a one-year project which has the following NCFs:
Year 0: $-£2m$; Year 1: £10m.

The nominal cost of capital for this project is $r_{nom} = 12\%$ and the expected annual rate of inflation is $r_{RPI} = 5\%$.

a) Calculate the real cost of capital.

b) Show that the NPV on this project is both a real and a nominal measure.

c) What error would have been made in calculating the real discount rate if the approximation had been used: real rate = nominal rate less expected inflation rate?

4 What is the difference between internal and external capital rationing?

5 If the benefit–cost ratio is to be used in a capital rationing situation, what assumptions are necessary?

6 Consider the following information on five independent projects:

Project	Net Investment Outlay (£s)	PV of Future NCFs (£s)
A	£500	£1000
B	£1000	£2500
C	£400	£300
D	£300	£400
E	£200	£300

a) Assuming no capital rationing, indicate which projects should be selected and calculate the total NPV of the selected projects.

b) Assume that a single-period internal capital constraint of £1600 has been imposed. Indicate which projects would be selected using the BCR and calculate the total NPV of the selected projects. Demonstrate that the PVI would produce the same choice.

c) Indicate which projects should be accepted, under this capital constraint, if each of the five projects was non-divisible.

7 Consider the following two projects:

	NCFs(£s)	
Year	A	B
0	−250	−1000
1	200	300
2	500	400
3		600
4		500

The discount rate is 10%.

a) Calculate the NPV of each project.

b) Calculate the NPV of each project under the common lifespan approach and indicate which project you would accept.

Exercises

1 Given the information in question 7, calculate, for each project, the NPV under Constant Scale Replication and the Annual Equivalent Value. What is the relationship between CSR and the AEV?

2 Sometimes the term marginal is used when referring to the corporate tax rate and the weights used in determining the average cost of capital. Why is this?

3 'Retained earnings normally represent a cheaper source of funds than new equity issues ...' Discuss.

Endnotes

1. Assuming perfect capital markets with no taxes, the capital structure of a company will have no effect on the overall, or average, cost of capital used in project evaluation. This is explored in the next chapter.

    Note also that this approach estimates the average cost of capital by assessing the overall β risk of a project and does not involve explicit calculation of the component costs of capital. An alternative, which will yield roughly the same answer, uses the CAPM and the risk adjusted component costs directly. This latter approach involves a considerable amount of tedious calculations and is not presented here.

2. A comparison of Equations 7.1 and 7.3 demonstrates the effects that are being taken into account. If, either, the company is not using any debt (B = 0), or its marginal tax rate is zero (t_c = 0), then the debt interest tax shield will not exist, in which case:

$$\left[\frac{S + B(1 - t_c)}{S + B} \right] = 1$$

    Further, if the project has the same β risk as the company, $\beta_{asset} = \beta_{project}$, Equation 7.3 reduces to Equation 7.1.

3. If the project is financed in terms of the existing capital structure and does not alter risk, then with β_{asset} = 0.972 the tax effect reduces the original cost of capital of 11.75% to approximately 10.39%. With β_{asset} = 0.972

$$r_{project} = 3.2 + [12 - 3.2][0.972][0.84] = 10.39\%$$

4. That NPV is both a nominal and a real measure can be seen by considering the nominal NCF in any period t; its present value is:

$$\frac{NCF_t}{(1 + r)^t}$$

    The real NCF is:

$$\frac{NCF_t}{(1 + r_{RPI})^t}$$

    To obtain its present value, the real cost of capital must be applied, that is, it must be divided by $(1 + r^*)^t$. However,

$$(1 + r^*)^t = (1 + r)^t/(1 + r_{RPI})^t$$

    therefore the present value of the real NCF in period t, is:

$$\frac{NCF_t/(1 + r_{RPI})^t}{(1 + r)^t/(1 + r_{RPI})^t} = \frac{NCF_t}{(1 + r)^t}$$

5. The relationship between the BCR and the PVI is easily demonstrated:

$$BCR = \frac{NPV}{I_0} = \frac{PVFNCF - I_0}{I_0}$$

$$= \frac{PVFNCF}{I_0} - 1 = PVI - 1$$

6. For example, a company in the private health care sector may have decided to provide a residential nursing home for the elderly in a particular geographical area. It is considering two alternatives, one which involves the renovation of an existing building and the other the construction of a complex on a greenfield site. It is likely that the renovation option will have a considerably shorter life than the greenfield option. The company assumes, given the future age structure of the population, that such accommodation will always be needed. Thus, in comparing these options, allowance must be made for the fact that each potential project will be replaced at the end of its life.

7. This formula is derived in the following way. Assume a project has a life of $t = n$ years and is to be exactly replicated at the end of each n years, to infinity; then given the discount rate, r,

$$NPV(CSR) = NPV(Std.) + \frac{NPV(Std.)}{(1 + r)^n} + \frac{NPV(Std.)}{(1 + r)^{2n}} + \cdots \qquad (i)$$

For simplicity let $U = 1/(1 + r)^n$, then Equation (i) can be re-expressed as

$$NPV(CSR) = NPV(Std.)[1 + U + U^2 + \ldots + U^n] \qquad (ii)$$

Multiply Equation (ii) by U, therefore

$$(U)NPV(CSR) = NPV(Std.)[U + U^2 + U^3 + \ldots + U^{n+1}] \qquad (iii)$$

By subtracting Equation (iii) from Equation (ii), most of the terms in the [ ] bracket on the right-hand side cancel, leaving

$$NPV(CSR)[1 - U] = NPV(Std.)[1 - U^{n+1}] \qquad (iv)$$

Since the project is being replicated to infinity, and since $U = 1/(1 + r)^n$, U^{n+1} tends to zero as $n \to \infty$ and Equation (iv) reduces to

$$NPV(CSR)[1 - U] = NPV(Std.) \qquad (v)$$

Finally, since $t = n$, $U = 1/(1 + r)^n = 1/(1 + r)^t$, which is the present value interest factor for t years at $r\%$. Thus the NPV of a project under constant scale replication is:

$$NPV(CSR) = \frac{NPV(Std.)}{1 - U}$$

$$= \frac{NPV(Std.)}{1 - PVIF_{t,r}}$$

8. The Constant Scale Replication approach, with a chain of projects to infinity, has an important role to play in determining optimal duration. This issue arises, for example, when considering afforestation projects where an estimate of the optimal time for harvesting trees is needed. Optimal duration is beyond the scope of this introductory text.

References

Ben-Horim, M., 'Comments on the Weighted Average Cost of Capital as a Cutoff Rate', Financial Management, 1979

Emery, G.W., 'Some Guidelines for Evaluating Capital Investment Alternatives with Unequal Lives', Financial Management, 1982

Hamada, R.S., 'The Effect of the Firms Capital Structure on the Systematic Risk of Common Stocks', Journal of Finance, 1972

Hoskins, C.G., 'Benefit–Cost Ratio Ranking for Size Disparity Problems', Journal of Business, Finance and Accounting, 1977

Hutchinson, R., *Economic Appraisal and the Prioritisation of Capital Projects*, Occasional Paper No. 23, Belfast, Policy Planning and Research Unit, Civil Service Economics Division, 1991

Levy, H. and M. Sariat, *Capital Investment and Financial Decisions*, New York, Prentice-Hall, 1990

Van Horne, J.C., 'A Note on Biases in Capital Budgeting Induced by Inflation', Journal of Financial and Quantitative Analysis, 1971

Weingartner, H.M., 'Capital Rationing: Authors in Search of a Plot', Journal of Finance, 1977

8 Capital structure and valuation

Introduction

Much of the content of the preceding chapters has been concerned with long-term asset investment decisions, where additions to value are created by undertaking projects with positive NPVs. While NPV takes account of how a project is financed, via the opportunity cost of capital used as the discount rate, the impact that the long-term financing decision might have on valuation has been largely ignored.

Avoidance of a financing effect was primarily based on the implicit assumption that investment and financing decisions were independent. Alternatively, to the extent that taxation was introduced into the cost of capital formulation (especially at the beginning of the last chapter) any potential impact that this might have had on the capital structure decision was side-stepped, by assuming that a company had already chosen the appropriate combinations of debt and equity financing.

Whether or not the financing decision has any relevance for valuation is a subject of considerable controversy, representing a central area of theoretical and empirical research in corporate finance. In this chapter, the main themes of this controversy – referred to as the capital structure, valuation debate, or the capital structure puzzle – are examined.

After some preliminary discussion, the main part of this chapter begins with a presentation of Modigliani and Miller's model of capital structure irrelevancy, in an environment where there are no personal or corporate income taxes. This model's implications are then discussed, in particular, those pertaining to the behaviour of the rate of return required by shareholders. Recall that, in equilibrium, this represents a company's cost of equity capital.

Modigliani and Miller's model, when first published, challenged the conventional or Traditionalist belief in an optimal capital structure. Consequently, before analysing the effects that corporate and personal taxes might have on the irrelevancy position, some of these Traditionalist arguments are outlined.

The final parts of the chapter are concerned with what is loosely referred to as the Modernist position. Taking the view that the main advantages of debt financing derive from a company's ability to set interest charges against corporate tax payments, the Modernist view focuses on the disadvantages associated with debt financing: bankruptcy, financial distress and agency costs. These advantages and disadvantages are likely to interact, to produce an optimal debt:equity ratio, minimising the average cost of capital and maximising a company's market value.

Preliminary considerations

Without doubt, it is the overall set of assets produced by a company's investment decisions, and the levels and timing of the resulting net cash flows, which are the primary determinants of a company's current market value. These expected net cash flows are partitioned to provide the income streams for the debt and equity holders who finance the assets. Ultimately, the extent to which the capital structure decision creates an additional market value effect depends on how each of these income streams is discounted.

The overall net cash flows, constituted by operating income or earnings before interest and taxes, are subject to risk. Since, however, debtholders receive fixed interest payments and have prior claim on assets, their income is virtually certain. The equity holders' income is not and is influenced mainly, but as it will be argued not exclusively, by the risk of the operating income stream. It is these risk differences which imply that the cost of equity capital exceeds the cost of debt capital.

The core issue in the capital structure/valuation debate is whether or not there is a specific combination of debt and equity which maximises the total market value of a company. Assuming that a company has only two sources of capital, long-term debt and equity, the current market value, V, can be measured by the sum of the current market values of its debt, B, and its equity, S, that is, as:

$$V = B + S \qquad\qquad (8.1)$$

In this context, the capital structure of a company can be measured by either the ratio of debt to total market value (B/V), or the ratio of debt to equity (B/S). These measures of financial leverage or financial gearing are used interchangeably.[1]

While the capital structure puzzle can be viewed in terms of whether or not there is an optimal leverage ratio which maximises market value, it can equivalently be viewed in terms of the average cost of capital. (Recall from Chapter 7, that the average cost of capital is a function of the component costs of debt and equity capital, weighted by the respective proportions of debt and equity in a company's capital structure.) From the principles of valuation it should now be clear that, other things being equal, the value of an asset varies inversely with its cost of capital. Consequently, since V is based on a company's overall assets and will vary inversely with its overall cost of capital, an optimal financial leverage ratio (if one exists) which maximises V, does so by minimising the average cost of capital.

Modigliani and Miller: a taxless environment

To get to grips with the capital structure puzzle, the ideal conditions under which capital structure will have no effect on value must be identified. Then, by attempting to assess the extent to which these conditions are violated in practice, it may be possible to assess the likelihood of there being optimal capital structures for individual companies. Further, to effectively demonstrate that under these conditions such a relationship does not exist, a simplified valuation model should be used. This avoids the technical complexities of discounting which are inconsequential to the central issues. It was with these views in mind that Modigliani and Miller (MM) published their seminal capital structure irrelevancy paper in 1958.

Assumptions

The perpetuity model, developed in Chapter 2 (Equation 2.6), represents the most basic valuation formula. Consequently, MM assume that a company's investment decision is given and produces zero growth, with its total asset base generating, in perpetuity, a constant annual expected operating income. Investors are rational and have homogeneous expectations in respect of this operating income's probability distribution. To abstract from any complicating effects that taxes and dividend policy might have on value, it is also assumed that there are no personal or corporate taxes and that all earnings, after interest payments, are paid out as dividends.

A change in capital structure is brought about by selling debt to repurchase equity (a rise in financial leverage), or by selling equity to repurchase debt (a fall in financial leverage). To avoid these buying and selling activities having their own impact on valuation, there are no market transactions costs and information is costlessly available to all. These latter conditions are part of MM's perfect capital market assumption. It includes the notion that the cost of debt capital represents a constant rate of interest at which both companies and individuals can borrow and lend funds.[2] Effectively, debt capital is viewed as risk free.

Value and the costs of financing

Under the above assumptions, with a company's annual fixed operating income, Y, being generated by its total asset base, a company's total market value is simply determined by dividing this income by the company's average cost of capital, r_a, that is:

$$V = \frac{Y}{r_a} \qquad (8.2)$$

In order to determine, via the average cost of capital, if capital structure has an effect on V, the component costs of capital must be related to r_a, through the weighted average cost of capital formula. In other words, the cost of debt capital, r_d, and the cost of equity capital, r_e, must be estimated under the above assumptions.

The component costs of capital

In a perpetuity context, only perpetual debt is used and since its opportunity cost of capital is constant, it will not vary with the amount of debt in a company's capital structure. In equilibrium, the market value of debt is determined by the annual and perpetual fixed interest payment, I, divided by r_d, that is:

$$B = \frac{I}{r_d} \qquad (8.3)$$

Thus the cost of debt capital can be expressed as:

$$r_d = \frac{I}{B} \qquad (8.3a)$$

The total annual interest charge which must be deducted from Y, before r_e can be estimated, is:

$$I = r_d B \qquad\qquad (8.3b)$$

With a 100% dividend payout policy, the total dividend income paid out to shareholders is therefore:

$$D = Y - r_d B \qquad\qquad (8.4)$$

Thus, given the equity capitalisation rate, the total market value of the shares in a zero growth company,[3] is:

$$S = \frac{D}{r_e} \qquad\qquad (8.5)$$

This defines the equity capitalisation rate as:

$$r_e = \frac{D}{S} \qquad\qquad (8.5a)$$

The average cost of capital

In this simplified environment, the weighted average cost of capital,[4] in the absence of a corporate tax rate, can be determined (from Equation 7.1, with $t_c = 0$) as:

$$r_a = r_d \left[\frac{B}{S + B}\right] + r_e \left[\frac{S}{S + B}\right] \qquad\qquad (8.6)$$

To illustrate, consider a company producing an operating income of Y = £0.8m. The company has a total market value of V = £10m. The market value of its debt is B = £4m, at an opportunity cost of r_d = 5%. With a total annual fixed interest charge (Equation 8.3b) of

$$I = (.05)(£4m) = £0.2m$$

the total dividend payout (Equation 8.4) is:

$$D = £0.8m - £0.2m = £0.6m$$

Given V = £10m and B = £4m, the market value of equity, determined from Equation 8.1, is:

$$S = £10m - £4m = £6m$$

The cost of equity capital (from Equation 8.5a) is, therefore,

$$r_e = \frac{0.6}{6} = 0.10 \text{ or } 10\%$$

With an average cost of capital (Equation 8.6) of

$$r_a = 0.05 \left[\frac{4}{4 + 6}\right] + 0.10 \left[\frac{6}{4 + 6}\right] = 0.08 \text{ or } 8\%$$

the company's current market value, given Y = £0.8m, is confirmed (Equation 8.2) as:

$$V = \frac{£0.8m}{0.08} = £10m$$

Changing the capital structure

Will a change in capital structure induce a change in market value? A superficial analysis of the above example could suggest that the answer to this question is yes: a change in capital structure does affect value. With V = £10m and B = £4m, the current financial leverage ratio is B/V = 0.4. Now consider an increase in leverage which raises B/V to 0.5. Equity, at r_e = 10%, is the more expensive source of funds, relative to debt at r_d = 5%. It seems logical that if a company increases the proportion of the cheaper source of financing (from 40% to 50%) and reduces the proportion of the more expensive source (from 60% to 50%), there will be valuation benefits. A change in the way the given assets are financed will not affect the income, Y, that these generate. Given, therefore, that r_d is constant and assuming that r_e does not change with capital structure, the average cost of capital falls to,

$$r_a = 0.05[.5] + 0.10[.5] = 0.075 \text{ or } 7.5\%$$

and the market value of the company rises to:

$$V = \frac{£0.8m}{0.075} = £10.67m$$

MM Proposition I

According to MM, however, the answer to the above question is an unambiguous no: capital structure does not affect value. They argue, by their Proposition I, that if two companies are identical in all respects except that their capital structures differ, they cannot, in equilibrium, have different market values. By implication, this proposition also applies to a single company which alters its capital structure: its market value will not change. In the above example, therefore, Proposition I implies that when B/V changes from 0.4 to 0.5, V will not rise to £10.67m but will remain at £10m.

Market value, under Proposition I, is independent of capital structure and operating income is constant. Thus, a company's average cost of capital must also be constant and independent of financial leverage, since from Equation 8.2:

$$V = \frac{Y}{r_a}$$

In the above example this implies that when B/V changes from 0.4 to 0.5, r_a will not fall to 7.5% but will remain at 8%. In terms of the weighted average cost of capital formula (Equation 8.6), this must imply that there is an adjustment effect, if leverage increases, to exactly offset a company's increased reliance on debt capital, the cheaper source of financing. Given that debt is riskless, so that r_d is constant, the adjustment must take place in terms of the cost of equity capital. Under the MM approach, r_e must rise, as leverage increases, by just a sufficient amount to keep r_a constant. (The two approaches in this example are in fact defining Durand's (1952) Net Income and Net Operating Income methods of valuation. These are outlined in Appendix 8.1.)

In the current example, to maintain r_a at 8% and, therefore, V at £10m, r_e must rise from 10% (when B/V = 0.4) to 11% (when B/V = 0.5). With $r_e = 11\%$,

$$r_a = 0.05[.5] + 0.11[.5] = 0.08 \text{ or } 8\%$$

If B/V increases to 0.6, then r_e must rise to 12.5%, that is:

$$r_a = 0.05[.6] + 0.125[.4] = 0.08 \text{ or } 8\%$$

The relationship between the equity capitalisation rate and financial leverage constitutes MM's second proposition. Before presenting this relationship in its general form, and exploring its implications, the rationale supporting the first proposition, and on which the whole of MM's analysis rests, is explained.

Arbitrage and 'home-made' leverage

MM support Proposition I through the concept of arbitrage. The argument is that if investors identify two identical companies which have different market values, they will have found two investments between which they can trade to earn profits at zero risk. This type of trading, or arbitrage, will drive market values into equality. Arbitrage is possible in a perfect capital market because, with the costs of debt financing faced by companies and individuals being identical, investors view personal and corporate leverage as perfect substitutes. This implies that, if the only difference between two companies is in relation to their corporate leverage levels, investors will view the companies as perfect substitutes, which must have identical market values.

This argument is reminiscent of one of the EMH implications in Chapter 5. Recall that, in an efficient market, investors are not willing to pay for something which they can costlessly do for themselves. Under MM, investors can create their own personal leverage, to match any level of corporate leverage, at no extra cost. They will not, therefore, be willing to place a premium on the value of one company, relative to another, solely on the basis that it has more debt in its capital structure.

An example explaining how the arbitrage process works is contained in Appendix 8.2.

MM Proposition II

With arbitrage opportunities, in a perfect capital market, fully supporting Proposition I, MM's second proposition specifies the relationship which must exist between the equity capitalisation rate and capital structure. By rearranging the weighted average cost of capital formula, Equation 8.6, this relationship is formally expressed as:[5]

$$r_e = r_a + (r_a - r_d)(B/S) \tag{8.7}$$

Capital structure is now defined in terms of the debt:equity ratio, B/S. Since, by assumption, r_d is constant and since r_a must also be constant under Proposition I, there is a linear and positive $(r_a > r_d)$ relationship between r_e and B/S. As the debt:equity ratio rises, the cost of equity capital rises, to exactly offset the increased reliance on debt capital. Recall that, in equilibrium, r_e also represents the equity holder's required rate of return.

Equation 8.7 states that this required rate of return is equal to the average cost of capital, plus a surcharge for risk. The risk surcharge effect, which is explained below, is equal to the spread between the average cost of capital and the debt interest rate, representing a measure of risk aversion, times the debt:equity ratio. In the above example, with r_a constant at 8% and r_d constant at 5%, r_e must rise from 10%, when B/V = 0.4, to 11% when B/V = 0.5. This is demonstrated by Equation 8.7 since, when B/V = 0.4, that is the B/S ratio is 2:3,

$$r_e = 8\% + (8\% - 5\%)(2/3) = 10\%$$

When B/V = 0.5, that is the B/S ratio is 1:1,

$$r_e = 8\% + (8\% - 5\%)(1) = 11\%$$

Note that (from endnote 1), B/S = B/V ÷ (1 − B/V). Thus, for example, when B/V = 0.4, B/S = 0.4/0.6 or 2/3.

The pure equity capitalisation rate

Notice, in Equation 8.7, that the average cost of capital has a very interesting meaning. It represents what is referred to as the rate of capitalising a pure equity stream. Consider the case of an all equity financed company where B/S = 0. Here, the equity capitalisation rate, denoted as r_e^*, is simply equal to the average cost of capital, that is

$$r_e^* = r_a + (r_a - r_d)(0.0) = r_a \qquad (8.7a)$$

Viewing this the other way round, a company's average cost of capital can be defined as the rate of return required by shareholders to discount a dividend income stream, produced by financing a company entirely by equity.

If, for example, a company with a given investment policy believes that, under an all equity financing plan, shareholders require a rate of return of $r_e^* = 12\%$, then this represents the company's average cost of capital and project discount rate. If the company employs a debt:equity ratio of 3:5, with $r_d = 4\%$, its average cost of capital would remain at 12%. Now, however, because it has used debt, it is required to offer shareholders a rate of return of 16.8% in compensation, that is:

$$r_e = 12\% + (12\% - 4\%)(3/5) = 16.8\%$$

If the debt:equity ratio is increased to 4:5, r_e rises to:

$$r_e = 12\% + (12\% - 4\%)(4/5) = 18.4\%$$

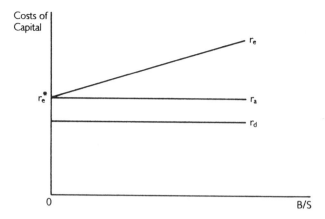

Figure 8.1   MM cost of capital schedules

The relationships between the component and average costs of capital and the debt:equity ratio are presented diagrammatically in Figure 8.1.

Equity valuation models

The above has profound implications for the all equity share valuation models presented in Chapter 3. There, the Gordon Growth dividend valuation approach and the investment opportunities approaches to share valuation were used to model a company under a hypothetical all equity financing policy. From the above, the required rate of return on equity, derived in each model, represents a pure equity capitalisation rate, and therefore an average cost of capital, providing that the MM capital structure irrelevancy propositions hold.

Note that these models were developed on the objective of maximising shareholder wealth through the maximisation of the price per share of a company. Given that the average cost of capital is equal to the pure equity capitalisation rate, the objective of maximising the total market value of a company, with debt in its capital structure, will result in the maximisation of its share price and hence shareholder wealth.

Financial leverage and financial risk

Why does the equity capitalisation rate behave in the manner depicted in Figure 8.1? A general feel for the answer should already be apparent, if it has been noted that there is a certain similarity between Equation 8.7 and the SML of the CAPM (Chapter 4, Equation 4.5). Recall, in the latter case, that an individual's investment decision was viewed in terms of a blend of investments in the market equilibrium portfolio of risky assets and the risk-free rate of interest. The positive and linear SML demonstrated that as systematic risk measured by a share's β increased, so the expected, and in equilibrium required, rate of return on equity increased. This was explained by individual investors increasing the proportion of their investments in the market portfolio and reducing the proportions of their lending (or increasing the proportions of their borrowing) at the risk-free rate of interest. In other words, the risk–return relationship was explained in terms of investors changing their exposures to personal leverage. The risk of the market portfolio did not of course change.

By companies engaging in corporate leverage, the amount of risk that shareholders are exposed to is increased. This must be the case, since personal and corporate leverage are perfect substitutes. Consequently, as corporate leverage is increased, the benefits to companies from the increased use of the cheaper source of debt capital are exactly offset by the increase in their cost of equity capital, which is necessary to compensate shareholders for additional risk. Companies which engage in corporate leverage do not alter the total risk that their assets are exposed to; therefore, their market values remain constant.

Equity βs

This can be further explained by considering the decomposition of an equity β into its relevant business risk and financial risk components. Given that shares will be held in a well-diversified portfolio, it is only the systematic risk of a company which is important from a valuation perspective. This systematic risk is primarily influenced by the nature of a company's business operations and the type of assets it has invested in to exploit its business opportunities. The nature of a company's business determines the total variation in its operating income but it is only how this co-varies with the market equilibrium portfolio which is important. It is the relevant risk inherent in a company's assets which defines its relevant business risk, measured by a company's asset β.

When debt is added to the capital structure, equity holders experience additional risk due to financing. Debtholders receive fixed interest payments and have a prior claim on assets. When operating income, after fixed interest payments, is fed through to shareholders, the relevant risk is amplified. The amplification represents financial risk.

This can be demonstrated using the asset β equation presented in Chapter 4 (Equation 4.8). The asset β is defined as a weighted average of a company's debt and equity βs, where:

$$\beta_{assets} = \beta_{debt}\left[\frac{B}{S+B}\right] + \beta_{equity}\left[\frac{S}{S+B}\right] \tag{8.8}$$

With debt, in the MM model, assumed to be risk free, $\beta_{debt} = 0$ and Equation 8.8 simplifies to:

$$\beta_{assets} = \beta_{equity}\left[\frac{S}{S+B}\right] \tag{8.8a}$$

Assume, initially, that a company is all equity financed. With no debt (B = 0), $\beta_{assets} = \beta_{equity}$. In other words β_{assets}, representing the relevant business risk of a company, measures the β of a pure equity stream and determines r_e^*, the rate of capitalising this stream, via the SML.

Once debt is introduced, the equity β rises above the asset β, reflecting the addition of financial risk. Rearranging Equation 8.8a:

$$\beta_{equity} = \beta_{assets} \left[\frac{S + B}{S} \right]$$ (8.8b)

Since $S + B > S$, for $B \neq 0$, $\beta_{equity} > \beta_{assets}$. Equivalently,

$$\beta_{equity} = \beta_{assets} \left[1 + \frac{B}{S} \right]$$ (8.8c)

That is, an equity β is equal to the asset β times one plus the company's leverage ratio.

If, for example, $\beta_{assets} = 0.8$ and the debt:equity ratio is 2:5 (that is B/S = 0.4),

$$\beta_{equity} = 0.8(1 + 0.4) = 1.12$$

A rise in the debt:equity ratio to, say 4:5 (or B/S = 0.8), increases β_{equity} to:

$$\beta_{equity} = 0.8(1 + 0.8) = 1.44$$

A rise in the equity β produces, via the SML, a rise in the cost of equity capital. In equilibrium, MM's cost of equity capital, framed in terms of financial leverage (Equation 8.7), produces identical results.

The technicalities of business and financial risk are further explored in Chapter 10 when the inter-relationships between investment and financing decisions are considered.

Unlevered and levered βs

When discussing, at the beginning of the last chapter, ways of estimating a project's cost of capital, the concept of unlevering and then relevering β coefficients was introduced; this can now be explained. Recall that Sellright plc wanted to expand into the health club industry and had identified Jimnasium plc as having the appropriate β for Sellright's new project. Jimnasium had a different capital structure from Sellright, therefore Jimnasium's β coefficient had to be unlevered to net out the effect of Jimnasium's financial risk. This unlevered asset β, or pure equity β, had then to be relevered to take account of Sellright's capital structure, and hence its financial risk, thus producing the appropriate project β. The unlevering and relevering process was somewhat more complex than the above because, in the Sellright/Jimnasium example, β_{debt} was not assumed to be zero.

MM Proposition III

The average cost of capital which is used as the discount rate in NPV investment appraisals is, under MM's Propositions I and II, independent of capital structure. This leads to MM's third and final proposition, that investment and financing decisions are independent.

Developing the base case model

The above has presented the MM base case, capital structure irrelevancy model and demonstrated its implications for the cost of equity capital. The model must now be appraised and extended, to determine the conditions which might invalidate the base case and produce an optimal debt:equity ratio, which would maximise the total market value of a company. In a practical sense, if an optimal debt:equity ratio exists, this must be identified by management and targeted in their day-to-day formulation of financial policy.

The Modernist approach focuses on taxation and its interplay with bankruptcy, financial distress and agency costs. Before examining these factors, the earlier Traditionalist[6] response to the MM irrelevancy position is briefly reviewed.

Some Traditionalist arguments

One of the early Traditionalist challenges to the MM position related to Proposition II. If shareholders, instead of responding in the manner implied by Equation 8.7, took a different attitude to financial risk then, it was argued, an optimal capital structure would exist. One view was that at very low levels of debt, shareholders would not view their risk of ownership as being materially affected, so that the cost of equity capital would initially remain constant when B/S was relatively low but increasing. (As an earlier example in the chapter showed, holding r_e and r_d constant causes r_a to fall.) Subsequently, however, as B/S rose beyond some point, the risk of ownership would be perceived as being affected, with the consequent rise in r_e 'pulling up' r_a. In other words, r_a has a minimum value which maximises V.

An alternative view, demonstrated in Figure 8.2, was that at very low levels of leverage, shareholders would respond to modest increases in debt by increasing r_e but in a less marked fashion than implied by MM's Proposition II. They would, however, exhibit a more marked increase in r_e, at high levels of leverage. This Traditionalist shape to the r_e function induces an optimal capital structure by causing the r_a function to become 'u' shaped and possess a minimum point.

Imperfect arbitrage
MM's capital structure irrelevancy arguments are, however, fundamentally based on the view that, in perfect capital markets, the perfect substitutability of corporate and personal leverage enables the arbitrage process to operate unhindered. This supports Proposition I. As a consequence Proposition II, which gives MM's formulation of the r_e function, must hold. Therefore, challenges to the independence of value and capital structure are primarily based on factors which would inhibit the arbitrage process, by making personal and corporate leverage imperfect substitutes.

If personal and corporate leverage are imperfect substitutes, shareholders may be willing to pay a premium for the shares in a levered company, if corporate leverage conveys benefits which shareholders cannot personally achieve for themselves. Given the inverse relationship between value and the discount rate, such a price premium would effectively imply that the required rate of return on equity would

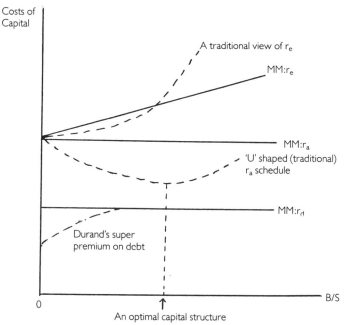

Figure 8.2   Some Traditionalist views

be lower than it otherwise would be in a perfect capital market. Capital structure would, therefore, affect the overall market value of a company and its average cost of capital.

Borrowing and transactions costs

This type of situation would arise if companies can borrow and lend funds at cheaper rates than shareholders. Similarly, if transactions costs are introduced, arbitrage will be impaired. This is especially the case if companies, through the size of their financial market dealings, experience economies of scale in the costs of using the market and, consequently, face lower transactions costs than private individuals.

Limited liability

The existence of limited liability in the corporate sector may also have an impact. Here, the risk facing shareholders exposing themselves indirectly to debt, by buying shares in a levered company, may be lower than the risk they face in obtaining personal leverage. In the former case, if a company defaults on its fixed interest payments, individual shareholders are limited in their liability to the size of their shareholdings in the company. They are not liable for the company's debt. In the case where personal leverage is used, a company default may expose shareholders to claims in respect of their personal borrowings.

Bankruptcy

Limited liability can only have this effect, however, if in responding to default, through either bankruptcy or company reorganisation, there are costs involved. In the case of bankruptcy, for example, these costs are associated with administration fees and the sale of assets at distress prices. In a perfect capital market there are no bankruptcy costs, so the full economic value of assets would be realised on liquidation and the proceeds equitably distributed between debt and equity holders. In a perfect capital market, value and capital structure are independent.

Institutional restrictions

Institutional restrictions may also play a part in inducing an optimal capital structure. One example is Durand's Super Premium Hypothesis. Recall from the discussion on corporate bonds, in Chapter 3, that there is a widespread practice of assigning ratings to corporate debt. Regulations sometimes restrict investment institutions to holding only high grade, Aaa or Aa, rated bonds. Since there is only a limited amount of this quality which can be issued by companies, excess demand may develop for high quality debt, thus placing a premium on its market value and, consequently, a discount on its cost. At modest levels of debt, therefore, the cost of debt capital may be lower than it otherwise would be under perfect capital markets. A 'u' shaped average cost of capital schedule would again be experienced, with its implications for an optimal capital structure. This is demonstrated in Figure 8.2.

Partitioning risk

Still focusing on the cost of debt schedule, an alternative situation accepts the constant cost of debt assumption over low to medium levels of leverage. This implies that debt is risk free, with no chance of a company defaulting on its fixed interest payments. After some critical level of leverage, however, the cost of debt rises, demonstrating that debtholders recognise the possibility of a company defaulting on its debt in the face of relatively large fixed interest payments. In this case, supporters of the MM position argue that the average cost of capital remains constant, with the rise in the rate of return required by debtholders being offset by a slower increase in the equity capitalisation rate. This is demonstrated in Figure 8.3. In other words, because financial leverage does not alter the total risk of a company's assets (that can only be effected by changing the investment decision)

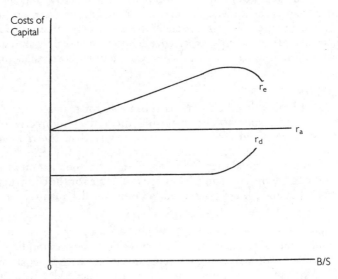

Figure 8.3   A variant of MM

financial leverage simply partitions risk between bondholders and equity holders. With the capital structure irrelevancy model in this form, there is a possibility that it implies irrational behaviour on the part of shareholders. As r_e increases, but at a decreasing rate, they become less risk averse in the face of default risk.

This rebalancing of risk between shareholders and debtholders is highly complex, however, because once default is introduced bankruptcy possibilities arise, with their associated costs. Before looking at this and other aspects of the Modernist approach, MM's model with its corporate tax adaptation is presented.

MM and corporate taxes

While the Traditionalist market imperfections examined above can be important, many would argue that they pale into insignificance when compared to the potential imperfections which are introduced by the taxation system. Indeed, one of MM's main purposes in developing their capital structure irrelevancy propositions was to demonstrate that it was the presence of corporate income taxes which, via capital structure, created a value effect. In these circumstances, the reason that companies exhibit a preference for debt capital is that they are able to set debt interest charges against their tax liabilities. To see this, consider MM's simple but penetrating corporate tax adaptation of their base case irrelevancy model. Analysis of the possible effects of personal taxes is deferred, for the moment.

Debt interest charges and corporate tax liabilities

First, assume that an all equity financed company is subject to a corporate income (or profits) tax rate, t_c. Instead of shareholders receiving all of the operating income as dividends, their income is reduced by the amount of the tax bill, $t_c Y$. With the annual income to shareholders reduced to

$$Y - t_c Y = Y(1 - t_c)$$

and a pure equity capitalisation rate of r_e^*, the market value of the unlevered company is:

$$V_u = Y \frac{(1 - t_c)}{r_e^*} \qquad (8.9)$$

This is illustrated in Table 8.1, where as a result of a corporate tax rate of 40% the dividend income available to shareholders is reduced, from the full operating income of £1.5m, to £0.9m. Given $r_e^* = 12\%$, the market value of the unlevered company is £7.5m.

Next, assume that debt is introduced into the capital structure. Since interest charges are tax deductible, the tax rate is levied on operating income less fixed interest charges; that is on $Y - r_d B$. Thus the income to be paid out to shareholders (adjusting Equation 8.4) is now:

$$D = (Y - r_d B)(1 - t_c) \qquad (8.10)$$

Table 8.1: Valuation with debt and corporate taxes

Assume $Y = £1.5m$, $r_e{}^* = 12\%$, $t_c = 40\%$, $B = 4m$ and $r_d = 3\%$

ALL EQUITY CASE

$$D = Y(1 - t_c) = £1.5m(1 - .40) = £0.9m$$

$$V_u = \frac{Y(1 - t_c)}{r_e{}^*} = \frac{£1.5m(1 - .40)}{0.12} = \frac{£0.9m}{0.12} = £7.5m$$

DEBT FINANCING

$$D = (Y - r_d B)(1 - t_c)$$
$$= (£1.5m - 0.03£4m)(1 - .40)$$
$$= £0.828m$$

An alternative expression for D:

$$Y(1 - t_c) - r_d B + t_c r_d B = £1.5m(1 - .40) - 0.03(£4m) + (.4)(.03)(£4m)$$
$$= £0.9m - £0.12m + £0.048m$$
$$= 0.828m$$

Earnings after taxes in the levered company:

$$EAIT = D + r_d B = Y(1 - t_c) + t_c r_d B$$

MARKET VALUE OF LEVERED COMPANY

$$V_L = \frac{Y(1 - t_c)}{r_e{}^*} + t_c B = V_u = t_c B$$
$$= £7.5m + 0.4(£4m) = £7.5m + £1.6m$$
$$= £9.1m$$

From the example in Table 8.1, the presence of £4m of debt capital at $r_d = 3\%$ causes a further reduction in dividend income, to £0.828m.

An alternative expression for Equation 8.10, achieved by simply multiplying out some of the terms in this equation, is:

$$D = Y(1 - t_c) - r_d B + t_c r_d B \qquad (8.10a)$$

In this latter form, shareholder income can be seen to be determined by three components:

- $Y(1 - t_c)$, the after tax income available in the all equity financing case;
- less $r_d B$, the debt interest charges paid to bondholders;
- plus $t_c r_d B$, a shield on tax payments resulting from interest charges.

This last term represents the annual income gain to shareholders from including debt in the capital structure:

$$\text{Annual Interest Tax Shield} = t_c r_d B \qquad (8.11)$$

In the example, with $t_c = 40\%$, $r_d = 3\%$ and $B = £4m$, the annual benefit from being able to set interest charges against tax payments is:

$$(.4)(.03)(£4m) = £0.048m$$

Market value and corporate taxes

To obtain the total market value of this levered company, the combined income stream of debtholders and shareholders must be determined and the appropriate costs of capital applied in the discounting process. Given the income to shareholders (defined in Equation 8.10a) and adding the income to debtholders, $r_d B$, the combined after-tax income of the company, EAT, is:

$$EAIT = Y(1 - t_c) - r_d B + t_c r_d B + r_d B$$

that is,

$$EAIT = Y(1 - t_c) + t_c r_d B \tag{8.12}$$

In Equation 8.12, two components in the after-tax income stream are identified. The first, $Y(1 - t_c)$, is identical to the income stream in the unlevered company. It should therefore be capitalised at r_e^*, as in Equation 8.9, giving, in terms of the example in Table 8.1:

$$V_u = \frac{Y(1 - t_c)}{r_e^*} = £7.5m$$

The second term, $t_c r_d B$, is the annual interest tax shield. Because debt is assumed to be risk free, this income stream is certain. By the principles of risk and return, it must be discounted at the risk-free rate of interest, r_d. Thus its present value is:

$$(t_c r_d B)/r_d = t_c B$$

that is:

$$\text{Present Value of the Tax Shield} = t_c B \tag{8.13}$$

In terms of the example, the annual interest tax shield was £0.048m. Given the debt interest rate, $r_d = 3\%$, the present value of these annual benefits is £0.048m/ $(.03) = £1.6m$. In other words, the present value of the tax shield, given $t_c = 40\%$ and $B = £4m$, is:

$$t_c B = (0.4)(£4m) = £1.6m$$

Summarising, in an environment with corporate taxes, the market value of a levered company, V_L, is:

$$V_L = \frac{Y(1 - t_c)}{r_e^*} + \frac{t_c r_d B}{r_d} \tag{8.14}$$

or

$$V_L = V_u + t_c B \tag{8.14a}$$

In other words, V_L, the market value of a levered company is equal to its market value under an all equity financing plan plus the present value of the tax shield. In the example (see Table 8.1):

$$V_L = £7.5m + £1.6m = £9.1m$$

Consider another example of a company with $Y = £2.5m$ and $B = £5m$. The company is subject to a corporate tax rate of $t_c = 35\%$ and has estimated its pure equity capitalisation rate at $r_e^* = 15\%$. From Equation 8.14a:

$$V_L = \frac{£2.5m(1 - .35)}{0.15} + 0.35(£5m) = £10.83m + £1.75m = £12.58m$$

The total market value of this company, £12.58m, which has a leverage ratio of $B/V = £5m/£12.58m = 0.4$, is equal to its value in an unlevered situation, £10.83m, plus the present value of the tax shield, £1.75m.

The cost of capital and tax adjustment

Note that Equation 8.13 explains the tax adjustment used at the beginning of Chapter 7, when calculation of the average cost of capital was discussed. There, the effective amount of debt financing used by a company was determined by subtracting what was defined as the Debt Interest Tax Shield (Equation 7.4) from the market value (that is the present value) of debt: $B(1 - t_c) = B - t_cB$ (see Equations 7.5 and 7.6). Clearly the Debt Interest Tax Shield is a present value measure based on MM's capital structure theory. Note also, as already explained, that when estimating the average cost of capital in this case, the debt:equity ratio was taken as given, so that discussion of what would constitute the optimal, or target, capital structure was avoided.

All debt financing

The problem with MM's formulation of the debt and corporate taxes model is that, while it indicates that it is the presence of corporate taxes which causes capital structure to have an effect on value, it implies an all debt, and no equity, optimal capital structure. Given Equation 8.14a, it is obvious that the greater the amount of debt used by a company, the greater the present value of the tax shield and the greater V_L. In the last example, if the amount of debt increases from £5m to £7m, other things being equal, the present value of the debt interest tax shield rises to $(.35)(£7m) = £2.45m$. Given $V_u = £10.83m$, V_L rises from £12.58m to £13.28m:

$$V_L = £10.83m + £2.45m = £13.28m$$

The leverage ratio has increased from 0.4 to $B/V = £7m/£13.28 = 0.53$. Thus, aiming for a target capital structure of 100% debt financing would be in pursuit of management's goal of maximising market value.

This relationship is depicted in terms of market value and the financial leverage ratio, defined in terms of debt to total market value, in Figure 8.4. Since 100% debt financing maximises market value, the implication must be that the average cost of

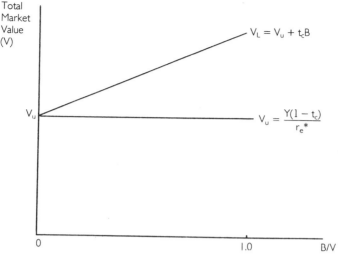

Figure 8.4   Market value with corporate taxes

capital declines continuously as leverage increases. In other words, r_a is minimised at r_d, the cost of the 100% debt financing.

Personal taxes

The vast majority of companies do not exhibit capital structures going anywhere near 100% debt financing. Accepting, however, the undoubted benefits of the presence of corporate taxes, in the form of debt interest tax shields, a search for associated costs which might offset some, or even all, of the tax benefits is required. An obvious area to begin this search is by extending the MM model to include the tax environment as a whole, that is, to consider both corporate and personal taxes.

A company's earnings are distributed, after taxes, to its debtholders and equity holders, many of whom will be subject to personal taxes. In the case of debtholders, the impact that personal taxes may have is straightforward. Payments to debt-holders are in the form of fixed interest income which is subject to each debtholder's marginal income tax rate. Defining this personal tax rate as t_p, an income tax payment of t_p is made on each £1 of interest income, leaving the debtholder with a net of tax interest income of £1$(1 - t_p)$. If, for example, $t_p = 30\%$, the net of tax interest income on each £1 is:

$$£1(1 - .30) = 70p$$

The effective tax rate on equity income

Where equity income is concerned, the effect of personal taxes is not so straight-forward. Equity holders receive their income in two forms: dividends, which are subject to t_p, the same personal income tax rate as debt interest income; and capital gains which are subject to a capital gains tax rate, t_g. In a number of countries the capital gains tax rate is less than t_p, meaning that the effective tax rate on overall equity income can be less than the personal tax rate. This effective tax rate, t_{ef}, will depend on how each £1 of equity income is split between dividends and capital gains and on the respective tax rates. (This breaks the MM assumption of 100% dividend payout policy.)

If, for example, $t_p = 30\%$, $t_g = 20\%$ and each £1 of equity income is composed of 60p of dividends and 40p of capital gains, the total tax payment is:

$$£0.60(.30) + £0.40(.20) = £0.26$$

This gives a net equity income per £1 of 74p which is higher than the net debt interest income per £1 of 70p. The effective tax rate on equity income is therefore determined as:

$$£1(1 - t_{ef}) = £0.74$$

That is,

$$t_{ef} = 1 - 0.74 = 0.26 \text{ or } 26\%$$

This is below the personal income tax rate of 30%.

With $t_{ef} < t_p$, there are potential disadvantages to the ownership of debt, relative to equity. While, therefore, the existence of corporate taxes provides tax shield benefits, these may be partly or wholly eroded if management have to increase the pre-tax required rate of return on debt, and thus the cost of debt capital, relative to the pre-tax rate of return on equity.[7] This would be necessary to compensate for the disadvantages that potential debtholders would otherwise perceive and to encourage the take-up of debt issues.

Even if there is no difference between personal income and capital gains tax rates, $t_p = t_g$, the effective tax rate on equity income is still likely to be less than t_p. Dividend income is normally paid annually but capital gains are only realised, and thus subject to tax, on the sale of shares. To the extent that part of equity income is received in terms of capital gains, and the sale of shares is postponed, the effective tax rate in any given year will be less than the personal income tax rate. In an extreme situation, if all earnings after interest and taxes are retained by a company, and shareholders never sell their shares, t_{ef} would be zero. In this latter case there are no dividends on which t_p can be levied and, with no share sales, t_g cannot be levied.

Miller's valuation equation

In this overall tax environment, the objective of management is to minimise the present value of all tax payments (corporate and personal) and so maximise their company's net after-tax income. In these circumstances, the valuation equation, developed on the assumption that only corporate taxes are levied (Equation 8.14a), is modified to take account of personal taxes, such that:

$$V_L = V_u + \left[1 - \frac{(1 - t_c)(1 - t_{ef})}{(1 - t_p)}\right] B \qquad (8.15)$$

To simplify this expression, let

$$V_L = V_u + [1 - \lambda]B, \tag{8.15a}$$

where

$$\lambda = \frac{(1 - t_c)(1 - t_{ef})}{(1 - t_p)} \tag{8.15b}$$

The implications of Miller's equation

This modification, while interesting, does not really resolve the capital structure puzzle because it predicts alternative extreme capital structure positions, depending on the value of λ. Table 8.2 illustrates different values that λ can take by varying the corporate, personal and effective tax rates.

Table 8.2: Illustrating Miller's valuation equation

$V_L = V_u + [1 - \lambda]B,$

where

$$\lambda = \frac{(1 - t_c)(1 - t_{ef})}{(1 - t_p)}$$

Assume $V_u = £10m$ and $B = £2m$, therefore, $V_L = £10m + [1 - \lambda]£2m$

Tax Rates (%)					Implied Target
t_c	t_{ef}	t_p	λ	$V_L (£m)$	Capital Structure
35	25	25	$\dfrac{(1 - .35)(1 - .25)}{(1 - .25)} = 0.65$	10.70	$V_L = V_u + t_c B$, therefore, 100% debt financing
35	20	25	$\dfrac{(1 - .35)(1 - .20)}{(1 - .25)} = 0.69$	10.62	$V_L < V_u + t_c B$ but $V_L > V_u$, therefore 100% debt financing
35	20	48	$\dfrac{(1 - .35)(1 - .20)}{(1 - .48)} = 1.00$	10.00	$V_L = V_u$, therefore, Capital Structure Irrelevancy[1]
35	20	55	$\dfrac{(1 - .35)(1 - .20)}{(1 - .55)} = 1.156$	9.69	$V_L < V_u$, therefore, 100% equity financing

[1] An alternative case demonstrating irrelevancy is where all earnings are retained and shares are never sold. Here t_{ef} is automatically zero and Miller's equilibrium model produces $t_c = t_p$ in which case $\lambda = 1$. With, at the margin, the personal and corporate tax rates being equal there is no optimal capital structure for the individual firm, although there is for the economy as a whole.

If there is no difference between the personal income tax rate and the effective tax rate on equity income, $t_p = t_{ef}$, then (from Equation 8.15b) $\lambda = 1 - t_c$. Consequently, Equation 8.15a reduces to the standard MM corporate tax position, where $V_L = V_u + t_c B$. A 100% debt financing policy is implied. This is exemplified in Table 8.2 where $t_p = t_{ef} = 25\%$.

Other things being equal, if $t_{ef} < t_p$, then $\lambda < (1 - t_c)$ and the valuation benefit of financial leverage, relative to the standard MM position, is reduced.[8] In other words, the reduction in corporate taxes, resulting from corporate leverage, is partly offset by the higher taxes on debt income, relative to equity income. Even in this case, however, since debt still has a positive effect on value, the implied target capital structure is 100% debt financing. This is exemplified in Table 8.2 with $t_{ef} = 20\%$ and $t_p = 25\%$.

When $\lambda = 1$, the original capital structure irrelevancy position is re-established. Here, by Equation 8.15b,

$$(1 - t_p) = (1 - t_c)(1 - t_{ef}) \tag{8.15c}$$

and the interaction of the corporate, personal and effective tax rates results, in equilibrium, in the tax advantages of corporate debt being eliminated. This is exemplified in Table 8.2 with $t_c = 35\%$, $t_{ef} = 20\%$ and $t_p = 48\%$.

Finally, if $\lambda > 1$, the $1 - \lambda$ in Equation 8.15a is negative, indicating that the presence of debt capital reduces value below the unlevered case. This implies an all equity target capital structure, as illustrated in Table 8.2.

Miller's treatment of corporate and personal income taxes has introduced a debate, in the $\lambda = 1$ case, as to whether in practice the tax system could produce a situation where capital structure is irrelevant to an individual company's market valuation. The details of this discussion are beyond the scope of this text but, except in this case, Miller's approach does not produce a plausible (non-extreme) target capital structure.

Risk and debt interest tax shields

One of the weaknesses in Miller's model is the implicit assumption that all fixed interest charges are tax deductible. In any given year, however, this is only possible to the extent that corporate taxes are incurred, which in turn depends on the level of profitability. If operating income becomes relatively low (or negative), the full amount of interest charges (or none at all) may not be capable of being offset against taxes. In practice, operating income varies on a year to year basis, thus the business risk of a company, related to variations in its operating income, will impart riskiness to its debt interest tax shield, and may represent one of the reasons for observing a (non-extreme) target capital structure.

Depreciation tax shields

This may be compounded by other competing tax shields. Recall, in Chapter 6 (Equation 6.10), the concept of a depreciation tax shield. The existence of this type of depreciation, in the form of capital allowances, reduces taxable income and, therefore, may impact on a company's ability to offset debt interest charges, thus further influencing the level of debt that management is willing to employ.

Bankruptcy, financial distress and agency costs

The current state of the debate on the capital structure puzzle suggests that, if there is an optimal capital structure, in the form of an optimal combination of debt and equity, it arises because of a trade-off effect. In particular, the benefits of the debt interest tax shield are eventually offset by the costs associated with expected bankruptcy and financial distress and by general costs associated with the agency problem.

Bankruptcy

Operating income, out of which fixed interest commitments are met, is subject to risk. As the amount of debt in the capital structure is increased, increasing the level of these commitments, there is an increasing probability that some future fall in operating income will be of a sufficient size to cause a company to default on its fixed interest payments. Assuming that this induces bankruptcy, the associated legal and administration fees must be met before any income is distributed to shareholders and bondholders. Since, in a bankruptcy situation, bondholders will exercise their prior claims over equity holders, these costs will represent a drain on the income available to the latter group. In addition, if assets on liquidation realise less than their economic value, by being sold at distress prices in secondhand markets, equity holders will be further penalised.

Consequently, as the amount of debt in the capital structure increases, the probability of bankruptcy will increase and equity holders will require compensation for the expected costs of bankruptcy, by raising their required rates of return. Also, to the extent that debtholders believe that high levels of leverage will jeopardise their chances of receiving the full market value of their debt, on liquidation, they too will raise their required rates of return.[9] This adds a further dimension to financial risk.

In this way, a target capital structure of less than 100% debt financing will emerge. Empirical studies have shown, however, that the costs of bankruptcy are relatively small at, on average, around 3% of a company's value. Consequently, the effect of these costs on the debt interest tax shield may in practice be insignificant. It is the indirect costs associated with the probability of financial distress which are argued to be much more significant.

Financial distress

Companies sometimes go through a period of persistent financial distress. In such a situation they can experience difficulties in adequately synchronising their cash inflows and outflows; difficulties in paying their input suppliers; and come close to not meeting their fixed interest obligations. While financial distress may be resolved by reorganising and restructuring operations (and possibly through some form of refinancing), the probability of financial distress occurring is obviously closely associated with the probability of bankruptcy, and may eventually result in this outcome.

Once it becomes apparent to employees, input suppliers and customers that a company is in, or is entering into, a period of financial distress, costs will be incurred. As the probability of financial distress increases with financial leverage, the expected costs of financial distress increase and erode corporate tax shield benefits. Some of the factors producing financial distress costs are:

- a fall in sales, arising from customers' concerns about a company's ability to maintain the quality of its products, spare parts and service 'back-up';
- production problems caused by increased risk surrounding the supply of raw

materials, since suppliers may withdraw credit terms and require cash on delivery (further complicating the timing of a company's cash flows);
- a loss of efficiency resulting from an exit of key management and technical personnel, motivated by job security fears;
- aggravated financial distress arising from difficulties with capital suppliers, especially banks, who may curtail overdraft facilities and general back-up lines of credit; and
- underinvestment resulting from the rejection of projects with positive NPVs which do not generate positive net cash flows in the short run and would, therefore, if accepted, further complicate financial distress.

Agency costs of debt

Financial distress is closely bound up with the agency problem and the costs incurred in attempting to resolve it. On the assumption that management act in the interests of shareholders, the agency costs of debt were described in Chapter 3, when the determinants of corporate bond yields were examined. Recall that, because of information asymmetries (management have more information on their company than debtholders), a company can use debt capital, in a period of financial distress, for projects other than those specified when the debt capital is raised. This defines the asset substitution problem, where riskier projects than warranted can be undertaken to the disadvantage of debtholders. If the high-risk projects pay off, the financial distress of the company may be significantly eased, to the benefit of equity holders, but debtholders only receive their fixed interest income. Alternatively, if the projects fail, it is the debtholders who bear the brunt of failure.

The underinvestment problem, described in the last section, may also be reinforced. Companies may reject positive NPV projects which have low risk, independent of the timing of their net cash flows, since in conditions of financial distress the relatively assured pay-offs of low risk projects would largely go to debtholders, at the expense of shareholders.

As explained in Chapter 3, there is a number of responses to this form of the agency problem: monitoring procedures, or a compensatory rise in the required rate of return on debt, and/or restrictive covenants built into loan agreements. All of these responses introduce costs which will be borne, ultimately, by the shareholders of a company. In the case of restrictive covenants, for example, while these help restrict a rise in the cost of debt capital, they introduce indirect costs in terms of limits on a company's financing flexibility. Indeed, where restrictive covenants involve pledging tangible assets as collateral, these in themselves may physically limit the debt financing capacity of a company to some proportion of its existing tangible asset base.

In essence, therefore, as financial leverage increases above a low to moderate level, the agency costs of debt come on stream and are argued to rise to a point where they eventually cancel the benefits of the debt interest tax shield.

Agency costs and equity

Agency costs are not restricted to debt; they can arise in respect of the relationship between management and shareholders where, because of the divorce of ownership from control, the objectives of these two groups can diverge. Once again, a core issue is the problem of asymmetric information, with the shareholders needing to monitor management. An interesting argument can be put forward in these circumstances: that issuing new debt (increasing financial leverage) can reduce some of these agency costs. The argument is that, since potential bond subscribers will analyse the company to determine if their required rate of return matches the prospective rate offered on the new debt issue, shareholders are provided with a 'free' monitoring service. Assuming management recognise this agency cost of equity and make new debt issues, then they are effectively signalling information to the market, other things being equal, that they believe their company's future prospects to be sound. Consequently, an increase in leverage, other things being equal, may have the effect of increasing a company's overall market value.

The discipline that debt provides has been further explored by Jensen (1989) and more recently Ofek (1993). They argue that high leverage can provide benefits in the dynamic sense that companies with high debt:equity ratios may respond more quickly to the development of adverse performance than companies with low debt:equity ratios. Ofek, for example, argues that:

> ... a choice of high leverage during normal operations ... appears to induce a firm to respond operationally and financially to adversity after a short period of poor performance, helping to avoid lengthy periods of losses with no response. The existence of debt in the capital structure may thus help to preserve the firms going concern value.

The above, however, are still considered to be insufficient to outweigh the agency costs of debt, so that, in net terms, agency costs reduce the benefits of the debt interest tax shield.

An optimal capital structure

Summarising the above discussion, the presence of bankruptcy, financial distress and net agency costs are likely to begin to offset the benefits of the debt interest tax shield, as financial leverage rises above some specific level. Eventually this will induce a fall in the total market value of a company. This is demonstrated in Figure 8.5, relative to the MM debt and corporate taxes valuation schedule. In other words, the MM case, in present value (PV) terms, is that:

$$V_L = V_u + PV\left(\begin{array}{c} \text{Tax} \\ \text{Shield} \end{array}\right) \qquad (8.16)$$

A major strand of the Modernist view is that:

$$V_L^* = V_u + PV\left(\begin{array}{c} \text{Tax} \\ \text{Shield} \end{array}\right) - PV\left(\begin{array}{c} \text{Bankruptcy} \\ \text{Costs} \end{array}\right) - PV\left(\begin{array}{c} \text{Financial} \\ \text{Distress} \\ \text{Costs} \end{array}\right)$$

$$- PV\left(\begin{array}{c} \text{Net} \\ \text{Agency} \\ \text{Costs} \end{array}\right) \qquad (8.17)$$

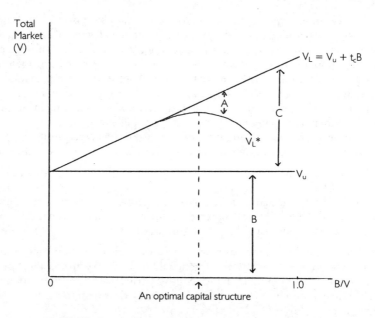

A: PV of Bankruptcy, Financial Distress and Net Agency Costs
B: PV of All Equity Financed (Unlevered) Company
C: PV of Debt Interest Tax Shield

Figure 8.5   *Market value with bankruptcy, financial distress and agency costs*

Myers' Pecking Order Model

Note that financial distress and agency costs, as factors creating an optimal capital structure, are not the only element in the Modernist view. An alternative argument is contained in Myers' Pecking Order Theory which implies that there is no optimal capital structure as such. Here, what appears to be an empirically observed optimal capital structure results from a company's cumulative requirement for external financing, after it has exhausted its preferences for internal financing.

Myers' model views retained earnings as management's first preference for financing investment projects. Retained earnings and dividends constitute a company's earnings after interest and taxes, EAIT. Given that retained earnings are jointly determined with a company's payout policy and that management aim for a target dividend payout ratio that remains relatively stable, there is a limit, at each level of EAIT, to the amount of retained earnings that can be used in any one year. (Dividend payout policy is discussed in the next chapter.)

In these circumstances the second preference in the pecking order will be debt capital, followed by external new equity issues. Thus a company's debt:equity ratio, at a given point in time, does not represent a conscious effort to meet a target capital structure but is simply the result of past excursions into the capital markets, when the first preference for retained earnings has been exhausted.

The Pecking Order Model can be explained in terms of management's desire to avoid both the financial distress and the implied monitoring and issue costs which would arise from external financing. Information asymmetries and information signalling also enter the explanation. If, for example, management have superior information on good investment projects and believe that their company's share price is undervalued in respect of these prospects, they will exhibit a preference for debt over equity when external finance is required. They will not want to raise new equity at an undervalued price. In these circumstances the market will interpret an increase in financial leverage as positive evidence of the company's prospects.

An ongoing debate

Empirical evidence on capital structure indicates that debt:equity ratios vary across industries and between firms within given industries. The capital structure puzzle arises because the distribution of debt:equity ratios could occur randomly, if capital structure is irrelevant; or be produced by each company's cumulative requirement for external financing, the Pecking Order Model; or result from each company's exposure to financial distress and agency costs; or be due to other complex tax factors. It is because there are elements in each of these approaches which can partially explain the debt:equity distribution, that the puzzle remains unresolved and is likely to provide continuing research stimulus in corporate finance.

Does the debate matter?

The answer to this question is: yes it does. If management believe that there is an optimal capital structure, they will devote resources to attempting to discover the appropriate debt:equity ratio for their own company and to monitoring and adjusting actual financial leverage, in relation to the target thus established.

The reasons for an optimal capital structure are ultimately based on imperfections in capital markets. To the extent that the capital structure debate can clarify which of these imperfections are significant, there is a rationale for government policy to attempt to ensure that these imperfections are minimised and capital market efficiency promoted.

Summary

The present chapter has attempted to present the main elements which have informed the capital structure, valuation debate over the past three decades – beginning with MM's irrelevancy propositions and ending with the contribution that agency theory and Myers' Pecking Order Model have made.

MM's capital structure irrelevancy propositions are effectively about the conservation of value in the face of capital structure changes. In their model, the value of a company depends on the expected net cash flows from its investments and the average cost of financing these investments. Value has nothing to do with how the net cash flows are distributed between interest income and dividend income. From a risk perspective, financial leverage partitions risk between corporate bondholders and equity holders but, by not affecting the total risk of a company's assets, once again leads to the conservation of value. Thus the average cost of capital must be independent of capital structure.

The presence of corporate income taxes clearly introduces advantages to debt financing. That this does not lead, on average, to companies exhibiting extremely high financial leverage ratios, suggests that, as leverage rises, there are costs, and non-debt tax shields, which eventually outweigh corporate tax shield benefits. Given the ambiguity surrounding the role of personal income taxes as a counter-balancing effect, most of the emphasis in the Modernist view is on the role of financial distress and agency costs as factors eroding corporate tax shield benefits and inducing an optimal leverage ratio.

This review of the capital structure, valuation debate presents another example of how financial economic models can be used to isolate and explain, under idealised conditions, some of the main factors which form part of a financial puzzle. By doing so, these models provide a systematic framework within which a problem can be examined; but it is only a framework and is not intended to produce hard and fast solutions in practical situations. Without doubt, the capital structure, valuation debate will remain a centrepiece of future research in corporate finance. New ways of examining the puzzle will be developed which further enrich and extend this framework.

Some of the issues raised in this chapter are taken up again, in Chapter 10, when the inter-relationships between investment and financing decisions are examined. Here empirical aspects of the capital structure puzzle are touched upon, in the context of the impact that investments in tangible and intangible assets can have on financial leverage. Investments in intangible assets tend to increase financial distress and agency costs; however, to the extent that these intangible assets are in the form of reputational assets (brand names and R and D), information signalling models suggest that these costs can be reduced, so increasing a company's debt financing capacity. Other aspects of the agency problem are explored in Chapter 14, when investment and financing issues, peculiar to small business entrepreneurs, are explored.

Before this, the next chapter presents another of the central controversies in corporate finance: the dividend puzzle or dividend, valuation debate. It is probably in this area that the role of information signalling can be best understood. Yes, you've guessed it, it's Miller and Modigliani again!

Questions

1 A company has an annual operating income of $Y = £1m$, in perpetuity, and a total market value of $V = £15m$. The market value of its perpetual debt is $B = £5m$, at $r_d = 3\%$. There are no taxes and all earnings after interest charges are paid out as dividends.
   a) Calculate the company's weighted average cost of capital.
   b) Assume that financial leverage changes to $B/V = 0.5$. Find the market value of the company under the Traditionalist approach.

c) Assuming that financial leverage changes to $B/V = 0.5$, find the market value of the company under the MM approach. What does this imply about the cost of equity capital?

2 Assume that a company becomes subject to a corporate tax rate of $t_c = 40\%$ and that the MM Debt and Taxes Model applies. The market value of debt is $B = £10m$, at $r_d = 5\%$. $Y = £2m$ and the equity capitalisation rate is $r_e^* = 15\%$.
   a) Find the company's annual interest tax shield and the present value of this tax shield.
   b) Find the total market value of the company.
   c) What is the target capital structure which would maximise the company's total market value?

3 Each £1 of equity income that an investor receives is composed of 70p in dividends and 30p in capital gains. The investor faces a capital gains tax of $t_g = 15\%$ and a personal tax rate of $t_p = 30\%$.
   a) Explain the concept of the effective tax rate on equity income.
   b) Find the effective tax rate on equity income, t_{ef}, in this case.

4 A company, without debt in its capital structure, has a market value of $V_u = £50m$. The company is considering changing its capital structure so that it can employ £20m of debt.
   a) State Miller's Valuation Equation.
   b) Apply Miller's Valuation Equation to find the market value of this company, under this new debt policy, when $t_c = 30\%$, $t_{ef} = 25\%$ and $t_p = 15\%$.
   c) Find the total market value of the company when $t_c = 50\%$ and $t_{ef} = t_p = 30\%$. In this situation, what other model would produce Miller's valuation result?

5 What are the main factors which are likely to offset the tax shield benefits of financial leverage and induce an optimal capital structure?

Exercises

1 What do you understand by the concept of the pure equity capitalisation rate?

2 Demonstrate how the CAPM can be used to explain the relationship between financial risk and corporate financial leverage. Illustrate your answer.

3 What are the main factors which are likely to produce financial distress?

Endnotes

1. The terms gearing and leverage are normally used interchangeably as are the ratios: B/S and B/V. Strictly speaking, financial leverage is defined as $FL = B/S$ and financial gearing as $FG = B/V$. Since, however, $V = B + S$,

$$FG = \frac{B}{B+S} = \frac{B/S}{(B/S)+1}, \text{ that is, } FG = \frac{FL}{FL+1}$$

In other words, in financial leverage terms,

$$FL = \frac{FG}{1 - FG}, \text{ that is, } \frac{B}{S} = \frac{B/V}{1 - (B/V)}$$

Note that these market value definitions of financial leverage differ from the accounting book value definition in Chapter 1.

2. In their original paper, MM assumed that companies could be placed into homogeneous risk classes. With the subsequent development of the CAPM, this assumption has become redundant.

3. This is based on the Gordon Growth Model, developed in Chapter 3 where, by Equation 3.3b,

$$P_0 = \frac{d_1}{r_e - g}$$

With zero growth ($g = 0$), a constant annual dividend per share ($d = d_1$), and n shares on issue, this equation is expressed in total equity value terms as:

$$nP_0 = \frac{nd}{r_e}$$

The market value of equity is $S = nP_0$ and the total dividend payout is $D = nd$.

4. The valuation equation specified in Equation 8.2, $V = Y/r_a$, is derived from the weighted average cost of capital formula, in Equation 8.6. Given (from Equation 8.1) that $V = B + S$, Equation 8.6 can be written as

$$r_a = \frac{r_d B}{V} + \frac{r_e S}{V}$$

Since $I = r_d B$ (Equation 8.3b) and $D = r_e S$ (rearranging Equation 8.5a),

$$r_a = \frac{I}{V} + \frac{D}{V} = \frac{I + D}{V}$$

With total interest and dividend payments constituting operating income, that is $I + D = Y$:

$$r_a = \frac{Y}{V}$$

hence

$$V = \frac{Y}{r_a}$$

5. Given Equation 8.6

$$r_a = r_d \left[\frac{B}{S + B} \right] + r_e \left[\frac{S}{S + B} \right]$$

Multiply the whole equation by $(S + B)/S$, therefore,

$$r_a \left[\frac{S + B}{S} \right] = r_d \frac{B}{S} + r_e$$

and

$$r_e = r_a \left[1 + \frac{B}{S} \right] - r_d \frac{B}{S}$$

$$= r_a + r_a \frac{B}{S} - r_d \frac{B}{S}$$

$$= r_a + (r_a - r_d) \frac{B}{S}$$

6. The term Traditionalist is used because the idea that there is an optimal capital structure, minimising the average cost of capital and maximising total market value, represented the consensus view, although generally ill defined, before MM's seminal paper. This paper 'forced' the Traditionalists to think about their position in a more formal and systematic way.

7. To illustrate, take a simple example where there is no risk so that the rates of return on debt and equity are equal at 15%. Next, introduce taxes and assume $t_{ef} = 26\%$. The after-tax rate of return on equity is:

$$r_e(1 - t_{ef}) = (.15)(1 - .26) = 0.111 \text{ or } 11.1\%$$

With $t_p = 30\%$, the after-tax rate of return on debt is

$$r_d(1 - t_p) = (.15)(1 - .30) = 0.105 \text{ or } 10.5\%$$

To make the after-tax rate of return on debt equal to the after-tax rate of return on equity, other things being equal, management would have to raise the pre-tax rate of return on debt to:

$$r_d{}^* = (0.111)/(1 - .30) = 0.1586 \text{ or } 15.86\%$$

8. Assuming $0 < t_c < 100\%$, then $0 < \lambda < 1$ and, therefore, $1 - \lambda > 0$.

9. The expected costs of bankruptcy are defined as the estimated level of these costs, in present value terms, times the probability of bankruptcy. Consider a company where $V_u = £10.75m$ and $t_c = 35\%$. The company has a market value of debt of $B = £5m$. Thus,

$$V_L = £10.75m + 0.35(£5m) = £10.75m + £1.75m = £12.5m$$

At this leverage ratio, $B/V = £5m/£12.5m = 0.4$, the probability of bankruptcy, P_b, is assumed to have been estimated at 0.1. The present value of the estimated bankruptcy costs, assumed constant, is £5.6m. Thus the expected costs are $(.1)(£5.6m) = £0.56m$. These are well below the present value of the debt interest tax shield of $t_cB = £1.75m$. $B/V = 0.4$ is, therefore, not an optimal capital structure. Assume B is increased to £8m, thus

$$V_L = £10.75m + 0.35(£8m) = £10.75m + £2.8m = £13.55m$$

At this level of leverage, where $B/V = £8m/£13.55m = 0.59$, assume that P_b rises to 0.5. The expected costs of bankruptcy are now: $(0.5)(£5.6m) = £2.8m$. These expected costs match the present value of the tax shield $(t_cB = £2.8m)$. Therefore, $B/V = 0.59$ is the optimal capital structure.

Appendix 8.1 Valuation: net income and net operating income methods

The two approaches described in the example at the beginning of this chapter are in fact defining Durand's (1952) Net Income (NI) and Net Operating Income (NOI) methods of valuation. MM's paper accepts the Net Operating Income approach and provides its theoretical rationale.

Under the NI approach, a company is valued by capitalising its net income after interest payments (given a constant r_d and r_e). To see this, assume an all equity financed company with $Y = £0.8m$ and $r_e = 10\%$. Therefore, with $NI = Y$

$$S_u = £0.8m/.10 = £8m$$

S_u is the value of equity in the unlevered company, hence $V_u = S_u$. Next, consider £4m of debt in the capital structure at $r_d = 5\%$. The interest charge is $0.05(£4m) = £0.2m$, leaving

$$NI = £0.8m - £0.2m = £0.6m$$

Thus the market value of equity in the levered company, S_L, is now,

$$S_L = £0.6m/.10 = £6m$$

and the total market value, $V_L = S_L + B$, is increased from £8m to £10m, that is:

$$V_L = £6m + £4m = £10m$$

Under the alternative Net Operating Income approach, the company is valued by capitalising its operating income or earnings before interest charges (not net of interest charges). Using the above example, in the all equity case, as under the NI approach,

$$V_u = S_u = £0.8m/.10 = £8m$$

Since NOI is defined to include interest charges it must be independent of capital structure, as must the discount rate at which it is capitalised. Thus when £4m of debt is introduced into the capital structure, total market value remains constant at:

$$V_L = £0.8/.10 = £8m$$

Given $B = £4m$, $S_L = V_L - B$, that is, $S_L = £8m - £4m = £4m$.

Superficially, this latter approach can seem unconvincing when compared to the Net Income approach. Given the arbitrage rationale that MM developed under their assumptions, the Net Operating Income approach can be the only valid approach to valuation. Arbitrage is explained in the main body of the chapter, with an example of how arbitrage operates being given in Appendix 8.2.

Appendix 8.2 The arbitrage process

To understand the arbitrage process, consider the two companies profiled in Table A8.2.1. Both have the same operating income, $Y = £1m$, and are identical in all respects except that company U is all equity financed, and hence unlevered (its $B/V = 0$), while company L has both debt and equity in its capital structure. Company L's market value is composed of 25% debt, at $r_d = 6\%$, which has a market value of $B = £2m$. Assume that, for some reason, the total market values of the two companies diverge, with $V_u = £7m$ and $V_L = £8m$. Since company U is unlevered, the market value of its equity, S_u, is equal to its total market value:

$$S_u = V_u = £7m$$

For the levered company:

$$S_L = V_L - B = £8m - £2m = £6m$$

Assume that you have invested only in the levered company, owning 10% of its equity. Given the difference in the market values, you are considering whether it would be worth while switching your investment from company L to company U.

Table A8.2.1: Levered and unlevered company profiles

	Company U £m	Company L £m
Operating Income (Y)	1.00	1.00
Market Value of Debt (B)		2.00
Debt Interest Rate (r_d)		6%
Debt Interest Charge:		
$r_d B$		0.12
Income paid out:		
$D = Y - r_d B$	1.00	0.88
Total Market Value (V)	7.00	8.00
Market Value of Equity:		
$S = V - B$	7.00	6.00

To determine this, you need to compare the annual income from your current investment with that on an alternative investment in the unlevered company.

In the case of the levered company, Table A8.2.1 indicates that its debt interest charge is £0.12m, leaving a total annual dividend payout of £0.88m. Since you own 10% of its equity, your annual income, INC_L, is:

$$INC_L = 0.10(£0.88m) = £0.088m$$

Putting this in the form of a general equation, with α representing the proportion of your investment:

$$INC_L = \alpha(Y - r_d B) \tag{8.2.1}$$

If you decide to switch investments, you will sell your shares in the levered company and invest in the same proportion, $\alpha = 10\%$, in the unlevered company. Given that $S_L = £6m$, you would raise £0.6m on the sale of these shares, but with $S_u = £7m$ the cost of purchasing 10% of company U is £0.7m. This implies a shortage of personal capital of £0.1m. Under the perfect capital market assumption, however, you can borrow these funds at the same rate as the corporate sector, $r_d = 6\%$, and produce 'home-made' leverage. In effect your personal borrowing would be £0.1m and the resulting personal interest cost $0.06(£0.1m) = £0.006m$. Generalising,

$$Personal\ Borrowing = \alpha(S_u - S_L) \tag{8.2.2}$$

and

$$Personal\ Interest\ Costs = \alpha(S_u - S_L)r_d \tag{8.2.2a}$$

What income would you derive from investing in the unlevered company? Since it is all equity financed, all of its operating income is paid out as dividends, consequently you would initially receive $0.10(£1m) = £0.1m$; but you must deduct the interest cost of your personal borrowings. This would give an annual income from company U of

$$INC_u = £0.1m - £0.006m = £0.094m$$

or in general terms

$$INC_u = \alpha Y - \alpha(S_u - S_L)r_d \qquad (8.2.3)$$

Now look at the difference between the two incomes, $INC_u - INC_L$, to determine whether or not it would be worth switching investments, from the equity in the levered company to the equity in the unlevered company. Subtracting Equation 8.2.1 from Equation 8.2.3,

$$INC_u - INC_L = £0.094m - £0.088m = £0.006m$$

Since this differential is positive and does not result from any extra risk, you, as a rational investor, would make the switch. The fact that you can do so is the result of your ability to substitute, at no extra cost, personal leverage for corporate leverage.

In terms of a generalisation, the subtraction of Equation 8.2.1 from Equation 8.2.3 produces the result:

$$INC_u - INC_L = \alpha(V_L - V_u)r_d \qquad (8.2.4)$$

(This is explained at the end of this appendix.)
Consequently, when the market value of the levered company exceeds the market value of the unlevered company ($V_L > V_u$), $Y_u - Y_L > 0$ and profitable arbitrage opportunities exist. All rational investors, in a perfect capital market with costless information, will recognise this and begin to switch investments from the levered company to the unlevered company. (If $V_u > V_L$, the switch would be in the opposite direction, with investors engaging in personal lending.)

The switch away from the levered company causes a reduced demand for its shares and the market value of its equity, S_L, to fall. The market value of company L's debt being unaffected, the result must be a fall in V_L. On the other hand, the preference for equity in the unlevered company would cause S_u to rise and hence V_u to increase, since $V_u = S_u$. Through this process, V_u will become equal to V_L. At this point all arbitrage opportunities will be exhausted, since by Equation 8.2.4

$$INC_u - INC_L = 0$$

and there will be no further incentive to switch investments.

Finally, with $V_L = V_u$ and operating income being identical in both companies,

$$V_L = V_u = \frac{Y}{r_a} \qquad (8.2.5)$$

implying that the average cost of capital is independent of capital structure.

Deriving Equation 8.2.4

From Equation 8.2.3

$$INC_u = \alpha Y - \alpha(S_u - S_L)r_d$$

From Equation 8.2.1

$$INC_L = \alpha(Y - r_d B) = \alpha Y - \alpha r_d B$$

Subtracting Equation 8.2.1 from Equation 8.2.3:

$$INC_u - INC_L = -\alpha(S_u - S_L)r_d + \alpha r_d B$$

Substituting for $S_u = V_u$ and $S_L = V_L - B$,

$$INC_u - INC_L = -\alpha(V_u - V_L + B)r_d + \alpha r_d B$$
$$= \alpha(-V_u + V_L - B)r_d + \alpha r_d B$$
$$= \alpha(V_L - V_u) - \alpha r_d B + \alpha r_d B$$
$$= \alpha(V_L - V_u)$$

Therefore if $V_L > V_u$, $INC_u - INC_L > 0$; but when $V_L = V_u$, $INC_u - INC_L = 0$.

References

Allen, D., 'The Pecking Order Hypothesis: Australian Evidence', Applied Financial Economics, 1993

Bank of England, 'Personal and Corporate Sector Debt', Quarterly Bulletin, 1994

Constanias, R., 'Bankruptcy Risk and Optimal Capital Structure', Journal of Finance, 1983

De Angelo, H. and R.W. Masulis, 'Optimal Capital Structure under Corporate and Personal Taxation', Journal of Financial Economics, 1980

Durand, D., 'Cost of Debt and Equity Funds for Business: Trends and Problems of Measurement', Conference on Research in Business Finance, National Bureau of Economic Research, New York, 1952

Durand, D., 'The Cost of Capital, Corporation Finance and the Theory of Investment': Comment, American Economic Review, 1959

Financial Management, 'Special Issue on Financial Distress', 1993

Haugen, R.A. and L.W. Senbert, 'Corporate Finance and Taxes: A Review', Financial Management, 1986

Jensen, M.C., 'Active Investors, LBO's and Privatisation of Bankruptcy', Journal of Applied Corporate Finance, 1989

Jensen, M.C. and W. Meckling, 'Theory of the Firm: Management Behaviour, Agency Costs and Ownership Structure', Journal of Financial Economics, 1976

Jensen, M.C. and C.W. Smith, 'Stockholder, Manager and Creditor Interests: Applications of Agency Theory', in E.I. Altman and M.G. Subrahmanyam (Eds.), Recent Advances in Corporate Finance, Homewood, Ill., Irwin, 1985

Leibowitz, L., S. Kogelman, and E. Lindenberg, 'A Short-fall Approach to the Creditor's Decision: How Much Leverage Can a Firm Support?' Financial Analysts Journal, 1990

Masulis, R.W. The Debt/Equity Choice, Cambridge, Mass., Ballinger, 1988

Miller, M.H., 'Debt and Taxes', Journal of Finance, 1977

Modigliani, F. and M.H. Miller, 'The Cost of Capital, Corporation Finance and the Theory of Investment', American Economic Review, 1958

Modigliani, F. and M.H. Miller, 'Taxes and the Cost of Capital: A Correction', American Economic Review, 1963

Myers, S.C., 'The Capital Structure Puzzle', Journal of Finance, 1984

Myers, S.C., 'The Search for Optimal Capital Structure', in J.M. Stern and D.H. Chew (Eds.), The Revolution in Corporate Finance, Oxford, Blackwell, 1992

Ofek, E., 'Capital Structure and Firm Response to Poor Performance', Journal of Financial Economics, 1993

9 Dividends and valuation

Introduction

The previous chapter has explored the controversy surrounding the capital structure decision. In this chapter another of the ongoing debates in corporate finance is examined: the dividend puzzle which addresses the issue of whether or not the dividend payout policy which management adopts has an effect on the market value of a company.

Once again, a number of simplifying assumptions are made in order to focus on the main factors in the dividend, valuation relationship. In particular, the analysis has tended to be carried out using all equity financing models. While financial leverage is, therefore, not explicitly considered, there is an implicit sense in which it is always present. Recall from Chapters 3 and 7 that retained earnings constitute one of the components of a company's capital structure. As retained earnings represent what remains of operating income, after interest and tax payments have been made and after dividends have been distributed to shareholders, dividends are closely associated with the capital structure decision. Assuming, however, that MM's capital structure irrelevancy propositions hold, the inclusion of debt capital does not influence the effect that dividends might, or might not, have on valuation.

There are two ways of thinking about the dividend policy issue. In one sense it is about whether or not the dividend payout ratio is a passive or an active decision variable. If it is a passive one, dividends are determined residually after a company has determined the amount of earnings, after interest and taxes (EAIT) it wishes to retain for investment purposes. In other words, focus is on the retention ratio

$$b = \frac{\text{Retained Earnings}}{\text{EAIT}}$$

with the payout ratio

$$1 - b = \frac{\text{Total Dividends}}{\text{EAIT}}$$

determined passively. If it is the payout ratio which is the active decision variable, then it is retained earnings which are determined residually, after management has chosen the value of $1 - b$ which they believe it is necessary to target in order to maximise market value.

Another way of looking at the dividend decision is in terms of the conservation of value principle. Under the MM capital structure irrelevancy propositions, how operating income is partitioned between debt interest income and equity income has no effect on a company's total market value. The analogy, in the dividend debate, is the Earnings Theorists' position that equity holders, who can receive equity income in any combination of dividends and capital gains, are concerned only with the total EAIT which are available to them. How these earnings are apportioned between dividends and capital gains has no effect on the total value of equity, thus dividend policy is irrelevant. The Dividend Theorists, or what is sometimes referred to as the Traditionalists, disagree with this and support the Theory of the Dividend Effect. The Dividend Theorists argue that the way shareholders receive their equity income does matter and that, consequently, dividend policy is relevant to valuation.

The main part of this chapter begins by reviewing the dividend valuation model in the light of the dividend controversy. This is followed by a presentation of Miller and Modigliani's (MM) dividend irrelevancy proposition. As a base case this MM model specifies the ideal conditions under which dividend policy is a passive residual, having no effect on valuation.

The rest of the chapter focuses on identifying which, if any, of the idealised conditions, when violated, produces a dividend effect. After looking at some of the Traditionalist arguments on risk and outlining some of the evidence on dividend policy in practice, the main potential source of a dividend effect, capital market imperfections, is examined. This Modernist position views agency costs, and in particular information asymmetries and signalling, as the most likely explanations for an observed relationship between share prices and dividend payouts. The dividend puzzle remains unresolved, however, since there is disagreement over whether the observed relationship is fundamentally determined by other, non-dividend related, factors.

The dividend valuation model

The idea of a dividend controversy can initially appear rather odd given, via the dividend valuation model, the fundamental role that dividends per share play in determining a share's price. Recall from Chapter 3 (Equation 3.3) that a share's price is equal to the discounted sum of the future series of expected dividends per share:

$$P_0 = \frac{d_1}{1 + r_e} + \frac{d_2}{(1 + r_e)^2} + \cdots + \frac{d_n}{(1 + r_e)^n} + \cdots \qquad (9.1)$$

In the dividend controversy the full validity of this model is accepted. What is questioned, however, is the nature of the timing of the dividend payments, that is, whether or not a redistribution of dividends over time affects P_0.

To understand what is meant by this, consider a situation where a company decides not to pay out the dividend per share, d_1, expected in year one. Instead, it decides to retain d_1 and invest it for one year only, at a rate of return k. In year two it pays out d_1, together with the return on this one-year investment, kd_1. As a result the total year two dividend payment is equal to d_2, as normally expected, plus $d_1(1 + k)$, and Equation 9.1 becomes:

$$P_0' = \frac{d_2}{(1 + r_e)^2} + \frac{d_1(1 + k)}{(1 + r_e)^2} + \cdots + \frac{d_n}{(1 + r_e)^n} + \cdots \qquad (9.1a)$$

The change in the current share price, $\Delta P_0 = P_0' - P_0$, resulting from this change in the timing of the dividend payout, is determined by subtracting Equation 9.1 from Equation 9.1a.

Most of the terms in the two equations cancel, leaving[1]

$$\Delta P_0 = \frac{d_1(1 + k)}{(1 + r_e)^2} - \frac{d_1}{1 + r_e}$$

$$= \frac{d_1}{(1 + r_e)^2}(k - r_e) \qquad\qquad (9.1b)$$

From Equation 9.1b it appears that the timing of the dividend payout does effect a change in share price, in all but the special case where $k = r_e$.

Consider an example where the year one dividend is expected to be $d_1 = 40p$, and where $r_e = 12\%$. If $k = 20\%$, the rate of return from investing the postponed dividend exceeds the equity cost of capital and ΔP_0 is positive, implying a rise in the share price:

$$\Delta P_0 = \frac{0.40}{(1.12)^2}(.20 - .12) = 2.55p$$

If $k = 6\%$, with $k < r_e$, ΔP_0 is negative, implying a fall in the share price:

$$\Delta P_0 = \frac{0.40}{(1.12)^2}(.06 - .12) = -1.91p$$

Only in the case where $k = r_e$ does $\Delta P_0 = 0$. In other words, dividend payout policy appears irrelevant when the rate of return at which the postponed dividend is invested is equal to the equity capitalisation rate.

It is this special case, however, which gives a clue to the dividend irrelevancy argument. In the former two cases it is not the postponement of the dividend payment in itself which produces the share price change but the fact that d_1 is being invested at different rates of return, which diverge from r_e.

Assuming an all equity financing model with, for the moment, sufficient retained earnings to cover all profitable investments, the special case illustrates a general principle: that providing a company's investment policy is optimal, dividend policy is irrelevant. An optimal investment position is achieved where earnings are retained up to the point where the marginal rate of return on investment (the rate of return on the last £ of investment undertaken) is equal to the shareholders' required rate of return. It is when this position is achieved that the dividend payout ratio is determined as a residual.

This investment argument becomes clearer, from a different angle, when the equity valuation analysis in Chapter 3 is considered. There, besides valuing shares in terms of a dividend model, two alternative investment opportunities approaches (Solomon's and MM's), based on retained earnings, were presented. These were shown to be identical to the dividend valuation model. Given, however, the alternative assumptions about the amount of earnings which were retained for investment purposes,[2] at attractive rates of return ($k > r_e$), a different dividend income stream was generated in each investment opportunities approach, creating a different share price. It may appear, therefore, that different streams of dividend payouts produce different share prices but this will be because they are based on different investment policies.

The Miller–Modigliani model

MM, in another seminal paper published in 1961, neutralised the investment effect to demonstrate that dividends in themselves do not affect value. They assume that an all equity financed company's investment policy is given and constituted by an investment outlay, in year t, of £I_t which produces an operating profit of π_t. (There is no debt or taxes so all operating income is available to shareholders.) As a base case model the assumption is made that capital markets are perfect with all that this implies, from the previous chapter, about the absence of transactions costs and other market imperfections. In addition, investors operate under conditions of certainty, so that any risk impact is avoided, and are rational. Under the rationality assumption, investors are indifferent to the form in which they receive their equity income; that is, to whether they receive £1 of income in terms of dividends or capital gains.

The MM irrelevancy model is developed in full for two reasons. First, it is only by considering the model in detail that the reason for the dividend decision not affecting the market value of a company becomes clear. Second, the model demonstrates, in an interesting way, the relationship between internal and external equity financing and shows how dividend policy can be formulated as a trade-off between the two.

Formulating the dividend decision

MM formulate the dividend decision by assuming that there are only two ways of financing investment: internally, through retained earnings, and externally, through a new issue of shares. Retained earnings are equal to the difference between operating profits π_t, and the total dividend payout D_t paid at the end of period t, that is, $\pi_t - D_t$.

At the end of the current year a company has to decide how to finance its given investment I_t. Given π_t, the decision on dividend payout determines retained earnings. Consequently, any shortfall between the given investment outlay and the amount of earnings retention, determines the size of the new equity issue at the end of year t, or equivalently, at the beginning of year t + 1. This new equity financing, NE_{t+1}, is:

$$NE_{t+1} = I_t - (\pi_t - D_t) \tag{9.2}$$

Consider, for example, a company with I_t = £10m and π_t = £6m. If it decides to pay out D_t = £2m, its retained earnings are £4m and it needs to raise £6m from a new issue of shares:

$$NE_{t+1} = £10m - (£6m - £2m) = £6m$$

In this way dividend policy is expressed in terms of the substitution of retained earnings for new equity issues and vice versa. A rise in dividends is accompanied by a rise in new issues to compensate for the fall in retained earnings. A fall in dividends is accompanied by a fall in new issues which, in turn, is compensated for by a rise in retained earnings.

Existing and new shareholders

In a slightly inexact sense, there are two sets of shareholders being identified. One set represents the existing, or 'original', shareholders[3] who receive all the current dividends before a new issue of shares is made. The second represents the additional set of shareholders when the new issue is made.

It is the current market value of equity, V_t, which is to be determined, that is the value before new shareholders are brought in. When, however, new shareholders are brought in, at the beginning of period $t + 1$, the market value of the company at this point in time, V_{t+1}, will represent total value for both the original and new sets of shareholders. At $t + 1$ the original shareholders' investment value, V^*_{t+1}, will be equal to the total market value, net of the new issue, that is:

$$V^*_{t+1} = V_{t+1} - NE_{t+1} \qquad (9.3)$$

Substituting for NE_{t+1}, from Equation 9.2,

$$V^*_{t+1} = V_{t+1} - I_t + \pi_t - D_t \qquad (9.3a)$$

If, for example, $V_{t+1} = £20.5m$, with a new issue of £6m, the value of equity for the original shareholders (those holding all of the outstanding shares at the beginning of period t) is now, in period $t + 1$:

$$V^*_{t+1} = £20.5m - £6m = £14.5m$$

The fundamental principle of valuation

To determine the current market value of a company, V_t, MM begin with the fundamental principle of valuation where the rate of return on a share, r, is equal to the dividend yield plus the capital gain (or loss). The latter is specified as the change in the share price between the beginning of periods t and $t + 1$. Thus:

$$r = \frac{d_t}{P_t} + \frac{P_{t+1} - P_t}{P_t} \qquad (9.4)$$

Under certainty, and in equilibrium, all investments must earn this rate of return because in the absence of risk all assets are perfect substitutes. (Although this is a single-period valuation concept it applies to a multi-period case, as demonstrated in Chapter 3.)

By rearranging Equation 9.4, the current price of a share is defined as:

$$P_t = \frac{1}{1 + r} [d_t + P_{t+1}] \qquad (9.4a)$$

Assume that there are currently (at the beginning of period t) n shares on issue, held by existing shareholders. The current total market value of equity, $V_t = nP_t$, is defined as:

$$V_t = \frac{1}{1+r}[D_t + V^*_{t+1}] \qquad (9.4b)$$

The total dividend payout to existing shareholders is $D_t = nd_t$ and the market value of the existing shareholders' equity, at the beginning of the next period, is $V^*_{t+1} = nP_{t+1}$.

Substituting Equation 9.3a into Equation 9.4b effectively integrates the dividend policy decision of a company into its valuation equation, and yields:

$$V_t = \frac{1}{1+r}[D_t + V_{t+1} - I_t + \pi_t - D_t] \qquad (9.4c)$$

By doing this, however, the total dividend payment automatically disappears, leaving MM's valuation equation in its final form:

$$V_t = \frac{1}{1+r}[V_{t+1} + \pi_t - I_t] \qquad (9.4d)$$

Explaining the current market value

In other words Equation 9.4d indicates that the current market value of a company is independent of the current dividend decision. The current market value is a function of:

- the discount rate, to which all assets are subject, and which is, therefore, independent of the current dividend payout;
- the level of investment, which is given and determines the level of profits, both of which must therefore be independent of D_t; and
- V_{t+1}, representing the present value, at $t + 1$, of the future prospects of the company, which are independent of current dividends.

If Equation 9.4d is generalised, for the multi-period case, V_{t+1} can be shown to be independent of D_{t+1}; V_{t+2} of D_{t+2}; and so on. The current market value of the company is, therefore, independent of the dividend policy decision, in general.

An illustration

A numerical illustration of the dividend irrelevancy position is provided in Table 9.1. As before, the company under consideration has a fixed investment of £10m, generating a profit of £6m. At the beginning of period t there are n = 10m shares outstanding, defining the holdings of existing shareholders, priced at £1.50. Thus the current market value of the company is £15m. This represents the wealth which existing shareholders have invested in this company. It is independent of the amount of dividends being paid out.

With a total dividend payout of £2m, at the end of period t, and a discount rate of 10%, MM's valuation equation implies that the total value of the company, at the beginning of period t + 1, is:

$$V_{t+1} = £20.5m$$

Table 9.1: Illustrating dividend irrelevancy

$I_t = £10m$, $\pi_t = £6m$ and $r = 10\%$
Beginning year t: n = 10m shares outstanding and $P_t = £1.50$

Current Market Value:

$$V_t = nP_t = (10m)(£1.50) = £15m$$

Dividend Decision[1]:

$$D_t = £2m$$

Required External Equity:

$$NE_{t+1} = I_t - (\pi_t - D_t) = £10m - (£6m - £2m) = £6m$$

MM Valuation Equation:

$$V_t = \frac{1}{1+r}[V_{t+1} + \pi_t - I_t] = \frac{1}{1.10}[V_{t+1} + £6m - £10m]$$

Implies[2]:

$$V_{t+1} = £20.5m$$

Therefore,

$$V^*_{t+1} = V_{t+1} - NE_{t+1} = £20.5m - £6m = £14.5m$$

Share Price: Period t + 1

$$P_{t+1} = V^*_{t+1}/n = £14.5m/10m = £1.45$$

New Share Issue, n*

$$n^* = NE_{t+1}/P_{t+1} = £6m/£1.45 = 4.14m$$

Shares Outstanding: Period t + 1

$$n + n^* = 10m + 4.14m = 14.14m$$

[1] End of period t + 1

[2] $V_t = \frac{1}{1.10}[V_{t+1} + £6m - £10m] = £15m$. Therefore, $1.10(£15m) = V_{t+1} - £4m$.

Implies: $v_{t+1} = 1.10(£15m) + £4m = £16.5m + £4m = £20.5m$

This must be the case if V_t is to be maintained at £15m. With a new equity issue of £6m, needed to cover investment expenditure, the market value of equity for existing shareholders at the beginning of period t + 1 is:

$$V^*_{t+1} = £20.5m - £6m = £14.5m$$

The wealth of existing shareholders has not changed, however, since they have just received a total dividend payment of £2m, taking their wealth at the beginning of t + 1 to £16.5m. Given the discount rate the present value of this wealth is £16.5m/ (1.10) = £15m, which is equal to V_t, the current market value of the company.

The share price and rate of return effects

With new shareholders being brought into the company, but with investment and hence operating profit remaining constant, the earnings of existing shareholders are diluted. This causes the share price to fall between periods t and t + 1. Given that the initial 10m shares are valued at the beginning of period t + 1 at £14.5m, the share price falls from £1.50 to £1.45. This represents a capital loss to the original shareholders of:

$$\frac{P_{t+1} - P_t}{P_t} = \frac{£1.45 - £1.50}{£1.50} \simeq -0.033 \text{ or } -3.3\%$$

This is compensated for, however, by the dividend yield. With $D_t = £2m$ and $n = 10m$, $d_t = 20p$ and the dividend yield is:

$$\frac{d_t}{P_t} = \frac{£.20}{£1.50} \simeq 0.133 \text{ or } 13.3\%$$

This maintains the 10% equilibrium rate of return, to which all assets under certainty are subject, that is:

$$r = \frac{d_t}{P_t} + \frac{P_{t+1} - P_t}{P_t} = 13.3\% - 3.3 = 10.0\%$$

Therefore, from another angle, dividend policy cannot have affected the current total market value of this company's equity, since the rate of return has not changed.

Note that, at any point in time in a perfect capital market, the price of an outstanding share and a new issue, which is just being made, must be equal. As Table 9.1 demonstrates, at the beginning of period $t + 1$, $P_{t+1} = £1.45$. Given the value of the new equity issue which is £6m, this indicates that the number of new shares, n^*, which have to be issued to help finance investment is:

$$n^* = £6m/£1.45 = 4.14m$$

This takes the total number of shares outstanding, at the beginning of period $t + 1$, to $n + n^* = 14.14m$.

The earnings dilution can now be seen. With $n = 10m$, EPS would have been π_t/n_t, that is: £6m/10m = 60p. With the addition of the new shares, EPS have fallen to $\pi_t/(n + n^*)$, that is: £6m/14.14m $\simeq$ 42p.

MM dividend irrelevancy

Summarising, the MM dividend irrelevancy proposition argues that once investment is neutralised, the level of dividends paid will not have an effect on the current market value of a company. By implication, a change in dividend policy will not have an effect either. If, for example, there is an increase in current dividend payments, these will be accompanied by a rise in new share issues. The wealth of existing shareholders will remain unaltered, however, since the increase in dividends is accompanied by a compensating capital loss. In addition, with the increase in new share issues exactly matching the increase in dividends (the reduction in retained earnings) and thus the capital loss to existing shareholders, the total market value of the company must remain unaltered.

Home-made dividends

An astute reader reviewing the above will come to the conclusion that the argument is tautological. The view that V_t is independent of D_t is merely a proposition. By accepting the proposition, all of the above analysis must automatically follow. The proposition needs to be supported by some fundamental mechanism operating in the capital markets.

Recall that in developing the explanation of dividend irrelevancy, it was stated that in a slightly inexact sense two groups of shareholders were being identified: existing shareholders and new shareholders. In a proper sense, of course, there is no distinction to be made between these groups since existing shareholders can purchase part or all of the new issue, if desired. This introduces, in support of MM's dividend irrelevancy proposition, the key concept that shareholders have the ability to freely declare their own home-made dividends.

The idea here is that shareholders require income for consumption purposes. Shareholders who receive insufficient dividends to cover their current consumption needs can, therefore, create their own dividends by selling part of their equity holdings. In a perfect capital market, with no transactions costs or taxes, this occurs at no cost to the shareholder and with no effect on the intrinsic value of a company. Similarly, for shareholders whose dividend payments exceed their current consumption needs, a home-made reduction in dividends is achieved by using the excess dividend income to purchase additional shares.[4]

Home-made dividends being perfect substitutes for corporate dividends, shareholders will not have a preference for particular corporate payout ratios and will not pay a premium for shares in a company which targets a particular payout ratio. The idea of an efficient market is here again. Thus, companies which are identical in all respects except that their payout ratios differ must have identical market values, in equilibrium. The analogy with the capital structure debate, where personal and corporate leverage are perfect substitutes, should be clear.

Traditionalist risk arguments

In the initial response to the MM position, the Dividend Theorists focused on their perception of the weakness of the certainty assumption, arguing that once this was relaxed, dividend policy would have an effect on value. The arguments are quite complex but effectively centre on the view that, in a risky environment, the time pattern of dividend payments will influence the discount rate and, therefore, cause shareholders to place different values on identical companies which have different dividend payout policies.

One way of thinking about the risk issue is to consider the dividend valuation model in Equation 9.1. Dividend Theorists would argue that near-term dividends, those dividends per share paid now or expected over the next two or three years, have less risk attached to them than more distant dividends expected perhaps in nine, ten or eleven years' time. As a result of this 'bird in the hand' argument, the rate at which dividends are discounted is viewed as an increasing function of time, reflecting higher future risk. On this basis, the dividend valuation model becomes:

$$P_0 = \frac{d_1}{1 + r_1} + \frac{d_2}{(1 + r_2)^2} + \cdots + \frac{d_n}{(1 + r_n)^n} + \cdots \qquad (9.5)$$

where $r_1 < r_2 \ldots < r_n < \ldots$ (The e subscript, denoting the equity discount rate, is dropped for simplicity.)

Now consider what is argued to happen if a near-term dividend is reduced to increase retained earnings. Through investment this creates additional future income which will lead to future, but more distant, dividend payments. With the discount rate increasing through time, however, future dividends will be discounted more heavily than near-term dividends. The shift from current dividends to future dividends will therefore cause a change in a company's share price, or so it would seem. Investors are exhibiting a preference for current dividends over future dividends, implying that relatively high current dividend payouts will have positive effects on share prices.

Another way of looking at this risk issue is in terms of the two equity income streams: dividends and capital gains. Since capital gains reflect future, more distant, and therefore more risky prospects, a higher discount rate will be applied to this income stream relative to the dividend income stream. This would appear to be the case according to empirical evidence which tends to suggest that management follow a consistent policy of attempting to provide a relatively stable, and therefore more predictable, pattern of dividends through time. Here investors are not indifferent to the receipt of £1 of income in the form of dividends or capital gains, rather they value £1 of dividends more highly than £1 of capital gains. With a lower discount rate applied to dividends, relative to capital gains, shareholders have a tendency to pay higher prices for shares which have relatively high payout ratios.

Despite the above arguments it has now been generally accepted that, in perfect capital markets, the introduction of risk does not affect MM's dividend irrelevancy position. In the dividend valuation model if the discount rate is an increasing function of time, this will affect future investment policy which, as already explained, is based on the relationship between the rate of return on investment and the cost of capital. Consequently, when risk is introduced, a changing dividend policy may appear to affect share prices when the underlying reason is on the investment side.

The view that investors might have a preference for dividends over capital gains is irrational,[5] given that in a perfect capital market investors can freely declare their own dividends. As MM point out, equity holders are interested in the total earnings stream which is available to them. Once investment is neutralised, the risk of this earnings' stream is given and cannot be affected by how earnings are apportioned between dividends and capital gains.

Imperfect capital markets

If dividend policy is to have an effect on share prices, it will result from factors which inhibit equity holders from freely declaring their own dividends. As this depends on the assumption of perfect capital markets, it is the factors which result in this assumption being broken, and the ways in which the markets deal with these factors, which constitute the source of any potential dividend effect.

The problem, however, is that different imperfections lead to conflicting predictions about the impact of dividend policy on share prices. Some imperfections, as discussed below, signify that a high payout policy will maximise share price. Some other imperfections suggest that a low (or even zero) payout will maximise share price and some suggest dividend irrelevancy.

One of the most interesting arguments, which goes some way to explaining observed dividend policy, is advanced in the context of dividends and information signalling. It is difficult to determine, however, whether the information content of dividend announcements, or dividend signals, implies anything about optimal dividend policy.

Before discussing these Modernist arguments a brief review of the evidence on practical dividend policy is presented. Some of the theoretical implications raised by capital market imperfections can then be related to this empirical evidence in an attempt to gain further insights into the dividend puzzle.

Evidence on dividend payout policy

The classic study on dividend policy was carried out by Lintner (1956), through a survey of managers in the United States. Subsequent studies have tended to generally confirm Lintner's results, one of the most recent being the 3i survey of 178 finance directors in the United Kingdom whose companies each had an annual turnover of more than £200m. Some of the 3i results are reported in the Bank of England Quarterly Review (1993).

A broad summary of the findings of various dividend policy surveys suggests that while there are companies which do not pay dividends, payout ratios are, on average, relatively high. In the US the average payout ratio has been reported to be around 50% of earnings per share (EPS), while in the UK the evidence suggests that the average has been between 30% and 35% during the 1980s.

In terms of managers' attitudes towards dividend policy, three main conclusions can be drawn. Managers appear to:
- have a strong aversion to cutting dividends, that is, to cutting the level of dividends per share;
- follow a stable or consistent payout policy, where a specific payout ratio is formulated as a long-run target; but
- over the short run, make gradual adjustments towards this long-run target.

Adjusting dividends per share
To explain the latter point, consider a company which has a long-run target payout ratio of 0.5, or 50% of EPS. Assume that EPS have been relatively stable over the past four or five years, at 40p, and that the most recent annual dividend per share, d_0, is: $d_0 = (0.5)(£0.4) = 20p$. Next, assume that EPS are expected to rise to 60p in the coming year, suggesting that, with $d_1 = (0.5)(£0.6) = 30p$, dividends per share will rise by 10p. This is unlikely to happen immediately. On the basis of the higher EPS, management will tend to adjust dividends per share gradually, moving possibly one-third of the way (each year) towards a target dividend per share of 30p. Thus, assuming that EPS remain at 60p over the next few years, dividends per share might

be increased annually by between 3p and 4p, providing a dividend income stream over the next three years of, say: $d_1 = 23.5p$, $d_2 = 27p$ and $d_3 = 30p$.

In practical terms EPS will not remain stable on an annual basis. Indeed one argument for observed dividend policy is that with EPS varying considerably from one year to the next, management are induced to formulate consistent dividend policies which provide relatively stable expected dividend streams. This is achieved by a target payout ratio based on management's view of the long-run trend in EPS. With EPS expected to vary in the short run, however, management make partial adjustments towards this trend in order to smooth out short-run variations.

Lest there be some confusion over what is happening to the different ways in which dividends can be measured, the above implies that if EPS are expected to trend upwards in the long run, a long-run upward trend in the level of dividends can be expected. The latter is determined by the long-run target payout ratio. Management, however, have a strong desire to avoid cuts in the level of dividends per share and a desire to stabilise the level of dividend payments, relative to short-run variations in EPS. Thus, while the long-term payout ratio may be relatively stable, the short-run payout ratio can vary considerably.

Transactions costs

When considering imperfections in capital markets, and the effect that these might have on the ability of shareholders to freely declare their own dividends, one of the first limitations is associated with the transactions costs of buying and selling shares. Brokerage fees of between 1% and 2% can be relatively significant, especially for private individuals. How transactions costs affect preferences for dividend payout ratios is hard to determine because, as explained later, the preference depends on investors' current income needs.

Flotation costs

Flotation costs can also impinge on the dividend irrelevancy proposition, inducing a shareholder preference for retained earnings. All other things being equal, a rise in dividends tends to be accompanied by a new share issue to help finance investment. New issues involve underwriting fees and costs associated with advertising and preparing prospectuses. With the available funds raised through new equity financing being net of flotation costs, shareholders may apply a higher required rate of return to companies exhibiting relatively high dividend payouts. Thus, with an implied negative relationship between share prices and payouts, share prices would be maximised by management pursuing relatively high retentions. This is contrary to the empirical evidence, reported above, of relatively high payout ratios.

Dividends and taxes

An important imperfection, which might lead to a preference for low or even zero dividend payout, relates to the taxation system. In the last chapter the concept of an effective tax rate on equity income was introduced. This was determined, in part, by a combination of the personal tax rate t_p, levied on dividend income, and the capital gains tax rate, t_g. If $t_p > t_g$, there will be a preference for receiving income in terms of capital gains, thus encouraging the use of retained earnings for profitable investment opportunities rather than new issues of equity and, hence, high dividend payouts. As explained, even if $t_p = t_g$, there can be a bias against dividends because the realisation of capital gains can be postponed beyond a given year.

One of the problems with attempting to interpret the tax effects is that different investors face different marginal tax rates. There may be investors whose marginal personal tax rates are sufficiently less than their capital gains tax rates, which results in them exhibiting a preference for dividends over capital gains. The tax effects would not operate at all, however, for some large tax-exempt investment institutions who would then be indifferent, other things being equal, to the payout policy of individual companies, thus supporting dividend irrelevancy.

Even in the case of tax-exempt institutions, different tax regimes can cause dividends to have different effects on share prices. The Bank of England (1993), for example, has commented on the increase in dividend payments (paralleled by an increase in share issues) made by UK industrial and commercial companies during the 1980s. The Bank argues that part of the explanation may have been associated with the UK's system of advance corporation tax:[6]

> The rise in the dividend payout ratio may in part reflect the provision for tax-exempt shareholders (including pension funds) to reclaim advance corporation tax on dividends. For companies paying mainstream corporation tax, there is a higher charge on retained than distributed profits. As profitability increased in the 1980s, it is likely that a greater proportion of firms paid mainstream corporation tax, and hence were able to take advantage of the difference in effective tax rates.

That specific tax regimes can have different effects is further demonstrated by Miller and Scholes (1982), who argued that tax laws in the US enabled investors to postpone tax payments through various counterbalancing loan schemes, with interest set against taxes. This lends support to the dividend irrelevancy proposition. The weakness here, however, is that taxes cannot be postponed indefinitely. On the other hand Feldstein and Green (1983), using a portfolio theory based argument, indicate that all companies must pay some dividends, even when there are tax-exempt institutions.

The clientele effect

The dividend irrelevancy position comes to the fore again, in the clientele argument, where individual investors can be viewed as belonging to different groups, or clienteles, defined by their current income needs. Senior citizens, for example, may have a strong preference for current income and hence high dividends; while other groups, in early to mid-career, may have a preference for capital gains and hence low dividend payout. Through the presence of transactions costs impairing investors' abilities to adjust current dividends to current income requirements, each clientele group can be identified with a particular payout ratio.

Management, by targeting a particular long-run payout ratio and stabilising the level of dividend payments (as empirical evidence suggests), can be seen to be targeting a particular clientele of investors. Providing that there is a sufficient range of payout ratios (to cover all clientele groups) and that there is a sufficient number of companies adopting a particular payout ratio (to meet the income needs associated with each group), the dividend policy adopted by individual companies is irrelevant. Only if there is excessive demand for particular payout ratios will a premium be placed on the share prices of companies pursuing these as targets. In such a situation a change in dividend policy will affect share prices.

A tax clientele argument applies when differences in investors' marginal tax rates create different preferences for low (or even zero) and high dividend payouts. In this case, Elton and Gruber (1970) provide evidence that there is a negative relationship between company payout ratios and the tax brackets faced by their investors.

Information signalling

The observation that management follow a consistent dividend policy, combined with a strong aversion to cutting the level of dividends, can also be interpreted in the context of information signalling.

In an early response to MM's dividend irrelevancy proposition, empirical tests were carried out on the effect that equal changes in retentions and dividends had on share prices. The evidence indicated that dividend increases had a much stronger positive effect on share prices than did increases in retained earnings. This suggested that investors placed a higher value on each £1 of dividends, relative to each £1 of retained earnings. In addition to serious doubt being cast on this evidence, because of weaknesses in the testing methodologies which were used, MM argue that it is not dividends in themselves which create relatively strong positive effects on share prices but the information they convey about the overall future performance of a company.

Under the MM Earnings Theorist approach, shareholders are concerned with their overall income stream which includes both dividends and capital gains. As already explained, in the short run, however, EPS can be highly volatile. Recognising this, management are concerned with conveying information to the market about the long-run trend in EPS. By choosing a target dividend payout ratio, based on this trend, any subsequent change in dividends reflects management's perception of how the long-run trend in EPS itself is likely to change. A rise in dividends, therefore, reflects an increase in this long-run trend and it is the latter which causes a share's price to rise.

A cut in dividends will convey negative information to the market on a company's future prospects and, therefore, cause a fall in its share price. Given that management wish to avoid conveying negative information, which could of course weaken their own positions, there is a strong aversion to responding to short-term difficulties by cutting the level of dividend payments in any given year. The market will interpret such a cut, not as a response to temporary difficulties, but as indicating that such difficulties are likely to persist.

This information signalling view is confirmed in the recent 3i survey of UK companies, where over 55% of finance directors agreed with the statement[7] that 'a cut in dividend payout sends adverse signals to markets and should be avoided'. Indeed there is other evidence which suggests that some companies will attempt to maintain their levels of dividend payments in the short run, even if dividends per share exceed EPS.

Dividends appear, therefore, to be used to signal information about a company's future prospects, their effect on share prices arising from the general problem of information asymmetries (management as insiders possessing a higher quality of information than shareholders as outsiders). Thus, in the sense that dividends are used as information signals, they do not necessarily imply that there is an optimal payout ratio which maximises share price.

Agency costs

The information signalling hypothesis can also be associated with the agency problem. Here an increase in dividends, accompanied by new equity issues, acts as a form of monitoring and has a tendency to reduce the agency costs that shareholders experience. In this situation a preference for dividends results from the benefits that shareholders derive from a company having to make regular use of the new issue market. This increases the frequency of external audits, with their agency cost reductions. In anticipation of the increased information that the market will require on each new share issue, management have less scope to pursue objectives which deviate from shareholder wealth maximisation. Additional benefits arise from the underwriting of each new share issue, since underwriters commit their own reputations to the issuer's assets and will require information before doing so.

This equity argument is similar to one of the positive effects identified between financial leverage and market value, where the market associates an increase in debt issues with improved monitoring.

Signalling ambiguity
In general the positive relationship between share prices and dividends, in the context of information signalling, is supported by empirical evidence although there can be some ambiguity over interpreting the signals. In the above, an increase in dividends conveys 'good news', a decrease 'bad news'.

It is possible, however, for an increase in dividends to convey 'bad news', indicating that a company has few profitable investment opportunities. In this context, therefore, it is possible for a decrease in dividends to convey 'good news' of highly profitable investment opportunities requiring increased use of retained earnings.

An ongoing debate

In the arguments and counter-arguments which have taken place between the Dividend Theorists and the Earnings Theorists, many interesting insights into the relationships between dividends and retained earnings, dividends and taxes, and dividends and information signalling have been uncovered. The dividend puzzle remains, however, and will continue to represent an important area for future research. Basically the problem is that dividend changes which appear to cause share prices to change, may indicate that there is an optimal payout policy which the management of a company are attempting to target, imperfectly, in a complex financial environment. Alternatively, an observed dividend effect may simply be superficial and be indicative of profound underlying changes in a company's future prospects.

Summary

This chapter has demonstrated, once again, the usefulness of building financial economic models on restrictive assumptions in order to focus attention on particular aspects of corporate behaviour.

By starting with MM's dividend irrelevancy proposition and then examining the assumptions on which it is based, it appears that if there is a dividend effect, it is most likely to be the result of imperfections in capital markets. The Modernist position is that the presence of differential taxes, information asymmetries and agency costs are the most important factors.

If there is an optimal dividend policy there will be managerial resource implications, in that financial managers will need to devote time and effort to identifying and targeting the payout ratio most likely to maximise market value.

But is there an optimal dividend policy? No definitive conclusions can be advanced in the light of the current state of theoretical and empirical knowledge. There is a consistent pattern to dividend payments in practice but the above factors can be interpreted in different ways: suggesting that it is a low (or even zero) payout which would maximise share price; or that a high payout is necessary; or that dividends are irrelevant. One part of the dividend puzzle is unambiguous: the important role that dividends play in information signalling.

This, and the last chapter, have effectively examined the conditions under which financing and investment decisions can be viewed independently. In imperfect markets, despite the continuing puzzles, there is a strong view that in practice the capital structure decision and (through the link with retained earnings) the dividend decision do impact on market value. Consequently there is a potential relationship between investment and financing. Some of the aspects of this relationship are examined in the next chapter.

Questions

1 Assume a company is expected to pay a dividend per share of 30p next year. The company's required rate of return on equity is 10%. The company decides to postpone this dividend payment, investing the retained amount for one year only

at a rate of return of 14% and then paying out the original dividend plus the investment return.
a) Calculate by how much the company's share price will rise as a result of this policy.
b) By how much would the share price change if the rate of return on the one-year investment is (i) 10% and (ii) 5%?
c) In terms of the MM dividend irrelevancy proposition how can these share price changes be explained?

2 Consider the following information on a company which has 20m shares outstanding at a current share price of £2.10. The company's fixed annual investment is £20m. It has current profits of £14m with a current payout ratio of 0.5. The company finances investment through a combination of retained earnings and new shares issue in a perfect capital market. The company's cost of equity capital is 8%.
a) Determine the amount of capital the company needs to raise by a new share issue.
b) What is the current market value of the company, V_t?
c) What is the implied market value of the company in period $t + 1$?
d) What amount of the $t + 1$ market value belongs to existing shareholders and what is the $t + 1$ share price?
e) How many shares are outstanding in period $t + 1$?

3 Given the information in question 2, assume that instead of maintaining the payout ratio at 0.5, management decides to increase it to 0.6.
a) Find the market value, in period $t + 1$, of the existing shareholders' wealth and the share price.
b) Explain why the current value of the existing shareholders' equity will not change as a result of this change in current dividend policy.
c) What is the rate of return to existing shareholders?

4 On what assumptions is the MM dividend irrelevancy proposition based?

5 In the capital structure debate it is the possibilities of arbitrage in a perfect capital market which ensure that the market value of a company is independent of capital structure. What mechanism, under perfect capital markets, ensures that the dividend decision of a company's management has no effect on the company's share price?

6 Briefly outline the risk arguments advanced by the Traditionalist supporters of the Theory of the Dividend Effect.

7 In practice, what appear to be the main guidelines governing the formulation of a company's dividend policy?

8 Under a consistent dividend policy how might the following be expected to behave?
a) the long-term payout ratio,
b) the short-term payout ratio,
c) short-term dividends per share relative to long-term dividends per share.

Exercises

1 How might the presence of taxes cause a management's dividend policy to have an effect on its company's share price?

2 How is Agency Theory used to explain the apparent effect that dividend policy has on share prices?

3 How is Information Signalling Theory used to explain management's pursuit of a consistent dividend policy and its desire to avoid dividend cuts?

Endnotes

1.

$$\Delta P_0 = \frac{d_1(1 + k)}{(1 + r_e)^2} - \frac{d_1}{1 + r_e}$$

Taking $(1 + r_e)^2$ as a common denominator,

$$\Delta P_0 = \frac{d_1(1 + k) - d_1(1 + r_e)}{(1 + r_e)^2} = \frac{d_1 k - d_1 r_e}{(1 + r_e)^2} = \frac{d_1(k - r_e)}{(1 + r_e)^2}$$

2. Recall that in the Solomon Model a constant proportion of earnings per share from a company's existing assets was retained and invested in each future year. In the MM investment opportunities approach, higher amounts of retained earnings were invested in each future year, since the constant retention ratio was applied to each future year's earnings per share.

3. This is slightly inexact because the original shareholders, at the beginning of period t, can, if they desire, subscribe to the new issue at the beginning of period t + 1. The importance of this lack of separation between original and new shareholders will be explored below, under the section of the chapter dealing with Home-made Dividends. For the moment, for the purposes of exposition, it is assumed that these two groups are separate.

4. In equilibrium, the demand for shares to create a reduction in home-made dividends will equal the supply of shares coming from investors who wish to increase their home-made dividends. Thus market values will not be affected by demand and supply forces induced by investors declaring their own dividends.

5. If a number of investors make irrational investment decisions which cause dividend changes to have an effect on share prices, the EMH would argue that providing some investors are rational, for example professional fund managers, a dividend effect could not persist. Rational investors would be encouraged to exploit observed irrationalities and would rapidly push the market prices of companies towards their intrinsic values, thus rendering changes in dividend policy irrelevant.

6. In the UK, companies are taxed via a corporate tax imputation system. Under this, when dividends are paid out they are viewed as having already been taxed at the basic personal income tax rate. Thus for tax-exempt investment institutions, or individuals whose marginal personal tax rate is zero, a tax refund can be claimed. When dividends are paid, companies have to make an advance corporate profits tax payment, which can be offset against the next normal corporate tax payment. The linking of the personal and corporate tax systems in this way creates circumstances favouring dividend payments.

7. The 3i survey also confirms the link between liquidity and dividend payments. In distress situations, where there are liquidity problems, the need for cash will have an important influence on determining a company's dividend policy. Liquidity problems can also be

experienced by companies with very good investment prospects which place an emphasis on earnings retention. Thus there is evidence to suggest that small to medium-sized rapidly growing companies exhibit relatively low payouts while large, mature companies are among those most likely to make relatively large payouts.

References

Ambarish, R. and J. Williams, 'Efficient Signalling with Dividends and Investments', Journal of Finance, 1987

Baker, K., G. Farrelly and R. Edelman, 'A Survey of Management Views on Dividend Policy', Financial Management, 1985

Bank of England, 'Company Profitability and Finance', Quarterly Bulletin, 1993

Born, J.A. and J.N. Rimby, 'A Test of the Easterbrook Hypothesis Regarding Dividend Payments and Agency Costs', The Journal of Financial Research, 1993

Elton, E. and M. Gruber, 'Marginal Stockholder Tax Rates and the Clientele Effect', Review of Economics and Statistics, 1970

Feldstein, M. and J. Green, 'Why Do Companies Pay Dividends?' American Economic Review, 1983

Gonedes, N., 'Corporate Signalling, External Accounting, and Capital Market Equilibrium: Evidence on Dividends, Income and Extraordinary Items', Journal of Accounting Research, 1978

Gordon, M.J., 'Optimum Investment and Financing Policy', Journal of Finance, 1963

Gordon, M.J., The Investment, Financing and Valuation of the Corporation, Homewood, Ill., Richard D. Irwin, 1964

Hansen, R.S., R. Kumar and D.K. Shome, 'Dividend Policy and Corporate Monitoring: Evidence from the Regulated Electric Utility Industry', Financial Management, 1994

Healy, P.M. and K.G. Palepu, 'Earnings Information Conveyed by Dividend Initiations and Omissions', Journal of Financial Economics, 1988

Kaloy, A., 'Signalling Information Content and the Reluctance to Cut Dividends', Journal of Financial and Quantitative Analysis, 1980

Lintner, J., 'Distribution of Incomes of Corporations Among Dividends, Retained Earnings and Taxes', American Economic Review, 1956

Miller, M.H., 'Dividends and Taxes', Journal of Financial Economics, 1978

Miller, M.H., 'Behaviour Rationality: The Case of Dividends', Journal of Business, 1986

Miller, M.H. and F. Modigliani, 'Dividend Policy, Growth and the Valuation of Shares', Journal of Business, 1961

Miller, M.H. and M. Scholes, 'Dividends and Taxes: Some Empirical Evidence', Journal of Political Economy, 1982

Pettit, R.R. 'Dividend Announcements, Security Performance and Capital Market Efficiency', Journal of Finance, 1972

Talmore, E. and S. Titman, 'Taxes and Dividend Policy', Financial Management, 1990

3i plc, 'Dividend Policy: Survey of Finance Directors', 1993

10 Investment and financing

Introduction

Analysis of the capital structure and dividend irrelevancy debates in the last two chapters indicate, respectively, that when arbitrage opportunities and the ability of investors to freely declare their own dividends are impaired, investment and financing decisions become interdependent.

This chapter explores some of the consequences of this interdependence, beginning with a discussion of the interrelationships between business risk and operating leverage, and financial risk and financial leverage.[1] With the exception of operating leverage, these concepts have already been introduced in the context of the capital structure debate in Chapter 8.

Operating leverage refers to the extent to which a company, when formulating its investment plans, builds fixed production costs into its operations. To the extent that a company has flexibility in choosing its operating leverage, it can influence the level of its business risk.

With financial risk representing the addition to business risk, consequent on the level of financial leverage, management may have a limited facility to combine investment and financing decisions to control the overall level of risk that a company is exposed to.

This chapter also examines, in the context of Agency Theory, how investment by asset type might influence the financing decision. Here, attention is focused on the distinction between tangible and intangible assets. In general, the higher the proportion of tangible assets in a company's total asset base, the lower its agency costs of debt. While intangible assets tend to increase these costs, recent research suggests that this is not the case where investments in advertising and research and development (R and D) are concerned. These intangible assets may reduce agency costs since intangible assets can have characteristics which enhance the reputation of a company in the capital markets.

The chapter concludes by returning to investment appraisal techniques. These were developed in Chapters 6 and 7 by making the assumption, in most cases, that investment and financing decisions are independent. The implications of interdependence are examined in the context of the weighted average cost of capital and the Adjusted Net Present Value method of investment selection. The latter adjusts a 'base case' NPV to take account of financing side-effects which may arise when capital markets are imperfect.

Leverage and risk

Throughout most of this book the assumption is made that management's objective is the maximisation of shareholder wealth. In other words, the ultimate consideration is how the investment and financing decisions of a company affect the income and wealth of a company's owners.

For any company a fundamental relationship exists between its sales and earnings before interest and taxes (EBIT), this relationship being primarily determined by the company's investment decision. Subsequently a fundamental relationship exists between EBIT and the shareholders' rate of return on equity, this relationship being primarily determined by a company's financing decision. Consequently, by developing models which demonstrate how these relationships might interact, a view of possible investment and financing interdependencies can be determined.

In addition these relationships are important in enabling a company to estimate how changes in the macroeconomic environment, and the level of competition it faces, are translated into changes in its stock market value. Changes in the rate of return on equity are ultimately determined, via a company's investment and financing decisions, by how macroeconomic factors and competition impact on a company's sales.

The above relationships involve risk–return trade-offs which are handled by assuming that each variable under consideration can be characterised by a normal probability distribution. The advantage of using a normal distribution, as explained in Chapter 4, is that it is fully described by two parameters: its mean and standard deviation. Thus, when examining sales or EBIT or the rate of return on equity, a company can focus on the expected level of each variable and its standard deviation. The purpose of the standard deviation, which is taken as a measure of risk, is to indicate the spread of possible outcomes around, that is, above and below, the mean or expected level of a variable.

Financial leverage and financial risk

In Chapter 8, when the capital structure decision was analysed, one of the key factors to emerge was that financial leverage had an impact on shareholder returns. Over a specific range of financial leverage, increases in the proportion of debt in the capital structure increased the rate of return on equity. It was also demonstrated, however, in terms of the CAPM β coefficient, that increases in financial leverage increased the financial risk that shareholders were exposed to and thus, when added to business risk, their total risk exposure.

In effect, when analysing financial leverage, it is its role in transforming EBIT into earnings after interest and taxes, EAIT, which is being considered. EAIT, which are available to common shareholders, can be expressed in terms of EPS where, with n shares outstanding:

$$EPS = \frac{EAIT}{n} \qquad\qquad (10.1)$$

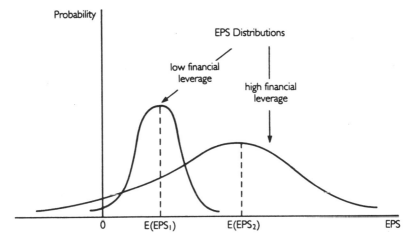

E(EPS₁): Expected level of EPS under low financial leverage

E(EPS₂): Expected level of EPS under high financial leverage

Figure 10.1   EPS probability distributions and financial leverage

Given a company's probability distribution of EBIT, the higher the level of financial leverage over a specific range, the higher both the expected level and standard deviation of EPS. This is illustrated in Figure 10.1, where two hypothetical probability distributions of EPS are shown for a relatively low, and a relatively high, level of financial leverage. In the former case there is only a small probability of negative EPS being experienced. While the higher level of financial leverage is shown to create a higher level of expected EPS, the spread of the EPS distribution, as measured by its standard deviation, has increased. This demonstrates that the shareholders' total risk exposure[2] has risen, the increase in the standard deviation being due to financial risk. Indeed, in the specific example, risk has increased to such an extent that there is now a significant probability of negative EPS.

The degree of financial leverage

Given a company's mean level of EBIT, that is, the level of EBIT which it expects to generate, it is important to understand how a rise (fall) above (below) this level will impact on its expected EPS. One way in which this can be summarised is through the use of an elasticity which measures the responsiveness of EPS to EBIT. This defines the Degree of Financial Leverage, DFL, at a given level[3] of EBIT, where:

$$DFL = \frac{\% \text{ Change in EPS}}{\% \text{ Change in EBIT}} \qquad (10.2)$$

or

$$DFL = \frac{\Delta EPS/EPS}{\Delta EBIT/EBIT} \qquad (10.2a)$$

with Δ representing the change in the level of a variable.

Table 10.1A: Financial leverage and earnings per share

$V = S + B = £60m, P = £1.50, r_d = 5\%$ and $t_c = 40\%$
Number of shares on issue: $N = S/P$
$EAI^I = EBIT - r_dB$
$EAIT = (EBIT - r_dB)(1 - t_c)$
$EPS = EAIT/n$

	Financial Structure FS1 All Equity	Financial Structure FS2 40% Debt	Financial Structure FS3 60% Debt
V	£60m	£60m	£60m
B		£24m	£36m
S	£60m	£36m	£24m
N = S/P	£60m/£1.50 = 40m	£36m/£1.50 = 24m	£24m/£1.50 = 16m
EBIT	£4.00m	£4.00m	£4.00m
r_dB	−£0.00m	−£1.20m	−£1.80m
EAI	£4.00m	£2.80m	£2.20m
EAIT = EAI(1 − .4)	£2.40m	£1.68m	£1.32m
EPS = EAIT/n	6p	7p	8.25p

^{I} EAI: Earnings after interest charges but before taxes

Table 10.1B: Illustrating the degree of financial leverage

Given the information in Table 10.1A, assume that EBIT turns out to be 25% above its expected level of £4m

	Financial Structure FS1 All Equity	Financial Structure FS2 40% Debt	Financial Structure FS3 60% Debt
EBIT	£5.00m	£5.00m	£5.00m
r_dB	−£0.00m	−£1.20m	−£1.80m
EAI	£5.00m	£3.80m	£3.20m
EAIT = EAI(1 − .4)	£3.00m	£2.28m	£1.92m
EPS = EAIT/n	7.5p	9.5p	12p

Calculating the Degree of Financial Leverage (DFL)

ΔEBIT/EBIT	(£5m − 4m)/£4m = 0.25	(£5m − £4m)/£4m = 0.25	(£5m − £4m)/£4m = 0.25
ΔEPS/EPS	(7.5p − 6p)/6p = 0.25	(9.5p − 7p)/7p = 0.357	(12p − 8.25p)/8.25p = 0.455
$DFL = \dfrac{\Delta EPS/EPS}{\Delta EBIT/EBIT}$	0.25/0.25 = 1.0	0.357/0.25 = 1.43	0.455/0.25 = 1.82

This concept is illustrated in Tables 10.1A and 10.1B. Three financial structures are considered: one where the company is all equity financed (financial structure FS1), one where it has 40% perpetual debt capital (FS2), and one where it has 60% perpetual debt capital (FS3). In the latter two cases the cost of debt capital is $r_d = 5\%$. For simplicity, it is assumed that the MM capital structure irrelevancy propositions hold so that the market value of the company, $V = £60m$, is invariate to capital structure. With a given share price of $P = £1.50$, this means that as the capital structure changes, the number of shares outstanding changes. With a corporate tax rate of $t_c = 40\%$, and an expected level to EBIT of £4m, Table 10.1A shows how EAIT are calculated and expressed in terms of EPS under each of the capital structures.

Table 10.1B calculates the effect on EPS, if EBIT turns out to be different from its expected level of £4m. As an example, a rise in EBIT to £5m is considered. With EBIT increasing by 25%, the respective increases in EPS under each capital structure are translated into Equation 10.2a, to give the DFL.

Under the all equity financing structure:

$$DFL_{FS1} = 1.0$$

This indicates that at the expected level of EBIT, a given percentage increase (decrease) in EBIT will be exactly matched by an equal percentage increase (decrease) in EPS.

Once debt is introduced, however, any change in EBIT has an amplifying effect on EPS. Under FS2, with a leverage ratio of B/V = 0.4,

$$DFL_{FS2} = 1.43$$

indicating, for example, that if EBIT turns out to be 1% above its expected level, EPS will have increased by 1.43% above its expected level, that is, by more than the 1% under the all equity case. The key point to realise, however, is that from a risk perspective the probability of EBIT turning out to be 1% below[4] its expected level, equals the probability of it turning out to be 1% above its expected level. If EBIT is 1% below its expected level, EPS will have fallen by 1.43%.

At the higher leverage ratio of B/V = 0.6, under FS3, the amplification of changes in EBIT on EPS is even higher, with

$$DFL_{FS3} = 1.82$$

In the all equity case it is business risk (defined below) which is the sole determinant of shareholder risk exposure. Thus, when only equity capital is used it is always the case that the DFL = 1.0. When debt is included, financial risk is added to business risk, so that the DFL exceeds 1.0.

The determinants of EBIT

The concepts of financial leverage and financial risk demonstrate how changes in EBIT are translated into changes in EPS. Taking one step back, the obvious question then arises: what are the factors which determine changes in EBIT, or operating profits? There are a number of these, including:

- the level of competition a company faces in its product and/or service markets;
- its pricing and promotional policies and how these are changed to cope with changes in competition;
- the potential variability in its input prices;
- other company-specific factors, for example, the state of its labour relations;
- government policy, and how it affects the general level of consumer confidence and exchange rate changes, among other macroeconomic factors.

To simplify, attention tends to be focused on two determinants of EBIT. The first and primary determinant is the probability distribution of sales, that is, sales volume as opposed to sales revenue. This is based on the assumptions that a company's performance ultimately rests on its ability to generate sales and that the probability distribution of sales will encapsulate most of the above interrelated factors. The second determinant relates to the flexibility a company has in carrying out its given investment intentions, in the form of its ability to influence the level of operating leverage it employs.

Operating leverage and business risk

Some companies, in making their investment decisions, have a range of ways in which they can combine their fixed and variable costs of production. In terms of this combination, operating leverage increases according to the extent to which a company builds fixed production costs into its operations. A car manufacturer, for example, which is considering establishing a plant in a high wage economy, may adopt a highly technological, robotic method of assembly. Alternatively, if establishing a plant in a low wage economy, it may opt for more labour-intensive methods. Comparing the two approaches, the former, because it is more capital intensive and will involve highly trained technical staff, may have a higher proportion of fixed costs than the latter. In the case of the labour-intensive method, the plant may rely more heavily on variable costs and thus have a lower level of operating leverage.

In the same way as a change in EBIT has a varying impact on EPS, according to the level of financial leverage (determined by fixed financing costs), so a change in sales has varying impacts on EBIT, according to the level of operating leverage (determined by fixed operating costs). In effect, at a company's operating level, there is a positive risk–return trade-off between its expected level of EBIT and the spread of the probability distribution of EBIT, the latter defining a company's business risk.

Examining this in more detail, a company's investment decision 'locks' it into specific product and/or service markets and, therefore, exposes it to a particular probability distribution of sales. In this sense the investment decision, by determining the expected level and standard deviation of sales, largely predetermines a company's expected level of EBIT and its business risk, measured by the standard deviation of EBIT.

To the extent, however, that a company can choose its operating leverage, it can influence the position of its probability distribution of EBIT. This is illustrated in Figure 10.2 where two such hypothetical distributions are shown for a relatively low, and a relatively high, level of operating leverage. In the former case there is only a small probability of negative EBIT being experienced. All other things being equal, the high level of operating leverage is shown to create a higher level of expected EBIT but also a higher standard deviation and hence business risk.[5] Indeed, in this specific example, risk has increased to such an extent that there is a significant probability of losses, that is, of negative operating profits.

In summary, given the underlying probability distribution of sales, a company can increase its expected level of EBIT by increasing its operating leverage; however, this is accompanied by an increase in business risk. Subsequently, at a given level of operating leverage, a company can increase its expected level of EPS by increasing

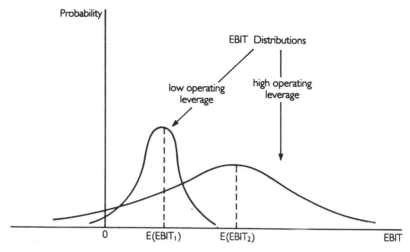

E(EBIT$_1$): Expected level of EBIT under low operating leverage

E(EBIT$_2$): Expected level of EBIT under high operating leverage

Figure 10.2   Probability distributions and operating leverage

its financial leverage; however, this is accompanied by an increase in financial risk which increases shareholders' total risk exposure above the level of business risk.

The degree of operating leverage

Given a company's mean level of sales, that is, the level of sales it expects to generate, it is important to understand how a rise (fall) above (below) this level will impact on its expected EBIT. One way in which this can be summarised is in terms of an elasticity, where the responsiveness of EBIT to sales, Q, is measured by the Degree of Operating Leverage, DOL. The DOL, at a given level of sales, is:

$$DOL = \frac{\% \text{ Change in EBIT}}{\% \text{ Change in Q}} \tag{10.3}$$

or

$$DOL = \frac{\Delta EBIT/EBIT}{\Delta Q/Q} \tag{10.3a}$$

This concept is illustrated in Table 10.2. To simplify the analysis, the price at which a company sells its product, P_p, is held constant. Three operating plans are defined in terms of the relationship between total fixed cost, TFC, and unit variable cost, v. Over the respective operating plans, OP1, OP2 and OP3, operating leverage increases.

The first half of Table 10.2 demonstrates how EBIT are calculated. With total variable cost, TVC, defined as unit variable cost times output, vQ, total cost is equal to total variable cost plus total fixed cost:

$$TC = vQ + TFC \tag{10.4}$$

Table 10.2: Illustrating the degree of operating leverage

Product Price: $P_p = £6.50$ Expected Sales: Q = 2m units
Expected Total Revenue (TR): $P_pQ = £13.00m$
Total Cost (TC) = Total Variable Cost (TVC) + Total Fixed Cost (TFC)

	Operating Plan OP1	Operating Plan OP2	Operating Plan OP3
TR	£13.00m	£13.00m	£13.00m
v	£2.80	£2.50	£1.00
TVC = vQ	£5.60m	£5.00m	£2.00m
TFC	£3.50m	£4.00m	£6.00m
TC = TVC + TFC	£9.10m	£9.00m	£8.00m
EBIT = TR − TC	£3.90m	£4.00m	£5.00m

Assume that sales turn out to be 10% above their expected level of 2m units. Thus with Q = 2.2m units, TR = (£6.50)(2.2m) = £14.3m

TR	£14.3m	£14.3m	£14.3m
v	£2.80	£2.50	£1.0
TVC = vQ	£6.16m	£5.50m	£2.20m
TFC	£3.50m	£4.00m	£6.00m
TC = TVC + TFC	£9.66m	£9.50m	£8.20m
EBIT = TR − TC	£4.64m	£4.80m	£6.1m

	Calculating the Degree of Operating Leverage (DOL)		
$\Delta Q/Q$	(2.2m − 2m)/2m = 0.1	(2.2m − 2m)/2m = 0.1	(2.2m − 2m)/2m = 0.1
$\Delta EBIT/EBIT$	(£4.64m − £3.90m)/£3.90m = 0.19	(£4.80m − £4.00m)/£4.00m = 0.2	(£6.10m − £5.00m)/£5m = 0.22
$DOL = \dfrac{\Delta EBIT/EBIT}{\Delta Q/Q}$	0.19/0.10 = 1.9	0.2/0.10 = 2.0	0.22/0.10 = 2.2

With total revenue, TR, equal to price times output,

$$TR = P_pQ \qquad (10.5)$$

EBIT equals TR − TC, that is:

$$EBIT = P_pQ - vQ - TFC = (P_p - v)Q - TFC \qquad (10.6)$$

As TFC in each operating plan is invariate to output changes (as is unit variable cost), $P_p - v$ is often referred to as the contribution margin, that is, the contribution which each additional unit of output makes to EBIT.

The second half of Table 10.2 calculates the effect on EBIT if sales volume turns out to be different from its expected level of 2m units. As an example a rise in sales above the mean, to 2.2m units, is considered. With sales volume increasing by 10%, the respective increases in EBIT are translated into Equation 10.3a, to give the DOL in each case.

Under OP1,

$$DOL_{OP1} = 1.9$$

This indicates that at the expected level of sales, a given percentage increase (decrease) in sales has an amplifying effect on EBIT. The DOL is higher in each subsequent plan:

$$DOL_{OP2} = 2.0$$

and

$$DOL_{OP3} = 2.2$$

In the latter case, for example, if sales volume turns out to be 1% above (below) its expected level, EBIT will have increased (decreased) by 2.2% above (below) its expected level.

Combined leverage

The DOL and the DFL can be brought together in a combined leverage concept to indicate the fundamental relationship which exists between a company's ability to generate sales, in its product and/or service markets, and the EPS made available to shareholders through the stock markets. The Degree of Combined Leverage, DCL, is simply the product of the DOL and the DFL:

$$DCL = DOL \times DFL \qquad\qquad (10.7)$$

Using Equations 10.2 and 10.3, the DCL measures the percentage change in EPS resulting from a percentage change in sales. That is, the DCL is defined, at a given level of sales, as:

$$DCL = \frac{\% \text{ Change in EBIT}}{\% \text{ Change in Sales}} \times \frac{\% \text{ Change in Sales}}{\% \text{ Change in EBIT}} \qquad\qquad (10.7a)$$

$$= \frac{\% \text{ Change in EPS}}{\% \text{ Change in Sales}} \qquad\qquad (10.7b)$$

or

$$DCL = \frac{\Delta EPS/EPS}{\Delta Sales/Sales} \qquad\qquad (10.7c)$$

Consider, for example, operating plan OP2 in Table 10.2. At an expected level of sales of 2m units, and an associated EBIT of £4m,

$$DOL_{OP2} = 2.0$$

At this level of EBIT, and assuming capital structure FS2 in Table 10.1B,

$$DFL_{FS2} = 1.43$$

Thus, on combining these two leverage levels,

$$DCL = 2.0 \times 1.43 = 2.86$$

indicating that, at the expected level of sales of 2m units, a 1% rise (fall) from the expected level of sales causes a 2.86% rise (fall) around the expected level of EPS.[6]

Joint investment and financing

To the extent that a company has flexibility in the choice of its operating leverage level and actively decides to combine it with specific levels of financial leverage, its investment and financing decisions are jointly determined. If, for some reason, a company wishes to limit the overall risk exposure of its shareholders, the combined leverage concept suggests that this can be achieved by choosing a relatively low level of financial leverage in association with a relatively high level of operating leverage, or vice versa. In other words, capital-intensive investments, which involve a company building a relatively large amount of fixed production costs into its operations, may encourage it to concentrate on equity financing and adopt a conservative debt financing policy. Alternatively, companies whose investments involve relatively high levels of variable operating costs may choose to rely on financing policies encompassing relatively high levels of debt.

Assume, for example, that in keeping with a policy to control the overall level of risk exposure, a company wishes to target its DCL at 2.83. If, in carrying out its given investment intentions, it could choose a DOL = 1.5, then in choosing its financing strategy it would aim for a DFL = 1.89 since DCL = 1.5 × 1.89 = 2.83. Alternatively, if it could, and did, choose a more capital-intensive operating plan, with, say, an associated DOL = 2.5, it would target a capital structure with a relatively low amount of debt capital which is likely to produce a DFL = 1.13 since DCL = 2.5 × 1.13 = 2.83. In a similar fashion if, because of capital market imperfections, a company faces limits on its debt financing capacity, the financing decision may dictate the choice of operating leverage, to the extent that this is possible.

Operating and financial leverage assumptions

The analysis of business risk[7] and operating leverage, and financial risk and financial leverage, is based on highly restrictive assumptions.

By assuming normality of the probability distribution of sales, normality is automatically implied for both the EBIT and the EPS distributions. If sales are not normally distributed, then the respective standard deviations of EBIT and EPS will not fully measure business risk or shareholders' total risk exposure.

In the case of operating leverage product and input prices are given and there is an assumed inverse relationship between unit variable cost and total fixed costs. This latter relationship, if it exists in practice, will only do so over a limited range. If this relationship is broken and/or product prices, input prices and other factors vary with sales, an operating leverage effect will become much more problematical.

In the case of financial leverage the effects which have been described are based on the assumption that market value is constant. In a strict sense, therefore, since the total market value of a company is independent of financial leverage, and thus the overall risk exposure of shareholders, the view that management may wish to combine particular levels of operating and financial leverage is irrational. However, once capital market imperfections are introduced, in the form of information, bankruptcy, financial distress and agency costs, specific combinations of operating and financial leverage may well be appropriate. In these cases, however, the calculation and interpretation of the DCL may become highly complex. As Prezas (1987) has shown, when investment and financing decisions are jointly determined, the level of debt influences not only the DFL but the DOL as well.

Despite the above, the value of using simplified models, at least to identify a particular aspect of corporate financing which can be important in complex financing and investment environments, has again been demonstrated.

Tangible and intangible assets

In presenting the Modernist view of the capital structure debate, in Chapter 8, the agency theory of debt was advanced as one of the important reasons for expecting companies to have optimal capital structures. This arose in the context of moral hazard where, because of information asymmetries and the difficulty of monitoring managers' behaviour, the asset substitution and underinvestment problems were encountered. These, in effect, demonstrated that investment and financing inter-dependencies could be induced by agency costs.

Agency costs and intangible assets

Further research into the agency problem has been carried out by considering the asset mix of a company. In particular, Myers (1984) points out that where firms are using a relatively high proportion of intangible assets, agency costs can become more acute. Intangible assets not only include human capital investment, but can be associated with advertising and R and D expenditures, all of which aid the development of the unique characteristics of a company. Once financial distress is encountered, however, it is these 'firm-specific' or intangible assets whose values become most problematical. Firm-specific assets are difficult to reallocate, have very limited secondhand markets (if any) and cannot be used as collateral for borrowing. On the other hand, tangible assets tend to reduce the agency costs of debt. They have reasonably active secondary markets so that their values are less uncertain in distress situations. Indeed debt covenants, which help mitigate some of the agency problems, are written in terms of tangible assets and often specifically exclude intangibles.

The intangibility problem also arises in respect of risky projects which involve substantial future growth potential. Growth potential initially increases Leibowitz and Kogelman's (1992) concept of the franchise value of a company: the value associated with potential pay-offs from investment opportunities which are expected to earn returns above a company's cost of capital. Franchise value, because it represents a potential which has not yet been realised, is an intangible asset. As growth potential is realised, however, the franchise value is transformed into tangible assets but there can be significant time lags in the transformation process.

Evidence by Chung (1993), based on an analysis of the debt policy of over 1000 US companies, lends support to the potential growth, agency cost argument, by demonstrating a negative relationship between financial leverage and price–

earnings ratios. Recall from Chapter 3 that growth potential is reflected in high price–earnings ratios with, as growth potential is transformed into tangible assets, price–earnings ratios declining towards their base levels.

The above may, therefore, imply that companies will constrain their levels of investments in intangible assets in order to limit the agency costs of debt. They may also pay more attention to the speed with which intangibles can be transformed into tangible assets, favouring projects with lower transformation times. While this aspect is automatically taken account of in the timing of net cash flows in an NPV investment appraisal, an assessment of the effects of intangibles on the cost of debt capital is also required.

Investment and business strategy decisions

While a high ratio of intangible:tangible assets can be expected to raise the cost of debt financing, recent and interesting refinements of this issue suggest that some forms of intangible assets, which were at one time argued to increase the agency costs of debt, can actually reduce them. Chauvin and Hirschey (1993) and Balakrishnan and Fox (1993) put forward this hypothesis by examining the links between investment and business strategy decisions.

Business strategy, which is formulated by companies to gain competitive advantages in their product and/or service markets, often involves investments in firm-specific assets. In terms of financial signalling models, investments in brand names, advertising and R and D, which are developed as part of business strategy, can create reputational characteristics which are interpreted by debt holders as a guarantee. As Balakrishnan and Fox state:

> ... once investments in brand names etc. become realised as reputational assets, they may require continued expenditure much like maintenance to keep physical facilities from depreciating too rapidly. The presence and maintenance of reputational assets may therefore be taken by lenders as commitment by the firm to be an aggressive competitor in its product market, leading to lower costs of debt financing. ...

Consequently, where sustained investments in these firm-specific assets demonstrate to capital markets a continued commitment to maintaining competitive advantage, they can be expected to have a positive effect on financial leverage. Empirical evidence presented by Balakrishnan and Fox supports this hypothesis as do Chauvin and Hirschey, who find that advertising and R and D expenditures have substantial positive influences on the market values of companies, especially large-sized companies.

By making this distinction between tangible and intangible assets, additional complexities in the investment and financing decisions of a company are revealed. In practical situations it may well be important to determine the appropriate mix between financing, investment and business strategy decisions, when both product and capital markets are imperfect.

In industrial economics, branding, advertising and R and D have always been identified as having an important role to play in the competitive process, through product differentiation and the creation of barriers to entry. In corporate finance these firm-specific investments are seen to have a capital market role. Thus firm-specific investments are not simply confined to explaining how super-normal profits are created through elements of monopoly power and, consequently, reflected in share prices. These intangible assets are now argued to extend directly into the finance function, influencing the cost of debt capital.

The asset intangibility issue, while of some significance to the finance functions of large companies, is of particular importance in explaining the relationships between small firms and their capital suppliers, mainly banks. This is explored in Chapter 14.

Investment appraisal

When examining project appraisal techniques in Chapters 6 and 7, much of the analysis was carried out on the assumption that investment and financing decisions were independent. At the beginning of Chapter 7, however, when calculating the overall cost of capital, implicit allowance was made for joint investment and financing effects in the risk adjusted, weighted average cost of capital formula.

The weighted average cost of capital approach

Recall from Equation 7.5 that this was used to determine a project discount rate,

$$r_{project} = r_f + [E(r_m) - r_f] \, \beta_{project} \left[\frac{S + B(1 - t_c)}{S + B} \right]$$

This equation takes into account the effect of taxation and financial risk on the investment decision.

From the subsequent analysis of the capital structure decision, in Chapter 8, it should now be apparent that this weighted average approach is based on restrictive assumptions. In particular, the above equation assumes that:
• a company's capital structure is given;
• debt and equity capital are valued as level perpetuities;
• the cash flows of a project are also constant and generated in perpetuity.

Providing that a potential investment project is relatively small in relation to a company's existing assets, and recognising that if the perpetuity assumption does not hold there will be some minor inaccuracies in calculation, this approach can be used with a reasonable level of confidence in obtaining a project's NPV.

Adjusted net present value

An alternative approach, which is argued to take a fuller account of investment and financing interactions, and which does not involve the perpetuity and given target capital structure assumptions, is the Adjusted Net Present Value, ANPV, method. It is effectively based on the principle that MM adopted in their debt and taxes valuation model. Adapting this principle, in the context of project appraisal, the ANPV method calculates the NPV of an investment on the assumption that it is to be financed purely by equity. The ANPV then adjusts this 'base case' NPV by adding the NPV of any debt financing side-effects. The NPV of these side-effects can, of course, be either positive or negative.

In calculating the all equity NPV the pure equity capitalisation rate, r_e^*, is applied to a project's unlevered net cash flows (UNCFs) to yield an unlevered NPV (UNPV). In calculating the NPV of financing side-effects (NPVFS), the discount rate appropriate to the risk associated with the side-effects is applied.

Note that there is nothing special in referring to project NCFs as being unlevered. Unlevered NCFs are simply NCFs without debt interest charges being deducted. This is consistent with the principles of calculating NCFs, discussed in Chapter 6. Having considered financial leverage in detail, it can now be understood that in the examples in Chapter 6 it was effectively unlevered NCFs which were being discounted.

Defining the ANPV as:

$$ANPV = UNPV + NPVFS \tag{10.8}$$

or

$$ANPV = \sum_{t=1}^{n} \frac{UNCF_t}{(1 + r_e^*)^t} - I_o + NPVFS \tag{10.8a}$$

the standard investment decision rule applies, where an independent project i can be accepted if:

$$ANPV_i \geqslant o \tag{10.9}$$

To illustrate, consider a very simple example where a project, which has an initial investment outlay of $I_o = £10m$, is expected to generate a constant annual operating profit of £2.5m in perpetuity. The corporate tax rate is $t_c = 25\%$ and there are no depreciation allowances. The company intends financing the project with £5m of debt capital, at $r_d = 7\%$, and has estimated its pure equity capitalisation rate at $r_e^* = 15\%$. Thus:

$$UNPV = \frac{£2.5m(1 - .25)}{0.15} - £10m = £12.50m - £10m = £2.5m$$

Assuming that there are no bankruptcy or financial distress costs, the financing side-effects in this case consist entirely of the annual debt interest tax shield:

$$r_d t_c B = (.07)(.25)(£5m) = £0.0875m$$

Thus, discounting this, at $r_d = 7\%$,

$$NPVFS = \frac{£0.0875}{.07} = £1.25m$$

and

$$ANPV = £2.50m + £1.25m = £3.75m$$

With ANPV > o, the project is acceptable.

In general, financing side-effects are not limited to debt interest tax shields. The side-effects will include, as the capital structure debate indicated, the costs associated with making new issues, bankruptcy, financial distress and other associated net agency factors. In the above example, assuming that issue costs are £0.1m and that the NPV of the other additional financing side-effects is −£0.75m, the ANPV would be reduced to:

$$ANPV = £2.50m + £1.25m - £0.1m - £0.75m = £2.9m$$

The ANPV method has its own weaknesses. It is based on the view that the separate cash flow streams of a project should be identified according to the risk classes into which they fall. In this respect practical problems can be encountered, particularly relating to the financing side-effects. While there is little ambiguity in respect of separating out any tax benefits and determining the discount rate which should be applied to these (the cost of debt capital), it may be difficult to discriminate properly between other side-effects and to estimate their appropriate discount rates.

The weighted average cost of capital and ANPV

The above simple example is chosen so that the equivalence of the ANPV and weighted average cost of capital approaches can be illustrated, under the perpetuity assumptions. Using the weighted average cost of capital approach the project discount rate is applied to the unlevered NCFs to give the conventional NPV:

$$NPV = \sum_{t=1}^{n} \frac{UNCF_t}{(1 + r_{project})^t} - I_o \qquad (10.10)$$

To calculate the weighted average cost of capital, an estimate is required of the relevant cost of equity capital when there is debt in the capital structure. Given the perpetuity example, this can be deduced from MM's Equation 8.7, adjusted for tax:

$$r_e = r_e^* + (r_e^* - r_d)(B/S)(1 - t_c) \qquad (10.11)$$

In the above example (excluding financial side-effects other than the debt interest tax shield), assume that the debt to total market value ratio is $B/V = 0.364$. This implies that $S/V = 0.636$ and that[8] $B/S = 0.571$. Thus with $r_e^* = 15\%$, $r_d = 7\%$ and $t_c = 25\%$

$$r_e = 0.15 + (.15 - .07)(.571)(1 - .25) = 0.1843 \text{ or } 18.43\%$$

Assuming the project has the same risk as the company's existing operations, the simpler version of the weighted average cost of capital given in Equation 7.1 can be used, where:

$$r_{project} = r_d(1 - t_c)\left[\frac{B}{S + B}\right] + r_e\left[\frac{S}{S + B}\right]$$

Therefore,

$$r_{project} = 0.07(1 - .25)[.364] + 0.1843[.636] = 0.1363 \text{ or } 13.63\%$$

With the project generating an annual operating profit of £2.5m in perpetuity, the weighted average cost of capital approach gives a conventional NPV, from Equation 10.10, which is equal to the ANPV, that is:

$$NPV = \frac{£2.5m(1 - .25)}{0.1363} - £10m = £3.75m = ANPV$$

Both the weighted average cost of capital and the ANPV approaches discount the unlevered net cash flows. The ANPV uses the pure equity capitalisation rate and then adds the NPV of the financing side-effects. In this example financing side-effects consist only of tax shield benefits which are discounted at the pre-tax cost of debt. The weighted average cost of capital approach applies one discount rate directly. It is based, however, on the component costs of capital, with the tax effects taken into account in terms of the after-tax cost of debt. For further discussion of these issues see Ross et al. (1993).

Maintaining the existing capital structure

In the above example it is assumed that the company has an existing capital structure, measured by its B/V ratio of 0.364, and that this is to be maintained if the new project is undertaken. The project has an investment outlay of £10m, of which £5m is to be financed with debt capital. This is the amount of debt which will maintain the existing capital structure. It is not the amount implied if the B/V ratio had been applied to I_o. In the latter case the amount of debt finance raised would have been (0.364)(£10m) = £3.64m. Why is this?

The financing structure of a company is related to its total market value measured by the value of its assets; therefore, to maintain the existing capital structure the amounts of any new debt and equity raised must be determined in relation to the total value of the project being undertaken. The total value of a project is equal to its NPV plus the present value of its investment outlay. In the current example the total value of the project is: £3.75m + £10m = £13.75m. Thus given B/V, the amount of new debt financing is 0.364(£13.75m) = £5m.

The above illustrates a general principle which must be adopted if a company's capital structure is to remain constant in the face of determining the additional amounts of debt and equity to be raised for a given project. This principle is based on the NPV concept. The NPV of a project, that is, its contribution over and above its initial investment outlay, goes to shareholders and so adds to the value of the new equity initially raised. To keep the capital structure constant this additional equity effect must be taken into account.

Only in special cases where a project's NPV = o, or where MM's capital structure irrelevancy propositions hold (perfect capital markets with no taxes), can the amounts of new debt and equity be determined directly by applying the existing capital structure weights to a project's investment outlay.

As an illustration of the general principle, assume that the total market value of the company in the above example, before the project is undertaken, is V = £100m. Given B/V = 0.364, the current market values of debt and equity are:

B = £36.4m and S = £63.6m

By undertaking the project the company raises £5m of new debt, taking B to £41.4m. Since I_o = £10m and B = £5m, the amount of new equity initially raised is £5m. The project, however, has an NPV = £3.75m, so that the market value of equity rises to £63.6m + £5m + £3.75m = £72.35m. With these new total values of debt and equity, the B/V ratio is maintained:

B/V = £41.4m/(£41.4m + £72.35m) = 0.364

Finally, note that this example reinforces yet another general principle of investment appraisal, developed in Chapter 6. Namely, by making investment decisions on the basis of maximising NPV, the net addition to shareholder wealth is maximised through the maximisation of the market value of equity.

Summary

Given the complex nature of corporate finance, analysis of the subject is largely carried out by making assumptions which isolate individual topics of interest. This enables attention to be focused on the factors which influence each topic, and on the identification of unresolved problems which are likely to determine the direction of future theoretical and empirical research. This methodological approach is pursued at a general level in the subject by taking the financing decision as given, and examining how the investment decision determines value, or by taking the investment decision as given, and examining how the financing decision determines value.

This chapter has attempted to explore some of the valuation consequences when investment and financing decisions are co-determined. Three areas were examined: the relationships between operating and financial leverage, the roles of tangible and intangible assets and the relevance of some investment appraisal techniques.

Under special conditions, which some would argue are highly restrictive, an inverse relationship exists between operating and financial leverage. This may enable management, in imperfect capital markets, to combine the levels of operating and financial leverage in a way which controls shareholder risk exposure.

Where asset intangibility is concerned, investment strategies which create large but intangible growth opportunities (or franchise values) may have adverse effects on a company's debt financing capacity. This can be partly offset, however, to the extent that investment is undertaken in R and D, branding and other promotional strategies which have reputational benefits and are, therefore, quasi-tangible.

Finally, in the presence of investment and financing interdependencies care has to be taken in appraising potential investment projects. While the weighted average cost of capital approach can be used, with appropriate recognition given to its limitations, the Adjusted Net Present Value method represents an interesting and, some would argue, more comprehensive approach to valuing financing side-effects in imperfect markets.

Questions _____

1 Explain the difference between operating leverage and financial leverage.

2 a) What does the degree of operating leverage measure?

   b) Consider a company which has an expected level of sales of 4m units. The unit price of its product is £2. On the production side, its unit variable cost is £1 and its total fixed cost is £0.25m. Calculate the company's degree of operating leverage at its expected sales level assuming sales increase above this level by 10%.

3 a) What does the degree of financial leverage measure?

   b) Given that the company described in question 2 faces a corporate tax rate of 30%, has £12.5m of debt outstanding at $r_d = 6\%$ and has 21m shares on issue, calculate its degree of financial leverage, at its expected level of EBIT, resulting from a 10% rise in EBIT.

4 What constitutes the intangible assets of a company? In what ways might the proportion of intangible assets influence the level of agency costs that a company is exposed to?

5 Consider a project with an initial capital outlay of £5m. It is expected to generate a constant annual operating profit of £1.2m in perpetuity. The company finances the project with £2m of debt capital at $r_d = 5\%$ and has a pure equity capitalisation rate of $r_e^* = 12\%$. The company's corporate tax rate is 30% and there are no depreciation allowances. Given that the costs of raising new finance represent 0.5% of the initial capital outlay on the project, calculate the project's adjusted net present value.

6 The existing market value of a company is £50m, made up of £10m of debt capital and £40m of equity capital. The company has decided to undertake a new project, costing £5m, which has an NPV of £8m.

   a) Calculate the amount of new debt and equity capital that the company must raise to finance the new project if the company wishes to maintain its existing capital structure.

   b) Demonstrate that, under this financing plan, when the new debt and equity is issued the capital structure of the company has not changed.

Exercises

1 What are the main factors determining the business risk of a company?

2 Assume that a company has a DOL = 2.5 and wants to maintain its DCL at 5.0.
   a) What degree of financial leverage should it aim for?
   b) What does this degree of combined leverage measure?
   c) On what assumptions is the measurement of the degree of operating leverage based?

3 Compare and contrast the weighted average and ANPV approaches to investment appraisal.

Endnotes

1. In a number of texts the relationships between business risk and operating leverage, and financial risk and financial leverage, are introduced prior to discussion of the capital

structure puzzle. This can cause confusion, especially since the analysis of these relationships presupposes, in the context of financial leverage, MM's capital structure irrelevancy propositions. It is hoped that by having postponed the present discussion to this stage such confusion is avoided and, in addition, that further insights into the importance of the financing decision, and its potential links with the investment decision, are provided.

2. As explained at the end of Chapter 1, the usual practice is to refer to the degree of total risk exposure, defined in terms of the coefficient of variation. The coefficient of variation is equal to the standard deviation of a variable (σ) divided by its mean or expected level denoted by E( ). In terms of EPS

$$\text{The Degree of Total Risk Exposure} = \frac{\sigma_{EPS}}{E(EPS)}$$

In Figure 10.1 the two distributions are drawn such that the coefficient of variation of the distribution associated with higher financial leverage exceeds that of the distribution associated with lower financial leverage. Thus the degree of total risk exposure is increasing with financial leverage.

3. Because an elasticity measure is being used, it is defined in relation to a given level of EBIT. Remember that the general nature of an elasticity is such that its magnitude depends on the point at which it is measured. Thus the DFL will change as the level of EBIT from which it is measured is changed. The present analysis measures the DFL at the expected or mean level of EBIT.

4. With a normal probability distribution being symmetric about its mean, the probability of an increase above the mean is equal to the probability of an identical decrease. This explains why the standard deviation, in relation to the mean of a normal distribution, can be used as a measure of risk.

5. The usual practice is to refer to the degree of business risk, defined in terms of the coefficient of variation of EBIT, where

$$\text{The Degree of Business Risk} = \frac{\sigma_{EBIT}}{E(EBIT)}$$

The degree of business risk measures the standard deviation of EBIT per £ of expected EBIT. In terms of Figure 10.2, the two distributions are drawn such that the coefficient of variation of the distribution associated with higher operating leverage exceeds that of the distribution associated with lower operating leverage.

6. In illustrating the calculation of the DCL, from Tables 10.1 and 10.2, only OP2 and FS2 can be used. OP2 creates the expected level of EBIT of £4m in FS2. In the other two financial structures the operating plans do not produce expected EBIT of £4m.

7. The discussion in this chapter has been carried out in terms of total business risk, as measured by σ_{EBIT}, as opposed to systematic business risk, as measured by an asset β coefficient. Given the assumptions, this does not materially affect the results of the analysis. For a technical discussion of the relationship between β and the degrees of operating and financial leverage, see Gahlon and Gentry (1982).

8. Assume B/V = 0.364; since V = B + S, S/V = 1 − B/V = 0.636, therefore, B/S = B/V ÷ S/V = 0.571.

References

Balakrishnan, S. and I. Fox, 'Asset Specificity, Firm Heterogeneity and Capital Structure', Strategic Management Journal, 1993

Barunch, L., 'On the Association between Operating Leverage and Risk', Journal of Financial and Quantitative Analysis, 1974

Chung, K., 'Asset Characteristics and Corporate Debt Policy', Journal of Business Finance and Accounting, 1993

Gahlon, J. and J. Gentry, 'The Relationship between Systematic Risk and the Degrees of Operating and Financial Leverage', Financial Management, 1982

Gailen, L., 'Leverage, Output Effects and the M-M Theorems', Journal of Financial Economics, 1977

Hutchinson, R. and L. Hunter, 'Determinants of Capital Structure in the UK Retailing Sector', International Journal of Retailing, Distribution and Consumer Research, 1995

Leibowitz, L. and S. Kogelman, 'Franchise Value and the Growth Process', Financial Analysts Journal, 1992

Levy, H. and R. Brooks, 'Financial Break-Even Analysis and the Value of the Firm', Financial Management, 1986

Long, M. and I. Malitz, 'The Investment-Financing Nexus: Some Empirical Evidence', in J. Stern and D. Chew (Eds.), The Revolution in Corporate Finance, Oxford, Blackwell, 1992

Myers, S., 'Interactions of Corporate Financing and Investment Decisions: Implications for Capital Budgeting', Journal of Finance, 1974

Myers, S., 'The Capital Structure Puzzle', Journal of Finance, 1984

O'Brien, T. and P. Vanderheiden, 'Empirical Measurement of Operating Leverage for Growing Firms', Financial Management, 1987

Prezas, A., 'Effects of Debt on the Degrees of Operating and Financial Leverage', Financial Management, 1987

Ross, S., R. Westerfield and J. Jaffe, Corporate Finance, Homewood, Ill., Irwin, 1993

Titman, S. and R. Wessels, 'The Determinants of Capital Structure Choice', Journal of Finance, 1988

11 Further issues in debt financing

Introduction

In Chapter 3 the principles involved in valuing debt and equity were examined in detail. Where debt financing was concerned the emphasis was on the pricing of standard or straight debt instruments, both gilt edged and corporate.

This chapter explores, as its central theme, some aspects of hybrid debt and lease financing. Hybrid debt involves marketable debt issues (bonds) which incorporate equity financing features, the two principal types being warrants and convertibles.

Warrants arise when a company issues standard debt and includes a future option, over a specified period, to purchase shares in the company at special option prices. Thus a warrant gives an investor the right to participate in the equity of a company. Convertible bonds give an investor the option to convert each bond into a specified number of shares. Convertibles have, therefore, similar features to warrants. They differ from the latter, however, in that when the option to convert is exercised, the outstanding debt is simply retired by being swapped, at no charge, for equity. In the case of warrants, if the option is exercised the equity is purchased at a special price but the debt issue remains outstanding to the end of its term to maturity.

Leasing is normally viewed as a form of debt financing. It involves a company gaining the use of an asset through some form of rental agreement, where the company makes regular fixed rental payments over the period of the lease. (In a number of cases the lease payments may be variable and tied to general interest rate changes or changes in the level of inflation.) Since the company has no ownership rights to the asset, the asset is relinquished (like repaying a principal amount borrowed) at the end of the lease period. One of the key aspects in determining a leasing strategy involves an NPV appraisal of a lease the asset versus a buy the asset decision.

Before examining aspects of hybrid debt and leasing, the chapter begins with a brief review of the features which may or may not be included in a bond's indenture provisions. A number of these have already been discussed. Brief comments are also included on debt financing through the banking system. This is followed by considering how NPV can be applied in assessing the appropriateness of a bond refunding strategy. After examining hybrid debt and leasing, the chapter draws to a close by giving further consideration to another aspect of financing which was introduced in Chapter 3: the term structure of interest rates. Alternative theories of the term structure are briefly reviewed, to determine whether management is indifferent to, or adopts a preference for, short-term relative to long-term borrowing strategies.

The debt contract

In Chapter 3 debt financing was examined in terms of corporate bond issues. From a company's point of view, since bonds make regular fixed interest payments and bondholders have a prior claim on assets over shareholders, the cost of debt capital is lower than the cost of equity capital. The indenture provisions of a bond, setting out the contract between borrower and lender, can be used to help determine the level of risk that the lender is exposed to. Given the positive risk–return trade-off, a company can lower its cost of debt capital by offering greater security to lenders. This can be achieved by backing bonds by some or all of the assets of a company and by including restrictive covenants which reduce agency costs.

Restrictive covenants can include special requirements that, for example, total debt should not exceed a specific percentage of total capital and/or that dividends should not be paid on common shares, unless earnings are maintained at or above a given level. Covenants may also include specified levels of financial ratios, for example, that the current ratio (current assets:current liabilities) should be maintained at or above some minimum level. The tighter the restrictive covenants, the lower the level of risk and the lower the cost of capital but the more restrictive is the future financing policy of the company while the particular bond issue remains outstanding.

Indenture provisions often include a sinking fund. This involves a company setting aside a fixed sum of money each year (or a given percentage of revenue or a given percentage of earnings) which, together with accrued interest, is generally sufficient to meet the repayments of the principal or face value of the bond on its redemption date. Again while reducing risk, a sinking fund can restrict a company's future financing strategy since it may represent a drain on internal investment funds.

In the UK, corporate bonds secured by assets are generally referred to as debentures, while corporate bonds which are unsecured are generally referred to as loan stock. Two broad types of secured debentures can be identified. The first is secured by a fixed charge over specific assets which cannot be disposed of while the bond is outstanding. In the event of default it is these assets which are sold to help pay off debt holders. The second, which is more risky and therefore can be expected to entail a higher cost of capital, is secured by a floating charge on all assets. These assets can be disposed of, but when default occurs the charge fixes on those assets which have not already been mortgaged. Loan stock, by being unsecured by either a fixed or floating charge, is in a higher risk category.

Bank financing

In the UK, relative to the US, companies are much less reliant on corporate bond issues, using bank lending as a major source of debt financing. Banks provide short-term funds in the form of overdrafts and back-up lines of credit, and medium and long-term funds in the form of term loans. Long-term bank loans are usually defined as having a life in excess of ten years. Most loans are offered at variable, as opposed to fixed, interest rates. The alternative ways of calculating loan interest were discussed, together with the concept of an APR, towards the end of Chapter 2.

Bank loans often have restrictive covenants of the type outlined above in order to reduce risk to the lender. The loan contract normally includes collateral in the form of a company's assets or, especially in the case of small businesses, personal assets of an owner-manager.

The restrictive covenants are included to deal with the agency problem of debt which applies to bank lending as well as bond financing. It can be argued, however, that a bank's costs of monitoring management's use of loans are less than the costs experienced by the more impersonal financial markets, especially when a company has a well-established relationship with a bank. In this respect, therefore, the cost of obtaining term loans may be less than the cost of obtaining debt capital through the bond markets. In addition personal banker–client relationships may enable restrictive covenants to be more precisely tailored to specific lending circumstances and may, especially for large-sized companies, create a better environment for renegotiating these restrictions as the trading conditions of a company develop and change.

Bank lending represents the main source of debt financing for small businesses and in many cases the dominant source of investment funds in the small firm's capital structure. Bank lending is explored in more detail in Chapter 14 which deals with some of the issues surrounding small business financing.

Call price features

Returning to the analysis of bond financing, the final factor to consider in the indenture provisions is a call price feature. This is a prominent aspect of corporate bond issues in the US and entails a company specifying a price at which it can call back a bond before its redemption date. The call can either be immediate, any time after a bond is issued, or deferrable; for example, the call might only be able to be exercised after the first five years of a bond's life. The call price is set above the face value of the issue and can be to the disadvantage of bondholders.

Consider a bond with a five-year deferred call feature which has a face value of $1000 and a call price of $1030. The bond has been outstanding for five years and interest rates are substantially below their level at the time of issue. The bond was initially sold at its par value but the fall in interest rates has caused its price to rise to $1040. If the call feature is exercised at $1030, bondholders lose $10 per bond. Consequently, in order to compensate for this type of disadvantage, callable, relative to non-callable, bonds require higher coupon payments.

Because of the inverse relationship between bond prices and interest rates, the inclusion of a call price feature only has a potential value to a company if a bond is issued during a period of cyclically high interest rates. If interest rates are cyclically low when an issue takes place, they can only be expected to rise, leading to a fall in the bond's price below its face value. In such circumstances exercising a call at a price above the bond's face value would be irrational.

There is considerable controversy over the value of a call feature. A call feature is said to give a company more flexibility in its financing strategy and to enable it to take advantage of a fall in interest rates through bond refunding. This assumes that managers can take an opinion, contrary to the EMH, on future interest rate movements. As discussed in Chapter 3, however, the EMH implies that the term structure of interest rates, at any given point in time, fully reflects the current state of knowledge on anticipated interest rate changes.

Even if the EMH does not hold, there could still be no advantage to including a call feature in a bond if management and the markets had the same ability to forecast interest rate changes. In these circumstances any interest cost advantage for the company would be exactly offset by the premium on the rate of return required by the market to take up the callable issue.

Kraus (1992) suggests that instead of these conventional arguments, the main value of including a call feature arises from the prospect of reducing interest rate risk (discussed in Chapter 3) which in turn may reduce a company's cost of equity capital. Thus the advantage of including a call feature in a bond can be explained in terms of a rise in the market value of equity.

In the UK this call price feature may only be included in perpetual bonds. In the case of bonds with finite redemption dates, only offers to repurchase can be made in the hope that they are sufficiently attractive to bondholders. A bondholder is not obliged to accept such an offer.

Bond refunding

The benefit of a call price feature is that it enables a company to call in an outstanding bond when it appears appropriate to adopt a refunding strategy. Bond refinancing occurs where a debt issue was made during a period of high interest rates and, therefore, required a company to offer a high coupon interest rate. If, before the bond has reached its maturity date, there are substantial falls in interest rates, the company can consider retiring the bond by making a new issue. Proceeds from the new issue are used to finance the repurchase of the original bond at the lower interest cost on the new issue. The life of the new bond is equal to the remainder of the original bond's term to maturity.

Tables 11.1A and 11.1B illustrate how NPV is applied to help determine whether or not a bond issue should be refunded. A US callable bond is used as an example. Consider a company which issued, five years ago, $50m worth of callable bonds with a 30-year maturity, offering a 14% coupon interest rate (r_c). The corporate tax rate, then as now, is 40% and it is assumed for simplicity that only annual end-of-year interest payments are made. The par value of each bond is $1000 and the call price is $1100, indicating a call premium over par value of $100. Current interest rates are relatively low and the company could issue a new 25-year bond, now, to raise $50m to repurchase the existing issue at its call price.

Given current interest rates, if the new issue is to be sold at par ($1000), a 10% coupon rate would be required to ensure that the new issue is taken up by the market. Thus $r_c = r_d = 10\%$ represents the cost of capital that the company uses in making its NPV assessment.[1] Assuming the new and existing issues have identical characteristics, this also represents the required rate of return for existing bondholders indicating, by Equation 3.1a, that the current market value of the existing bond is:

Table 11.1A: Bond refunding

Funding: $50m, Corporate tax rate: 40%
Existing bond: $r_c = 14\%$, par value $1000, initial term 30 years, currently 25
    years outstanding, issue costs 0.6% of funding.
Potential new bond: $r_c = 10\%$, par value $1000, term 25 years, issue cost 0.8%
    of funding.
After tax discount rate for refunding appraisal: $r_d(1 - t_c) = .10(1 - .4) = 6\%$

Bond Refunding Benefits
Annual interest after tax
    Existing bond: $(.14)(\$50m)(1 - .4) = \$4.20m$
    New bond: $(.10)(\$50m)(1 - .4) = \$3.00m$
    Interest savings: $\$4.20m - \$3.00m = \$1.20m$

Present value of interest savings
    $\$1.20m \, (PVIFA_{25,6}) = \$1.20m(12.783) = \$15.34m$

$$BV_0 = \$140 \, PVIFA_{25,10} + \$1000 \, PVIF_{25,10}$$
$$= \$140(9.077) + \$1000(0.092) = \$1362.78$$

It can therefore be seen that, other things being equal, there is a considerable disadvantage to existing bondholders if the call is exercised and they receive only $1100 for each bond.

The NPV of refunding

The NPV takes account of the present value of the costs and benefits of the potential refunding. The main benefit is in interest cost savings. These are shown in Table 11.1A. Because debt financing is being used, interest costs are tax deductible and the company uses its after-tax cost of debt capital as the discount rate: $0.10(1 - .4) = 0.06$ or 6%. The present value of the interest savings if refunding takes place is $15.34m.

The main costs of refunding are associated with the call premium to be paid and the net issue costs associated with the existing bond and the potential new bond. The latter costs arise from underwriting fees, etc.

With a call price of $1100, the call price premium represents 10% of the par value of the existing bond. Thus the total after-tax cost of exercising the call premium is, as Table 11.1B indicates, $0.10(\$50m)(1 - .4) = \$3m$.

In general, issue costs are tax deductible but since the tax benefits arise because the company has use of the funds raised over the life of a debt issue, these costs are capitalised and amortised, that is, effectively depreciated, for tax purposes.

In the case of the new bond the issue costs are assumed to be 0.8% of the funds raised, that is $(0.008)(\$50m) = \$0.4m$. As Table 11.1B shows, these are amortised over a 25-year period to determine the present value of the tax benefits. These benefits are then deducted from the current cash outlay of $0.4m in order to determine the net present issue costs of the new bond.

When the existing bond was originally floated issue costs represented 0.6% of the funds raised, $(0.006)(\$50m) = \$0.30m$, and were treated in exactly the same way for

Table 11.1B: Bond refunding

Bond Refunding Costs

Call premium after tax
  $(.10)(\$50m)(1 - .4) = \$3.00m$
New bond issue costs: $0.40m
  Amortised: $\$0.40/25 = \$16,000$
  PV annual tax benefit: $\$16,000(.4)(12.783) = \$0.082m$
Net present issue costs of new bond: $\$0.40 - \$0.082 = \$0.318m$
Existing bond issue costs: $\$0.30m$
  Amortised: $\$0.30/30 = \$10,000$
  PV tax benefit lost remaining 25 years: $\$10,000(.4)(12.783) = \$51,132$
  Costs amortised to date (after 5 years): $5(\$10,000) = \$50,000$
  Cost write-off: $\$0.30m - \$0.05m = \$0.25m$
  Tax benefit from cost write-off: $\$0.25m(.4) = \$0.1m$

Net present issue costs of existing bond: $\$51,132 - \$100,000 = -\$48,868$
Overlapping interest cost for one month:
$1/12$ of annual interest cost original bond $= (0.0833)(\$4.2m) = \$349,860$

NPV of Refunding Strategy

	$
Present value of interest savings	15,340,000
Call premium	−3,000,000
Net present issue costs new bond	−318,000
Net present issue costs old bond	48,868
Overlapping interest	−349,860
	NPV = 11,721,008

tax purposes as the issue costs on the new bond. Now, however, the existing bonds are to be refunded. The company must, therefore, calculate the present value of the tax benefits which would have accrued had the existing bond been outstanding for the remaining 25 years of its life, and treat these as lost tax benefits. The appropriate calculations are shown in Table 11.1B.

On the other hand there will be a current tax advantage to consider in respect of the existing bonds because the unamortised issue costs will be written off. Annually, over the 30-year period, the issue cost on the existing bond is $\$0.30m/30 = \$10,000$; therefore, with costs of $\$0.30m - 5(\$10,000) = \$0.25m$ to be written off, a current tax saving of $(.4)(\$0.25m) = \$0.1m$ arises.

Finally, there may be a short period after the new bond is sold before the funds raised can be paid out on the bond which has been recalled. During this overlapping period the interest on the recalled bond represents a cost to the company. Assuming, in this example, that the overlapping period is one month, this cost is equal to approximately one-twelfth of the annual interest cost of the original bond.

Bringing all of the above benefits (from Table 11.1A) and costs together in the last part of Table 11.1B, the NPV of this refunding strategy is approximately $11.72m. While the NPV is positive, the actual decision on refunding might be deferred. This would depend on management's opinion, if they could take one, on whether and when further falls in interest rates are due.

If the call price operated, as in the case of a UK bond, through a company only being able to offer to repurchase an existing issue, rejection of the offer would depend on the view existing bondholders take of the likelihood and timing of future interest rate falls. Anticipated falls in interest rates would probably induce rejection of the offer since falls in interest rates would induce further capital gains (in relation to the par value). Alternatively, if existing bondholders' assessments indicate a rise in interest rates, and therefore a fall in bond prices, bondholders might be encouraged to take up the offer. In opportunity cost terms they would be able to invest the proceeds at higher rates of interest, assuming that the anticipated rise in interest rates occurs.

Warrants

Warrants entail the right, but not the obligation, to purchase a given number of shares in a company at a specified option price. If issued, they are usually accompanied by an offer of straight debt capital. At the time of issue the option price is set between 15% and 25% above a company's current share price, with the right to exercise the warrant having an expiry date.[2]

Consider a company whose current share price is £1.80. It has decided to issue bonds with 25 years to maturity. Each bond has a warrant attached with the option to purchase one share in the company at an option price, P_{opt}, of £2.20. This option expires after six years. Assuming that the issue is taken up by the market, the implication is that the market believes the company to have good, but risky, future growth prospects. These growth prospects, as and if they are realised, will result in the company's share price rising over time and exceeding the option price. Providing this occurs before the expiry of the option, investors who choose to exercise their warrant options can make significant gains.

The value of exercising the option, at any time before the expiry date, is referred to as the exercise value, EV_t, and simply defined as:

$$EV_t = (P_t - P_{opt})(\text{Number of Shares on Option}) \qquad (11.1)$$

In the above example, if the share price at the end of three years has risen to £3.20 then the EV of the warrant will be

$$EV = (£3.20 - £2.20)(1) = £1$$

Note that if the share price falls below the option price, the EV will not be negative. By definition it will be zero since there would be no reason to exercise the warrant, and pay £2.20 for a share, when the share could be bought on the market at a lower price.

Because of this potential to take an equity stake in the company at an advantageous price (when the market price of equity exceeds the option price), warrant holders have the potential right to a share in the company's future dividend income and capital gains. Consequently, when bonds are issued with warrants, debt is raised at a lower coupon interest rate than would be the case if a hybrid feature had been excluded; that is, if the bonds had been issued without warrants.

The market price of a warrant

One of the features of warrants is that they can be detached from the bond issue and sold separately. Because they have a speculative appeal, deriving from the probabilities of the share price rising above the option price (and potentially falling

Table 11.2: Illustrating warrants

XYZ company warrant: one share on option at option price of £1.50
Assume market price of warrant = exercise value of warrant

Exercise Value = (Share Price − Option Price)(Number of Shares on Option)

Share Investment	Warrant Investment
Current share price £3.20	EV = (£3.20 − £1.50)(1) = £1.70
Share price rises to: £6.40	EV = (£6.40 − £1.50)(1) = £4.90
Capital gain: (£6.40 − £3.20)/£3.20 = 100%	Capital gain: (£4.90 − £1.70)/£1.70 = 188%
Maximum possible loss if share purchased: £3.20	Maximum possible loss if warrant purchased: £1.70

Share Investment	Warrant Investment
Current share price £6.00	EV = (£6 − £1.50)(1) = £4.50
Share price rises to: £12.00	EV = (£12 − £1.50)(1) = £10.50
Capital gain: (£12 − £6)/£6 = 100%	Capital gain: (£10.50 − £4.50)/£6 = 133%
Maximum possible loss if share purchased: £6.00	Maximum possible loss if warrant purchased: £4.50

again), warrants sell in the market at a premium over their exercise value. To understand why, assume initially that a warrant's market price is equal to its exercise value and consider the example in the first half of Table 11.2.

In Table 11.2 an investor has two alternative strategies: to purchase a share in the XYZ company, at a current price of £3.20, or an XYZ warrant. The option price on this warrant is £1.50. The warrant has one share on option, therefore

EV = (£3.20 − £1.50)(1) = £1.70

and, assuming that the warrant sells at its EV, its market price is £1.70.

Table 11.2 shows how the investor can compare the returns on each of the above strategies under a rise in the share's price. No dividends are paid on the share over this return period and the share, if purchased, or the warrant, if purchased, is sold at the end of the return period so as to realise the capital gains.

As Table 11.2 indicates, if the share price doubles the capital gain from purchasing the share is considerably less than the capital gain from purchasing the warrant. On the other hand, if the share price falls the maximum loss from purchasing the share is £3.20, when the share price completely collapses. This is considerably more than the maximum loss from purchasing the warrant, which is limited to its price of £1.70.

In this example, if the warrant is priced at its exercise value there is an enhanced capital gains feature and a limited loss protection feature from holding the warrant, relative to the share. Consequently the market will place a positive value on these features thus explaining why, in practice, the market will price the warrant at a premium above its exercise value.

As the company's share price rises, however, the premium over exercise value will decline. This occurs for a number of reasons. First, the higher the share price, the smaller both the enhanced capital gain and limited loss protection features, as demonstrated in the second half of Table 11.2. Second, the rise in a company's share price will indicate that its growth potential is being realised and that the risk surrounding its future performance is being reduced. Warrant holders will, there-

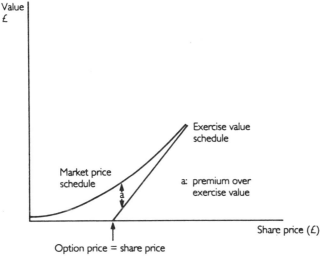

Figure 11.1   The market price and exercise value of a warrant

fore, be increasingly motivated to exercise their options. This will enable them to partake in future dividend payouts, which are likely to be increased, and in capital gains from further share price rises. Once a warrant is actually exercised it can only be worth its exercise value. Third, as the share price rise takes place in a time dimension, it will be associated with a shortening of the interval to the expiry date of the warrant. This again increases the probability that the warrant will be exercised (before it is too late to do so) and, therefore, reduces the value of the premium.

The relationships between the market price and exercise value of a warrant and the price of the underlying equity are shown in Figure 11.1. (The exercise value schedule is based on the illustration in Table 11.2.)

Reasons for issuing warrants

The circumstances under which a company will prefer to issue straight debt capital with warrants were at one time argued to arise from a company's desire to issue equity. The company was considered to believe, contrary to the EMH, that its share price was considerably undervalued. It therefore chose hybrid debt, which gave it the ability to set the option price above its current share price so as to more closely reflect the intrinsic value of its equity.

Modern arguments in favour of issuing warrants focus on companies with high risk, high growth potential which want to issue debt. Because of their risk, however, a straight debt issue would incur a relatively high cost of capital. By issuing bonds with warrants the cost of debt capital can be reduced since the market value of a warrant, because of its speculative appeal, increases with risk. In other words, the hybrid nature of combining straight debt with equity provides a substitution effect of a higher warrant value against a lower cost of debt. This implies that the value of this financing instrument is less sensitive to the risk of a company's operations.

Bonds with warrants also help mitigate some of the agency costs of debt which arise in a high risk situation. In, for example, the presence of the asset substitution problem, straight bondholders require compensation in the form of higher returns. As this problem is to the potential advantage of equity holders, warrants give holders a potential equity participation feature. Warrants may also enable a company to avoid some of the limitations on their future financing flexibility which otherwise would have to be imposed through restrictive covenants. In particular, warrants are often issued with unsecured loan stock.

Convertibles

A convertible bond is an alternative form of hybrid debt financing. It is issued for mainly the same reasons as warrants. In the case of a convertible the bond is accompanied by the right to convert the bond, over a specific period, into a specified number of shares.[3] While warrants can be detached from an outstanding bond issue and sold separately, this facility is not available for convertibles. Consequently, the market value of a convertible, which is explained below, is determined both by its straight debt feature and its conversion feature.

In setting the terms of a convertible issue a company's main decision, in relation to the conversion feature, is specifying the implicit share price at which conversion can take place. It is an implicit price because each bond is swapped for a specified number of shares. At the time of issue the conversion price is likely to be set between 15% and 25% above a company's current share price.

Consider a company which is raising debt by issuing a convertible bond with a par value of £100. Its current share price is £2.20 and it sets its conversion price, P_c, at £2.78. The conversion ratio, R, which determines the number of shares into which each bond can be converted, is defined by the par value of the bond, M, divided by the conversion price; that is:

$$R = \frac{M}{P_c} \tag{11.2}$$

In the present example,

$$R = \frac{£100}{£2.78} = 36$$

indicating that, on the conversion of each bond, an investor will receive 36 shares in the company in question.

Conversion value

At a given point in time, over the conversion period, the conversion value, CV_t, is measured by the conversion ratio times the share price in period t, thus:

$$CV_t = P_t R \tag{11.3}$$

If, for example, two years after the above issue is made the issuing company's share price has risen from £2.20 to £2.35, the conversion value will have risen from its initial level of

$$CV_0 = £2.20(36) = £79.20$$

to

$$CV_2 = £2.35(36) = £84.60$$

If at the end of four years the share price rises to £3.00, the conversion value will exceed the price at which the convertible was originally sold, its par value of £100, since

$$CV_4 = £3.00(36) = £108.00$$

If the market has taken up a convertible, one of the reasons will be its belief that there is a reasonable probability that the company's risky high growth strategy will pay off. Consequently, a conversion value schedule is often specified, theoretically, in terms of the expected growth rate in the company's share price. Assuming that the share price at the time of issue, P_0, will grow at an annual compound rate g, Equation 11.3 can be rewritten as:

$$CV_t = P_0(1 + g)^t(R) \qquad (11.3a)$$

Straight debt value

The convertible's straight debt feature is valued using the bond pricing principles in Equation 3.1, where the bond value, in any year t, with n years to maturity is:

$$BV_t = \sum_{t=1}^{n} \frac{I_t}{(1 + r_d)^t} + \frac{M}{(1 + r_d)^n} \qquad (11.4)$$

To illustrate, assume in the above example that the convertible at the time of issue had an n = 20-year term to maturity and was offered with a coupon rate of $r_c = 8\%$. With M = £100, the annual end-of-year interest payments are £8 per bond. The convertible bond was initially sold at its par value of £100. If this had been a straight debt issue, the coupon rate would have had to have been set equal to the required rate of return on an outstanding bond of similar risk and term to maturity. Because the bond has a conversion feature, however, the coupon rate was set below the required rate, assumed to be $r_d = 10\%$. Thus at the time of issue the straight debt value of the convertible is below its par value (as is its conversion value of £79.20). At the time of issue the straight debt value is:

$$BV_0 = \sum_{t=1}^{20} \frac{£8}{(1.10)^t} + \frac{£100}{(1.10)^{20}}$$

$$= £8 \ PVIFA_{20,10} + £100 \ PVIF_{20,10}$$

$$= £8(8.514) + £100(0.149) = £83$$

The straight debt value will rise, assuming r_d remains constant, as time elapses. At the end of six years, for example, with a 14-year term to maturity:

$$BV_6 = £8 \ PVIFA_{14,10} + £100 \ PVIF_{14,10} = £8(7.786) + £100(0.263) = £88.59$$

At the end of its life, assuming it is not converted, it will approximate its par value.

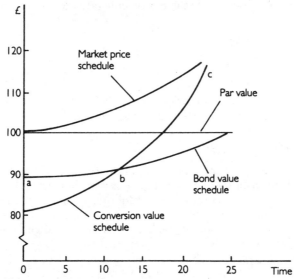

Figure 11.2   Bond value, conversion value and market price schedules of a convertible loan stock

The market value of a convertible

In Figure 11.2 the straight debt and conversion values are illustrated in relation to a convertible's market price. Figure 11.2 is based on the example given in Table 11.3. This example is used to explain the concept of the market value floor of a convertible and to demonstrate why a convertible's market price is at a premium above both its bond and conversion values.

The market value floor

In the example in Table 11.3, $BV_0 = £88.32$ and $CV_0 = £80.40$, both of which are below the issue price of £100. At the end of year one, all other things being equal, the bond value will have risen to $BV_1 = £88.51$ because of the pure time discounting effect, and the conversion value will have risen to £82.01 because the share price will have increased by 2% over the first year.

Now consider an investor who wishes to buy a straight bond at the end of year one. If the market price of this convertible is below its value as a straight debt instrument, that is, below £88.51, the investor will view the convertible as a bargain and purchase it. In an efficient bond market, however, all bond investors will take this view, so that the forces of supply and demand will always ensure that the convertible never sells below its bond value.

Consider another situation, illustrated in Table 11.3, where at the end of year eight an investor wishes to buy equity in this company. If the market price of the convertible is below its conversion value, that is, below £94.23, the investor will view the convertible as a bargain, purchase it, and exercise the right to convert into 67 shares per convertible bond. In an efficient equity market all equity investors will take this view, so that the forces of supply and demand will ensure that the convertible never sells below its conversion value.

Table 11.3: Illustrating convertibles

Convertible bond initially issued with n = 25 years to maturity.
Par value M = £100, Coupon interest rate r_c = 6%, Discount rate r_d = 7%
Annual fixed interest payment $I = r_c M$ = £6
Share price at time of issue: P_o = £1.20, Conversion price P_c = £1.493
Annual compound rate of growth in share price, g = 2%
  Conversion ratio: $R = M/P_c$ = £100/£1.493 = 67

$$\text{Bond value: } BV_{t-1} = \sum_{t=1}^{n} \frac{I}{(1 + r_d)^t} + \frac{M}{(1 + r_d)^n} = I(PVIFA_{n,rd}) + M(PVIF_{n,rd})$$

Conversion value: $C_t = P_o(1 + g)^t(R)$
(Use future value interest factors to compute $(1 + g)^t$)

Bond Value	Conversion Value
At time of issue	
$BV_o = £6(PVIFA_{25,7}) + £100(PVIF_{25,7}) = £88.32$	$CV_o = £1.20(FVIF_{n,7})(67) = £80.4$
At end of year 1	
$BV_1 = £6(PVIFA_{24,7}) + £100(PVIF_{24,7}) = £88.51$	$CV_1 = £1.20(FVIF_{1,2})(67) = £82.01$
At end of year 8	
$BV_8 = £6(PVIFA_{17,7}) + £100(PVIF_{17,7}) = £90.28$	$CV_8 = £1.20(FVIF_{8,2})(67) = £94.23$
At end of year 15	
$BV_{15} = £6(PVIFA_{10,7}) + £100(PVIF_{10,7}) = £92.94$	$CV_{15} = £1.20(FVIF_{15,2})(67) = £108.2$

In the light of these two examples the market value floor of a convertible can be defined, in Figure 11.2, by the line abc. In other words the market value floor specifies the minimum price below which a convertible will never sell. It is determined by BV_t when $BV_t > CV_t$, and by CV_t when $CV_t > BV_t$. The market value floor can vary as market rates of interest vary and as expectations in respect of a company's growth rate vary.

Explaining a convertible's premium
The convertible sells at a premium above its market value floor (that is, above both its bond and conversion values) because of the speculative appeal of its equity feature, combined with limited loss protection. This is explained next.

Consider an investor who wishes to purchase £100 of shares in the company, characterised in Table 11.3, at the end of year zero. The investor has a choice of purchasing the shares directly from the market, or purchasing the convertible at £100. If, just after purchase, the share price halves, the direct purchase of shares will have led to a 50% capital loss. On the other hand if the convertible is purchased, its market price can only fall, at maximum, to its straight debt value[4] of £88.32, indicating a maximum capital loss of (£88.32 − £100)/£100 = 11.68%. The market places a value on this limited loss protection feature; consequently the convertible sells at a premium above its bond and conversion values.

For roughly the same reasons as a warrant's premium declines with respect to its exercise value as the underlying share price rises, so a convertible's premium declines with respect to its conversion value as time elapses. Assuming in the case of a convertible that its share price grows through time, holders of the convertible will be increasingly attracted to exercise their conversion rights so that they can partake in the future capital gains from equity ownership and in dividend income. Once actual conversion takes place the value of a convertible can only be equal to its conversion value; thus as the probability of conversion increases, the premium over conversion value will decline. In addition, as the share price rises and the conversion value exceeds the straight debt value, the benefits of the limited loss protection feature decline relatively.

Lease financing

Up to this point in the book it has been assumed that when a company determines the projects it wants to invest in, it acquires ownership rights in the associated tangible assets. Consequently, the financing decision has focused on the types of capital, long-term debt and/or equity used to purchase plant, equipment, land and buildings. As an alternative to acquiring ownership rights a company can finance assets through leasing. Lease financing involves borrowing an asset for a specified period; making regular rental payments on it, often fixed but sometimes variable; and then returning it to its owner at the end of the leasing period. Hire purchase has similar characteristics but, unlike leasing, results in a company acquiring the ownership rights to an asset when the hire-purchase agreement terminates.

Types of leasing

There are many forms of leasing involving short, medium and long-term contracts. In the short to medium term, for example, a company in the construction industry may lease particular items of equipment which are specific to one-off construction projects. At a more general level, large numbers of companies negotiate leasing agreements in respect of their car fleets of between two and four years duration. These types of contract are often referred to as service leases since their terms and conditions involve the lessor, the company who owns and lends the asset, arranging the asset's insurance cover and undertaking its repair and maintenance. Charges for these services are built into the lease payments made by the lessee, the company who borrows the asset. A service lease usually gives the lessee a right to cancel before the end of the lease's term, subject to the payment of a cancellation fee.

Longer-term leasing agreements are usually associated with assets which a lessee expects to utilise for considerable periods of time: land, buildings, office space and capital equipment. In most of these cases, but not all, there is no service lease element involved since it is the lessee who is under a contractual obligation to maintain and insure the asset.

Leases can also be categorised as operating or financial leases according to how the lessor intends utilising the asset when it is returned at the end of the leasing agreement. In the case of an operating lease the lessor may use the asset as the basis for a subsequent lease.

A service lease is a special type of operating lease since it often involves assets, such as office equipment and cars, which are not operated for their full economic life during their initial leasing period. These assets have to be leased again (or sold) before the lessor company can recover its investment. This partly explains why the lessor takes on the responsibility of maintaining and insuring the asset in order to ensure that it is in reasonable condition at the end of each leasing term.

Alternatively, a financial or capital lease involves a lessee having effective use of an asset for the main part of the asset's economic life. Thus the lessor normally disposes of the asset, at the end of the first leasing agreement, for a 'scrap' value and has no incentive to undertake responsibilities for service and maintenance. In addition, financial leases cannot be cancelled by either the lessee or the lessor. A financial lease is, therefore, closest in its characteristics to debt financing.

Two other forms of leasing are important: sale and leaseback and a leveraged lease. Sale and leaseback involves a company raising capital by selling assets which it owns but, as part of the sale agreement, leasing the assets back for a specified period. A company may, for example, sell an office block and lease the whole or part of the office space back for a specified number of years. A leveraged lease involves a third party who supplies funds to the lessor to purchase an asset. The asset is then leased, usually under a financial leasing agreement.

Reasons for leasing

There are a number of reasons which have been advanced for preferring to lease an asset as opposed to purchasing it. In the case of a service lease the main reasons relate to the convenience of passing servicing and insurance responsibilities to the lessor. There is also the potential flexibility that cancelling the lease provides if a company's trading conditions change or the asset becomes obsolete through technical progress.

In an efficient market, however, these reasons are somewhat weak. First, the lease payments will include direct insurance and service costs and indirect administration costs. Lessees would have incurred these costs themselves if they had arranged these services on their own behalf. Second, the lease payments and cancellation fees will include an element of compensation for the lessor in respect of the risk that the lessee might cancel the leasing agreement. Under the purchase of an asset the risk that the company might default on, for example, the debt raised to finance it would be included in the company's cost of capital. Third, in a perfect market a company which purchased an asset and had to sell it in a secondhand market, before the end of its useful economic life, would realise the asset's intrinsic value. There would, therefore, be no real advantage to be gained from the potential to cancel a leasing agreement.

There may, however, be some advantages in service leasing, especially for small firms or large companies using specialised pieces of equipment. In these cases scale economies in servicing and administration costs may only be available to the lessor, who operates a relatively large pool of similar assets. There may also be advantages to lessees who, because of limited knowledge of the technical nature of the equipment, believe that leasing, with a service agreement, is the only viable option available.

Off-balance sheet items
Another questionable reason for preferring to lease an asset, especially under an operating lease agreement, is the effect it has, or effectively does not have, on a

company's balance sheet. The argument in favour of an operating lease arises when a company is close to its target debt:equity ratio, and supposedly has difficulty raising further debt capital because of restrictions imposed by existing bond covenants. Independently, a rise in its debt:equity ratio may increase its cost of capital.

As an operating lease is an off-balance sheet item, it is not included as part of a company's assets and liabilities and will not change a company's recorded capital structure. Thus existing covenants can supposedly be circumvented and the debt:equity ratio maintained at its target level. A financial lease is recorded in the balance sheet and will be interpreted as a form of debt financing thus changing the capital structure.

In an efficient market, however, both debt and equity holders, and indeed lessors, would be aware of the real capital structure impact of operating leases. Thus any change in the total market value of a company would reflect any change in the company's intrinsic value independently of the differences in the accounting treatment between straight debt capital, operating leases and financial leases.

Both operating and financial leases have been said to provide greater financing flexibility when they substitute for debt capital because neither form of lease will include covenants restricting a company's future financing policy. This again is a dubious argument in the context of the EMH.

Tax asymmetries

The main and unambiguous advantage in leasing lies in tax asymmetries between lessees and lessors and the potential each has to create a depreciation tax shield on a given asset. Recall, from Chapter 6, that the purchase of an asset enables a company to set allowable depreciation charges against its tax payments. In the extreme, a company which is not subject to tax cannot create a depreciation tax shield by purchasing an asset. In this case such a shield can only be activated by leasing an asset from a company which is subject to tax. The incentive for both lessee and lessor is to share the benefits of activation in negotiating the lease payment schedule. In general the potential exists to maximise depreciation tax shields, by leasing as opposed to buying, providing that the lessee's marginal tax rate is less than the lessor's.

Ultimately the only way of determining whether there is a preference for a lease or a buy decision is through formal investment appraisal. This is illustrated next, in terms of a financial lease.

The lease versus buy decision

Following the principles of investment appraisal set out in Chapter 6, the lease versus buy decision involves discounting the incremental net cash flows between these two options to obtain an NPV. On the initial hypothesis that the buy decision is to be rejected, the NPV is interpreted as the net advantage to leasing, NAL. Thus, for a given asset i, leasing is advantageous if

$$NAL_i > 0 \qquad\qquad (11.5)$$

Alternatively, if

$$NAL_i < 0 \qquad\qquad (11.5a)$$

the initial hypothesis is overturned and a buy decision is made. If $NAL_i = 0$, a company will be indifferent between the lease v. buy decision.

With the NPV formulated in this way, the current price (or cost of purchase) of an asset, I_0, represents a saving or benefit to a company. The other principal incremental NCFs occurring over the n year term of a lease are primarily made up of costs and are:
- the annual depreciation tax shield forgone by not purchasing the asset (a cost);
- the residual value of the asset forgone at the end of the leasing term (a cost);
- the lease payments (costs); and
- the incremental operating costs between the lease and buy alternatives (which can either represent costs or benefits).

Since a financial lease is a form of debt financing, the lease versus buy option can be interpreted as a lease versus purchase the asset with, in the latter case, 100% debt capital being used. Therefore the appropriate discount rate in determining the NAL would be the required rate of return on debt of the same maturity and risk as the lease.[5] Assuming that a financial lease has no restrictive covenants and is not secured in any way, the appropriate debt instrument would be an unsecured bond (in UK terms, loan stock).

In summary the NAL can be defined, on an after-tax basis, as:

$$NAL = I_0 - \sum_{t=0}^{n} \frac{\text{Incremental After-tax NCF}_t}{[1 + r_d(1 - t_c)]^t} \qquad\qquad (11.6)$$

The summation runs from $t = 0$, instead of the usual $t = 1$, to allow for the fact that lease payments are made in advance, the first lease payment being made at t_0 when the asset is initially borrowed.

Consider an example where a company has made a project investment decision requiring use of a piece of capital equipment costing £30,000. The equipment has a five-year life, has no residual value and its operating costs are identical under either a lease or buy option. If the company purchases the equipment, straight-line depreciation applies for tax purposes.

The company is considering either buying the equipment or entering into a five-year financial lease, with annual lease payments of £7000. The first lease payments, at the beginning of year one, can be effectively treated as occurring at the end of year zero. Like fixed interest charges, the lease payments are tax deductible, however, it is assumed that tax is paid on an end of year basis. The cost of debt capital is $r_d = 10\%$, and the after-tax discount rate, assuming that the company's marginal tax rate is 30%, is:

$$r_d(1 - t_c) = 0.10(1 - .3) = 0.07 \text{ or } 7\%$$

The incremental after-tax net cash flows, in this lease versus buy example, are set out

Table 11.4: A lease versus buy decision

Purchase price of equipment: £30,000
Annual depreciation: £30,000/5 = £6000
Annual payment on 5-year financial lease: £7000
$t_c = 30\%$, $r_d = 10\%$ thus $r_d(1 - t_c) = 7\%$

Year End	Lease payments[1] £	Tax allowance on lease payments £	Net of tax lease payments £	Depreciation £
0	7000		7000	
1	7000	2100	4900	6000
2	7000	2100	4900	6000
3	7000	2100	4900	6000
4	7000	2100	4900	6000
5		2100	−2100	6000

Present Value of After-Tax Lease Payments:
  $£7000 + £4900(PVIFA_{4,7}) - £2100(PVIF_{5,7})$
  $= £7000 + £4900(3.387) - £2100(0.713) = £22,099$

Present Value of Depreciation Tax Shield:
  $(.3)(£6000)(PVIFA_{5,7})$
  $= (.3)(£6000)(4.10) = £7380$

NAL = I_0 − PV after-tax lease payments − PV depreciation tax shield
  $= £30,000 - £22,099 - £7380 = £521$

[1] Annual lease payments made in advance, thus the first lease payment of £7000 is made at the beginning of year one, to all intents and purposes, at the end of year 0.

in Table 11.4. The NAL is equal to the purchase price of the equipment (the benefit from not buying the asset) minus the present value of the net of tax lease payments minus the present value of the depreciation tax shield forgone by not purchasing the equipment, that is:

  · NAL $= £30,000 - £22,099 - £7380 = £521$

As the NAL > 0, the company should lease the asset.[6]

The term structure of interest rates

In considering the financing decision attention has been focused on long-term sources of capital, a major theme being whether or not a company needed to identify, and therefore target, a particular capital structure which would maximise its market value. If, as Chapter 3 indicated, the term structure of interest rates[7] tends to slope upwards for most periods of time, there would appear to be a strong rationale for including a significant proportion of short-term debt in the capital structure. An upward sloping yield curve implies that short-term gilt rates (and hence the general level of short-term interest rates) are lower than long-term gilt rates (and hence the general level of long-term interest rates). Consequently the cost of a company's short-term capital appears to be less than the cost of its long-term capital, or does it?

The maturity structure of assets and liabilities

The issue of the relationship between short-term and long-term interest rates is potentially important. This is not just because the costs of financing may differ on a short-term, relative to a long-term, basis but because short-term debt capital can be used to finance assets with relatively long terms to maturity.

Consider, for example, a new piece of equipment which has an economic life of 15 years. This could be financed with a 15-year bond or a 15-year bank loan or a 15-year financial lease. Alternatively, a company could choose to finance the equipment with a series of one-year bank loans over a 15-year period, renegotiating the terms and conditions of short-term borrowing as each one-year loan matures. In other words a company does not need to match the maturity structure of its assets and liabilities: it does not need to finance a building which has a 50-year life with a 50-year loan, or a piece of equipment which it needs for six months with a six-month bank loan or a six-month operating lease. The maturity structure of assets and liabilities can diverge; indeed there is nothing to stop a company financing short-term assets with long-term capital.

The view which a company takes on short-term versus long-term financing depends crucially on the theories explaining the shape of the term structure of interest rates. There are three main theories: the pure expectations hypothesis, the capital risk (or liquidity premium) hypothesis and the market segmentation hypothesis. Under the first of these, a company would be indifferent about choosing between long-term and short-term financing but might not be indifferent if either of the latter two hypotheses hold.

The pure expectations hypothesis

The pure expectations hypothesis argues that long-term interest rates exceed short-term interest rates only because the market expects short-term interest rates to rise in the future.

Consider a company which wants to borrow a given sum of money for two years. It can negotiate a two-year term loan at an annual rate of interest of $r_2 = 8\%$. (The 'two' subscript refers to the fact that this rate of interest is negotiated on a two-year term.) Alternatively, the company could negotiate a one-year loan at a rate of interest of $_0r_1 = 7\%$, that is, a rate of interest now (negotiated at the end of period zero) for year one. If this latter financing route is taken, the company would negotiate, at the end of year one, a further one-year loan. The company will, however, have an expectation now of what the single period or short-term rate of interest will be in year two. Assume the company expects this to be $_1r_2 = 9\%$.

Under the pure expectations hypothesis the financial markets will have produced a situation where

$$(1 + {_0r_1})(1 + {_1r_2}) = (1 + r_2)^2 \tag{11.7}$$

That is, a loan of £1 now, borrowed for two years at an annual rate of interest of r_2, will be identical to two one-year loans at a rate of interest of $_0r_1$ for the first year and at an expected rate of interest of $_1r_2$ for the second year. For a three-period case, under the pure expectations hypothesis,

$$(1 + {_0}r_1)(1 + {_1}r_2)(1 + {_2}r_3) = (1 + r_3)^3 \qquad (11.7a)$$

The above example has been set up under the pure expectations hypothesis. Thus, by Equation 11.7,

$$(1.07)(1.09) = (1.08)^2 = 1.17$$

In other words, £1 will compound to £1.17 under the two-year loan and also £1.17 under two one-year loans.

Now consider the pure expectations hypothesis in respect of a three-year loan where $r_3 = 10\%$. Given ${_0}r_1 = 7\%$ and ${_1}r_2 = 9\%$, it must be the case that the expected short-term interest rate in year three is ${_2}r_3 = 14.1\%$, since, from Equation 11.7a,

$$(1.07)(1.09)(1.141) = (1.10)^3 = 1.33$$

Therefore, under the pure expectations hypothesis, the only reason that the yield on the three-year loan (or bond), $r_3 = 10\%$, exceeds that on the two-year loan, $r_2 = 8\%$, is that the market expects future short-term interest rates to rise. In other words the term structure is upward sloping, $r_3 > r_2$, purely because the market expects ${_0}r_1 < {_1}r_2 < {_2}r_3$. Consequently there is no advantage to be gained from borrowing at short-term rates of interest, even if they are lower than long-term rates.

If short-term rates were expected to fall, such that ${_0}r_1 = 7\%$, ${_1}r_2 = 6\%$ and ${_2}r_3 = 2.1\%$, then the term structure would be downward sloping. A period of 'tight money' would be indicated, with current short-term rates exceeding long-term rates. In this example the rate on a two-year loan exceeds that on a three-year loan, $r_3 < r_2$. For the two-year loan:

$$(1 + r_2)^2 = (1.07)(1.06) = 1.1342$$

implying

$$(1 + r_2) = \sqrt{1.1342} = 1.065$$

so that

$$r_2 = 1.065 - 1.0 = 0.065 \text{ or } 6.5\%$$

For the three-year loan,

$$(1 + r_3)^3 = (1.07)(1.06)(1.021) = 1.158$$

implying

$$r_3 = \sqrt[3]{1.158} - 1.0 = 1.05 - 1.0 = 0.05 \text{ or } 5\%$$

There is no advantage in borrowing at lower long-term interest rates, however, since yield curves are downward sloping, purely because future short-term interest rates are expected to fall.

If short-term interest rates are expected to remain constant, for example, ${_0}r_1 = {_1}r_2 = {_2}r_3 = 7\%$, the yield curve will be flat, that is, horizontal, with $r_2 = r_3 = 7\%$ since

$$(1 + r_2)^2 = (1.07)(1.07)$$

and

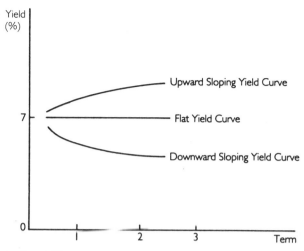

Figure 11.3   Illustrating yield curves

$$(1 + r_3)^3 = (1.07)(1.07)(1.07)$$

The three alternative yield curves implied above are sketched in Figure 11.3.

The capital risk/liquidity premium hypothesis

Another explanation for the yield curve is based on the capital risk or liquidity premium hypothesis. It argues that long-term rates of interest will exceed short-term rates of interest, not just because future short-term rates are expected to rise but also because there is a congenital weakness on one side of the bond market. As Chapter 3 indicated, investors are interested in the capital value of their bonds as well as in interest income. The capital value, however, is sensitive to interest rate changes, with interest rate risk causing a greater variation in a bond's price the longer its term to maturity. Consequently, because of risk aversion, suppliers of debt capital (those who buy bonds) have a preference to lend short term; whereas borrowers (those who issue bonds) have a preference to borrow long.

The only way that supply and demand can be matched in this situation is by borrowers offering premiums on long-term rates relative to short-term rates, and the longer the term to maturity, the greater the premium. The equation expressing the term structure has, therefore, to be modified to include the adjustment for liquidity in the long-term market. Equation 11.7a, for example, expressing the three-year yield becomes

$$(1 + r_3)^3 = (1 + {}_0r_1)(1 + {}_1r_2 + L_1)(1 + {}_2r_3 + L_2) \qquad (11.7b)$$

$L_1 < L_2$ represents the liquidity premiums.[8] This equation indicates that long-term rates are the product of short-term rates plus liquidity premiums.

In an earlier example, under the pure expectations hypothesis, a three-year yield of 10% was produced, assuming ${}_0r_1 = 7\%$, ${}_1r_2 = 9\%$ and ${}_2r_3 = 14.1\%$. Under the capital risk hypothesis with, for example, liquidity premiums of $L_1 = 0.5\%$ and

$L_2 = 0.75\%$, this yield would be exceeded by 0.4% since it would not be based purely on the expected future rise in short-term rates. That is,

$$(1 + r_3)^3 = (1.07)(1.09 + 0.005)(1.141 + 0.0075) = 1.3456$$

implying,

$$r_3 = \sqrt[3]{1.3456} - 1.0 = 1.105 - 1.0 = 0.104 = 10.4\%$$

In technical terms the yields and expected future short-term interest rates are referred to as spot rates of interest. The expected future spot rates, with added liquidity premiums, are referred to as implied forward rates of interest. The latter are the future short-term rates of interest implied by observed spot yield curves, that is, by observing yields at a given point in time on bonds of different maturities.

Under the pure expectations hypothesis, expected forward rates are equal to expected future spot rates. Under the capital risk or liquidity premium hypothesis, expected future spot rates are less than the implied forward rates, by the amounts of the liquidity premiums.

A fuller analysis of the term structure of interest rates is beyond the scope of this text. A good advanced introduction is provided by Russell (1992).

Short-term borrowing risks

The liquidity premium hypothesis implies that even if macroeconomic changes in an economy cause current short-term interest rates to rise, with the expectation that future short-term rates will fall, the term structure may remain upward sloping. This occurs because future short-term rate expectations are offset by liquidity premiums.[9] Only if there is a very strong rise in current short-term rates will the term structure slope downwards. (Here the relatively large expected falls in future short-term rates will be sufficient to offset liquidity premiums.) Consequently, for most periods of time, the term structure of interest rates is upward sloping with the cost of short-term borrowing being less than the cost of long-term borrowing. Companies may not, therefore, be indifferent between short-term and long-term borrowing strategies.

Even if the costs of short-term borrowing are less than the costs of long-term borrowing, for most periods of time, the benefits of financing long-term assets on a short-term basis must be weighed against the risks involved. The risks arise in two senses: first, from the potential difficulty in meeting higher interest charges if events in the future cause short-term interest rates to rise; and second, from the possibility that short-term funds might become unavailable in the future.

Under the EMH it is not possible to predict future changes in the term structure of interest rates since the term structure, at a given point in time, reflects the market's consensus view of the future. A company borrowing short term, with a view to 'rolling over' short-term debt, may find itself suddenly and unexpectedly in a period of 'tight money'. This type of situation is often associated with the start of a recession, as exemplified in the case of the UK in the late 1980s. In such circumstances, companies facing general declines in their business activities in a recession may experience extreme difficulties in meeting higher interest charges associated with renegotiating their short-term borrowings. By borrowing long term, certainty is created in respect of coupon interest payments over the term of a loan.

In addition, the risks surrounding a company's operations in a recession may rise to a point where capital suppliers are unwilling to re-lend. This, for example, has been argued to have been one of the serious problems facing the small business sector in the UK in the early 1990s, an issue pursued in Chapter 14.

In summary, empirical evidence suggests that the term structure of interest rates is upward sloping for most periods of time so that the costs of short-term financing are less than the costs of long-term financing. The balance which a company strikes between the short and long-term debt components in its capital structure depends on the costs and risks of short-term financing and on the strategy the company adopts towards matching the maturity structure of its assets and liabilities. Further consideration is given to these factors in the context of working capital policy, which is explored in the next chapter.

The market segmentation hypothesis

This third theory, explaining the term structure, is based on the view that financial institutions want to minimise interest rate risk. One way of achieving this is through matching the maturity structure of their assets and liabilities. Banks, for example, with short-term deposit liabilities tend to match these by investing in short-term assets; while insurance companies, with long-term pension fund liabilities, tend to match these by investing in long-term assets.

Given that market participants have strong maturity preferences, financial markets become segmented in line with each maturity. The result is imperfect arbitrage between segments, with premiums developing according to the supply and demand for each maturity. Empirical evidence tends to suggest that while imperfect arbitrage may exist in the short run, long-run market segmentation will not persist.

Summary

This chapter has been used, in one sense, to 'tie up' some loose ends in the analysis of debt financing. It has concentrated primarily on long-term corporate bonds. A brief discussion of bank financing, which tends to be concentrated on short and medium-term lending, was included to illustrate the similarities with bond financing in the context of Agency Theory. Lease financing, which again can be of a short and medium-term nature, was included because it has a number of features in common with debt financing. NPV was, as usual, shown to be an important tool in investment appraisal, this time in the context of bond refunding decisions and analyses of lease or buy decisions.

Warrants and convertibles were introduced to illustrate hybrid debt instruments with potential equity participation features. Warrants are closely related to a relatively new field of financial investments: traded options. An introduction to this topic, and financial futures, is presented in Chapter 16.

The term structure of interest rates, drawing out the links between short, medium and long-term interest rates, represents a point of departure, for the moment, from essentially long-run analysis in corporate finance. In the following chapter, on working capital management, some of the major issues in short-term investment and financing are introduced.

Questions

1 If a bond has a call price feature, what are the implications for investors?

2 A bond with a par value of $1000 has 20 years to maturity. It was issued five years ago with a 10% coupon interest rate to raise $15m in debt for a company. The company then, as now, faces a corporate tax rate of 25%. Current interest rates are low and the company could refinance the existing outstanding issue at a coupon rate of 4%. The call price on the existing bond is $115. The issue costs of the new bond are 1% of the funds raised. In the case of the existing bond the issue costs were 0.5%. Determine whether it would be advantageous for the company to refinance the existing bond.

3 Outline the main reasons for issuing convertibles and bonds with warrants.

4 What do you understand by the concept of the market value floor of a convertible bond?

5 What legitimate reasons can be given for leasing?

6 A company can purchase a piece of capital equipment, which has a four-year life, for £20,000. Depreciation for tax purposes is on a straight-line basis and the equipment has no residual value. The company's cost of debt capital is 8.33% and its corporate tax rate is 40%. As an alternative, the company could lease the asset for four years at annual lease payments of £6000. The equipment's operating costs are identical under either a lease or buy option. Calculate the net advantage to leasing and indicate which option, lease or buy, the company should choose.

7 What do you understand by the pure expectations hypothesis of the term structure of interest rates?

8 The rate of interest on a three-year loan is 12%. The short-term interest rate for the coming year is 5% and that expected for the following year is 7%. Under the pure expectations hypothesis, what is the expected short-term rate for year three?

9 Assume that the current one-year interest rate is 8% and that the expected single-period rate for year two is 9%, with a liquidity premium of 0.5%.
a) Find the yield to maturity on a two-year investment.
b) All other things being equal, what would the two-year yield be if the single-period rate of interest for year two fell to 7%?

Exercises

1 What short-term borrowing risks is a company likely to be exposed to?

2 An AB Company's share is currently priced at £2.20. The company has warrants outstanding with one share on option, per warrant, at an option price of £1.60.

a) What is the current exercise value of the warrant?

b) Explain why the warrant is likely to sell at a premium above its exercise value.

3 Explain the liquidity premium, or capital risk, hypothesis of the term structure of interest rates.

Endnotes

1. Some argue that the discount rate should be the company's average cost of capital. Majority opinion tends to favour the after-tax cost of refunding the debt. The arguments in favour of the latter are similar to those in the MM debt and taxes model. Here, the cost of debt capital was applied to determine tax shield benefits (in Chapter 8) because these arose directly from the use of debt capital and were subject to a lower level of risk than a company's operating cash flows. In the bond refunding case, one debt issue substitutes for another, hence NCFs associated with refunding are subject to much lower levels of risk relative to the company's overall operations.

2. Often the warrant will specify particular dates before the expiry date when the option to purchase can be exercised.

3. Often a convertible will specify particular dates when conversion rights can be exercised. The conversion feature may have an expiry date less than the initial term to maturity on the bond. For simplicity, it is assumed that conversion can take place at the end of each year throughout the life of the convertible bond.

4. This assumes that whatever causes the share price to fall does not jeopardise the fixed interest payments on the company's debt capital, otherwise the bond value of the convertible would change.

5. It can be argued that the cost of debt capital should be applied to all the incremental NCFs with the exception of the expected residual value of the asset. Where the residual value is likely to be significant, it might be more appropriate to apply a company's average cost of capital in determining its present value, since residual value will be subject to a higher level of risk than the other incremental NCF elements.

6. In this example it is assumed that the company has already made its project investment decision and subsequently wishes to determine whether or not it should buy or lease the asset. The NAL measures the financing side-effects of leasing and there can be situations where projects with a conventionally calculated, but negative, NPV become acceptable when the NAL is added. For a discussion of this and other methods of appraising the lease versus buy decision, see Emery and Finnerty (1991).

7. Recall that the term structure of interest rates shows the relationship between gilt yields and their term to maturity, holding all other factors constant.

8. Yield curves extend to maturities of more than 30 years and it is unlikely that liquidity premiums, in practice, will be significant over short to medium-run periods of three or four years. To keep the analysis simple, however, the present example assumes premiums to be significant over short to medium-run periods.

9. Another explanation views the premiums as being partly determined by inflation risk. Inflation risk arises in respect of uncertainty about future inflation rates, that is, about future unanticipated inflation as opposed to future anticipated inflation. Inflation risk increases with term to maturity.

References

Altman, E., 'The Convertible Debt Market: Are Returns Worth the Risk?', Financial Analysts Journal, 1989

Blake, D., *Financial Market Analysis*, London, McGraw-Hill, 1990

Brennan, M. and E. Schwartz, 'Convertible Bonds: Valuation and Optimal Strategies for Call and Conversion', in K. Ward (Ed.), *Strategic Issues in Finance*, Oxford, Butterworth-Heinemann, 1994

Cason, R., 'Leasing, Asset Lives and Uncertainty: A Practitioner's Comments', Financial Management, 1987

Drury, C. and S. Braund, 'The Leasing Decision: A Comparison of Theory and Practice', Accounting and Business Research, 1990

Emery, D. and J. Finnerty, *Principles of Finance with Corporate Applications*, New York, West Publishing Company, 1991

Holland, J., 'Bank Lending Relationships and the Complex Nature of Bank–Corporate Relations', Journal of Business Finance and Accounting, 1994

Kraus, A., 'An Analysis of Call Provisions and the Corporate Refunding Decision', in J. Stern and D. Chew (Eds.), *The Revolution in Corporate Finance*, Oxford, Blackwell, 1992

Russell, S., 'Understanding the Term Structure of Interest Rates: The Expectations Theory', Federal Reserve Bank of St Louis, 1992

Schall, L., 'Analytic Issues in Lease vs. Purchase Decisions', Financial Management, 1987

Schwartz, E., 'The Valuation of Warrants: Implementing a New Approach', Journal of Financial Economics, 1977

Shiller, R.J., 'The Term Structure of Interest Rates', in B. Friedman and F. Hahn (Eds.), *Handbook of Monetary Economics*, Vol. 1, North Holland, 1990

12 Working capital

(This chapter has been prepared in conjunction with Ken Dyson)

Introduction

The major part of the analysis in the preceding chapters has been concerned with long-term investment and financing decisions. It is a company's long-term commitment to its product and/or service markets, through capital investment, which is fundamental to generating stock market expectations about its future long-term annual net cash flows. It is this expected future series when discounted at an overall cost of capital primarily influenced by the long-term capital structure decision which is the principal determinant of a company's total market value.

In the short term, however, a considerable amount of managerial resources is devoted to day-to-day decision making in respect of working capital. Working capital, which also has an effect on a company's total market value, consists of short-term (current) assets and short-term (current) liabilities which, by definition, have terms to maturity under one year. Current assets can be funded wholly or in part on a short-term basis, with net working capital measured as current assets less current liabilities.

This chapter begins by defining the main components of current assets and current liabilities and by describing the role of working capital in a company's operations.

Attention is then turned to the core element in working capital: the management of cash flows. In long-run analysis, the focus of attention is on annual net cash flows. In short-run analysis, a key issue is how the current year's net cash flows are expected to take shape on a daily or weekly basis. The expected short-term behaviour of net cash flows involves a company in developing strategies to avoid financial distress and bankruptcy, especially if the company anticipates sustained periods over which cash outflows will exceed cash inflows.

Following this, some of the basic principles involved in modelling the components of working capital are described. These relate to the management of cash and marketable securities, inventory, and accounts receivable (or trade debtors). In terms of current liabilities, there are two main components: accounts payable (or trade creditors) and short-term debt financing. Only the former is analysed in any detail. Short-term debt, which is normally provided by bank loans and overdrafts, is discussed in Chapter 14.

Finally, overall working capital policy is examined in terms of a company's overall level of investment in current assets and in respect of the strategy the company adopts in matching the maturity structure of its assets and liabilities.

The nature of working capital

The principal components of current assets are:
- inventories of raw materials, work in progress, finished goods and spare parts;
- payments yet to be received for goods and services already supplied to customers, accounts receivable;
- cash and marketable securities, the latter referring to tradable investments in financial assets which are close substitutes for cash.

These assets are essential to the current operations of a company. In particular, inventory and accounts receivable can have an important impact on a company's ability to maintain, and indeed increase, its level of sales. Cash and marketable securities have an important role in relation to liquidity.

Inventories of raw materials ensure that production runs can be maintained in the face of unexpected shortages of inputs. Inventories of finished goods play a role in meeting expected variations, and unanticipated increases, in sales. Spare parts inventories are important in creating good back-up services which maintain and enhance the credibility of the product and foster customer goodwill.

The trade credit policy of a company, determining the terms on which goods are sold to its customers, also has a bearing on sales. Most large companies do not operate a cash on delivery system but offer customers delayed payment terms which often include special discounts if accounts are paid within a specified period of the goods being received. A relaxation of trade credit terms is one method of improving sales but it results in the value of accounts receivable increasing.

Current assets can be financed on a long-term basis, as explained at the end of this chapter; however, in practice significant parts of current assets are financed by current liabilities. The two principal sources of short-term financing are:
- bank loans and overdrafts; and
- payments yet to be made to suppliers for goods and services already received, accounts payable.

If, for example, an increase in sales requires an increase in the various components of a firm's inventory, these components can be financed by increasing short-term (or long-term) borrowings, and/or by relying more heavily on trade credit offered by suppliers. In the latter case this increases the value of accounts payable.

Cost and benefits

Decisions on working capital involve applying the principles of corporate finance to determine the optimal level of each component of current assets that is consistent with maximising the total market value of a company. Analogously the costs of short-term financing should be minimised in the context of a company's overall capital structure.

In the case of current assets the optimal level of inventory is determined by setting inventory ordering, warehousing and financing costs against sales revenue, and ultimately profit, benefits. There is an optimal level of trade credit which is determined by sales revenue benefits set against the opportunity costs of: offering customers discounts for prompt payment, interest forgone on delayed receipts and, ultimately, any persistent bad debt problems. There are also costs to be considered in administering, or paying for, credit evaluation services. These services assign credit ratings to customers to help reduce the probability of incurring bad debt.

The optimal level of investment in cash and marketable securities is similarly determined in a cost-benefit framework. Of all the components of current assets this one, because of its liquidity implications linked to the probabilities of financial distress and bankruptcy, has the most significant impact on a company's market value. Liquidity implications are discussed below.

In general the optimal level of a component of current assets is determined by investing up to the point where the marginal cost of holding the asset is equal to its marginal benefit. In practice, while it is relatively straightforward to determine the holding and financing costs associated with investing in current assets, it is much more difficult to isolate their individual benefits in terms of their potential contribution to sales revenue. This, which will be demonstrated later, has resulted in attention being focused on the management of given levels of current assets from the point of view of minimising their holding and financing costs.

Managing short-term net cash flows

In the short term, how net cash flow takes shape on a daily or weekly basis has an important bearing on value.

Cash outflows

Over a year, cash outflows will consist of regular payments to meet wages and salaries, and bills furnished by suppliers. Cash outflows will also occur in respect of tax demands, interest payments and fees which can be expected at specific times during the year and in respect of the purchase of plant and machinery for long-term capital investment. These constitute what is referred to as the transactions motive for holding cash.

There may also be unanticipated events over a year which require a company to have immediate access to cash resources. This constitutes the precautionary motive for holding cash. A speculative motive can exist to enable a company to take advantage of undervalued inputs or equipment which come up for sale due, for example, to a competitor going bankrupt. There is a fourth reason for holding cash known as a compensating balance motive. Here a company's bank may require it to hold minimum balances in its current account in order to indirectly cover the bank's costs of administration. If a company receives no interest on its current account, its bank receives all of the income earned on the company's balances through the bank's own investment strategies. Recently there has been a tendency to move away from compensating balances, with companies negotiating transactions fees with banks and receiving current account interest payments, or investing their surplus cash elsewhere.

Cash inflows

Where cash inflows are concerned, these can be expected to occur at regular intervals over the year largely as a result of the pattern of sales. This pattern can, however, be uneven if sales are seasonal. For example, in the cases of toy manufacturers and department stores the majority of sales, and hence cash inflows, can be expected to occur in the months around Christmas. In the case of a clothing manufacturer a significant proportion of orders can be expected during the weeks in which this industry has its national and international fashion shows.

In addition, anticipated cash inflows may be disrupted due to sudden and unexpected changes in the economy. If, for example, there is an unanticipated rise in interest rates, short-term trade debtors who also have high levels of bank debt may respond by delaying settlement of their invoices, using their own cash inflows to meet higher bank interest charges. Further, a major customer of a company may fail leaving significant amounts of unpaid debts.

Net cash flow policy

Given the opportunity costs of cash, in terms of borrowing and lending rates, it is in the interests of a company to:

- delay its expected cash outflows as long as possible, subject to minimising the risks of jeopardising input supplies;
- maximise, at a current point in time, its expected cash inflows, subject to minimising the risk of jeopardising customer goodwill;
- avoid significant periods when excess cash balances earning no interest are likely to increase as a result of cash inflows exceeding cash outflows; and
- avoid incurring costs associated with using short-term bank loans or overdrafts to cover significant periods when cash outflows exceed cash inflows.

In the short term in order to cope with periods when net cash flows are expected to be negative and to avoid, at other times, holding excessive amounts of idle cash balances, a company can invest in a portfolio of marketable securities which earns interest. Investment in this portfolio is increased when short-term net cash flows are positive. When cash outflows exceed incoming cash receipts, some of the short-term marketable securities are sold to meet the deficit.

There are problems of capital, or interest rate, risk involved in holding a portfolio of marketable securities. Recall from Chapters 3 and 11 that unexpected rises in interest rates lead to falls in the capital value of marketable securities. Consequently companies, in seeking to avoid financial distress, tend to invest surplus cash balances in short-term marketable securities[1] whose prices, in response to a given interest rate change, vary less than those of long-term marketable securities. This minimises interest rate risk but entails a cost since, with the term structure of interest rates sloping upwards for most periods of time, short-term marketable securities earn a lower rate of return than long-term marketable securities.

In general the optimal level of cash and marketable securities will be determined in a much wider risk–return trade-off context, where the risk of not being able to meet short-term cash outflows is set against the opportunity costs of foregoing investments in long-term physical assets. On average, returns on the latter exceed the returns which companies can earn on both short-term and long-term financial assets.

Liquidity

The above introduces the concept of liquidity which is defined as the ability to realise value in cash. It has two components:
- the conversion time of an asset, that is, the time lag between deciding to sell an asset and receiving payment for it; and
- its conversion price.

Cash has zero conversion time and no conversion price risk. Marketable securities, providing they are actively traded, have zero conversion time but have significant conversion price risk associated with interest rate risk.

The optimal level of liquidity, that is, a level which is not too low so as to produce significant probabilities of financial distress and bankruptcy, and not too high so as to reduce the rate of return on long-term investment, is difficult to determine. As a rough guide a number of short-term financial ratios can be examined to determine if an optimal liquidity policy is being pursued. Beginning with cash and marketable securities ratios, these are:

$$\frac{\text{Cash} + \text{Marketable Securities}}{\text{Current Assets}}$$

and

$$\frac{\text{Cash} + \text{Marketable Securities}}{\text{Current Liabilities}}$$

Reasonably large values of the former indicate that cash and marketable securities can provide substantial sources of funds to finance any increases in current assets which might occur with increased sales. Reasonably high levels of the latter measure the ability to meet current liabilities without the need to liquidate other current assets, for example inventory, or without recourse to external sources of finance.

It would be wrong, however, to determine the liquidity position of a company purely in cash ratio terms. As indicated, inventory can be sold directly for cash, but it may have a relatively long conversion time and have a conversion price which is significantly less than the inventory's intrinsic value. The latter will occur especially if it is known that inventory is being offered for sale in a situation of financial distress.

Banks and financial institutions provide factoring services in respect of inventory and invoice discounting in respect of accounts receivable so as to eliminate conversion time. Here, a part or a whole of a company's inventory and/or its accounts receivable are purchased by a factoring company which, consequently, provides an immediate infusion of cash. Again, however, the conversion price will be below the intrinsic value of the current asset being purchased since factors earn their returns from obtaining assets at significant discounts and then reselling them or, in the case of accounts receivable, collecting payments due.

Two, more broadly based liquidity measures take some of the above points into account. The first is the current ratio defined as:

$$\text{Current Ratio} = \frac{\text{Current Assets}}{\text{Current Liabilities}}$$

This encompasses net working capital (current assets less current liabilities) and is a measure of a company's capacity to meet its liabilities, due within one year, out of current assets. Because a substantial proportion of current assets includes inventory which, assuming factoring services are not used, has a positive conversion time and significant conversion price risk, a desirable level for this ratio is taken, on average, to be 2:1. The second liquidity measure is referred to as the Acid Test or Quick ratio. This ratio nets out the effect of inventory and is defined as:

$$\text{Quick Ratio} = \frac{\text{Current Assets} - \text{Inventory}}{\text{Current Liabilities}}$$

On average, its optimal level is considered to be 1:1.

These cash, current and quick ratios are unlikely to give a full picture of a company's liquidity position. Back-up lines of credit which may not be explicitly observable can be important, for example, a bank's willingness to vary the overdraft ceiling that it has placed on a company's current account and a bank's willingness to provide additional short-term loans at short notice. These factors will help to determine a company's financing flexibility which, as explained in Chapter 11, partly depends on the levels of short-term and long-term tangible assets already pledged in existing loan contracts. Indeed the ability of a company to provide a near-term cash flow forecast, and the variability surrounding near-term cash flows, also play a part in determining the effect of liquidity on a company's market value.

The above introduces a dynamic aspect to liquidity which is not normally picked up in static (at a point in time) short-term financial ratios. The dynamic aspect involves the speed with which a company can alter its short-term position to avoid a crisis. It has been argued that one possible way of accommodating this is by considering a ratio based on a company's earnings power, that is, the ratio of:

$$\frac{\text{Current Liabilities} - \text{Quick Assets}}{\text{Operating Funds Expected to be Generated over a Year}} \times 365$$

This ratio gives the number of days required to pay off net current debt, that is, current debt not covered by liquid or quick assets. If, for example, this ratio exceeds 365 a company will be unable to meet its net current obligations out of its current year's expected earnings. Alternatively, if the ratio is significantly below 365 and short-term difficulties arise, the indication may be that additional short-term finance will be obtainable since banks would view such funding as entailing low risk. Expected earnings over the current year are not, however, a substitute for a short-term cash flow forecast which provides better evidence of the ability to repay net current debt.

Examples of how the above, and other ratios, can be used in the analysis of a company's overall performance are presented in the concluding chapter of this book.

Cash management models

Focusing attention on the management of cash, there is, as already explained, an opportunity cost to holding idle cash balances in terms of the returns foregone by not investing cash in short-term marketable securities. This suggests that a company should develop a policy which, given its need for cash, minimises the amount of cash balances it holds over a given period. The simplest approach to this problem is set out by Baumol (1952) who adapted what is referred to as the Economic Order Quantity Model. In effect, by selling and thus converting the appropriate amount of short-term marketable securities into cash, a company creates (orders) its optimal (economic) cash balance.

The Baumol model

Under the Economic Order Quantity Model it is assumed that a company determines its transactions demand for cash, £T, over a specified period, say one year.[2] This overall period is broken into sub periods of equal length by dividing a company's total transactions demand for cash by the cash balance, £C, which it holds at the beginning of each sub-period. This cash balance is run down smoothly to meet the company's cash outflow requirements, reaching zero at the end of each sub-period. Each time the cash balance needs replenishing, at the beginning of each sub-period, £C is realised through the sale of the appropriate amount of marketable securities.

Given the transactions demand for cash, the number of sub-periods, T/C, is found by determining the optimal level of C in respect of:
- the opportunity cost of holding cash in terms of the interest rate, i, foregone by not investing in marketable securities; and
- the market trading costs, b, involved each time the company converts a proportion of its marketable securities into cash.

With the average cash balance over each sub-period expressed as £C/2, the total interest foregone is i[£C/2] and, given the number of sub-periods, the total conversion cost is b[£T/£C]. The total fixed cost of holding cash, TCC, is therefore:

$$TCC = i[C/2] + b[T/C] \qquad (12.1)$$

To determine the optimal cash balance, C*, this cost function is minimised[3] with respect to C, producing what is known as the square root formula where:

$$C^* = \sqrt{\frac{2bT}{i}} \qquad (12.2)$$

Consequently the optimal number of sub-periods, determining the number of times short-term marketable securities are converted, is T/C*.

Mathematically, because the optimal cash balance is expressed in terms of a square root formula, transactions economies of scale are indicated. That is, the optimal cash balance, C*, increases less than in proportion to any increase in the overall transactions demand, T, for cash. A similar conclusion applies to the market transactions costs, b, of converting marketable securities. Alternatively, as would be expected, the optimal cash balance varies inversely with the rate of return, i, available on marketable securities.

To illustrate, consider a company whose transactions demand for cash for the coming year is T = £1m. Assume i = 5% and b = £100; therefore, by Equation 12.2:

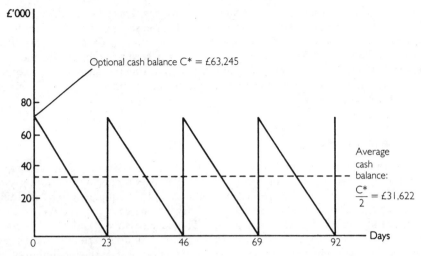

Figure 12.1   Illustrating the economic order quantity model

$$C^* = \sqrt{\frac{2(£100)(£1m)}{.05}} = £63,245$$

With an optimal cash balance of £63,245, the number of sub-periods, and hence marketable security conversions over the year, is $T/C^* \simeq 16$. This implies that the company runs its cash balance to zero at approximately the end of every 23 days, that is, 365/16 days. This example is illustrated graphically in Figure 12.1. The cash balance is shown to decline smoothly over each sub-period, 'jumping' to the optimal level at the start of each subsequent sub-period.

If the transactions demand for cash in the above example doubles to T = £2m, all other things being equal, the optimal cash balance increases, but by less than 100%, to:

$$C^* = \sqrt{\frac{2(£100)(£2m)}{.05}} = £89,442$$

This indicates transactions economies of scale. At this new level of transactions demand a rise in the costs of converting marketable securities, to b = £120, produces an optimal cash balance of:

$$C^* = \sqrt{\frac{2(£120)(£2m)}{.05}} = £97,979$$

Alternatively, a rise in i to 10%, given T = £2m and b = £120, reduces the optimal cash balance from £97,979 to:

$$C^* = \sqrt{\frac{2(£120)(£2m)}{.10}} = £69,282$$

In this latter case there are £2m/£69,282 $\simeq$ 29 sub-periods implying that the cash balance requires replenishing approximately every 13 (365/29) days.

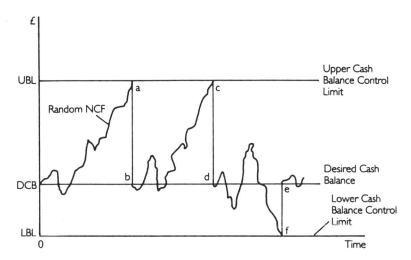

ab and cd represent cash investments in short-term marketable securities

ef represents the amount of short-term marketable securities converted into cash

Figure 12.2   The Miller–Orr model

The Baumol model captures the essence of the cash management problem, however, the explicit assumption that cash outflows occur smoothly over time is unreasonable. There is also the additional implicit assumption that, at the beginning of the overall transactions period, cash inflows match the subsequent transactions period cash outflow. In practice, as explained, there are unpredictable elements in cash inflows and outflows. If this unpredictability is not too significant the Baumol model can be adapted by including a minimum cash balance to cover risk. This minimum balance prevents cash holdings falling to zero at the end of each sub-period.

The Miller–Orr model

Where unpredictability is a serious problem a more sophisticated approach to cash flow management is required. One such model, based on optimal control theory, has been developed by Miller and Orr (1966). This model assumes that net cash flow behaves in a random fashion over time and introduces optimal cash control limits in relation to investments in short-term marketable securities. An upper cash balance limit, UBL, and a lower cash balance limit, LBL, are established together with a desired cash balance level, DCB.

Positive net cash flows are held in the form of idle cash balances until the net cash flow reaches the upper control limit. When this occurs, the cash balance is immediately reduced to its desired level by purchasing short-term marketable securities equal in value to the difference between UBL and DCB. This is illustrated in Figure 12.2. When net cash flows reach their lower control limit, the cash balance is immediately brought to its desired level by converting a proportion of marketable securities into cash equal in value to DCB − LBL. For simplicity it is assumed, as illustrated in Figure 12.2, that LBL = 0; in other words, that net cash flows are allowed to fall to zero before the desired cash balance is replenished.

Relative to the Baumol model the additional feature introduced in the Miller–Orr model is the variance, σ^2, of the daily net cash flow series. This replaces the notion of the transactions demand for cash. Given the rate of return on short-term marketable securities, i, and their fixed market trading conversion costs, b, the desired cash balance is determined in terms of a cube-root formula:

$$DCB = \sqrt[3]{\frac{3b\sigma^2}{4i}} \qquad\qquad (12.3)$$

The optimal value of the upper control limit is:

$$UBL = 3(DCB) \qquad\qquad (12.3a)$$

The average cash balance is approximately equal to:

$$\text{Average Cash Balance} = (UBL + DCB)/3 \qquad\qquad (12.3b)$$

Consider an example where i = 5% and b = £100. The daily standard deviation of a company's net cash flow is £25,820; hence its variance is $\sigma^2 = (£25,820)^2$. From Equation 12.3 the company's desired cash balance is:

$$DCB = \sqrt[3]{\frac{3(£100)(£25,820)^2}{4(.05)}} \approx £10,000$$

With an upper control limit (Equation 12.3a) of

$$3(£10,000) = £30,000$$

each time net cash flow reaches this limit the company purchases short-term marketable securities worth:

$$£30,000 - £10,000 = £20,000$$

When net cash flows fall to zero the company converts £10,000 of short-term marketable securities into cash.[4] The average cash balance in this example is:

$$(£30,000 + £10,000)/3 = £13,333$$

Managing inventory

Cash and marketable securities are a form of inventory; therefore, when considering inventory in the wider context of raw materials, finished goods and spare parts, the basic principles used in cash management are applied. Indeed the Economic Order Quantity Model was developed originally with physical inventory in mind. Here for example, the optimal level of raw materials over an inventory holding period is determined in relation to the demand for a company's product and the holding and ordering costs of stock. Holding costs include the opportunity costs of financing inventory and of warehousing space together with any insurance costs.

As in the case of running out of cash, there are costs involved in running out of raw materials and spare parts in terms of potential disruptions to production runs and sales patterns. Additional physical inventory costs can include the danger of a deterioration in the quality of inventory if it is held for too long; obsolescence, especially if the inventory is of a technical nature; and lead time variations, that is, the time lag between ordering and receiving new inventory. An important potential benefit from holding inventory is associated with possible price discounts on bulk purchases. Moving beyond the Economic Order Quantity Model, optimal control theory can be used to take account of unpredictability in product demand patterns.

A recent approach to inventory management in companies with repetitive manufacturing systems has involved near elimination of stock holdings. This just-in-time inventory system requires suppliers to provide the relevant inputs, in their relevant quantities, at the precise points in time when they are needed in a manufacturing operation. There are costs in attempting to ensure that the just-in-time system works. These involve developing, co-ordinating and monitoring operating plans between a company and its suppliers.

In practical terms a typical ratio which can be examined to help assess a company's inventory policy is the inventory turnover ratio:

$$\text{Inventory Turnover} = \frac{\text{Costs of Goods Sold}}{\text{Inventory}}$$

A relatively high inventory turnover ratio may suggest that a company is managing this current asset relatively efficiently. It could suggest, for example, that excessive amounts of stock, which would incur a significant probability of obsolescence and high warehousing costs, are not being held. On the other hand a relatively high ratio could indicate that not enough stocks are being held to support future potential sales growth. In effect a company's inventory turnover ratio should be judged in relation to the nature of the stock being held and in respect of a base point, such as the average inventory turnover ratio for the industry in which the company is located.

Managing accounts receivable

A company which grants trade credit to its customers creates current assets in the form of accounts receivable or trade debtors. It also influences its average collection period, that is, the average time lag between supplying customers and receiving cash payments in settlement of invoices. As explained, granting trade credit can have an important effect in stimulating a company's sales and thus, given its average collection period, its sales revenue.

The average collection period is important in an opportunity cost sense since it involves a company in foregoing interest on cash which could have been invested in marketable securities. An important additional factor in offering trade credit is the probability of incurring bad debt, that is, selling to customers who significantly delay or even default on their payments. Granting trade credit can be analysed in terms of NPV.

As an investment decision, while the factors influencing the trade credit decision are complex, two simple examples are presented below to illustrate the basic principles. This is followed by a brief discussion of consumer credit evaluation.

The average collection period

Looking at the average collection period, one way of reducing this is by changing or introducing, if not already in existence, discounts on the list price of goods sold, the discounts only being available to customers who settle their accounts within a specified period. (Such a policy can also influence sales.) While a reduction in the average collection period has a benefit in that it reduces interest foregone on accounts receivable, it has a cost to the extent that discounts are taken up by customers and, consequently, profits from increased sales are reduced.

To illustrate these concepts, consider a company which has monthly sales of £2m and annual sales of £24m. Its average collection period is 30 days, indicating that there is approximately one month between it supplying its products and receiving payments for them. The company has, therefore, an average investment in accounts receivable of £2m. In terms of its annual sales the company has an accounts receivable turnover ratio:

$$\text{Receivables Turnover} = \frac{\text{Annual Sales}}{\text{Average Receivables Balance}} = \frac{£24m}{£2m} = 12$$

Note that the ratio for the average collection period is formally defined on 365 days in the year, as:

$$\text{Average Collection Period} = \frac{\text{Accounts Receivable}}{\text{Sales}} \times 365$$

In the present example this ratio is (365)(£2m/£24m) = 30.4 days. Normally in accounting terms this would be rounded to 31 days.

The NPV of offering discounts

The company is currently not offering discounts but is considering introducing a discount policy to reduce its investment in accounts receivable. To assess the viability of such a new policy the company must calculate the NPV of offering discounts. This NPV is composed of benefits, in terms of a reduction in the average investment in accounts receivable, and costs, in terms of profit foregone by customers taking up discounts.

The company estimates that it can reduce its average investment in accounts receivable by £1m, representing a benefit, by introducing a '2/10 net 25' trade credit policy. This trade credit policy means that the company wants settlement of its invoices within 25 days and will give a 2% discount to customers who settle within 10 days. To abstract from other complicating factors, assume that the introduction of this policy will not affect sales volume, the cost of sales or the company's risk exposure. Consequently, if the company reduces its average investment in accounts receivable to £1m, its receivables turnover ratio will increase to £24m/£1m = 24, with its average collection period falling to (365)(£1m/£24m) = 15.2 days, on rounding, 16 days.

In terms of the costs arising from the potential introduction of the new trade credit policy the company estimates, on the basis of the proportion of customers expected to settle accounts within 10 days and, therefore, take up discounts, that annual profits will fall by £100,000 in perpetuity. Thus, using the perpetuity valuation principle and assuming that the rate of return required on trade credit financing is 20%, the present value of these costs is:

$$\frac{£100,000}{0.20} = £500,000$$

The benefit of introducing the potential new trade credit policy is a once-for-all reduction of £1m in the average investment in accounts receivable. The resulting present value of benefits minus present value of costs is:

$$NPV = £1m - £0.5m = £0.5m$$

As this NPV is positive the '2/10 net 25' trade credit policy should be introduced.

Granting trade credit to a new customer

NPV can also be used to determine whether or not to grant trade credit to a new customer. Consider an example where a company has the prospect of gaining a new long-term customer in perpetuity. The company estimates that if it accepts the new customer on a trade credit basis, annual profits will increase by £20,000 but that there is only a 70% chance of the customer paying. Thus the probability of the customer paying, and the company increasing profit, is 0.70. If the customer does not pay, the company's losses will be determined by the cost of goods sold, not the sales revenue losses. The annual cost of goods to be sold is £30,000, with the probability of incurring losses, or this customer not paying, being equal to one minus the probability of the customer paying, that is, $1.00 - 0.70 = 0.30$.

All other things being equal, should the potential new customer be granted trade credit? Assuming that the appropriate discount rate for financing trade credit is 20%, the expected NPV (ENPV) of this decision is:

$$ENPV = PV \text{ of Profits} \begin{bmatrix} \text{Probability} \\ \text{of Payment} \end{bmatrix} - PV \text{ of Losses} \begin{bmatrix} \text{Probability of} \\ \text{of Non-payment} \end{bmatrix} \quad (12.4)$$

That is,

$$ENPV = \frac{£20,000}{0.20} [0.7] - \frac{£30,000}{0.20} [0.3] = £70,000 - £45,000 = £25,000$$

As the expected NPV is positive the customer should be accepted, even though there is a 30% chance of the customer being a bad debtor.

Customer credit evaluation

In making decisions on offering trade credit, a company may wish to assess the creditworthiness of its customers in order to screen out those who would potentially create a serious bad debt problem. In the case of existing customers, probabilities indicating the likelihood of payment can be based on a company's records which show past payment histories, although some view must be taken of an existing customer's future trading position.

The main difficulties of credit evaluation come in respect of new customers. Initially assessment can be handled through a company's own credit department using, for example, credit scoring analysis. Here a new customer may be requested to complete a questionnaire, the information given being processed through a credit scoring function. This function gives an overall credit score. The company will have processed its records on existing customers through this function in order to determine a critical score value that discriminates between customers who have proved to be bad risks and those who have not. The new customer's credit score is compared to this critical value and a decision made on whether or not to offer new credit.

Companies can use external sources of credit evaluation by obtaining bank references or approaching professional credit rating agencies. Whether internal or external methods are used, there are costs involved in making credit evaluations. These involve paying fees to external agencies or meeting administration and salary costs if a company uses its own credit evaluation systems. These costs must be weighed against the benefits which can arise from using these systems to limit bad debt problems while at the same time increasing sales by successfully selecting new creditworthy customers.

Accounts payable as a source of short-term finance

There are two sides to trade credit. For the company offering trade credit, accounts receivable are a current asset, while for the company taking trade credit accounts payable are a current liability and, therefore, a source of short-term financing.

When accounts payable do not involve discounts they are effectively a costless source of finance. In this case the settlement of accounts should be delayed as long as possible, subject to not jeopardising the goodwill of the creditor company. A ratio which can be used as a general guide in determining a company's debt payment policy is:

$$\text{Debtor Turnover} = \frac{\text{Annual Sales}}{\text{Average Balance of Accounts Payable}}$$

The opportunity cost of accounts payable
If discounts are involved and the accounts payable of a company are not settled within the period when the discount is available, an opportunity cost may be incurred with this source of financing.

Consider an example where accounts are payable on a '2/10 net 30' basis. That is, accounts should be settled within 30 days of the receipt of an invoice but will be subject to a 2% discount if settled within 10 days. Assume that a company decides not to take the discount and settles at the end of 30 days. If the company had taken the 2% discount it would have paid 98p per £1 of invoiced goods. It has decided to defer payment to 20 days after the end of the discount period. Using the interest rate principles developed in Chapter 2, the 20-day period interest rate is $r_p = 2/98 = 0.0204$ or 2.04%. Formally (from Chapter 2) the interest rate is determined on the 'discount' principle, that is:

$$\frac{\text{Interest}}{\text{Principle} - \text{Interest}} = \frac{\%\text{Discount}}{100 - \%\text{Discount}} = \frac{2}{100 - 2} = \frac{2}{98} = 2.04\%$$

To calculate the annual, or effective, rate of interest, r_{ef}, the future value interest factor is used in a slight adaptation of Equation 2.9 where:

$$r_{ef} = FVIF_{m,r_p} - 1 \qquad\qquad (12.5)$$

With a 20-day interest rate and assuming 360 days in the year, the number of compounding periods is m = 360/20 = 18. Thus,

$$r_{ef} = FVIF_{18,2.04} - 1 = (1 + .0204)^{18} - 1 \approx 0.438 \text{ or } 43.8\%$$

In other words what might appear as a relatively costless method of financing (not taking a 2% discount) is, in effect, highly expensive. Especially for small firms which tend to rely heavily on trade credit financing, a policy of not taking discounts but settling invoices within the overall specified period (30 days in this example) exposes the firm to a high component cost of capital.[5]

However, if a company can delay payment beyond the overall settlement date, the opportunity cost of not taking discounts declines. In the '2/10 net 30' example assume that payment is delayed to day 60, without incurring a loss in creditor goodwill in the form of a future refusal of trade credit. On payment taking place 50 days after the discount could have been taken up, m = 360/50 = 7.2. Thus the effective rate of interest is reduced to:

$$r_{ef} = (1 + .0204)^{7.2} - 1 \approx 0.157 \text{ or } 15.7\%$$

Other sources of short-term finance

Other sources of short-term finance include bank loans and overdrafts. In recent years some large companies have issued their own commercial paper, or short-term unsecured notes, for which there is no secondary market. This confirms the growing role of disintermediation (discussed in Chapter 1) where companies have realised that they do not have to use banks in all cases as intermediaries between borrowers and lenders. Companies can borrow directly from other companies or institutional investors.

The cash operating cycle

Having introduced some of the ratios associated with current asset and liability management, it is useful to return to cash management and consider the cash operating cycle. This indicates the net time interval between cash inflows from goods sold and cash outflows for the purchase of resources. It is a measure of the length of time a company has funds tied up in working capital, an increase (decrease) in the cycle indicating an increase (decrease) in working capital needs.

A company's cash operating cycle is equal to:
• the average number of days a given inventory is held, measuring the length of time required to purchase and sell its product;
  plus
• the average collection period on its accounts receivable, measuring the length of time required to collect sales revenue;
  minus

Table 12.1: The cash operating cycle

Annual sales	£100,000
Cost of goods sold	£40,000

	Balances £s			Ratios		
Inventory	5000	Inventory Turnover	=	$\dfrac{\text{Cost of Goods}}{\text{Inventory}}$ =	$\dfrac{£40,000}{£5000}$	= 8
Accounts Receivable	10,000	Receivables Turnover	=	$\dfrac{\text{Sales}}{\text{Receivables}}$ =	$\dfrac{£100,000}{£10,000}$	= 10
Accounts Payable	5000	Debtor Turnover	=	$\dfrac{\text{Sales}}{\text{Accounts Payable}}$ =	$\dfrac{£100,000}{£10,000}$	= 10

- the average period of its accounts payable, measuring the length of time payments can be deferred on its purchase of resources.

That is, the cash operating cycle is equal to:

$$365\left[\frac{1}{\text{Inventory Turnover Ratio}} + \frac{1}{\text{Receivables Turnover Ratio}} - \frac{1}{\text{Debtor Turnover Ratio}}\right]$$

Since each of these ratios measures, respectively, the number of times in a year that inventory, accounts receivable and accounts payable are 'turned over', dividing each ratio into the number of days in a year measures the average number of days each of these components of working capital is held.

To illustrate, consider a company which has average annual sales of £100,000 at an average annual cost of goods sold of £40,000. Given the average balances in its inventory, accounts receivable and accounts payable and the relevant ratios, as indicated in Table 12.1, the cash operating cycle is:

$$365\left[\frac{1}{8} + \frac{1}{10} - \frac{1}{10}\right] = 365[0.125 + 0.1 - 0.1] = 45.6 \text{ days.}$$

If, for example, the company reduced its investment in accounts receivable there would be, all other things being equal, an improvement in liquidity as measured by the cash operating cycle. Assuming accounts receivable are reduced to £6000, the receivables turnover ratio falls to £100,000/£6000 = 16.7. Thus the cash operating cycle is reduced from 45.6 days to 31 days; that is, in the latter case:

$$365\left[\frac{1}{8} + \frac{1}{16.7} - \frac{1}{10}\right] = 365[0.125 + 0.06 - 0.1] = 365[0.085] = 31 \text{ days.}$$

Overall working capital policy

To bring this chapter to a close it is important to consider the overall policy which a company might adopt in respect of its working capital. There are two aspects to this, one involving the investment decision and the other involving the financing decision. The former is examined first.

Current asset policy

In an earlier part of this chapter, when discussing cash and marketable securities, the importance of the risk–return relationship was identified. It was argued that the benefits of liquidity, in terms of producing low risk but low returns, should be weighed against relatively higher returns but higher risk produced by investing in long-term physical or fixed assets.

This risk–return principle applies to a company's investment decision in respect of its overall current assets. In this context there are three alternative strategies which can be adopted. They involve average, conservative and aggressive approaches to risk management. Under the conservative strategy, relative to the average, there is a relatively high proportion of investment in current assets. This produces below average risk and below average total return. Under the aggressive strategy, relative to the average, there is a relatively low proportion of investment in current assets, producing above average risk and above average total returns.

The choice of strategy varies from industry to industry depending on the nature of the product and/or service being supplied and, among other factors, on sales variation and the degree of operating leverage. Sales variation and operating leverage determine business risk and hence the variation in net cash flows. The overriding objective should be to determine the ratio of current assets to total assets which maximises the total market value of a company.

Current and long-term liability policy

Once the investment decision has been made, strategies for financing current assets must be addressed. These strategies involve choosing the term structure of liabilities appropriate to a given term structure of assets. The analysis is aided by considering a company's cumulative capital requirement at a given point in time, that is, the total capital necessary to fund a company's total investment. The cumulative capital requirement is determined by fixed, or long-term, assets; permanent current assets; and spontaneous, or fluctuating, current assets.

The division of current assets into permanent and spontaneous components arises to the extent that a company can predict its long-term trend in sales. To the extent that it can do this, the proportions of its current assets necessary to support this trend can be considered to be long term and, therefore, effectively permanent. The remaining proportions of current asset investments (in cash and marketable securities, inventories and accounts receivable) are spontaneous. They are spontaneous in that these current assets fluctuate to facilitate unanticipated changes in sales and as a result of the innate variation in the current asset components themselves. The cumulative capital requirement is illustrated in Figure 12.3.

There are three alternative financing strategies which involve average, aggressive and conservative hedging approaches to financial risk management.

The average hedging approach consists of matching the maturity structure of assets

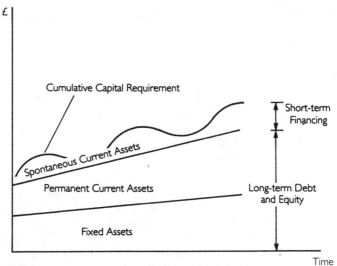

Figure 12.3   The cumulative capital requirement and average hedging

and liabilities, on the assumption that permanent current assets can be treated as long-term investments. Here all fixed and permanent current assets are funded by long-term debt and equity, with spontaneous current assets being financed by short-term debt and accounts payable. This approach exposes a company to 'average' risk with 'average' expected returns. The average hedging approach is illustrated in Figure 12.3.

Given that the term structure of interest rates slopes upwards for most periods of time, a company could increase its expected returns by financing its spontaneous, and most of its permanent, current assets on a short-term basis and, if desired, part of its fixed assets as well. This constitutes the aggressive hedging strategy since, as explained at the end of Chapter 11, short-term financing increases a company's risk exposure. That is, given the need to 'roll over' short-term debt, a company may find itself suddenly and unexpectedly in a period of 'tight money' with steep rises in the costs of short-term financing. Thus, under an aggressive strategy, difficulties may be experienced in:

● meeting high interest rate payments on renegotiated loans; and
● even obtaining short-term funds.

Alternatively, since borrowing long term creates certainty in respect of interest payments, a company may opt for a conservative hedging strategy. Here, in addition to financing fixed and permanent current assets with long-term debt and equity, these financing sources are used to meet most of a company's spontaneous current asset commitments.[6] While involving lower than average risk, because long-term interest payments are usually fixed and dividend payments are made at the discretion of management, the higher cost of long-term financing produces lower than average expected returns.

There are complex factors influencing hedging strategy choice. If an average hedging approach is adopted it should be consistent with a company's desired exposure to business and financial risk. Although average hedging produces 'average' returns, it does not imply that a company's total market value is not being maximised.

Where financing flexibility is important to the maximisation of market value, a movement towards an aggressive hedging strategy may be more appropriate.

Finally, the above financing strategies have been examined on the assumption that a company's investment policy is given. As explained in Chapter 10 investment and financing decisions may be made on a joint basis if capital markets are imperfect. In this case an aggressive current asset strategy could, for example, be combined with a conservative hedging approach to financing so as to achieve a company's desired risk exposure.

Summary

Working capital management involves the day-to-day management of current assets and current liabilities. The objective of working capital management is to ensure that the optimal levels of cash and marketable securities, other non-financial inventories and accounts receivable are determined with a view to maximising the total market value of a company.

In many cases of financial distress the underlying problem can be traced to poor working capital policy. In particular there is often a failure to appreciate the need, especially in the case of small firms, to develop a sound approach to forecasting short-term net cash flows. This arises both in terms of identifying cash inflows and outflows, which can be anticipated with a reasonable level of confidence, and making allowance for unanticipated elements.

Current liabilities can have a significant role to play in financing a company's current assets but must be viewed in the broader context of a company's overall financing strategy. With regard to the risk–return trade-off, management need to identify and target the optimal combination of short, medium, and long-term financing appropriate to the maximisation of their company's total market value.

Questions _____

1 What role have current assets to play in the sales policy of a company?

2 What are the main objectives which a company should pursue in managing its cash inflows and its cash outflows?

3 Consider a company with an annual transactions demand for cash of £0.5m. The opportunity cost of holding cash is 4% and financial market trading costs are £50 per transaction.
Using the Economic Order Quantity Model, determine:
a) The optimal cash balance.
b) The number of times over a year that short-term marketable securities are converted into cash.
c) The average holding period of each optimal cash balance.

4 Given question 3 illustrate transactions economies of scale by doubling the transactions demand for cash, all other things being equal.

5 Given the information in question 3 and assuming that the standard deviation of the company's daily net cash flow is £15,179, determine using the Miller–Orr model:
   a) The company's desired cash balance.
   b) The level of the company's cash balance which triggers investment in short-term marketable securities and the amount of such an investment.
   c) The company's average cash balance.

6 A company has an annual sales turnover of £50,000 at an average annual cost of goods sold of £18,000. It has the following average balances:
Inventory £1000
Accounts receivable £8000
Accounts payable £2000
   a) Find the company's cash operating cycle.
   b) What would happen to the cash operating cycle and what would be the implications for liquidity if, all other things being equal, the company halved its investment in inventory?

7 In terms of financing, what is an aggressive hedging strategy? What risks are involved in adopting an aggressive hedging strategy?

Exercises

1 What ratios, and other factors, should be examined when making an assessment of a company's liquidity position?

2 A company is purchasing goods from a supplier who offers credit on a 3/15 net 45 basis. The company settles its invoices only at the end of each 45-day period. Assuming a 360-day year, find the effective cost of this source of financing.

3 Assume that the company in exercise 2 is a small business whose only other source of finance is a short-term bank loan at an effective rate of interest of 15%. This loan represents 60% of the company's financing. Ignoring taxation, what is the company's average cost of capital? Given this cost of capital, what conclusions might you come to about the 'sensibleness' of this company's financing strategy?

4 In terms of investments in current assets, what constitutes an aggressive strategy and what constitutes a conservative strategy?

Endnotes

1. Short-term marketable securities are also chosen because they are traded in active secondary markets which give them a high level of liquidity. In the UK, companies will

usually choose short-term securities with low default risk such as Treasury Bills, Bank Bills, Certificates of Deposit and short-term local authority loans. Cash can also be invested in the overnight money markets.

2. The overall transactions period does not have to be one year, it can be a month, a two-month period, etc. The transactions period may be determined by a major cash inflow at a given point in time. Here, with a company using this inflow to meet expected future cash outflows, the transactions period is determined by the time it is expected to take to deplete the inflow.

3. TCC is minimised with respect to C by setting the first derivative of Equation 12.1 equal to zero. That is

$$\frac{d(TCC)}{dC} = \frac{i}{2} - \frac{bT}{C^2} = 0$$

Assuming the second derivative $d^2(TCC)/dC^2 > 0$,

$$C^2 = \frac{2bT}{i}, \text{ hence } C* = \sqrt{\frac{2bT}{i}}$$

4. More sophisticated versions of this model allow for investment in long-term marketable securities. Here a portfolio of short-term marketable securities is held because of interest rate risk, however, it is subject to optimal control limits. If, as a result of sustained increases in net cash inflows, investments in short-term marketable securities have been increasing and reach the upper control limit, any additional excess cash is placed in a portfolio of long-term marketable securities. Recall that the latter will, on average, earn higher returns than the short-term portfolio. If, as a result of persistent net cash outflows, the lower control limit of the short-term investment portfolio is reached, investment is switched from the long-term portfolio to raise short-term investment to its desired level.

5. A very approximate formula for calculating the annual effective rate of interest is:

$$\frac{\%Discount}{100 - \%Discount} \times \frac{360}{Days \text{ of Credit Outstanding} - Discount \text{ Period}}$$

In the present example with a discount of 2%, a discount period of 10 days and 30 days of credit outstanding, the approximate annual rate of interest is:

$$\frac{2\%}{100 - 2\%} \times \frac{360}{30 - 10} = .0204 \times 18 = 0.367 \text{ or } 36.7\%$$

6. In extreme cases, all the cumulative capital requirement is financed with long-term funds. Here, when the cumulative capital requirement falls below the funds available, a company's cash and marketable securities investments increase. When the requirement rises, part of the marketable securities are liquidated.

References

Adams P., S. Wyatt and Y. Kim, 'A Contingent Claims Analysis of Trade Credit', Financial Management, 1992

Altman E., 'Financial Ratios, Discriminant Analysis and the Prediction of Corporate Bankruptcy', Journal of Finance, 1968

Baumol W., 'The Transactions Demand for Cash: An Inventory Theoretic Approach', Quarterly Journal of Economics, 1952

Chambers D. and N. Lacey, *Modern Corporate Finance*, Harper Collins, 1994

Galligner G. and A. Ifflander, 'Monitoring Accounts Receivable Using Variance Analysis', Financial Management, 1986

Gilmer R., 'The Optimal Level of Liquid Assets: An Empirical Test', Financial Management, 1985

Kim Y. and J. Atkins, 'Evaluating Investments in Accounts Receivables: A Wealth Maximising Framework', Journal of Finance, 1978

Miller, M. and D. Orr, 'A Model of the Demand for Money by Firms', Quarterly Journal of Economics, 1966

Miller T. and B. Stone, 'Daily Cash Forecasting: Alternative Models and Techniques', Journal of Financial and Quantitative Analysis, 1985

13 Mergers and reorganisation

(This chapter has been prepared in conjunction with Ken Dyson)

Introduction

As it should be evident from the share price models discussed in Chapter 3, companies are not static organisations. They operate in a continuously changing environment, with their future growth prospects, whether positive or negative, having a major impact on their value. Up to this point growth prospects have been examined in terms of a company creating net new investment by adding to its existing capital stock or, in the case of negative growth, deciding not to replace some of its existing assets as these depreciate. In many instances, however, companies seek rapid change in the size and/or structure of their assets in order to: defend positions in existing markets, and/or exploit future profit potential in these markets, and/or expand into new areas of activity. The vehicles used to achieve rapid change are mergers and acquisitions which create external growth, as opposed to the internal growth process implicit in the preceding chapters.

In the short run at least, merger and acquisition activity does not represent net new investment, but simply a reorganisation of the ownership of assets. In the medium term, however, since the decision to merge with, or acquire, another company will be a significant part of a management's business and investment strategies, mergers and acquisitions are likely to have an effect on capital stock. Whether or not the effect is positive or negative depends, however, on the reasons for the merger or acquisition. In some cases a merger can be viewed as an essential phase in a company's strategy of creating rapid external growth. In other cases a merger can be a necessary prelude to rationalising investment and reducing overcapacity in an industry in long-run decline.

Individual companies may also reorganise their operations to achieve rapid contraction, through 'demerger' or disinvestment. This involves a company selling off parts of its existing assets to avoid, for example, financial distress and/or to concentrate operations, and future new investment, on its core areas of business.

With major merger waves occurring in the UK throughout this century[1] (the most recent peaks being over the periods 1967–73 and 1986–89) and disinvestment being a feature of the 1980s, this chapter examines some of the principal issues in these forms of company reorganisation.

The discussion begins by identifying the two main elements in the merger investment decision: synergy and the wealth effects anticipated by shareholders in each of the companies involved in a potential merger. The main arguments in favour of mergers are then presented before outlining the principal issues in financing a merger. This is followed with a discussion of some of the defensive tactics which companies can attempt to use to avoid becoming takeover targets. Finally, some company restructuring issues are examined in the context of management and leveraged buyouts.

Note that a merger involves two companies mutually agreeing to fully integrate their operations, while an acquisition occurs when one company bids for, and acquires, another company, sometimes against the wishes of the company being acquired or targeted. In practice, because of the complex factors involved, it is extremely difficult to distinguish between these two forms of activity; therefore, the terms merger and acquisition are used interchangeably.

The merger investment decision

Mergers are investment decisions and as such should be analysed on an NPV basis. Their underlying rationale is founded in synergy, where the value created by two companies which merge exceeds the sum of their individual pre-merger market values. The concept of synergy can be expressed simply as '2 + 2 = 5'.

Formally, defining the pre-merger values of two companies as V_B, for the bidder, and V_T for the target, and the value that the merger creates as V_{BT}, the potential synergy effect, SYN, is:

$$SYN = V_{BT} - (V_B + V_T) \qquad (13.1)$$

Note that V_{BT} does not necessarily represent the market value of the combined companies. This depends, as explained later, on whether on the one hand the owners of the target become shareholders in the bidding company or on the other receive a cash payment for their equity.

Normally a bidder will seek professional advice from a financial institution, such as a merchant bank, on the prospects of a potential merger and on the appropriate methods of financing it. The advisory fees and any market transactions costs, where for example a potential merger is to be financed by a new issue of capital, must be subtracted from Equation 13.1 in order to determine the economic value, or net synergy effect, NSYN, of the merger. With total fees and charges of FTC:

$$NSYN = V_{BT} - (V_B + V_T) - FTC \qquad (13.1a)$$

One of the central issues in executing a merger concerns the price which the bidder pays for the target company. Once a target's shareholders become aware that a potential merger is in prospect, the market value of their equity normally rises, adding a premium to the pre-merger market value of the target. If this premium, V_{TP}, turns out to be the actual premium paid on acquisition, it will represent the benefits of the merger to the target company's shareholders in terms of the increase in their wealth. From the bidding company's point of view this premium represents a cost. Consequently the NPV of a merger, from a bidding company's point of view, is determined by subtracting the premium from the net synergy effect. This NPV, which measures the potential increase in wealth of the bidder's shareholders, is:

$$NPV = V_{BT} - (V_B + V_T) - FTC - V_{TP} \qquad (13.1b)$$

Consider an example where two companies have market values, before there is any suggestion of a merger, of: $V_B = £60m$ and $V_T = £35m$. The bidder investigates the prospects of taking over the target company and estimates that the value created by the merger would be $V_{BT} = £120m$. The synergy effect is:

$$SYN = £120m - (£60m + £35m) = £25m$$

With estimated fees and market trading costs of $FTC = £6m$, the net synergy effect is

$$NSYN = £25m - £6m = £19m$$

indicating that the merger is economically justifiable.

The bidding company estimates that when its interest in the target company becomes known, the market value of the target's equity will rise[2] by £12m. On the assumption that this is the eventual premium paid by the bidder to execute the acquisition, the bidder views the acquisition as viable since:

$$NPV = £19m - £12m = £7m$$

Despite the net synergy gains of a potential merger, it is possible that a bidding company might expect to eventually pay too high a premium for a target company. In such a situation V_{TP} exceeds the net synergy gain and results in a negative NPV, indicating, from the bidding company's point of view, that the merger is not viable. In the above example if $V_{TP} = £22m$:

$$NPV = £19m - £22m = -£3m$$

Thus despite a potential net synergy gain of £19m the bidding company's shareholders would, if the merger went ahead, experience a reduction of £3m in their wealth.

Given the complexities in potential merger evaluation, this type of situation has turned out in practice with acquiring companies, after the event, realising that they have paid too much for an acquisition and made a negative NPV investment. There can, however, be legitimate cases where the wealth of shareholders in one of the companies involved in a merger does decline. This would arise where the management of the company in question embark on a merger, in anticipation of avoiding increasing problems of financial distress, which would otherwise lead to bankruptcy.[3]

In general, empirical evidence indicates that the gains to shareholders in acquired companies are relatively large, while gains to shareholders in acquiring companies are quite modest, and sometimes short-lived. Jensen and Ruback (1983), for example, have shown that the gains for shareholders in acquired companies in the US can be as much as 26%. Similar gains of around 30% have been reported for UK mergers by Franks et al. (1978) who found, in contrast, the gains for shareholders in acquiring companies to be between only 2.5% and 4%.

In summary there are two distinct aspects to the merger investment decision:
- the net gains from synergy, indicating whether or not a merger is economically viable; and
- how these net gains are to be distributed between the shareholders of each of the companies involved in the potential merger.

In the case where a bidding (acquiring) company and a target (to be acquired) company can be identified, even if the net synergy gains are positive, the acquisition decision depends largely on the premium to be paid for the target company, that is, on the distribution of expected gains between the shareholders in both the bidding and target companies.

Synergy gains from horizontal and vertical mergers

A significant factor in creating synergy, via a merger, is the ability to exploit production scale economies. By rationalising plants a merged company can move down its long-run average cost curve with, other things being equal, the fall in long-run average cost increasing the merged company's future expected net cash flows. Scale economies are most likely to be achieved in horizontal mergers, that is, mergers within a given industry. In addition, the ability to exploit scale economies can enhance market power, and thus supernormal profits. The enhancement of market power may be achieved if scale economies create barriers to entry to potential new competitors and force existing competitors out of the merged company's markets. In the latter situation existing competitors would experience relative cost disadvantages in relation to the merged company.

Scale economies can also be a feature of vertical mergers, where companies integrate backwards in the stages of production, or integrate forwards towards distribution channels and retail outlets. Additional benefits can be achieved, in the case of backwards integration, by securing sources of supply and internalising transfer prices. These benefits can arise when a company purchases inputs from a supplier who has elements of monopoly power, and/or when a company experiences high costs of search for alternative and cheaper sources of inputs. By acquiring an input supplier the price of the input is internalised, and market search costs are avoided. Also, the bidding company may be able to restrict access to competitors who use this source of inputs, again enhancing the bidding company's position in its core markets.

Similar arguments apply to forwards integration, where the control of channels of distribution and/or retail outlets can enable bidding companies to exclude access to competitors' products. Also, where the final demand for a company's product is variable, forward integration can enable the acquiring company to gain more information on this variability and thus enhance efficiency. Efficiency gains can be achieved in, for example, the management of current assets (inventory, accounts receivable and accounts payable) and production runs. In addition forwards integration can produce better planning in respect of future capital investment.

There can be other gains from both horizontal and vertical mergers through, for example, streamlining management.

Conglomerate mergers

It is in the case of conglomerate mergers, where two companies in separate vertically unrelated industries merge, that scale economies and market power have little or no explanatory role.

Superficial reasons
Superficially, risk reduction might appear as an obvious benefit from conglome-

ration since conglomerates diversify across unrelated markets. This reduces company-specific risk and may make management more secure in their employment, but it is not, by itself, a valid argument for mergers in an efficient market. Recall (from Chapter 4) that investors can remove all of a company's specific risk by holding its shares in a well-diversified portfolio and consequently (from Chapter 5), that investors in an efficient stock market will not pay a premium for an activity they can achieve for themselves at no extra cost.

More recent risk arguments, relevant to conglomerate mergers, relate to the agency costs of debt, with the suggestion that company diversification reduces the risk of debtholders. However, with systematic risk being unchanged and overall market value, in this risk context, being unaffected, the implication is that shareholders are made worse off since risk must be transferred from debtholders to shareholders.

Another questionable risk proposition relates to R and D. Here there is evidence to suggest that large companies confine their R and D activities to projects with modest risk, leaving small-sized firms to take on high-risk research. When the latter has been developed to a stage where risk has been significantly reduced, the small firm becomes the target of a large bidder who has sufficient capital to develop a project to its full commercial potential. In an efficient market, however, the bid premium on the target would match any net synergy gains, creating a zero NPV investment for the bidding company.

Benefits of conglomerate mergers

There are unambiguous benefits to conglomerate mergers where, for example, they enable a bidding company to enter new profitable markets quickly and, in the process, acquire an existing management team and/or surmount market entry barriers.

While the R and D argument, related to risk, may be questionable, both R and D and marketing expertise can provide intangible links across vertically unrelated markets. If expertise in these functions has been built up in a company's core business, and the core has reached its mature, relatively slow growth stage, excess capacity develops in marketing and R and D which can be exploited through diversification. Similarly, if a dominant position has been established in the core business, supernormal profits will be available for investment.

General reasons for mergers

Supernormal profits are closely related to Jensen's (1986) hypothesis that the level of free cash flow in a company is an important factor explaining acquisition activity. Free cash flow arises where a company generates net cash flows, after interest and taxes, in excess of the funds' requirements necessary to exploit available profit opportunities in its existing markets. Free cash flow can be used to increase dividends, repurchase a proportion of a company's shares, embark on an acquisition strategy, or build up large reserves of cash and marketable securities. According to Jensen, companies tend to avoid using free cash flow to increase dividend payments or repurchase shares. They also tend to avoid using it to build up high levels of cash and marketable securities, which could indicate inefficient management of liquidity, and place a company itself under the threat of takeover. Consequently management has a tendency to use free cash flow for acquisitions.

Taxation

Explanations supporting the use of free cash flow for merger activity relate to the personal taxes faced by shareholders in the bidding company, to corporate taxes and to information signalling.

As explained in Chapters 8 and 9, when personal tax rates are in excess of capital gains tax rates, shareholders may have a bias against dividends. This on its own would suggest that free cash flow should be used for either acquisitions or share repurchases. The market might, however, interpret share repurchases as negative information on company performance, encouraging management to adopt an acquisitions strategy.[4] Also share repurchases create realised capital gains which become subject to tax, whereas an acquisition has the potential to create capital gains which do not have to be realised by the bidder's shareholders.

Where corporate taxes are concerned, acquisition of a loss-making enterprise may be encouraged if the losses can be set against the acquiring company's profits, thus reducing its tax burden. This approach is permitted by tax laws in the US; however, in the UK the tax-loss provision is much more restrictive. Losses incurred on an acquisition in the UK cannot be set against an acquiring company's profits, only against the acquired company's future profits if it continues to operate in the same line of business. Increases in the present value of tax shields may also be achieved by bidders acquiring companies with underused debt capacity, with a view to increasing the financial leverage ratio in the merged enterprise.

Size arguments

There is a size argument favouring mergers. This relates to the costs of financing where, post-merger, large-sized companies achieve economies of scale in market transactions costs associated with subsequent new capital issues. Similarly it has been suggested that the average cost of capital is negatively related to the size of a company. In this case, however, there is an implicit view that size reduces financial risk but, in the context of the capital structure debate, this is a spurious reason for mergers. A more plausible suggestion is that management may embark on acquisition activity to increase their company's size as a defensive strategy aimed at reducing the probability of their own company becoming an acquisition target.

Managerial inefficiency

Finally, the ability to correct managerial inefficiency has been put forward as a significant reason for mergers. According to Marris (1964) and others, the threat of acquisition can act as a discipline on management by forcing management to operate a company in the best interests of shareholders, thus reducing the agency costs of equity.

When a company is run inefficiently by, for example, overmanning or an inefficient use of technology or with excessive liquidity, the stock market values it on the basis of its existing management. A bidding company may therefore see profit potential in an acquisition, achievable by creating redundancies or using excess cash and marketable securities for more profitable long-term investments. In an efficient market, however, once a bid appears likely, the target's share price would rise to reflect the efficient utilisation of assets under new management. In other words the

Table 13.1: Comparing an aquisition by cash with an offer of shares

	Pre-merger	
	Bidding company	Target company
Share price	£1.25	£1.00
No. shares outstanding	80m	50m
Market value	£100m	£50m
Bid premium		£10m

Post-merger

Total value created by acquisition: £180m

Financed by a cash offer
  Cash offer: £50m + £10m = £60m
  Market value of merged company: £180m − £60m = £120m
  Shares outstanding[1] in merged company: 80m

Share price post-merger: £120m/80m = £1.50

Financed by share offer
  Market value merged company[2]: £180m
  Bid price per share on target: £60m/50m = £1.20
  Exchange ratio: £1.20/£1.25 = 0.96:1
  No. shares exchanged by bidder: 0.96(50m) = 48m
  No. shares outstanding in merged company: 80m + 48m = 128m

Share price post-merger: £180m/128m = £1.406

[1] With a cash acquisition, the number of shares in the bidding company remain unchanged since the target company's shareholders have been 'bought' out for cash.
[2] On a share offer the target company's shareholders become part owners of the bidding company, after acquisition, so that the whole of the value created by the merger is reflected in the merged company's market value.

bid premium on the target would match the net synergy gains, creating a zero NPV investment for the bidder.

Financing an acquisition

There are a number of ways in which a company can finance an acquisition by:
• a cash purchase of the target company's equity;
• an issue of shares;
• an issue of long-term debt; or
• a combination of all three methods.

An all cash offer is relatively straightforward. In the case of issuing shares, however, careful attention has to be paid to the exchange ratio, that is, the number of shares the bidding company exchanges for shares in the target company.

A cash offer

Consider the two companies, detailed in Table 13.1, which before any thought of a merger have market values: $V_B = £100m$ and $V_T = £50m$. For the sake of simplicity it is assumed that both companies are all equity financed and that there are no fees or transactions costs (FTC = 0) in completing the acquisition. The bidding company concludes that the acquisition of the target will create a total value of £180m. The bid premium on the target is $V_{TP} = £10m$, and is accepted by the target company's directors.

This merger is economically viable since, by Equation 13.1a, the net synergy effect is:

$$NSYN = V_{BT} - (V_B + V_T) = £180m - (£100m + £50m) = £30m$$

The bid premium is acceptable to the bidding company's shareholders since, by Equation 13.1b, the bidding company's NPV for this investment is:

$$NPV = £30m - £10m = £20m$$

If the acquisition is paid for by cash the cost of the target, as shown in Table 13.1, is its pre-merger market value plus the bid premium, that is,

$$Cost\ of\ Acquisition = £50m + £10m = £60m$$

After the acquisition the target's assets become an integral part of the bidding company. The bidding company's value increases to £120m, that is, the total value created by the merger (£180m) less the cash expenditure on the acquisition (£60m).

Under a cash acquisition the number of shares outstanding in the bidding company remains constant, post-merger. With a £20m increase in wealth for the bidding company's shareholders, determined by this investment's NPV, and with 80m shares outstanding, the bidding company's shareholders experience a capital gain per share of £20m/80m = £0.25. This raises their company's share price from £1.25 pre-merger, to £1.50 post-merger, and the market value of their equity from £100m to £120m. In other words, as Table 13.1 indicates, the share price, post-merger, is £120m/80m = £1.50.

Purchasing by a share issue

As an alternative the bidding company may decide to purchase the target with an exchange of shares between the bidding company and the target company, which is achieved by a new share issue. In this case the target company's shareholders become part owners of the bidding company so that the market value of the merged enterprise reflects the total value of £180m created by the merger. The number of shares exchanged is determined by the exchange ratio.

The exchange ratio and pre-merger prices

Using the cash price of £60m as a base, and given the number of shares outstanding in the target company (50m), the bidding company could decide to pay £60m/50m = £1.20 for each of the target's shares. This gives a per share bid premium of 20p, equivalent to the total bid premium of £10m.

The exchange ratio is determined as:

$$Exchange\ Ratio = \frac{Bid\ Price\ per\ Share}{Bidder's\ Current\ Share\ Price} = \frac{£1.20}{£1.25} = 0.96:1$$

In other words the bidding company exchanges 0.96 of its shares for each of the shares in the target, or 96 shares per 100 of the target's.

Given the number of shares outstanding in the target company, the exchange ratio implies that the bidding company must raise $.96(50m) = 48m$ new shares. Assuming this can be achieved at the bidding company's share price of £1.25, the exchange appears, on face value, to be equivalent to purchasing the target for the cash price of £60m, since $48m(£1.25) = £60m$. This is not the case.

To understand why this share exchange is not equivalent to the cash purchase, the share price of the bidder, after it has acquired the target, must be considered. The market value of the new enterprise is £180m but under the share exchange, relative to the cash offer, the number of shares outstanding will have increased from 80m to $80m + 48m = 128m$. The target company's shareholders now have a stake in the merged enterprise equal to 37.50% of its equity (48m/128m). The bidding company's shareholders experience a reduction of their share of equity, relative to the cash offer position, from 100% to 62.50%. With 128m shares on issue the share price under this given share exchange ratio is £180m/128m $=$ £1.406 (see Table 13.1), that is, approximately 9p below the merged company's share price under the cash offer.

Under the share exchange, however, the bidder has paid more than £60m, the cash price of the target. The target company's shareholders have effectively received the post-merger share price times the number of shares exchanged by the bidding company, that is:

$$48m(£1.406) = £67.50m > £60m \text{ cash price.}$$

The increase in wealth of the bidding company's shareholders, £20m under the cash offer, has now been reduced. The pre-merger value of their shareholding was £100m but is now

$$80m(£1.406) = £112.50m$$

indicating a reduction in gain, relative to the cash offer:

$$£112.50m - £100m = £12.50m < £20m$$

This result arises because the exchange ratio is based on the pre-merger prices of the two companies. Since the target company's shareholders gained a stake in the bidding company's equity, and the bidding company's share price rose on acquisition, from £1.25 to £1.406, the cost of the acquisition increased above the cash offer.

If, alternatively, the share price of the company falls on acquisition, the cost of acquisition will decline below its cash price. Assume, in the above example, that the bidding company's pre-merger share price falls, after merger, to £1.22. Given the total number of shares outstanding, the market value falls to $(128m)(£1.22) =$ £156.16m. With the target company's shareholders holding 37.5% of the equity, the effective cost of the acquisition is $0.375(£156.16m) = £58.56m$. Had a cash offer of £60m been made and accepted, the target company's shareholders would not have shared in the subsequent loss in value after the merger. By financing through a share exchange, however, both sets of shareholders experience losses, the bidding company's shareholders experiencing a decline in their equity value, from the pre-merger value of £100m, to .625(£156.16) = £97.60m.

The exchange ratio and post-merger value

It is possible to set the exchange ratio in relation to the expected post-merger value in order to achieve equivalence between a share offer and a cash offer. In the above example the expected post-merger value is £180m. If the target shareholders are to receive £60m of this equity, their share, post-merger, will be:

$$\alpha_T = \frac{£60}{£180m} = 0.33 \text{ or } 33\%$$

Expressing this in terms of the number of shares they will receive,

$$\alpha_T = \frac{NN}{NN + NOB} \qquad (13.2)$$

where,

NN is the number of new shares issued, and
NOB is the number of shares outstanding in the bidding company prior to the bid.

Solving Equation 13.2 for NN yields:

$$NN = \frac{\alpha_T}{1 - \alpha_T} NOB \qquad (13.2a)$$

Thus with NOB = 80m and α_T = 0.33, the number of new shares to be issued by the bidding company is:

$$NN = \frac{.3333}{1 - .3333} 80m \approx 40m$$

As there are 50m shares outstanding in the target company, pre-merger, the exchange ratio is 40m/50m = 0.8:1. That is, when expressed equivalently in terms of the relevant share prices:

$$\text{Exchange Ratio} = \frac{\text{Bid Price Per Share}}{\text{Expected Share Price of Merged Company}}$$

$$= \frac{£1.20}{£1.50} = 0.8:1$$

Given the total number of shares outstanding after the merger, 40m + 80m = 120m, and given the expected post-merger value of £180m, the post-merger share price is equivalent to that which would have been achieved under the cash offer (£180m/120m = £1.50). Thus the target company's shareholders have effectively received, in equity, 40m(£1.50) = £60m. This exchange ratio is of course based on an expected post-merger value which the market, when the merger is completed, may not agree with.

Another example
Consider a second example summarised in Table 13.2. The companies involved

Table 13.2: An acquisition example

	Pre-merger	
	Bidding company	Target company
Share price	£3.0	£0.70
No. shares outstanding	50m	100m
Market value	£150m	£70m
Bid premium		£15m

Post-merger

Value created by acquisition £270m

Cash Offer

If cash offer made: Cash price = £70m + £15m = £85m
Bid price per share = £85m/100m = £0.85
Value of equity in merged company = £270m − £85m = £185m
Expected share price in merged company = £185m/50m = £3.70

Share Offer
Exchange ratio based on pre-merger share prices
Exchange ratio = £0.85/£3.00 = £0.2833:1

No. of shares offered by bidder to target = 0.2833(100m) = 28.33m
Total number of shares on issue = 28.33m + 50m = 78.33m
Expected share price of merged company £270m/78.33m = £3.45
Value to target shareholders = 28.33m(£3.45) = £97.74m > Cash price

Exchange ratio: based on cash equivalent

$$a_T = \frac{\text{Bid price}}{\text{Expected market value of merger}} = \frac{£85m}{£270m} = 0.3148$$

No. of shares offered by bidder to target = $\frac{a_T}{1 - a_T}$ 50m = 22.97m

Total number of shares on issue = 22.97m + 50m = 72.97m
Expected share price of merged company = £270m/72.97m = £3.70

$$\textbf{Exchange ratio} = \frac{\textbf{Bid price per share}}{\textbf{Expected share price of merged company}} = \frac{£0.85}{£3.70}$$

$$= 0.2297:1$$

---

have pre-merger market values of $V_B = £150m$ and $V_T = £70m$. The bid premium is $V_{TP} = £15m$ and the total value created, if the merger takes place, is $V_{BT} = £270m$. With net synergy of

$$NSYN = £270m - (£150m + £70m) = £50m$$

and an NPV to the bidding company of

$$NPV = £50m - £15m = £35m$$

the acquisition is viable.

On the basis of a cash offer the acquisition costs £85m, that is, a bid price per share of 85p, and the market value of the merged company is £185m. With 50m shares outstanding in the bidding company, the post-merger share price is £3.70.

Where a share offer is concerned, two cases are illustrated in Table 13.2, the first where the exchange ratio is based on the pre-merger share prices of the two companies and the second where the exchange ratio is based on the expected post-merger value.

Using the pre-merger share prices the exchange ratio is 0.2833:1, indicating that the bidding company exchanges 0.2833 of its shares for every share in the target. With 28.33m new shares issued to execute the exchange, and a total number of shares outstanding, post-merger, of 78.33m, the post-merger share price is £3.45. In terms of their proportion of equity in the merged company, the target shareholders have 28.33m/78.33m = 0.3617, or 36.17%. They have received, in effect, 28.33m(£3.45) = £97.74m. In other words an extra £12.74m, relative to the cash offer of £85m.

The second case uses Equation 13.2a to determine the number of new shares which should be issued, if equivalence with the cash offer is to be established. Here, as the last section of Table 13.2 indicates, $a_t = 0.3148$ and the number of new shares to be issued is:

$$NN = \frac{.3148}{1 - .3148}\ 50m = 22.97m$$

The bid price for the target is £85m/22.97m = £3.70. As there will now be 72.97m shares outstanding, post-merger, this is equal to the post-merger share price of £3.70. Thus, relative to the cash position, the bidding company has not overpaid for its acquisition. Given the original bid price per share in the target, the exchange ratio is 0.2297:1. The respective equity shares, post-merger, are 22.97m/72.97m = 0.3148 or 31.48% for the target's shareholders, and 100 − 31.48 = 68.52% for the bidder's shareholders.

Of course if the market does not agree, after merger, with a value of £270m, the target company's shareholders will gain or lose, relative to the cash position, depending on how the market has moved. If the share price rises above £3.70 the target company's shareholders gain; if it falls below £3.70 they appropriate part of the losses, along with the bidding company's shareholders.

Complexities in financing

The above illustrates some of the complexities in deciding how to finance a merger and, indeed, the implicit difficulties involved in determining whether or not a merger will benefit shareholders. At the announcement of a bid the prices of the respective companies involved can react in different ways during the negotiation process. This, and the uncertainty surrounding the expected market price of the merged entity, complicates the determination of the appropriate exchange ratio, in the case of a share issue. Agreement on the exchange ratio is essential if 'fair' appropriation of potential gains, or potential losses, is to be achieved between the sets of shareholders in the merger.

Anticipation of how the market might react post-merger may also influence the method of financing. From the bidding company's point of view, a cash offer, if sufficient funds are available, might be favoured if there is a reasonable probability that the post-merger share price will rise significantly. Here the bidding company's

Table 13.3: Acquisitions and earnings per share

| | Pre-merger | | Bidder post-merger |
	Bidder	Target	
No. shares outstanding	150,000	150,000	225,000
Share price	£3.00	£1.50	£3.00
Market value	£450,000	£225,000	£675,000
Earnings	£30,000	£30,000	£60,000
Earnings per share	£0.20	£0.20	£0.267
Price–earnings ratio	15	7.5	11.23

shareholders can expect to appropriate all the additional gains, with the target shareholders receiving a fixed cash sum.

Conversely a share offer might be appropriate where there is uncertainty about how the price will settle after merger. While in this case the target company's equity holders would share in any gains, they would also experience part of the losses from a fall in the bidder's share price, post-merger.[5]

The bidding company also has to consider how an equity issue and/or a debt issue might affect capital structure and, in the case of any cash that is offered, how liquidity in the merged company might be affected.

Earnings per share

There might be a temptation to abandon proper investment appraisal techniques when considering an acquisition and concentrate on the effect a merger might potentially have on earnings per share, EPS. When there are real economic gains from an acquisition, overall EPS in the merged company will improve.

There are situations, however, due to the accounting methods of recording a merger, where improvements in EPS can be entirely illusory. To understand this, consider the two companies in Table 13.3. While both companies have equal current EPS, their price–earnings ratios differ. Recall from Chapter 3 that the higher PE ratio for the bidding company reflects the market's expectation that it will experience a significantly higher expected future growth in earnings, relative to the target. Here, if the bidding company and the target company merge, there are assumed to be no synergy gains; thus the total market value of the bidding company, after the merger, is the sum of the individual companies' market values, that is:

$$V_{BT} = V_B + V_T = £450,000 + £225,000 = £675,000$$

Further, assuming for simplicity that the bidding company does not pay a premium for the target, the bidding company will have made a zero NPV transaction.

In this example the acquisition is completed by a share offer based on the pre-merger prices of the two companies, thus the exchange ratio is,

$$\frac{£1.50}{£3.00} = 0.5{:}1$$

The exchange ratio indicates that the bidding company exchanges one of its shares for every two of the target's. Given the number of shares in the target, 150,000, the bidding company must issue 75,000 new shares, 0.5(150,000), bringing the total number of shares outstanding, post-merger, to 150,000 + 75,000 = 225,000.

Concentrating on EPS, with no synergy, earnings in the merged company are simply determined by combining the pre-merger earnings of the separate companies. The resulting EPS of 26.7p appear, however, to indicate that EPS have increased by approximately 34%. In an efficient market, since the bidding company has made a zero NPV investment, its share price would not be expected to change, post-merger, so that the increase in EPS would be judged by the market to have no effect on value. The illusion simply comes about because, although the earnings in the merged company have doubled, the number of shares has only increased by 50%. As the share price of the bidding company on merger remains unchanged, the price–earnings ratio falls from 15 to 11.23 to reflect this new situation.

Price–earnings ratios

Another way of analysing mergers, which was once considered to be useful, was to focus on PE ratios. The argument was that if a company with a high PE ratio adopted a merger strategy based on the acquisition of companies with low PE ratios, value would be increased. The analysis was based on the implicit assumption that the PE ratio of the bidding company would remain unchanged after the merger.

In the example in Table 13.3, if this was the case and the post-merger PE ratio remained at 15, then with EPS = 26.7p the share price of the merged company would rise. The share price would rise from £3.00 to £4.005, the latter determined as 15(26.7p) = £4.005, taking the market value to 225,000(£4.005) = £901,125. In an efficient market, since there are no economic benefits to the merger, this could not happen and a major error would have been made by management who adopted such a strategy.

Reducing the probability of acquisition

The above analysis is based on the assumption that a merger will be undertaken if there are viable synergy gains, and if the bidding company's shareholders are satisfied with the distribution of gains between themselves and the target company's shareholders. Some managements, however, who view their companies as possible future acquisition targets, are conscious of the impact that acquisition might have on their own employment positions. The managements may, therefore, attempt to take steps to defend their companies against 'unwelcome' bids.

In a number of cases a company's ownership structure is sufficient to significantly reduce, but never eliminate, the probability of it becoming an acquisition target. This is likely to occur where share ownership of a publicly quoted company is concentrated in the hands of one individual; a close family group; a financial institution, such as an insurance company; or a group of employees. Privately owned companies are even less likely to become vulnerable to an unwanted takeover.

If a management has as one of its objectives the avoidance of unfriendly bids for their company, they can attempt to ensure that the above types of ownership structure are maintained, or they can take their own initiatives. As already indicated, there is some evidence that size and the threat of acquisition are inversely related. Consequently management may initiate its own acquisition policy as a method of rapidly achieving a size commensurate with a defensive position. Alternatively management may attempt to introduce what are referred to as 'poison pills', with the intention of raising the cost of acquisition faced by a potential bidder and, therefore, discouraging a bid.

A 'poison pill' often involves giving existing shareholders the option, only exercisable on an acquisition, of purchasing additional shares at a discount. This would bias the distribution of any synergy gains towards the target company's shareholders, to the disadvantage and disapproval of the potential bidder's shareholders.

If an unwanted bid is made the management of a target company might seek legal action to stop an eventual acquisition. Alternatively management might seek a buyer for a particular set of the company's assets which the bidder views as 'crown jewels', that is, as essential to the success of the eventual merger. Another strategy is for management of the target company to seek an alternative 'friendlier' company with which to merge. The latter is often referred to as the 'white knight' strategy but can become highly complex. Under the UK's City Code on Mergers and Acquisitions, for example, any information provided to the 'white knight' by the target must, on request, be passed to the original bidder.

Other defensive tactics might be a reverse takeover bid, with the target company bidding for, and threatening the management of, the company which initiated the idea of the merger in the first place. In some instances the management of a target company have issued a revised profits forecast in an attempt to demonstrate that the target's future performance is better than expected. The belief is that the target's share price will rise, thus raising the potential cost of the acquisition. In an efficient market, however, such a tactic could not be expected to work since the market price of the target will already fully reflect its intrinsic value, on the assumption that it remains an independent company. This strategy has been adopted by some companies in the UK, for example, Foseco which attempted to thwart acquisition by Burmah Castrol in 1990. This bid was ultimately successful.

Yet another strategy is referred to as 'golden parachutes'. These may be negotiated by management to enhance their compensation packages in the event of redundancy created by a successful merger. The idea, again, is to raise a bidder's potential acquisition costs and thus reduce the probability that a company with 'golden parachutes' will become a target. Recent research by Born et al. (1993) casts doubt on this argument, suggesting that such arrangements may signal negative information to the market about existing management efficiency, and thus increase the possibility of acquisition. The 'golden parachute' and other tactics raise the more general issue of the agency costs of equity and whether it is appropriate for management, from the point of view of shareholders, to employ defensive tactics to avoid acquisitions and secure their own employment positions.

Mergers and regulation

There are statutory instruments and stock market self-regulatory codes which may limit the feasibility of a merger. Because of the monopoly power connotations, especially associated with vertical and horizontal mergers, the US, the UK and, indeed, the Commission of the European Union have statutory monopolies and restrictive practices policies aimed at preventing mergers which would be against the public interest. Public interest is interpreted in a number of ways. At one extreme, for example, a merger can be deemed to be against the national interest where international mergers in the defence industry are under consideration. In general, however, the public interest criteria refer to the potential gains and losses in consumer, or economic, welfare arising from an intended merger.

Where, for example, the UK's Monopolies Commission is concerned, potential mergers which are referred to it are examined on a public interest basis. This takes account of expected price and output effects, post-merger investment intentions, potential cost efficiency gains and expected benefits from future technical progress, among a host of other costs and benefits. The Monopolies Commission then makes a recommendation to the President of the Board of Trade in favour of or against the merger, the President making the final decision.

In the UK self-regulatory issues are largely associated with the City's Panel on Takeovers and Mergers. This Panel's code of practice is voluntary, in the sense that it has no statutory powers, but companies breaking the code can be excluded from a quotation on the stock market. The main objective of the Panel is to protect shareholder interests when merger negotiations and acquisitions are in progress, in particular the interests of minority shareholders in target companies.

Disinvestment and other forms of restructuring

Although the major part of this chapter has been concerned with mergers, these are not the only form of restructuring activity undertaken by companies. In recent years a number of companies have decided to disinvest, particularly target companies during or after an unsuccessful merger bid. Disinvestment involves selling off, or separating, parts of the assets of a company, a recent example being ICI. After an unsuccessful bid from Hanson plc, ICI undertook disinvestment in July 1993 by selling its acrylic division to the DuPont Corporation in exchange for the latter's European nylon interests and £235m in cash. Another example is Boots which in 1994 sold its pharmaceuticals division to BASF, the German chemicals giant.

There are a number of reasons for disinvestment. First, there may be a belief that the parts of an existing company when added as separate entities are worth more than the whole. This essentially represents reverse synergy, where '5 − 1 = 5'. Second, a company may want to dispose of assets which it believes it cannot operate efficiently and which, in some way, detract from the company's ability to run its core business. A number of UK conglomerate mergers during the 1960s eventually proved unsuccessful and led them to pursue disinvestment strategies during the 1980s. Third, a company may perceive a need to improve liquidity, especially in a crisis, or want to realise cash resources for attractive new investments. Disinvestment of part of a company's assets may, therefore, stave off bankruptcy in the former situation, and in the latter provide investment funds.

Sell-offs, spin-offs and going private

Disinvestment can be achieved in a number of ways: through a sell-off of assets for cash and/or shares, through a spin-off, or by going private.

Spin-offs do not, however, provide cash resources since they normally involve a division of a holding company being given to the company's existing shareholders. In effect existing shareholders are given equity to provide them with a direct interest in the spin-off division, which then operates as a separate company with its own board of directors. The rationale for the spin-off is that greater control will be exercised over its operating, investment and financing decisions.

Going private means a group of individuals, often the existing management of a company, buying the company's equity and taking the company off the stock market. This, for example, occurred in the UK when Richard Branson purchased the shares of Virgin, a company he had originally founded and previously launched as a public company. A company which goes private can go public again in the future. Also, going private can apply in a sell-off.

According to De Angelo et al. (1984) a number of motives can be identified for going private. First, it enables a company to avoid annual registration costs and administration expenses (for example administrative expenses associated with dividend payments) incurred when it is publicly quoted. Second, it enables management to avoid problems which might arise at shareholder annual general meetings. Third, if there is a problem of short-termism in the stock market, discussed in Chapter 5, management of a public company may be discouraged from undertaking long-term investments which have relatively low rates of return but are nevertheless viable. Fourth, where management and/or employees become the owners of a company, they will have a greater incentive to work more effectively and efficiently, thus minimising the agency problem in respect of equity.

Buyouts, buy-ins and leverage

One of the dominant ways of going private is through a management buyout where the existing management of a company, or a division in the case of a sell-off, buys the relevant equity and acquires control. Examples of management buyouts in the UK are Kingfisher, MFI and Cookson. The latter is an industrial and metals conglomerate, which sold part of its engineering products operation for £84.5m to a management team. While buyouts are usually management based, all employees can be involved, as in the case of the National Freight Consortium buyout, for example. A buy-in occurs where a company or a division goes private through a group of outsiders purchasing the relevant equity.

Management buyouts (and buy-ins), as the Cookson example illustrates, can require substantial funds. They can be financed partly by cash (received for example in redundancy payments) and short-term bank loans, but often a large proportion of the equity purchase is financed by raising long-term debt capital. This results in high levels of financial leverage, giving rise to the concept of a leveraged buyout (or leveraged buy-in). The debt is normally backed by the assets which have been purchased in the buyout (buy-in).

There are different forms of debt in a leveraged buyout, but in general the debt is high risk with a high default rating. Junk bond issues were a prominent feature of early US management buyouts. Mezzanine finance is another form of high risk/ high interest rate debt. Here the debt has a convertible equity feature which can only be exercised in the future when specified requirements have been met by the company which has gone private.

Two principal motives have been identified for management/leveraged buyouts. First, value is added in going private by the tax shields arising from the use of financial leverage. Second, since leveraged buyouts often mean management become the owners of a company, their incentive to improve efficiency and raise the rate of return on investment is increased. This incentive tends to be reinforced since the use of high-risk debt is associated with a high required rate of return on debt and therefore necessitates relatively high levels of operating income. Operating income must be adequate to cover debt interest payments and to produce significant levels of earnings after interest and taxes in order to provide a return to the owner-managers. Thus, management buyouts, effected by high financial leverage, reduce the agency costs of equity but tend not to increase the agency costs of debt, as might otherwise be expected.

Liquidation

The most severe form of disinvestment is a liquidation where an entire company is sold off in individual parts. The rationale is the belief that the sum of the values of the individual parts, as independent entities, is greater than the value of the company before liquidation.

Summary

Mergers, acquisitions, disinvestments and, ultimately, liquidations are important vehicles for restructuring assets, especially in a highly competitive environment where there is rapid technological change, a need to be innovative, and a need to be both cost and price competitive. These means of reorganising business activity and business resources can be essential instruments facilitating the development of management strategy for the future.

Like any investment decision mergers (and disinvestments) must be viewed in the context of NPV assessments. The major difficulty, however, is that two sets of shareholders are normally involved, the gains for one of the sets, ironically shareholders in the bidding company, being somewhat problematical.

Public policy to stop mergers which are deemed to be against the public interest is relatively well founded. Strategies developed by individual management teams to reduce the probability that the companies they work for will become takeover targets may not be well founded. Only defensive strategies which can be shown to be in the interests of shareholder wealth maximisation are legitimate.

Finally, the recent developments in management and leveraged buyouts (and buy-ins) can be seen, to some extent, as interesting resolutions of aspects of the agency problem.

Questions

1 Consider the ABC company which has a market value of £75m. It is considering taking over the XYX company which has a market value of £50m. ABC estimates that the value of the merged company, V_{AZ}, would be £140m, but that there will be a bid premium of £10m if the merger is executed. The estimated fees and market trading costs of the merger are £3m. ABC has 125m shares outstanding and XYZ has 125m shares outstanding. Indicate whether the merger is economically viable and whether it is viable from the bidding company's point of view.

2 Ignoring the £3m transactions costs in question 1, assume that ABC decides to purchase XYZ by a cash offer. Both companies are all equity financed.
   a) What is the cash offer?
   b) What is the total value of ABC after the merger?
   c) What is the post-merger share price of ABC?

3 Ignoring the £3m transactions costs, assume that ABC makes a share offer to the equity holders in XYZ based on an exchange ratio determined by ABC's pre-merger share price and a bid price for XYZ based on the cash price that would be paid for XYZ.
   a) Show that the post-merger share price of ABC is below what it would have been under the cash offer in question 2.
   b) How much do the shareholders in XYZ gain relative to the cash offer?
   c) How much do the original shareholders in ABC lose relative to the cash offer?
   d) What proportion of shares do the shareholders of ABC and XYZ own in the merged enterprise?

4 Given question 1 and ignoring the £3m transactions costs, what proportion of shares in the merged company should XYZ shareholders have if the post-merger share price is to be equal to the post-merger share price under the cash offer in question 2?

5 What do you understand by the concept of a management/leveraged buyout? What are the principal motives for such a buyout?

6 What role does the concept of 'free cash flow' play in explaining the motives for mergers?

7 What are the main reasons for horizontal and vertical mergers?

Exercises

1 In what ways can the management of a company attempt to reduce the probability of their company becoming a target for a takeover?

2 Under what conditions might a cash offer for a company be preferred to a share offer?

3 What are the major reasons for disinvestment?

Endnotes

1. Evidence in the UK between 1969 and 1990 indicates, for example, that apart from the period 1974–85 average annual expenditure on mergers and acquisitions by industrial and commercial companies accounted for at least 39% of gross fixed capital formation.

2. The bidder's share price, as well as the target's share price, can vary during merger negotiations, especially if the negotiations are protracted and there is resistance on the part of the target company.

3. Here the announcement of the intended merger would be interpreted, in a signalling context, as indicating the possibility of future financial distress, leading to a fall in share price.

4. Recall from Chapters 8 and 9 that even if there is no difference between the personal income and capital gains tax rates, that is, $t_p = t_g$, there can be a bias against dividend payments in favour of capital gains to the extent that the sale of shares is postponed to the future. Using free cash flow to repurchase shares would create a realised capital gain, thus the tax argument may also represent a reason favouring the use of free cash flow for acquisitions as opposed to share repurchases. The really complicating factor in this argument is the tax position of a target when this company's shareholders are receiving cash for their shares. In this case the bid premium may include some compensating payment to meet personal tax liabilities, the payment effectively being made by the bidding company's shareholders.

5. All of this analysis assumes of course that the same shareholders remain in the respective companies after a bid is announced.

References

Born, J.E., H. Trahan and H. Faria, 'Golden Parachutes: Incentive Aligners, Management Entrencher, or Takeover Bid Signals?', Journal of Financial Research, 1993

Cowling, K.A., P. Stoneman and J. Cubbin, *Mergers and Economic Performance*, Cambridge, Cambridge University Press, 1980

DeAngelo, H., L. DeAngelo and E. Rice, 'Going Private: Minority Freezeouts and Stockholder Wealth', Journal of Law and Economics, 1984

Franks, J., J. Broyles and M. Hecht, 'An Industry Study of the Profitability of Mergers in the United Kingdom', Journal of Finance, 1978

George, K., 'Do We Need a Merger Policy?', in J. Fairburn and J. Kay (Eds.), *Mergers and Merger Policy*, Oxford, Oxford University Press, 1989

Hite, G. and J. Owners, 'Security Price Reactions Around Corporate Spin-Off Announcements', Journal of Financial Economics, 1983

Hughes, A., *Mergers and Economic Performance in the UK: A Survey of the Empirical*

Evidence, 1950–1990, University of Cambridge, Department of Applied Economics Working Paper No. 9118, 1991

Jensen M., 'Agency Costs of Free Cash Flow, Corporate Finance and Takeovers', American Economic Review, 1985

Jensen, M. and R. Ruback, 'The Market for Corporate Control, the Scientific Evidence', Journal of Financial Economics, 1983

Kim, E. and J. Schatzberg, 'Voluntary Corporate Liquidations', Journal of Financial Economics, 1987

King, M., 'Takeover Activity in the UK', in J. Fairburn and J. Kay (Eds.), *Mergers and Merger Policy*, Oxford, Oxford University Press, 1989

Lev, B., 'Observations on the Merger Phenomenon', in J. Stern and D. Chew (Eds.), *The Revolution in Corporate Finance*, Oxford, Basil Blackwell, 1992

Marris, R., *The Economic Theory of Managerial Capitalism*, London, Macmillan, 1964

McConnell, J. and C. Muscarella, 'Corporate Capital Expenditure Decisions and the Market Value of the Firm', Journal of Financial Economics, 1985

Myers, S., 'A Framework for Evaluating Mergers', in *Modern Developments in Finance*, New York, Praeger, 1976

Newbould, A., *Management and Merger Activity*, Gulthstead Press, 1970

Palepu K., 'Predicting Takeover Targets: A Methodological and Empirical Analysis', Journal of Accounting and Economics, 1986

Roll, R., 'The Hubris Hypothesis of Corporate Takeovers', Journal of Business, 1986

Shliefer, A. and L. Summer, 'Breach of Trust in Corporate Takeovers', in A. Auerbauch (Ed.), *Corporate Takeovers: Causes and Consequence*, Chicago, University of Chicago Press, 1988

Stableton, R., 'Mergers, Debt Capacity, and the Valuation of Corporate Loans', in M. Keenan and L. White (Eds.), *Mergers and Acquisitions*, Heath Lexington MA, 1982

14 Investment, financing and the small firm[1]

Introduction

Attention having been focused in the preceding chapters on large publicly traded companies, this chapter explores some of the issues peculiar to the investment and financing activities of small privately owned businesses.

In advanced economies small businesses, or what are often referred to as small to medium-sized enterprises (SMEs), have received increasing attention in recent years. First, because this sub-sector of the corporate economy makes a highly significant contribution to employment and output.[2] Second, because there has been considerable concern about the ability of small businesses or firms to raise sufficient funds, at fair and competitive costs of capital, to finance future growth and/or sustain existing operations in times of financial distress. This concern arises in part from attempts to explain three observations:
- the reliance of small firms on short-term debt capital provided by the banking system;
- the relatively high failure rate among small firms; and
- the tendency for the majority of surviving small firms to exhibit slow growth.[3]

It must be stressed, however, that any weaknesses which can be identified in the corporate finance functions of small firms can only represent part of the explanation for these observations. High failure rates, for example, occur especially among recently established small firms. These firms tend to fail because of managerial inexperience, the innate risks associated with developing new ideas, and the small firm's concentration on a very limited range of products, which makes it highly vulnerable to recessionary phases of the business cycle.

In the case of the finance function the main concerns are with the small firm's limited use of equity capital and the costs it faces in using debt financing. In respect of the latter, the areas of controversy relate to the extent to which excessive interest rates and loan handling charges are levied by banks. They also relate to the possibility that small firms are required to cover their borrowings with unnecessary amounts of tangible assets, that is, with collateral whose value is significantly in excess of the amount of funds being borrowed. In the case of equity capital the controversy centres on whether or not there is an equity gap. This arises where small firms experience difficulties in accessing relatively small amounts of equity and, even when such sums are available, have to face prohibitively high required rates of return.

A major difficulty in analysing these controversies concerns the extent to which the behaviour of small firms has its origins, on the one hand, in imperfections in the supply of finance and, on the other, in the objectives of small firm owners. In the latter case these objectives may influence small firm investment strategies and their relative demand for debt and equity and make it appear, superficially, that small firms face major financing constraints. This difficulty is briefly discussed in the next section.

The chapter then proceeds on the initial assumption that the small firm is run by an owner-manager whose overriding objective is to retain control of his/her business. In the light of this objective the corporate finance principles developed in the preceding chapters are applied in order to show how a small firm might choose to rely on debt financing and, consequently, opt for a slow growth strategy to limit the effects of agency costs. Empirically the majority of small firms do not seek growth. These firms are often referred to as 'lifestyle' businesses since they have been established to meet the lifestyle aspirations of their founders.

This demand side perspective provides a benchmark against which some of the practical issues associated with small firm financing can be examined. These issues are illustrated in the present chapter by reviewing the recent debate on small firm financing in the UK. The aim is to determine the extent to which the problems which have been identified are supply side in nature, arising from restrictions imposed by financial institutions.

The chapter draws to a close with a discussion of some of the policy initiatives which have been introduced in the UK to improve small firm access to debt and equity, and to reduce the component costs of these sources of capital. For the minority of small firms which seek to exploit significant growth opportunities, and therefore subject themselves to increased risk exposures, these costs can be relatively high.

Owner-manager objectives

From a corporate finance point of view the interpretation that is placed on the financing difficulties which small firms may experience depends on whether those difficulties are supply side or demand side induced. Often there is an implicit assumption that owner-managers act to maximise value.[4] Given this assumption there is a desire to invest in all available projects whose expected future net cash flows, when discounted at the appropriately determined risk adjusted cost of capital, are positive. Consequently imperfections in the supply of finance tend to be highlighted as a contributory cause of any SME sector tendency to invest suboptimally, exhibit slower than average growth and/or experience higher than average bankruptcy rates.

Alternatively, if it is assumed that an owner-manager has an overriding objective to retain control of his/her business, equity aversion may be exhibited. That is, the owner-manager may have an aversion to extending the firm's equity base beyond the point where diversification of ownership jeopardises his/her control. In these circumstances an owner-manager, by limiting demand for equity, makes the explicit choice of relying largely on debt financing. Since this can expose the small firm to agency problems, with their associated implications for the costs of debt financing, the owner-manager may seek to reduce these costs by limiting the small firm's overall risk exposure.

As Knight (1965) and Kilstrom and Laffont (1979) argue, it is a small firm's willingness to be exposed to risk which has a critical bearing on its size and future expansion. For many small firms the owner-manager's initial motivation in starting up a business may have resulted from a desire for independence, which produces a strong risk-averse attitude and a movement away from maximising the current market value of the firm. Indeed, as Chamberlin and Gordon (1989 and 1991) argue, the maximisation of the current market value of the firm is only an appropriate objective for shareholders who are portfolio investors with relatively small stakes in individual companies. For owner-managers of small firms, who are exposed to both systematic and unique risk, current market value maximisation has to be balanced against the overriding objective of long-run survival.[5]

Investment and debt financing

For most owner-managed firms, therefore, the emphasis on the need to finance operations through debt capital provided by the banking system arises from ownership and long-run survival objectives. These, at least in the early stages of a firm's development, limit the demand for equity capital to an owner-manager's own resources and/or his family's contributions.

Given a small firm's reliance on debt capital the owner-manager may be able to commit the small firm to a level of debt which takes account of the need for a flexible response to unanticipated changes in operating income. If this is the case agency costs may not be significant enough to warrant excessive interest rate premiums over base rates or excessive collateral requirements. Owner-managers may, however, have to contemplate high debt:equity ratios, especially in crisis situations, and thus encounter the standard agency costs associated with financial distress.

In an effort to anticipate and/or ease such a situation, the small firm may attempt to reduce its overall risk exposure by reducing business risk. This may result in a general investment policy exhibiting low levels of innovation, and a business strategy aimed at relatively well-established but slow-growing markets. In addition a small firm may adopt a low level of operating leverage.

Recall, in the context of the joint investment and financing strategies explored in Chapter 10, that at a given level of risk exposure a lower level of operating leverage permits a company to increase its financial leverage. Mills and Schumann (1985) argue that small firms have a tendency to employ low levels of operating leverage, as evidenced by their concentration on labour-intensive production techniques. The rationale is that the small firm acquires greater flexibility in adapting to unexpected demand changes, with the resulting potential cost advantages compensating for cost disadvantages experienced from remaining small and not exploiting economies of scale.

Proprietorship and equity financing

Along with, or as an alternative to, changes in its investment policy the owner-manager can attempt to increase the small firm's equity base. This can enable the small firm to reduce its current debt:equity ratio and, therefore, the agency costs of debt. Increasing the equity base can also have the added advantage of increasing the small firm's potential debt financing capacity, thus creating a form of financial slack which can be used in future situations of financial distress. (Alternatively, if the small firm is close to its target financial leverage ratio, an increase in equity would facilitate a proportionate expansion in bank debt financing.)

Once an owner-manager has contributed his/her desired proportion of personal wealth, including retained earnings, to the small firm, the main route for increasing the supply of equity is through attracting partners into the business. On the basis of a proprietorship model where, as Chamberlin and Gordon argue, 'ownership and control are completely joined', partners can only be attracted by offering them a higher rate of return than would be available from investing in publicly traded shares. This premium on the small firm's cost of equity capital arises to compensate for the conflicting objectives which may exist among new partners[6] and for the difficulties they can expect to experience should they seek to sell their partnerships in the future. Without an active secondary market the sale of partnerships becomes complicated by search costs for buyers and by special tailormade conditions which may have been written into partnership agreements. These may not be suitable for subsequent investors.

In addition signalling and agency problems, linked to moral hazard, apply to privately owned small firms as well as to publicly quoted companies. As explained, with regard to the dividend debate in Chapter 9, signalling models suggest that publicly quoted companies are averse to issuing new equity since the market, in the presence of information asymmetries, interprets a new issue as forecasting an increase in business risk. This in turn can increase the probability of financial distress. The result is a depression in the price at which new shares can be issued and a consequent increase in the cost of equity capital.

For small firms these agency and information issues are still present even when equity is being supplied by family and/or friends. Family and friends will experience problems in understanding the nature of the business and, consequently, have difficulties with monitoring investments. In some senses these difficulties can be more acute when subjective personal relationships are involved.

From the small firm founder's point of view, therefore, expanding the equity base in this manner induces a rise in the equity cost of capital. The small firm may attempt to reduce this cost by, again, altering its investment strategy to lower business risk and consequently its total risk exposure.

Jointly, or as an alternative strategy, the small firm may take the opportunity, when expanding its equity base, to move towards a more conservative debt:equity ratio and thus reduce total risk exposure via a reduction in financial risk. This approach is favoured by Chamberlin and Gordon. They argue, under the proprietorship model, that the small firm's long-run survival objective will encourage it to adopt a debt:equity ratio which is below the level consistent with the maximisation of its market value.

Thus the objectives of the small firm proprietorship can cause small firms not only to avoid high-risk projects but also, except in crisis situations, to engage in levels of borrowing which are significantly below their debt capacity.

Equity capital via a market listing

Moving away from the proprietorship model, an owner-manager can obtain equity via a market listing. Here, while exposing the firm to outside shareholders, the objective would be to leave managerial control to a group of inside shareholders. This raises the same issues, in respect of the cost of equity capital, as discussed above. A premium on the return on equity, in the form of a discount on the price of the issue which facilitates listing, may be required. Such a discount would need to take account of the agency costs resulting from the partial divorce of ownership from control. These agency costs can be expected to increase as the dilution of inside control increases, since the willingness of managers to work hard and take risks in launching new products will fall as their proportion of equity ownership declines.

Anticipation of these extra equity costs – either in terms of proprietorship or a market listing – may of course simply reinforce an owner-manager's aversion to new equity, stemming initially from a desire to remain independent and in control of the firm. Thus any apparent failure of small firms in the equity capital market may be ultimately demand induced.

This point is reinforced by Burke (1992) who argues that there is an important distinction to be made between the voluntary and involuntary capital constraints faced by small firms. Agency costs, combined with the high fixed costs of flotation, can prevent small firms taking the direct market listing route, leading to the conclusion that they face an involuntary capital constraint. In these circumstances merger or acquisition represents a viable alternative. Since such alternatives are often rejected by small firms the implication may be, as Burke argues, 'that many small firms may be voluntarily capital constrained', preferring to trade off independence against capital availability.'

Retained earnings

The small firm owner has another way of expanding the equity base: internally through profit retention. Here equity capital still has an opportunity cost. From the owner-manager's point of view, however, this may be significantly below the rate of return required to bring partners into the business or obtain a market listing. The major reason, as Pratten (1991) argues, is that an owner-manager does not require a competitive return on his human, and consequently intangible, capital investment which represents a substantial part of a small firm's assets. If, however, an owner-manager pursues a combination of investment and debt policy which produces relatively low risk, and hence a low return on personal equity, the tendency to earn low profits will narrow the base from which retained earnings can be supplied.

Utilising debt capacity

The above has argued that risk aversion and ownership objectives limit a small firm's demand for equity and may explain its reliance on debt capital as the principal source of external funding. Given this reliance it is important to examine the small firm's debt decision, holding the equity base constant. The arguments are similar to those developed in relation to the capital structure debate in Chapter 8, with the corollary that a small firm may choose a sub-optimal financial leverage ratio consistent with the objective of long-run survival.

Recall that there is a positive incentive to increase the amount of debt in the capital structure when debt interest costs are tax deductible. Recall also, however, that these benefits are eventually offset by financial distress and agency costs associated with monitoring for the asset substitution and underinvestment problems. In the case of large companies part of the monitoring problem is solved by restrictive covenants included in bond contracts. In the case of small firms this monitoring problem is partially solved through the provision of loan collateral, although, as in the case of restrictive covenants, this can reduce future financing flexibility.

For small firms who are heavily reliant on debt capital, further reductions in the opportunity cost of debt financing, including collateral commitments, are possible. These reductions can be achieved by creating conditions which signal to debt suppliers, banks, that the asset substitution and underinvestment problems are being minimised. Conditions conducive to this are the avoidance of major growth opportunities and the maintenance of an investment strategy which exposes the small firm to only moderate levels of business risk. In other words the small firm may:
• avoid the asset substitution problem by actively demonstrating that high-risk projects are being rejected; and
• avoid the underinvestment problem by actively demonstrating that low-risk projects are being undertaken.

Debt policy and asset intangibility

The key issue in adopting the above investment strategy is to convince debt suppliers that these problems are being minimised. The demonstration effect is partly based on the small firm's past record, but is also linked to its mix of tangible and intangible assets and to the speed with which intangible assets can be transformed into tangible assets. As it was explained in Chapter 10, once financial distress is encountered it is intangible assets, closely linked to potential growth opportunities, whose values become most problematic.

For the small owner-managed firm, a significant proportion of investment is in the owner-manager's intangible human capital. While owner-managers may not, as Pratten argues, require a competitive return on this component, its presence raises the cost of debt capital, the very source of funds on which the small firm is heavily reliant. In addition banks, in securing their small firm loan portfolios, formulate their collateral requirements in terms of tangible assets. Thus for small firms there will be a further rationale for avoiding risky projects with significant growth potential. This is especially the case, as Brewer and Genay (1994) argue, for those firms which are newly established in trade and service industries and tend to have high ratios of intangible assets.

In addition there can be a significant time lag in the process of transforming projects with substantial growth opportunities into tangible assets. Hence owner-managers may elect to pursue investment in relatively safe and non-innovative projects which can be demonstrated to have relatively short transformation processes. This, once again, will permit the small firm to limit the cost of debt financing. Also, by concentrating on projects which are transformed into tangible assets in a relatively short period of time, the firm can improve its ability to offer collateral and thus expand its debt financing capacity.

Banker–client relationships

While, in general, asset intangibility will tend to limit debt capacity, the argument was made in Chapter 10 that part of this investment in large companies may become realised as reputational assets. In the case of the small firm the equivalent factor is the development of its banker–client relationship. This enables the small firm to establish its credibility.[8] Thus the reliance on bank financing by small firms does not simply arise from what Shapiro (1992) suggests as lower bank monitoring costs, relative to bondholders. It is integrally bound up with the ability it gives the small firm, through interpersonal contact, to demonstrate the proportion of its intangible assets which have a reputational base. Also there are advantages to being able to tailor and renegotiate terms and conditions in a face-to-face situation.

Short-term debt financing

Further possibilities exist for reducing the cost of debt financing by using short-term maturities. These advantages are partly due to the term structure of interest rates. As it was explained in Chapter 11, the term structure is upward sloping for most time periods, implying that the interest costs of short-term debt financing are lower than those of long-term debt financing. In addition, however, by using short-term debt the small firm is provided with an environment where there is, as Myers (1977) argues, 'a setting for the continuous and gradual renegotiation' of the terms and conditions between borrowers and lenders. This implies that the owner-manager can be more efficient and flexible in exploiting any improvements, through time, in the small firm's reputational asset base. The use of medium to long-term debt results in greater rigidities and negotiating costs, if attempts are made to alter existing debt contracts.

There is also, according to Myers, a desire to match the maturity structure of assets and liabilities in an attempt to reduce the agency costs of debt arising from the underinvestment problem. Assuming that small firms have, on the asset side, a preference for low-risk projects with short gestation/transformation periods, the propensity to exploit short-term, relative to long-term, financing possibilities is again enhanced.

There are offsetting costs associated with short-term financing, as explained in Chapter 11. In periods of 'tight money', when the term structure of interest rates becomes downward sloping, the interest costs of short-term debt can become prohibitive. Also, in recessionary periods, the attempt to roll over short-term debt contracts may become increasingly difficult. Banks may perceive a steeper increase in the risks of financing small firms. Where these risks rise beyond banks' risk tolerance levels, consistent with their overriding responsibilities to their risk-averse depositors, there is a rationale for refusing to supply extra finance and in some cases for refusing to renew existing loan and overdraft commitments when their term expires.

A re-cap

The key aim of the theoretical discussion above has been to illustrate that, where small firms appear to experience underfunding in terms of equity and indeed debt capital, part of the explanation can be traced to decisions made by owner-managers. On the demand side, when an owner-manager's attitude is risk averse and accompanied by a desire to retain control of the firm in some form, limits may be actively placed on the use and growth of equity. These limits may be applied not only in the small firm's early, but also in its later, phases of development. Where there is a desire and an ability to maintain production cost flexibility in the face of unanticipated demand changes, relatively low levels of operating leverage may be adopted which enhance a preference for increased reliance on debt capital.

Given this reliance on debt financing, agency problems which tend to be reinforced by a relatively high ratio of intangible to tangible assets may induce small firms to control the opportunity cost of debt financing. This can be achieved by choosing low-risk projects and avoiding product market opportunities with high growth potential. These factors may reinforce the small firm's propensity for short-term debt financing.

From the agency point of view further reductions in debt financing charges – in terms of interest rate premiums, collateral requirements and loan handling charges – may be achieved. These reductions are possible if the interdependent investment and debt financing policies adopted by small firms can be used to establish and develop banker–client relationships. In effect this does not represent an attempt by small firms to cope with explicit imperfections in the supply of finance, but with distortions created by inefficiencies in the information flows between borrowers and lenders.

Even allowing for the small firm's reliance on debt financing, its underlying attitude to its return on equity and its long-run survival objective may imply that the level of debt, consistent with market value maximisation, is not reached. That is, except in crisis situations, the small firm may choose a conservative debt:equity ratio.

Small business financing in the UK

In practice small firms in the UK obtain most of their equity capital from the personal resources of owner-managers, their families and/or friends. Most of the small firms' debt capital is obtained from the banking system. There are, however, alternative sources of capital available. In institutional terms formal venture capital companies provide funds for relatively high-risk projects, with public bodies providing some equity but mainly subsidised loans and grants. The public bodies range from commercial organisations such as Enterprise Boards financed by local authorities, to regional financial agencies such as the Welsh Development Agency and the Northern Ireland Local Enterprise Development Unit.

In recent years an informal network of venture capitalists known as 'business angels' has arisen. These are private high net-worth individuals, often self-made entrepreneurs, whose past experience gives them a particular flair for assessing the risk and expected return associated with small firm projects. Business angels provide risk capital directly to small firms with which they have had no family or other prior association.

There is also the Unlisted Securities Market (USM), whose continued existence is currently being reviewed by the Stock Exchange. The USM was developed in the early 1980s to improve SME access to equity capital and to enable those SMEs who sought external equity, via a flotation of shares, to achieve a market listing at relatively low issue costs. Improved access and lower issue costs are achieved since, under the USM, companies are not subject to the full requirements of a formal Stock Exchange listing.

Two central government schemes, aimed at stimulating investment in small privately owned firms, have also been available. On the equity side the Business Expansion Scheme (BES) provided special tax relief to individual investors in small firms or via an approved BES venture capital fund. On the debt side there is a Loan Guarantee Scheme (LGS) where part of the risk associated with an approved small firm bank loan is underwritten by the government.

Bank financing

Beginning with a review of the evidence on bank financing, there are four main issues: interest charges, collateral requirements, loan handling fees and the approach taken by banks in assessing the financing needs of small firms.

Interest rates
Where interest rates are concerned, the premiums charged to small firms are generally judged in relation to either base rates or the prime rates charged to large companies. On average prime or blue chip rates are highly competitive in relation to base rates. Using the London Inter-Bank Offer Rate (LIBOR) to approximate the latter, large companies throughout the 1980s were charged around a premium of 1%. This premium rose in 1991, at the height of the most recent recession, to about 1.5% for companies with an annual turnover of over £10m. In 1991 the average margin for firms with less than £1m annual turnover was around 3%, or between 1.5% and 2% above the blue chip rate.[9]

The above suggests that the interest rate premiums faced by small firms have remained relatively stable over the past 20 years. This conclusion is based on the Wilson Committee's (1979) argument that during the 1970s small firms paid, on average, 2% above the rate charged to large companies.[10] In one sense, however, it is just conceivable that the small firm premium has fallen in risk adjusted terms. The rapid growth of the SME sector in the UK took place during the 1980s, after the late 1970s/early 1980s recession, and during a period of significant structural change in the UK economy. Consequently the average level of risk in financing the small business sector may have increased over the past 10 years.

Collateral requirements

While it would not appear, on average at least, that interest rate premiums faced by small firms are excessive, this conclusion does not seem to apply in respect of collateral requirements. Collateral:loan ratios appear excessive, even when account is taken of:

- the high proportion of intangible assets in a small firm's total asset base;
- the price risk surrounding the secondhand value of its tangible assets; and
- its general reliance on debt financing.

Bannock and Morgan (1988), for example, suggest that for firms with less than nine employees, collateral:loan ratios in the UK are over three times their equivalent in the US.

Capital gearing versus income gearing

With respect to the initial decision on whether or not to grant a term loan or provide overdraft facilities, banks have been argued to rely too heavily on collateral, that is, on what is referred to as the capital gearing approach. In terms of the principles of valuation it has been suggested that greater emphasis should be placed on an income gearing approach. In other words banks should concentrate on assessing the expected future net cash flows from the projects for which funding is being sought and make more effort to assess project risk. In this way, by being able to set individual loan interest rates in the context of the risk–return relationship, banks can place less reliance on obtaining security in lending.

As competition within the banking sector itself has increased, there is some evidence that banks are moving away from the security in lending approach and developing corporate financing strategies based on the analysis of future product and service market trends. In the end, however, because of the monitoring problems already discussed, banks face costs in acquiring information on the future prospects of small firm projects. These costs can be particularly acute: first, for start-up firms where a banker–client relationship has not been established, and second, for the minority of non-lifestyle small firms which seek funding to actively exploit high-risk growth potential. In both cases information costs can only be compensated for by charging relatively high loan arrangement fees and/or by increasing interest rates on loans. Alternatively they can be avoided by requiring increased security in lending, based on a small firm's existing tangible assets.

Bank fees

Where loan handling fees are concerned, most of the recent surveys of small firms indicate that the complex ways in which banks appear to arrive at fee charges cause more anxiety among small firms than the levels of fees themselves.

Recessions

Finally, banks tend to be criticised for increasing interest rates and loan collateral requirements during periods of recession. When these increases occur, in respect of additional financing and/or refinancing packages, they are often warranted by rises in the levels of risk associated with a recession. Existing financing agreements should not, however, as Hutchinson and McKillop (1992) argue, be altered beyond what was explicitly, or implicitly, negotiated when these were first entered into. Banks, when initially determining the terms and conditions of each loan facility, should make their assessments in respect of each small firm's project-specific risk and in the wider context of systematic risk. In the latter case banks should concentrate on assessing the expected trends in the business cycle over the term of a loan or overdraft. If risk has not been properly assessed, with loan interest rates and collateral:loan ratios having been underestimated, the resulting assessment and information failures should be absorbed by the lender, without the borrower being penalised.

The financing gap

A bank's ultimate concern is with its depositors who use banking facilities for a convenient money transmission service and as a relatively safe repository for their funds, hence the low return (due to low risk) on deposit accounts. In the light of this, banks have an absolute risk tolerance limit in lending. They may, therefore, in a proper commercial sense, refuse to undertake high-risk lending to small firms.

This identifies a need for other sources of small firm financing. The most appropriate in accommodating high risk is equity finance, but, it has been argued, the majority of small firms have an aversion to this source of capital in an external form. In addition, the minority of small firms which have no aversion to external equity and who wish to exploit high-risk growth potential face issue costs and disclosure requirements which prohibit raising relatively small sums on the main stock market. Some attempt was made to rectify this situation by introducing the USM in the early 1980s, however, with minimum issue costs in this market of around £100,000, it is still costly to obtain an amount of new capital below £10m. This problem has led to an under-usage of the USM and, when combined with thin trading in companies which have already accessed this market, has led the Stock Exchange authorities to review the USM's operations with a view to closure.

There are, therefore, some difficulties faced by small firms which wish to raise small amounts of equity, difficulties which point to the wider problem of a financing gap. This is sometimes referred to as an equity gap but includes problems in raising loan capital as well.

The financing gap was identified over 50 years ago by the Macmillan Committee (1931) and in subsequent reports by the Radcliffe Committee (1959), the Bolton Committee (1971) and the Wilson Committee (1979). The most recent estimates in the CBI Report suggest that the gap over which most companies experience difficulties in raising funds is in the range £50,000 to £500,000. In real terms, however, the gap has declined significantly in recent years.

In response to the financing gap, formal venture capital companies emerged in the late 1940s with the intention of providing small amounts of relatively high-risk capital. All the recent evidence suggests, however, that formal venture capitalists have concentrated their investments on corporate restructuring. According to the CBI Report, management buyouts and buy-ins have represented over 25% of venture capital deals and over 50% of their investment. One of the reasons is that formal venture capitalists are primarily motivated by capital gains as opposed to dividend income, and search out rapid growth projects with expected future annual returns, depending on risk, of between 30% and 60%. As Harrison and Mason (1993) argue:

> Reviews of the institutional venture capital industry in the UK have demonstrated that only government and local authority backed funds have consistently focused their investment in a size range anywhere near that associated with the equity gap, and funds are continuing to move away from the small-scale financing of . . . early stage and start-up ventures.

There has been growth in the informal venture capital market, in terms of business angels, or high net-worth individuals, who provide funds under £50,000 on an individual project basis. This source of capital is still underdeveloped, one of the reasons being poor information networks which make it difficult for business angels to be matched with small firms seeking high-risk capital. Another reason may be a lack of investment opportunities so that, once again, there is a problem in assessing the extent to which apparent difficulties faced by some small firms are supply side, relative to demand side, determined.[11]

Policy initiatives

A number of policy initiatives have been introduced in an attempt to cope with the financing gap. From an equity perspective the Business Expansion Scheme, introduced in 1983, gave tax relief to individual investors on their top marginal tax rate, up to a maximum of £40,000 of new equity investment in unquoted companies. There were two major strands to the scheme: direct investment through a public offer or private placement and indirect investment through a managed BES fund, the latter being aimed at achieving portfolio diversification. On balance, as Stanworth and Gray (1991) conclude, this scheme failed to address the equity gap and in particular failed to provide investment for high technology projects which are important in terms of the future growth and development of the economy in general. The BES was discontinued in 1993. Efforts to address the relative failure of investment in technological projects, and to generally encourage new firm formation, are being made through the Enterprise Allowance Scheme; SMART, the Special Merit Award for Research and Technology; and Regional Enterprise Grants.

On the debt side the Loan Guarantee Scheme was introduced in 1981. Its primary intention is to assist with the provision of small firm loans for high-risk projects which, under normal commercial criteria, would be rejected by the private sector. Under the latest revision in the March 1993 Budget, small firms have an opportunity to apply to a bank participating in the scheme for up to £250,000, with the government guaranteeing 85% of the loan. Borrowers pay an interest rate premium to the Department of Employment of 1.5% on the whole value of the loan, where the bank lending rate is variable, and 0.5% for fixed rate loans. The interest rate determined by the bank, which has the responsibility under the LGS of making the project risk assessment, takes account of the government guarantee. The LGS is an interesting example of a policy initiative based on the risk–return trade-off principle. Guaranteeing part of the loan is a method of risk reduction.

Recent proposals for new policy initiatives in the CBI Report suggest, among other things, that more favourable tax breaks should be introduced and lower premiums charged on the LGS. Management education, improved information networks in respect of business angels and caution in considering closure of the USM are also advanced as important ways of coping further with the financing gap.

Other financial management aspects

In completing this chapter, it is instructive to summarise some of the other factors which differentiate small firms from large publicly quoted companies. In general one of the problems of small size is that scale economies cannot be achieved in the management function, so that division and specialisation of managerial tasks is extremely limited. Owner-managers may have particular expertise but this is usually confined to marketing or production management. In the main, owner-managers lack experience in financial management and specifically lack understanding of cash flow management.

Small firms rely much more heavily on short-term working capital than do large-sized firms and, in particular, on taking trade credit from suppliers and offering trade credit to customers. The latter is argued to be highly significant to small firms, especially in recessionary periods, since delays in payments disrupt cash inflows and can be a major underlying cause of financial distress.

Because of their aversion to equity and reliance on debt capital, small firms may have a greater preference for borrowing assets and, therefore, for using operating and financial leases than large-sized companies.

Finally, surveys which examine the financing problems faced by small firms have also tended to highlight their concern with 'paperwork'. The costs of 'form filling', administering salaries and wages, complying with health and safety requirements and other bureaucratic regulations can be proportionately heavier for small, relative to large-sized, firms. This is again a function of the inability to exploit scale economies in management.

Summary

The available evidence on the small firm financing debate in the UK suggests that if there is a problem on the supply side, it is most likely to be connected with difficulties in raising both loan and equity capital in the range £50,000 to £500,000. While there may also be a tendency, especially among banks, to focus too narrowly on security in lending, the general costs of bank financing appear, at least on the average, to reflect the higher risks and monitoring costs associated with the SME sector.

Many of the apparent financing difficulties of small firms – their reliance on short-term debt, their limited use of equity, and their failure to exploit growth opportunities – may well stem from the attitude of small firm owners. It appears that the great majority are lifestyle owners who wish to remain in control of their firms, and their objectives do not necessarily coincide with value maximisation.

Once again, by using investment and financing principles, it has been possible to present in the first half of this chapter a structured analysis of an important issue in corporate finance. That analysis helped to give a theoretical focus to the demand side aspects of the small firm financing debate. The relative weights which should be given to demand and supply side explanations are, in the end, however, an important empirical question, given the significance of the SME sector in all major economies.

Attention having been focused on the special aspects of small firm investment and financing activities, the next chapter examines some of the factors unique to companies which operate in international markets and develop international investment and financing strategies.

Questions

1 What is likely to be the main objective of the owner-managers of most small firms? What implications is this objective likely to have for the owner-managers' demand for debt and equity capital?

2 Why is the banker–client relationship important to a small firm?

3 What is meant by capital gearing and income gearing?

4 Apart from the underlying objectives of owner-managers, what other factors might dissuade the small firm from seeking external equity capital via a market listing?

Exercises

1 Why is it important to attempt to distinguish between demand side and supply side factors when considering the debate on small firm financing?

2 What roles do venture capitalists and business angels play in the small business sector?

Endnotes

1. Part of this chapter is based on an article published by Robert Hutchinson (1995) in *Small Business Economics* (Kluwer Academic Publishers) pp. 231–9. The article is entitled: 'The Capital Structure and Investment Decisions of the Small Owner-Managed

Firm: Some Exploratory Issues'. Relevant parts of the article are reprinted by permission of Kluwer Academic Publishers.

2. A recent Confederation of British Industry Report (1993) estimates that 98% of firms in the UK employ fewer than 200 people. While this chapter is concerned with the SME sector in general, it concentrates its attention on small firms. Although it does not enter the debate on the size definition which should be used in specifying small, it is helpful, from a conceptual point of view, to have some idea of what this means. In practical terms small firms are usually defined as those with an annual revenue below £1m, or in employment terms (which will not necessarily result in the same set of firms) as those with fewer than or equal to 10 employees. Using the latter definition, small firms in the UK accounted for approximately 25% of total employment towards the end of the 1980s. If a definition of under 50 employees is used, this rises to approximately 40%.

3. The great majority of small firms grow slowly because they are 'lifestyle' businesses. As it will be explained in the main body of this chapter, the founders of these lifestyle businesses may have long-run survival objectives which result in them having an aversion to equity and moving away from the objective of value maximisation. On the growth point in general it is interesting to note, given the employment size definition in endnote 2, that the CBI Report references research which has identified a growth corridor of firms with between five and 50 employees. The Report indicates that while '20% of small firms enter this corridor, only 2% emerge from the other end. The rest either remain within the corridor or fail.'

4. For the small privately owned firm, market value is largely determined by the current value of its tangible assets. Unlike publicly quoted companies, however, the intrinsic value of these assets can be difficult to determine in practice, if the assets are not normally traded in relatively active secondhand markets.

5. For a fuller discussion of the reasons why current market value maximisation for the privately owned firm is not consistent with a long-run survival objective, see Chamberlin and Gordon (1991).

6. Under the proprietorship model additional partners may not take an active role in the business. If they do not, they leave control in the hands of the original owner-manager who acts as their agent. In these circumstances potential agency problems imply that further compensation is required in terms of the return offered to passive partners.

7. The main thrust of the arguments on voluntary capital constraints is not that there are no supply side problems, but rather that these may have been overestimated.

8. See, for example, Petersen and Rajan (1994) for a recent review and development of empirical work on banker–client relationships.

9. Note that this discussion is in terms of averages. A number of large companies can negotiate loan interest rates which are approximately equal to the LIBOR rate. In the case of small firms the premium over LIBOR can vary considerably, largely due to the risk levels attached to particular small firm projects.

10. The Wilson Committee argued that the 2% premium was in part a reflection of the higher lending risks and credit evaluation costs that banks experienced in making loans to small, relative to large, firms. The Committee nevertheless concluded that the premium was too high.

11. Another factor complicating the supply side/demand side issue is the crowding-out hypothesis, where the availability of development agency grants, especially in the 'remoter' regions of the UK (Scotland, Wales and Northern Ireland), may be used by small firms as a form of 'free' equity, crowding out some private sector supply.

References

Bannock, G. and E. Morgan, *Banks and Small Businesses: An International Perspective*, London, The Forum for Private Business, 1988

Bolton Committee, *Report of the Committee of Inquiry on Small Firms*, Cmnd. 4811, London, HMSO, 1971

Brewer, E. and H. Genay, 'Funding Small Businesses through the SBIC Programme', Economic Perspectives, Federal Reserve Bank of Chicago, 1994

Burke, A., 'The Impact of Capital Grants on Entrepreneurship: A Model of the Supply of General Entrepreneurs', University College Dublin, Working Paper 92/16, 1992

Chamberlin, T. and M. Gordon, 'Liquidity, Profitability and Long-run Survival: Theory and Evidence on Business Investment', Journal of Post-Keynesian Economics, 1989

Chamberlin, T. and M. Gordon, 'The Investment, Financing and Control of the Firm: A Long-run Survival View', Cambridge Journal of Economics, 1991

Confederation of British Industry, 1993, *Finance for Growth: Meeting the Needs of Small to Medium Sized Enterprises*, Report for the CBI Smaller Firms' Council, London, CBI

Harrison, R. and C. Mason, 'Finance for the Growing Business: The Role of Informal Investment', National Westminster Bank Quarterly Review, 1993

Hughes, A., 'The "Problems" of Financing Smaller Businesses', University of Cambridge, Small Business Research Centre, Working Paper No. 15, 1992

Hutchinson, R., 'The Capital Structure and Investment Decisions of the Small Owner-Managed Firm: Some Exploratory Issues', Small Business Economics, 1995

Hutchinson, R. and D. McKillop, 'Banks and Small to Medium Sized Business Financing in the United Kingdom: Some General Issues', National Westminster Bank Quarterly Review, 1992

Keasey, K. and R. Watson, 'Banks and Small Firms: Is Conflict Inevitable?' National Westminster Bank Quarterly Review, 1993

Kilstrom, R. and J. Laffont, 'A General Equilibrium Entrepreneurial Theory of Firm Formation based on Risk Aversion', Journal of Political Economy, 1979

Knight, F., *Risk, Uncertainty and Profit*, New York, Harper and Row, 1965

Macmillan Committee, *Report of the Committee on Finance and Industry*, Cmnd. 38971, London, HMSO, 1931

Mills, D. and L. Schumann, 'Industry Structure and Fluctuating Demand', American Economic Review, 1985

Myers, S., 'Determinants of Corporate Borrowing', Journal of Financial Economics, 1977

Petersen, M.A. and R.G. Rajan, 'The Benefits of Lending Relationships', Journal of Finance, 1994

Pratten, C., 'The Competitiveness of Small Firms', University of Cambridge, Department of Applied Economics, Occasional Paper No. 57, 1991

Radcliffe Committee, *Report of the Committee on the Working of the Monetary System*, Cmnd. 827, London, HMSO, 1959

Shapiro, A., 'Guidelines for Corporate Financing Strategy', in J. Stern and D. Chew (Eds.), *The Revolution in Corporate Finance*, Oxford, Blackwell, 1992

Stanworth, J. and C. Gray (Eds.), *Bolton 20 Years On: The Small Firm in the* 1990s, London, Paul Chapman, 1991

Wilson Committee, *The Financing of Small Firms, Interim Report of the Committee to Review the Functioning of the Financial Institutions*, Cmnd. 7503, London, HMSO, 1979

15 Investment and financing: the international dimension

(This chapter has been prepared in conjunction with Kate McCaffery)

Introduction

The great majority of both publicly and privately owned companies, irrespective of their size, operate in international markets. For the SME sector, with its production activities largely confined to the domestic economy, international business is primarily in the form of exports of goods and services and imports of raw materials, semi-finished goods and capital equipment. For large-sized companies, two additional aspects of international business are often important: international investment and international financing. It is direct foreign investment, in terms of plant and equipment, indirect foreign investment, in terms of financial assets, and the partial funding of domestic and international operations, in terms of foreign sources of finance, which give many large-sized companies their distinctive multinational character.

Once a company is involved in international business, its management is confronted by a much more complex environment than that experienced domestically, the added complexity being largely determined by foreign currency exposure. The level and range of a company's international transactions determine the income it receives initially, and the payments it has to make ultimately, in foreign currencies. In addition its ownership of foreign subsidiaries determines the proportion of its assets denominated in foreign currencies. It is how a company's future series of foreign currency net cash flows, and the assets of its foreign subsidiaries, translate into its domestic currency which has a significant impact on its total market value. This impact depends principally on the currency exchange rates between the foreign and domestic economies in which the company operates and on its exposure to exchange rate risk. The latter, which is similar in concept to interest rate risk, refers to the valuation effects of unanticipated changes in exchange rates.

Given that foreign currency transactions are at the core of a company's international business policy, this chapter proceeds by explaining how exchange rates are measured and by examining the nature and role of exchange rate risk. This is followed by an introduction to the Purchasing Power Parity and Interest Rate Parity theorems of exchange rate determination and by a brief discussion on international sources of finance.

The chapter draws to a conclusion by specifying the additional factors which have to be taken into account, for example political risk, when investment appraisal is applied in an international context.

Throughout this chapter it is assumed that the companies being analysed are registered in the UK. This defines a company's domestic economy to which, for example, its profits from foreign investments are repatriated, and the domestic currency in which its value is ultimately measured: sterling.

Exchange rates

The price at which currencies are traded against each other is known as the foreign exchange rate. This rate, at a given point in time, measures the relative value of one currency in terms of another. Exchange rates can be quoted in two ways: directly and indirectly.

The indirect method of quotation expresses the number of units of a foreign currency in terms of one unit of the domestic currency. In the case of the relationship between sterling and the deutschmark (DM), for example, the value of DMs is expressed per £. Thus an exchange rate of DM2.50/£ indicates that £1 is worth DM2.50. If, at this exchange rate, a UK company wished to pay cash for a German company valued at DM250m, it would purchase DMs on the foreign exchange. Ignoring foreign exchange transactions charges, the requisite DMs would cost £100m since £100m(DM2.50/£) = DM250m.

The direct method of quotation expresses the number of units of a domestic currency in terms of one unit of the foreign currency. In the above example the indirect exchange rate of DM2.50/£ becomes, in its direct form, £0.4/DM, indicating that one DM is worth £0.40. The direct method is simply the reciprocal of the indirect method:

$$£/DM = 1 \div DM/£ = 1 \div 2.50 = £0.40$$

In the situation where the German company is being acquired, the amount of £s needed to purchase DM250m is obtained, directly, by multiplying the number of DMs by the £/DM exchange rate: (£0.4/DM)(DM250) = £100m.

In the UK and the Republic of Ireland (where the currency is the Irish £) exchange rates are always quoted indirectly. In the rest of the European Union, the rates are quoted directly. This chapter is based on the indirect method of quoting exchange rates.

Quoting exchange rates

Just as in the case of shares and bonds, foreign exchange dealers quote two exchange rates: the rate at which they are willing to buy one currency in terms of another (the bid price), and the rate at which they are willing to sell that currency in terms of the other (the offer price). The bid–offer spread determines the foreign exchange dealer's margin or profit.

In the case of the Japanese yen, for example, the indirect exchange rate in London might be Yen/£ = 167–169. A company who wishes to buy yen, using £s, will do so at the bid price of Yen167/£. At this price, a foreign exchange dealer is willing to buy £1 by selling Yen167. A company who wishes to buy £s, using yen, will do so at the offer price Yen169/£. At this price, a foreign exchange dealer is willing to sell £1 by buying Yen169.

To illustrate the difference between the bid–offer prices, consider a UK company which wishes to purchase capital equipment from Japan costing Yen334m. It decides to use part of its sterling cash and marketable securities balances to do so. At the above exchange rate the £ cost of yen, at the foreign exchange dealer's bid price of Yen167/£, is Yen334m ÷ Yen167/£ = £2m. Alternatively, if another company wishes to buy £s with Yen334m, it would do so at the offer price of Yen169/£ and only receive Yen334m ÷ Yen169/£ = £1.976m. The margin for the foreign exchange dealer, from two such transactions, is: £2m − £1.976m = £0.024m.

For ease of exposition the middle rate, that is, the average of the bid and offer prices, is used in the examples in the rest of this chapter.

Exchange rate risk

Companies which operate internationally are exposed to foreign currency, or exchange rate, risk. Exchange rate risk arises where unanticipated changes in exchange rates affect the £ value of those parts of a company's assets and cash flows which are denominated in foreign currencies. Three principal factors are involved in exchange rate risk: transactions exposure, translation exposure and economic exposure.

Transactions exposure

Transactions exposure arises where changes in exchange rates affect the £ value of a company's future series of expected foreign currency net cash flows. These flows are created by transactions which involve not only foreign receipts and payments for, respectively, exports and imports, but capital flows created by direct foreign investment and borrowing and lending in foreign currencies.

Consider an exporting example where a UK company exports goods to Germany, on a trade credit basis, to the value of DM20,000. The UK company expects payment in DMs in three months time. The current exchange rate is DM2.40/£ which, if it remains constant, will produce DM20,000 ÷ DM2.40/£ = £8333 when payment is received. If, in three months time, however, the exchange rate turns out to be DM2.35/£, the DM will have appreciated in value against the £ (the £ will have depreciated in value against the DM) causing the £ value of these exports to rise to DM20,000 ÷ DM2.35/£ = £8511. Here, because it now takes fewer DMs to purchase £1, the UK exporter gains on this transaction.[1] Conversely if the DM depreciates against the £ (the £ appreciates against the DM) the exporter will lose, relative to the current exchange rate of DM2.40/£. If, for example, in three months time the exchange rate is DM2.50/£, the DM cash inflow, valued in £s, will be: DM20,000 ÷ DM2.50/£ = £8000.

Note, as a general rule, that when the exchange rate falls (rises), the first currency in the quoted rate appreciates (depreciates) against the second currency. When the exchange rate rises in the above example, the first currency, the DM, depreciates against the second currency, the £. When the exchange rate falls, the DM appreciates against the £. The opposite holds for the second currency: a rise in DM/£ indicates an appreciation of the £ against the DM, and a fall in DM/£ indicates a depreciation of the £ against the DM.

For the business sector as a whole, transaction exposure is likely to be the dominant element in exchange rate risk, because of the frequency of transactions and the propensity of exchange rates to vary considerably over short periods of time.

Translation exposure

Translation exposure arises because of accounting regulations. Here companies have to translate income and expenses, as well as the book value of assets, from foreign subsidiaries into their domestic currency when drawing up their annual accounts. This form of exposure is most likely to be of importance to companies which are involved in direct foreign investment and then only if the relevant exchange rates vary considerably from one reporting date to the next. Where assets of foreign subsidiaries have been used as collateral for domestic loans, however, translation exposure can influence financial distress and the probability of bankruptcy, especially if the £ value of foreign assets declines as a result of the £ appreciating against the relevant foreign currencies.

Economic exposure

While transaction exposure refers to the effect of exchange rate changes on a given set of transactions, arising from a company's existing activities, economic exposure refers to the impact of exchange rate movements on the future competitiveness of a company. The depreciation of the £ against other European Union currencies in 1992, when the UK government withdraw from the ERM, is an extreme example of this type of exposure. At least in the short run this devaluation caused an increase in demand for UK produced goods in countries like Germany and France. Other things being equal, the DM and French franc prices of UK goods being sold in these countries became cheaper relative to the close substitutes produced and sold in Germany and France. Of course imports into the UK from these economies became more expensive, making it difficult to determine the extent of the short-run net benefits from this devaluation.

Managing foreign exchange exposure

Consider a UK importer who is agreeing, now, to purchase goods from a German exporter to the value of DM2m, with payment expected at the end of one month. The current exchange rate is DM2.50/£. This is referred to as a spot exchange rate, since dealing at this rate involves 'on the spot' delivery of currencies. The UK importer could decide to:
- buy DMs now, at this spot exchange rate; or

- wait and purchase the DMs at the spot exchange rate ruling at the end of one month.

The choice between these two strategies depends on the opportunity cost of purchasing DMs now, in terms of the interest rate differentials between the UK and Germany, and on the importer's ability to take an opinion on the spot exchange rate expected at the end of one month.

If the importer uses part of his current cash balances to purchase DMs now, he loses the opportunity to earn a return at the domestic interest rate. The importer can, however, invest DMs in Germany, for example in a bank account, earning a return for one month at the prevailing German interest rate. (Alternatively the cash to purchase DMs now could be borrowed, with the same opportunity cost implications.)

Assuming for the moment that the importer estimates the interest rate differential to be zero, his choice of strategy will be based on whether he expects the £, at the end of one month, to appreciate or depreciate against the DM. If the £ is expected to appreciate, that is, the spot rate is expected to rise, the given number of DMs will be purchased for fewer £s one month from now, leading the importer to postpone purchase of DMs for one month. If the £ is expected to depreciate, each DM will cost more at the end of one month, relative to the spot rate, leading the importer to purchase DMs now, at the current spot exchange rate. If no change is expected the importer will be indifferent between the two strategies.

A relevant example is shown in Table 15.1. With imported goods costing DM2m in one month's time, the cost of DM2m, now, is £0.8m at a spot rate of DM2.50/£. In one month's time the cost is £0.769m at an expected spot rate, $E(DM/£)_t$, of $E(DM/£)_1 = 2.60$. The time period t is defined in months. The £ is expected to appreciate, so the importer will want to purchase DMs in one month's time. Alternatively, the cost is £0.833m at an expected spot rate of $E(DM/£)_1 = 2.40$. In this case the £ is expected to depreciate, so the importer will buy the DMs now. If the exchange rate is expected to stay constant, at $E(DM/£)_1 = 2.50$, the importer is indifferent to the purchase, now, or at the end of one month.

In the above example, if the importer is faced with exchange rate risk he may be unwilling to take his own opinion on how future exchange rates might change. In

Table 15.1: Illustrating foreign exchange exposure

Purchase of goods by a UK importer from a German exporter. Payment in one month's time DM2m

Spot exchange rates	Cost of DM2m
Current: DM2.50/£	DM2m ÷ DM2.50/£ = £0.8m
Expected appreciation of £: One month spot rate DM2.60/£	DM2m ÷ DM2.60/£ = £0.769m
Expected depreciation of £: One month spot rate DM2.40/£	DM2m ÷ DM2.40/£ = £0.833m
One-month forward rate DM2.55/£$_{(f.1)}$	DM2m ÷ DM2.55/£$_{(f.1)}$ = £0.784m

this circumstance, if he decides to buy DMs now, he undertakes what is known as a money market hedge. He hedges exchange rate risk by buying DMs at the current spot exchange rate, which is known with certainty, and invests the DM sum for one month in the money markets. This strategy would turn out to his disadvantage if the spot exchange rate at the end of one month is greater than the current spot rate. If the one-month spot rate turns out to be below the current spot rate, he has the extra advantage of not having to buy DMs which have appreciated in value.

Other hedging strategies are available using forward exchange rates.

Forwards and options

The markets for major currencies not only quote spot rates for immediate delivery of currencies, but also forward rates. Under forward rates, currencies can be bought and sold, now, for delivery in the future at a specified future price. Forward rates are usually quoted for one, three, six, nine and twelve months forward. These are standard forward dates but a forward rate can be arranged at any time up to one year.

Forward exchange rates
In the above example, if the exchange rate one month forward, $DM/£_{(f.t)}$, is $DM2.55/£_{(f.1)}$, the importer can contract, now, to buy DM2m at the end of one month by paying, at that time, $DM2m \div DM2.55/£ = £0.784m$. The difficulty here is that the spot rate in one month's time may not be equal to the forward rate. If it turns out to be above it, say $DM2.60/£$, the importer, as shown in Table 15.1, would only have paid £0.769m, if he had decided to use the spot market in the future rather than a forward contract. In other words the forward contract goes against the importer. If, alternatively, the spot rate at the end of one month is below the forward rate of $DM2.55/£_{(f.1)}$, say $DM2.40/£$, the importer would have paid £0.833m (that is, more for DMs) if he had used the future spot market rather than the forward contract. In other words the forward contract is favourable to the importer.

In effect, the forward purchase of DMs protects against an unanticipated deterioration of the spot exchange rate, from the importer's point of view. That is, it protects against a fall in the $DM/£$ spot exchange rate below the forward rate. In the above example protection is shown under the case where the spot rate falls from $DM2.50/£$ to $DM2.40/£$, to be below the forward rate of $DM2.55/£_{(f.1)}$, that is, the DM appreciates, the £ depreciates. The importer cannot, however, gain if the spot rate improves, relative to the forward rate, because he has contracted at the forward rate.[2] To deal with this situation the importer can take out an options contract, instead of irrevocably committing himself to a forward rate.

Using exchange rate option contracts
In the case of an options contract the UK importer of the German goods has the option, for which he pays a premium, to purchase or not to purchase DMs at the one-month forward exchange rate of $DM2.55/£_{(f.1)}$. Under an options contract this forward exchange rate is known as the exercise price.

If the spot rate in one month's time exceeds the exercise price, say it is $DM2.60/£$, the importer will not exercise the option but purchase DMs in the spot market. The

Table 15.2: Comparing forwards and options

Purchase of goods by a UK importer from a German exporter. Payment in one month's time DM2m

Using the Future Spot Market	Using a Forward Contract	Using an Options Contract
	One-month forward rate: DM2.55/£	One-month option rate: DM2.55/£
One-month spot rate: DM2.60/£ ∴ Cost of DM2m is: £0.769m	Must purchase at DM2.55/£ ∴ Cost of DM2m is: £0.784m	Do not exercise option, buy at spot ∴ Cost of DM2m is: £0.769m
One-month spot rate: DM2.40/£ ∴ Cost of DM2m is: £0.833m	Must purchase at DM2.55/£ ∴ Cost of DM2m is: £0.784m	Exercise option and buy at option price ∴ Cost of DM2m is: £0.784m

cost in the spot market is DM2m ÷ DM2.60/£ = £0.769m, against the cost at the option price, DM2m ÷ DM2.55/£ = £0.784m. There is, therefore, a gross saving of:

£0.784m − £0.769m = £0.015m

This example assumes that the cost of taking out the option is less than £0.015m. Alternatively, if the spot rate in one month's time is less than the option price, say it is DM2.40/£, the importer will exercise his option to purchase DM2m at the option price of DM2.55/£. The cost of purchase (excluding the option premium) is £0.784m, while the cost at the spot rate is: DM2m ÷ DM2.40/£ = £0.833m. This results in a gross saving of

£0.833m − £0.784m = £0.049m

relative to the DM2.40/£ spot rate.

In effect, the option contract protects against an unanticipated deterioration (fall) in the spot exchange rate from the importer's point of view, that is, an appreciation of the DM relative to the forward rate. At the same time, unlike the forwards contract, the option holder has the possibility of benefiting from using the spot market in the future if there is an improvement in the spot rate relative to the forward rate.[3] A summary of the above example, comparing forwards and options, is presented in Table 15.2.

Options are not confined to currencies but include shares and bonds. The basic principles underlying options trading are presented in the next chapter.

Other forms of hedging

Other forms of hedging exist in terms of foreign currency swaps, for example. Here a foreign currency is purchased, now, at a spot exchange rate and simultaneously sold for future delivery at a forward rate. In this case both the spot and forward rates are known with certainty.[4] Also futures contracts, which are different from forwards contracts, can be used. The basic principles underlying futures contracts are presented in the next chapter.

Current assets and liabilities

As a general rule if a UK company is operating internationally and believes that the currency of a country with which it is trading will appreciate against the £ (that is, the £ will buy fewer units of the foreign currency), it should increase its current assets in the foreign currency. In other words it should increase its foreign currency holdings in terms of cash and marketable securities, inventories and accounts receivable. On the liability side the company should minimise foreign short-term borrowings and accounts payable in the appreciating currency. Effectively the company's net working capital (current assets less current liabilities), in terms of foreign currency translation exposure, should be increased. Where a depreciation of the foreign currency is expected, net working capital exposure in the foreign currency should be decreased.

If a company believes that, in the face of exchange rate risk, it cannot anticipate future exchange rate changes better than the market, a policy of matching assets and liabilities in foreign currencies might be pursued in an attempt to hedge, or neutralise, the effect of exchange rate risk. Alternatively, hedging strategies using forwards and options might be advisable.

The value of hedging

Whether or not companies can hedge their transaction, translation and economic exposures is a subject of considerable debate. Under perfect and fully integrated international capital markets, and given assumptions (discussed below) about the prices of internationally traded goods and services, hedging currency exposures would be of no benefit. This view, which is similar in context to the EMH discussed in Chapter 5, sees foreign currency markets as fully reflecting all relevant information on the expected future behaviour of exchange rates, with forward exchange rates being unbiased estimates of expected future spot rates. All future changes in spot rates are, therefore, fully anticipated. Under economic exposure, for example, the implication is that the prices of goods and services adjust to exactly offset any changes in exchange rates. Interest rate differentials between countries are also fully anticipated so that, for example, money market hedges would have no value.

International parity relationships

The view that hedging has no value is based on equilibrium relationships linking international product, foreign exchange and money markets via relationships between international inflation rates, exchange rates and interest rates. Two central explanations are involved: the Purchasing Power Parity Theorem and the Interest Rate Parity Theorem. These, together with two other international parity relationships, are outlined below. As explained later, however, empirical evidence indicates that these parities are impaired in practice and that there is, therefore, a rationale for attempting to develop strategies to manage currency exposure.

Purchasing power parity

The Purchasing Power Parity Theorem (PPP) is based on the notion that a good, or more generally a basket of goods, in one country will cost the same, in a common currency, as in another country. For example, if a car in Germany is priced today at DM30,000, goods arbitrage across international borders ensures, under PPP, that the same model can be purchased in the UK for DM30,000. This only happens, however, if the exchange rates between two economies, for example Germany and the UK, adjust through time to reflect differences in these economies' inflation rates. In other words, in equilibrium the ratio of the expected spot exchange rate 12 months from now, $E(DM/£)_t$, to the spot exchange rate today, $DM/£$, must perfectly reflect the differences in the expected annual rates of inflation. Defining the expected annual inflation rates for the UK and Germany as $E(\theta_{UK})$ and $E(\theta_G)$, respectively, PPP states:[5]

$$\frac{1 + E(\theta_G)}{1 + E(\theta_{UK})} = \frac{E(DM/£)_t}{DM/£} \qquad (15.1)$$

Consider an example where the spot exchange rate is DM2.50/£ and the expected annual inflation rates are: $E(\theta_G) = 6\%$ and $E(\theta_{UK}) = 4\%$. Since, by the PPP relationship in Equation 15.1,

$$\frac{1 + 0.6}{1 + .04} = \frac{E(DM/£)_t}{2.50}$$

the expected future spot rate must be $E(DM/£)_{12} = 2.548$, to preserve parity. That is,

$$E(DM/£)_{12} = (2.50)[(1.06)/(1.04)] = 2.50[1.0192] = 2.548$$

In other words, since inflation in Germany is expected to be higher over the coming year than in the UK, the DM is expected to depreciate against the £. At the current spot exchange rate of DM2.50/£, the DM purchase price of a basket of goods in Germany is expected to rise relative to the DM purchase price of the same basket in the UK. German consumers tend, therefore, to be dissuaded from purchasing their goods domestically and tend to be encouraged to purchase them in the UK. Arbitrage between goods markets therefore causes an excess demand for £s relative to DMs, leading to an appreciation of the £ against the DM, a depreciation of the DM against the £.

In the example of the car costing DM30,000 in Germany, at the spot exchange rate of DM2.50/£, it can be purchased in the UK, now, for £12,000. That is, DM30,000 ÷ DM2.50/£ = £12,000. One year from now, given the expected German inflation rate, the car is expected to cost DM30,000(1.06) = DM31,800 in Germany. In the UK, given its expected inflation rate, the car is expected to cost £12,000(1.04) = £12,480. Under PPP, with an expected spot exchange rate one year from now of $E(DM/£)_{12} = 2.548$, the car can be expected to be bought in DMs, in either country, for DM31,800. The expected UK price in DMs one year from now is £12,480(DM2.548/£) = DM31,800.

Interest rate parity

In discussing the exchange rate strategies open to a company, the opportunity cost of buying a foreign currency, now, for transactions in the future, was identified in terms of the interest rate differential between the domestic and foreign country's

Table 15.3: Illustrating the interest rate parity theorem

UK company considers investing £1m cash for one year in either:

UK government bond $r_{UK} = 10\%$

or

German government bond $r_G = 12\%$

Exchange rates: spot DM2.39/£, twelve months' forward: DM2.41/£$_{(f.12)}$

Comparison of Investments

UK investment

End of one year, UK bond investment: £1m(1 + r_{UK}) = £1m(1 + .10) = £1.1m

German investment:

(i)   Purchase DMs, now, at spot exchange rate

$$£1m(DM2.39/£) = DM2.39m$$

(ii)   Contract now to purchase £s at the 12-month forward exchange rate: DM2.41/£$_{(f.12)}$

(iii)   Invest DMs, now, at $r_G = 12\%$

$$DM2.39m(1 + r_G) = DM2.39m(1 + .12) = DM2.677m$$

(iv)   Convert DMs received in one year at DM2.41/£$_{(f.12)}$ (the contracted forward rate under (ii))

$$DM2.677m \div DM2.41/£_{(f.12)} = £1.1108m$$

End of one year, German bond investment, in £s, is: £1.1108m

Since £1.1m < £1.1108m, undertake German investment.

Interest Rate Parity

If the IRP relationship of Equation 15.2 holds, there would be no difference between the two investments. Given $r_{UK} = 10\%$, $r_G = 12\%$ and DM/£2.39, the forward rate would have to be DM2.433/£$_{(f.12)}$, since

$$\frac{1.12}{1.10} = \frac{DM/£_{(f.12)}}{2.39} = \frac{2.433}{2.390}$$

In this situation the DM2.677m received at the end of the year would be exactly equal to the UK investment sum received of £1.1m since

$$DM2.677m \div DM2.433/£_{(f.12)} = £1.1m$$

money markets. Just as there is arbitrage across international goods markets under PPP, arbitrage takes place across international money markets in respect of interest rate differentials. Under the Interest Rate Parity Theorem (IRP), the differential between the spot and forward exchange rates between two economies must offset, in equilibrium, the difference in their interest rates.

Consider an example where a UK company is viewing the alternative opportunities for investing £1m cash, for one year, in short-term marketable securities. A UK government bond with a one-year term to maturity is available, offering a yield of $r_{UK} = 10\%$. The company compares this to the yield on a German government bond, $r_G = 12\%$, of identical risk and term to maturity. The spot exchange rate is DM2.39/£ and the 12-month forward rate is DM2.41/£$_{(f.12)}$. The steps the company uses in comparing these two investments are recorded in Table 15.3. Note that in the German investment the company buys DMs, now, to convert the principal and interest, at the end of one year, from DMs to £s at the forward rate.

The comparison between these investments indicates that the German investment would be preferable since, at the end of one year, the company would have £1.1108m, as against £1.1m from investing in the UK government bond. As both the current spot and forward exchange rates are known with certainty, there is, at these rates, a riskless arbitrage profit of £0.0108m.

Many companies and foreign exchange dealers would recognise the above opportunity, however, so that with the demand for DMs increasing relative to £s, the foreign exchange markets would adjust the forward exchange rates appropriately. In equilibrium, under IRP, the forward exchange rate would have to be DM2.433/£$_{(f.12)}$, as the last section of Table 15.3 indicates, if there is to be no difference between these two investments. Generalising, the IRP equilibrium relationship states that:[6]

$$\frac{1 + r_G}{1 + r_{UK}} = \frac{DM/£_{(f.t)}}{DM/£} \qquad (15.2)$$

In terms of the example in Table 15.3, with $r_G = 12\%$, $r_{UK} = 10\%$, DM2.433/£$_{(f.12)}$ and DM2.39/£, the parity relationship of Equation 15.2 is:

$$\frac{1 + r_G}{1 + r_{UK}} = \frac{1.12}{1.10} = \frac{DM/£_{(f.12)}}{DM/£} = \frac{2.433}{2.390}$$

Discounts and premiums

Under IRP, if interest rates in the foreign economy exceed those in the domestic economy, the foreign currency (DMs in the above example) depreciates against the £. In this case the £ buys more DMs forward, that is, £1 buys DM2.433 forward as against the spot buy of DM2.39. In practice the foreign currency is said to sell at a discount in the forward market relative to the spot market. In the present example the discount on the forward rate is DM0.043. To get the forward rate, the discount is added to the spot rate:

$$DM/£ + \text{forward discount} = DM2.390/£ + DM0.043 = DM2.433/£_{(f.12)}$$

The discount, under IRP, exactly offsets the higher interest rate in the foreign country relative to the domestic country.

Conversely, if domestic interest rates exceed foreign interest rates, the foreign currency is said to sell at a premium in the forward market relative to the spot market. For example, if $r_{UK} = 14\%$, $r_G = 8\%$ and the spot exchange rate is DM2.39/£, the forward exchange rate exceeds the spot rate. That is, the forward rate under IRP must be DM2.264/£$_{(f.12)}$ since, by the parity expressed in Equation 15.2,

$$\frac{1 + r_G}{1 + r_{UK}} = \frac{1.08}{1.14} = \frac{DM/£_{(f.12)}}{DM/£} = \frac{2.264}{2.390}$$

The premium in this case is DM0.126. To obtain the forward rate the premium is subtracted from the spot rate:

$$DM/£ - \text{forward premium} = DM2.390/£ - DM0.126 = DM2.264/£_{(f.12)}$$

To familiarise the discount/premium concept, some examples are presented in Table 15.4 using bid–offer prices.

Table 15.4: Illustrating forward discounts and premiums

	Bid Price	Offer Price
Illustrating Discounts		
DM/£ spot	1.572	1.579
1 month forward	DM0.079	DM0.082 discount
6 months forward	DM0.101	DM0.192 discount

The forward market indicates that the DM is at a discount and is expected to depreciate against the £

The forward rates are: DM/£ + discount

1 month forward DM/£:	1.651	1.661
6 months forward DM/£:	1.673	1.771

	Bid Price	Offer Price
Illustrating Premiums		
Yen/£ spot	167	169
1 month forward	Yen10	Yen11 premium
3 months forward	Yen12	Yen13 premium

The forward market indicates that the Yen is at a premium and is expected to appreciate against the £

The forward rates are: Yen/£ − premium

1 month forward Yen/£:	157	158
3 months forward Yen/£:	155	156

Expectations theory

Recall, from the options example, that another strategy consideration for a company is how the actual spot rate turns out, say in six months or 12 months, in relation to the six-month forward rate or 12-month forward rate that could be contracted now. Under the expectations theory of forward exchange rates the expected spot rate is equal to the forward rate, that is:[7]

$$E(DM/£)_t = DM/£_{(f.t)} \qquad (15.3)$$

In the example just completed, where the 12-month forward rate is $DM2.264/£_{(f.12)}$, the 'best' unbiased estimate of the spot rate, expected in 12 months' time, is $E(DM/£)_{12} = 2.264$. Note that this is an expectations theory so that, on average, the forward exchange rate for period t equals the expected spot rate for that period. The expected spot rate can turn out to be above, equal to, or below the forward rate but that occurrence will be purely random under international parity relationships.

Implications of the international parity relationships

If, in equilibrium, the above three relationships hold, then there is no value in developing hedging strategies.

Consider a company which is to pay DM10m in three months' time. The spot exchange rate, now, is DM2.55/£ and the three months' forward rate is $DM2.60/£_{(f.3)}$. Under PPP, IRP and the expectations theory, the best estimate of the spot rate expected in three months' time is $E(DM/£)_3 = 2.60$. Thus the company's best estimate is that the DM will depreciate against the £, therefore, its optimal strategy is to wait for three months and buy the DMs at an expected sterling cost of DM10m ÷ DM2.60/£ = £3.846m. At the current spot rate the cost would be DM10m ÷ DM2.55/£ = £3.922m.

The spot rate in three months' time might be above or below the forward rate. While, as a result of chance, the company might gain in the short run by hedging, repeated transactions in foreign currencies over a period of time would see short-run gains offset by short-run losses. In other words the company could not consistently beat the market's quoted forward exchange rate since it is an unbiased estimate of the expected future spot rate.

Alternatively, if the three months' forward rate is quoted at DM2.50/£$_{(f.3)}$, the company's best estimate is that the DM will appreciate against the £ and its optimal strategy is to make its sterling purchase of DM10m now.

The International Fisher Effect

The final international parity relationship is the International Fisher Effect (IFE). Recall, from the end of Chapter 2, that the domestic Fisher Effect showed how nominal interest rates in an economy would reflect both real rates of interest and expected inflation rates. The IFE extends this concept in an international context.

With r as the nominal rate of interest, r* as the real rate of interest and θ as the expected rate of inflation, the domestic Fisher Effect is stated (in a variant of Equation 2.11) as:

$$1 + r^* = \frac{1 + r}{1 + \theta}$$

Under PPP, IRP and the expectations theory, an IFE must hold, so that nominal interest rates and expected inflation rates between countries, for example the UK and Germany, conform to the parity relationship:

$$\frac{1 + r_G}{1 + r_{UK}} = \frac{1 + E(\theta_G)}{1 + E(\theta_{UK})} \qquad (15.4)$$

In the case where $E(\theta_G) = 6\%$ and $E(\theta_{UK}) = 4\%$, IFE must hold, so that:

$$\frac{1 + r_G}{1 + r_{UK}} = \frac{1.06}{1.04} = 1.019$$

This is shown to be so, approximately, when $r_G = 12\%$ and $r_{UK} = 10\%$, that is:

$$\frac{1 + r_G}{1 + r_{UK}} = \frac{1.12}{1.10} = 1.018$$

Check with Table 15.3; these are the respective interest rates used in the example illustrating the IRP.

A general example
Consider an example illustrating all of the above parities in terms of the UK and

Table 15.5: Illustrating international parity relationships

Annual expected inflation rate: $E(\theta_{UK}) = 8\%$, $E(\theta_J) = 3\%$
Spot exchange rate: Yen190/£; 12-month forward rate Yen181.20/£$_{(f.12)}$
One-year government bond rate: $r_{UK} = 10\%$, $r_J = 4.91\%$

Purchasing power parity

$$\frac{1 + E(\theta_J)}{1 + E(\theta_{UK})} = \frac{E(Yen/£)_t}{Yen/£} = \frac{1.03}{1.08} = \frac{181.20}{190.00} = 0.9537$$

Expectations theory

$$E(Yen/£)_t = Yen/£_{(f.t)} = 181.20$$

Interest rate parity

$$\frac{1 + r_J}{1 + r_{UK}} = \frac{Yen/£_{(f.t)}}{Yen/£} = \frac{1.0491}{1.10} = \frac{181.20}{190.00} = 0.9537$$

International Fisher Effect

$$\frac{1 + r_J}{1 + r_{UK}} = \frac{1 + E(\theta_J)}{1 + E(\theta_{UK})} = \frac{1.0491}{1.10} = \frac{1.03}{1.08} = 0.9537$$

Real rate of interest: $(1 + r)/(1 + \theta) - 1.0$
Japan: $(1.0491)/(1.03) - 1.0 = 1.01854 - 1.0 = 0.01854$ or 1.854%
UK: $(1.10)/(1.08) - 1.0 = 1.01852 - 1.0 = 0.01852$ or 1.852%
The real rates are approximately equal

Japan. The details are presented in Table 15.5. It is assumed that $E(\theta_{UK}) = 8\%$ and $E(\theta_J) = 3\%$, and that the spot exchange rate is Yen190/£. Under PPP the expected spot exchange rate in one year's time is $E(Yen/£)_{12} = 181.20$. As the UK has a higher expected inflation rate, the £ is expected to depreciate against the yen, that is, the yen is expected to appreciate against the £. Under expectations theory this expected spot rate is the 12-month forward rate. In other words the forward price of yen, now, indicates that the yen is selling at a premium in the forward market relative to the spot price. Under IRP this premium reflects interest rate differentials, with UK interest rates exceeding Japanese rates. In terms of the IFE, exchange rates adjust to reflect differences in expected inflation and equate real rates of return on investment between the two economies.

Validity of the international parity relationships

In general, empirical evidence indicates that the forward exchange rate is not an unbiased estimator of the expected future spot rate and that currency markets are not efficient. In addition, transport costs and other imperfections indicate that international arbitrage across goods markets is impaired, implying that PPP does not hold. Similarly, the existence of differences in transactions costs in using international financial markets and international differences in tax regimes, among other factors, imply that there are deviations from IRP. All of this suggests that companies can gain advantages by taking forwards, options and futures positions in exchange rate dealings. In other words these and other hedging strategies, developed to cope with exchange rate risk in the form of unanticipated changes in exchange rates, are worthwhile.

International financing

Companies can finance both their foreign and domestic operations by combinations of capital raised domestically and internationally.

Financing domestic operations

Raising foreign capital to fund domestic investments results in exposure to exchange rate risk since the associated dividends, interest and loan repayments are made in foreign currencies. Where medium to long-term foreign debt is used, the problems of currency management can be quite serious. Here the standard difficulty of accurately assessing how any economic variable, in this case an exchange rate, will change beyond a three or four-year period, is confronted. When considering foreign equity for domestic use similar problems are likely to be experienced, although it may be possible to phase dividend payments on foreign equity to coincide with 'favourable' movements in exchange rates. In the case of debt finance, remember, fixed interest obligations must be met on contract dates.

Short-term foreign borrowing for domestic purposes can be more easily managed, through currency hedging, since forward exchange rates are quoted, for most major currencies, up to 12 months forward. Forward rates are not often quoted beyond 12 months, a factor which further complicates the medium to long-term foreign financing decision. Using foreign sources of short-term financing for domestic purposes can, however, raise problems in respect of refinancing. 'Rolling over' short-term debt involves interest rate risk in the economy in which the short-term funds are being borrowed, and introduces a longer-term exchange rate risk dimension.

Even if IRP does not hold exactly, it indicates that if interest rates in a foreign economy are rising, relative to the domestic economy, the forward exchange rate will be at a discount to the spot exchange rate. By implication future spot exchange rates can be expected to rise, leading to depreciation of the foreign currency relative to the domestic currency. With inexact IRP the rise in the foreign interest cost of short-term borrowing might not be fully defrayed by the exchange rate change.[8]

A company might, on the one hand, be able to avoid higher short-term loan costs because of the flexibility of short-term financing: the ability to switch international sources of financing at the end of each loan agreement. On the other hand it may be difficult to predict the movement of the term structure of interest rates in a foreign economy, relative to the domestic economy.

Financing foreign subsidiaries

Using domestic capital markets to fund a company's foreign investments (or using foreign capital from sources other than the foreign economy in which investment is being undertaken) also raises currency exposure problems. In both these cases, however, by funding investments in a foreign economy through that economy's capital markets, transactions exposure can be eliminated. This can be achieved by making foreign currency dividend and interest payments out of the cash inflows generated in that currency. Also, translation exposure can be handled by attempting to match the maturity structure of assets and liabilities in the foreign currency. If, for example, a UK company is purchasing capital equipment with a 25-year life for its French subsidiary, it could use a 25-year loan raised in French francs. An appreciation (depreciation) of the £ against the FF, which would reduce (increase) the sterling value of the French plant, would be matched by a decrease (increase) in the sterling value of the loan liability. Avoidance of the costs of exchange rate risk in these ways must, however, be carefully balanced against the costs of capital which could be raised from other foreign sources.

Often a reason for raising capital internationally is that it can be obtained at relatively low required rates of return, especially where foreign capital markets have relatively low levels of financial market regulation. These are major factors explaining the significant growth of the eurobond market. Here bonds are sold in a foreign country but not in terms of that country's currency. A eurodollar bond can be issued in France, for example, in US dollars. In contrast, a French foreign bond would be issued in France in FFs.

International investment appraisal

The decision whether or not to invest in a foreign project is based on the standard appraisal techniques developed in Chapters 6 and 7. Basically a company must estimate the future series of incremental net cash flows associated with a potential foreign project and apply the appropriate discount rate in order to compute the project's NPV. Providing that the project's NPV ≥ 0 and that there is no capital rationing, the project should be undertaken.

The NCFs must include tax effects in the foreign country and any domestic tax effects if the foreign NCFs are being remitted to the parent company's headquarters. Also, the relevant tax and depreciation shields available in the foreign country must be assessed, together with subsidies and other incentives which the foreign country is offering to attract inward investment.

In some cases, especially in third-world economies, there may be legal restrictions on the amount of profit that can be remitted to a foreign subsidiary's parent's headquarters. In such cases a company may be required to reinvest a given percentage of its foreign subsidiary profits in the foreign economy. Whether or not these restrictions need to be taken into account depends on the other investment opportunities available in the foreign country. The discount rate used in a foreign project assessment is an opportunity cost which, under perfect capital markets, reflects the alternative investment opportunities available in the foreign economy. Reinvestment at this rate would not, therefore, affect the total market value of the multinational company concerned.

If capital markets are not perfect, the reported profits from a foreign subsidiary may be capable of being 'manipulated' in some way through a parent company's transfer pricing policy. This type of opportunity arises where, for example, the parent company supplies raw materials or semi-finished goods from its other plants, located in countries which do not impose repatriation restrictions. In this case the NPV of the project can still be based on the actual expected NCFs generated in the foreign economy.

If capital markets are not perfect and reported profits cannot be altered, then in order to determine whether a project would be acceptable to the parent company's investors, its NPV must be calculated by taking explicit account of these restrictions in the foreign currency NCF series.

Currency net cash flows

A major difficulty in determining a foreign project's NPV is deciding the appropriate point at which to convert the appraisal's calculations from the foreign currency into the domestic currency. Basically, the future annual NCF series calculated in the foreign currency can be:
- converted to the domestic currency and then discounted at the company's domestic discount rate, using the future expected spot exchange rate at the end of each year; or
- the foreign discount rate can be applied to the foreign currency NCFs to obtain the project's NPV, the latter being converted to a company's domestic currency value at the current spot exchange rate.

The main difficulty with the first method should be obvious: forecasting the expected series of future spot exchange rates. The second method, however, involves forecasting the future series of expected annual interest rates in the foreign country. These form a significant element in the determination of the foreign discount rates which have to be applied to each future year's NCF. If the international parity relationships hold, either method gives the same result.

To demonstrate that each method gives the same result, if international parity relationships hold, consider a potential two-year project that a UK company can undertake in Germany. The initial cost of the project and its annual NCFs are expressed in DMs in Table 15.6. The spot exchange rate is DM2.50/£. The company estimates that its project cost of capital should be based entirely on one-year government bond rates. For Germany these are expected to be 10% and 15% for years one and two respectively.

Table 15.6: Estimating a foreign project NPV

Year	NCF in DMs	German discount rate	PVIF$_{t,r}$	PVNCF in DMs
0	−100.00		1.0	−100.00
1	500.00	10%	0.909	454.50
2	1000.00	15%	0.756	756.00
			NPV = DM	1110.50

Sterling value of NPV = DM1110.50 ÷ DM2.50/£ = £444.20

Year	NCF in DMs	Spot exchange rates DM/£	NCF[1] in £s	UK discount rate	PVIF$_{t,r}$	PVNCF in £s
0	−100.00	2.50	−40.0		1.0	−40.00
1	500.00	2.546	196.39	8%	0.926	181.86
2	1000.00	2.614	382.56	12%	0.797	304.90
					NPV =	£446.76

[1] DM(NCF) ÷ DM/£

To calculate the project's NPV in DMs these German rates are applied, in the first half of Table 15.6, to the NCFs denominated in DMs, producing an NPV = DM1110.50. At the spot exchange rate the sterling value of this NPV is:

$$DM1110.50 \div DM2.50/£ = £444.20$$

Alternatively the NPV can be calculated by converting the DM net cash flows into sterling net cash flows. The company estimates that UK government bond rates for years one and two are 8% and 12%, respectively, and believes that IRP holds. Thus at the end of year one it determines the 12-month forward exchange rate, using Equation 15.2, as

$$\frac{1.10}{1.08} = \frac{DM/£_{(f.12)}}{2.50}$$

that is, $DM2.546/£_{(f.12)}$. Under the expectations theory this is the expected spot exchange rate at the end of year one. Using the German and UK interest rates expected in year two, and the year one expected spot exchange rate, the spot exchange rate expected at the end of year two is,

$$\frac{1.15}{1.12} = \frac{DM/£_{(f.24)}}{2.546}$$

that is, $E(DM/£)_{24} = DM2.614/£_{(f.24)}$. These expected spot exchange rates are applied, in the second half of Table 15.6, to calculate the sterling value of the DM NCFs. Finally, applying the UK discount rates produces an NPV = £446.76. This is equivalent (apart from rounding errors) to the sterling value of the NPV produced in the first half of the table.

As explained above, empirical evidence indicates that international parity relationships do not hold and that foreign exchange markets are not efficient. Consequently these two approaches to estimating a foreign project's NPV are likely to give different results. Given that expected future spot exchange rates are possibly more difficult to forecast than the future spot rates of interest expected within a foreign economy, the first method may on balance be more appropriate. In other words the NPV of a foreign project should be calculated in the foreign currency, and then converted to the domestic currency at the current spot exchange rate.

Project costs of capital

To illustrate a point, the above example was based on a highly simplified case where interest rates were used as project discount rates. A project's discount rate must, however, be based on the component costs of capital, taking account of a company's capital structure. In other words a risk adjusted weighted average cost of capital must be used in project appraisal. While a company investing abroad faces additional risk, in terms of currency exposure, its cost of capital may be lower, other things being equal, than if it confined its investment to its domestic economy. This arises because of the possibilities of reducing systematic risk below the level associated with its domestic economy.

Empirical evidence, for example Lessard (1976), suggests that the stock exchange indices in major international equity markets (Japan, the UK, the US, France,

Germany, etc.) are less than perfectly positively correlated. Thus, following the principles of diversification developed in Chapter 4, an international version of the CAPM produces lower required rates of return.

Using the CAPM approach for estimating a project cost of capital, as suggested at the beginning of Chapter 7, a foreign project β can be calculated by:
- identifying a company of similar risk in the foreign economy;
- calculating its return variation in relation to an international portfolio of equities, that is, its β; and
- unlevering and relevering the estimated β appropriately.

Political risk

In addition to exchange rate risk, multinational companies must also consider political, or country, risk. This is related to the unanticipated actions of foreign governments in, for example, unexpectedly changing their tax laws, or their rules on profit remittance, or their degree of financial market regulation. Political risk is to some extent picked up in exchange rate movements and so will already be included in a project's cost of capital but political risk can take extreme forms. A government's political philosophy might change and lead, for example, to confiscation of foreign owned assets within its jurisdiction or to nationalisation, with poor compensation paid for the assets acquired by the state in the latter case. The probability of civil war and revolution might also be important considerations in some potential multinational investments.

Adjusted net present value

Finally, from the discussion on international financing, it becomes clear that the way in which a foreign project is financed may be partly influenced by the strategy a company adopts towards managing its currency exposure. This implies that, in an international context, investment and financing decisions may become interdependent. In these cases the ANPV method of investment appraisal might be more appropriate than the standard application of NPV. The ANPV approach was discussed in detail at the end of Chapter 10. Recall that it identifies separate elements in a project's NCF series and discounts each element at the appropriate risk adjusted rate.

Holland (1986) presents a summary of the research which has examined how the ANPV can be applied in an international context. One possibility, which takes account of some of the above factors, is to specify the ANPV of a foreign project as:

$$\text{ANPV} = \text{PV[Capital Outlays]} + \text{PV[Remittable NCFs]}$$
$$+ \text{PV[Tax and Depreciation Shields]} + \text{PV[Financial Subsidies]}$$

(15.5)

Summary

This chapter has demonstrated that a company which extends its operations beyond the borders of its domestic economy faces an additional set of variables dominated by currency exposure. While these add to the complexity of decision making, international operations are analysed using the basic principles of investment and financing. The key consideration is exchange rate risk which is amenable to reduction if at least two of the international parity relationships do not hold exactly.

Hedging foreign currency exposure can be achieved in a number of ways, for example, by using forward exchange rates, which are usually quoted up to 12 months forward, in a forwards or futures contract; or by using options; or by matching assets and liabilities in a foreign currency.

Both futures and options are not restricted to foreign currencies; they have much wider application. The general principles underlying these instruments are presented in the next chapter.

Finally, remember that the indirect exchange rate is interpreted as follows:
- if the rate rises, for example the DM/£ rate, the first currency (DMs) depreciates, the second (£s) appreciates;
- if the rate falls, the first currency appreciates, the second depreciates.

Where forward rates are concerned, they are quoted:
- at a discount to the spot rate, if the forward rate is above the spot rate; and
- at a premium to the spot rate, if the forward rate is below the spot rate.

Thus discounts are added to a spot rate to obtain a forward rate and premiums are subtracted from a spot rate to obtain a forward rate.

Questions

1 The ABC company has just exported goods to Germany to the value of DM10,000. The current exchange rate is DM2.33/£ but ABC won't receive payment in DMs for one month.
   a) Assuming that the exchange rate remains constant, what is the £ value of ABC's exports one month from now?
   b) What is the £ value of exports one month from now if the £ appreciates against the DM by 10% over this period?
   c) What is the £ value of ABC's exports one month from now if the DM depreciates against the £ by 10% over this period?
   d) What is the £ value of ABC's exports if the £ depreciates by 10%?

2 A company is purchasing capital equipment from the US for $2.5m and will settle the invoice in dollars in two months' time. The spot exchange rate is $1.47/£ and the forward rate is $1.49/£$_{(f.2)}$.
   a) All other things being equal, should the company contract at the forward rate to purchase dollars?
   b) If the company expects the two-month future spot rate to be $E(\$/£)_2 = 1.46$, when should it purchase dollars, now or in two months' time? What market should it use?
   c) Repeat part (b) assuming $E(\$/£)_2 = 1.52$.
   d) Repeat part (b) assuming $E(\$/£)_2 = 1.44$.

3 In question 2 the spot exchange rate is $1.47/£ and the forward rate is $1.49/£$_{(f.2)}$.

Assume that the company decides to use the forward market. What problem has the company faced if $E(\$/\pounds)_2 = 1.52$? How could the company have attempted to avoid this problem?

4 A company can buy a piece of capital equipment, now, from the US at a cost of $2.5m. The spot exchange rate is $1.50/£. The company is considering delaying purchase for one year and wants to know the £ cost of the equipment one year from now. It estimates that the price of the equipment is subject to the US annual inflation rate which is expected to be 5%. It expects the UK's annual inflation rate to be 8%. Assuming purchasing power parity holds, what is the expected £ cost of the equipment one year from now?

5 Assume that the spot rate of exchange is DM2.32/£ and that one-year yields on government bonds in the UK and Germany are, respectively, 8% and 6%. What would the 12-month forward rate of exchange have to be under the International Parity Theorem?

6 In general what does empirical evidence indicate about international parity relationships?

7 Consider the following information: the spot exchange rate between the UK and the US is $1.48/£ and respective annual rates of inflation are 4% and 2%.
   a) Assuming that PPP and the expectations theory hold, calculate the rate of foreign exchange expected in 12 months' time and the 12-month forward rate.
   b) If the rate of interest in the UK is 7%, what is the rate of interest in the US, given IRP?
   c) Given (a) and (b) demonstrate that the International Fisher Effect must hold and calculate the approximate real rates of interest in each economy.

Exercises

1 A UK company is considering undertaking a project in the US at a cost of $10m. The project has a two-year life and its NCFs are: year one $8m and year two $12m. The year one interest rate in the US is 10% and the year two rate is expected to be 15%. The spot exchange rate is $1.50/£.
   a) Calculate the $ NPV of the project and convert it to a sterling value.
   b) Assume that the UK interest rate in year one is 9% and that it is expected to be 12% in year two. Calculate the sterling value of the project's NCFs, assuming IRP holds, and show that the sterling NPV of the project is equal to that achieved under (a).

2 What do you understand by the concept of political risk?

3 Explain the terms transaction and translation exposure.

Endnotes

1. Note that the reverse holds for a UK importer of goods from Germany. Since the DM has appreciated, he has to pay more £s per DM to purchase the imports.

2. Note that the reverse holds if this example is applied to a UK company receiving DMs in the future. Here the forward purchase of £s for DMs creates protection against an unanticipated depreciation of the DM (appreciation of the £), that is, a rise in the spot exchange rate from DM2.50/£ to DM2.60/£, for example. The company receiving DMs in the future cannot, however, gain if the spot rate falls.

3. Note that the reverse would hold if this example applied to a company wanting to sell DMs.

4. An importer buying a foreign currency at the spot exchange rate, or at a relevant forward rate, knows that the payment in £s for the foreign currency is certain. By waiting to buy in a future spot market, uncertainty about payments in £s is created. Another way an importer could create certainty is to agree with the foreign country supplier a price for his product or service in sterling. Here any exchange rate risk is transferred from the domestic importer to the foreign exporter. In practice domestic importers agree prices with foreign exporters in the foreign currency while domestic exporters agree prices with foreign importers in the domestic currency.

5. Recall that this chapter is using indirect exchange rates. If the direct exchange rate was being used, that is, the inverse or reciprocal of the indirect rate, PPP would be expressed as:

$$\frac{1 + E(\Theta_G)}{1 + E(\Theta_{UK})} = \frac{£/DM}{E(£/DM)_t}$$

6. Like endnote 5, if the direct exchange rate is being used, IRP is expressed as:

$$\frac{1 + r_G}{1 + r_{UK}} = \frac{£/DM}{£/DM_{(f.t)}}$$

7. Under the direct exchange rate, the expectations theory states:

$$E(£/DM)_t = £/DM_{(f.t)}$$

8. In the ERM, of which the UK is not now a part, the IRP is likely to hold almost exactly.

References

Buckley, A., *Multinational Finance*, London, Philip Allan, 1986

Eiteman, D., A. Stonehill and M. Moffett, *Multinational Business Finance*, Reading, Addison-Wesley, 1992

Fisher, I., *The Theory of Interest*, New York, Augustus M. Kelly, 1965

Henning, C., W. Pigott and R. Scott, *International Financial Management*, New York, McGraw-Hill, 1978

Herring, R. (Ed.), *Managing Foreign Exchange Risk*, Cambridge, Cambridge University Press, 1983

Holland, J., 'The International Dimensions of Corporate Financial Management', in M. Firth and S. Keane (Eds.), *Issues in Finance*, London, Philip Allan, 1986

Husted, S. and M. Melvin, *International Economics*, New York, Harper and Row, 1990

Lessard, D., 'World, Country and Industry Relationships in Equity Returns: Implications for Risk Reduction through International Diversification', Financial Analysis Journal, 1976

Levi, M., *International Finance: Financial Management and the International Economy*, New York, McGraw-Hill, 1983

Maloney, P., 'Managing Currency Exposure: The Case of Western Mining', in D. Chew (Ed.), *New Developments in Commercial Banking*, Oxford, Blackwell, 1991

Melvin, M., *International Money and Finance*, New York, Harper and Row, 1989

Shapiro, A., 'Capital Budgeting for the Multinational Corporation', Financial Management, 1978

Valdez, S., *An Introduction to Western Financial Markets*, London, Macmillan, 1993

Watson, A., *Finance of International Trade*, The Institute of Bankers, London, 1981

16 Futures and options

(This chapter has been prepared in conjunction with Kate McCaffery)

Introduction

The management of risk forms a significant part of corporate finance. Up to this point in the text, risk analysis has concentrated on portfolio diversification in the context of a company's cost of capital. Assuming that equity investors hold broadly based portfolios to avoid specific risk, only the systematic risk that a company is exposed to has a bearing on its required rate of return.

The other main method of managing risk is hedging. This concept was briefly introduced when considering working capital management and foreign currency exposure in Chapters 12 and 15 respectively.

One way in which hedging can be achieved is by matching the maturity structure of assets and liabilities. Here unanticipated changes in the future price of an asset, generally referred to as financial price risk, are offset by unanticipated changes in the future value of a closely associated liability.

Financial price risk can also be hedged by agreeing to deal in an asset in the future at a price negotiated now. This agreement forms a contract which, in the case of futures and options, can be traded in its own right in the financial markets. Such a contract is known as a derivative financial instrument, in the sense that it derives its value from the underlying asset it trades. It is because the spot price of an asset, at some future date, cannot be known with certainty that a contract to hedge the future is entered into.

Hedging is like insurance in that the aim is to protect against losses associated with uncertain future events. Unlike insurance, which is based on the principle of risk pooling, hedging, using derivatives, is based on the principle of risk transference. Here the risks associated with cash, or spot, market transactions are transferred to the derivatives markets.

In this chapter the principles governing the two derivative instruments, futures and options, whose trading has expanded dramatically over the past 20 years, are examined. The analysis begins with a brief review of forwards, which are in some respects quite similar to futures. The presentation on futures includes an explanation of the main features of a futures contract and descriptions of margin accounts and marking to market. Margin accounts and marking to market are the main mechanisms ensuring that formal Futures Exchanges are well capitalised.

The second half of the chapter introduces the basic ideas behind options. Call and put option contracts are defined and some illustrations on hedging with options presented. There is a very brief review of option pricing and the chapter closes by discussing some of the general applications of option theory.

Forwards

The previous chapter introduced forward contracts in respect of foreign currency. Recall, for example, that if the spot exchange rate between deutschmarks and sterling is DM2.50/£ and the three-month forward rate is DM2.53/£$_{(f.3)}$, a company can contract, now, to purchase DMs for £s in three months' time at the forward exchange rate. Under the forwards contract, assuming that the company requires DM1m, it agrees to take delivery of DM1m in three months, making a payment at that time of DM1m ÷ DM2.53/£ = £0.395m.

The main benefit of the forward contract is that the agreed, and therefore certain, future price transfers the risk associated with cash market transactions to the forwards derivative market. It protects against a rise in the spot purchase price of an asset above the forwards price (from the buyer's point of view), and protects against a fall in the spot price of an asset below the forwards price (from the seller's point of view).

If, in the above example, the spot exchange rate in three months' time is DM2.60/£, the company experiences a loss (the foreign exchange dealer a gain) because DM1m would only cost DM1m ÷ DM2.60/£ = £0.385m in the spot market compared to £0.395m under the forwards contract. The reverse happens, with the company gaining (the foreign exchange dealer losing) relative to the spot market transaction, if the spot exchange rate in three months' time, say DM2.45/£, is below the forward rate of DM2.53/£$_{(f.3)}$.

Forward rate agreement

Another relatively popular forward contract is a Forward Rate Agreement, or FRA, made in respect of interest rates. It is designed to hedge against interest rate risk.

Consider a company which needs to borrow, in two months' time, £1.5m for a subsequent three-month period. It agrees to borrow this sum from Bank A at a variable rate of interest. While the current annual rate of interest is 8%, the company is concerned that when it comes to draw down £1.5m short-term interest rates may have risen, increasing its cost of short-term debt financing. To hedge interest rate risk exposure, the company enters an FRA with Bank B.[1] Under this agreement it borrows, notionally, £1.5m for three months at an agreed annual rate of interest of 10%, the FRA taking effect two months from now. The FRA results in Bank B compensating the company if the future spot rate of interest rises above the agreed forward rate. Alternatively, if the spot rate turns out to be below the forward rate, the company compensates Bank B.

A rise in interest rates
Assume that in two months' time the annual spot rate of interest rises to 12% and remains at this level for the subsequent three months. The company's actual borrowings of £1.5m from Bank A incur an approximate interest cost over the three-month period of:

$$£1.5m \left(12\% \times \frac{3 \text{ months}}{12 \text{ months}} \right) = £0.045m$$

Under the FRA this unanticipated rise in interest rates is hedged, since the notional borrowing of £1.5m from Bank B, at a fixed annual rate of interest of 10%, only incurs an interest charge of:

$$£1.5m \left(10\% \times \frac{3}{12}\right) = £0.0375m$$

Consequently Bank B compensates the company by making payments, based on the three-month period, equal to the interest rate differential between the spot rate on the actual sum borrowed and the agreed forward rate on the notional sum borrowed. On the notional borrowing of £1.5m, Bank B therefore pays the company:

£0.045m − £0.0375m = £0.0075m

In effect the FRA ensures that the company's actual borrowings of £1.5m are made at an effective fixed annual rate of interest of 10%.

A fall in interest rates
Alternatively, if the spot rate of interest falls below the FRA, to say 6%, the company is disadvantaged in that it has locked into an effective annual rate of interest of 10%. Although the company borrows the actual sum of money from Bank A at a three-monthly interest cost of

$$£1.5m \left(6\% \times \frac{3}{12}\right) = £0.0225m$$

the company must now compensate Bank B by making a payment on the notional borrowing, equivalent to the interest differential. Because spot rates have fallen below the FRA, the FRA now favours the other party, Bank B, as opposed to the company. The compensation paid by the company to Bank B is:

£0.0375m − £0.0225m = £0.015m

Weaknesses of forward contracts
In general a forward contract, which can be negotiated in respect of a financial asset or commodity (such as oil, tea or coffee), is a private agreement with its terms and conditions tailormade to the requirements of the parties concerned. It is the most popular way of hedging currency risk, with forward currency contracts negotiated between companies and banks. The main weakness of a forward contract, on any underlying asset, is that it is subject to a high degree of credit risk. There are two reasons for this. First, there is no initial cost to entering into a forward contract. Second, all gains and losses between the parties are realised when the contract matures and the assets or goods are exchanged at the previously agreed price. There is, therefore, quite a strong incentive for the party experiencing losses, or for a party which no longer needs to exchange the asset in the forward agreement, to default on the forward contract.

Futures contracts

A futures contract is similar to a forwards contract in that it deals with the future purchase and sale of an asset at a price agreed now. It is fundamentally different from a forward contract, however, in that the buyer of the asset enters into an agreement directly with an organised Futures Exchange. Simultaneously a contract to sell the identical amount of the asset is entered into, with the Exchange, by the seller. The two parties, one agreeing to deliver the asset to the Exchange and the other agreeing to take delivery of the asset from the Exchange, negotiate the futures price, the Exchange does not. The purpose of the Futures Exchange is to ensure that default on delivery and payment does not take place. The Exchange eliminates credit risk by providing standardised legal agreements which are traded in a well-capitalised market. It thus enables the parties to a futures contract, if they desire, to 'unwind', or terminate, the agreement before the delivery date. Also, if one party to an agreement does default, the Exchange will deliver the asset in place of the original buying (selling) trader.

In effect, futures are forward contracts which are tradable through formal Exchanges, for example, the London International Financial Futures Exchange (LIFFE), the Singapore International Monetary Exchange (SIMEX) and the Irish Futures and Options Exchange (IFOX). Futures contracts are limited to a small selection of assets; for example, short-term and long-term interest rate futures, equity futures and stock index futures which are available on LIFFE. The strong preference for trading foreign currencies through forward contracts resulted in dealings in foreign currency futures being suspended on LIFFE in 1990.

A typical Futures Exchange organises its contracts by specifying:
- a standard contract size;
- a delivery date for the underlying asset;
- a system of margin accounts; and
- a daily marking to market settlement.

An illustration
To illustrate, consider an IFOX example where Irish government long-term gilt-edged securities are being traded in futures contracts. Recall from Chapter 3 that a gilt-edged security has a nominal, face or par value of £100 but that the spot price varies inversely with the level of interest rates. (In the case of Irish government gilts, the face value is in Irish £s as opposed to sterling £s.)

IFOX has a typical contract size where gilts are traded in lots of £50,000 nominal. With each gilt having a par value of £100, each contract contains 500 gilts, that is, £50,000/£100 = 500. The futures price of each gilt is quoted at £x per £100 par. Thus if the current spot price of gilts is £98 and three-month gilt futures are priced today at £95, a company buying one contract agrees to take delivery of 500 gilts, directly from IFOX, on the settlement day at an agreed price of 500(£95) = £47,500. (In this example, because the gilt is selling at a futures price below the current spot price, the implication is that the market expects interest rates to rise in the future.) Since a Futures Exchange runs a 'balanced book', there will be a futures contract by which another party agrees to deliver 500 gilts to IFOX for £47,500.

Because gilt futures are traded, the futures price for a given future delivery date, or settlement date, can change through time as new contracts are negotiated. The prices of the new contracts will take into account the recent daily changes in the spot price of the underlying asset and the market's estimate of how the spot price is likely to change in the future. The market may, for example, revise its view on future interest rate changes. As explained below, the prices on existing contracts are marked to the prices on new contracts in what is referred to as marking to market.

Margins and marking to market

A Futures Exchange operates on an initial margin and a marking to market system. The initial margin is not a downpayment but a form of security bond to ensure commitment of the parties to the futures contract. The initial margin can be set between 5% and 15% of the initial value of the contract, with a minimum margin specified over the life of the contract. The margin account is held by the Exchange.

As the settlement price on a given futures contract changes on a daily basis, the value of outstanding contracts are marked to market, that is, revised upwards or downwards as appropriate. Traders who experience a loss may find that their margin accounts fall below the minimum permissible limit, in which case they receive a margin call from the Exchange. This call requires the trader to restore the margin. If this is not possible, the trader's position is wiped out. Thus margin accounts and marking to market ensure the continuing liquidity of the parties, or traders, in the futures contracts, and provide a well-capitalised market in which there can be confidence.

To illustrate the above points, consider the following hypothetical IFOX example. It is 14 June and futures contracts, in long-term Irish gilts, have a settlement date of 19 June. The XYZ company decides to purchase 10 contracts, each at a nominal value of £50,000. The quoted selling price is £97, which implies that on 19 June XYZ will take delivery on 10 gilt futures contracts (5000 gilts) at 5000(£97) = £485,000. A 5% initial margin is required on the nominal value of the gilts. This cash payment of 0.05(£0.5m) = £25,000 must be made to IFOX on 15 June. The transaction is recorded in Table 16.1.

On 15 June other new contracts are entered into at £97.20. This implies that the XYZ company's gilt contracts rise in value to 5000(£97.20) = £486,000. Under marking to market, XYZ has a profit of £1000, that is:

$$£486,000 - £485,000 = £1000$$

This profit is paid by IFOX, in cash, to XYZ's margin account on 16 June.

At close of trade on 16 June assume that the price of June contracts in Irish gilts has fallen to £96.50 implying, under marking to market, that with the value of XYZ's contracts now at 5000(£96.50) = £482,500, XYZ has made a loss:

$$£482,500 - £486,000 = -£3500$$

XYZ therefore must make a cash payment of £3500 to the Exchange on 17 June. The payment is taken out of XYZ's margin account. If, as a result, the margin account fell below its minimum permissible level, a margin call would be made by the Exchange to restore the margin account to the initial margin of £25,000.

Trading in June contracts ceases at 11.00 a.m. on 17 June. At this time, marking to market gives a settlement price of £96.10, that is, 5000(£96.10) = £480,500. This indicates that XYZ has made a further loss of

Table 16.1: Illustrating marking to market on a futures contract

XYZ company purchases 10 Irish long gilt futures contracts. Size of each contract, £50,000 nominal. Given that the nominal, or par value, of a gilt is £100, 500 gilts will be delivered, per contract, by IFOX on the settlement date. The futures price is quoted per £100 par and an initial margin of 5% is required on par.

Date	Quoted settlement[1] (futures price)	Implied value XYZ's contracts[2]	Initial margin	Marking to market settlement
14 June (XYZ contract)	£97.00	£485,000	£25,000	
15 June	£97.20	£486,000		
16 June	£96.50	£482,500		£1000
17 June	£96.10	£480,500		−£3500
(Trade in June futures close)				
18 June	£96.10	£480,500		−£2000
			Cumulative	
19 June	£96.10	£480,500	marking	−£4500
(Settlement/delivery date)			to market	

[1] The price movement on a contract is known as a 'tick'. With a 'tick' defined as 0.01, the price has changed, between 14 and 15 June, by 20 tick movements. Thus the value of XYZ's contracts, between 14 and 15 June, has risen by 20 (tick movements) × £5 (tick value) × 10 (contracts) = £1000. The tick value is the value of a tick per contract. With 500 gilts in a contract, the tick value is 500(.01) = £5. Between 16 and 17 June, the value of XYZ contracts falls by 70(£5)(10) = £3500.
[2] There are 10 contracts, each with 500 gilts, therefore, the implied value of XYZ's contracts is determined by multiplying each day's quoted settlement price by 5000.

$$£480,500 − £482,500 = −£2000$$

which is deducted from its margin account.

On 19 June, which is settlement day, XYZ receives 5000 gilts from IFOX at £96.10 per £100 nominal, that is, at a cost of 5000(£96.10) = £480,500. On the basis of the cumulative marking to market settlement, XYZ has already paid £4500 (see Table 16.1), thus the price for XYZ June contracts is:

$$£480,500 + £4500 = £485,000$$

In other words the contract price of £485,000 entered into on 14 June has been paid. In practical terms XYZ makes a payment of £460,000 to the Exchange on 19 June. This is determined as:
- the initial contract price of £485,000, less
- the cumulative marking to market settlement of £4500, which has already been paid out of XYZ's initial margin, less
- the net initial margin, £25,000 − £4500 = £20,500.

In other words:

$$£485,000 − £4500 − £20,500 = £460,000$$

A balanced book
Note that, because a Futures Exchange runs a balanced book, 10 contracts to supply

5000 gilts must have been entered into with the Exchange on 14 June, with the supplier required to make a 5% margin payment. In the supplier's case, the marking to market settlement would have resulted in the reverse of the payment flows indicated in Table 16.1. On 17 June, for example, the debit of £3500 from XYZ's margin account would have been credited to the supplier's margin account. Note also that on the date on which trading in June contracts finishes, 17 June, the spot price of Irish long gilts would be equal to the futures price of £96.10.

Long and short positions
The above example illustrates in a simple way the mechanics of marking to market adjustment of the settlement price on a futures contract. Generalising, if subsequent trading in a particular contract results in higher settlement prices, all old contracts are marked to the higher price. The number of outstanding contracts at any point in time is referred to, technically, as open interest.

Participants with a long position, that is, those who contract to buy the underlying asset, are then required to pay a greater amount on the settlement date than agreed on their contract date. They will, however, have already received in cash the difference between the settlement price and the contract price.

Conversely, participants with a short position, that is, those who contract to sell the underlying asset, receive a higher payment on the settlement date, when they deliver the underlying asset to the Futures Exchange. In this case, however, they have already paid the difference, in cash, to the Exchange.

The reverse situation arises for both sets of participants if trading results in lower settlement prices.[2]

Unwinding

The practice of marking futures contracts to market on a daily basis makes it easy to liquidate, or unwind, a futures position before the final settlement date. For example, if the XYZ company decided, on 16 June, that it did not wish to take delivery of its long position in Irish gilts, it could open a matching short position on 16 June. In other words it would contract with IFOX to deliver on 10 gilt futures contracts, at the settlement price, on the close of trade on 16 June. XYZ still has to pay the marking to market settlement of £3500 resulting on 16 June from its original contract. As indicated in Table 16.1, this is paid on 17 June. IFOX now cancels XYZ's matching positions. XYZ, after 16 June, has no remaining obligation to IFOX. XYZ does not have to deliver cash (under its original futures contract to buy gilts); nor does it have to deliver gilts (under its matching contract). Also, it is not subject to any further marking to market settlements.

Imperfect hedging

On the settlement date the price of gilt futures, or any futures contract, always equals the spot price on the underlying asset, on that date. In ideal conditions, therefore, futures can be used to obtain a perfect hedge. Conditions are never ideal, however, since over the term of a futures contract spot market prices on an underlying asset will be less than perfectly positively correlated with the prices at which the futures contract trades. Therefore if a company unwinds a futures contract before the settlement date, spot and futures settlement prices may diverge, resulting in an imperfect hedge.

Even when the settlement date is reached, perfect hedges may in practice be difficult to achieve. This arises because the settlement date in a futures contract is pre-specified. This specific date, on which a company is required by an Exchange to take (or make) delivery of the underlying asset, will not usually coincide exactly with the date on which the company itself wants to trade the underlying asset. The spot price on this latter date may, therefore, differ from the price on the settlement date.

Short-term interest rate futures

In an earlier section of this chapter an example of a forwards contract on interest rates, an FRA, was given. As an alternative to an FRA, short-term interest rate futures (SIRFs) are available for hedging interest rate risk. Indeed interest rate futures account for over 90% of all futures trading on LIFFE. These futures contracts, which are of three months' duration, have four delivery months per year: March, June, September and December. LIFFE trades four short-term time deposit contracts: sterling, eurodollars, eurodeutschmark and ECU (European Currency Unit).

The SIRFs are priced on an index basis of 100, minus the annual rate of interest. For example, if a company buys a three-month sterling time deposit contract for 88.00, the company fixes on an annual rate of interest of 12% (that is, the price is 100.00 − 12.00 = 88.00). This implies that the company locks into a three-month interest rate of 3%. Using the index approach means that the price of a SIRF varies inversely with changes in spot rates of interest. Therefore, through marking to market, the company receives profits if the price of a SIRF rises, implying spot rates fall, and incurs losses if the price of a SIRF falls, implying spot rates rise. These profits or losses offset the spot versus fixed interest rate positions, thus hedging interest rate risk. In the case of SIRFs the minimum margin always equals the initial margin, the initial payment being made to the Exchange when the SIRF contract is initially agreed.

An illustration
To illustrate the principles of SIRFs, without going into too much detail on how LIFFE organises the trades, consider the XYZ company which wishes to borrow £1.5m for three months from the beginning of July, at a variable interest rate. It expects short-term interest rates to rise over this period. To hedge its position, XYZ decides to sell short-term September sterling interest rate futures contracts. The contract size is £500,000 nominal, so it sells three contracts at a nominal value of 3(£0.5m) = £1.5m. The price of each contract is 93.00, indicating that XYZ has locked into an annual interest rate of 7%, since 100.00 − 7.00 = 93.00. This implies a three-month rate of interest of 1.75%. At this interest rate the cost of borrowing £1.5m is:

$$(0.0175)£1.5m = £26,250$$

Table 16.2: Illustrating short-term interest rate futures

XYZ company sells three sterling interest rate futures contracts.

Contract size: £500,000   Price: 93.00

With price at 93, implied annual rate of interest is 7%, that is, $100 - 7 = 93$
Implied quarterly (90-day) rate of interest is 1.75%, that is, $7\% \div 4 = 1.75\%$

Assume interest rate rises to 10%

Price of interest rate futures falls to 90, that is, $100 - 10 = 90$

Tick Movement
Interest rate has risen by 3 percentage points.
LIFFE defines a minimum permissible change in the interest rate as 0.01.
This change is known as a tick movement.
There are, therefore, on the basis of a 3 percentage point rise:

$$3 \div 0.01 = 300 \text{ tick movements in this example.}$$

Tick Value
A tick movement, on a nominal contract of £500,000, produces a change in interest cost, over three months, of:

$$0.0001 \left(\frac{3}{12}\right) £500,000 = £12.50$$

This defines the tick value of a contract.

Overall change in interest cost
Tick Movement $\times$ Tick Value $\times$ Number of Contracts $= 300(£12.50)(3) = £11,250$

Margin Payment
LIFFE pays this amount, £11,250, into XYZ's margin account.
As explained in the text, this achieves a perfect interest rate risk hedge for XYZ.

Assume that just after XYZ obtains the actual loan from a bank at the beginning of July, annual interest rates rise to 10% and remain at this level to the end of September. On a three-month rate of 2.5%, the interest cost is:

$$(0.025)(£1.5m) = £37,500$$

This produces an increase in borrowing costs, relative to the 7% annual interest cost on the futures contract:

$$£37,500 - £26,250 = £11,250$$

The sale of the three futures contracts has, however, offset this extra cost, producing a perfect hedge which allows XYZ to borrow, effectively, at the fixed annual rate of 7%. To see this, consider what has happened to XYZ's futures contracts.

XYZ sold three September sterling interest rate futures contracts at the beginning of July at a settlement price of 93.00, with a nominal value of £1.5m. The only initial payment is the initial margin, normally £750 per contract, which is returned at the end of the contract period. The rise in interest rates, from 7% to 10%, produces a fall in the price of September sterling interest rate futures to $100.00 - 10.00 = 90.00$. Since XYZ is selling these futures contracts it gains, the profit being paid by LIFFE into XYZ's margin account. The profit is £11,250, which exactly offsets the extra interest cost on the actual loan.

Table 16.3: Hedging and an interest rate fall

XYZ company sells three sterling interest rate futures contracts.

Contract size: £500,000   Price: 93.00

With price at 93, implied annual rate of interest is 7%, that is, $100 - 7 = 93$
Implied quarterly (90-day) rate of interest is 1.75%, that is, $7\% \div 4 = 1.75\%$

XYZ company bank borrowings
XYZ borrowings of £1.5m for three months
Interest cost at an annual rate of interest of 7%

$$(0.07)\left(\frac{3}{12}\right)(£1.5m) = £26,250$$

Assume interest rate falls to 5%
Interest cost at an annual rate of interest of 5%

$$(0.05)\left(\frac{3}{12}\right)(£1.5m) = £18,750$$

Saving in interest cost, 5% relative to 7%,

$$£26,250 - £18,750 = £7500$$

September short-term interest rate futures contract
Interest rate falls from 7% to 5%, since price rises from 93 to 95.
  Tick Movement 200
  Tick Value £12.50 (see Table 16.2)
XYZ loss on 3 futures contracts
  200(12.50)(3) = £7500

Margin Payment
XYZ is required to make cash payment of £7500 to LIFFE, exactly offsetting gain from borrowing, at annual spot rate of 5%, relative to fixed annual rate of 7%.

The profit is calculated on ticks, tick values and the number of contracts. This is illustrated in Table 16.2. Assuming that no further interest rate changes take place, the September contracts are closed out on the final settlement date in September, with the XYZ company receiving £11,250 (plus the return of its initial margin).[3] Table 16.3 illustrates how a perfect hedge would have been achieved if the interest rate, instead of rising from 7% to 10%, had fallen to 5%.

Note that the XYZ company felt confident enough (did it not believe in the EMH?) to take an opinion that interest rates would rise. Therefore, it contracted to sell September interest rate futures to offset, through the expected gains from futures trading, the higher interest charges on its loan.

Imperfect hedging
The above showed cases where interest rate risk could be perfectly hedged through the use of interest rate futures. There are two main reasons why this may not be possible in practice. First, futures deal in standard contract sizes. If a company wanted to borrow £1.8m then, with a contract size of £500,000, only three futures contracts could be entered into. The additional £0.3m would have to be hedged in some other way. Second, when interest rates changed, for example from 7% to 10%, the short-term sterling interest rate futures price matched the cash market change by going from 93.00 to 90.00. Interest rate futures are, however, based on underlying fixed interest securities, for example gilts, whose prices respond to

factors in addition to changes in interest rates. If, therefore, interest rates change by three percentage points, the SIRF's price may not change identically. If the change in the price had been from 93.00 to, say 90.05, then the implied change in the futures contract would only have been 295 ticks, as opposed to 300. Because of the cash market change being inexactly matched, an imperfect hedge would result.

Options

When discussing forwards and futures it became apparent that one of the short-comings of these derivatives is that the respective forward and settlement prices may not necessarily equal the future spot price of the relevant underlying asset. Thus companies (or individuals) wishing to take delivery of an underlying asset, using either of these two derivative instruments, would have been better off using the future spot, or cash, market if the spot price had turned out to be below the guaranteed price. The spot market cannot be used, however, since under a forwards or futures contract there is an obligation to the agreed price. Alternatively the seller of an underlying asset would have been better off executing trade through the spot market, if the spot price had turned out to be above the guaranteed price.

This problem of limited flexibility in choice can be tackled through another derivative instrument: an option. An option involves the sale by contract of the right to buy or sell an underlying asset, at a price agreed now: the exercise or strike price. An option has an expiry date, and the exercise of any rights under the contract terminates thereafter. There are two general forms of options: a European option, where the right to buy or sell an underlying asset can only be exercised on the expiry date; and an American option, where this right is exercisable at any time during the term of the option contract.

Initially only equity options existed, but the option markets have expanded to include, for example, stock indices, debt, currency and futures. In this chapter examples are restricted to equities, which still form the dominant underlying asset class. In London, for example, LIFFE trades[4] American options of nine months' duration on approximately 70 UK listed companies.

Calls and puts

Option contracts come in two basic types: a call option and a put option.

A call option contract gives the holder the right to purchase or not to purchase a given number of shares in a company at an exercise price. On LIFFE the standard contract size is 1000 shares (on US Options Exchanges 100 shares). While the holder of a call option is not under an obligation to purchase the underlying shares, the other party to the contract, known as a call option writer, is under an obligation to sell at the exercise price if the call is exercised by the option holder. The similarity between call options and the discussion on warrants in Chapter 11 should be obvious. Recall that warrants are a form of hybrid debt giving the holder the right to purchase a specified number of shares in a company, at an exercise price.

A put option gives the holder of this contact the right to sell or not to sell a given

Table 16.4: Quoting call and put options[1]

		Calls			Puts		
		Jan	April	July	Jan	April	July
Unilever	1100	52	$73\frac{1}{2}$	88	$5\frac{1}{2}$	24	36
(1141)	1150	$19\frac{1}{2}$	$44\frac{1}{2}$	60	$23\frac{1}{2}$	48	$59\frac{1}{2}$
Grand Met	390	$19\frac{1}{2}$	$30\frac{1}{2}$	37	13	19	$24\frac{1}{2}$
(401)	420	7	$17\frac{1}{2}$	24	$32\frac{1}{2}$	$36\frac{1}{2}$	$41\frac{1}{2}$
Brit Telecom	360	$26\frac{1}{2}$	37	44	4	$7\frac{1}{2}$	$13\frac{1}{2}$
(378)	390	$9\frac{1}{2}$	$19\frac{1}{2}$	$27\frac{1}{2}$	17	$20\frac{1}{2}$	$27\frac{1}{2}$
Thorn EMI	1000	15	$49\frac{1}{2}$	$74\frac{1}{2}$	1	$22\frac{1}{2}$	$30\frac{1}{2}$
(1013)	1050	–	25	$48\frac{1}{2}$	$36\frac{1}{2}$	$49\frac{1}{2}$	$55\frac{1}{2}$

Source: Financial Times: 21/11/94
[1] Note that when the exercise price exceeds the share price, for example, Unilever 1150 > 1141, the option is said to be in the money. When below, Unilever 1110 < 1141, the option is said to be out of the money.

number of shares in a company at an exercise price. While the holder of a put option is not under an obligation to sell the underlying asset, the other party to the contract, known as a put option writer, is under an obligation to buy at the exercise price if the put is exercised by the option holder.

Quoting options

The prices at which options contracts are bought and sold on formal Options Exchanges vary over their term to expiry. These prices are referred to as option premiums. In the case of a call option the premium paid by the call option holder represents the cost of his right (but not obligation) to buy the underlying asset at the exercise price. This premium is paid to the call option writer as his charge for being potentially obligated to sell at the exercise price. The premium at which a put option is traded is similarly interpreted. For the moment the option premium is assumed given.

Table 16.4 illustrates how equity calls and puts are quoted on LIFFE. The first column in the table indicates the company's name and the current, or spot, price of its shares. Options run in nine-month cycles, with three expiry dates available, depending on the current point in a year. In Table 16.4 the option expiry dates occur in January, April and July. 'On-the-spot' trading in options contracts between January and March would see expiry dates of April, July and October.

The exercise prices on each option are shown in the second column of Table 16.4, with the option premiums, that is, the prices of the call and put contracts, quoted in the remaining columns in relation to their expiry dates.

Consider the case of Unilever as an example. Its current share price (on 21/11/94) is £11.41. The option premium on Unilever April call contracts, with an exercise price of £11.00, is 73.5p per share. An investor purchasing this call contract (on 21/11/94) has the right, up to the expiry date in April 1995, to purchase 1000 Unilever shares at an exercise price per share of £11.00. For this right the investor pays an option premium of 73.5p per share. In other words in order to buy the call option contract, the investor pays 1000(£0.735) = £735. Unilever's April call contracts, with an exercise price of £11.50, have an option premium of 44.5p.

The profit potential on a call

As shown below, one important feature of options is the potential profit that can be made, for example, from buying a call and exercising it when the market price of the share exceeds the call option contract's exercise price. In Unilever's case, for example, assume that an investor purchased the April call contract at 73.5p. Assume also that the market price of Unilever rises significantly above its 'current' share price of £11.41 to, say, £12.41. By exercising the call the investor can purchase Unilever shares at £11.41. If the investor then sells these shares on the market at £12.41, a gross profit is made, per share, of £12.41 − £11.41 = £1.00. After deducting the price, per share, of the option contract, the net profit is: £1.00 − £0.735p = £0.265. Market transactions costs are ignored. Unilever's share price could, of course, fall substantially.

In general, the lower the exercise price on a call contract, other things being equal, the higher the profit potential. Consequently the premiums at which call contracts can be bought and sold are inversely related to the exercise prices on the underlying assets.

The profit potential on a put

Conversely, put option premiums vary directly with the exercise price. The profit potential from holding a put comes from the right to sell the underlying asset at an exercise price which may, within the contract period, exceed the underlying asset's market price.

Consider the case of British Telecom (Table 16.4). BT's 'current' share price is £3.78. The option premium on its July puts, which have an exercise price of £3.60, is 13.5p. At the exercise price of £3.90, the option premium on July puts is 27.5p. In the latter case, for example, the holder of this put contract has the right to sell, up to the expiry date in July 1995, 1000 BT shares at £3.90 each. This right is bought at an option premium of 27.5p, that is, at a cost per contract of 1000(£0.275) = £275.

Note that for both calls and puts the option premium is higher, the longer the date to expiry. In the case of Thorn EMI calls, at an exercise price of £10.00, the option premiums are respectively, 15p January, 49.5p April and 74.5p July.

Profit profiles

The reasons for the relationships between option premiums and exercise prices and option premiums and expiry dates are outlined towards the end of this chapter. Before this a deeper understanding of profit profiles, and the use of options as hedging instruments, is necessary.

Call option holders

Consider a hypothetical example where an investor now (1 November) wishes to buy, in two months' time, shares in the XYZ company. The investor can buy a January call option at an option premium of 25p per share, with an exercise price of

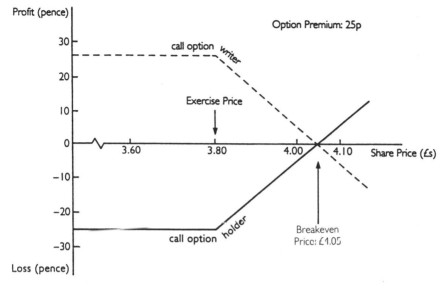

Figure 16.1   Profit profiles on XYZ call options

£3.80. Under this contract the investor has the right to purchase 1000 XYZ shares in early January (a European option is assumed for simplicity) at £3.80 per share, paying £250 now, that is, 1000(25p) for the contract.

Exercising the option

Assume that by the beginning of January the market price of XYZ shares has risen to £4.10. The investor would, therefore, exercise the option at £3.80 on the expiry date, rather than purchase shares in the January spot market at £4.10. The investor's profit, on a per share basis, from exercising the option would be

Market Price − Exercise Price − Option Price,

that is,

£4.10 − £3.80 − £0.25 = £0.05

If the difference between the January market price and the exercise price had been equal to the option premium, profit on the contract would have been zero. This would occur at a market share price of £4.05 which defines, in profit profile terms, the breakeven market price, since

£4.05 − £3.80 − £0.25 = £0.00

Alternatively, if the market/exercise price differential had been below the option premium, profits would have been negative. In this case, for example, a market price of £3.90 would still have resulted in the call option being exercised, but at a loss of

£3.90 − £3.80 − £0.25 = −£0.15

The profit profile in this example is illustrated in Figure 16.1.

Buying in the spot market

Note that the option premium on the call contract is like a sunk cost to the call option holder. The call holder has already paid the option premium. If the holder wants the asset on the expiry date, and the exercise price is less than the market price of the underlying asset, the call is exercised and the share is purchased at the exercise price of £3.80. However, if the market price of the share is below the exercise price, the option will not be exercised since the share can be purchased at a lower cost through the spot market. In this case, however, the loss the investor experiences on the call option contract is limited to the option premium of 25p per share which he/she has already paid.

In effect, by buying a call option on an underlying share an investor limits losses to a maximum, equal to the option premium, but has the potential to make profits by buying the underlying share at the exercise price. As Figure 16.1 indicates, the profit potential rises as the share price rises above the breakeven level and is, theoretically, unlimited.

Call option writers

A mirror profit profile exists for the writer of the above call option on XYZ shares. It is illustrated in Figure 16.1, assuming that the writer takes a naked position in the underlying share, that is, that the writer does not already own the share.

If the call is not exercised, and it will not be if the market price is less than the exercise price, the call option writer's profit equals the option premium he/she has received for writing the call. Once the market price exceeds the exercise price the call will be exercised, with the writer obligated to deliver. The naked call option writer must, therefore, purchase the underlying share in the spot market, the writer's profit declining as the share price rises above the exercise price.

Note that since the writer does not own the underlying share the profit profile, when the market price of the share exceeds the exercise price, is determined by:
- the option premium (already received)
  plus
- the exercise price
  less
- the price the writer has to pay in the market (to buy the share).

Thus the breakeven market price on the share, at which the call option writer's profit is zero, is £4.05 in the present example, that is,

$$£0.25 + £3.80 - £4.05 = £0.00$$

Losses can eventually be experienced and are, theoretically, unlimited.

Hedging and a covered call

The direct purchase of an underlying share in the spot market can be combined with writing a call. This provides a covered, as opposed to a naked, position for the call option writer and, over the term of the call option contract, a hedge on holding the share.

The profit profile of a covered call option writer, in the XYZ share example, is

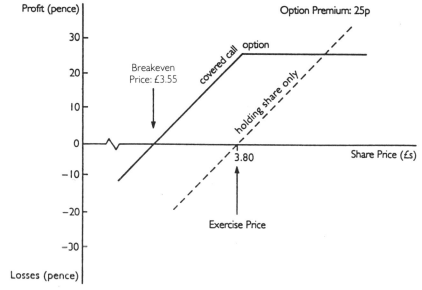

Figure 16.2   Profit profile on a covered call option

shown in Figure 16.2, assuming that the share is purchased by the writer at the exercise price. The call option writer agrees to sell at £3.80, the exercise price.

If the market price on expiry is less than £3.80 the call option holder will not exercise the call, and the writer can only sell at the spot market price. Figure 16.2 demonstrates, however, that as the share price declines the writer of a covered call is partly compensated by the premium paid to him for writing the call. This compensation is nullified when the share price declines to £3.55, that is, the breakeven point of £3.80 − £0.25.

As the share price rises above the breakeven point, the call option writer makes profits. Since, however, the holder of the call will exercise his option when the market price of the share exceeds the exercise price, the maximum profit of the writer (who is obligated to sell) is limited to the option premium of £0.25 per share.

By holding shares alone and not writing the covered call, there is unlimited profit potential as the share price rises. This is indicated, for an XYZ share, by the dashed line in Figure 16.2. Thus the covered call hedges, in respect of potential losses, at the expense of placing an absolute limit on profit potential.

Profit profiles on puts

A call option holder has the right to buy shares at the exercise price; therefore, as already demonstrated, profits increase as the share's market price rises above the breakeven point. Conversely, since a put option holder has the right to sell a share, the put option holder's profits rise as the share price falls below the breakeven market price on the put's underlying asset.

The holder of a put will only make profits if the exercise price, less the option premium paid by the holder of the put, is above the share's market price. Thus the

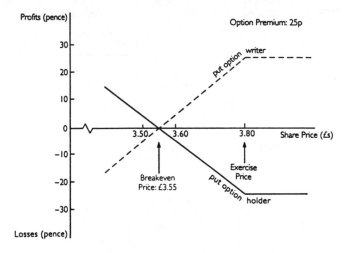

Figure 16.3　Profit profiles on XYZ put options

breakeven market price is £3.55 in the XYZ share example. In other words, with an exercise price of £3.80 and a put option premium of 25p:

$$£3.80 - £0.25 = £3.55$$

The profit profile for the put option holder is shown in Figure 16.3. If the market price of the share exceeds the exercise price, the put option holder will not exercise his right to sell the underlying share and is therefore subject to a maximum loss. This maximum loss is equal to the option premium which the put option holder has already paid.[5]

A mirror profit profile for the put option writer, who is obligated to buy if the put option is exercised, is also shown in Figure 16.3. If the put option holder does not exercise his/her right to sell the underlying share, the writer's maximum profit is equal to the option premium the writer has already received.

In the extreme case, when on expiry of the put contract the underlying share's price is zero, the put option holder will exercise his right to sell the share at £3.80. In this situation the maximum loss for the put writer, who is obligated to buy at the exercise price, is equal to the exercise price less the put option premium which he/she has already received. This maximum loss to the put option writer represents the maximum gain to the put option holder.

Hedging and bull spreads

It should be clear from the above that calls and puts can be used separately to hedge particular positions. The holder of a share, for example, can hedge the risk that the share's price will fall in the future by writing a covered call option or by buying a put option. An investor who wishes to buy a share in the future can hedge the risk that the share's price will rise by buying a call option.

Hedging can also be achieved by buying and selling options simultaneously on the same underlying asset. These bull spreads (and bear spreads) arise when options on

Table 16.5: Illustrating a bull spread strategy

January Calls (Standard contract size: 1000 shares)

Exercise Price	Call Premiums
£2.20	15p
£2.00	25p

Bull Spread Strategy

Buy the 'expensive' call at 25p. Cost of contract:

$$1000(25p) = £250$$

Sell the 'cheap' call at 15p. Receive for contract sale:

$$1000(15p) = £150$$

Net contract cost of bull spread:

$$£250 - £150 = £100$$

Assume share price rises above £2.20

Investor holds 'expensive' call, exercises it and buys 1000 shares at cost:

$$1000(£2.00) = £2000$$

Investor has written 'cheap' call, which is exercised, therefore investor obligated to sell 1000 shares, receiving:

$$1000(£2.20) = £2200$$

Profit on share trading:

$$£2200 - £2000 = £200$$

Net profit on bull spread strategy

Profit on share trading – net contract cost:

$$£200 - £100 = £100$$

a common underlying asset, with a common exercise price, have different expiry dates. Alternatively options on the common underlying asset can have the same expiry date but different exercise prices. In either situation the result is that the options on the common underlying asset have different premiums.

A bull spread strategy involves buying a call and simultaneously selling (writing) a call. It is used when the future spot price of the underlying asset is expected to rise, and provides a hedge against an unanticipated fall in this spot price.

Consider a company whose calls have the same expiry date (January) but different exercise prices of £2.00 and £2.20, with respective option premiums of 25p and 15p. An investor using a bull spread strategy would:
- buy the more expensive call (becoming a call option holder), paying 25p on a per share basis, and
- sell the cheaper call (becoming a call option writer), receiving 15p on a per share basis.

Note that the higher the exercise price, the lower the call's value, or premium. This arises, other things being equal, because there is less profit potential to be realised the higher the exercise price is.

If it turns out that the share price rises above £2.20, both calls will be exercised. The resulting profit is calculated in Table 16.5. Given that the investor has undertaken two call option contracts of 1000 shares each, he/she buys (as a call option holder) 1000 shares at a cost of £2000, and is obligated to sell (as a call option writer) 1000 shares for £2200. The net contract cost per share is 25p − 15p = 10p or, on the standard contract size of 1000 shares, £250 − £150 = £100. Thus net profit gain is equal to:

- the cash inflow, from the writer's share sale,
  minus
- the cash outflow on his/her purchase of the shares,
  less
- the net contract cost.

That is:

$$£2200 − £2000 − £100 = £100$$

This is the maximum potential net profit gain on the bull spread strategy.

If, alternatively, the price on the underlying share falls below £2.00, neither contract will be exercised and the investor's maximum loss would be equal to the net contract cost of £100.

Buy a call only versus a bull spread strategy

Assume that an investor, in the belief that the underlying share price will rise, excludes selling a call and restricts his/her strategy to buying a naked call contract. On this strategy, if the price of the underlying share rises above the breakeven point, the potential profit gain could be unlimited. The investor would purchase the call with the lowest exercise price: in the above example, the call at 25p with an exercise price of £2.00. The breakeven point, on this buy a call only strategy, is the exercise price plus the option premium, that is, £2.00 + £0.25 = £2.25. If the call holder does not exercise the call, the loss on the single contract is 1000(£0.25) = £250.

In comparison, under the bull spread strategy, while net profit gains are restricted to a maximum of £100, the maximum loss, if neither contract is exercised, is reduced from £250 (under the buy a call only strategy) to £100.

Another way of viewing this bull spread strategy, relative to the buy a call only strategy, is in terms of breakeven points. Under the buy a call only strategy, the breakeven point is £2.25. Thus if the price of the underlying share rises above (falls below) £2.25, profits are made (losses are incurred). On the bull spread strategy the net cost, or net option premium, is £0.10, so that the breakeven point is brought down to £2.00 + £0.10 = £2.10. Profits, although limited to a maximum of £100 under the bull spread strategy, now occur when the share price rises above £2.10. Also losses, which are limited to a maximum of £100, are not only reduced under the bull spread strategy, but now do not occur until the price of the share falls below £2.10.

Hedging and bear spreads

The importance of the bull spread strategy is reflected in a number of Exchanges offering this buy/sell combination in a single option contract. The bull spread strategy provides a hedge against the risk of an unanticipated fall in the price of an underlying asset, when the anticipation is, on balance, of a price rise. When, on

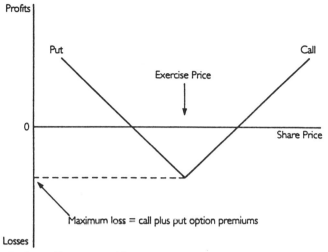

Figure 16.4   Profit profiles on a straddle

balance, the anticipation is of a price fall in the underlying asset, a bear spread strategy provides a hedge against the risk of an unanticipated rise in the price. The bear spread strategy involves combining puts: an investor buying the cheaper put and selling (writing) the more expensive one.

Speculating with a straddle

Other option strategies are available which combine puts and calls. In these cases, however, the strategies are often speculative, as opposed to hedging, in nature. One such speculative strategy is a straddle.

A straddle is used when an investor believes that an underlying asset's price will become relatively volatile. The investor, in other words, expects the price to either rise substantially or fall substantially. The straddle involves simultaneously purchasing a put and a call option on the underlying asset, where the put and the call have the same exercise prices and expiry dates.

If the price of the underlying asset on the expiry date is significantly above the exercise price, the call option is exercised and profits are made, since the underlying asset is delivered to the call option holder at the exercise price. If the price of the underlying asset on the expiry date is significantly below the exercise price, the put option is exercised and profits are made, since the underlying asset is sold by the put option holder at the exercise price.

A straddle profit profile is shown in Figure 16.4. This profit profile is a function of the combination of a call option holder's profit profile (see, for example, Figure 16.1) and a put option holder's profit profile (see, for example, Figure 16.3).

The problem with the straddle is that it is a costly instrument on which to base speculation, especially if neither contract is exercised on the expiry date. This would occur if, on the expiry date, the spot price of the underlying asset equalled its exercise price. Here the maximum loss would be equal to the call and put option premiums paid by the holder of the straddle. Losses, although lower, are still incurred if the price of the underlying asset is relatively close to the exercise price on the date of expiry. If these prices are close on the expiry date it would not be unreasonable to infer that the price volatility on the underlying asset has turned out, over the term of the straddle contract, to be significantly lower than expected.

Option pricing

The pricing of option contracts is complex. In this section the main factors determining option premiums are identified but not brought together in any formal way in an option pricing formula. Such a pricing formula has been developed by Black and Scholes (1973) but it is too technical for an introductory text. It is interesting to note, however, that it was the theoretical work of Black and Scholes, and its suitability for practical application, that facilitated the growth of trading in derivative instruments.

At an early stage in this chapter, when discussing how American option prices are quoted on LIFFE, attention was drawn to two important factors in respect of option premiums:

(i) given the price of the underlying share and the expiry date on the option contract, the call premium varies inversely (the put premium directly) with the exercise price; and

(ii) given the price of the underlying share and the exercise value on the option contract, the option premium on both calls and puts varies directly with the term to expiry.

Return to Table 16.4 to confirm these factors.

Option premiums and exercise prices
Point (i) should now be clear from the analysis of profit profiles. (Although these profiles were shown, for simplicity, in relation to European options, their principles apply equally to American options.) Because a call gives the holder the right to purchase an underlying asset at the exercise price, the lower the exercise price in the call contract, other things being equal, the greater the potential profit (the lower the potential loss). The call premium partly reflects this potential value.

In the case of puts, the option premium and exercise price are positively related, other things being equal, because the put option holder has the right to sell the underlying asset at the exercise price.

Option premiums and terms to expiry
Under point (ii) there is a positive relationship, for both calls and puts, between option premiums and the term to expiry. This arises because the longer the term to expiry, the greater the possibility that the market price of the underlying asset will move favourably in relation to the exercise value in the option contract.

Option premiums and other factors
In drawing out other factors influencing option premiums, it is implicit, in the above two points, that the relationship of the exercise value to the market price of

the underlying asset is important. So is the future expected movement in the underlying asset's market price over the remaining term of a contract. From portfolio principles, developed in Chapter 4, the risk associated with future price rises, or falls, can be measured by the variance, or standard deviation, of returns on the underlying asset.

Also, given the time value of money, initially developed in Chapter 2, an opportunity cost interest rate has a role to play. This arises because an option contract effectively postpones the purchase or sale of an underlying asset. Thus the option holder is enabled to 'free' cash to earn interest on a naked call or put, or lend the underlying asset if a covered position is taken. The opportunity cost is measured by the risk free rate of interest. In addition there is an opportunity cost in respect of any dividends on an underlying asset.

In general, therefore, the principal factors determining option premiums, at any point in time over the life of an option contract, are:
• the exercise value of the option;
• the term to expiry of the option;
• the current market price of the underlying asset;
• the risk free rate of interest;
• the standard deviation of the market price of the underlying asset; and
• any relevant dividend 'type' payments associated with the underlying asset.

The general application of option pricing theory

Option pricing theory has been applied to interpret corporate financial decisions in general. As already explained, bonds issued with warrants represent a call option where the holder of a warrant has the right to purchase shares at a specified price. The company issuing the warrant is a call option writer. In a similar vein, convertible bondholders, who have the right to convert their debt into equity, are call option holders. ·

Where straight debt is concerned, bondholders can be considered as put option writers with the shareholders of a company buying the put. The shareholders have, in effect, purchased the right to default on interest payments. Recall from Chapter 3 that the required rate of return on a corporate bond includes a default risk premium. In terms of option theory this default premium represents the option premium paid to straight bondholders, as put option writers.

Owning equity in a levered company can also be interpreted as shareholders owning a call option. Consider a company which has debt to the face value of £10m. This debt is to be repaid one year from now. Assuming that the value of the company's assets turns out to be below £10m one year from now, shareholders will simply abandon the company to the debtholders. If, however, the value of the assets exceeds £10m, shareholders will exercise their call option, making the repayment of the debt principal, this repayment representing the exercise price on the shareholders' call option. Shareholders' 'profit' would be the excess in the value of the company's assets over £10m.

A rights issue, where a company offers existing shareholders the right to purchase additional shares at a discount, is equivalent to a company writing a call option. Underwriting of share issues, where the underwriter agrees to take up, for a fee, part of a new issue which has not been sold, can be interpreted in terms of a put option. The underwriter is the put option writer, the fee received for his services representing the put option premium paid by the company, which then becomes the put option holder.

Summary

Because of an increase, during the 1970s and 1980s, in the price volatility of a wide range of financial assets, there was a pressing need to develop more sophisticated ways of hedging financial price risk. The result has been both an expansion of trade in derivative instruments and the development of strategies based on complex combinations of forwards, futures and options contracts.[6]

Forwards and futures lock companies, now, into agreed forward or future prices on underlying assets which are to be delivered at some forward or future date. Options improve flexibility by enabling holders of option contracts to trade underlying assets in the future, at future prices agreed now, or at future spot prices.

In general, risk management has been one of the major development areas in corporate finance. This development has not simply been confined to the theoretical analysis and practical application of derivatives; it also encompasses, as earlier chapters in this book have demonstrated, the application of modern portfolio theory, including the capital asset and arbitrage pricing models.

Finally, because this text focuses on corporate finance, the emphasis in this chapter has been on the use of futures and options as hedging instruments. The equally important role that these derivatives play in speculation, together with formal models of futures and options pricing, are topics more appropriate to investment analysis in modules on financial institutions and markets.

Questions

1 Consider a company which wishes to borrow £1m, in one month's time, for a subsequent two months. It agrees to borrow this sum at a variable rate of interest from Bank A. The current annual rate of interest is 9% and the company enters an FRA with Bank B at a current annual rate of interest of 11%. Explain how this agreement will operate if, in one month's time, the spot rate of interest:
   a) rises to 12% and remains at this level for two months;
   b) falls to 8% and remains at this level for two months.

2 Explain the concepts of margins and marking to market in futures contracts.

3 A company decides to borrow £3m, at a variable rate of interest, for three months from the beginning of October. It sells six sterling interest rate futures contracts at 92. When the company borrows the actual £3m, at the beginning of October, it is faced with an annual borrowing rate of 12% which remains at this level to the

end of December. Demonstrate how this interest rate futures contract has hedged risk.

4 Explain the difference between an American and a European option and the difference between a call option and a put option.

5 The XYZ company's current share price is £4.50. An investor purchases one October call on XYZ shares from LIFFE, at 38p, which has an exercise price of £4.65. Assuming that this is a European option, explain whether or not the call will be exercised if the XYZ share price on the expiry date of the call option is:
a) £5.30
b) £4.60
c) £4.68
What is the profit, in each of these cases, of the call option writer?

6 A company's April calls have exercise prices of £4.80 and £5.10, with respective option premiums of 35p and 25p.
a) Explain how an investor would establish a bull spread strategy.
b) Explain how the investor would react if in April the company's share price is:
(i) £5.40; (ii) £4.85; (iii) £4.75.

7 Explain why bondholders in a company can be considered as put option writers who have sold a put to the shareholders in the company.

Exercises

1 What are the main weaknesses of a forward contract?

2 The ABC company's current share price is £7.40. An investor purchases from LIFFE, for 29p, one January put on ABC shares at an exercise price of £7.60. Assuming that this is a European option, explain whether or not the put will be exercised if the ABC share price on the expiry date of the put option is:
a) £7.90
b) £7.62
c) £7.42
What is the profit, in each of these cases, of the put option writer?

3 Explain why owning equity in a levered company can be interpreted as share-holders owning a call option.

Endnotes

1. A company can arrange a loan and enter into an FRA with the same bank, if desired. The loan and the FRA are, however, negotiated separately.

2. The margin account normally earns interest. Also the cash flows between the Exchange and the traders are subject to interest rate opportunity cost. This makes the actual analysis of the values involved in futures trading more complex.

3. Note that in the above example a cash settlement was made and no delivery of an 'underlying' asset was required. Alternatively a delivery could have been required of actual time deposits of £500,000, earning the specified interest rate. Those interested in this aspect of interest rate futures are referred to Blake (1990) or Kolb (1988).

4. There are also over-the-counter options which are not initially traded on LIFFE but agreed directly between two parties.

5. Naked positions in the underlying asset are again assumed.

6. Another important instrument used in hedging is a swap agreement. Swap contracts are private agreements between two parties to exchange cash flows over specified time periods in the future. In many respects they are merely a series of forwards contracts. Swaps are negotiated in respect of interest rates, currency and other financial assets.

References

Black, F. and M. Scholes, 'The Pricing of Options and Corporate Liabilities', Journal of Political Economy, 1973

Blake, D., Financial Market Analysis, London, McGraw-Hill, 1990

Cox, J. and M. Rubinstein, 'Option Pricing: A Simplified Approach', Journal of Financial Economics, 1985

Fabozzi, F. and F. Modigliani, Capital Markets: Institutions and Instruments, Englewood Cliffs, Prentice-Hall, 1992

Fuller, R. and J. Farrell, Modern Investments and Security Analysis, New York, McGraw-Hill, 1987

Hull, J., Introduction to Futures and Options Markets, Englewood Cliffs, Prentice-Hall, 1991

Kolb, R., Understanding Futures Markets, Englewood Cliffs, Scott, Foresman and Company, Glenview, Illinois, 1988

Mason, S. and R. Merton, 'The Role of Contingent Claims Analysis in Corporate Finance', in E. Altman and M. Subrahmanyam (Eds.), Recent Advances in Corporate Finance, Homewood, Ill., Richard D. Irwin, 1985

Redhead, K. and S. Hughes, Financial Risk Management, London, Gower, 1988

Rutterford, J., Introduction to Stock Exchange Investments, London, Macmillan, 1993

Smith, C., 'Managing Financial Risk', in D. Chew (Ed.), New Developments in Commercial Banking, Oxford, Blackwell, 1991

17 Review and conclusions

Introduction

The main principles of corporate finance having been presented, this final chapter provides an overall view of their application in terms of ratio analysis. This is followed by a discussion on the alternatives to the main objective of market value maximisation and an overall conclusion.

Ratio analysis

To help obtain a summary view of a company's overall performance a number of ratios, based on a company's income statements and balance sheets, can be specified. Income statements and balance sheets were explained in Chapter 1. As a refresher, the profit and loss account and balance sheets for Hopefully Viable plc are recorded in Tables 17.1 and 17.2 respectively.

Ratios can be divided into five categories:
- liquidity ratios;
- asset management or activity ratios;
- debt management ratios;
- profitability ratios;
- market ratios.

Table 17.1: Hopefully Viable plc: profit and loss account[1]

For the year end 31 December 1994	£m
Turnover	100.00
Cost of sales	(60.00)
Gross profit	40.00
Distribution/administrative expenses	(25.00)
Operating profit: EBIT	15.00
Interest payable	(7.00)
Profit on ordinary activities before tax: EAI	8.00
Tax on ordinary activities	(2.00)
Profit on ordinary activities after tax: EAIT	6.00
Ordinary dividends on equity income	(4.00)
Transferred to reserves	2.00
Dividends per share £4.00m/30m	13.33p
Earnings per share £6.00m/30m	20.00p

[1] Number of shares outstanding: n = 30m

Table 17.2: Hopefully Viable plc: balance sheets

At 31 December 1994	£m
Fixed assets	35.00
Current assets	
Stocks (inventory)	12.00
Debtors (accounts receivable)	20.00
Cash + marketable securities	21.00
	53.00
Total assets	88.00
Current liabilities	
Accounts payable	(20.00)
Other creditors	(10.00)
	(30.00)
Creditors: amounts falling due after more than one year	(15.00)
Total liabilities	(45.00)
Net assets: total assets − total liabilities	43.00
Capital and reserves	
Called up share capital[1]	15.00
Share premium account	9.00
Other reserves	19.00
Shareholders' funds = book value of equity	43.00

[1] 30m ordinary shares at 20p

The main ratios, grouped by category, are defined in Tables 17.3A and 17.3B, together with illustrations of how these ratios are calculated. The illustrations use the information on Hopefully Viable plc reported in Tables 17.1 and 17.2. Most of these ratios have already been introduced in previous chapters.

Normally a given company's ratios are examined through time, in relation to the principal industry in which the company operates. For the most part industry averages are taken as rough measures of the target ratios which a company should be aiming to achieve.

Consider Hopefully Viable plc which has its principal operations in industry x. It is February 1995 and you want to analyse its performance. You have already calculated, in Tables 17.3A and 17.3B, Hopefully Viable's ratios for 1994. You have obtained copies of its accounts for 1992 and 1990 and have calculated the company's, and industry's average, ratios for these periods. The relevant information is reported in Table 17.4.

Hopefully Viable's ratios are examined below, together with a summary discussion of the importance of each category of ratios.

Liquidity ratios

From the discussion on working capital in Chapter 12, the key short-term factors influencing value are liquidity, trade credit and inventories. A reasonable level of liquidity needs to be maintained to avoid short-term financial distress. Too high a level of liquidity implies, however, that a company has too much of its resources

Table 17.3A: Definitions of basic ratios

		Hopefully Viable plc Ratios 1994	

Liquidity ratios

Current ratio:	$\dfrac{\text{Current Assets}}{\text{Current Liabilities}}$	$\dfrac{£53\text{m}}{£30\text{m}}$	$= 1.767$
Quick ratio:	$\dfrac{\text{Current Assets} - \text{Inventory}}{\text{Current Liabilities}}$	$\dfrac{£53\text{m} - £12\text{m}}{£30\text{m}}$	$= 1.367$
Cash ratios:	$\dfrac{\text{Cash} + \text{Marketable Securities}}{\text{Current Assets}}$	$\dfrac{£21\text{m}}{£53\text{m}}$	$= 0.396$
	$\dfrac{\text{Cash} + \text{Marketable Securities}}{\text{Current Liabilities}}$	$\dfrac{£21\text{m}}{£30\text{m}}$	$= 0.700$

Activity ratios

Average collection period:	$\dfrac{\text{Accounts Receivable}}{\text{Sales}}$	$\dfrac{£20\text{m}}{£100\text{m}} \times 365 = 73$ days	
Debtor turnover:	$\dfrac{\text{Sales}}{\text{Accounts Payable}}$	$\dfrac{£100\text{m}}{£20\text{m}}$	$= 5.000$
Inventory turnover:	$\dfrac{\text{Cost of Goods sold}}{\text{Inventory}}$	$\dfrac{£60\text{m}}{£12\text{m}}$	$= 5.000$
Total asset turnover:	$\dfrac{\text{Sales}}{\text{Total Assets}}$	$\dfrac{£100\text{m}}{£88\text{m}}$	$= 1.136$

Cash operating cycle:

$$365\left[\frac{1}{\text{Inventory Turnover}} + \frac{1}{\text{Receivables Turnover}^1} - \frac{1}{\text{Debtor Turnover}}\right] = 365\left[\frac{1}{5.0} + \frac{1}{5.0} - \frac{1}{5.0}\right] = 73 \text{ days}$$

^{1} Receivables Turnover = Sales/Accounts Receivable = £100m ÷ £20m = 5.0

concentrated in short-term cash, marketable securities and other current assets, earning, on average, lower rates of return than on long-term investments.

In Hopefully Viable's case, the current ratio for 1994 is below what is generally argued to be its desired level of 2:1 and the quick ratio is above its desired level of 1:1. However, since 1990 there has been a gradual improvement in both ratios, in terms of Hopefully Viable's ability to bring them towards their industry averages, or target values.

Between 1990 and 1994 the ratio of cash plus marketable securities to current assets has remained approximately equal to the industry average. When this is viewed against the marked improvement in the ratio of cash plus marketable securities to current liabilities, the implication is that Hopefully Viable's working capital position has been improved. The improvement appears to have been achieved through more efficient management of its current liabilities, although, as indicated below, when discussing the cash operating cycle, there is some evidence of more efficient management of current assets.

Activity ratios

Inventory and accounts receivable are important aids in generating sales. Where accounts receivable are concerned, however, a high average collection period has

Table 17.3B: Definitions of basic ratios

		Ratios for Hopefully Viable plc 1994

Debt management ratios

Gross leverage: $\dfrac{\text{Total Debt}}{\text{Total Assets}}$ $\dfrac{\text{£45m}}{\text{£88m}} = 0.511$

Times interest earned: $\dfrac{\text{EBIT}}{\text{Interest}}$ $\dfrac{\text{£15m}}{\text{£7m}} = 2.143$

Fixed charge coverage : $\dfrac{\text{EBIT} + \text{Lease Payments}}{\text{Interest} + \text{Lease Payments}}$ $\dfrac{\text{£15m} + \text{£1m}}{\text{£7m} + \text{£1m}} = 2.000$

Profitability ratios

Net profit margin: $\dfrac{\text{EAIT}}{\text{Sales}}$ $\dfrac{\text{£6m}}{\text{£100m}} = 0.060$

Return on assets: $\dfrac{\text{EAIT}}{\text{Total Assets}}$ $\dfrac{\text{£6m}}{\text{£88m}} = 0.068$

Return on equity: $\dfrac{\text{EAIT}}{\text{Book Value of Equity}}$ $\dfrac{\text{£6m}}{\text{£43m}} = 0.140$

Earnings power: $\dfrac{\text{EBIT}}{\text{Total Assets}}$ $\dfrac{\text{£15m}}{\text{£88m}} = 0.170$

Market ratios

Dividend yield: $\dfrac{\text{Dividends per Share}}{\text{Share Price}}$ $\dfrac{13.33\text{p}}{\text{£3.50}} = 0.038$

Price–earnings ratio: $\dfrac{\text{Share Price}}{\text{Earnings per Share}}$ $\dfrac{\text{£3.50}}{20\text{p}} = 17.500$

[1] Assumes company has off-balance sheet operating lease payments of £1m
[2] Share price 31/12/94: £3.50

opportunity cost implications in terms of interest income foregone on outstanding credit. There are also opportunity costs from holding too much inventory, in terms of financing and stock obsolescence.

The average collection period and inventory turnover are part of the set of asset management, or activity, ratios which measure how a company's resources are being utilised. These two ratios refer to specific short-term assets. The total asset turnover ratio (introduced in Chapter 1) measures a company's overall asset productivity, in terms of its ability to generate sales.

In Hopefully Viable's case, the 1994 average collection period of 73 days is above the average for the industry but has been reduced towards the industry average and, therefore, improved since 1990. Inventory turnover is stable but higher than the industry average. Thus relatively lax trade credit and inventory policies may partly explain why Hopefully Viable's total asset turnover ratio has exceeded the industry average over the five-year period.

Cash operating cycle
Looking at the cash operating cycle, which measures the length of time a company has funds tied up in working capital, Hopefully Viable's liquidity position has improved over the period under analysis. The cash operating cycle has fallen from

Table 17.4: Company and industry ratios

	Hopefully Viable plc			Industry X		
	1994	1992	1990	1994	1992	1990
Current ratio	1.78	1.61	1.49	1.95	2.10	2.10
Quick ratio	1.37	0.95	0.83	1.20	1.29	1.32
Cash ratios:						
$\dfrac{\text{Cash + Marketable Securities}}{\text{Current Assets}}$	0.40	0.38	0.37	0.39	0.38	0.39
$\dfrac{\text{Cash + Marketable Securities}}{\text{Current Liabilities}}$	0.70	0.41	0.45	0.71	0.71	0.70
Average collection period (days)	73	82	90	68	70	72
Debtor turnover	5.00	6.00	6.00	5.00	5.20	5.10
Inventory turnover	5.00	5.00	5.20	4.50	4.50	4.50
Total asset turnover	1.14	1.19	1.20	1.11	1.12	1.11
The cash operating cycle (days)	73	80	85	74	75	76
Gross leverage	0.51	0.64	0.60	0.51	0.52	0.51
Times interest earned	2.14	2.16	2.18	2.17	2.15	2.19
Fixed charge coverage	2.00	2.01	2.11	1.99	2.11	2.11
Net profit margin	6.00%	4.13%	4.79%	5.59%	6.21%	6.62%
Return on assets	6.82%	4.91%	5.75%	6.21%	6.96%	7.35%
Return on equity	13.95%	13.63%	14.37%	12.65%	14.5%	15.00%
Earnings power	17.00%	16.5%	17.00%	16.00%	15.50%	16.10%
Dividend yield	3.80%	4.60%	4.45%	4.50%	4.51%	4.55%
Price–earnings ratio	17.50	14.00	13.50	16.41	17.42	16.50

85 days in 1990 to 73 days in 1994 and is now around the industry average, having previously been above it. This has resulted from two factors. First, improvements in debtor turnover from 6.0 in 1990 to 5.0 in 1994, that is, an improvement in the accounts payable period,[1] which has lengthened from 61 days in 1990 to 73 days in 1994. Second, improvements in the average collection period,[2] that is, a reduction in the average collection period, from 90 days in 1990 to 73 days in 1994.

Debt management ratios

There has been extensive discussion of the impact that debt capital may have on valuation, particularly in Chapter 8 which dealt with the capital structure, valuation debate. Gross leverage is an overall measure of capital structure, with the times interest earned and fixed charge coverage ratios measuring a company's ability to meet its fixed charge obligations out of its annual operating income.

If, because of financial distress and agency costs, the view is taken that there is an optimal capital structure, excessive gross leverage may indicate that a company has not managed to target its debt financing policy as well as it should. This conclusion might also be reflected in low levels of the times interest earned and fixed charge coverage ratios. In consequence a company's performance, in terms of its profitability and market value, might well be below the levels associated with the deployment of optimal investment and financing strategies.

In Hopefully Viable's case, there may well have been concern about its past capital structure. The gross leverage ratio suggests that, up to recently, Hopefully Viable plc pursued an 'excessive' debt financing policy relative to the industry average. Again this may have reinforced concern in the early 1990s about the current and quick ratios, which for that period demonstrate a possible over-reliance on short-term liabilities relative to current assets. On the available evidence the recent improvement in Hopefully Viable's gross leverage (it has moved down towards the industry average) may have come about through a reduction in short-term debt. At this stage, however, further investigation of Hopefully Viable's accounts would be necessary in order to determine how the ratio of long-term debt to equity has behaved.

Although gross leverage before 1994 was above the industry average, the times interest earned and fixed charge coverage ratios were around the industry averages. This would tend to suggest that the company was able to raise debt capital at relatively low rates of interest and/or generate above average operating income. The latter argument is supported by the above average earnings power of Hopefully Viable's assets, which in turn may have been reinforced by the above average asset turnover ratio. Again, however, attention needs to be drawn to the possibility that the asset turnover ratio was unduly influenced by other than average trade credit and inventory policies.

In the above circumstances 'excessive' gross leverage in the early 1990s, combined with an above average collection period, could have exposed Hopefully Viable to financial distress, had economic conditions turned seriously against the company. Such difficulties could have exposed the company to increasing problems of bad debt. It would also have increased the probability of Hopefully Viable not being able to meet its fixed interest charges, if there had been a recession-induced decline in its operating income.

As it is, Hopefully Viable has recently been able to reduce its reliance on debt capital.

Profitability ratios

Recall that profitability ratios were first introduced in Chapter 1, under the DuPont system. Here the return on equity (ROE) is expressed as the product of the return on assets (ROA) and financial leverage (L), that is:

$$ROE = ROA \times L \qquad\qquad (17.1)$$

Leverage, under the DuPont system, is defined as total assets (A) divided by the book value of equity (EQ), that is $L = A/EQ$. The definition of gross leverage (GL) in this chapter's tables is, $GL = $ total debt $\div$ total assets, that is, $GL = (A - EQ)/A$. In terms of the DuPont system:[3]

$$L = 1/(1 - GL) \qquad\qquad (17.2)$$

The idea of the DuPont system is to determine which factors have most influence on the return on equity. In Hopefully Viable's case, ROE has remained relatively stable and close to its industry averages over the period under analysis. As Table 17.4 indicates, however, the company has strengthened its position, especially between 1992 and 1994, by, on the one hand, reducing its financial leverage while, on the other, increasing its return on assets.

This underlying improvement in the company's performance is further under-scored when the way in which the ROA has been increased is examined. From Chapter 1, the ROA can be expressed as the product of the net profit margin (PM) and the total asset turnover ratio (ATR), that is:

$$ROA = PM \times ATR \tag{17.3}$$

Over the period of analysis, while there has been a reduction in the asset turnover ratio, the net profit productivity of sales has increased.

Earnings power and the average interest cost of debt

There is one cautionary point in this relatively strengthened position: the breakeven point between the earnings power of Hopefully Viable's assets and its average interest cost of debt. From Equation 1.14a in Chapter 1, the ROE can be expressed as a function of the corporate tax rate (t_c), the average interest rate on debt (i), financial leverage (L) and earnings power (EP), that is:

$$ROE = (1 - t_c)[i + L(EP - i)] \tag{17.4}$$

Recall that when EP > i, an increase in financial leverage increases the ROE, whereas when EP < i, an increase in financial leverage reduces ROE.

In Hopefully Viable's case, the latest available information (for 1994) indicates that with total debt of £45m (see Table 17.2) and interest charges of £7m (see Table 17.1) the implied average interest rate on debt is: i = £7m/£45m = 0.1556 or 15.56%. Thus although EP > i, the margin over the breakeven point is quite low. At EP − i = 17.00% − 15.56%, the margin is 1.44 percentage points. Thus the ROE may be vulnerable to, for example, future recession-induced falls in Hopefully Viable's EP and/or increases in its average interest rate on debt.

Note that with a tax charge of £2m in 1994 and EAI of £8m (see Table 17.1), the implied corporate tax rate is t_c = £2m/£8m = 25%. In addition, given gross leverage of 0.51, Equation 17.2 produces an L value of L = 1/(1 − .51) = 2.04. Substituting the values of t_c and L into Equation 17.4, together with EP = 0.17 and i = 0.1556, produces the return on equity for 1994 of:

$$ROE = (1 - .25)[0.1556 + 2.04(0.17 - 0.1556)] = 0.1387$$

This is the approximate return on equity for Hopefully Viable plc of 13.95% recorded in Table 17.4.

Market ratios

The two main market ratios which are normally examined are the dividend yield and the price–earnings ratio. Recall from Chapter 3 (on debt and equity valuation) that the PE ratio measures the current price that the market is willing to pay for each £ of current earnings per share. The PE ratio is a measure of the market's anticipation of the future growth prospects of a company.

Recall too that PE ratios and dividend yields tend on average to be negatively correlated. This arises because the expected return on a share includes an income (dividend) yield and a measure of expected capital gains (losses). A low dividend yield indicates that a company may be pursuing a high retentions policy, to exploit 'good' future investment opportunities, as reflected in relatively high PE ratios.

The market's interpretation of the improvements which Hopefully Viable plc has made over the early 1990s appears to have been positive. Hopefully Viable's PE ratio was below the industry's average in 1990 but is now above it in 1994. In addition, if the above interpretation of Hopefully Viable's ratios is accepted, it appears that improvements in working capital and debt management are being accompanied by better investment prospects in the future. The fall in dividend yield, below the industry average, combined with the rise in the company's PE ratio, might suggest that retentions are being used to finance new investment. Alternatively retentions might be being used purely to reduce the level of financial leverage. Again further investigation of Hopefully Viable's accounts would be necessary to clarify this issue.

Subjectivity

Recall from Chapter 3 that financial analysts use a range of techniques to make inferences about the current and future prospects of a company. Ratios are an important element in the fundamental analyst's tool kit, but different analysts may interpret a given company's set of ratios in different ways. In other words analysts' estimates of intrinsic, relative to market, values are based on their specific past experience, intuition and specialist investment appraisal techniques. This leads to variations, across analysts, on buy and sell recommendations with respect to given companies. The important point to note from this is that there is a significant element of subjectivity in interpreting ratios. Thus the above analysis of Hopefully Viable plc is open to debate.

Note also that there are significant limitations to ratio analysis stemming largely from their accounting number, historic cost basis. It is the expected future performance of a company, and how expectations are likely to influence current and future market values, that are of primary interest in corporate finance. Nevertheless ratio analysis can provide an overall view of a company's past ability to maintain 'sound' and relatively consistent investment and financing strategies.

Such strategies are evident when a company's ratios are relatively stable and close to their industry averages and when there is past evidence indicating a company's capability to adjust its ratios rapidly to any new targets implied by unanticipated changes in the economic environment. It is in these senses that the examination of the historic behaviour of a company's ratios can give a reasonably fair picture of how a company is likely to prosper, at least in the short-term future.

It is also important to mention that special statistical techniques, such as discriminant analysis, have been applied to ratios. The main purpose has been to predict corporate failure. Using past data on bankruptcy, critical ratio values are identified. It is argued that it is those existing companies which cannot consistently meet these critical values that are the ones which have the highest probability of failing in the future.

Alternatives to market value maximisation

Most of the analysis in corporate finance is based on the underlying assumption that the management of a company are committed to shareholder objectives. On the premise that these objectives focus on the maximisation of wealth, managerial investment and financing decisions are taken with the aim of maximising the total current market value of a company.

Managerial objectives

In the presence of the divorce of ownership from control, management have the possibility of pursuing their own objectives which may conflict with shareholder wealth maximisation. Managerial objectives are associated with personal power and prestige, managerial income, expense preferences and job security.

In the literature on industrial economics the models which take these types of objectives into account come under the general title of the Managerial Theories of the Firm. The most prominent of these theories are Baumol's (1959) Sales Revenue Maximising Model, Williamson's (1964) Managerial Discretion Model and Marris's (1963) Model of Managerial Enterprise.

These managerial models make different predictions about the behaviour of the firm. They generally conclude, however, that management deviate from the profit maximising objective common to the neoclassical theories of the firm, with the result that firms are of a larger size than would be consistent with managers meeting shareholder objectives. This result holds, on balance, irrespective of whether size is measured in terms of assets, employment or sales revenue. (Behaviouralist theories of the firm, which deal with conflicting objectives within a managerial structure, come to the same general conclusions on size.) To the extent, therefore, that the pursuit of managerial objectives produces these results, the implications must be that sub-optimal investment and financing decisions are being made, from the shareholders' point of view.

Minimum profits constraint

In practical terms it is difficult to determine how far management objectives can deviate from those of shareholders. Managerial theories recognise that management must meet a level of profits which satisfies shareholders and avoids jeopardising management's own job security. This minimum profit constraint, when translated into corporate finance terms, represents a minimum required rate of return on equity.

The constraint is positively influenced by a number of factors. First, by the extent to which shareholders are aware of the potential agency costs associated with information asymmetries and moral hazard. Second, by the concentration of share ownership. Third, by the extent to which information which is publicly available is reflected in the current market prices of financial assets, that is, by the degree of capital market efficiency.

Given the above, the probability that market value maximisation dominates managerial decision making is increased when:
• the required rate of return on equity includes a premium to compensate

shareholders for potential agency costs and/or shareholders require management to adopt information signalling devices;

- financial institutions and managed funds, which aim to maximise their own wealth, have significant shareholdings in individual publicly traded companies; and
- the threat of takeover is an integral mechanism promoting market efficiency.

Shareholder objectives

Shareholders themselves may not fully concentrate on the maximisation of their wealth. They may have philanthropic motives and take into consideration moral and ethical issues in respect of the use of limited resources. The 'green' debate, for example, with its global warming and other environmental aspects may enter shareholder utility functions.

In the final analysis, however, while such objectives are not inconsequential, they are side issues. The great majority of the investing public who own shares directly, or indirectly through managed investment and pension funds, aim to maximise their return, subject to the level of risk they wish to be exposed to. This objective can only be achieved if management make investment and financing decisions which, with appropriate consideration given to the risk–rate-of-return trade-off, maximise the current total market value of the company they operate.

Conclusions

In the preceding chapters the focus of attention has been on large publicly traded companies. It was assumed that their shares and long-term debt were actively traded in efficient stock markets. Thus the expected future outcomes, associated with investment and financing decisions, could be translated into current market prices. In the context of the divorce of ownership from control it was also assumed, subject to the agency problem and the special circumstances of the small privately owned firm, that management acted in the interests of shareholders by maximising the current total market value of a company's assets. It was on this basis that the principles of investment and financing, which are summarised below, were developed.

These principles involve specifying NPV investment appraisal techniques and estimating component and average costs of capital, taking into account risk, tax, financial distress and agency costs. Given the financing decision, the fundamental investment principle is to choose investments on the basis of maximising NPV. Given the investment decision, the fundamental financing principle is to choose the optimal capital structure, if one exists, which minimises the appropriately determined average cost of capital.

The possibilities of investment and financing interactions were also considered. Here, agency costs, particularly relating to the debt financing decision, have an important impact on value in terms of the asset substitution and underinvestment problems and in terms of investments in tangible and intangible assets.

The general principles of investment and financing apply to all aspects of corporate finance, for example, short-term working capital, longer-term acquisition and reorganisation activities and international operations, including exposure to foreign exchange risk and foreign project investment. All of the decisions in these areas are made with the aim of maximising the current total market value of a company.

The preceding chapters have also demonstrated that the role and management of risk is central to the development of optimal investment and financing strategies. In general terms the CAPM provides a simple but very powerful base for analysing the risk–rate-of-return trade-off.

Where risk management principles are concerned, these can be applied in terms of portfolio theory and its risk diversification objectives, and in terms of risk hedging. Risk hedging is achieved by matching the maturity structure of assets and liabilities or by using derivatives: forwards, futures and options.

It is the tension between the desire to achieve higher returns from investment and financing and the need to control risk that is one of the major factors continuing to motivate the study and application of corporate finance. The other primary factors are the controversies regarding the effects that the capital structure and dividend decisions have on valuation.

Questions

1 What non-value-maximising objectives do management tend to pursue?

2 What factors are likely to limit management's ability to pursue their own objectives?

Endnotes

1. The accounts payable period is equal to

$$\frac{\text{Accounts Payable}}{\text{Sales}} \times 365$$

or 365(1/Debtor Turnover). In 1994, for example, the accounts payable period for Hopefully Viable is 365(1/5) = 73 days.

2. In addition to the average collection period on accounts receivable, the average period on accounts payable may convey useful information. If, in general, this ratio is above the industry average, it suggests that a company is unduly delaying payments for goods and services received. This could jeopardise future supplies to the company and, in a general recession, cause creditors to activate bankruptcy proceedings. In Hopefully Viable's case, debtor turnover was above the industry average, implying that the average payment period was below the industry average. In 1990, for example, with Hopefully Viable's debtor turnover equal to 6.0, its average payment period was 365(1/debtor turnover) = 61 days. For the industry, the average payment period was 365(1/5.10) = 72 days.

3. To obtain the relationship $L = 1/(1 - GL)$, consider the definition of $L = A/EQ$. A is composed of debt (D) and equity (EQ). Thus with $A = D + EQ$, $EQ = A - D$. Therefore,

$$L = \frac{A}{A - D}$$

Dividing the right-hand side of this equation, above and below, by A yields:

$$L = \frac{(A/A)}{(A/A) - (D/A)} = \frac{1}{1 - GL}$$

References

Altman, E., 'Financial Ratios, Discriminant Analysis and the Prediction of Corporate Bankruptcy', Journal of Finance, 1968

Baumol, W., *Business Behaviour, Value and Growth*, London, Macmillan, 1959

Cyert, R. and J. March, *A Behaviouralist Theory of the Firm*, Englewood Cliffs, Prentice-Hall, 1963

Foster, G., *Financial Statement Analysis*, Englewood Cliffs, Prentice-Hall, 1986

Johnson, W., 'The Cross-sectional Stability of Financial Ratio Patterns', Journal of Financial and Quantitative Analysis, 1979

Marris, R., 'A Model of Managerial Enterprise', Quarterly Journal of Economics, 1963

Williamson, O., *The Economics of Discretionary Behaviour: Managerial Objectives in a Theory of the Firm*, Englewood Cliffs, Prentice Hall, 1964

General Appendices

Appendix A

Table A.1: Future value interest factor: $FVIF_{t,r} = (1 + r)^t$

t\r	1%	2%	3%	4%	5%	6%	7%	8%	9%	10%	12%	15%	20%	25%	30%	35%
1	1.010	1.020	1.030	1.040	1.050	1.060	1.070	1.080	1.090	1.100	1.120	1.150	1.200	1.250	1.300	1.350
2	1.020	1.040	1.061	1.082	1.102	1.124	1.145	1.166	1.188	1.210	1.254	1.322	1.440	1.562	1.690	1.822
3	1.030	1.061	1.093	1.125	1.158	1.191	1.225	1.260	1.295	1.331	1.405	1.521	1.728	1.953	2.197	2.460
4	1.041	1.082	1.126	1.170	1.216	1.262	1.311	1.360	1.412	1.464	1.574	1.749	2.074	2.441	2.856	3.321
5	1.051	1.104	1.159	1.217	1.276	1.338	1.403	1.469	1.539	1.611	1.762	2.011	2.488	3.052	3.713	4.484
6	1.062	1.126	1.194	1.265	1.340	1.419	1.501	1.587	1.677	1.772	1.974	2.313	2.986	3.815	4.827	6.053
7	1.072	1.149	1.230	1.316	1.407	1.504	1.606	1.714	1.828	1.949	2.211	2.660	3.583	4.768	6.275	8.172
8	1.083	1.172	1.267	1.369	1.477	1.594	1.718	1.851	1.993	2.144	2.476	3.059	4.300	5.960	8.157	11.032
9	1.094	1.195	1.305	1.423	1.551	1.689	1.838	1.999	2.172	2.358	2.773	3.518	5.160	7.451	10.604	14.894
10	1.105	1.219	1.344	1.480	1.629	1.791	1.967	2.159	2.367	2.594	3.106	4.046	6.192	9.313	13.786	20.106
11	1.116	1.243	1.384	1.539	1.710	1.898	2.105	2.332	2.580	2.853	3.479	4.652	7.430	11.642	17.921	27.144
12	1.127	1.268	1.426	1.601	1.796	2.012	2.252	2.518	2.813	3.138	3.896	5.350	8.916	14.552	23.298	36.644
13	1.138	1.294	1.469	1.665	1.886	2.133	2.410	2.720	3.066	3.452	4.363	6.153	10.699	18.190	30.287	49.469
14	1.149	1.319	1.513	1.732	1.980	2.261	2.579	2.937	3.342	3.797	4.887	7.076	12.839	22.737	39.373	66.784
15	1.161	1.346	1.558	1.801	2.079	2.397	2.759	3.172	3.642	4.177	5.474	8.137	15.407	28.422	51.185	90.158
16	1.173	1.373	1.605	1.873	2.183	2.540	2.952	3.426	3.970	4.595	6.130	9.358	18.488	35.527	66.541	121.71
17	1.184	1.400	1.653	1.948	2.292	2.693	3.159	3.700	4.328	5.054	6.866	10.761	22.186	44.409	86.503	164.31
18	1.196	1.428	1.702	2.026	2.407	2.854	3.380	3.996	4.717	5.560	7.690	12.375	26.623	55.511	112.45	221.82
19	1.208	1.457	1.753	2.107	2.527	3.026	3.616	4.316	5.142	6.116	8.613	14.232	31.948	69.389	146.19	299.46
20	1.220	1.486	1.806	2.191	2.653	3.207	3.870	4.661	5.604	6.727	9.646	16.366	38.337	86.736	190.05	404.27
21	1.232	1.516	1.860	2.279	2.786	3.399	4.140	5.034	6.109	7.400	10.804	18.821	46.005	108.42	247.06	545.76
22	1.245	1.546	1.916	2.370	2.925	3.603	4.430	5.436	6.658	8.140	12.100	21.644	55.205	135.53	321.18	736.78
23	1.257	1.577	1.974	2.465	3.071	3.820	4.740	5.871	7.258	8.954	13.552	24.891	66.247	169.41	417.53	994.65
24	1.270	1.608	2.033	2.563	3.225	4.049	5.072	6.341	7.911	9.850	15.178	28.625	79.496	211.76	542.79	1342.8
25	1.282	1.641	2.094	2.666	3.386	4.292	5.427	6.848	8.623	10.834	17.000	32.918	95.395	264.70	705.63	1812.8
30	1.348	1.811	2.427	3.243	4.322	5.743	7.612	10.062	13.267	17.449	29.960	66.210	237.37	807.79	2619.9	8128.4

Table A.2: Present value interest factor: $PVIF_{t,r} = 1/(1 + r)^t$

t \ r	1%	2%	3%	4%	5%	6%	7%	8%	9%	10%	11%	12%	15%	20%	25%	30%	35%
1	.990	.980	.971	.962	.952	.943	.935	.926	.917	.909	.90	.893	.870	.833	.800	.769	.741
2	.980	.961	.943	.925	.907	.890	.873	.857	.842	.826	.812	.797	.756	.694	.640	.592	.549
3	.971	.942	.915	.889	.864	.840	.816	.794	.772	.751	.731	.712	.658	.579	.512	.455	.406
4	.961	.924	.888	.855	.823	.792	.763	.735	.708	.683	.659	.636	.572	.482	.410	.350	.301
5	.951	.906	.863	.822	.784	.747	.713	.681	.650	.621	.593	.567	.497	.402	.328	.269	.223
6	.942	.888	.837	.790	.746	.705	.666	.630	.596	.564	.535	.507	.432	.335	.262	.207	.165
7	.933	.871	.813	.760	.711	.665	.623	.583	.547	.513	.482	.452	.376	.279	.210	.159	.122
8	.923	.853	.789	.731	.677	.627	.582	.540	.502	.467	.434	.404	.327	.233	.168	.123	.091
9	.914	.837	.766	.703	.645	.592	.544	.500	.460	.424	.391	.361	.284	.194	.134	.094	.067
10	.905	.820	.744	.676	.614	.558	.508	.463	.422	.386	.352	.322	.247	.162	.107	.073	.050
11	.896	.804	.722	.650	.585	.527	.475	.429	.388	.350	.317	.287	.215	.135	.086	.056	.037
12	.887	.789	.701	.625	.557	.497	.444	.397	.356	.319	.286	.257	.187	.112	.069	.043	.027
13	.879	.773	.681	.601	.530	.469	.415	.368	.326	.290	.258	.229	.163	.093	.055	.033	.020
14	.870	.758	.661	.577	.505	.442	.388	.340	.299	.263	.232	.205	.141	.078	.044	.025	.015
15	.861	.743	.642	.555	.481	.417	.362	.315	.275	.239	.209	.183	.123	.065	.035	.020	.011
16	.853	.728	.623	.534	.458	.394	.339	.292	.252	.218	.188	.163	.107	.054	.028	.015	.008
17	.844	.714	.605	.513	.436	.371	.317	.270	.231	.198	.170	.146	.093	.045	.023	.012	.006
18	.836	.700	.587	.494	.416	.350	.296	.250	.212	.180	.153	.130	.081	.038	.018	.009	.005
19	.828	.686	.570	.475	.396	.331	.277	.232	.194	.164	.138	.116	.070	.031	.014	.007	.003
20	.820	.673	.554	.456	.377	.312	.258	.215	.178	.149	.124	.104	.061	.026	.012	.005	.002
21	.811	.660	.538	.439	.359	.294	.242	.199	.164	.135	.112	.093	.053	.022	.009	.004	.002
22	.803	.647	.522	.422	.342	.278	.226	.184	.150	.123	.101	.083	.046	.018	.007	.003	.002
23	.795	.634	.507	.406	.326	.262	.211	.170	.138	.112	.091	.074	.040	.015	.006	.002	.001
24	.788	.622	.492	.390	.310	.247	.197	.158	.126	.102	.082	.066	.035	.013	.005	.002	.001
25	.780	.610	.478	.375	.295	.233	.184	.146	.116	.092	.074	.059	.030	.010	.004	.002	.001
30	.742	.552	.412	.308	.231	.174	.131	.099	.075	.057	.044	.033	.015	.004	.001	.001	.001

Table A.3: Present value interest factor of an annuity: $PVIFA_{t,r} = \left[\dfrac{1 - (1+r)^{-t}}{r}\right]$

t \ r	1%	2%	3%	4%	5%	6%	7%	8%	9%	10%	11%	12%	15%	20%	25%	30%	35%
1	.990	.980	.971	.962	.952	.943	.935	.926	.917	.909	.901	.893	.870	.833	.800	.769	.741
2	1.970	1.942	1.913	1.886	1.859	1.833	1.808	1.783	1.759	1.736	1.713	1.690	1.626	1.528	1.440	1.361	1.289
3	2.941	2.884	2.829	2.775	2.723	2.673	2.624	2.577	2.531	2.487	2.444	2.402	2.283	2.106	1.952	1.816	1.696
4	3.902	3.808	3.717	3.630	3.546	3.465	3.387	3.312	3.240	3.170	3.102	3.037	2.855	2.589	2.362	2.166	1.997
5	4.853	4.713	4.580	4.452	4.329	4.212	4.100	3.993	3.890	3.791	3.696	3.605	3.352	2.991	2.689	2.436	2.220
6	5.795	5.601	5.417	5.242	5.076	4.917	4.767	4.623	4.486	4.355	4.231	4.111	3.784	3.326	2.951	2.643	2.385
7	6.728	6.472	6.230	6.002	5.786	5.582	5.389	5.206	5.033	4.868	4.712	4.564	4.160	3.605	3.161	2.802	2.508
8	7.652	7.326	7.020	6.733	6.463	6.210	5.971	5.747	5.535	5.335	5.146	4.968	4.487	3.837	3.329	2.925	2.598
9	8.566	8.162	7.786	7.435	7.108	6.802	6.515	6.247	5.995	5.759	5.537	5.328	4.772	4.031	3.463	3.019	2.665
10	9.471	8.983	8.530	8.111	7.722	7.360	7.024	6.710	6.418	6.145	5.889	5.650	5.019	4.192	3.570	3.092	2.715
11	10.368	9.787	9.253	8.760	8.306	7.887	7.499	7.139	6.805	6.495	6.207	5.938	5.234	4.327	3.656	3.147	2.752
12	11.255	10.575	9.954	9.385	8.863	8.384	7.943	7.536	7.161	6.814	6.492	6.194	5.421	4.439	3.725	3.190	2.779
13	12.134	11.348	10.635	9.986	9.394	8.853	8.358	7.904	7.487	7.013	6.750	6.424	5.583	4.533	3.780	3.223	2.799
14	13.004	12.106	11.296	10.563	9.899	9.295	8.745	8.244	7.786	7.367	6.982	6.628	5.724	4.611	3.824	3.249	2.814
15	13.865	12.849	11.938	11.118	10.380	9.712	9.108	8.560	8.061	7.606	7.191	6.811	5.847	4.675	3.859	3.268	2.825
16	14.718	13.578	12.561	11.652	10.838	10.106	9.447	8.851	8.313	7.824	7.379	6.974	5.954	4.730	3.887	3.283	2.834
17	15.562	14.292	13.166	12.166	11.274	10.477	9.763	9.122	8.544	8.022	7.549	7.120	6.047	4.775	3.910	3.295	2.840
18	16.398	14.992	13.754	12.659	11.690	10.828	10.059	9.372	8.756	8.201	7.702	7.250	6.128	4.812	3.928	3.304	2.844
19	17.226	15.679	14.324	13.134	12.085	11.158	10.336	9.604	8.950	8.365	7.839	7.366	6.198	4.843	3.942	3.311	2.848
20	18.046	16.352	14.878	13.590	12.462	11.470	10.594	9.818	9.129	8.514	7.963	7.469	6.259	4.870	3.954	3.316	2.850
21	18.857	17.011	15.415	14.029	12.821	11.764	10.836	10.017	9.292	8.649	8.075	7.562	6.312	4.891	3.963	3.320	2.852
22	19.661	17.658	15.937	14.451	13.163	12.042	11.061	10.210	9.442	8.772	8.176	7.645	6.359	4.909	3.970	3.323	2.853
23	20.456	18.292	16.444	14.857	13.489	12.303	11.272	10.371	9.580	8.883	8.266	7.718	6.399	4.925	3.976	3.325	2.854
24	21.244	18.914	16.936	15.247	13.799	12.550	11.469	10.529	9.707	8.985	8.348	7.784	6.434	4.937	3.981	3.327	2.855
25	22.023	19.524	17.413	15.622	14.094	12.783	11.654	10.675	9.823	9.077	8.422	7.843	6.464	4.948	3.985	3.329	2.856
30	25.808	22.396	19.601	17.292	15.373	13.765	12.409	11.258	10.274	9.427	8.694	8.055	6.566	4.979	3.995	3.332	2.857

Table A.4: Future value interest factor of an annuity: $\text{FVIFA}_{t,r} = \left[\dfrac{(1+r)^t - 1}{r}\right]$

t\r	1%	2%	3%	4%	5%	6%	7%	8%	9%	10%	12%	15%	20%	25%	30%	35%
1	1.000	1.000	1.000	1.000	1.000	1.000	1.000	1.000	1.000	1.000	1.000	1.000	1.000	1.000	1.000	1.000
2	2.010	2.020	2.030	2.040	2.050	2.060	2.070	2.080	2.090	2.100	2.120	2.150	2.200	2.250	2.300	2.350
3	3.030	3.060	3.091	3.122	3.152	3.184	3.215	3.246	3.278	3.310	3.374	3.472	3.640	3.813	3.990	4.172
4	4.060	4.122	4.184	4.246	4.310	4.375	4.440	4.506	4.573	4.641	4.779	4.993	5.368	5.766	6.187	6.633
5	5.101	5.204	5.309	5.416	5.526	5.637	5.751	5.867	5.985	6.105	6.353	6.742	7.442	8.207	9.043	9.954
6	6.152	6.308	6.468	6.633	6.802	6.975	7.153	7.336	7.523	7.716	8.115	8.754	9.930	11.259	12.756	14.438
7	7.214	7.434	7.662	7.898	8.142	8.394	8.654	8.923	9.200	9.487	10.089	11.067	12.916	15.073	17.583	20.492
8	8.286	8.583	8.892	9.214	9.549	9.897	10.260	10.637	11.028	11.436	12.300	13.727	16.499	19.842	23.858	28.664
9	9.368	9.755	10.159	10.583	11.027	11.491	11.978	12.488	13.021	13.579	14.776	16.786	20.799	25.802	32.015	39.696
10	10.462	10.950	11.464	12.006	12.578	13.181	13.816	14.487	15.193	15.937	17.549	20.304	25.959	33.253	42.619	54.590
11	11.567	12.169	12.808	13.486	14.207	14.972	15.784	16.645	17.560	18.531	20.655	24.349	32.150	42.566	56.405	74.696
12	12.682	13.412	14.192	15.026	15.917	16.870	17.888	18.977	20.141	21.384	24.133	29.001	39.580	54.208	74.326	101.84
13	13.809	14.680	15.618	16.627	17.713	18.882	20.141	21.495	22.953	24.523	28.029	34.352	48.496	68.760	97.624	138.48
14	14.947	15.974	17.086	18.292	19.598	21.015	22.550	24.215	26.019	27.975	32.392	40.504	59.196	86.949	127.91	187.95
15	16.097	17.293	18.599	20.023	21.578	23.276	25.129	27.152	29.361	31.772	37.280	47.580	72.035	109.69	167.29	254.74
16	17.258	18.639	20.157	21.824	23.657	25.672	27.888	30.324	33.003	35.949	42.753	55.717	87.442	138.11	218.47	344.90
17	18.430	20.012	21.761	23.697	25.840	28.213	30.840	33.750	36.973	40.544	48.883	65.075	105.93	173.64	285.01	466.61
18	19.614	21.412	23.414	25.645	28.132	30.905	33.999	37.450	41.301	45.599	55.749	75.836	128.12	218.05	371.51	630.92
19	20.811	22.840	25.117	27.671	30.539	33.760	37.379	41.446	46.018	51.158	63.439	88.211	154.74	273.56	483.97	852.74
20	22.019	24.297	26.870	29.778	33.066	36.785	40.995	45.762	51.159	57.274	72.252	102.44	186.69	342.95	630.16	1152.2
21	23.239	25.783	28.676	31.969	35.719	39.992	44.865	50.422	56.764	64.002	81.598	118.81	225.02	429.68	820.20	1556.5
22	24.471	27.299	30.536	34.248	38.505	43.392	49.005	55.456	62.872	71.402	92.502	137.63	271.03	538.10	1067.3	2102.2
23	25.716	28.845	32.452	36.618	41.430	46.995	53.435	60.893	69.531	79.542	104.60	159.27	326.23	673.63	1388.4	2839.0
24	26.973	30.421	34.426	39.082	44.501	50.815	58.176	66.764	76.789	88.496	118.15	184.17	392.48	843.03	1806.0	3833.7
25	28.243	32.030	36.459	41.645	47.726	54.864	63.248	73.105	84.699	98.346	133.33	212.79	471.98	1054.8	2348.8	5176.4
30	34.784	40.567	47.575	56.084	66.438	79.057	94.459	113.28	136.31	164.49	241.33	434.74	1181.9	3227.2	8729.8	23221.0

Appendix B: Some technical issues

This appendix presents some very basic revision on those technical and quantitative issues that are an important feature of this book. The revision covers the concept of summations, the reciprocal of a number, a linear equation and some basic rules on statistics.

Summations

A summation is simply a way of summarising an expression of a series of numbers which are added to each other. Summations are used extensively in Chapter 2, which deals with the time value of money. If there is a series of n numbers, each represented by an X, and the sum of the series is required, then the sum, S, is:

$$S = X_1 + X_2 + X_3 + \ldots + X_n$$

Using a summation, this rather long expression can be simplified and written as:

$$S = \sum_{t=1}^{n} X_t$$

This states that the X's should be summed (Σ), or added, over the X values with the subscripts $t = 1, 2, \ldots, n$. If, for example, $n = 6$, that is, there are six X values to be added, then:

$$S = \sum_{t=1}^{6} X_t = X_1 + X_2 + X_3 + \ldots + X_6$$

If each X has the following values, $X_1 = 2, X_2 = 4, X_3 = 5, X_4 = 1, X_5 = 10, X_6 = 7$, then

$$S = \sum_{t=1}^{6} X_t = 2 + 4 + 5 + 1 + 10 + 7 = 29$$

If only the last three numbers were required to be added, then the summation would be specified as:

$$S = \sum_{t=4}^{6} X_t = X_4 + X_5 + X_6 = 1 + 10 + 7 = 18$$

Reciprocals

Another technical aspect of Chapter 2 relates to taking the reciprocal, or the inverse, of a number. In technical terms the reciprocal of a given number is one over the number in question. If, for example, you want the reciprocal of 20, you need to divide 1 by 20, that is:

$$\frac{1}{20} = 0.05$$

Sometimes you might want the reciprocal of a number which is being squared. Consider, for example, 10 squared, that is, $(10)^2$ or verbally 10 to the power of 2. If you want the reciprocal of this number it is:

$$\frac{1}{10^2} = \frac{1}{100} = 0.01$$

Mathematically, this can be written in a different way, as $(10)^{-2}$, that is, 10 to the power of minus 2. Thus

$$(10)^{-2} = \frac{1}{(10)^2} = \frac{1}{100} = 0.01$$

If you had a number which you were cubing, say 5, then the cube of 5 is simply $5 \times 5 \times 5 = 125$. Notationally this can be written as $(5)^3$, that is, 5 to the power of 3. If you wanted the reciprocal of this number, it would be 1 divided by 5 cubed, that is, 1 divided by 5 to the power of 3. That is:

$$\frac{1}{(5)^3} = \frac{1}{125} = 0.008$$

This could alternatively be written as 5 to the power of minus 3, that is:

$$(5)^{-3} = \frac{1}{(5)^3} = \frac{1}{125} = 0.008$$

In Chapter 2, when discounting is encountered, cash flows are discounted by dividing a cash flow by 1 plus the rate of interest, r, raised to a power. Thus a cash flow to be received three years from now, X_3, is divided by $(1 + r)$ to the power of 3, that is:

$$\frac{X_3}{(1 + r)^3}$$

Using the above, this can be written as:

$$\frac{X_3}{(1 + r)^3} = X_3(1 + r)^{-3}$$

Similarly if a cash flow, X_7, is to be received seven years from now and is being discounted, the discount factor is

$$\frac{1}{(1 + r)^7} = (1 + r)^{-7}$$

Applying this to the cash flow:

$$\frac{X_7}{(1 + r)^7} = X_7(1 + r)^{-7}$$

In other words the cash flow to be received in seven years' time can either be divided by $(1 + r)$ to the power of 7, or multiplied by $(1 + r)$ to the power of minus 7.

Generalising, a cash flow to be received t periods from now is discounted by dividing X_t by $(1 + r)^t$, that is:

$$\frac{X_t}{(1 + r)^t} = X_t(1 + r)^{-t}$$

A linear equation

The equation of a straight line relates one variable to another. The form that everyone should be familiar with is,

Y = a + bX,

where Y and X are variables and a and b are parameters, that is constants, or fixed values. The intercept of this equation is represented by 'a' and gives the value of Y when X = 0, that is

Y = a + b(0) = a

Diagrammatically, if Y and X are graphed as in Figure B.1, the intercept is the point where the equation cuts the Y axis. If, for example, a = 4 and b = 2, then when

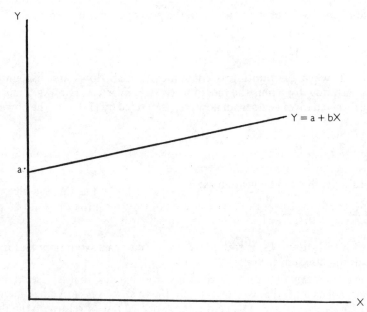

Figure B.1   A linear equation

X = 0, Y = 4 + 2(0) = 4 = a. The slope of the equation is given by 'b' and measures how a small change in X causes Y to change. Consider the above example, where a = 4 and b = 2, then:

$$Y = 4 + 2X$$

Assume that initially X = 6, then the Y value is:

$$Y = 4 + 2(6) = 16$$

Next assume that the X value rises by one unit, from X = 6 to X = 7. Then the Y value becomes:

$$Y = 4 + 2(7) = 18$$

In other words Y has increased by two units, from Y = 16 to Y = 18, as a result of a one unit change in X. This change is measured by 'b', the slope coefficient which, in this example, is b = 2.

Assume, for example, that the change in Y is required, resulting as a consequence of a rise in X from 29 to 30. This is automatically measured by the slope coefficient b = 2. That is, when X = 29,

$$Y = 4 + 2(29) = 4 + 58 = 62$$

When X = 30,

$$Y = 4 + 2(30) = 4 + 60 = 64$$

Therefore, the change in Y is equal to 64 − 62 = 2 = b.

In introductory corporate finance two simple linear equations occur regularly: the risk–rate-of-return trade-off of the Capital Asset Pricing Model, first encountered in Chapter 4, and the cost of capital functions which are a prominent feature of Chapter 8.

The capital asset pricing model

In this case the relationship between the expected rate of return on a share (the Y variable) is expressed as a linear function of a measure of risk (the X variable). Specifically

$$E(r_i) = r_f + [E(r_m) - r_f]\beta_i$$

where $E(r_i)$ is the expected rate of return on the ith share (the Y variable) and β_i is a measure of the ith share's risk (the X variable).

The intercept, that is, the 'a' coefficient, is what is known as the risk-free rate of interest: $a = r_f$. It measures the expected rate of return on the ith share when this share has no risk, that is, when $\beta_i = 0$. In other words:

$$E(r_i) = r_f + [E(r_m) - r_f](0) = r_f = \text{'a'}$$

The slope of the relationship, that is, the 'b' coefficient, $b = [E(r_m) - r_f]$, measures how the expected rate of return on the ith share changes, that is, rises (falls) as a result of a small change, that is, rise (fall), in the ith share's risk. A small increase in risk, that is, a small increase in β_i, causes the expected rate of return on the share to rise by an amount equal to $b = [E(r_m) - r_f]$. As indicated in Chapter 4, this slope measures what is known as the market risk premium, that is, the difference between the expected rate of return on the market, $E(r_m)$, minus the risk-free rate of interest, r_f.

The cost of capital

One of the important cost of capital relationships in Chapter 8 expresses the cost of equity capital, r_e (the Y variable), as a linear function of a company's debt:equity ratio, B/S (the X variable). Specifically,

$$r_e = r_a + (r_a - r_d)B/S$$

The intercept term, the 'a' coefficient, measures the cost of equity capital when there is no debt in a company's capital structure, that is, when $B = 0$ and, therefore, $B/S = 0$. In this case the equity cost of capital is equal to the average cost of capital, r_a, that is:

$$r_e = r_a + (r_a - r_d)(0) = r_a = \text{'a'}$$

The slope coefficient measures the impact that a small change in capital structure, for example a small increase in debt relative to equity, has on the cost of equity capital. In the case of a small increase in the debt:equity ratio, a small rise in B relative to S increases the size of B/S. This causes r_e to rise by an amount equal to $(r_a - r_d) = \text{'b'}$.

In this formulation of the cost of capital relationship, the slope coefficient is measured by the difference between the average cost of capital (r_a) and the cost of debt capital (r_d).

Some statistical expressions

In Chapter 4, on Modern Portfolio Theory and the Capital Asset Pricing Model, the main technical issues involve variances. There are three basic rules in using variances.

First, the variance of a constant, or fixed number, is zero since by definition a constant cannot vary. Thus if 'a' is a constant:

$$\text{Var}(a) = 0$$

Second, while the variance of a constant by itself is zero, the variance of a constant times a variable, for example the variance of aX, becomes:

$$\text{Var}(aX) = a^2\text{Var}(X)$$

Note that in notation form a variance is represented by σ^2. Its standard deviation, which is the square root of the variance, is $\sigma = \sqrt{\sigma^2}$.

Third, if X and Y are two random variables, then the variance of $X + Y$ is equal to the variance of X plus the variance of Y plus twice the co-variance of X and Y. Notationally,

$$Var(X + Y) = Var(X) + Var(Y) + 2Cov(XY)$$

The co-variance is a key element in portfolio analysis. The co-variance measures the degree of association between two variables, a positive co-variance indicating that high values of one variable are associated with high values of the other variable; or that low values of one variable are associated with low values of the other variable.

In terms of the share prices of two companies, a positive co-variance would indicate that when the price of one company's shares is relatively high, the price of the other company's shares will also be relatively high. Should the price of one company's shares fall to a relatively low level, the implication is that the share price of the other company will have fallen to a relatively low level as well.

A negative co-variance indicates that high (low) values of one variable are associated with low (high) values of another variable.

The co-variance of two variables is unbounded, that is, it has no upper or lower limit. By standardising the co-variance, that is, by dividing it by the product of the standard deviations of the two variables in question, the correlation coefficient is obtained:

$$Cor(XY) = \frac{Cov(XY)}{\sigma_x \sigma_y}$$

The correlation coefficient between two variables lies between -1 and $+1$.

If, for two variables X and Y, $Cor(XY) = 1$, this indicates that X and Y are perfectly positively correlated. The implication is that increases (decreases) in one variable are exactly matched by increases (decreases) in the other. If $Cor(XY) = -1$, the variables are perfectly negatively correlated, indicating that increases (decreases) in one variable are exactly matched (or more appropriately exactly offset) by decreases (increases) in the other variable. If $Cor(XY) = 0$, then the implication is that there is no statistical relationship between the two variables in question. In the latter case a movement in one variable will not in any way be associated with a movement in another. A good illustration of this is in relation to a variable and a constant. The correlation between a single variable and a constant must be zero since, by definition, the variable's values can change but the constant's cannot.

As explained in Chapter 4, the key to diversification of the risk of a portfolio lies in the fact that the prices, or rates of return, between shares are less than perfectly positively correlated, so that a change in the price of one share is not exactly matched by the change in the price of another.

The above rules of variances are applied in Chapter 4 to the determination of the risk of a two-asset portfolio. With the rate of return on a share representing a random variable, the return on a portfolio (r_p) is expressed as a simple weighted average of the returns on the two assets (1 and 2) comprising the portfolio. Thus,

$$r_p = w_1 r_1 + w_2 r_2$$

where w_1 represents the proportion of wealth invested in asset 1 and w_2 the proportion of wealth invested in asset 2, $w_1 + w_2 = 1.0$. These proportions are initially held fixed, therefore they represent constants. Hence in taking the variance of the portfolio, given the above rules,

$$Var(r_p) = (w_1)^2 Var(r_1) + (w_2^2)Var(r_2) + 2(w_1 w_2)Cov(1,2).$$

Since,

$$Cor(1,2) = \frac{Cov(1,2)}{\sigma_1 \sigma_2}$$

$$Cov(1,2) = \sigma_1 \sigma_2 Cor(1,2)$$

Substituting, for the co-variance, into the above expression for the variance of the portfolio, gives:

$$\sigma_p^2 = (w_1)^2 \sigma_1^2 + (w_2)^2 \sigma_2^2 + 2\sigma_1 \sigma_2 (w_1 w_2) Cor(1,2)$$

The risk of the portfolio is then defined in terms of its standard deviation of returns, that is:

$$\sigma_p = \sqrt{(w_1)^2 \sigma_1^2 + (w_2)^2 \sigma_2^2 + 2\sigma_1 \sigma_2 (w_1 w_2) Cor(1,2)}$$

Appendix C:
Answers to questions

Chapter 1

1 In terms of their economic life there are two broad categories of assets: long-term assets and short-term, or current assets. Long-term assets consist of physical plant and equipment, etc., while current assets consist of inventories, cash and marketable securities and accounts receivable. Assets can also be classified as tangible and intangible. Intangible assets are related to goodwill and represent value which is created by investments in, for example, education and training and R and D.

2 Gross profits are equal to turnover less the cost of sales. Operating income is equal to gross profits less distribution and other expenses. It is from operating income, or earnings before interest and taxes, that interest payments on debt are made. Since interest payments on debt are tax deductible, the amount of tax a company is liable to is determined on the basis of operating income, net or interest payments. Operating income less both interest and tax payments defines earnings after interest and taxes. EAIT belong to the shareholders of a company.

3 While EAIT are owned by shareholders, management are given discretion over the amount of EAIT they pay out to shareholders as dividends and the amount they retain for investment. The retention ratio, b, measures the proportion of EAIT which are retained by a company. The payout ratio, $1 - b$, measures the proportion of EAIT which are paid out in dividends.

4 a) EBIT = £250m − £100m − £50m = £100m
   b) EAIT = £100m − £15m − £37m = £48m, thus the payout ratio is: $1 - b$ = £19.20m/£48m = 0.4 or 40%
   c) Since $1 - b$ = 0.4, b = 0.6 or 60%
   d) EPS = EAIT/n = £48m/100m = 48p
   e) d = £19.20m/100m = 19.2p

5 a) Net assets = total assets − total liabilities
   total assets = £600m + £400m = £1000m
   total liabilities = £300m + £620m = £920m
   Thus, net assets = £1000m − £920m = £80m

   b) Net working capital = current assets − current liabilities
   $$= £400m - £100m = £300m$$
   c) Net assets = the book value of equity (EQ) = shareholders' funds = £80m.
   EAIT = £70m − £30m − £20m = £20m
   Total assets, A = £1000m
   ROE = EAIT/EQ = £20m/£80m = 0.25 or 25%
   ROA = EAIT/A = £20m/£1000m = 0.02 or 2%

d)

A/EQ = £1000m/£80m = 12.5

This ratio represents one of the ways of measuring financial leverage, that is, the use of debt financing relative to equity financing. In this case the ratio measures the book value of debt + the book value of equity:the book value of equity.

6 a)   From the answers to question 5,

L = A/EQ = 12.5 and ROA = 0.02

thus

ROE = ROA × L = 12.5 × 0.02 = 0.25 or 25%

b)   The net profit margin is:

PM = EAIT/turnover = £20m/£200m = 0.10

The asset turnover ratio is:

ATR = Turnover/A = £200m/£1000m = 0.2

Thus

ROA = PM × ATR = 0.10(0.2) = 0.02, or 2%.

c)

EP = EBIT/A = £70m/£1000m = 0.07 or 7%

Since EQ = £80m and A = £1000m, the book value of debt is A − EQ = £1000m − £80m = £920m. With fixed interest charges of I = £30m, the average interest rate on the book value of debt is: i = £30m/£920m = 3.26%. Corporate taxes of £20m have been levied on operating income less fixed interest charges, that is, on £70m − £30m = £40m. Thus the implied corporate tax rate is, t_c = £20m/£40m = 50%. Finally,

ROE = (1 − .5)[.0326 + 12.5(0.07 − .0326)]
    = (1 − .5)[.0326 + 12.5(.0374)]
    = (1 − .5)[.0326 + .4675] = 0.25 or 25%

7 Marketability refers to the ability to buy and sell assets after they have been initially issued. An active secondary market is one where regular daily trade in an asset takes place, thus ensuring that an asset can be bought or sold at very short notice. Marketability is important in two senses:
• it enhances the prospects of companies being able to make new issues in primary markets; and
• promotes capital market efficiency in the sense of helping to ensure that the current market prices of assets reflect their 'true', or intrinsic, values.

Chapter 2

1 a)   £1000(FVIF$_{5,15}$) = £1000(2.011) = £2011
   b)   £1000(FVIF$_{10,8}$) = £1000(2.159) = £2159

c) $£1000(FVIF_{30,6}) = £1000(5.743) = £5743$

2 Present value of cash flow series:

$$PV = 500(PVIF_{0,5}) + 3000(PVIF_{1,5}) + 6000(PVIF_{2,5}) + 1000(PVIF_{3,5})$$
$$+ 500(PVIF_{4,5})$$
$$= 500(1.0) + 3000(.952) + 6000(.907) + 1000(.864) + 500(.823)$$
$$= £10,073.50$$

a) If the discount rate rises to 7% the present value of the cash flow falls to:

$$PV = 500(1.0) + 3000(.935) + 6000(.873) + 1000(.816) + 500(.763)$$
$$= £9740.50$$

b) If the discount rate falls to 3% the present value of the cash flow series rises to:

$$PV = 500(1.0) + 3000(.971) + 6000(.943) + 1000(.951) + 500(.888)$$
$$= £10,466$$

3 $£4000(PVIFA_{10,6}) = £4000(7.360) = £29,440$
$£4000(PVIFA_{15,8}) = £4000(8.560) = £34,240$
$£4000/0.08 = £50,000$

4 a) For annuity A:

$£7360 = £1000(PVIFA_{10,r_A})$.

Thus $PVIFA_{10,r_A} = 7.360$ which produces $r_A = 6\%$.

For annuity B:

$£9266 = £1200(PVIFA_{10,r_B})$.

Thus $PVIFA_{10,r_B} = £9266/£1200 = 7.722$ which produces $r_B = 5\%$.
Since annuity A offers the higher rate of return it is, all other things being equal, of 'better value'.

b) With a personal opportunity cost of funds of 8%, which is above the rate of return offered on annuity A, you would reject this annuity outright. In other words, you require a higher rate of return (8%) than you can expect (6%). A similar conclusion would arise if you viewed this annuity in terms of NPV. Annuity A costs £7360. Given your opportunity cost of funds of 8% you would value it at:

$£1000(PVIFA_{10,8}) = £1000(6.710) = £6710$

Thus with a negative NPV $= £6710 - £7360 = -£650$, annuity A would be rejected.

5 The annual fixed instalment on the four-year loan is determined as:

$£10,000 = I(PVIFA_{4,10})$

Thus $I = £10,000/3.170 = £3154.57$.
The loan amortisation schedule is as follows:

Year	Instalment (£)	Loan interest (£)	Capital repayment (£)	Loan outstanding (£)
1	3154.57	1000.00	2154.57	7845.43
2	3154.57	784.54	2370.03	5475.40
3	3154.57	547.54	2607.03	2868.37
4	3154.57	286.84	2867.73	0.0

6 a) $£500(FVIF_{3,8}) = £500(1.260) = £630.00$
   b) $£500(FVIF_{6,4}) = £500(1.265) = £632.50$
   c) $£500(FVIF_{24,1}) = £500(1.270) = £635.00$

The effective rate of interest in each case is
   a) $r_e = FVIF_{1,8} - 1 = 1.080 - 1.0 = 8\%$
   b) $r_e = FVIF_{2,4} - 1 = 1.082 - 1.0 = 8.2\%$
   c) $r_e = FVIF_{8,1} - 1 = 1.083 - 1.0 = 8.3\%$

7 With the nominal rate of interest quoted on a semi-annual basis and the loan taken out over two years, the total interest charge is:

$$£4000(.147)(2)(2) = £2352$$

Each monthly instalment over two years is

$$(£4000 + £2352)/24 = £264.67$$

Thus

$$£4000 = £264.67(PVIFA_{24,r_p})$$

This gives a $PVIFA_{24,r_p} = 15.11$ and therefore $r_p \simeq 4\%$. Thus with a monthly rate of 4% the APR = 12(4%) = 48%.

8 a) The approximate real rate of interest is:

$$r^* \simeq 9\% - 4.81\% = 4.19\%$$

   b) The exact real rate is:

$$1 + r^* = \frac{(1 + .09)}{(1 + .0481)} = 1.04$$

Thus $r^* = 1.04 - 1.0 = 0.04$ or 4%.

Chapter 3

1 a) To ensure that the bond sells at its par value, r_c must equal r_d. With M = £100 and r_c = 5%, I = £5. Thus the bond sells at its par value since:

$$BV_o = £5(PVIFA_{20,5}) + £100(PVIF_{20,5})$$
$$= £5(12.462) + £100(.377) = £100$$

   b) (i) if $r_d = 5\%$ then since $r_d = r_c$ $BV_o = £100$. That is:

$$BV_o = £5(PVIFA_{10,5}) + £100(PVIF_{10,5})$$
$$= £5(7.722) + £100(.614) = £100$$

(ii) if $r_d = 10\%$ the bond sells below par:

$$BV_o = £5(PVIFA_{10,10}) + £100(PVIF_{10,10})$$
$$= £5(6.145) + £100(.386) = £69.33$$

(iii) if $r_d = 3\%$ the bond sells above par:

$$BV_o = £5(PVIFA_{10,3}) + £100(PVIF_{10,3})$$
$$= £5(8.530) + £100(.744) = £117.05$$

2 a) Bond A: $BV_A = £10(PVIFA_{15,10}) + £100(PVIF_{15,10})$
$$= £10(7.606) + £100(.239) = £100$$
Bond B: $BV_B = £10(PVIFA_{5,10}) + £100(PVIF_{5,10})$
$$= £10(3.791) + £100(.621) = £100$$

b) Bond A: $BV_A = £10(PVIFA_{15,6}) + £100(PVIF_{15,6}) = £138.82$
Bond A: $BV_B = £10(PVIFA_{5,6}) + £100(PVIF_{5,6}) = £116.82$

c) As a result of a four percentage point fall in yields, both bonds' prices rise. The longer dated bond A, however, experiences a greater price rise than the shorter dated bond B. Bond A's price rises by (£38.82)/£100 = 38.82%. Bond B's price rises by (£16.82)/£100 = 16.82%. This illustrates the concept of interest rate risk where the responsiveness of a bond's price to a given percentage change in yields increases with its term to maturity.

3 Both gilt-edged securities and corporate bonds have the common features that they are usually issued for a fixed term to maturity, offer a known fixed interest payment and are subject to interest rate, or price, risk. The main distinguishing feature between these two types of bonds is that corporate bonds are subject to default risk, that is, the risk that the company which has issued a corporate bond might, at some stage over the bond's life, be unable to meet its fixed interest payment obligations. The probability that a government of an advanced capitalist democracy would default on its fixed interest obligations is negligible.

4 Bond rating agencies assign default risk ratings to corporate bonds. These ratings indicate the likelihood that the companies issuing these bonds will experience financial distress which ultimately might jeopardise their ability to meet their fixed interest obligations, at some future date. Rating agencies monitor a company's performance in terms of its financial ratios, the types of products it produces, the foreign markets in which it operates, etc. As the future prospects for the company change, rating agencies may alter their default risk ratings.

5

Gordon Growth Model: $P_0 = \dfrac{d_1}{r_e - g}$

Scenario A

$$P_0 = \frac{.15}{.05 - .03} = £7.50$$

Scenario B

$$P_0 = \frac{.18}{.08 - .04} = £4.50$$

6

Solomon's Model: $P_0 = \dfrac{E}{r_e} + \dfrac{bE}{r_e}\left[\dfrac{k}{r} - 1\right]$

Thus

$$P_0 = \frac{.5}{.10} + \frac{(.35)(.5)}{.10}\left[\frac{.13}{.10} - 1\right] = £5.525$$

The present value of EPS from existing assets is

$$\frac{E}{r_e} = \frac{.5}{.10} = £5.00$$

The price of the share in question would be £5 if the company was expected to experience zero growth in the future. This would arise if no earnings were retained for investment purposes (b = 0), or if the rate of return on new investment equalled the equity capitalisation rate ($k = r_e$) or both.

7 Both share price models use internal financing only and express a company's share price in terms of earnings per share arising from existing assets and potential new investments. The Solomon Model assumes that in each future year a constant proportion of EPS from existing assets is invested. The MM model assumes that in each future year a constant proportion of EPS generated in each future year is invested.

$$P_0 = \frac{(1 - b)E}{r_e - bK}$$

Thus

$$P_0 = \frac{(1 - .35)(.5)}{.10 - (.35)(.13)} = £5.96$$

In question 6 the Solomon Model produced a share price of £5.525. The MM Model's share price is higher because higher amounts of EPS are invested in future years, relative to the Solomon investment strategy.

8 The required rate of return represents the minimum rate of return that an investor requires to hold a particular share. The expected rate of return is the investor's estimate of the rate of return that the share will yield, given its market price and market expectations about its future performance in terms of, for example, expected dividends and growth rates. In equilibrium the expected and required rates of return are equal. In the context of the MM Model the expected and required rate of return can be expressed as the expected dividend yield plus the expected growth rate. The growth rate is defined as the retention ratio times the rate of return on new investment. That is

$$r_e = \frac{d_1}{P_0} + bK$$

All other things being equal, if the required rate of return exceeds the expected rate of return, the market produces a fall in the share price of sufficient magnitude to bring the expected rate of return up to the level of the required rate. Vice versa in the case where the required rate of return is less than the expected rate.

9 Fundamental analysts study the fundamentals of a company, its financial accounts and the expected future trends in the markets in which it operates in order to determine the company's intrinsic value. They may achieve this directly by estimating the parameters of a formal share valuation model or indirectly using, for example, the justified price–earnings ratio approach. Fundamental analysts then compare their estimates of intrinsic value with the current market price of a share. If their estimate exceeds the market price, a buy recommendation might be made. If it is below the market price, a sell recommendation might be made.

Chapter 4

1 a) $E(r_p) = (.3)(.08) + (.7)(.12) = 0.108$ or 10.8%
   b) Simple weighted average of asset risks

   $(.3)(.10) + (.7)(.16) = 0.142$ or 14.2%

   c)
   $$\sigma_p = \sqrt{w_1^2\sigma_1^2 + w_2^2\sigma_2^2 + 2w_1w_2Cor(1,2)\sigma_1\sigma_2}$$
   $$= \sqrt{(.3)^2(.10)^2 + (.7)^2(.16)^2 + 2(.3)(.7)(.10)(.16)COR(1,2)}$$
   $$= \sqrt{0.0009 + 0.01254 + 0.00672COR(1,2)}$$
   $$= \sqrt{0.01344 + 0.00672COR(1,2)}$$

   With $COR(1,2) = 1.0$

   $$\sigma_p = \sqrt{0.02016} = 0.1419 \text{ or } 14.2\%$$

   There are no benefits to diversification in this case since, with a perfect positive correlation between the two assets, the risk of the portfolio is a simple weighted average of the risks of the two assets. See the answer to part (b) of this question to confirm.
   d) With $COR(1,2) = 0.6$

   $$\sigma_p = \sqrt{0.01344 + 0.00672(.6)} = 0.132 \text{ or } 13.2\%$$

   There are benefits to diversification in this case. The expected return on the portfolio is always a simple weighted average of the expected returns on the individual assets. With less than perfect positive correlation between the assets' returns, the risk of the portfolio is less than a simple weighted average of the individual asset's risks. Consequently since risk is reduced more than in proportion to expected return, when $COR(1,2) < 1$, risk diversification benefits arise.

2 In deriving the portfolio equilibrium condition for the individual investor, it is assumed that rates of return on all assets are normally distributed, that the returns between pairs of assets are less than perfectly positively correlated, that borrowing

and lending can be undertaken at a common risk-free rate of interest and that individual investors are risk-averse expected utility maximisers.

The additional assumptions necessary to produce equilibrium for the whole capital market are that capital markets are perfect and investors have homogeneous expectations over their one-period time horizons. The perfect capital market assumption implicitly includes a common borrowing and lending rate and additionally a taxless environment, with infinitely divisible assets, no transactions costs and costlessly available information which all investors have access to.

3 $E(r_A) = 6\% + [16\% - 6\%](1.0)$
$\quad\quad = 6\% + [10\%](1.0) = 16\%$
$\quad E(r_B) = 6\% + [10\%](2.5) = 31\%$
$\quad E(r_c) = 6\% + [10\%](0.2) = 8\%$

Share A is an average share and therefore is expected to earn the average return available on the market. Share B is an aggressive share, possessing above average market risk. In order to hold this share in a portfolio an investor will require and expect it to earn a rate of return in excess of the market's average rate. Share C is a defensive share, possessing below average market risk. Thus an investor does not require or expect this share's rate of return to be above, or even equal to, the market's average rate.

4 In equilibrium, under the CAPM, shares are priced according to their risk. Consequently shares with identical risk, as measured by β, have, in equilibrium, identical rates of return which, given β, are determined from the SML. In equilibrium these rates of return are both expected and required rates. The SML indicates the rate of return that the capital markets require if a share, with a given β, is to be held in a well-diversified portfolio. If, for a given β, a share's expected rate of return is above the SML, the share is 'underpriced'. Its price will rise to bring its expected rate of return back onto the SML.

5 The implications of the absence of the perfect capital markets assumption depend on what parts of this assumption are broken. In equilibrium, with the presence of the assumption all rates of return lie along the SML.

If the perfect capital market assumption is broken by the presence of transactions costs or the absence of infinite divisibility, investors may not always 'fine tune' their portfolios, in which case rates of return may lie off the SML. The presence of taxes may cause investors to exhibit preferences for particular shares, those for example which pay high dividends (or low dividends depending on the individual's tax circumstances). In this case specific risk may be present in an individual's portfolio. If borrowing and lending rates differ, the linearity property of the CAPM is lost.

6 a)

$$\beta_p = \sum_{i=1}^{n} w_i \beta_i$$

$$= (.49)(.05) + (.7)(.10) + (1.09)(.20) + (1.26)(.35) + (1.2)(.30) = 1.11$$

This is an aggressive portfolio, since $\beta p > 1$. In an upward trending market the portfolio can be expected to 'outperform' the market average. In a downward trending market this portfolio can be expected to 'underperform', that is, its return can be expected to fall by a greater amount than the fall in the market average.

b)

$$\text{Market Risk} = \sqrt{\beta_p^2 \sigma_{FT}^2} = \sqrt{(1.11)^2 (16^2)} = \sqrt{315.42} = 17.76$$

$$\text{Specific Risk} = \sqrt{\sum_{i=1}^{5} (w_1 \delta_i)^2} = \sqrt{211.52} = 14.54$$

$$\text{Total Risk} = \sqrt{(\text{Market Risk})^2 + (\text{Specific Risk})^2} = 22.96$$

c) The specific risk of this portfolio is less than the total risk of any one of the shares because of risk diversification.

d) The specific risk of this portfolio has not been totally removed because there is not a sufficient number of different shares in the portfolio to achieve the full effects of diversification and bring portfolio risk down to the level of market risk.

Chapter 5

1 In equilibrium, in the context of the CAPM, individual assets and portfolios of assets are priced according to their risk. Given an asset's risk, as measured by its β coefficient, the SML determines the rate of return that the market requires the asset to earn. 'Beating the market' implies that an investor can earn a higher rate of return on an asset relative to the rate required by the market, and that the positive abnormal return can be earned over a consistent period of time.

The EMH does not imply that abnormal returns cannot be earned. It implies that abnormal returns cannot be earned consistently. In other words, over a period of sufficient length positive abnormal returns are cancelled by negative abnormal returns, with an investor earning an expected return (required by the market) which is appropriate to the level of risk he/she is exposed to.

2 The EMH implies that accounting information which is publicly available, that is, accounting information which is published in company financial statements, will be fully reflected in a share's price. In addition it implies that cosmetic information which is irrelevant to valuation will be ignored by the markets.

Smith identifies a number of accounting practices which may have been used by companies to 'artificially' boost their share prices. These practices may or may not have had the desired effect which the companies which used them hoped for. It is only possible to assess this by statistical analysis. Smith's study does not do this; therefore, it constitutes neither evidence in support of, nor against, the EMH.

3 The 'small firm effect' has been advanced as an explanation for one of the important market anomalies 'discovered' in empirical research on the EMH. It relates to the apparent ability to earn abnormal returns by trading shares in the month of January. Some research has tended to suggest that these abnormal returns result specifically from trading in small-sized firms, that is, firms with small

capitalisations. The argument is that if small firms are more risky than large firms, then these abnormal January returns are indeed anomalous since they represent a proper market determined risk premium. Problems over empirical estimates of risk, in the small firm case, and the link between PE ratios and small capitalisations have tended to cloud the small firm explanation.

4 The paradox of the EMH is that while market participants cannot beat the market and earn consistent abnormal returns from information based trading rules, active participation to try and beat the market is apparently necessary if capital markets are to be efficient markets. It is only by making buy and sell decisions on the basis of relevant new information that new information can be fully reflected in current market prices. The paradox itself may be more apparent than real, in the sense that market participants may simply need to act on new information in order to enable them to earn consistent normal returns appropriate to their desired level of risk exposure. In other words investors need to act on relevant new information to avoid being beaten by an efficient market.

5 If both corporate debt and equity are 'fairly' priced in efficient capital markets, then the yields to maturity on corporate debt and the expected rates of return on equity, at a given point in time, represent 'fair' and best available estimates of the component costs of debt and equity capital.

Chapter 6

1 Given the cost of capital, all independent projects whose NPVs are greater than or equal to zero are acceptable. Similarly all independent projects, with conventional NPV schedules, whose internal rates of return are equal to, or in excess of, the cost of capital are acceptable.

2 a)

$$NPV_A = \frac{£1250}{1 + IRR} - £1000 = 0, \text{ thus } 1 + IRR = \frac{£1250}{£1000} = 1.25$$

Therefore, $IRR_A = 25\%$

$$NPV_B = \frac{£1024}{1 + IRR} - £800 = 0, \text{ thus } 1 + IRR = \frac{£1024}{£800} = 1.28$$

Therefore, $IRR_B = 28\%$. Since $IRR_A > IRR_B > 10\%$, direct application of the IRR suggests that project B is preferred to project A.

b)

$NPV_A = £1250(PVIF_{1.10}) - £1000 = £1250(.909) - £1000 = £136.25$

$NPV_B = £1024(.909) - £800 = £130.82$

Since $NPV_A > NPV_B \geq 0$, the NPV suggests that project A is preferred to project B.

c) As evident from (a) and (b) there is a conflict of choice between the NPV and IRR investment appraisal methods. This is resolved by considering the incremental cash flows between the two projects. Assume (incorrectly) that project B had been chosen using the direct application of IRR. Notionally, by rejecting project A, the following incremental cash flows have been given up:

Year 0: −£200   Year 1: £226

The IRR on this incremental project is:

$$NPV = \frac{£226}{1 + IRR} - £200 = 0, \text{ thus } 1 + IRR = \frac{£226}{£200} = 1.13$$

Therefore IRR = 13%.

Since IRR on this incremental project is greater than the opportunity cost of capital, the project is acceptable. By accepting project A, this incremental project's cash flows plus project B's cash flows are implicitly included. Therefore, project A, under this amended IRR approach, is preferable. This was indicated under the direct application of the NPV decision rule.

Accepting project A in preference to project B creates a greater addition to wealth. This is confirmed by considering the NPV of the incremental project, which is:

$$NPV = £226(.909) - £200 = £5.43$$

Adding this NPV to the NPV of project B yields the NPV of project A, that is:

$$NPV_A = £130.83 + £5.43 = £136.26$$

d) The rough sketch of the three NPV schedules will indicate that the schedules for A and B cross over. The crossover point occurs at a discount rate of 13% which is the IRR on the incremental project, that is, the discount rate which makes the NPV on the incremental project zero. The NPV schedule on the incremental project is equal to the NPV schedule of project A less the NPV schedule of project B.

3

$$NPV = \frac{40}{1 + IRR} + \frac{-27.83}{(1 + IRR)^2} - 13.9 = 0$$

Multiply by $(1 + IRR)^2$, thus

$$+40(1 + IRR) - 27.83 - 13.9(1 + IRR)^2 = 0$$

This is equivalent to the quadratic

$$aX^2 + bX + c$$

where

$$X = 1 + IRR, a = -13.9, b = 40, c = -27.83$$

Therefore,

$$1 + IRR = \frac{-b + \sqrt{b^2 - 4ac}}{2a}$$

which has a solution since $b^2 < 4ac$, that is, $(40)^2 < 4(-13.9)(-27.83)$, that is, $1600 < 1547.35$

$$1 + IRR = \frac{-40 - \sqrt{1600 - 1547.35}}{2(-13.9)}$$

$$= \frac{-40 - \sqrt{52.65}}{-27.8} = \frac{-40 - 7.26}{-27.8} = 1.70 \therefore IRR = 70\%$$

or

$$1 + IRR = \frac{-40 + 7.26}{-27.8} = 1.1778 \therefore IRR = 17.78\%$$

The NPV on this project is

$$£40(PVIF_{1,10}) - £27.83(PVIF_{2,10}) - £13.9$$
$$£40(.909) - £27.83(.826) - £13.9 = -£0.52$$

The project should be rejected as it has a negative NPV, despite the fact that both IRRs > 10%.

The multiple roots problem arises because cash flows have changed sign more than once, creating a 'non-conventional' cash flow schedule.

4 a) Applying PVIFs at 7% to the cash flows of each of the projects produces the following NPVs:

$$NPV_A = £4849.20 \qquad NPV_B = -£6105.50 \qquad NPV_C = £2340.00$$

Projects A and C should be accepted creating a total net addition to wealth of NPV = £4849.20 + £2340.00 = £7189.20

b) Since $PB_A = 4$ and exceeds $PB^{Max} = 3$, project A, despite its positive NPV, would be rejected. Projects B and C would be accepted since $PB_B = 3$ and $PB_C = 2$. This is despite project B having a negative NPV. The total NPV of selected projects under the payback appraisal method is −£6105.50 + £2340.00 = −£3765.50.

c) The project selection under the PB is incorrect because PB is a non-discounting method and, therefore, does not consider the time value of money. The PB also only considers the NCFs arising within the payback period ignoring, for example, the large negative NCFs occurring in periods four and five in project B's case.

5 When determining a project's cash flows all relevant cash flows should be taken into account at the time they occur. Only incremental cash flows should be considered. Sunk costs should be excluded and double counting avoided. All project interlinkages should be considered as should all opportunity costs. Any tendency, in estimating incremental NCFs, to be over-optimistic or over-pessimistic should be avoided.

Chapter 7

1 Under the constant risk assumption, the cost of capital is:

$$r_a = r_d(1 - t_c)\left[\frac{B}{S + B}\right] + r_e\left[\frac{S}{S + B}\right]$$

With a debt:equity ratio of 7:11, there is £7 of debt for every £11 of equity, therefore, $B/(S + B) = 7/(18) = 0.389$.

$$r_a = 4\%(1 - .4)[0.389] + 12\%[0.611] = 8.27\%$$

2 Food Processors plc has first to calculate the project's risk, based on the asset β of Holiday and Conference plc. It does this by using the data given on Holiday and Conference plc.

$$\beta_{project} = \beta_{assets} = \beta_{debt}\left[\frac{B(1 - t_c)}{S + B(1 - t_c)}\right] + \beta_{equity}\left[\frac{S}{S + B(1 - t_c)}\right]\frac{B}{S}$$

Therefore

$$r_{project} = 0.3\left[\frac{6(1 - .35)}{4 + 6(1 - .35)}\right] + 2.2\left[\frac{4}{4 + 6(1 - .35)}\right]$$

$$= 0.3[.494] + 2.2[.506] = 1.26$$

Food Processors plc has now unlevered Holiday and Conference plc's β. Food Processors now relevers this β to determine its project cost of capital, using its own capital structure and tax rates.

$$r_{project} = r_f + [E(r_m) - r_f]\beta_{project}\left[\frac{S + B(1 - t_c)}{S + B}\right]$$

$$= 5\% + [15\% - 5\%](1.26)\left[\frac{7 + 3(1 - .25)}{10}\right] = 16.66\%$$

Note that its own debt and equity βs are not used in determining its project β.

3 a) The real cost of capital is

$$1 + r_{real} = \frac{(1 + r_{nom})}{(1 + r_{real})} = \frac{1.12}{1.05} = 1.0667$$

That is, $r_{real} = 6.67\%$

b)

$$NPV(Nom) = \frac{£10m}{(1.12)} - £2m = £8.929m - £2m = £6.929m$$

To determine the real NPV, the NCFs must be discounted by the rate of inflation:

$$NCF(Real) = \frac{£10m}{1.05} = £9.524m$$

Thus

$$NPV(Real) = \frac{£9.524m}{(1.0667)} - £2m = £6.928m$$

c) Using the approximation

$$r_{real} \simeq r_{nom} - r_{RPI}$$
$$r_{real} \simeq 12.0\% - 5\% = 7.00\%$$

The error would have been an overestimate of the real rate of interest by .23 percentage points.

4 Internal capital rationing involves a company's management imposing its own limits on the amount of capital expenditure in any one period. The company is capable, at the given cost of capital, of raising any amount of funds that it might require externally from the capital markets. Under external capital rationing, it is the capital markets themselves that impose limits on the amount of capital that a company can raise at a given cost of capital. Either the external constraint can be breached but only by being willing to pay a higher cost of capital for funds in excess of the constraint; or the constraint can be absolute with no funds available over a specified limit.

5 To use the benefit–cost ratio, the following assumptions are necessary: capital is internally rationed for a single period only and projects are independent and infinitely divisible.

6 From the information in the question the following can be calculated.

Project	NPV	BCR	BCR ranking	PVI	PVI ranking	Net outlay
A	£500	1.0	2	2.0	2	£500
B	£1500	1.5	1	2.5	1	£1000
C	−£100	−0.25	5	0.75	5	£400
D	£100	0.33	4	1.33	4	£300
E	£100	0.5	3	1.5	3	£200

NPV = PV future NCFs − net investment outlay
BCR = NPV ÷ net investment outlay
PVI = PV future NCFs ÷ net investment outlay

a) Select all projects where $NPV_i \geqslant 0$, therefore reject project C. Total NPV of investment = NPVs of project A, B, D and E = £2200.
b) With an expenditure constraint of £1600, ranked projects accepted under BCR: B, A, 0.5E. This just exhausts the capital constraint. Total NPV = £2050. Note that under BCR only projects with BCR ⩾ 0 are acceptable. As the above shows, PVI gives exactly the same ranking.
c) If each of the five projects is non-divisible, those projects which maximise NPV, subject to the capital constraint, must be accepted. These projects are A and B, giving NPV = £2000. Expenditure is £1500 leaving £100 of the capital constraint unused.

7 a)
$$NPV_A = -£250 + £200(PVIF_{1,10}) + £500(PVIF_{2,10})$$
$$= -£250 + £200(.909) + £500(.826) = £344.80$$

$$NPV_B = -£1000 + £300(.909) + £400(.826) + 600(.751) + £500(.683)$$
$$= £395.20$$

Under this standard application of NPV, since $NPV_B > NPV_A$, project A would be accepted.

b) To use the common lifespan approach, project A is repeated once, to give it a common lifespan with project B. Project B's NPV remains as before at £363.70. The NCFs for Project A under the CLS approach are:

NCFs(£s)

Year 0	-250	
1	200	
2	500	-250
3		200
4		500

NPV for the repeated project is:

$$NPV = -£250 + £200(.909) + £250(.826) + £200(.751)$$
$$+ £500(.683) = £630.00.$$

NPV(CLS) for project A now exceeds that of project B, so project A would be accepted. Under the standard application of NPV, however, project B would have been accepted and project A rejected.

Chapter 8

1 a) Use Equations 8.1 and 8.3b to 8.6. With $V = £15m$ and $B = £5m$, the market value of equity is $S = V - B = £15m - £5m = £10m$. The interest charge on debt is $i(B) = 0.03(£5m) = £0.15m$. Dividends are $D = Y - r_dB = £1m - £0.15m = £0.85m$. Thus the cost of equity is $r_e = D/S = £0.85m/£10m = 8.5\%$. This gives an average cost of capital of:

$$r_a = r_d \frac{B}{S+B} + r_e \frac{S}{S+B} = 0.03\left(\frac{5}{15}\right) + 0.085\left(\frac{10}{15}\right) = 6.667\%$$

The total market value of the company is, therefore, as stated: $V = Y/r_a = £1m/0.0667 = £15m$.

b) From above $B/V = 0.333$. If B/V changes to 0.5 then, under the Traditionalist approach, r_a and r_e remain constant. With $S/V = 1 - B/V = 0.5$, r_a falls to 5.75%, that is:

$$r_a = 0.03(0.5) + 0.085(0.5) = 0.0575$$

V rises to:

$$V = £1m/0.0575 = £17.39m$$

c) Under the MM approach, a change in capital structure does not affect V, which remains at £15m, and does not affect r_a, which remains at 6.667%. By Equation 8.7, the implication is that r_e rises to exactly offset any benefits from increased reliance on the cheaper source of capital (debt). In other words r_e rises from 8.5%, when $B/V = 0.333$, to 10.34% when $B/V = 0.5$, that is:

$$r_e = r_a + (r_a - r_d)B/S = 0.0667 + (0.0667 - 0.03)(1) = 13.04\%$$

Note that from endnote 1 in Chapter 8:

$$B/S = \frac{B/V}{1 - B/V} = \frac{0.50}{1 - 0.50} = 1.00$$

2 a) By Equation 8.11, the annual interest tax shield is equal to: .

$$t_c r_d B = (0.4)(.05)(£10m) = £0.2m$$

By Equation 8.13, since debt is assumed riskless and perpetual, the annual interest tax shield is a riskless perpetuity; therefore, its present value is:

$$t_c r_d B \div r_d = t_c B = (0.4)(£10m) = £4m.$$

   b) The total market value of the company is found using Equation 8.14 where:

$$V_L = V_u + t_c B$$

V_u, the unlevered value of the company, is needed. From Equation 8.14:

$$V_u = \frac{Y(1 - t_c)}{r_e^*} = \frac{£2m(1 - .4)}{0.15} = £8m$$

Therefore $V_L = £8m + £4m = £12m$.

   c) Since $V_L = V_u + t_c B$, the target capital structure under the MM debt and taxes model is 100% debt financing.

3 a) Equity income is usually received in the form of both capital gains and dividends. Capital gains and dividend income may be subject to different tax rates, in which case the effective tax rate will depend on how each £1 of income is split between dividends and capital gains and on the respective tax rates.

   b) For each £1 of equity income received, shareholders pay 70p(.30) = 21p tax in respect of dividends and 30p(.15) = 4.5p in respect of capital gains. Thus the total tax payment per £ is 25.5p and the effective tax rate on equity income is $t_{ef} = 25.5\%$.

4 a) From Equation 8.15, Miller's Valuation Equation is:

$$V_L = V_u + \left[1 - \frac{(1 - t_c)(1 - t_{ef})}{(1 - t_p)}\right] B$$

   b)

$$V_L = £50m + \left[1 - \frac{(1 - .30)(1 - .25)}{(1 - .15)}\right] £20m$$

$$= £50m + [1 - .6176]£20m = £50m + £7.648m = £57.648m$$

   c)

$$V_L = £50m + \left[1 - \frac{(1 - .50)(1 - .30)}{(1 - .30)}\right] £20m$$

$$= £50m + [1 - .50]£20m = £60m$$

In this case, the effective and personal tax rates on equity income are equal. This produces the same result as MM's debt and taxes model where:

$$V_L = V_u + t_c B = £50m + 0.50(£20m) = £60m$$

5 The Modernist approach to the capital structure puzzle identifies three main

costs which are likely to reduce the present value of the tax shield. These are the present values of: bankruptcy costs, financial distress costs and net agency costs. As the debt:equity ratio increases, these costs are likely to increase and eventually equal the present value of the tax shield. The debt:equity ratio, at which this equality occurs, is the optimal debt:equity ratio indicating the optimal capital structure for the relevant company.

Chapter 9

1

$$\Delta P_0 = \frac{d_1(1 + k)}{(1 + r_e)^2} - \frac{d_1}{1 + r_e}$$

$$= \frac{d_1}{(1 + r_e)^2} (k - r_e)$$

a)
$$\Delta P_0 = \frac{0.30}{(1.10)^2} (.14 - .10) \simeq 1p$$

b) (i)
$$\Delta P_0 = \frac{0.30}{(1.10)^2} (.10 - .10) = 0.0p$$

(ii)
$$\Delta P_0 = \frac{0.30}{(1.10)^2} (.05 - .10) = -1.24p$$

c) These share price changes might appear to be the result of a change in the timing of dividend policy but are the result of the company's underlying investment policy.

2 a) With $1 - b = 0.5$ and thus $b = 0.5$, the company retains $0.5(£14m) = £7m$ for investment purposes. This means that it needs to raise $£20m - £7m = £13m$ via a new equity issue.

b) $V_t = 20m(£2.10) = £42m$

c) Under the MM valuation principle

$$V_t = \frac{1}{1 + r} [V_{t+1} + \Pi_t - I_t]$$

Thus

$$£42m = \frac{1}{1.08} [V_{t+1} + £14m - £20m]$$

Hence $V_{t+1} = £42m(1.08) - £14m + £20m = £51.36m$.

d) The amount of the $t + 1$ market value belonging to existing shareholders equals V_{t+1} less the amount of the new share capital raised, thus

$V^*_{t+1} = £51.36m - £13m = £38.36m$

With existing shareholders having 20m shares the share price at the beginning of $t + 1$ is

£38.36m/20m = £1.918

e) Since the total market value in $t + 1$ is £51.36m, and in a perfect capital market the new share issue in period $t + 1$ must be priced at £1.918, there are £51.36m/£1.918 = 26.78m shares outstanding in $t + 1$.

3 a) With a payout ratio of $1 - b = 0.6$, now only 40% of the £14m profits are retained. This implies that with £5.6m retentions the company needs to raise a higher amount of capital via a new issue:

£20m − £5.6m = £14.4m

By the fundamental principle of valuation, since profits, investment expenditure and the discount rate do not change as a result of the change in the dividend policy, V_{t+1} remains unchanged at £51.36m as does the current market value at £42m. Now however, the market value, in period $t + 1$, of the existing shareholders' equity does change to

V^*_{t+1} = £51.36m − £14.4m = £36.96m

This implies that the share price in period $t + 1$ is £36.96m/20m = £1.848 and that there are £51.36m/1.848 = 27.79m shares outstanding in period $t + 1$.

b) As a result of the change in dividend policy, the existing shareholders' value of equity has fallen from £38.36m (in question 2) to £36.96m; however, their dividend payout, at the end of period t, has risen from £7m to £8.4m, taking their wealth at the beginning of period $t + 1$ to £45.36m. The present value of this is £45.36m/(1.08) = £42m.

c) The rate of return to existing shareholders is their dividend yield plus the growth rate in the share price (that is, the capital gain/loss). With P_0 = £2.10, a total dividend payment of £8.4m on existing shareholdings of 20m, the dividend per share is £8.4m/20m = 42p, thus the dividend yield is .42/£2.10 = 20%. The capital loss over the period is (£1.848 − £2.10)/£2.10 = −12%. Thus the expected rate of return, in equilibrium, is equal to the cost of equity capital

r = 20% − 12% = 8%

4 The dividend irrelevancy proposition is based on the assumptions of certainty, perfect capital markets, rationality and given investments.

5 In a perfect capital market it is the ability of investors to declare 'homemade' dividends which ensures the irrelevancy of dividend policy. If current dividends are insufficient for current income needs additional 'dividends' can be created by selling, at no disadvantage, an appropriate amount of shares. If dividends exceed current income needs, the excess can be invested by purchasing an additional amount of shares without affecting the price or the rate of return.

6 The Traditionalist risk argument is that forming distant future expectations is more risky than forming near-term expectations. Consequently a policy which reduces near-term dividends, albeit to increase investment to create higher dividend payments in the more distant future, affects a company's share price. The reason is not, according to the Traditionalists, because investment policy is changing but because a change in the time pattern of dividend payments alters the risk pattern as well.

7 Empirical studies of dividend policy suggest that management target a relatively high long-term payout ratio with a view to convincing the markets that they are pursuing a consistent dividend policy. They also appear to have a strong aversion against cutting dividends, at least in the short run.

8 a) A relatively stable long-term payout ratio is pursued and apparently linked to management's view of the long-term trend in EPS.
  b) Because of quite substantial short-term variations in EPS and a desire to limit the short-term variations in dividends per share, the short-term dividend payout ratio can be expected to show significant variations.
  c) While the short-term variation in dividends per share is contained it may still show greater variation than the long-term trend, at least to the extent that the long-term trend is tied, through a long-term target payout ratio, to a long-term trend in EPS which is relatively stable.

Chapter 10

1 Financial leverage refers to the extent to which a company, through the use of debt capital, builds fixed interest costs into its capital structure. Operating leverage refers to the extent to which a company builds fixed costs into its production operations.

2 a) The degree of operating leverage is an elasticity concept which measures, at a given level of sales, the responsiveness of EBIT to a change in sales, that is,

$$DOL = \frac{\Delta EBIT/EBIT}{\Delta Q/Q}$$

  b)
$$TR = PQ = £2(4m) = £8m$$
$$TC = vQ + TFC = £1(4m) + £0.25m = £4.25m$$
$$EBIT = £8m - £4.25m = £3.75m$$

Assuming sales increase by 10% to 4.4m

$$TR = £8.8m \qquad TC = £4.65m$$

Therefore EBIT = £4.15m. Thus

$$DOL = \frac{£0.4m/£3.75m}{0.4/4} = 1.067$$

This indicates that a 10% rise in sales above the expected level produces a 10.67% increase in EBIT.

3 a) The degree of financial leverage is an elasticity concept which measures, at a given level of EBIT, the responsiveness of EPS to a change in EBIT, that is,

$$DFL = \frac{\Delta EPS/EPS}{\Delta EBIT/EBIT}$$

b) The expected level of EBIT in question 2 is £3.75m. With debt of £12.5m, at an interest rate of 6%, interest charges are 0.06(£12.5m) = £0.75m, thus

$EAI = £3.75m - £0.75m = £3m$

With $t_c = 30\%$ and n = 21m shares outstanding

$$EPS = \frac{EAIT}{n} = \frac{£3m(1 - .3)}{21m} = 10p$$

A rise in EBIT by 10% produces EBIT = £4.125m. Thus

$EAI = £4.125m - £0.75m = £3.375m$

and

$$EPS = \frac{£3.375m(1 - .3)}{21m} = 11.25p$$

Thus

$$DFL = \frac{£0.0125/£.10}{£0.375m/£3.75m} = 1.25$$

This indicates that a 10% rise in EBIT above the expected level produces a 12.5% increase in EPS.

4 Intangible assets can include investments in human capital, advertising, general marketing and R and D. Since these assets are not tangible and have no realisable value in circumstances of financial distress, the greater the proportion of intangible assets in a company's total asset base, the greater the potential agency costs of debt and equity. To the extent, however, that these intangible assets have reputational value and are an integral part of a company's business strategy decisions, they can have a tendency to reduce agency costs. These reputational assets are recognised by the capital markets as essential to the maintenance and development of a company's competitive strategy.

5 With $r^*_e = 12\%$, the perpetual annual operating profit of £1.2m produces an unlevered NPV of

$$UNPV = \frac{£1.2m}{.12} - £5m = £5m$$

To find the ANPV, the financing side-effects must be subtracted. The costs of raising new finance are:

$0.05(£5m) = £0.25m$

The annual tax shield is

$t_c r_d B = (.3)(0.05)(£2m) = £0.03m$

This is in perpetuity, hence the present value of this tax shield is

$$\frac{t_c r_d B}{r_d} = (.3)(£2m) = £.6m$$

Thus

$$ANPV = £5m - £0.25m - £0.6m = £4.15m$$

6 a) The existing capital structure, measured in terms of debt capital to total market value, is £10m/£50m = 0.2.

$$NPV + I_o = £8m + £5m = £13m$$

Thus 0.2(£13m) = £2.6m of debt capital must be raised and £5m − £2.6m = £2.4m of new equity capital.

b) As a result of the new project being undertaken the company adds £2.6m to its debt capital, thus raising the total amount of debt capital to £12.6m. The equity value of the company rises by the £2.4m of new share issues; however, the NPV of the project, which belongs to shareholders, adds a further £8m to equity, raising the total amount of equity capital to £50.4m. With the total market value of the company now at £63m, the proportion of debt in the capital structure is

$$\frac{£12.6m}{£63m} = 0.2$$

The existing capital structure has been maintained.

Chapter 11

1 A call price feature gives a company in the US the right to buy back a bond at a specified price, which is normally above the bond's par value. In the UK a call price feature enables a company to offer to buy back a bond at a specified price, but bondholders in this case are not obligated to accept the offer; in the US they are. When this feature is included in US corporate bonds, bondholders can be disadvantaged if the call is exercised when the call price is below the market value of the bond. In recognition of this risk, callable bonds normally have a premium on their yields to maturity, relative to non-callable bonds, all other things being equal.

2 If refunding takes place there is an interest cost saving determined as follows:

Annual Interest After Tax
Existing bond: (.10)($15m)(1 − .25)   = $1.125m
New bond: (.04)($15m)(1 − .25)   = $0.45m
Interest savings   = $0.675m
After tax discount rate: 0.04(1 − .25)   = 0.03 or 3%
PV Interest Savings $0.675m(PVIFA$_{20,3}$) = $0.675m(14.878)
                                         = $10.04265m

Main Costs of New Issue
Call price premium (after tax): (.15)($15m)(1 − .25) = $1.6875m
Issue costs new bond: (.01)($15m) = $0.15m

These are amortised over 20 years giving a PV of tax benefits of:

$$\frac{\$0.15m}{20}(.25)(14.878)\ \$0.027896m$$

Thus the net present issue costs of new bond are:

$$\$0.15m - \$0.027896m = \$0.122104m$$

Main Costs of Existing Bond Issue
Amortised: $(.005)(\$15m)/25 = \$0.003m$
PV tax benefit lost remaining 20 years: $\$0.003m(.25)(14.878) = \$.011159m$
Costs amortised to date (after 5 years): $5(\$0.003m) = \$0.015m$
Cost write-off: $0.005(\$15m) = \$.075 - \$.015m = \$.06m$
Tax benefit from cost write-off: $(.25)(\$.06m) = \$.015m$

Net Present Issue Costs of Existing Bond: $\$.011159m - \$.015m = -\$.003841$

Overlapping Interest Cost for one month:

$$\frac{1}{12}(\$1.125m) = \$93750m$$

NPV of Refunding Strategy:

	$(m)
PV Interest savings	10.042650
Call Premium	−1.687500
NPV New Bond Issue Costs	−0.122104
NPV Old Bond Issue Costs	0.003841
Overlapping Interest	−0.093750
	8.143137

With the NPV of refunding being positive, it would be advantageous for the company to refinance the bond issue.

3 Because of their hybrid feature, warrants and convertibles give their holders the potential to take a future equity stake in a company. This potential helps to reduce some of the agency costs of debt and enables companies, when first issuing bonds with warrants or convertible bonds, to avoid having to offer a premium on a bond's anticipated yield to compensate for these costs. A company's debt financing flexibility may also be enhanced, to the extent that fewer restrictive covenants have to be built into a hybrid's indenture provisions. These issues are closely associated with the investment potential of a company and may be significant when a company has a high expected growth rate combined with high risk.

4 The market value floor of a convertible bond is determined by two factors: the bond's straight debt value and its conversion value. The market value floor is the value below which a convertible bond's price will not fall. A convertible bond will never sell below its value as a straight debt instrument since, in an efficient market, investors interested in buying straight debt would view a convertible as a bargain in this situation. Similarly a convertible will never sell below its conversion value. In this case investors interested in equity would view the convertible as a bargain, buy it, and convert immediately into equity.

5 The main reasons for leasing arise, in the case of a service lease for example, from the potential the lessor has to achieve economies of scale in servicing and administration of a large pool of specialised assets. A general advantage of leasing arises when a company, by purchasing an asset, cannot take advantage of a depreciation tax shield. By leasing an asset from a lessor who can take advantage of depreciation tax shields, the benefits of these tax shields can be shared with the lessee when agreeing the terms of the leasing agreement. Other arguments favouring leasing over purchase do not generally hold up, at least in an efficient market.

6 After tax cost of debt: $(8.33\%)(1 - .4) = 5\%$

Year end	Lease Payments £'s	Tax Allowance £'s	Net of Tax Lease Payments £'s	Depreciation £'s
0	6000		6000	
1	6000	2400	3600	5000
2	6000	2400	3600	5000
3	6000	2400	3600	5000
4		−2400	−2400	5000

PV of after-tax lease payments at $5\% = £13,829.27$
PV depreciation tax shield: $(.4)£5000(PVFA_{4,5}) = £7092$
$NAL = I_o - $ PV after-tax lease payments $- $ PV depreciation tax shield
$= £20,000 - £13,829.27 - £7092$
Therefore $NAL = -£921.27$
Since $NAL < 0$ the buy the asset option would be chosen.

7 The pure expectations hypothesis expresses long-term interest rates as a function of expected future short-term interest rates. According to this hypothesis the only reason that yield curves slope upwards, with long-term rates exceeding short-term rates, is because the market expects short-term rates to rise in the future. A downward sloping yield curve arises because the market expects short-term rates to fall in the future.

8 Under the pure expectations hypothesis:

$$(1 + r_3)^3 = (1 + {}_0r_1)(1 + {}_1r_2)(1 + {}_2r_3)$$

Thus

$$(1.12)^3 = (1 + .05)(1 + .07)(1 + {}_2r_3)$$

Therefore,

$$1 + {}_2r_3 = \frac{1.4049}{(1.05)(1.07)} = 1.25$$

that is,

$${}_2r_3 = 25\%$$

9 With liquidity premiums:
a)
$$(1 + r_2)^2 = (1 + .08)(1 + .09 + .005) = 1.1826$$

Thus $(1 + r_2) = \sqrt{1.1826} = 1.0875$ and $r_2 = 8.75\%$

b)

$(1 + r_2)^2 = (1 + .08)(1 + .07 + .005) = 1.161$

Thus $(1 + r_2) = \sqrt{1.161} = 1.0775$ and $r_2 = 7.75\%$

Chapter 12

1 Current assets are essential to maintaining existing levels of sales and may have an important role in supporting any desire to increase sales volume. If sales are to be increased, it may be necessary to increase the range of inventory holdings of raw materials, spare parts, etc. Also, an increase in accounts receivable, or a relaxation of the trade credit offered to customers, may help support a policy of increasing sales.

2 Given that money has an opportunity cost, a company, while being careful not to disrupt relationships unnecessarily with its customers and suppliers, should attempt to:
- delay cash outflows for as long as possible;
- speed up cash inflows;
- avoid persistent periods of excess cash balances; and
- avoid persistent periods when cash outflows exceed cash inflows.

3 a) The optimal cash balance is:

$$C^* = \sqrt{\frac{2(£50)(£0.5m)}{.04}} = \sqrt{1250} = £35,355$$

b) The number of times short-term marketable securities are converted into cash over the year is £0.5m/£35,355 $\approx$ 14.

c) Assuming 360 days in the year, the average holding period is 360/14 $\approx$ 26 days.

4 If the transactions demand for cash is doubled it increases by 100% and C^* becomes

$$C^* = \sqrt{\frac{2(£50)(£1m)}{.04}} = £50,000$$

This indicates that the optimal cash balance increases by less than 100%.

5 a) Under the Miller–Orr Model the desired cash balance is

$$DCB = \sqrt[3]{\frac{3(£50)(£15,179)^2}{4(.04)}} = £60,000$$

b) The upper control, or balance limit, is

$$UBL = 3(DCB) = £180,000$$

When this limit is reached, $UBL - DCB = £120,000$ is invested in short-term marketable securities.

c) The average cash balance is

(UBL + DCB)/3 = £80,000

6 a) The cash operating cycle is

$$365 \left[\frac{1}{\text{Inventory Turnover Ratio}} + \frac{1}{\text{Receivables Turnover Ratio}} \right.$$
$$\left. - \frac{1}{\text{Debtor Turnover Ratio}} \right]$$

$$\text{Debtor Turnover} = \frac{£50,000}{£2000} = 25.0$$

$$\text{Receivables Turnover} = \frac{£50,000}{£8000} = 6.25$$

$$\text{Inventory Turnover} = \frac{£18,000}{£1000} = 18$$

The cash operating cycle, measuring the length of time a company has funds tied up in working capital, is

$$365 \left[\frac{1}{18} + \frac{1}{6.25} - \frac{1}{25} \right] = 365[.17] = 62 \text{ days}$$

b) A halving of investment in inventory would increase the inventory turnover ratio to £18,000/500 = 36. As a result, the cash operating cycle becomes

$$365 \left[\frac{1}{36} + \frac{1}{6.25} - \frac{1}{25} \right] = 365[.148] = 54 \text{ days}$$

The cash operating cycle has been reduced because there has been a reduction in one of the current asset components, indicating that the company has reduced the amount of funds tied up in working capital so, other things being equal, improving liquidity.

7 An aggressive hedging strategy involves a company in financing its spontaneous and permanent current assets on a short-term basis. Given that the term structure of interest rates is upward sloping for most periods of time, this implies that a company can increase its expected rate of return on assets above the average. The main risks in using an aggressive hedging strategy concern the prospects of an unanticipated switch in yield curves from an upward sloping to a downward sloping position. This would imply a significant rise in the short-term costs of financing. Also, there is a risk in a period of 'tight money' that there might be an absolute limit placed on the amount of short-term funding available to a company.

Chapter 13

1 The synergy effect of the potential merger is

SYN = £140m − (£75m + £50m) = £15m

and the net synergy effect

$$NSYN = £15m - £3m = £12m$$

Therefore, the merger is economically viable. From ABC, the bidding company's point of view,

$$NPV = £12m - £10m = £2m$$

and the merger is viable.

2 a) The cost of the acquisition is £50m + £10m = £60m which would represent the cash offer.
   b) Since a cash offer is made the value of ABC, after the merger, is £140m − £60m = £80m.
   c) Under the cash offer the number of shares in ABC remain constant; therefore, the post-merger share price is £80m/125m = 64p, that is, 4p above the pre-merger price of £75m/125m = 60p.

3 a) Given the number of shares outstanding in XYZ and the value of the cash offer, ABC bids £60m/125m = 48p per share for XYZ. The exchange ratio is therefore

$$\frac{\text{Bid Price per Share}}{\text{ABC Current Share Price}} = \frac{48p}{60p} = 0.8{:}1$$

That is, ABC offers XYZ shareholders 40 shares in ABC for every 50 shares in XYZ. Thus ABC raises 0.8(125m) = 100m new shares. After the merger the total number of shares outstanding in ABC = 225m. Thus with a post-merger value of £140m, the share price is £140m/225m = 62.2p which is below the share price of 64p on the cash offer.
   b) The pre-merger share price of XYZ is £50/125m = 40p, therefore, the shareholders in XYZ have gained approximately 22.2p per share, or a total value of £22.2m, well over twice the bid premium of £10m under the cash offer.
   c) The original shareholders in ABC which, pre-merger, was valued at £75m, now have total equity valued at 125m(62.2p) = £77.75m. Under the cash offer their gain is £80m − £75m = £5m. Thus relative to the cash offer they lose £2.25m.
   d) XYZ shareholders have a share of 100m/225m = 44.4%, ABC shareholders have a share of 125m/225m = 55.6%.

4 Given the cash offer of £60m, XYZ shareholders should have

$$\alpha_T = \frac{£60m}{£140m} = 42.86\%$$

of the shares in the merged company. Given that

$$NN = \frac{\alpha_T}{1 - \alpha_T} NOB,$$

the number of new shares to be issued by ABC is

$$NN = \frac{.4286}{.5714} (125m) = 93.76m$$

This is equivalent to an exchange ratio of 93.76m/125m = 0.75:1. The bid price per share is £60m/125m = 48p. In other words the exchange ratio is

$$\frac{48p}{64p} = 0.75:1$$

There are now 218.76m shares outstanding in the merged company which, with a market value of £140m, implies that the post-merger share price is £140m/218.76m = 64p, which is equivalent to the post-merger share price under the cash offer.

5 A management buyout is one way in which a company or a division of a company can go private. The management of the company/division buy the company, often with high-risk debt capital, and take control. The principal motives for this form of going private arise from the tax shields created by the debt financing, and the reduction in the agency costs of equity arising from ownership of the company being conferred on its managers. With the incentive to achieve high efficiency and relatively high levels of operating income, to provide a 'good' return after interest payments to the 'owner-managers', the agency costs of debt also tend to be avoided.

6 Free cash flow arises when a company generates net cash flows, after interest and taxes, in excess of investment requirements in its existing markets. These free cash flows are unlikely to be used to increase dividends, to make share repurchases or to increase investments in cash and marketable securities. There are tax and information signalling reasons for avoiding use of free cash flows in these ways. Consequently the main alternative is to use free cash flow by developing a mergers and acquisition strategy.

7 The main reasons for vertical and horizontal mergers are to exploit economies of scale, to create cost disadvantages for existing and potential competitors, to secure sources of supply (in the case of vertical integration specifically) and to achieve efficiency gains in, for example, the management of current assets.

Chapter 14

1 The owner-managers of most small firms want to retain control of their businesses. They run what the CBI has referred to as lifestyle businesses and may, therefore, have other objectives than value maximisation. Because of the desire to retain control of their businesses, their demand for equity tends to be met from their own resources, those of family and friends and retained earnings. Since these sources of equity are limited, owner-managers have a preference for obtaining much of the capital that they need to expand their businesses from banks, in the form of term loans and overdraft facilities.

2 Just as in the case of large-sized firms, there are potential agency costs of debt associated with the loan finance received by small firms. This problem can be accentuated in the small firm's case, given its reliance on intangible assets. The establishment of good banker–client relationships between the small firm and its

bankers can help reduce the risk surrounding the agency problem and, conse-quently, reduce the debt interest rate premiums necessary to compensate for potential agency costs.

3 Capital gearing refers to the use of collateral in providing security for lending. Income gearing refers to the future expected net cash flows, or income, that potential projects are expected to generate in relation to the value of the loan which is being sought to finance the project.

4 Apart from wishing to avoid the diversification of ownership and the consequent dilution of control that a market listing would produce, owner-managers may find a market listing prohibitively expensive. The expense arises in two senses. First, because the issue costs associated with raising small sums of equity from the market may be disproportionately large. In other words, the small firm may be too small to benefit from economies of scale in transactions costs. Second, a stock exchange listing, especially a full listing, involves ongoing compliance costs in terms of the standards to be met for annual reporting purposes, etc.

Chapter 15

1 a) At DM2.33/£, the value of ABC's exports one month from now is DM10,000 ÷ DM2.33/£ = £4291.85.
   b) An appreciation of the £, the second currency, causes the indirect exchange rate to rise, therefore a 10% appreciation of the £ produces an exchange rate of DM2.563/£ and a fall in the £ value of exports, one month from now, to DM10,000 ÷ DM2.563/£ = £3901.68.
   c) A depreciation of the DM, the first currency, causes the indirect exchange rate to rise. Thus a 10% depreciation of the DM is equivalent to a 10% appreci-ation of the £ giving the answer to part (b).
   d) If the £ depreciates by 10%, the exchange rate falls from DM2.33/£ to DM2.097/£ and the £ value of exports rises from £4291.85, in part (a), to DM10,000 ÷ DM2.097/£ = £4768.71.

2 a) At the spot exchange rate of $1.47/£, the cost of $2.5m dollars now is $2.5m ÷ $1.47/£ ≈ £1.7m. At the forward rate the cost is $2.5m ÷ $1.49/£$_{(f.2)}$ ≈ £1.678m, hence the company should purchase dollars in two months' time, rather than now, at the forward rate and so enter a forward contact now.
   b) If using the spot market in two months' time, at an expected exchange rate E($/£)$_2$ = 1.46, the cost of dollars would be $2.5m ÷ £1.46/£ ≈ £1.712m. Since dollars can be bought in the forward market for £1.678m, which is cheaper than the current spot market price of $1.47/£, dollars should be purchased in two months' time using the forwards market.
   c) At E($/£)$_2$ = 1.52, the purchase of dollars in the spot market, two months from now, would be expected to cost $2.5m ÷ $1.52/£ ≈ £1.645m; thus dollars should be purchased in two months' time using the spot market.
   d) If E($/£)$_2$ = 1.44, the purchase of dollars in the spot market two months from now would be expected to cost $2.5m ÷ $1.44/£ = £1.736m. In this case the two-month forward market would be used.

3 By using the forward market, the £ cost of $2.5m is:

$$\$2.5m \div £1.49/£_{(f.2)} \simeq £1.678m$$

If the spot rate in two months' time turns out to be $1.52/£, the cost of dollars would have been

$$\$2.5m \div \$1.52/£ \simeq £1.645m,$$

which is cheaper than using the forward market. The company is already locked into the $1.49/£ exchange rate, in two months' time, because it entered a forwards contract at this rate and cannot avail itself of the benefits of using the spot market.

The company could have attempted to avoid this problem by using an option contract at the forward rate of $1.49/£_{(f.2)}. Under this contract it would not have been obligated to purchase at this rate and could have chosen not to exercise its option, using, instead, the spot market in two months' time, if this had been advantageous.

4 Under PPP

$$\frac{1 + E(\Theta_{US})}{1 + E(\Theta_{UK})} = \frac{E(\$/£)_{12}}{\$/£}$$

Thus $\dfrac{1.05}{1.08} = \dfrac{E(\$/£)_{12}}{1.50}$ and

$$E(\$/£)_{12} = 1.458$$

In one year's time, the $ cost of the US equipment is expected to be $2.5m(1.05) = £2.625m. Consequently the £ cost can be expected to be £2.625m ÷ $1.458/£ ≃ £1.80m.

5 Under IRP

$$\frac{1 + r_G}{1 + r_{UK}} = \frac{DM/£_{(f.12)}}{DM/£}$$

Thus $\dfrac{1.06}{1.08} = \dfrac{DM/£_{(f.12)}}{2.32}$ and

$$DM/£_{(f.12)} = 2.277$$

6 Empirical evidence tends to suggest that international parity relationships do not hold. Since currency markets are not efficient the expected future spot exchange rate is not equal to its equivalent forward rate. Similarly, because of transport costs and market transactions costs, PPP and IRP do not hold exactly.

7 Under PPP

$$\frac{1 + .02}{1 + .04} = \frac{E(\$/£)_{12}}{1.48} \therefore E(\$/£) = 1.452$$

Under the pure expectations hypothesis

$$E(\$/£)_{12} = \$/£_{(f.12)} = 1.452$$

$$\frac{1 + r_{US}}{1.07} = \frac{1.452}{1.48} \therefore 1 + r_{US} = 1.0498 \therefore r_{US} = 4.98\%$$

Under the International Fisher Effect

$$\frac{1 + r_{US}}{1 + r_{UK}} = \frac{1.0498}{1.07} = 0.981 = \frac{1 + E(\Theta_{US})}{1 + E(\Theta_{UK})} = \frac{1.02}{1.04} = 0.981$$

US real rate of interest: $\dfrac{1 + r_{US}}{1 + E(\Theta_{US})} = \dfrac{1.0498}{1.02} = 1.0292$

therefore the real rate of interest in the US $\simeq 2.9\%$

UK real rate of interest: $\dfrac{1.07}{1.04} = 1.0288$

therefore the real rate of interest in the UK $\simeq 2.9\%$

Chapter 16

1 a) Actual cost of borrowings from Bank A:

$$£1m \left(12\% \times \frac{2}{12}\right) = £0.02m$$

This unanticipated rise in interest rates from the 11% FRA rate to 12% is hedged since, under the FRA, the notionally borrowed sum from Bank B would cost:

$$£1m \left(11\% \times \frac{2}{12}\right) = £0.018333m$$

Therefore, Bank B compensates the company by paying

£0.02m − £0.018333m = £0.001667m

b) If the rate of interest falls to 8% the actual borrowings from Bank A cost:

$$£1m \left(8\% \times \frac{2}{12}\right) = £0.013333m$$

Now the company compensates Bank B by

£0.018333m − £0.013333m = £0.005m

2 The initial margin in a futures contract represents a 'down-payment' and is normally based on a fixed percentage of the value of the futures contract. Marking to market involves crediting/debiting an investor's margin account with the daily profit/loss arising from daily changes in the market value of the futures contract. If losses cause the margin account to fall below its minimum permissible level, then a margin call is made and the investor must immediately restore the margin to its minimum level.

3 With each SIRF contract valued at £500,000, the company has sold six SIRF

contracts to hedge its interest rate risk. At a price of 92, the company has locked into an annual interest rate of $100 - 92 = 8\%$, that is, 2% on the three-month basis. The initial margin payment is normally £750 per contract, so the company pays $6 \times £750 = £4500$ to the futures exchange. This sum is returned at the end of the contract period. The cost of borrowing under the 8% annual interest rate is:

£3m(0.02) = £0.06m

At the beginning of October interest rates rise to 12% so that the actual borrowing cost is:

£3m(0.03) = £0.09m

Thus the extra cost is:

£0.09m − £0.06m = £0.03m

This extra cost has been hedged, however, since the SIRFs fall in price to $100 - 12 = 88$. The profit of £0.03m is paid into the company's margin account. This profit is determined as:

Tick movement × Tick value × Number of contracts

Interest rates have risen by four percentage points, therefore the tick movement is $4 \div .01 = 400$. The tick value is $0.0001(3/12)£500,000 = £12.50$. There are six contracts, therefore the profit is:

400(£12.50)(6) = £0.03m

4 An American option can be exercised at any time over the duration of the option contract whereas a European option can only be exercised on the expiry date. A call option gives the holder the right to buy a share at the exercise price. A put option gives the holder the right to sell a share at the exercise price.

5 a) Profit on call = Share price − Exercise price − Call premium. Therefore, on a per share basis,

Profit = £5.30 − £4.65 − £0.38 = £0.27

Since a contract on LIFFE has 1000 shares, the profit on the contract is £270. The option is exercised.

b) Profit per share: −£0.38. Since the share price is below the exercise price the share would be purchased in the spot market and the option allowed to lapse.

c) Profit per share: £4.68 − £4.65 − £0.38 = −£0.35. On contract: −£350. The option is exercised.

6 a) An investor would establish a bull spread strategy by buying the more expensive call at 35p and selling the cheaper call at 25p.

b) (i) If the share price is £5.40, both calls are exercised. The investor buys 1000 shares at £4.80 at a cost of £4800, and sells 1000 shares at £5.10, receiving £5100. In the latter case the investor is a call option writer and it is in the interests of the holder of this call to exercise it. The net contract cost is 1000(35p − 25p) = £100 and the net profit £5100 − £4800 − £100 = £200.

   (ii) If the share price is £4.85, the investor would exercise the more expensive call and buy at £4.80, selling at the market price of £4.85. With a profit per share of 5p and a profit on the contract of £50 the net profit after deducting the net contract cost is £50 − £100 = −£50.

(iii) If the share price is £4.75, the investor will not exercise his right to buy at £4.80 and the holder of the call which the investor has written will not exercise the right to buy at £5.10. Thus the loss, which is at a maximum, is −£100.

7 Bondholders in a company can be considered as put option writers, with shareholders buying the put since the shareholders have purchased the right to default on interest payments.

Chapter 17

1 Management, in the presence of a divorce of ownership from control, tend to pursue personal power and prestige, managerial income, expense preferences, job security and size objectives.

2 The pursuit of managerial objectives tends to be constrained by the concentration of share ownership, the effective threat of acquisition, the availability of information and shareholders' abilities to impose information signalling constraints on management.

Index